THE CANADIAN YEARBOOK OF INTERNATIONAL LAW

1992

ANNUAIRE CANADIEN DE DROIT INTERNATIONAL

The Canadian Yearbook of International Law

VOLUME XXX 1992 TOME XXX

Annuaire canadien de Droit international

Published under the auspices of
THE CANADIAN BRANCH, INTERNATIONAL LAW ASSOCIATION
AND
THE CANADIAN COUNCIL ON INTERNATIONAL LAW
*with the financial support of the Social Sciences
and Humanities Research Council of Canada*

Publié sous les auspices de
LA SECTION CANADIENNE DE L'ASSOCIATION DE DROIT INTERNATIONAL
ET
LE CONSEIL CANADIEN DE DROIT INTERNATIONAL
*avec l'appui financier du Conseil de recherches
en Sciences humaines du Canada*

UBC Press

VANCOUVER, B.C.

ISBN 0-7748-0438-6
ISSN 0069-0058

Canadian Shared Cataloguing in Publication Data

Main entry under title:

The Canadian yearbook of international law

Vols. for 1963-   published under the
auspices of the Canadian Branch, International
Law Association and the Canadian Council on
International Law
    Editor: 1963-   C. B. Bourne.
    ISSN 0069-0058

    1. International Law — Yearbooks
I. International Law Association. Canadian
Branch and the Canadian Council on
International Law. II. Bourne, Charles B.
    JX21.C3   341'.05

UBC Press
University of British Columbia
6344 Memorial Road
Vancouver, BC V6T 1Z2
(604) 822-3259

The Board of Editors, the Canadian Branch of the International Law Association, the Canadian Council on International Law, and the University of British Columbia are not in any way responsible for the views expressed by contributors, whether the contributions are signed or unsigned.

Les opinions émises dans le présent *Annuaire* par nos collaborateurs, qu'il s'agisse d'articles signés, ou non signés, ne sauraient en aucune façon engager la responsabilité du Comité de rédaction, de la Section canadienne de l'Association de droit international, de la section canadienne du Conseil canadien de droit international ou de l'Université de Colombie Britannique.

Communications to *The Yearbook* should be addressed to:
Prière d'adresser les communications destinées à l'*Annuaire* à:

THE EDITOR, THE CANADIAN YEARBOOK OF INTERNATIONAL LAW
FACULTY OF LAW, COMMON LAW SECTION
UNIVERSITY OF OTTAWA
57 LOUIS PASTEUR
OTTAWA, ONTARIO K1N 6N5
CANADA

INTERNATIONAL LAW ASSOCIATION (CANADIAN BRANCH)
ASSOCIATION DE DROIT INTERNATIONAL (BRANCHE CANADIENNE)

Officers / Membres du bureau 1992-94

Life Honorary Presidents / *Présidents honoraires à vie*	Nicolas M. Matte Émile Colas Jean-Louis Magdelénat
Honorary Vice-Presidents *Vice-présidents honoraires*	Charles B. Bourne Maxwell Cohen
President / Président	Cameron DesBois
Vice-Presidents / *Vice-présidents*	Harry Bloomfield Armand De Mestral Brian Dickson Leslie Green Jennie Hatfield Lyon Valerie Hughes Mark Jewett Martin Low Jacques-Yvan Morin Gerald Morris Anne-Marie Trahan
Honorary Secretary-Treasurer / *Secrétaire-Trésorier honoraire*	Jean-Marc Fortier
Executive Committee / *Comité exécutif*	Cameron DesBois Harry Bloomfield Martin Low Jean-Marc Fortier Émile Colas Nicolas M. Matte Anne-Marie Trahan
Councillors / *Conseillers*	Charles B. Bourne Armand De Mestral Allan Gotlieb John Humphrey Edward McWhinney Daniel Turp Ivan Vlasic
International Officers / *Membres du bureau international*	Charles B. Bourne Émile Colas Jean-Louis Magdelénat Nicolas M. Matte

Editor-in-Chief of the Canadian Yearbook of International Law
Editeur-en-chef de l'Annuaire canadien de Droit international
D. M. McRae

Contents / Sommaire

CHARLES B. BOURNE xi *Preface*

Articles

ROSS HORNBY ET
VALERIE HUGHES
3 L'affaire de la délimitation maritime
Canada / France

41 Summary

PATRICIA K. WOUTERS 43 Allocation of the Non-Navigational Uses
of International Watercourses: Efforts at
Codification and the Experience of
Canada and the United States

88 Sommaire

WOLFF H. VON HEINEGG 89 Visit, Search, Diversion, and Capture in
Naval Warfare. Part II: Developments
since 1945

136 Sommaire

KATIA BOUSTANY 137 L'investigation dans le programme
nucléaire irakien

163 Summary

BRYAN SCHWARTZ AND
ELLIOT LEVEN
165 International Organizations: What Makes
Them Work?

194 Sommaire

VILAYSOUN
LOUNGNARATH, JR.
197 Les cadres juridiques de la capitalisation
des dettes commerciales des États

232 Summary

NORMAN P. FARRELL 233 The American Convention on Human
Rights: Canada's Present Law and the
Effect of Ratification

Notes and Comments / Notes et commentaires

EDWARD MCWHINNEY 261 The International Court as
Emerging Constitutional Court and the
Coordinate UN Institutions (Especially
the Security Council): Implications of the
Aerial Incident at Lockerbie

272 Sommaire

FRANKLYN P. 273 Consultation Procedures under UN Rules
SALIMBENE for the Control of Restrictive Business
Practices

290 Sommaire

CHRISTIAN JOLIVET 291 Récents développements dans le domaine
des services

ROSS HORNBY 301 State Immunity. *Re Canada Labour Code*:
A Common Sense Solution to the
Commercial Activity Exception

316 Sommaire

*Chronique de Droit international économique
en 1991 / Digest of International Economic
Law in 1991*

317 Commerce, préparé par Martin St-Amant

329 Le Canada et le système monétaire
international en 1991, préparé par
Bernard Colas

337 Investissement, préparé par Pierre Ratelle

Practice / La pratique

Canadian Practice in International
Law / La pratique canadienne en matière
de droit international public

347 At the Department of External Affairs in
1991-92 / Au ministère des Affaires
extérieures en 1991-92, compiled
by / préparé par Barry Mawhinney

365 Parliamentary Declarations in
1991-92 / Déclarations parlementaires en
1991-92, compiled by / préparé par
Maureen Irish

385 Treaty Action Taken by Canada in
1991 / Mesures prises par le Canada en
matière de traités en 1991, compiled
by / préparé par Céline Blais

Cases / La jurisprudence

403 Canadian Cases in International Law in
1991-92 / La jurisprudence canadienne
en matière de droit international en
1991-92, compiled by / préparé par
Joost Blom

427 *Book Reviews / Recensions de livres*

467 *Analytical Index / Index analytique*

474 *Index of Cases / Index des Affaires*

BOOK REVIEWS/RECENSIONS DE LIVRES

PAGE

*From Coexistence to Cooperation: International Law and
Organization in the Post-Cold War Era*
Edited by Edward McWhinney, Douglas Ross, Gregory
Tunkin, Vladlen Vereshchetin   JOHN N. HAZARD   427

International Law in Theory and Practice
by Oscar Schachter   IVAN I. HEAD   430

*International Human Rights: Problems of Law, Policy and
Practice.* 2nd Edition
by Richard B. Lillich   L. C. GREEN   431

International Human Rights Law
by Anne F. Bayefsky   L. C. GREEN   433

The Nuremberg Trial and International Law
Edited by George Ginsburgs and
V. N. Kudriavtsev   L. C. GREEN   436

Mine Warfare at Sea
by Howard S. Levie   W. J. FENRICK   438

Maritime Terrorism and International Law
Edited by Natalino Ronzitti   L. C. GREEN   440

Settlement of International and Inter-State Water Disputes in India
by B. R. Chauhan   C. B. BOURNE   443

Yearbook of International Environmental Law, Vol. 1 (1990)
Edited by Günther Handl   CRAIG SCOTT   446

Basic Documents of International Environmental Law, 3 vols.
Edited by Harald Hohmann   C. B. BOURNE   454

Basic Legal Documents of the Russian Federation
Edited by William E. Butler   L. C. GREEN   456

Aspects of Extradition Law
by Geoff Gilbert   L. C. GREEN   458

International Labour Law Reports, Vols. 7, 8, and 9
Edited by Zvi H. Bar Niv et al.   M. A. HICKLING   462

Preface

VOLUME 1 OF *The Canadian Yearbook of International Law* was published in 1963. Since then the *Yearbook* has appeared annually, the present volume being number XXX (1992). Throughout the intervening years, I have had the privilege of serving as its editor-in-chief.

Recently, I have increasingly felt that it was desirable to place the responsibility for the *Yearbook* in fresh and younger hands, and the Board of Editors has now accepted my recommendation that this be done. Accordingly, I am happy to announce that Professor D. M. McRae, presently Dean of the Faculty of Law, Common Law Section, of the University of Ottawa, has been appointed editor-in-chief of this *Yearbook*, beginning with Volume XXXI (1993).

I take this opportunity to thank all those who have supported me and the *Yearbook* most loyally during the years of my editorship. Chief among these are the members of the Canadian international law community who have made available the fruits of their scholarship for publication in the *Yearbook*. The granting agencies, especially the Social Sciences and Humanities Research Council of Canada, also deserve special mention, as do the Department of External Affairs, Ottawa, and the University of British Columbia's Press and its Faculty of Law. I urge that all of these persons and other bodies continue to support the *Yearbook*, for its future without this support will be bleak.

At this turning point in the life of the *Yearbook*, I am convinced that the *Yearbook* will endure and prosper under the editorship of Professor McRae. May it be so!

CHARLES B. BOURNE

THE CANADIAN YEARBOOK OF INTERNATIONAL LAW

1992

ANNUAIRE CANADIEN DE DROIT INTERNATIONAL

L'affaire de la délimitation maritime Canada/France

ROSS HORNBY ET VALERIE HUGHES*

INTRODUCTION

L E 10 JUIN 1992, un tribunal d'arbitrage ad hoc a fixé, à la demande du Canada et de la France, la frontière maritime appelée à commander tous droits et juridictions que le droit international reconnaît aux deux pays au voisinage des îles françaises de Saint-Pierre-et-Miquelon, situées à proximité de la côte méridionale de la province canadienne de Terre-Neuve. (Voir la Figure 1.) La décision du Tribunal mettait fin à un différend vieux de plus de vingt-cinq ans, et issu à l'origine des revendications concurrentes des deux Parties quant à la juridiction sur le plateau continental. Même si, dans ses motifs, le Tribunal rejette les prétentions de l'une et l'autre, la décision donne satisfaction pour l'essentiel au Canada.

Sur le plan du droit, la décision, en mettant comme elle le fait l'accent sur le couple "principes équitables/résultat équitable," est en tous points conforme à la jurisprudence établie au cours des vingt dernières années en matière de délimitation maritime. Le Tribunal a refusé d'adopter une démarche fondée exclusivement sur les règles rigides — ce qui l'aurait amené à privilégier

* Les auteurs sont avocats au ministère de la Justice (Ottawa). Ils ont représenté le Canada comme conseils dans l'affaire concernant la délimitation de la frontière maritime (Canada/France) et comme conseillers juridiques dans l'affaire concernant la délimitation dans la région du golfe du Maine (Canada/États-Unis, Cour internationale de Justice, 1984). Les opinions exprimées dans le présent article sont celles des auteurs et ne reflètent pas nécessairement celles du gouvernement du Canada.

Les auteurs tiennent à remercier M. Ronald Gélinas du ministère des Pêches et Océans (Ottawa) pour son aide dans la préparation des cartes ainsi que pour ses précieux commentaires.

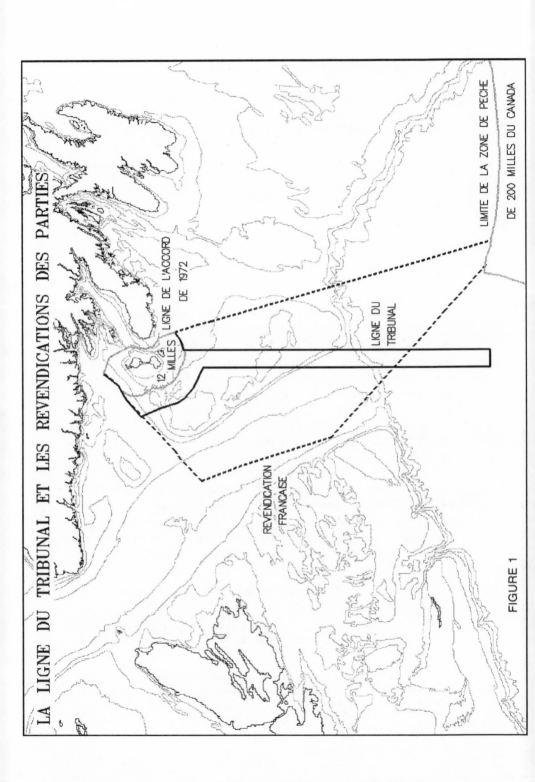

LA LIGNE DU TRIBUNAL ET LES REVENDICATIONS DES PARTIES

LIGNE DE L'ACCORD DE 1972

12 MILLES

LIMITE DE LA ZONE DE PÊCHE
DE 200 MILLES DU CANADA

LIGNE DU TRIBUNAL

REVENDICATION FRANÇAISE

FIGURE 1

l'équidistance, au détriment des intérêts du Canada dans la région. Le tracé dont il a décidé donne au Canada le contrôle de la plupart des ressources halieutiques d'importance commerciale dans la zone précédemment en litige, au grand soulagement des collectivités situées tout le long de la côte méridionale de Terre-Neuve où l'on dépend de ces ressources depuis des siècles. La France n'a donc pas réussi comme elle l'espérait à se faire attribuer, grâce à son pied-à-terre nord-américain, une vaste zone économique autonome à l'intérieur de la limite de 200 milles du Canada.

L'HISTORIQUE DU DIFFÉREND

La décision est venue trancher un différend qui datait du milieu des années 1960, lorsque le Canada et la France avaient tous deux commencé à délivrer des permis de recherche d'hydrocarbures pour les mêmes secteurs du plateau continental. (Le différend sur les droits de pêche ne devait se déclarer qu'après que les deux Parties eurent étendu à 200 milles leurs zones maritimes en 1977.) La Convention de Genève sur le plateau continental,[1] entrée en vigueur en 1964, avait fixé les règles régissant les droits des États sur le plateau continental. Elle comprenait la disposition suivante sur la délimitation du plateau en cas de différend:

Article 6
1. Dans le cas où un même plateau continental est adjacent aux territoires de deux ou plusieurs États dont les côtes se font face, la délimitation du plateau continental entre ces États est déterminée par accord entre ces États. À défaut d'accord, et à moins que des circonstances spéciales ne justifient une autre délimitation, celle-ci est constituée par la ligne médiane dont tous les points sont équidistants des points les plus proches des lignes de base à partir desquelles est mesurée la largeur de la mer territoriale de chacun de ces États.
2. Dans le cas où un même plateau continental est adjacent aux territoires de deux États limitrophes, la délimitation du plateau continental est déterminée par accord entre ces États. À défaut d'accord, et à moins que des circonstances spéciales ne justifient une autre délimitation, celle-ci s'opère par application du principe de l'équidistance des points les plus proches des lignes de base à partir desquelles est mesurée la largeur de la mer territoriale de chacun de ces États.

Cette règle de délimitation est communément appelée "règle de l'équidistance et des circonstances spéciales." La France a adhéré à

[1] R.T.C., 1970, n° 4. La Convention a été adoptée à Genève en 1958.

la Convention en 1965. Le Canada a signé la Convention en 1958 et l'a ratifiée en 1970.[2]

C'est en 1966 que le Canada a fait d'abord connaître sa position officielle relativement à sa prétention sur le plateau continental au large de Terre-Neuve, à l'occasion de discussions initiales tenues avec les représentants français, et dans la correspondance diplomatique échangée à ce sujet.[3] La relation géographique entre Saint-Pierre-et-Miquelon et le territoire canadien constituait, aux yeux du Canada, une "circonstance spéciale" justifiant une délimitation différente de celle qui résulterait de la ligne médiane. Mais la France rejeta l'approche des "circonstances spéciales" au profit de la théorie de l'équidistance.[4] Des négociations se tinrent sporadiquement et, en 1972, les représentants des deux pays signèrent un Relevé de conclusions,[5] qu'ils soumirent *ad referendum* à leurs gouvernements. Dans ce document, la France se disait prête à accepter un plateau continental "réduit" au large de Saint-Pierre-et-Miquelon (une carte annexée au Relevé montre une zone française de 12 milles marins au large des îles), et à renoncer à ses prétentions sur d'autres espaces, en échange de droits d'exploration et d'exploitation d'hydrocarbures dans un secteur plus grande pendant dix-huit ans. Le gouvernement canadien n'accepta pas l'entente *ad referendum* — malgré les nombreuses requêtes de la France — parce qu'il estimait excessifs les droits accordés à la France quant aux hydrocarbures sur une vaste étendue du plateau continental canadien. Des négociations eurent lieu de temps à autre, mais les deux Parties ne se sentaient pas pressées de régler le

---

[2] La France a toutefois, au moment de son accession, fait une déclaration qui avait trait entre autres à l'article 6. Il y était noté qu'à défaut d'accord spécifique, une délimitation opérée par l'application du principe de l'équidistance ne serait pas opposable à la France dans trois circonstances:
— si la délimitation est calculée à partir de lignes de bases instituées postérieurement au 29 avril 1958;
— si elle est prolongée au-delà de l'isobathe de 200 mètres de profondeur;
— si elle se situe dans des zones où il existe des "circonstances spéciales" au sens de l'article 6, à savoir: le golfe de Gascogne, la baie de Granville et les espaces maritimes du Pas-de-Calais et de la mer du Nord au large des côtes françaises.
Au moment de la ratification, le Canada a fait objection aux deux premiers éléments de la déclaration française et il a réservé sa position à l'égard du troisième.

[3] *Notes verbales* du Canada portant les dates du 22 février 1966, 4 mai 1966 et 2 novembre 1966.

[4] *Aide-mémoire* français du 29 juillet 1966.

[5] Annexes au *mémoire du Canada*, Volume I, Annexe B-2.

différend puisqu'elles avaient convenu de n'autoriser aucune activité de forage dans la zone contestée.[6]

Le différend prit une dimension nouvelle en 1977 lorsque le Canada établit une zone de pêche de 200 milles le long de ses côtes et que la France déclara une zone économique de 188 milles au large de sa mer territoriale de 12 milles, donnant ainsi naissance à une vaste étendue où se chevauchaient les prétentions des deux Parties.[7] Le Canada reconnut à la France une zone maritime de 12 milles au large de Saint-Pierre-et-Miquelon, appuyant sa position sur l'évolution du droit de la mer et sur la décision rendue par le Tribunal en 1977 dans l'*Arbitrage franco-britannique*.[8] Quant à la France, elle ne précisa pas les limites de sa revendication, mais indiqua que la ligne devait être tracée selon la méthode de l'équidistance. (Voir la Figure 1.)

Même si l'on n'a pas encore procédé à l'exploitation des hydrocarbures dans l'ancienne zone en litige, les eaux au large de Terre-Neuve sont, depuis des siècles, des lieux de pêche privilégiés. Depuis 1972, la pêche française en eaux canadiennes est régie par l'Accord relatif aux relations réciproques entre le Canada et la France en matière de pêche,[9] le dernier en date d'une série d'accords de pêche bilatéraux conclus avec ce pays depuis le début du dix-huitième siècle. À l'article 1, la France y renonce à ses droits conventionnels antérieurs; en contrepartie, à l'article 2, le Canada reconnaît aux ressortissants français le droit de pêcher dans les eaux canadiennes en cas de changement au régime juridique maritime, qui, en 1972, ne prévoyait qu'une zone de 12 milles.[10] Après l'extension de la juridiction canadienne à 200 milles, la France se limita pendant quelques années à la part des captures que le Canada l'autorisait à prendre dans le secteur s'étendant au-delà de

---

6 Le Canada et la France se sont entendus en 1967 pour décréter un moratoire sur les activités de forage dans la zone contestée.

7 *Décret sur les zones de pêche du Canada (Zones 4 et 5)*, C.P. 1977-1, le 1er janvier 1977, DORS/77-62; *Décret n° 77-169 du 25 février 1977 portant création, en application des dispositions de la loi du 16 juillet 1976, d'une zone économique au large des côtes du département de Saint-Pierre-et-Miquelon.*

8 *Arbitrage entre le Royaume-Uni de Grande-Bretagne et d'Irlande du Nord et la République française sur la délimitation du plateau continental,* Décision du 30 juin 1977, Nations Unies, *Recueil des sentences arbitrales (RSA)*, vol. XVIII, p. 3 (ci-après: *Arbitrage franco-britannique*, avec mention du numéro du paragraphe pertinent).

9 R.T.C., 1979, n° 37.

10 L'Accord traite aussi des droits de pêche de la France dans le golfe du Saint-Laurent.

12 milles des îles françaises. Au milieu de la décennie 1980, toutefois, elle commença à établir ses propres quotas, sans tenir compte des contingents fixés par le Canada, et son effort de pêche dépassa largement sa part traditionnelle des captures.[11]

La présence d'une immense étendue contestée au coeur même de la zone de 200 milles du Canada cessait donc de n'être qu'un simple inconvénient. Les autorités canadiennes estimèrent que la santé à long terme des ressources halieutiques serait compromise si l'effort de pêche ne diminuait pas. La France, pour sa part, n'était pas prête à réduire ses captures au niveau prescrit par le Canada et les relations furent ponctuées de différends de pêche acrimonieux. En 1986, il était devenu évident que les deux pays ne pourraient parvenir à une solution négociée. En janvier 1987, le Canada et la France signèrent donc des "Conclusions agréées," par lesquelles ils s'engageaient à négocier deux accords, soit un compromis d'arbitrage fixant les modalités du renvoi du différend à une procédure de règlement par tierce partie, et une entente intérimaire destinée à régir les activités de pêche de la France durant la procédure. Les deux accords furent signés le 30 mars 1989.

L'ÉTABLISSEMENT DU TRIBUNAL D'ARBITRAGE

Le Canada et la France avaient convenu de renvoyer le différend de délimitation maritime à un tribunal d'arbitrage ad hoc. Le Canada nomma comme juge national Allan Gotlieb, qui avait été diplomate et haut fonctionnaire durant la majeure partie de la Troisième Conférence des Nations Unies sur le droit de la mer. La France de son côté nomma Prosper Weil, un grand spécialiste en matière de délimitation maritime.[12] Les Parties désignèrent conjointement Eduardo Jiménez de Aréchaga de l'Uruguay, un expert

[11] La Communauté européenne a établi les contingents de 1982 et 1983 aux mêmes niveaux que les contingents fixés par le Canada. En 1984 et 1985, le contingent de la CE dépassait celui du Canada. En 1986, lorsque l'archipel de Saint-Pierre-et-Miquelon cessa d'être un *département d'outre-mer* pour devenir une *collectivité territoriale*, la responsabilité en matière de pêche passa de la Communauté à la France, laquelle ne fixa pas de contingent cette année-là. La France a établi des contingents pour les années subséquentes, contingents qui comprenaient une modeste part pour le Canada.

[12] Le professeur Weil était conseil du Canada dans l'affaire du *Golfe du Maine* entre le Canada et les États-Unis, tranchée par la Cour internationale de Justice en 1984: *Délimitation de la frontière maritime dans la région du Golfe du Maine (Canada c. États-Unis d'Amérique), C.I.J. Recueil 1984*, p. 246 (ci-après: affaire du *Golfe du Maine*, avec mention du numéro du paragraphe pertinent).

de la délimitation et ancien président de la Cour internationale de Justice, comme président du Tribunal; furent de même désignés Gaetano Arangio-Ruiz, un spécialiste italien du droit de la mer,[13] et Oscar Schachter des États-Unis, une autorité dans le domaine du droit international. Le greffier fut Felipe Paolillo de l'Uruguay, et le commandant Peter Beazley du Royaume-Uni servit d'expert au Tribunal pour les questions hydrographiques et techniques.

Dans le Compromis d'arbitrage, les Parties énoncèrent en ces termes la question soumise au Tribunal:

> Statuant conformément aux principes et règles du droit international applicables en la matière, le Tribunal est prié de procéder à la délimitation entre les Parties des espaces maritimes relevant de la France et de ceux relevant du Canada. Cette délimitation sera effectuée à partir du point 1 et du point 9 de la délimitation visée à l'article 8 de l'Accord du 27 mars 1972 et décrite dans son annexe. Le Tribunal établira une délimitation unique qui commandera à la fois tous droits et juridictions que le droit international reconnaît aux Parties dans les espaces maritimes susvisés.

Le Tribunal était donc prié de fixer une frontière maritime unique appelée à régir les diverses formes de juridiction que les États ont le droit d'exercer dans les espaces maritimes relevant d'eux. À cet égard, la question est analogue à celle qu'avaient soumise le Canada et les États-Unis à une Chambre de la Cour internationale de Justice en 1984, dans l'affaire du *Golfe du Maine*, où, pour la première fois, une instance judiciaire internationale était appelée à tracer une limite maritime unique et polyvalente. On notera que le Tribunal devait effectuer la délimitation en partant des points terminaux de la ligne établie à l'article 8 de l'Accord de pêche de 1972 pour diviser le chenal entre les îles françaises et la côte de Terre-Neuve, dont le tracé relève pour l'essentiel de la méthode de l'équidistance.

Il était convenu dans le Compromis que le Canada et la France supporteraient à égalité les dépenses générales de l'arbitrage, ainsi que la rémunération des membres du Tribunal et celle du greffier.

Les Parties échangèrent leurs pièces écrites le 1er juin 1990 (mémoires) et le 1er février 1991 (contre-mémoires). Selon le Compromis, celles-ci ne pouvaient être communiquées au public qu'une fois les audiences commencées, et chacune des Parties ne pourrait alors mettre en circulation que ses propres écritures. Le

---

[13] M. Arangio-Ruiz était conseil de l'Italie lorsque celle-ci a présenté sa requête d'intervention dans l'affaire du Plateau continental (Jamahiriya arabe libyenne/Malte), C.I.J. Recueil 1984, p.3.

Canada en a remis des exemplaires aux différentes bibliothèques juridiques du pays. Si la France choisissait de ne pas rendre publiques ses plaidoiries — ce qui serait conforme à sa pratique habituelle — il serait néanmoins possible de reconstruire sa thèse à partir de la critique qu'en fait le Canada dans ses documents.

La procédure orale se déroula à New York du 29 juillet au 21 août 1991. Les ministres de la Justice du Canada et de la France prononcèrent les déclarations liminaires. La procédure fut ouverte au public sur invitation, solution de compromis entre la position du Canada, qui préconisait des audiences publiques, et celle de la France, qui préconisait le huis clos.

Enfin, il était stipulé dans le Compromis que la sentence du Tribunal serait définitive et obligatoire.

Les conclusions des Parties

Pour le Canada, la délimitation devait s'effectuer conformément à des principes ou critères équitables, en tenant compte de toutes les circonstances pertinentes, afin d'aboutir à un résultat équitable. Il fit valoir que, pour cela, il fallait tout particulièrement respecter le principe de non-empiétement sur les espaces constituant le prolongement maritime naturel de l'une ou l'autre des Parties et faire en sorte qu'aucun des accidents géographiques de la zone pertinente n'exerce un effet disproportionné sur la délimitation. Parmi les circonstances pertinentes à prendre en compte figuraient les suivantes: la position des îles Saint-Pierre-et-Miquelon à proximité immédiate de la côte méridionale de Terre-Neuve, dont elles constituent une particularité non essentielle, les projections maritimes convergentes produites par deux grandes façades côtières canadiennes (Terre-Neuve et l'île du Cap-Breton), l'extrême disparité entre les longueurs côtières des Parties, la très forte dépendance du Canada à l'égard des ressources de la région, enfin, le rôle prédominant joué par le Canada quant aux activités d'État dans la région, en ce qui concerne entre autres les aides à la navigation, les opérations de recherche et de sauvetage et la protection de l'environnement.

Selon le Canada, une délimitation formée par une ceinture de 12 milles marins dans les espaces non encore délimités, ladite ceinture joignant les points terminaux de la ligne de délimitation établie en 1972, représentait une solution équitable.

La France, pour sa part, soutenait que le résultat ne pourrait être équitable que si le Tribunal tenait compte de toutes les circonstances pertinentes; elle proposait une délimitation fondée pour l'essentiel sur la méthode de l'équidistance. Au nombre des circonstances pertinentes, elle citait le cadre géographique du secteur en cause, qui, à son avis, était d'une "grande simplicité" du fait de l'absence d'États tiers dans la région. En outre, selon la thèse française, le principe de l'égalité souveraine des États conférait à Saint-Pierre-et-Miquelon le droit à une zone de 200 milles, et le principe de l'effet partiel était inapplicable en l'espèce puisque les îles, loin d'être une anomalie géographique, faisaient partie intégrante de la délimitation. La France chercha aussi à convaincre le Tribunal de tenir compte de certaines circonstances non géographiques, dont la dépendance économique française à l'égard des ressources halieutiques, et de considérations relatives à la navigation et à la sécurité. À ce dernier égard, elle fit valoir que les prétendus "pouvoirs de police" exercés par le Canada dans sa zone de 200 milles nuisaient à la liberté de navigation, et qu'il était essentiel que la zone française s'étendît au-delà de la limite canadienne des 200 milles pour que la France puisse jouir d'un accès sûr à la haute mer.[14] C'est dans ce secteur sud de la revendication française que le tracé s'écarte de la méthode de l'équidistance.

LA LIGNE ÉTABLIE PAR LE TRIBUNAL

Le Tribunal a indiqué clairement qu'à son avis ni la solution de l'enclave proposée par le Canada ni la ligne d'équidistance élargie préconisée par la France ne fournissait "ne serait-ce qu'un point de départ pour la délimitation."[15] La revendication du Canada déniait à la France une projection maritime au-delà de la mer territoriale de 12 milles et le Tribunal l'écarta sans autre forme de procès. La revendication française était, quant à elle, incontestablement exagérée, puisque la ligne d'équidistance utilisée pour construire la majeure partie du tracé amputait la projection en mer de longs

---

14 Une zone de 200 milles autour de Saint-Pierre-et-Miquelon serait enclavée dans la zone canadienne de 200 milles, qui s'avance bien davantage dans l'océan Atlantique en raison de la saillie formée par le cap Race, à Terre-Neuve, et par l'île de Sable au large de la Nouvelle-Écosse. Les allégations de la France selon lesquelles le Canada empiéterait sur la liberté de navigation dans la zone de 200 milles n'ont été évoquées que brièvement par le Tribunal, qui a pris note de la concordance de vues des Parties relativement au principe de la liberté de navigation énoncé dans l'article 58 de la Convention de 1982 sur le droit de la mer. *Décision du Tribunal d'arbitrage du 10 juin 1992* (ci-après appelée la *Décision*), par. 88.

15 *Décision*, par. 65.

segments de la côte terre-neuvienne, plus étendue, des deux côtés des îles françaises. Dans le secteur extérieur, le prolongement de la zone revendiquée par la France au-delà des 200 milles était dénué de crédibilité, puisqu'il faisait abstraction du long littoral de la presqu'île d'Avalon, à Terre-Neuve, tout en donnant plein effet à la minuscule ouverture côtière de l'île de Sable vers le nord. En fait, la demande d'accès direct à la haute mer au-delà de la zone cana-dienne de 200 milles semble avoir été fondée sur une éventuelle "territorialisation" de la zone économique exclusive qui n'est justi-fiée ni par le droit ni par les faits. Il n'est donc pas étonnant que le Tribunal ait estimé qu'il lui fallait formuler sa propre solution, indépendamment des propositions mises de l'avant par les Parties.

Pour y parvenir, il a adopté une approche en deux étapes, au motif que Saint-Pierre-et-Miquelon compte deux façades côtières faisant face au large: la côte ouest de Miquelon, plus longue, et l'étroite ouverture côtière de cette île et de Saint-Pierre vers le sud.[16] De l'avis du Tribunal, pour aboutir à un résultat équitable, il fallait appliquer une méthode qui reflète les circonstances géographiques particulières présentes dans chaque secteur.

S'agissant du premier secteur (le secteur occidental), le Tribunal a jugé qu'il serait équitable d'accorder à Saint-Pierre-et-Miquelon, comme zone économique exclusive, une ceinture de 12 milles marins supplémentaires à partir de sa mer territoriale. Le Canada avait soutenu que toute extension vers l'ouest au-delà de 12 milles marins amputerait la projection maritime vers le sud de la côte de Terre-Neuve, située tout près au nord. Le Tribunal considéra toutefois que "[T]oute extension vers le large des côtes françaises au-delà de la mer territoriale entraînerait inévitablement un certain empiétement sur la projection vers le large en direction du sud à partir de points situés sur la côte méridionale de Terre-Neuve et une certaine amputation de cette projection."[17] Ce qui l'amena à conclure: "Une extension limitée de l'enclave au-delà de la mer territoriale dans ce secteur occidental répondrait dans une certaine mesure à l'attente raisonnable par la France d'un titre au-delà de l'étroite bande de mer territoriale, quand bien même cette exten-sion provoquerait quelque empiétement sur certaines projections canadiennes vers le large."[18]

En réalité, le fait d'empiéter sur la projection maritime de la côte

16 *Décision*, par. 66.
17 *Décision*, par. 67.
18 *Décision*, par. 68.

sud de Terre-Neuve préoccupait davantage le Tribunal que ne le donnent à penser ces constatations. En effet, la ceinture de juridiction maritime qu'il a accordée à la France dans le secteur occidental ne génère pas une zone française de 24 milles. Placé devant deux possibilités — l'équidistance entre les côtes des Parties et la méthode consistant à tirer des arcs de cercle de 24 milles depuis les points de base de la mer territoriale française — le Tribunal a plutôt appliqué tour à tour, en partant du point terminal de la ligne de mi-canal entre Saint-Pierre-et-Miquelon et la côte de Terre-Neuve derrière les îles, la méthode susceptible de faire *le moins* obstacle à l'extension du littoral terre-neuvien. (Voir la Figure 1.)

Le juge national nommé par la France, Prosper Weil, a vivement critiqué cette façon de procéder, arguant que le Tribunal avait récusé l'équidistance lorsqu'elle pouvait bénéficier à la France mais l'avait acceptée lorsqu'elle limitait l'étendue de la zone française.[19] Même si l'analyse n'est pas tout à fait fausse, il est difficile d'imaginer comment on pourrait justifier une extension de la zone française au-delà de la ligne d'équidistance dans la partie du secteur occidental la plus proche du littoral terre-neuvien. Ce serait là une violation flagrante du principe du non-empiétement, qui aurait pour effet d'étendre la zone économique française pratiquement jusqu'à la limite de 12 milles de la mer territoriale du Canada.[20] Quoi qu'il en soit, le problème que l'équidistance posait au Tribunal tenait au "ballonnement" qu'elle entraîne dans les situations de stricte adjacence comme celle qui se présente à mesure qu'on avance vers le large à partir des îles françaises. Le recours à l'équidistance peut toutefois produire un résultat équitable lorsque les côtes se font face ou qu'elles se trouvent dans un rapport mixte d'opposition et d'adjacence, comme c'est le cas de la configuration à angle droit formée par la côte ouest des îles et la côte sud de Terre-Neuve dans la partie intérieure du secteur occidental. Par conséquent, toute critique de la ligne définie par le Tribunal dans cette partie du secteur occidental risque d'être davantage influencée par la perception individuelle du résultat global que par les avantages ou les inconvénients inhérents à l'utilisation de l'équidistance faite par le Tribunal dans cette zone particulière.

Certes, le Canada a plaidé contre tout recours à la méthode de l'équidistance dans la délimitation. Toutefois, il existe un précé-

---

[19] *Opinion dissidente de M. Prosper Weil,* par. 6.

[20] Malcolm D. Evans, *Relevant Circumstances and Maritime Delimitation.* pp. 154-55 (Oxford, Clarendon Press, 1989).

dent canadien où cette méthode a été utilisée dans une configuration semblable à la partie intérieure du secteur occidental (quoique beaucoup plus vaste). À l'intérieur du golfe du Maine, les côtes du Canada et des États-Unis forment aussi un angle droit. Dans cette région, la ligne établie par la Chambre de la Cour internationale de Justice est une ligne d'équidistance simplifiée.[21] De la même façon, à l'ouest de Saint-Pierre-et-Miquelon, l'équidistance appliquée dans les limites des côtes à angle droit de la partie intérieure du secteur en cause produit un résultat équitable. Ce n'est qu'au-delà de l'angle droit qu'apparaît l'explosion spatiale créée par l'équidistance lorsqu'une petite île fait saillie à proximité d'une côte continentale avec laquelle elle est alignée latéralement.

La Figure 2 illustre cet effet. Elle montre les propriétés géométriques d'une ligne d'équidistance appliquée à une petite île située à proximité d'une côte continentale. Comme l'a soutenu le Canada, une méthode qui permet de "créer autant avec si peu"[22] est de toute évidence inappropriée. Il est donc normal que le Tribunal ait abandonné l'équidistance à 24 milles marins des lignes de base servant à mesurer la mer territoriale française. C'est en effet à cet endroit que la position en saillie de Saint-Pierre-et-Miquelon provoque un ballonnement de la ligne d'équidistance, amputant la projection en mer de la côte terre-neuvienne de part et d'autre des îles.

Pour ce qui est du second secteur, au sud de Saint-Pierre-et-Miquelon, le Tribunal a conclu qu'aucun littoral canadien, opposé ou aligné latéralement, ne faisait obstacle à la projection des côtes des îles françaises. Il a donc rejeté l'argument du Canada selon lequel la zone française devait s'arrêter à la limite de 12 milles, précisant par ailleurs qu'il ne fallait "pas laisser une telle projection vers le large empiéter sur une projection frontale parallèle de segments adjacents du littoral sud de Terre-Neuve ou amputer leur projection."[23] C'est pourquoi il a limité la largeur du corridor à l'ouverture côtière de 10,5 milles marins de Saint-Pierre-et-Miquelon en direction du sud. Il en est résulté un long et étroit couloir qui, ajouté à la zone accordée aux îles dans le secteur occidental, crée une zone de juridiction maritime ayant l'appar-

---

[21] Affaire du *Golfe du Maine*, par. 216.

[22] *Contre-mémoire du Canada*, par. 406.

[23] *Décision*, par. 70.

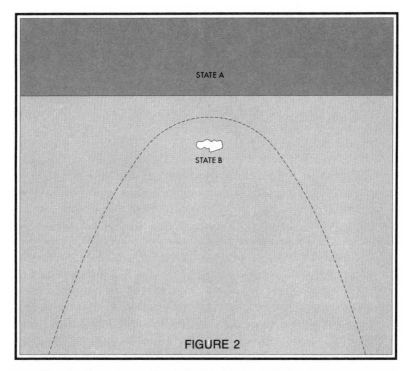

FIGURE 2

ence d'un "champignon" à l'allure déséquilibrée, pour reprendre l'expression utilisée par le juge Weil, dans son opinion dissidente.[24]

Le Canada avait fait valoir que les projections chevauchantes de ses littoraux plus longs de Terre-Neuve et de l'île du Cap-Breton (Nouvelle-Écosse) justifiaient d'amputer la projection vers le sud de Saint-Pierre-et-Miquelon. Le Tribunal a toutefois rejeté l'argument selon lequel tout l'espace maritime au sud des îles est compris à l'intérieur des projections convergentes des deux littoraux canadiens. Il a plutôt jugé que la côte de l'île du Cap-Breton donne au sud sur des espaces océaniques ouverts, ce qui confère au Canada une zone de juridiction maritime intégrale de 200 milles à partir de cette côte. Comme le Canada lui-même avait fait valoir que les côtes

[24] *Opinion dissidente de M. Prosper Weil*, par. 7. La raison de l'"allure déséquilibrée" du champignon est que, dans le secteur est, le Tribunal n'a pas accordé à la France l'équidistance ou 24 milles marins, selon la moindre de ces formules, comme il l'a fait dans le secteur ouest. Il a plutôt fermé la zone française avec la limite de 12 milles de la mer territoriale. Cette décision du Tribunal de ne pas donner à la France une zone économique à l'est des îles a pour conséquence que la "tête" et le "pied" du champignon présentent un déséquilibre.

ont tendance à se projeter frontalement dans la direction à laquelle elles font face, on peut comprendre que le Tribunal ait opté pour une solution n'attribuant à la côte de l'île du Cap-Breton qu'un rôle subordonné par rapport à celle de Terre-Neuve dans la phase initiale de la délimitation. (Dans la seconde phase, celle de la vérification de l'équité du résultat, la côte de l'île du Cap-Breton devait cependant jouer un rôle crucial, comme on le verra plus loin.)

On peut supposer que la France, de son côté, n'est guère satisfaite de la forme allongée de sa zone, qui reste bien en deçà de sa revendication et qui ne peut vraiment soutenir une pêche viable sous contrôle français. La France avait toutefois fait du titre des îles à une projection de 200 milles le leitmotiv de son argumentation. La solution du corridor n'est donc que la réponse logique du Tribunal à la thèse juridique française concernant l'égalité souveraine des États et à son corollaire, à savoir que toutes les côtes ont un titre égal, qu'elles appartiennent à des îles dépendantes ou à des pays continentaux indépendants. Le Tribunal aurait-il opté pour une solution plus pratique, par exemple une enclave de plus de 24 milles marins autour des îles, si la France n'avait pas tant insisté sur le principe des 200 milles? Bien sûr, la France a pu vouloir par là établir le principe de la distance, ayant à l'esprit les intérêts de ses nombreuses possessions insulaires dans le monde plutôt que ceux de Saint-Pierre-et-Miquelon. D'autre part, le Tribunal savait sans doute qu'il existe dans la pratique française des précédents pour le couloir de 200 milles. Dans la délimitation intervenue entre la Dominique et la France (en ce qui concerne la Martinique et la Guadeloupe), un tel couloir a été préféré à l'équidistance. La frontière maritime entre la France et Monaco est elle aussi formée d'un couloir de 200 milles, dont la largeur est égale à celle de l'enclave territoriale monégasque.[25] Ainsi donc, quand on l'examine à la lumière des arguments et de la pratique de la France, la solution du couloir semble moins bizarre que ne le laisse supposer une analyse superficielle.

---

25 Le Canada a évoqué devant le Tribunal ces exemples de la méthode du corridor, ainsi que d'autres, pour expliquer son concept de "portée relative," c'est-à-dire son argument selon lequel toutes les côtes n'ont pas un titre égal, parce que leur projection maritime devrait être proportionnelle à leur longueur. Le Tribunal rejeta l'argument, mais fit sienne la méthode du corridor dans un autre contexte. *Procédure orale*, le 14 août 1991, exposé du professeur Derek Bowett, c.r., p. 1139 et suivantes.

LA THÉORIE JURIDIQUE QUI SOUS-TEND LA LIGNE

Dans le second secteur, ou secteur méridional, la délimitation repose sur la théorie selon laquelle les côtes se projettent frontalement, dans la direction à laquelle elles font face.[26] Le Tribunal a jugé qu'il faut laisser à un État les espaces qui constituent le prolongement naturel ou l'extension en mer de ses côtes, de façon à éviter tout effet indu d'amputation ou d'empiétement sur les espaces situés juste devant le littoral de cet État. La jurisprudence considère comme synonymes l'amputation et l'empiétement. Ces deux concepts ont été développés, à partir des affaires de la *Mer du Nord* en 1969, dans le contexte d'une critique de la méthode de l'équidistance.[27] Dans les affaires de 1969, aussi bien les écrits de l'Allemagne que l'arrêt de la Cour ont montré l'amputation que produit une ligne d'équidistance latérale en déviant devant la côte d'un État adjacent. Cela tient au fait que l'équidistance amplifie l'effet exercé par des particularités non essentielles (caps et autres saillants), comme Saint-Pierre-et-Miquelon. Des concepts d'amputation et de non-empiétement à la théorie de la projection frontale — qui en est d'ailleurs la conséquence logique — il n'y a qu'un pas, qu'il est aisé de franchir. Dans l'affaire *Canada/France*, le Tribunal a donc appliqué la théorie, non pas comme une critique de l'équidistance, mais comme un fondement du titre et un facteur déterminant dans le choix de la méthode appropriée. C'est peut-être la première fois que la théorie est aussi clairement énoncée, mais il reste que le concept de la projection frontale est implicite dans les délimitations effectuées dans les affaires *Libye/Malte* et *Guinée/Guinée-Bissau*.[28]

Le juge Weil observe que, en s'appuyant sur la théorie de la

---

[26] *Décision*, par. 73.

[27] Affaires du *Plateau continental de la Mer du Nord (République fédérale d'Allemagne/Danemark; République fédérale d'Allemagne/Pays-Bas)*, Recueil C.I.J. 1969, p. 3 (ci-après: affaires de la *Mer du Nord*, avec mention du numéro du paragraphe pertinent).

[28] Dans l'affaire *Libye/Malte*, l'*Opinion conjointe de MM. Ruda, Bedjaoui et Jiménez de Aréchaga*, en particulier dans son paragraphe 6, souligne l'importance de la projection frontale dans cette délimitation: Affaire du *Plateau continental (Jamahiriya arabe libyenne/Malte)*, C.I.J. *Recueil 1985*, p. 13 (ci-après: l'affaire *Libye/Malte*, avec mention du numéro du paragraphe pertinent). Dans l'affaire *Guinée/Guinée Bissau*, le tribunal a représenté la façade maritime par une ligne droite, la zone maritime se projetant perpendiculairement à cette façade. *Tribunal arbitral pour la délimitation de la frontière maritime Guinée/Guinée Bissau*, sentence du 14 février 1985, I.L.M., vol. XXV, 1986.

projection frontale, le Canada semblait contredire la thèse de la projection radiale qu'il avait défendue dans l'affaire du *Golfe du Maine*.[29] Selon cette thèse, une côte irradie dans toutes les directions sur toute sa largeur, créant une "ceinture" de juridiction maritime constituée d'arcs de cercle de 200 milles tirés à partir des lignes de base de la mer territoriale. Le concept de la projection radiale est l'un des fondements théoriques de l'équidistance, puisqu'une ligne tracée selon ce concept permet, en cas de projections égales qui se chevauchent, de faire en sorte que les étendues les plus proches du littoral d'une Partie se retrouvent dans la zone maritime de cette Partie.

Pour expliquer l'apparente contradiction entre la position qu'il avait soutenue dans l'affaire du *Golfe du Maine* et celle qu'il mettait de l'avant dans l'espèce considérée, le Canada a invoqué trois arguments. D'abord, il a fait valoir que la Chambre avait rejeté la projection radiale au profit de la théorie de la projection perpendiculaire proposée par les États-Unis. Le Canada s'était donc aligné sur le droit en vigueur. Deuxièmement, il a soutenu qu'il fallait distinguer entre la délimitation et l'opération qui consiste à tracer des arcs de cercle pour déterminer la limite extérieure de la zone de 200 milles. Autrement dit, la méthode radiale dont on se sert pour établir les limites extérieures n'a rien à voir avec la délimitation entre États, car les règles applicables à chaque cas "diffèrent radicalement":[30] les premières sont d'application mécanique et automatique, tandis que les secondes sont flexibles et doivent s'appliquer en tenant compte de toutes les circonstances pertinentes de manière à produire un résultat équitable. À la lumière de ces critères fondamentaux de la délimitation, le Canada a affirmé que, pour aboutir à une solution équitable, le Tribunal devait respecter le principe du non-empiétement, et donc ne pas permettre à la zone française d'amputer la projection en mer des côtes canadiennes, plus longues. Troisièmement, et c'était là son argument le plus important, le Canada avait rejeté la projection radiale au profit de la projection frontale dont s'était servi son adversaire dans l'affaire du *Golfe du Maine*, parce que les circonstances géographiques de l'espèce considérée commandaient une approche différente.

Dans l'argumentation canadienne relative à la géographie, la disparité des longueurs côtières des Parties a été de loin la circons-

29 *Opinion dissidente de M. Prosper Weil*, par. 10.

30 *Contre-mémoire du Canada*, par. 315.

tance pertinente la plus importante. Le Tribunal a d'ailleurs fait de la longueur des côtes le pivot de sa décision. La place très grande qu'il a attribuée à ce facteur lui vaudra sans doute les reproches des tenants de l'équidistance, pour qui la configuration — et la configuration pratiquement seule — doit être le facteur déterminant de la délimitation. La décision est néanmoins tout à fait dans la ligne des affaires, en nombre toujours croissant, où la longueur des côtes et la configuration se voient accorder une importance égale pour l'atteinte d'un résultat équitable. Dans l'affaire du *Golfe du Maine*, la longueur des côtes a été un facteur fondamental. La Chambre a non seulement ajusté sa ligne pour prendre en compte la plus grande longueur du littoral américain, mais elle a aussi inclus la baie de Fundy dans son calcul du littoral canadien, ce qui a été capital pour l'attribution d'une partie des pêcheries du banc de Georges au Canada.[31] Dans l'affaire *Libye/Malte* également, la Cour a ramené la ligne médiane vers Malte afin de tenir compte de la disparité des longueurs côtières des Parties. Elle a jugé que "la méthode d'équidistance non corrigée peut laisser en dehors du calcul d'appréciables longueurs de rivage et attribuer à d'autres une influence exagérée en raison simplement de la physionomie des relations entre les côtes."[32] Mais, pour en revenir à l'affaire qui nous occupe, le poids accordé à la longueur des côtes et, partant, à l'amputation et à l'empiétement, soulèvera moins la controverse que l'application faite par le Tribunal, pour la première fois depuis l'affaire *Tunisie/Libye*,[33] d'un test de proportionnalité chiffré pour vérifier l'équité du résultat.

LE TEST DE PROPORTIONNALITÉ

Non content de faire de la disparité entre les côtes des Parties une circonstance pertinente, le Tribunal a en outre, comme l'y avait invité le Canada, appliqué un test de proportionnalité et comparé

---

[31] Affaire du *Golfe du Maine*, par. 221-22. Voir L. H. Legault et D. M. McRae, "The Gulf of Maine Case," (1984) XXII *Annuaire canadien de droit international* 267, p. 286.

[32] Affaire *Libye/Malte*, par. 56. Pour l'ajustement de la ligne médiane et la prise en considération de la disparité des longueurs de côte de la Libye et de Malte, voir les paragraphes 68 et suivants.

[33] Affaire du *Plateau continental (Tunisie/Jamahiriya arabe libyenne), C.I.J. Recueil 1982*, p. 18 (ci-après affaire *Tunisie/Libye*, avec mention du numéro du paragraphe pertinent), par. 131.

les ratios des longueurs côtières et des superficies maritimes pour vérifier l'équité du résultat. Bien entendu, le Canada ne s'était pas privé, dans ses écritures et plaidoiries, de souligner l'énorme disparité présentée par les littoraux des Parties dans la vaste configuration concave ou semi-circulaire formée par la côte sud de Terre-Neuve et la côte de l'île du Cap-Breton faisant face à l'Atlantique, que le Canada a appelée les approches du golfe et la France, l'antichambre du golfe.[34] Toutefois, le Tribunal ayant décidé, conformément à la théorie de la projection frontale, que les projections en mer des côtes de Saint-Pierre-et-Miquelon et de l'île du Cap-Breton ne se chevauchaient pas, on aurait pensé qu'il ne tiendrait plus compte de cette dernière dans l'opération de délimitation. En fait, le Tribunal a inclus la côte de l'île dans son calcul des côtes pertinentes et dans la définition de la zone à considérer aux fins du test de proportionnalité.

Le Tribunal s'est sans doute estimé justifié d'agir ainsi pour deux raisons. D'abord, tant le Canada que la France avaient soutenu que la côte de l'île du Cap-Breton était pertinente, bien que pour des raisons différentes.[35] Dès lors, on ne pouvait guère lui reprocher d'avoir pris en considération un facteur dont les Parties elles-mêmes avaient fait état. Deuxièmement, comme il a déjà été précisé, le Tribunal semble avoir pris en compte la côte de l'île non pas comme facteur indépendant de délimitation, mais plutôt comme caractéristique géographique objective pour mesurer les côtes des Parties aux fins du test de proportionnalité.

Prenant appui sur les deux extrémités des approches du golfe qu'avaient identifiées les Parties — le cap Race à Terre-Neuve et le cap Canso en Nouvelle-Écosse — le Tribunal s'est rangé à la thèse canadienne de l'énorme disparité entre les littoraux en cause. La France, pour sa part, prétendait que seuls étaient pertinents de courts segments des côtes canadiennes, s'étendant de part et d'autre des points qu'elle avait pris comme bases pour sa méthode

---

[34] Le Canada appelle cette zone les approches du golfe parce qu'elle marque une zone de transition entre les eaux libres de l'Atlantique et les eaux du golfe du Saint-Laurent proprement dites. *Contre-mémoire du Canada*, par. 49.

[35] Le Canada affirmait que la projection maritime de la côte de l'île du Cap-Breton recouvrait en partie les projections de Terre-Neuve et de Saint-Pierre-et-Miquelon. La France s'est servie de points de base sur la côte de l'île du Cap-Breton pour construire sa ligne d'équidistance, et elle a utilisé des segments de cette côte pour définir les côtes pertinentes aux fins de la délimitation. *Contre-mémoire du Canada*, par. 35.

de l'équidistance.[36] Bien qu'ayant rejeté cet argument, le Tribunal a toutefois, comme le demandait la France, exclu des côtes à prendre en considération le littoral de Terre-Neuve situé derrière les îles françaises, celui-ci ayant "déjà servi" en 1972 pour l'établissement de la ligne de mi-canal entre les îles et la masse terrestre canadienne.[37] Le Canada avait fait valoir que ce littoral devait intervenir pour le tracé de la frontière au large des îles puisque, dans l'*Arbitrage franco-britannique*, le tribunal avait permis à la côte française de "sauter" en quelque sorte pardessus les îles Anglo-Normandes. Par ailleurs, le Tribunal a inclus dans son calcul du littorial les 56 milles marins de la ligne de fermeture du détroit de Cabot, estimant que c'était là une façon commode de tenir compte du littoral canadien à l'intérieur du golfe faisant face à Saint-Pierre-et-Miquelon.[38] Pour ce qui est des côtes des îles françaises, le Tribunal a accepté le point de vue du Canada quant à leur longueur, mesurant toutefois leur direction générale au moyen de deux segments plutôt que par une ligne unique. Mais comme le Canada lui-même avait ouvert la voie à cette approche dans son *contre-mémoire*,[39] on peut dire que, grosso modo, la vision canadienne de la géographie pertinente l'a emporté sur celle de la France. Ainsi, le Tribunal en est arrivé à un rapport côtier de 15,3:1 en faveur du Canada. Ce rapport est certes inférieur à celui de 21:1 mis de l'avant par le Canada, mais il en est beaucoup plus proche que du rapport de 6,5:1 proposé par la France.

Ayant établi le ratio des longueurs côtières, il ne restait plus au

[36] Dans l'argumentation de la France, les côtes du Canada comprises dans les approches du golfe étaient littéralement gommées, ce qui a permis au Canada de saper la crédibilité de la thèse géographique de la France en présentant des cartes et des graphiques sur un système informatisé de données géographiques (appelé système SIG) installé dans la salle d'audience. Selon la France, les côtes pertinentes du Canada n'étaient guère plus que de courts segments autour de points de base pris sur la côte sud de Terre-Neuve, l'île du Cap-Breton et l'île de Sable et ayant servi à construire la ligne d'équidistance française. En superposant les côtes réelles des approches du golfe aux fragments côtiers jugés pertinents par la France, les plaideurs canadiens ont cherché à montrer que la France "refaisait la géographie," au sens le plus radical, pour appuyer ses prétentions.

[37] *Décision*, par. 30.

[38] Le Tribunal jugea que cette ligne de fermeture en travers du détroit de Cabot représentait "des lignes de côte à l'intérieur du golfe qui sont en opposition directe avec Saint-Pierre-et-Miquelon et qui se trouvent à une distance de moins de 400 milles marins." *Décision*, par. 29.

[39] *Contre-mémoire du Canada*, fig. 4.

Tribunal qu'à déterminer les limites extérieures de la zone à considérer pour la comparaison des superficies maritimes conférées au Canada et à la France par l'opération de délimitation. Pour ce faire, il a tracé une ligne du cap Canso au point d'intersection des limites de 200 milles de l'île du Cap-Breton et de Saint-Pierre-et-Miquelon, puis de la limite de 200 milles des îles françaises au point d'intersection avec la limite de 200 milles de Terre-Neuve à un point droit au sud du cap Race. (Voir la Figure 3.) Il en est résulté une zone de 63 051 milles marins carrés (mesurée jusqu'aux lignes de direction générale des côtes) dans laquelle la comparaison des espaces maritimes attribués aux Parties a fait apparaître un rapport de 16,4:1, ce qui est fort acceptable compte tenu du ratio de 15,3:1 déterminé par le Tribunal pour les longueurs côtières.

Dans son opinion dissidente, le juge nommé par la France déplore que le Tribunal ait recouru au test de proportionnalité "sous sa forme chiffrée."[40] Par cette expression, il faut entendre l'application du critère de proportionnalité pour comparer *a posteriori* les ratios des longueurs côtières et des superficies maritimes et s'assurer ainsi que le résultat n'est pas disproportionné. En somme, ce qu'on reproche à cette utilisation de la proportionnalité comme test d'équité, c'est son caractère arbitraire: quelles côtes faut-il inclure et quelle doit être l'étendue maritime pertinente? Le Tribunal est resté muet sur ce point, même s'il avait sans doute prévu les critiques. Pour sa part, le Canada a formulé dans son *Contre-mémoire* quelques principes directeurs qui pourront être utiles à l'avenir pour déterminer le cadre d'application de la proportionnalité:

(a) l'étendue visée ne doit pas être définie arbitrairement, mais plutôt en fonction des caractéristiques prédominantes de la géographie côtière ou d'autres facteurs objectifs;
(b) l'étendue à laquelle s'applique le test doit refléter une appréciation raisonnable de l'extension maritime des côtes des Parties;
(c) il n'est pas nécessaire que l'étendue visée englobe la totalité des zones revendiquées par les Parties.[41]

Le Tribunal a trouvé une solution particulièrement ingénieuse au problème que pose la détermination des limites extérieures sur la base de critères rationnels. En utilisant à cette fin des arcs de cercle de 200 milles qui se recoupent, il est peut-être venu le plus près de formuler une méthode objective, qui permette d'établir les

---

[40] *Opinion dissidente de M. Prosper Weil,* par. 23.

[41] *Contre-mémoire du Canada,* par. 514.

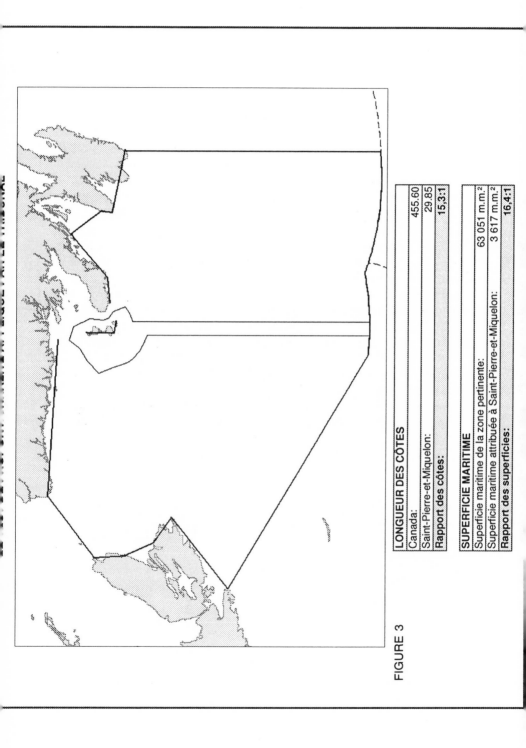

LONGUEUR DES CÔTES
Canada: 455.60
Saint-Pierre-et-Miquelon: 29.85
Rapport des côtes: 15,3:1

SUPERFICIE MARITIME
Superficie maritime de la zone pertinente: 63 051 m.m.²
Superficie maritime attribuée à Saint-Pierre-et-Miquelon: 3 617 m.m.²
Rapport des superficies: 16,4:1

FIGURE 3

limites extérieures de la zone pertinente dans les régions maritimes où il n'y a pas de caractéristiques naturelles pouvant servir de cadre de référence.

LES RÉPERCUSSIONS DU TRACÉ SUR LES RESSOURCES

Hydrocarbures

Comme on l'a déjà vu c'est un conflit concernant le plateau continental, réputé avoir un important potentiel en hydrocarbures, qui a donné naissance au différend de juridiction sur les espaces maritimes au large de Terre-Neuve et de Saint-Pierre-et-Miquelon. Le gouvernement canadien avait délivré des permis de recherche d'hydrocarbures à Gulf Resources Inc. et à Mobil Oil Canada, Ltd. en 1967, puis à Texaco Canada Resources Ltd. en 1971. Pétropar et Elf-Aquitaine obtinrent de la France, en 1966 et 1986 respectivement, des permis couvrant une partie du même secteur. Les fonds marins visés par les permis s'étendaient pour l'essentiel à quelque 50 milles marins au sud de Saint-Pierre-et-Miquelon. Même si plusieurs études géophysiques ont fait état de la présence possible d'hydrocarbures, il n'y a encore eu aucune découverte puisqu'un moratoire sur les activités de forage a été décrété en 1967.

Le Canada n'a pas beaucoup insisté, dans ses écritures et plaidoiries, sur le potentiel en hydrocarbures de la zone en litige, ni d'ailleurs sur l'intérêt qu'il y porte. La France, de son côté, ne s'est guère étendue sur ce point dans ses écrits. Toutefois, dans les derniers jours de la procédure orale, elle devait manifester un regain d'intérêt pour la question. Elle cherchait ainsi, en apparence, à convaincre le Tribunal de lui allouer des étendues situées bien au sud des îles françaises, où il est possible que se trouvent des hydrocarbures. Mais elle visait certainement aussi un autre objectif, puisque c'est dans cette même partie de la zone contestée que se rassemblent les importants stocks de morue en hiver, au moment du frai, quand il est le plus facile de capturer le poisson.

Comme la ligne établie par le Tribunal traverse le secteur visé par les permis, certains des permis canadiens et français devront être annulés. Si la superficie ainsi compromise du côté canadien est minime, il n'en va pas de même des détenteurs de permis français qui ont perdu une bonne part du territoire sur lequel ils prétendaient avoir des droits. En fait, les secteurs qui demeurent sous permis français — d'une largeur d'au plus 10,5 milles marins — ne pourront probablement être viables que dans le cadre de coentreprises avec les détenteurs de permis voisins.

Le Tribunal a noté dans sa décision que les Parties avaient fait connaître leur intérêt pour l'exploitation éventuelle d'hydrocarbures dans les zones où leurs revendications se chevauchaient et que les deux gouvernements avaient délivré des permis. Il a aussi mentionné qu'aucun forage n'avait été entrepris. Écartant ces considérations sans plus ample analyse, il a conclu que "[d]ans les circonstances actuelles, le Tribunal n'a[vait] aucune raison de considérer que les éventuelles ressources minérales [avaient] une incidence sur la délimitation."[42] On peut en inférer que si des activités de forage avaient eu lieu et que des découvertes importantes avaient été faites, ces considérations auraient pu jouer un rôle en tant que circonstances pertinentes aux fins de la délimitation. Cette hypothèse est corroborée par les affaires *Mer du Nord*, *Tunisie/Libye* et *Libye/Malte*, dans lesquelles la Cour internationale de Justice avait conclu que la présence dans la région à délimiter de puits de pétrole ou de ressources naturelles, "pour autant que cela soit connu ou facile à déterminer," pourrait effectivement constituer une circonstance pertinente à prendre en compte.[43]

Pêches

Les ressources halieutiques étaient, en fait, au coeur du différend. C'est en effet la juridiction à long terme sur la morue, le pétoncle et les autres stocks situés dans le secteur de gestion des pêches appelé "3Ps"[44] qui a provoqué le conflit. Et c'est le souci d'assurer la durabilité des ressources halieutiques très convoitées de ce secteur qui a incité le gouvernement du Canada à obtenir l'accord de la France pour le renvoi du différend à l'arbitrage. La Figure 4 montre la répartition des ressources halieutiques d'importance commerciale dans le secteur 3Ps.

Le Canada et la France ont tous deux beaucoup insisté, dans leurs écritures et plaidoiries, sur la dépendance économique de leurs populations respectives à l'égard des ressources halieutiques

---

42 *Décision*, par. 89.

43 Affaires de la *Mer du Nord*, par. 101 (D) (2); affaire *Tunisie/Libye*, par. 107; affaire *Libye/Malte*, par. 50.

44 En 1953, les eaux de l'Atlantique Nord-Ouest ont été partagées par la Commission internationale pour les pêcheries de l'Atlantique Nord-Ouest (CIPAN) en une série de zones désignées selon un code alphanumérique. Les eaux situées au large de la côte sud de Terre-Neuve se trouvent dans la subdivision 3Ps.

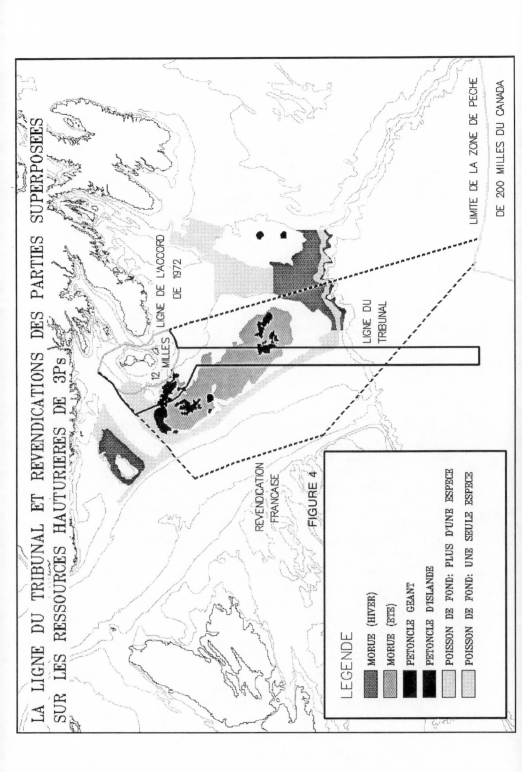

LA LIGNE DU TRIBUNAL ET REVENDICATIONS DES PARTIES SUPERPOSEES
SUR LES RESSOURCES HAUTURIERES DE 3Ps

LIGNE DE L'ACCORD DE 1972

12 MILLES

LIGNE DU TRIBUNAL

LIMITE DE LA ZONE DE PECHE DE 200 MILLES DU CANADA

REVENDICATION FRANCAISE

FIGURE 4

LEGENDE

MORUE (HIVER)

MORUE (ETE)

PETONCLE GEANT

PETONCLE D'ISLANDE

POISSON DE FOND: PLUS D'UNE ESPECE

POISSON DE FOND: UNE SEULE ESPECE

de la zone contestée, et cela bien que les tribunaux répugnent en général à accorder, du moins directement, un poids significatif aux considérations économiques dans les affaires de délimitation maritime.[45] On estime en effet qu'il ne serait pas équitable d'établir une frontière permanente en fonction de circonstances économiques souvent passagères. Les facteurs géographiques, en revanche, sont de nature moins éphémère, et ils peuvent donc commander une délimitation devant aboutir à une frontière permanente.

Il a déjà été reconnu toutefois que les considérations économiques offraient un moyen de vérifier l'équité d'une délimitation établie sur la base de facteurs autres qu'économiques. La Chambre de la Cour internationale de Justice tenait les propos suivants dans l'affaire du *Golfe du Maine:*

[les] données fournies par la géographie humaine et économique ... ne peuvent pas entrer en considération en tant que critères à appliquer à l'opération de délimitation elle-même, mais ... on peut [s'en] servir ... pour juger du caractère équitable de la délimitation établie à l'origine sur la base de critères empruntés à la géographie physique et politique.[46]

La Chambre a formulé le critère suivant pour savoir si les activités de pêche d'une Partie peuvent entrer en ligne de compte dans une délimitation:

Il est donc évident ... que l'ampleur respective de ces activités humaines liées à la pêche . . . ne saurait entrer en considération en tant que circonstance pertinente ou ... en tant que critère équitable à appliquer à la détermination de la ligne de délimitation. Le scrupule que la Chambre estime justifié d'avoir est celui de s'assurer que le résultat global, bien qu'issu de l'application de critères équitables et de l'utilisation de méthodes appropriées destinées à les traduire concrètement, ne se révèle pas d'une manière inattendue comme radicalement inéquitable, c'est-à-dire comme susceptible *d'entraîner des répercussions catastrophiques pour la subsistance et le développement économique des populations des pays intéressés.*[47] (italique ajouté)

Dans l'affaire *Canada/France,* le Canada a soutenu que les considérations économiques n'étaient pas de nature temporaire,

45 En 1982, par exemple, la Cour internationale de Justice estima, dans son arrêt concernant l'affaire *Tunisie/Libye,* au par. 107, que les "considérations économiques ne sauraient être retenues pour la délimitation des zones de plateau continental relevant de chaque Partie." Plusieurs décisions subséquentes ont confirmé que les considérations économiques ne peuvent influer de façon indue sur une délimitation.

46 Affaire du *Golfe du Maine,* par. 232.

47 *Ibid.,* par. 237.

puisqu'elles étaient le résultat direct des circonstances géographiques de la région. Historiquement, c'est la pêche qui est à l'origine du peuplement de la région, et c'est grâce à la pêche que la région a subsisté pendant des siècles. La terre ingrate de la côte méridionale de Terre-Neuve n'offre qu'un faible potentiel commercial pour ce qui est de l'agriculture, de l'exploitation forestière ou de l'extraction minière. Les habitants de cette côte sont par conséquent devenus extrêmement dépendants des ressources halieutiques de la zone contestée, et une délimitation qui mettrait en péril l'accès à ces ressources pourrait avoir des "répercussions catastrophiques" pour la plupart des collectivités de la côte sud. De l'avis du Canada, le volet économique de son argumentation corroborait ses prétentions, en venant appuyer et renforcer la solution dictée par la géographie.[48]

La France a elle aussi invoqué la dépendance économique des îles pour faire valoir sa thèse, revendiquant à ce titre "un minimum" de ressources économiques permettant le maintien de la collectivité de Saint-Pierre-et-Miquelon. Elle affirmait que, pour assurer l'avenir de la pêche française, il lui fallait obtenir une vaste zone maritime. Le Canada rejeta cet argument, faisant observer qu'il avait déjà accepté de pourvoir aux intérêts de pêche de la France dans l'Accord de pêche de 1972, indépendamment de la délimitation.

Le Tribunal, adoptant l'orientation générale de la jurisprudence, refusa d'attribuer quelque importance que ce soit aux considérations économiques dans l'établissement de la ligne de délimitation: "[L]a dépendance économique et les besoins n'ont pas été pris en considération dans le processus de délimitation."[49] Il n'a donc manifestement accordé aucun poids aux arguments des deux Parties, pour qui, dans ce cas particulier, les considérations économiques devaient entrer en ligne de compte parce que la dépendance à l'égard de la pêche était une caractéristique permanente de la région et ne pouvait par conséquent être écartée comme facteur passager. Il n'a pas davantage prêté attention à la pratique des États, dont le Canada a donné plusieurs exemples dans ses écritures et plaidoiries, et qui montre que les gouvernements ont déjà tenu

48 On se rappellera que, selon le tribunal saisi de l'*Arbitrage franco-britannique*, des considérations non géographiques "peuvent étayer et renforcer les conclusions déjà déduites des éléments géographiques, politiques et juridiques de la région . . . mais elles ne sauraient les annuler"; par. 188.

49 *Décision*, par. 83.

compte de considérations économiques dans la conclusion d'accords de délimitation.[50] En optant pour le courant traditionnel, le Tribunal montrait son hésitation à embrasser la nouvelle tendance selon laquelle les intérêts économiques devraient jouer un rôle dans la délimitation des frontières maritimes. Le professeur Derek Bowett, une autorité en la matière, mentionne que la Convention des Nations Unies de 1982 sur le droit de la mer[51] fait souvent référence aux intérêts économiques des États. Il s'exprime en ces termes:

(TRADUCTION) La proposition selon laquelle on ne saurait procéder à une délimitation sans tenir compte des intérêts économiques des États concernés repose donc sur un fondement juridique raisonnable. On pourrait même dire qu'une délimitation ne devrait pas être dissociée de l'intérêt que présente pour la communauté mondiale le bien-être économique des États qui connaissent le sous-développement économique ou qui sont défavorisés sur le plan de l'accès aux ressources.[52]

Dans son opinion dissidente, le juge Weil dit regretter que le Tribunal n'ait pas saisi l'occasion de "faire progresser l'épineux problème du caractère juridiquement pertinent, ou non, des facteurs économiques . . ."[53] Le juge Weil reconnaît que le tracé d'une délimitation maritime ne peut être dicté par le souci de partager les ressources, étant donné que leur importance est très variable. Toutefois, selon lui:

Il n'en demeure pas moins que l'on ne saurait, sous peine de verser dans l'artifice et la fiction, éliminer complètement les considérations économiques et socio-économiques de la balance des équités; cela serait d'autant plus paradoxal que l'exploration et l'exploitation des ressources sont à la

50 Les exemples cités sont l'accord Islande-Norvège concernant Jan Mayen (1980), l'accord Australie-Papouasie-Nouvelle-Guinée (1978) et l'accord URSS-Suède (1988).

51 Montego Bay, le 10 décembre 1982.

52 D. W. Bowett, "The Economic Factor in Maritime Delimitation Cases," 2 *International Law at the Time of Codification: Essays in Honour of Roberto Ago* pp. 45, 61-62 (Milan, 1987), cité dans L. D. M. Nelson, "The Roles of Equity in the Delimitation of Maritime Boundaries," (1990) 84 *American Journal of International Law* 837, p. 856. Voir aussi Malcolm D. Evans, "Maritime Delimitation and Expanding Categories of Relevant Circumstances," 40 I.C.L.Q., pp. 1-33; S. P. Sharma, "The Relevance of Economic Factors to the Law of Maritime Delimitation between Neighboring States," dans E. D. Brown et R. R. Churchill, éditeurs, *The UN Convention on the Law of the Sea: Impact and Implementation*, Travaux, Institut du droit de la mer, 19ᵉ Conférence annuelle, Hawaï, Institut du droit de la mer, 1987, pp. 248-65.

53 *Opinion dissidente de M. Prosper Weil*, par. 33.

racine des concepts de plateau continental, de zone de pêche et de zone
économique exclusive.[54]

Le juge Weil croit que les considérations économiques ont directement influé sur l'issue de certaines affaires de délimitation — "sans
que cela ait été dit"[55] — et il se réfère en particulier aux affaires de
la *Mer du Nord* et du *Golfe du Maine*. Il admet que la prise en
considération de facteurs économiques dans la balance des équités
risque de "rapprocher dangereusement la décision judiciaire de la
conciliation," mais, pour lui, c'est là "le prix à payer pour l'abandon de l'équité géographique concrétisée par la méthode simple et
neutre de l'équidistance au profit d'une équité largement
entendue."[56]

Le Tribunal d'arbitrage et d'autres tribunaux avant lui affirment
tous que les facteurs économiques sont sans effet sur l'opération de
détermination d'une frontière, mais les États continuent, dans leurs
écritures et leurs plaidoiries, d'invoquer à l'envi ces facteurs. Le
Canada et la France n'ont pas fait exception à cette pratique. Les
nombreuses données économiques et scientifiques déposées à
l'appui de l'argumentation du Canada donnent même à penser
que, de l'avis du Canada, ces facteurs pourraient jouer dans la
délimitation un rôle beaucoup plus grand que celui que leur
attribue la jurisprudence.

Il est vrai que le Tribunal n'a pas refusé d'emblée de tenir compte
des facteurs économiques. Il a déclaré qu'il ne saurait "ignorer les
arguments et les informations fournis par l'une et l'autre Partie au
sujet de l'incidence des droits et des pratiques de pêche sur le bien-
être économique des populations les plus touchées par la délimitation,"[57] et il estimait avoir "l'obligation de s'assurer que la solution à
laquelle il a abouti [sur la base des facteurs géographiques] n'est pas
radicalement inéquitable."[58] Néanmoins, selon les propos du Tribunal, "la solution que le Tribunal a adoptée en se fondant sur les
faits géographiques, sur des critères équitables et sur les principes du
droit n'aura assurément pas de répercussions catastrophiques pour
l'une ou l'autre Partie."[59]

[54] *Ibid.*, par. 34.

[55] *Ibid.*

[56] *Ibid.*, par. 36. Le juge Weil mentionne que l'on devrait aussi tenir compte des
considérations de sécurité, de navigation et d'environnement. Voir *infra*.

[57] *Décision*, par. 84.

[58] *Décision*, par. 84.

[59] *Décision*, par. 87.

Dans la pratique, la décision du Tribunal n'aura probablement pas d'incidences notables sur les activités de pêche du Canada, puisque la zone accordée à la France contient peu de ressources présentant de l'intérêt pour les pêcheurs canadiens. Plusieurs espèces sont pêchées par les Canadiens dans le secteur 3Ps, mais la plus importante pour les pêcheurs de Terre-Neuve est la morue. La plus grande partie des captures de morue sont le fait de pêcheurs opérant près de la côte dans des bateaux de petites dimensions, lorsque les stocks ont migré vers les eaux côtières après avoir passé l'hiver dans les profondeurs du large. Les eaux que revendiquait la France englobaient une bonne partie de la région que, semble-t-il, la morue traverse au cours de sa migration vers le littoral. La France aurait pu ainsi pratiquer une pêche d'interception à partir de gros chalutiers hauturiers, avec ce résultat qu'il y aurait eu moins de poissons à capturer dans les eaux côtières de Terre-Neuve. La menace qui pesait sur les pêcheurs côtiers était considérable, puisque la revendication française visait plus de la moitié de la biomasse (poids total) de la morue pour le secteur 3Ps. Les espaces maritimes adjugés à la France renferment moins de 9 p. 100 de la biomasse totale de la morue, ce qui permet au Canada de gérer désormais comme il l'entend le stock de morue du secteur 3Ps.[60] Le Canada conserve également le contrôle des autres stocks de poisson de fond du secteur 3Ps, à savoir le sébaste et la plie du Canada (sole), deux espèces qui, avec la morue, représentent une valeur annuelle totale d'environ 6,4 millions$.[61]

La côte méridionale de Terre-Neuve, qui compte quelque 80 000 habitants, est la région qui, dans les provinces de l'Atlantique, dépend le plus de la pêche. Environ 8 000 personnes, soit à peu près la moitié de la population active, travaillent dans l'industrie de la pêche. (Ce chiffre ne tient pas compte des pêcheurs et des travailleurs d'usine qui sont en chômage.) La plupart des collectivités sont des petits ports de pêche qui reposent sur un seul secteur; sans la pêche, une poignée seulement d'entre elles pourraient survivre.[62]

[60] La valeur annuelle moyenne des prises de morue des pêcheurs canadiens dans la zone revendiquée par la France était d'environ 1,7 million $ (dollars de 1990); pour la zone attribuée à la France, la valeur annuelle moyenne est d'environ 145 000 $ (dollars de 1990).

[61] Le Canada conserve le contrôle de 97 p. 100 de la biomasse du sébaste et de 90 p. 100 de la biomasse de la plie du Canada.

[62] *Mémoire du Canada*, par. 151.

La frontière établie par le Tribunal laisse au Canada le contrôle sur environ 90 p. 100 de la biomasse du pétoncle géant, une ressource de grande valeur qui présente un intérêt particulier pour les pêcheurs de la Nouvelle-Écosse. En 1988, la valeur totale des pétoncles géants pris dans le secteur 3Ps a dépassé 8millions$ (dollars de 1990). En 1987, cette valeur était d'environ 800 000 $, ce qui correspond davantage à la norme.

La France a succombé dans sa prétention à de précieux bancs de pêche que fréquentaient de façon irrégulière les bateaux français depuis des siècles. Au milieu de la décennie 1980, les prises françaises de la morue dans la zone contestée étaient évaluées à 10 millions $ par année, mais c'est seulement depuis 1989 que, à la suite de pressions politiques, les bateaux de Saint-Pierre-et-Miquelon n'ont plus l'obligation de partager ces prises avec les navires de pêche lointaine immatriculés en France métropolitaine. L'effet possible de la nouvelle délimitation sur la pêche française ressort nettement de la comparaison suivante: au cours des années 1980, les navires français ont capturé une moyenne annuelle de 12 000 tonnes métriques de morue dans la zone que la France revendiquait, soit une valeur annuelle de 7 millions $;[63] au cours de la même période, les captures annuelles moyennes de la France dans la zone française nouvellement définie ont été d'environ 1 500 tonnes métriques de morue, soit *un peu plus de 800 000 $ seulement par année.*

La nouvelle zone française renferme un pourcentage important d'un stock qui depuis peu présente de l'intérêt pour les pêcheurs de Grand Bank, à Terre-Neuve. Depuis 1991, ceux-ci capturent le pétoncle d'Islande dans un secteur qui se trouve juste à l'ouest de la ceinture de 12 milles au large de Saint-Pierre-et-Miquelon. Cette espèce était jusqu'alors négligée parce qu'elle est plus petite que le pétoncle géant traditionnel mentionné précédemment, et donc plus coûteuse à transformer. Elle présente de l'intérêt depuis la fermeture de l'usine de transformation du poisson de fond de Grand Bank, une épreuve qu'ont connue plusieurs petits ports de Terre-Neuve ces dernières années. La revendication française englobait la quasi-totalité de la biomasse du pétoncle d'Islande, tandis que la nouvelle zone française représente environ la moitié

[63] En 1986, les captures françaises de morue dans la zone contestée ont atteint environ 19 000 tonnes métriques, soit une valeur de plus de 10 millions $ (dollars de 1990). La France ne s'est jamais beaucoup intéressée aux espèces autres que la morue.

de cette biomasse. Grâce à la délimitation maintenant établie, la France pourra donc gérer à sa guise une partie importante du stock de pétoncles d'Islande du secteur 3Ps. La France n'a jamais été intéressée par la pêche du pétoncle. Toutefois, le contrôle qu'elle a acquis sur la moitié de la ressource lui donne la possibilité de "troquer" le pétoncle pour la morue, dans le contexte des droits de pêche réciproques prévus par l'Accord de pêche de 1972.[64]

La France a obtenu beaucoup moins que le Canada pour ce qui est des ressources halieutiques. Toutefois, le niveau de dépendance économique est beaucoup moins marqué pour la France que pour le Canada. Contrairement à ce qu'on observe pour la côte sud de Terre-Neuve, la pêche n'est pas le mode de vie de la majorité des 6 000 habitants des îles françaises. Près de la moitié de la population active travaille dans le secteur public. Quant à l'industrie de la pêche, elle compte moins de 500 personnes.[65]

La délimitation de la frontière ne signifie pas, bien évidemment, que les bateaux français cesseront de pêcher dans les eaux du Canada. L'Accord de pêche de 1972, qui ne comporte pas de date d'expiration, continue de régir la pêche française dans la zone canadienne nouvellement confirmée. Le Tribunal d'arbitrage, conscient du poids donné par lui aux faits de l'espèce, a estimé que la délimitation ne changerait pas de façon radicale la structure habituelle de la pêche dans la région. Il a vérifié l'équité de la délimitation et, selon lui, cette délimitation n'aura pas de "répercussions catastrophiques" pour les populations qui sont tributaires de la pêche. C'est là une conclusion qui a son importance. Le Tribunal semble faire allusion à l'argument du Canada selon lequel la France ne pouvait invoquer la dépendance économique à l'appui de ses prétentions, puisque le Canada avait déjà pourvu aux intérêts de pêche français dans l'Accord de 1972, indépendamment de la délimitation. Le Tribunal fait aux Parties cette admonition voilée: "Le Tribunal ne doute pas qu'en se conformant de bonne foi à l'accord de 1972, les Parties réussiront à gérer et à exploiter de manière satisfaisante les ressources halieutiques de la région."[66] Sans doute peut-on qualifier cette remarque de simple *obiter dictum*,

---

64 L'Accord prévoit, en son article 2, que le Canada reconnaît le droit des ressortissants français de pêcher dans les eaux canadiennes. Au surplus, le gouvernement français doit accorder la réciprocité aux ressortissants canadiens au large des côtes de Saint-Pierre-et-Miquelon.

65 *Mémoire du Canada*, par. 44, 158.

66 *Décision*, par. 87.

et le Tribunal lui-même a reconnu qu'il ne lui appartenait pas d'appliquer ou d'interpréter l'Accord de 1972, mais elle est tout de même significative.

AUTRES POINTS

L'affaire *Canada/France* soulevait une grande diversité de questions secondaires, dont quelques-unes seulement ont été abordées par le Tribunal dans les motifs de sa décision.

Le plateau étendu

Il est un aspect des motifs de la décision qui laisse perplexe. Ce sont les propos du Tribunal relativement à la question qu'il appelle "la question du plateau étendu." Dans leurs écritures et plaidoiries, les deux Parties avaient mentionné que le rebord externe de la marge continentale se situe dans cette région au-delà de 200 milles des lignes de base à partir desquelles est mesurée la mer territoriale. La France, arguant de ce fait, fit porter ses prétentions — du moins pour le plateau continental — au-delà de 200 milles de Saint-Pierre-et-Miquelon et même au-delà de la limite canadienne de 200 milles. L'objectif de la France était d'obtenir son propre corridor vers la haute mer, de telle sorte que ses navires soient dispensés de traverser les eaux canadiennes pour gagner des ports non canadiens ou en revenir. Par ailleurs, un corridor français vers le sud donnerait à la France juridiction sur d'importants secteurs de pêche. Le Canada rejeta la revendication française élargie, en affirmant que la France ne possédait aucune preuve quant à l'emplacement du rebord externe de la marge. Il était possible en effet que la revendication française excède la limite.

Les Parties ne semblent pas avoir considéré cette question comme ayant une importance particulière dans l'arbitrage; d'ailleurs, leurs écritures et plaidoiries n'en font guère état. Le Tribunal s'est pourtant donné beaucoup de mal pour l'esquiver, dans les motifs de sa décision. Plutôt que d'ignorer la question, comme il l'a fait pour bien d'autres aspects de l'affaire, ou de l'écarter pour absence de bien-fondé juridique, le Tribunal invoque deux motifs pour justifier son incapacité de la trancher. Le premier est assez singulier. Le Tribunal déclare qu'il ne peut rendre une décision engageant une partie absente du litige et que, s'il tranchait la question, il se trouverait alors à se prononcer sur une délimitation entre les Parties d'une part et la communauté internationale de l'autre, les fonds marins situés au-delà des juridictions nationales ayant été déclarés patrimoine commun de l'humanité. Le Tribunal explique aussi que le rebord externe de la marge continentale doit être déterminé sur la base des recommandations de la Commission des limites du plateau continental, dont la création est prévue par la Convention sur le droit de la mer mais qui n'est pas encore constituée.[67]

Le deuxième motif donné par le Tribunal pour refuser de statuer sur la question du plateau étendu apparaît plus valable. Selon le Tribunal, le Compromis d'arbitrage visait l'établissement d'une frontière maritime unique devant commander tous droits et juridictions qui peuvent être exercés par les Parties. En conséquence, le Tribunal ne pouvait statuer sur une délimitation qui ne s'appliquerait qu'au plateau continental et non à la fois au plateau et à la colonne d'eau.[68]

Ces motifs ne laissent pas d'être préoccupants. Le Tribunal semble dire que la question du plateau étendu est encore ouverte, et il invite en fait la France à maintenir ses prétentions sur le plateau continental au-delà de sa nouvelle zone maritime, dans des secteurs où le Canada exerce actuellement la juridiction en matière de pêche. Cette façon d'envisager la question du plateau étendu est regrettable, et il est probable qu'elle soulève une controverse. Les deux opinions dissidentes critiquent le raisonnement du Tribunal sur ce point. Le juge Weil estime que, dans l'état actuel du droit international et de l'information géomorphologique, le Tribunal ne pouvait en effet statuer sur l'étendue des fonds marins au-delà de 200 milles. Il affirme cependant que le Tribunal est allé trop loin en paraissant, sinon considérer la Convention de 1982 sur le droit de la mer comme un instrument liant le Canada et la France, du moins regarder l'article 76 de la Convention comme relevant du droit international coutumier. Le juge Gotlieb soutient quant à lui que le Tribunal aurait dû rejeter d'emblée toute prétention de la France à un plateau continental au-delà de la zone qui lui a été accordée pour le motif qu'une telle prétention est sans fondement, indépendamment de l'existence ou de l'inexistence d'une Commission des limites du plateau continental.

L'article 6 de la Convention de 1958 sur le plateau continental

D'après la France, l'article 6 de la Convention de 1958 sur le plateau continental était pertinent aux fins de la délimitation. Le

[67] *Décision*, par. 78-79.
[68] *Décision*, par. 82.

Tribunal signifia son désaccord, mais sans effectuer d'analyse juridique, se contentant de citer la conclusion de la Chambre de la Cour
internationale de Justice dans l'affaire du *Golfe du Maine*, selon
laquelle l'article 6 n'est pas applicable à la délimitation d'une
frontière maritime devant servir à toutes fins.[69]

La pratique des États

Le Canada et la France ont tous deux consacré une bonne partie
de leurs écritures et de leurs plaidoiries aux arguments se rapportant à la pratique des États en matière de délimitation maritime,
chacun donnant des exemples d'accords qui, selon lui, appuyaient
sa propre thèse sur la frontière la plus appropriée compte tenu des
circonstances géographiques de l'espèce. La décision semble indiquer que les arguments des Parties ont quelque peu influé sur le
raisonnement du Tribunal, même si celui-ci ne mentionne dans ses
motifs aucun des exemples cités.

Le relevé de conclusions

Le Tribunal a rejeté les arguments du Canada relatifs au Relevé
de conclusions, *l'accord ad referendum* entre les Parties mentionné
plus haut. Le Canada a tenté de montrer que la France elle-même
avait jugé acceptable une zone française de 12 milles au large de
Saint-Pierre-et-Miquelon. En effet, la décision rendue dans
l'*Arbitrage franco-britannique* laisse entendre que la France avait
invoqué le Relevé pour appuyer ses arguments en faveur d'une
enclave autour des îles Anglo-Normandes situées à proximité des
côtes françaises. Le Tribunal est avare de commentaires sur la façon
dont il analyse juridiquement la question, mais il est manifeste que
les arguments du Canada ne l'ont pas convaincu. Les motifs de la
décision mentionnent simplement que le Relevé ne pouvait être
invoqué parce qu'il traitait uniquement du plateau continental et
que, en tout état de cause, n'ayant jamais été ratifié par les deux
gouvernements, il n'avait pas valeur d'accord entre les Parties.[70]

L'arbitrage franco-britannique

Le Canada a voulu donner valeur de précédent à l'*Arbitrage
franco-britannique* de 1977, en faisant remarquer surtout que la

69 *Décision*, par. 40.

70 *Décision*, par. 91.

France avait réussi dans ce cas à faire admettre la solution de l'enclave pour les îles Anglo-Normandes. (La France préconisait une enclave de 6 milles, mais le tribunal attribua aux îles une enclave de 12 milles.) Le Canada a soutenu également que, selon le tribunal saisi de l'*Arbitrage franco-britannique,* le statut politique des îles Anglo-Normandes était pertinent et que par conséquent la dépendance politique de Saint-Pierre-et-Miquelon devait être prise en considération. Le Tribunal rejeta ces arguments. Selon lui, l'*Arbitrage franco-britannique* n'avait pas valeur de précédent pour l'espèce considérée, d'abord en raison de la proximité du littoral anglais, et aussi parce que les îles Anglo-Normandes étaient une caractéristique secondaire aux fins d'une délimitation entre deux côtes principales de mêmes proportions.[71] Mais le Tribunal n'explique pas pourquoi ces faits ne pouvaient étayer la thèse du Canada, qui les invoquait précisément pour démontrer le caractère équitable d'une enclave.[72] Le Tribunal ne fait aucune référence à l'*Arbitrage franco-britannique* de 1977 sur la question du statut politique. Selon lui, l'argument n'a pas d'application dans la délimitation maritime puisque le droit conventionnel est silencieux sur ce point.[73]

Les activités des États

Le Tribunal d'arbitrage ne semble pas avoir été influencé par les arguments du Canada sur le rôle prédominant exercé par lui dans la région pour ce qui est de la sécurité, de la navigation, de la recherche et du sauvetage, de la protection de l'environnement et de la conservation et de la gestion des pêches. Le Canada s'est appliqué aussi à faire ressortir l'importance de la délimitation sur le plan de la sécurité, c'est-à-dire l'effet qu'elle pourrait avoir sur le contrôle des grandes voies de navigation conduisant au coeur industriel de l'Amérique du Nord. Plusieurs affaires de délimitation, telles l'*Arbitrage franco-britannique* et l'affaire *Tunisie/Libye,* ont accordé un certain poids à la conduite des Parties dans les activités de ce genre, mais la question n'est pas abordée dans les motifs de la décision qui nous occupe. Cependant, le juge Weil tient les propos

---

[71] *Décision,* par. 42.

[72] Le Canada a soutenu qu'il n'y avait aucun fondement à la thèse selon laquelle l'absence d'une côte française face à Terre-Neuve devrait accroître le droit de Saint-Pierre-et-Miquelon par rapport à celui des îles Anglo-Normandes. *Mémoire du Canada,* par. 377.

[73] *Décision,* par. 49.

suivants dans son opinion dissidente: "Plus importante toutefois que la composante économique de l'équité spatiale est sa composante politique, avec ses considérations de sécurité, de navigation, d'environnement, etc."[74]

Les traités du XVIIIe siècle

L'un des arguments plus inédits du Canada concernait l'effet de certains traités du dix-huitième siècle et d'instruments connexes sur l'opération de délimitation. Le Canada soutenait que la revendication française était incompatible avec l'objet original de la cession des îles, lesquelles devaient servir d'"abri" aux pêcheurs français, aussi bien qu'avec les engagements souscrits à l'époque, selon lesquels les îles ne deviendraient pas "un objet de jalousie entre les deux nations." Avec raison, le Tribunal rejeta ces arguments, affirmant que les instruments en question ne pouvaient raisonnablement être interprétés comme limitant les droits de la France aux termes du droit de la mer contemporain,[75] mais non sans que la France s'appliquât d'abord, dans ses écritures et plaidoiries, à réfuter longuement les arguments du Canada.

LES OPINIONS DISSIDENTES DES JUGES NATIONAUX

Comme on l'a dit, les deux Parties ont nommé des juges nationaux au Tribunal d'arbitrage: Allan Gotlieb, pour le Canada, et Prosper Weil, pour la France. Les deux juges nationaux ont voté contre la décision majoritaire du Tribunal d'arbitrage et rédigé chacun une opinion dissidente.

Bon nombre des critiques formulées par le juge Weil contre la décision du Tribunal ont déjà été abordées ci-dessus. Essentiellement, le juge Weil refuse de souscrire à la théorie de la projection frontale élaborée par le Tribunal, et il rejette l'application faite du critère de proportionnalité. Il n'indique pas avec précision ce qui, selon lui, aurait été un résultat équitable. Cependant, comme il le fait dans ses ouvrages,[76] il préconise le recours à l'équidistance comme point de départ de la délimitation, quitte à l'ajuster pour tenir compte des circonstances pertinentes, par exemple la nécessité pour le Canada de contrôler les voies de navigation vers le golfe

---

[74] *Opinion dissidente de M. Prosper Weil*, par. 35.

[75] *Décision*, par. 55.

[76] Voir par exemple Prosper Weil, *Perspectives du droit de la délimitation maritime* (Paris, Éditions A. Pédone, 1988).

du Saint-Laurent ou la nécessité de reconnaître à la France "un territoire maritime digne de ce nom."[77] Le juge Weil ne dit pas jusqu'où il aurait ramené la ligne en direction de Saint-Pierre-et-Miquelon. Toutefois, faisant taire ses convictions juridiques, qui seraient en faveur d'une délimitation normative plutôt que d'une délimitation exposée "aux grands vents des principes équitables et du résultat équitable,"[78] il mentionne qu'il aurait accepté de souscrire à une solution ne faisant pas appel à l'équidistance, même à titre de premier pas, "si du moins le tribunal, choisissant la logique de l'équité largement entendue, avait tracé la frontière maritime de manière à ce que chaque partie puisse être rassurée sur sa sécurité (au sens géopolitique le plus large du terme) et sur l'avenir économique des régions concernées."[79]

Le juge Gotlieb, pour sa part, soutient que la décision du Tribunal n'est pas conforme au droit international. Toutefois, son désaccord concerne surtout la façon dont le Tribunal apprécie les faits géographiques. Il croit que le Tribunal a sous-estimé la longueur du littoral canadien et qu'il a indûment élargi la zone maritime pertinente au-delà des approches du golfe. Le Tribunal en serait ainsi arrivé à un résultat disproportionné, par conséquent inéquitable, et contraire au droit puisque contraire à la norme fondamentale selon laquelle toute délimitation doit être effectuée conformément à des principes équitables et en tenant compte de toutes les circonstances pertinentes, afin d'aboutir à un résultat équitable. Pour le juge Gotlieb, un résultat équitable aurait été une enclave de 24 milles, "sans rien d'autre (sans un corridor) . . ."[80]

CONCLUSION

Comme le Tribunal ne s'est pas montré particulièrement expansif sur le plan du raisonnement juridique, on pourrait croire que la décision, même si sans doute elle satisfait les Parties et s'accorde aux circonstances de l'espèce, ne constituera pas un réel jalon dans l'évolution de la jurisprudence.

En quoi on aurait tort, et cela pour deux raisons: d'abord, la décision contient plusieurs conclusions éclairantes sur des points de droit jusqu'à maintenant incertains. Ainsi, elle enrichit la juris-

---

[77] *Opinion dissidente de M. Prosper Weil*, par. 37.

[78] *Ibid.*, par. 36.

[79] *Ibid.*, par. 37.

[80] *Opinion dissidente de M. Allan Gotlieb*, par. 47.

prudence en ce qui concerne le rôle des îles dans la délimitation, elle rejette sans équivoque l'idée d'une délimitation unique dans laquelle seraient examinées séparément les équités du plateau continental et celles de la zone de pêche, et elle confirme que la masse terrestre et le statut politique devraient être sans effet sur le titre. D'autre part, elle donne à penser que l'affaire *Libye/Malte* ne marquait pas le tournant qu'ont voulu y voir certains auteurs, pour qui le balancier s'éloignait enfin du relativisme et de la multiplicité de méthodes des principes équitables pour revenir à la règle de l'équidistance.[81] Ceux-là semblent avoir fait erreur, car le droit de la délimitation maritime donne encore au juge un vaste pouvoir discrétionnaire dans un cadre assez librement défini de principes équitables. Il ne faut pas croire toutefois que la délimitation maritime soit dépourvue de contenu juridique.[82] Il y a des facteurs reconnus dont un tribunal doit tenir compte. Parmi ceux-là figurent au tout premier plan les facteurs géographiques, par exemple l'obligation d'éviter toute amputation des espaces revenant aux Parties et donc tout empiétement sur la projection de leurs côtes en mer, ou encore le lien entre un résultat proportionné (au sens large) et un résultat équitable. La décision rendue dans l'affaire *Canada/France* s'accorde avec ces paramètres juridiques. Elle entre dans le cadre discrétionnaire autorisé par la jurisprudence, et elle évalue, de façon équilibrée et raisonnable, les circonstances propres à la zone que se disputaient le Canada et la France.

La frontière maritime établie par le Tribunal doit, bien sûr, être aussi évaluée selon une perspective non juridique. Le Canada voulait que le différend frontalier soit réglé par arbitrage, en vue de mettre fin à une source de friction qui empoisonnait les relations bilatérales franco-canadiennes. Sans doute, la décision du 10 juin 1992 a-t-elle permis de régler le différend juridique, et une frontière permanente est-elle maintenant établie qui reconnaît la juridiction du Canada sur la plupart des ressources d'importance commerciale de la région, mais il est ironique de constater que le contentieux de la pêche entre le Canada et la France persiste. Jusqu'à maintenant, il n'a pas été possible de parvenir à une entente sur les quotas de pêche qui seront alloués à chacune des

[81] Cette idée est implicite dans l'étude de Prosper Weil, *Perspectives du droit de la délimitation maritime*, à la p. 20, où l'auteur constate qu' "un palier d'une importance cruciale a été atteint avec l'arrêt *Libye/Malte . . .*"

[82] L. A. Willis, "From Precedent to Precedent: The Triumph of Pragmatism in the Law of Maritime Boundaries," (1986) XXIV *Annuaire canadien de droit international* 3.

Parties dans la zone maritime nouvellement définie de l'autre. Toutefois, grâce à la décision du Tribunal, on sait maintenant quel État a juridiction sur quels secteurs, et il n'y aura plus de mêlée générale dans des eaux qui sont d'une importance cruciale pour l'avenir de la côte sud de Terre-Neuve. Les relations des Parties s'inscrivent maintenant dans un cadre nouveau, un cadre au reste plus en harmonie avec leurs intérêts respectifs dans la région. Si le Tribunal avait imposé une solution davantage favorable à la France, on peut supposer que le risque de détérioration des relations bilatérales entre les deux pays aurait été beaucoup plus élevé.

Summary

The Canada/France Maritime Boundary Case

The authors contend that the ad hoc Court of Arbitration established by Canada and France to delimit the maritime boundary off the French islands of St. Pierre and Miquelon has come up with an equitable solution, fully consistent with the applicable international law. They argue that the decision of June 10, 1992 properly rejected the extreme claims of the Parties, and correctly applied the law in adopting a method that gave predominance to geographical factors, in particular the enormous disparity in the lengths of the Parties' coasts, with a view to arriving at a proportionate result. Although the decision leaves the bulk of the fisheries resources under Canadian control, with a view to arriving at a proportionate result. Although the decision leaves the bulk of the fisheries resources under Canadian control, the authors consider this to be commensurate with the relative interests of the Parties in the area, and suggest that the judgment has facilitated the ongoing management of both the resources and Franco-Canadian relations. In their view the emphasis in the judgment on the tendency of coasts to project in the direction in which they face, and the application of the corridor method to allow a full 200-mile zone to the French islands, finds support in both the jurisprudence and in State practice.

Allocation of the Non-Navigational Uses of International Watercourses: Efforts at Codification and the Experience of Canada and the United States

I INTRODUCTION

IN JULY 1992, the International Law Commission (ILC)[1] adopted on first reading a set of Draft Articles entitled The Law of the Non-Navigational Uses of International Watercourses.[2] Governments have been asked to comment on this document by January 1993. The Draft Articles raise important issues for Canada and the United States, which share a border crossed by more than 300 rivers and lakes.[3]

---

* Assistant at the Faculty of Law, University of Geneva; Graduate Student for the Ph.D. degree at the Institute of International Studies, Geneva. The author thanks Professor Lucius Caflisch and Professor Charles Bourne for their helpful comments and suggestions.

---

[1] The International Law Commission, established by General Assembly Resolution 174(II) of Nov. 21, 1947, has for its main task "the promotion of the progressive development of international law and its codification." See the Statute of the International Law Commission, UN Doc. A/CN.4/4/Rev.2 (1982).

[2] UN GAOR, 43d Sess., at 1, UN Doc. A/CN.4/L.463/Add.4 (1991) [hereinafter Draft Articles]. The Draft Articles are reprinted in the "Doman Colloquium on the Law of International Watercourses," 3 Colorado J. Int'l Environmental L. and Pol., 1-11 (1992), [hereinafter Doman Colloquium].

[3] D. G. Lemarquand, "Preconditions to Cooperation in Canada-U.S. Boundary Waters," 26 Natural Res. J. 221-42 (1986).

This article focuses on the rules governing allocation of the non-navigational uses of international watercourses; more specifically, it examines the two norms: "equitable utilization" and "no appreciable harm." The ILC, while asserting that these rules are complementary, has expressly endorsed the latter as the governing rule of the Draft Articles.

Following consideration of the relevant parts of the Draft Articles, and a brief summary of the work in the area by the International Law Association (ILA) and the Institute of International Law (IDI), these efforts at codification and progressive development of international watercourse law will be compared to the practice followed by Canada and the United States.

How states agree (or disagree) to allocate the rapidly diminishing quantities of quality water resources is an important, perhaps, crucial issue. Attention to the law regarding the allocation of the non-navigational uses of international watercourses, however, is of relatively recent origin.[4] The dual pillars of international relations, state sovereignty and sovereign equality have, to a large extent, determined the parameters of the law on the subject.[5] But growing interdependence in a world with limited pristine resources and

---

[4] L. A. Teclaff, *The River Basin in History and Law* 15 (1967). For a survey of the law in the area, see S. C. McCaffrey, Second Report on the Law of the Non-Navigational Uses of International Watercourses, Doc. A/CN.4/399 and Add.1 and 2, in II Yearbook of the International Law Commission, part 1, at 87-144 (1986), especially at 110-34; also, L. Caflisch, "Principes généraux du droit de cours d'eaux internationaux," 219 Recueil des cours de l'Académie de droit international de La Haye, 1989-VII (forthcoming) [hereinafter Recueil des cours]; C. B. Bourne, "The Right to Utilize the Waters of International Rivers," 3 *Canadian Yearbook of International Law*, 187-264 (1965), [hereinafter Bourne, "International Rivers"]. For the law in Canada and the United States, see: J. Austin, "Canadian-United States Practice and Theory Respecting the International Law of International Rivers: A Study of the History and Influence of the Harmon Doctrine," 37 Can. Bar Rev. 393-443 (1959); C. B. Bourne, "Canada and the Law of International Drainage Basins," in R. Macdonald, G. Morris, and D. M. Johnston (eds.), *Canadian Perspectives on International Law and Organization*, 468-99 (1974) [hereinafter Bourne, "Law of Drainage Basins"]; and M. Cohen, "The Regime of Boundary Waters: The Canadian-United States Experience," 3 Recueil des cours, 221-338 (1975) [hereinafter Cohen, "Boundary Waters"].

[5] Teclaff, *supra* note 4, at 80, traces the origins of international water use allocation rules. International relations have moved from the laws of "co-existence" to "co-operation"; see W. Friedmann, *The Changing Structure of International Law* 60-63 (1964).

ever-increasing environmental problems has sharpened the edge of the problem.

II EFFORTS AT CODIFICATION

Of the five theories of international watercourse use allocation most commonly advanced, the limited territorial sovereignty theory has come to prevail.[6] It is closely linked with the principles of equitable utilization and no harm, and appears to have its foundation in the concept of *bon voisinage*.[7] The theory holds that a state's right to use international waters located on or passing through its territory is not absolute, but is limited by the recognition of similar rights in co-basin states.

The no harm rule, based on the maxim *sic utere tuo ut alienum non laedas* ("so use your own property as not to injure another's property"), limits a state's territorial rights in general: a state cannot use its territory in any way that would harm other states. It is debatable whether the *sic utere tuo* maxim has crystallized into a generally recognized principle of international law, but it is clear that the no harm principle has influenced state practice.[8] By contrast, the equitable utilization rule applies specifically to international water-

---

6 These theories are: absolute territorial sovereignty (also referred to as the "Harmon Doctrine"), absolute territorial integrity, prior appropriation, community of interests, and limited territorial sovereignty. See J. Lipper, "Equitable Utilization," in A. H. Garretson, R. D. Hayton, and C. J. Olmstead (eds.), *The Law of International Drainage Basins* 15-89, at 18-62 (1967); B. A. Godana, *Africa's Shared Water Resources* 32-65 (1985).

7 See J. Andrassy, "Les relations internationales de voisinage," 79 Recueil des cours, 1951-II, 73-182, and C. Bédard, *Le Régime juridique des Grands Lacs* 130-38 (1966).

8 A. Lester, "Pollution," in A. H. Garretson et al., *supra* note 6, at 89-123, states at 96: "*sic utere tuo* has been generally recognized in the literature as a principle of international river law." J. G. Lammers, *Pollution of International Watercourses* (1984) states at 570, "there exists considerable uncertainty about the origin, legal nature, content, feasibility of application or even the very existence of the principle," and concludes, "it is better for the sake of clarity of legal argument to avoid the maxim . . . in discussions about the rights and duties of States regarding the use of the waters of international watercourses." Professor Bourne classifies the *sic utere* maxim as part of a "primitive system of law": see C. B. Bourne, "Principles and Planned Measures" in the Doman Colloquium, *supra* note 2, at 65-92, 84-88 [hereinafter, Bourne, "Principles"]. While all agree that there are limits on a state's rights to use its international waters, the foundation and definition of these limits differ.

courses; it was developed primarily in domestic courts (notably in the United States) and its foundations lie in customary international law.[9] Both principles have had an important influence on the development of the law governing international watercourse allocation problems; this is evident upon examination of the work of the ILC, the ILA, and the IDI.

THE INTERNATIONAL LAW COMMISSION

The ILC's Draft Articles aim to provide states with rules to assist them in the peaceful resolution of issues involving the non-navigational uses of international watercourses. The twin cornerstones of the Draft are Articles 5 and 7.[10] The ILC has decided that the latter is the governing rule.[11]

Article 7, entitled "Obligation not to cause appreciable harm," provides as follows: "Watercourse states shall utilize an international watercourse in such a way as not to cause appreciable harm to other watercourse states." In its commentary on this article, the ILC states that it is

a specific application of the principle of the harmless use of territory expressed in the maxim *sic utere tuo ut alienum non laedas*, which is itself a reflection of the sovereign equality of states. That is, the exclusive competence that a watercourse state enjoys within its territory is not to be exercised in such a way as to interfere with the competence of those other watercourse states over matters within their territories.[12]

---

[9] See McCaffrey, Second Report, *supra* note 4; Bourne, "Law of Drainage Basins," *supra* note 4, at 475. G. Handl, "The Principle of 'Equitable Use' as Applied to International Shared Resources," 14 Revue belge de droit international 40-62, at 47 (1978-79), quotes the OECD Directorate's definition of equitable use as a maxim that implies "that the use of a common resource by each country, while aiming in principle at optimum exploitation, must be compatible with the safeguard of the interests of other countries concerned, on the basis of the conjunction of a series of criteria which vary according to the particular situation."

[10] S. C. McCaffrey, "The Law of International Watercourses: Some Recent Developments and Unanswered Questions," 17 Denver J. Int'l L. and Pol. 505-26, 508 (1989) [hereinafter McCaffrey, "Recent Developments"].

[11] The primacy of the no appreciable harm rule was not readily adopted; in fact, each of the three last Special Rapporteurs had different views on the issue. See Bourne, "Principles," *supra* note 8, at 73-79 for a summary of this evolution.

[12] Commentary, 1988 ILC Report, 83.

The no harm rule was not adopted by a consensus of the Commission;[13] in fact, in his Second Report, Special Rapporteur McCaffrey had recommended that the no harm article should

> be redrafted in such a way as to bring it into conformity with . . . the principle of equitable utilization. . . . [T]he focus should be on the duty not to cause legal injury (by making a non-equitable use) rather than on the duty not to cause factual harm. . . . [I]n the context of watercourses, suffering even significant harm may not infringe the rights of the harmed state if the harm is within the limits allowed by an equitable utilization.[14]

His recommendation did not prevail. In his Fourth Report, however, McCaffrey recommended that, in matters involving pollution harm, "no appreciable harm" should be the fundamental rule.[15] He now finds certain advantages in adopting this rule as the primary rule of the Draft Articles.[16]

---

13 McCaffrey, Second Report, *supra*, note 4, at 94-95 refers to the divided views of the Sixth Committee of the General Assembly. See Report of the International Law Commission on the Work of its Thirty-Ninth Session, UN GAOR Supp. (No.10), UN Doc.A/42/10 (1987), reprinted in II Yearbook of the International Law Commission, part 1, at 1, 20, 23, UN Doc. A/DN.4/SER.A/1987/Add.1; on the Sixth Committee discussions, see A/C.6/43/SR, Nov. 18, 1988, at 13.

14 See McCaffrey, in Second Report, *supra* note 4, at 133 proposed the following Draft Article: "In its use of an international watercourse, a watercourse State shall not cause appreciable harm to another watercourse State, except as may be allowable within the context of the first State's equitable utilization of that international watercourse." In support, he argued that "The particular advantage of this formulation is that it embodies in express terms the duty not to cause harm, but makes clear that this duty is subject to the rights a State may have by virtue of its equitable utilization of the international watercourse." McCaffrey's predecessors, Evensen and Schwebel, each had their own approach to the issue. See Bourne, "Principles," *supra* note 8, at 79-82; L. Caflisch, "*Sic Utere Tuo Ut Alienum Non Laedas.* Règle prioritaire ou élément pour déterminer le droit d'utilisation équitable et raisonnable d'un cours d'eau international?" Festschrift für Walter Müller, forthcoming [hereinafter Caflisch, "Sic Utere Tuo"].

15 S. C. McCaffrey, Fourth Report on the Law of the Non-Navigational Uses of International Watercourses, UN GAOR, International Law Commission, 40th Session, at 14, UN Doc. A/CN.4/412/Add.2 (1988) [hereinafter McCaffrey, Fourth Report].

16 See McCaffrey, "Recent Developments," *supra* note 10, at 510, in which he asserts:
> First the ILC's approach affords a measure of protection to the weaker State that has suffered harm. It is not open to the stronger State to justify a use giving rise to the harm on the ground that it is "equitable." A second, and

What qualifies as "appreciable"[17] harm? The Commentary to Article 7 explains:

"appreciable harm" embodies a factual standard . . . [it] must be capable of being established by objective evidence. There must be a real impairment of use, i.e., a detrimental impact of some consequence upon, for example, public health, industry, property, agriculture or the environment in the affected state. "Appreciable" harm is, therefore, that which is not insignificant or barely detectable but is not necessarily "serious".[18]

The equitable utilization rule, provisionally adopted in 1987 (one year before Article 7), is set out in Article 5 of the Draft Articles as follows:

1. Watercourse states shall in their respective territories utilize an international watercourse in an equitable and reasonable manner. In particular, an international watercourse shall be used and developed by watercourse states with a view to attaining optimum utilization thereof and benefits therefrom consistent with adequate protection of the watercourse.

---

related, point is that it is far simpler to determine whether the "no harm" rule has been breached than is the case with the obligation of equitable utilization. Thus, primacy of the "no harm" principle means that the fundamental rights and obligations of States with regard to their uses of an international watercourse are more definite and certain than they would be if governed in the first instance by the more flexible (and consequently less clear) rule of equitable utilization. And finally, the "no harm" rule is preferable in cases involving pollution and other threats to the environment. While a State could conceivably seek to justify an activity resulting in such harm as being an "equitable use," the "no harm" principle would — at least *prima facie* — require abatement of the injurious activity.
See also S. C. McCaffrey, "The International Law Commission and its Efforts to Codify the International Law of Waterways," 67 Annuaire suisse de droit international 32-55, 50-52 (1990) [hereinafter, McCaffrey, "The ILC"].

17 The ILC concluded that "appreciable" is the preferred qualifier, since it provides the most factual and objective standard; 1987 ILC Report, 86-101. For a critique of the ILC's choice of this term, see the ILA's discussion in its Seoul Report, ILA, Sixty-Second Report, Seoul 1986, at 275-83 [hereinafter Seoul Complementary Rules], and also discussion in K. Sachariew, "The Definition of Thresholds of Tolerance for Transboundary Environmental Injury under International Law: Development and Present Status," 37 Netherlands Int'l L. Rev. 193-206, (1990); D. B. Magraw, "Transboundary Harm: The International Law Commission's Study of 'International Liability'," 80 Am. J. Int'l L. 305-30, at 322 (1986); J. J. A. Salmon, "La pollution des fleuves et des lacs dans le droit international" (provisional report), 58-I Annuaire de l'Institut de droit international 193-380, 218-28 (1979).

18 The meaning of the term "appreciable" (it is not used in the sense of "substantial") is found in paras. 15 and 16 of the Commentary to Article 3 of the Draft Articles.

2. Watercourse states shall participate in the use, development and protection of an international watercourse in an equitable and reasonable manner. Such participation includes both the right to utilize the watercourse and the duty to co-operate in the protection and development thereof, as provided in the present articles.

For the ILC, the equitable utilization rule "finds its limit in the duty ... not to cause appreciable harm. ....[A] watercourse state may not justify a use that causes appreciable harm to another watercourse state on the ground that the use is 'equitable,' in the absence of an agreement between the watercourse states concerned."[19] Where a conflict of uses occurs,[20] "adjustments or accommodations [to be arrived at on the basis of equity] are required in order to preserve each watercourse state's equality of right."[21]

Article 6, entitled "Factors relevant to equitable and reasonable utilization," provides a non-exhaustive list of six factors to be considered in the assessment of an equitable and reasonable utilization. Neither harm nor injury are included in this list.

Part IV (Articles 20-23) of the Draft Articles focuses on the protection and preservation of the "ecosystem of the international watercourse." In this context, the ILC continues to recognize the primacy of Article 7, using appreciable harm as the governing guideline, especially in matters of pollution.[22]

THE INTERNATIONAL LAW ASSOCIATION

The Helsinki Rules of 1966,[23] and to a lesser extent the New York Resolution of 1958,[24] form the basis for the ILA's ongoing work in international watercourse law. The ILA has expressly refused to deviate from the basic principles espoused in these two texts, deciding instead to update and clarify them through complementary

19 Commentary to Article 7.

20 The Commentary to Article 6 provides: "Where the quantity or quality of the water is such that all of the reasonable and beneficial uses of all watercourse States cannot be fully realized, what is termed a 'conflict of uses' results."

21 Commentary to Article 5.

22 See the Commentary to Article 23, "Prevention, Reduction and Control of Pollution."

23 ILA, Report of the Fifty-Second Conference, Helsinki 1966, at 477 [hereinafter Helsinki Rules].

24 ILA, Report of the Forty-Eighth Conference, New York 1958, at 99-102 [hereinafter New York Resolution].

rules and guidelines. It has chosen equitable utilization as the governing rule,[25] and "no substantial injury" is only one of the many factors to be considered in determining what qualifies as an equitable use. The meaning of substantial injury is expanded upon in Article 1 of the Complementary Rules of 1986.[26] The ILA reiterates the primacy of the equitable utilization rule in its commentary to the Article[27] and also in its work on pollution.[28]

THE INSTITUTE OF INTERNATIONAL LAW

The Institute of International Law, in Article 2 of its Salzburg Resolution of 1961,[29] provides that every state has a limited right to use its international waters; the rules of international law, the provisions of the Resolution, and the similar rights of co-basin states limit

[25] Article 4 of the Helsinki Rules provides: "Each basin State is entitled, within its territory, to a reasonable and equitable share in the beneficial uses of the water of an international drainage basin." Article 5 provides: "What is a reasonable and equitable share . . . is to be determined in the light of all the relevant circumstances in each particular case." Paragraph 2 to the same article lists the "relevant factors" to be considered in the assessment of "a reasonable and equitable share."

[26] Seoul Complementary Rules, *supra* note 17. Under Article 1 of the Complementary Rules of 1986: "A basin State shall refrain from and prevent acts or omissions within its territory that will cause substantial injury to any co-basin State, provided that the application of the principle of equitable utilization as set forth in Article IV of the Helsinki Rules does not justify an exception in a particular case. Such an exception shall be determined in accordance with Article V of the Helsinki Rules."

[27] The Commentary to Article 1 of the Seoul Complementary Rules provides: "The ILA considers it to be evident that the duty to refrain from activities that would cause substantial injury to other basin States, as well as the exceptions from that duty, must be accommodated to the principle of equitable utilization . . . In order to reach an equitable balance between the uses and needs of all the basin States also the injurious consequences of the undertaking should be assessed."

[28] Article 10 of the Helsinki Rules, which deals with pollution, begins, "Consistent with the principle of equitable utilization"; the Commentary to this provision provides: "Any use of water . . . that denies an equitable sharing of uses by a co-basin State . . . is a violation of international law." See also ILA, Report of the Fifty-Ninth Conference, Belgrade 1980, at 373; ILA, Report of the Sixtieth Conference, Montreal 1982, at 535.

[29] The Salzburg Resolution on the Use of International Non-Maritime Waters, 49-II Annuaire de l'Institut de droit international, Session de Salzbourg 1961, at 381-84 [hereinafter Salzburg Resolution].

use entitlement.[30] Disputes over the extent of state rights are to be resolved on the basis of equity.[31] Uses that seriously affect other uses might be allowed in accordance with equitable considerations but may require the payment of compensation.[32] The Salzburg Resolution tacitly endorses the equitable utilization rule with the proviso that compensation may be required in certain cases.

CONCLUSION

The ILC, the ILA, and the IDI have based their work on international watercourse allocation on the general principles of equitable utilization and no harm. What distinguishes their approaches is the role assigned to each of these principles. The ILC has taken the view that the governing rule is "no appreciable harm," thereby differing from both the ILA and the IDI, which have considered "equitable utilization" to be the overarching principle.

The foregoing sections of this article have examined the approaches chosen by three expert bodies to deal with the complex issues relating to the allocation of the non-navigational uses of international watercourses. But, as H. A. Smith noted, "[t]he practical value of legal discussion is in direct proportion to its concern with actual facts, and experience has shown that all attempts to solve river problems by dogmatic insistence upon abstract legal

---

30 Article 2 of the Salzburg Resolution runs as follows: "Every State has the right to utilize waters which traverse or border its territory, subject to the limits imposed by international law and, in particular, those resulting from the provisions which follow. This right is limited by the right of utilization of other States interested in the same watercourse or hydrographic basin." See also the IDI's Resolution, "The Pollution of Rivers and Lakes and International Law," 58-II *Annuaire de l'Institut de droit international, Session d'Athènes* 1979, 196-203 [hereinafter Athens Resolution]. Article II thereof prohibits transboundary pollution.

31 Article 3 of the Salzburg Resolution provides: "If the States are in disagreement over the scope of their rights of utilization, settlement will take place on the basis of equity, taking particular account of their respective needs, as well as of other pertinent circumstances."

32 Article 4 of the Salzburg Resolution provides: "No State can undertake works or utilizations of the waters of a watercourse or hydrographic basin which seriously affect the possibility of utilization of the same waters by other States except on condition of assuring them the enjoyment of the advantages to which they are entitled under Article 3, as well as adequate compensation for any loss or damage." Article VI of the Athens Resolution refers to compensation for "victims of transboundary pollution."

principles have been either futile or mischievous."[33] It is now
necessary to turn to the "hard anvil of practice."[34] Following a
description of state practice in Canada and the United States, that
practice will be confronted with the no harm and equitable utilization rules formulated by the ILC. The case studies, which vary in
many respects, represent the diversity of international watercourse
problems that have been encountered in relations between Canada
and the United States. While the 1909 Boundary Waters Treaty[35]
provides some indication on how the two countries have agreed to
resolve their international watercourse disputes, it does not tell the
whole story.

III   Case Studies: Canada and the United States

As one author has stated, "[i]t is in the nature of things that
water will always be an important issue in Canada-United States
relations. This is so because those who fixed the boundary between
the two countries took no account of the geographical unity of
drainage basins."[36] Water forms the boundary for more than one-
half of the 8,900-kilometre border between Canada and the United
States.[37] Before Canada became independent, the United States
dealt with Great Britain in matters concerning the regime of international waters.[38] In 1905, following an initiative by the United
States, the International Waterways Commission (IWC) was created.[39] It was active for some eight years, and its recommendations

[33] H. A. Smith, *The Economic Uses of International Rivers vi* (1931).

[34] *Ibid.*, 151.

[35] Treaty between the United States and Great Britain relating to Boundary
Waters, and Questions Arising between the United States and Canada, signed
at Washington, Jan. 11 1909 [hereinafter Boundary Waters Treaty or 35.1909
Treaty].

[36] Bourne, "Law of Drainage Basins," *supra* note 4, at 468.

[37] At least 3,200 kilometres of the Canada-U.S. border is composed of navigable
and non-navigable waters: L. M. Bloomfield and G. F. FitzGerald, *Boundary
Waters Problems of Canada and the United States* 1 (1958); G. Graham, "International Rivers and Lakes: The Canadian-American Regime," in Zacklin and
Caflisch (eds.), The Legal Regime of International Rivers and Lakes 3 (1981).

[38] Canada was afforded full treaty-making powers in 1923: D. C. Piper, The
International Law of the Great Lakes 6 (1967).

[39] N. Ely and A. Wolman, "Principal Legal Problems of International Drainage
Basins: Administration," in A. H. Garretson et al. (eds.), *supra* note 6, at
124-59. Cohen, "Boundary Waters," *supra* note 4, at 249, states: "The IWC

led to the conclusion of the 1909 Boundary Waters Treaty.[40]

The Boundary Waters Treaty realized three broad goals: it resolved some outstanding issues regarding two shared watercourses;[41] it provided general guidelines along which the two countries could approach other, existing and future, international watercourse disputes;[42] and it established the International Joint Commission (IJC).[43] The purpose of the Treaty is set out in its Preamble.[44]

A quick survey of the 1909 Treaty reveals an assured freedom of navigation on all boundary waters,[45] an established hierarchy of uses,[46] and restrictions on certain undertakings.[47] Pollution is prohibited,[48] and equal access to foreign courts for injured private

---

arose out of disputes concerning the Niagara River and the Niagara Falls, the need for finding a place for hydro-electric power in the scheme of boundary waters interests, and the need to explore other critical waterways, particularly in the dry West." See also G. V. LaForest, "Boundary Waters Problems in the East," in D. R. Deener (ed.), *Canada-United States Treaty Relations* 28-50, 33 (1963).

[40] Cohen, *supra* note 4.

[41] These watercourses are the Niagara River (Article 5), and the St. Mary and Milk rivers (Article 6).

[42] Article 8 of the Boundary Waters Treaty.

[43] *Ibid.*, Article 7.

[44] The preamble provides that the United States and Great Britain "being equally desirous to prevent disputes regarding the use of boundary waters and to settle all questions which are now pending between the United States and the Dominion of Canada involving the rights, obligations, or interests of either in relation to the other or to the inhabitants of the other, along their common frontier, and to make provision for the adjustment and settlement of all such questions as may hereafter arise, have resolved to conclude a treaty in furtherance of these ends. . . ."

[45] Article 1 appears to place navigational interests in the forefront. See Cohen, *supra* note 4, at 250.

[46] Article 8 describes three broad categories: (1) uses for domestic and sanitary purposes; (2) uses for navigation, including the service of canals for the purposes of navigation; and (3) uses for power and for irrigation purposes.

[47] Articles 3 and 4; see *infra* notes 51 and 52. The priority of uses has not been followed in practice: F. J. E. Jordan, "The International Joint Commission and Canada-United States Boundary Relations," in Macdonald et al. (eds.), *supra* note 4, at 539.

[48] Article 4 (para. 2) provides: "It is further agreed that the waters defined as boundary waters and waters flowing across the boundary shall not be polluted on either side to the injury of health or property of the other."

individuals is offered.[49]

The Treaty defines three categories of waters: boundary waters, tributary waters (defined in the Preliminary Article),[50] and "waters flowing from boundary waters"/"waters at a lower level than the boundary in rivers, flowing across the boundary" (defined in Article 4).[51] Articles 2, 3,[52] and 4 govern the uses that affect the natural flow or level of these waters.

Article 2, often referred to erroneously as a codification of the Harmon Doctrine,[53] provides that each state has "exclusive jurisdiction and control over the use and diversion . . . of all waters on its own side of the line," subject to a remedial provision on equal access for individuals.

[49] Article 2 provides that "any interference with or diversion from their natural channels of such waters on either side of the boundary, shall give rise to the same rights and entitle the injured parties to the same legal remedies as if such injury took place in the country where such diversion or interference occurs. . . ." See also Article 8, which allows the IJC to make provisions for the "protection and indemnity" against injury of any interests on either side of the boundary.

[50] The preliminary article provides: "boundary waters are defined as the waters from main shore to main shore of the lakes and rivers and connecting waterways, or the portions thereof, along which the international boundary between the United States and Dominion of Canada passes, including all bays, arms, and inlets thereof, but not including tributary waters which in their natural channels would flow into such lakes, rivers, and waterways, or waters flowing from such lakes, rivers, and waterways, or the waters of rivers flowing across the boundary."

[51] Article 4 provides that, failing special agreement, the parties will "not permit the construction or maintenance on their respective sides of the boundary of any remedial or protective works or any dams or other obstructions in waters flowing from boundary waters or in waters at a lower level than the boundary in rivers, flowing across the boundary, the effect of which is to raise the natural level of waters on the other side of the boundary unless . . . approved by the IJC. . . ."

[52] Article 3 prevents unilateral action that would "materially affect" the level or flow of the boundary waters on the other side of the border, although the "ordinary use of such waters for domestic and sanitary purposes" is protected.

[53] The Harmon Doctrine holds that, in accordance with the notion of state sovereignty, each state has a right to use freely those waters located on, or passing through its territory. Article 2 of the Boundary Waters Treaty restricts the "absoluteness" of this doctrine by granting access to remedies across the border to private citizens injured as a result of uses undertaken by the foreign state. See also Bloomfield and FitzGerald, *supra* note 37, at 43-46; McCaffrey, Second Report, *supra* note 4, at 106, especially note 97; and I. U. Reinumägi, 20 Valparaiso University L. Rev. 299-347, 310, note 66 (1986).

Article 4, in addition to requiring the approval of the IJC for works downstream that would raise the level upstream in "flowing boundary waters," prohibits pollution on either side of the border "to the injury of health or property on the other." This provision has grown in importance as concerns over pollution have come to the fore.

The IJC, which was established under Article 7 of the Boundary Waters Treaty, is vested with investigative, administrative, quasi-judicial, and arbitral powers.[54] In view of these extensive powers, it is submitted that most transboundary disputes could be resolved under the auspices and direction of the IJC.[55] However, as regards international watercourses, the IJC's jurisdiction is limited by the provisions of Articles 3, 4, and 8 of the 1909 Treaty.[56]

The Commission, guided by the general principles set out in Article 8,[57] receives applications for use approval and references on questions raised by the two states. Canada and the United States have adopted the practice of making joint references to the IJC, reflecting perhaps their non-adversarial approach to the use of this international institution. The Commission has been very active throughout its history, and its influence on the peaceful resolution of international water disputes between the two countries can be clearly demonstrated.[58]

The case studies that will now be undertaken against this background cover a range of use allocation problems: upstream-downstream conflicts, common pool resources, and integrated river basin development,[59] including, *inter alia*, pre- and post-1909 cases, the Chicago diversion question, the Columbia River dispute, and the recent Flathead River development proposal.

[54] See Articles 7 through 12, and Articles 3 and 4 of the 1909 Treaty. The IJC is comprised of six Commissioners, three appointed from each state, who meet a minimum of twice annually. For further discussion, see W. R. Willoughby, *The Joint Organizations of Canada and the United States* 17-64 (1979).

[55] Article 10 of the Boundary Waters Treaty.

[56] Under Articles 2 and 8 of the 1909 Treaty, the IJC does not have adjudicatory authority over tributary waters.

[57] Article 8 sets out five principles to be followed by the IJC in the performance of its work and provides, *inter alia*, that: "[t]he . . . Parties shall have, each on its own side of the boundary, equal and similar rights in the use of the waters hereinbefore defined as boundary waters."

[58] Cohen, "Boundary Waters," *supra* note 4, at 267-87; and, in general, Bloomfield and FitzGerald, *supra* note 37.

[59] B. Sadler, "The Management of Canada-U.S. Boundary Waters: Retrospect and Prospect," 26 Natural Res. J. 359-76, 361 (1986).

THE LAKE OF THE WOODS

In 1904, the Minnesota Canal and Power Company proposed the construction of reservoirs on Birch Lake in Minnesota.[60] The scheme involved a diversion of tributaries of the Rainy Lake/Lake of the Woods system. Canada objected, claiming that the proposed development would seriously impair its right to free navigation, and asked that the matter be referred to the IWC.[61] Following review of the matter, the IWC recommended that no permit be granted, although it admitted that:

[I]t was settled international law, recognized by both the United States and Great Britain, and lucidly stated by Attorney General Harmon . . . that, in the absence of treaty stipulations, a country through which streams had their course or in which lakes existed could, in the exercise of its sovereign power, rightfully divert or otherwise appropriate the waters within its territory for purposes of irrigation, the improvement of navigation, or for any other purpose which the Government might deem proper. . . . [S]uch an exercise of sovereign power over waters within the jurisdiction of a country could not be questioned even though the exercise of such sovereign power would be injurious to another country through which the same stream or lake passed.[62]

Despite this statement, the Commission maintained that comity required the United States to seek the consent of Canada before undertaking any unilateral action that might result in injury to that country or its citizens.[63] The United States agreed to negotiate "for the purpose of arriving at some mutually acceptable adjustment of the questions involved"[64] before granting the permit requested.

The Lake of the Woods diversion problem was abated temporarily by the remedial provision on equal access that is set out in Article 2 of the 1909 Treaty. This provision extends to individuals injured by actions taken in a foreign state the rights and legal remedies granted to citizens of the offending state. Although the Minnesota Power Company received its permit, concerns in Canada

60 J. Simsarian, "The Diversion of Waters Affecting the United States and Canada," 32 Am. J. Int'l L. 488-518, 488 (1938).

61 Navigation was a conventional right arising from the Webster-Ashburton Treaty, 1842, 8 U.S. Stat. 572, which provided in its Article 2 that the boundary waters in question be "free and open to the use of the citizens and subjects of both parties. . . ."

62 Simsarian, *supra* note 60, at 494.

63 J. Q. Dealey, "The Chicago Drainage Canal and St. Lawrence Development," 23 Am. J. Int'l L. 307-28, 314 (1929).

64 Simsarian, *supra* note 60, at 496.

persisted, and in 1912 the matter was referred to the IJC by the two governments. The task of the Commission was to investigate and report on the possibility and feasibility of regulating the water level of the Lake of the Woods.[65]

The IJC recommended that, "as a matter of sound international policy, neither nation should permit the permanent or temporary diversion of any waters within its jurisdiction that are tributary to the boundary waters under consideration, without first referring the proposed diversion to the Commission for recommendation."[66] The two governments agreed that a separate agreement should be drafted to deal with the issues, and in 1925 a Treaty and Protocol were entered into between the United States and Great Britain regarding the regulation of the level of the Lake of the Woods.[67] Article 11 of this Treaty codifies the recommendations of the IJC: "No diversion shall henceforth be made of any waters from the Lake of the Woods watershed to any other watershed except by authority of the United States or . . . Canada within their territories and with the approval of the International Joint Commission."

Although the Boundary Waters Treaty distinguished between boundary and tributary waters, the Lake of the Woods Convention placed the two on an equal footing: neither type was available for unilateral diversion. This clearly departed from the notion of absolute territorial sovereignty as articulated in Article 2 of the 1909 Treaty. The IJC was thus burdened with the task of examining all diversion issues relating to the Lake of the Woods.

THE ST. MARY AND MILK RIVERS

The St. Mary and Milk rivers have their sources in Montana (the St. Mary rises in the mountains, the Milk, in the foothills), and they both cross the international border into Alberta.[68] In 1891 the

---

65 Bloomfield and FitzGerald, *supra* note 37, at 42-44 and 72-75.

66 T. A. Kalavrouziotis, "U.S.–Canadian Relations Regarding Diversions from an International Basin: An Analysis of Article II of the Boundary Waters Treaty," 12 Fordham L. J. 658-81, 666 (1989), referring to the IJC, Final Report on the Lake of the Woods Reference, 1917, at 38.

67 Treaty and Protocol Between the United States and Great Britain in Respect of Canada to Regulate the Level of the Lake of the Woods, Feb. 24, 1925, 44 Stat. 2108; T.I.A.S. No. 6, 14 [hereinafter Lake of the Woods Treaty].

68 M. M. Whitemann, 3 *Digest of International Law* 831. The St. Mary River flows north, crosses the international boundary, and eventually drains into the Hud-

Montana legislature requested that the U.S. Congress conduct a feasibility study regarding the possible diversion of waters from the St. Mary into the Milk River; Canada reacted to this by considering her claims.[69] By 1902 the U.S. Congress had passed a Reclamation Act, which permitted the proposed diversion. Canada objected, claiming that the interference with the waters affected the northern course of the St. Mary basin waters, which were required for irrigation of Canadian land. Reaction in Canada included the construction of the "Spite Canal," which diverted the waters of the Milk River as it passed throught Canada.[70]

The dispute over the two diversions drew attention in Ottawa and Washington. After much discussion and numerous diplomatic exchanges, the two states agreed that "the waters . . . should be conserved for the beneficial use of the owners of agricultural and ranch lands through which these rivers flow."[71] The first draft treaty submitted by the U.S. Secretary of State, Elihu Root, was not satisfactory to Canada. After some time, however, the dispute was settled and the solution incorporated into Article 6 of the Boundary Waters Treaty, which reads as follows:

> The High Contracting Parties agree that the St. Mary and Milk Rivers and their tributaries [in the State of Montana and the Provinces of Alberta and Saskatchewan] are to be treated as one stream for the purposes of irrigation and power, and the waters thereof shall be apportioned equally between the two countries, but in making such equal apportionment more than half may be taken from one river and less than half from the other by either country so as to afford a more beneficial use to each . . . The channel of the Milk River in Canada may be used at the convenience of the United States for the conveyance, while passing through Canadian territory, of waters diverted from the St. Mary River.[72]

---

son Bay basin. The tributaries of the Milk River flow northeast, converging in Canada before returning south and draining into the Missouri River basin. See M. E. Wolfe, "The Milk River: Deferred Water Policy Transitions in an International Waterway," 32 Natural Res. J. 55-76 (1992).

[69] Wolfe, *supra* note 68, at 66-67.

[70] *Ibid.*, 67.

[71] Simsarian, *supra* note 60, at 492.

[72] Each state receives an equal share of the combined flows of the two rivers during irrigation season; Canada receives three quarters of the natural flow of the St. Mary, and one-quarter of the Milk and the United States is entitled to the balance from each (the original allocations provided for in Article 6 were changed by agreement in 1921). See Bloomfield and FitzGerald, *supra* note 37, at 87-93.

The United States would later argue that this water dispute had been resolved on the basis of equitable apportionment.[73] What is important here is that the two states took a co-operative approach to resolving common problems by agreeing to apportion the waters of the two river basins equally, and this was done in the face of the heated negotiations of Article 2 of the Boundary Waters Treaty.[74] If the rules established by Article 2 had been applied, the result would have been very different.

DIVERSION OF THE NIAGARA RIVER AND FALLS

The United States and Canada settled another important international water dispute through Article 5 of the 1909 Treaty. Under that special provision, the diversion of the Niagara River above the Falls is controlled so as to preserve the beauty of the Falls with minimum detriment to hydroelectric concerns in Ontario and New York State.

Canada was allowed a diversion that was almost double that allotted to the United States. This unequal apportionment was based on recognition of the status quo and on the understanding that the additional hydroelectric power generated from the upstream Ontario diversion would be sold to the United States.[75] Within a decade, however, the United States wanted to increase the amount of its diversion rights to a level equal to that allowed to Canada. After lengthy negotiations and the creation of an international regulatory board to monitor the diversion issue, the two countries concluded a new agreement in 1950 that altered Article 5 of the 1909 Treaty.[76]

73 R. W. Johnson, "The Columbia Basin," in A. H. Garretson et al. (eds.), *supra* note 6, at 167-255, 204, reviews the American arguments.

74 A. Patry, *Le régime des cours d'eau internationaux* 67 (1960) asserts: "Cet article du traité 1909 fut peut-être la première application du principe de l'unité du bassin fluvial."

75 Piper, *supra* note 38, at 88-89. Dealey, *supra* note 63, at 312, 315, suggests that the unequal division in Canada's favour was meant to counterbalance the disadvantages suffered by it in the Chicago diversion matter.

76 Treaty between Canada and the United States of America concerning the Diversion of the Niagara River, signed at Washington Feb. 27, 1950, and entered into force Oct. 10, 1950, 132 UN Treaty Series, 223, C.T.S. 1950/3 [hereinafter Niagara River Treaty]. The Treaty effectively terminates paras. 3, 4, and 5 of Article 5 of the Boundary Waters Treaty and provides for an increased diversion of the Niagara River. A provision aimed at preserving the beauty of the Falls limits the amounts of the diversion during certain times and periods.

Article 3 of the 1950 Niagara River Treaty prescribes that "[t]he amount of water which shall be available for [power purposes] shall be the total outflow from Lake Erie to the Welland Canal and the Niagara River (including the Black Rock Canal) less the amount of water used and necessary for domestic and sanitary purposes and for the service of canals for the purpose of navigation"; all excess waters not necessary for "scenic purposes" could be diverted for power uses by each state.[77]

The Niagara River Treaty also provides that remedial works be completed to preserve the beauty of the Falls. The costs would be shared equally between the two countries, and the IJC was requested to make recommendations regarding the construction of these works.[78] The International Niagara Board of Control was established to supervise the level of Lake Erie and the flow over the Falls.[79]

THE CHICAGO DIVERSION

The Chicago diversion involves Lake Michigan, which lies entirely in the United States[80] and thus, under Article 2 of the Boundary Waters Treaty, is within the exclusive jurisdiction of the United States. The dispute relating to it is an old one, dating back to 1848 when the Illinois and Michigan Canal was completed.[81] In 1889 the Illinois legislature created the Sanitary District of Chicago Corporation which, shortly after the coming into force of the 1909 Treaty, diverted water in excess of the limit prescribed by the U.S. Secretary of War; Britain responded on behalf of Canada with a

[77] Articles 5 and 4 of the Niagara River Treaty.

[78] *Ibid.*, Article 2. The works were completed in 1957.

[79] Piper, *supra* note 38, at 90. The Control Board, which evolved from the Niagara River Control Board created in 1923 by the two governments, measures the diversion amounts.

[80] Lake Michigan is one of the five lakes comprising the Great Lakes Basin international waters, which are "approximately, fifty-nine per cent Canadian," and which constitute the "largest single supply of fresh water in the world"; S. A. Williams, "Public International Law and Water Quantity Management in a Common Drainage Basin," 18 Case Western Reserve J. Int'l L. 155-201, 155 (1986).

[81] IJC, Great Lakes Diversions and Consumptive Uses, 15 (1985), [hereinafter IJC, Great Lakes Diversions Report]. See also IJC, Further Regulation of the Great Lakes 22-23 (1976) [hereinafter IJC, Great Lakes Further Regulation Report].

note of protest.[82] The diversion was intended originally for sanitation purposes, but later hydroelectric power and other uses were also accommodated.[83] When Chicago pushed for additional diversion rights, the U.S. Congress resisted by stipulating in its authorizing Bill "that nothing in this Act shall be construed as authorizing any diversion of water from Lake Michigan."[84]

Under Article 2 of the 1909 Treaty, the uses of the waters of Lake Michigan were an exclusively domestic concern. Only material injury to navigation rights might affect the diversion issue, but in this respect, the problem was twofold: what constitutes "material injury," and what weight is to be given to Canada's complaint?[85] The 1909 Treaty does not provide guidelines for answering these questions, and neither do the rules of customary international law.[86]

The matter fell within the exclusive jurisdiction of the U.S. Supreme Court. After federal/state struggles in court,[87] a permit was issued by the U.S. federal government to the state of Illinois in 1925, allowing for diversion so long as there was "no unreasonable interference with navigation." Significant diversion from Lake Michigan did occur, however, which "worked grave injury to Canadian interests."[88] But instead of settling the issues by treaty, as had been done with the Lake of the Woods problem, the United States insisted on the unilateral diversion of the waters of Lake Michigan. That diversion was claimed to be permitted under Article 2 of the 1909 Treaty; in this context, Canada's only legal interest in Lake Michigan related to navigation rights.

The unhappy situation persisted, but soon negotiations commenced. Canada argued that Lake Michigan was an integral part of the Great Lakes system and should be considered as such. In 1932,

---

82 IJC, Great Lakes Diversions Report, *ibid.*

83 The Chicago diversion consists of three components: "(a) water supply withdrawn directly from Lake Michigan for domestic and industrial purposes and then discharged into the Illinois River as treated sewage; (b) runoff that once drained to Lake Michigan but is now diverted into the Illinois River; and (c) water diverted directly from Lake Michigan into the Illinois River and canal system for navigation and dilution purposes in the Chicago area": *ibid.*

84 H. A. Smith, "The Chicago Diversion," 10 Brit. Y. B. Int'l L. 144-57, 145 (1929).

85 Piper, *supra* note 38, at 95.

86 *Ibid.*, 101.

87 The U.S. federal government brought injunction proceedings against Illinois.

88 Smith, *supra* note 84, at 147.

a Treaty on the Great Lakes/St. Lawrence system, which stated that no further diversion from the Great Lakes system could be made without authorization of the IJC, was concluded between the two countries, but it was never ratified,[89] owing to its failure to win approval in Congress.[90]

Worth noting is the attitude of the U.S. Assistant Secretary of State, Mr. James Grafton Rogers, chief American negotiator. He declared that he was concerned with the practical considerations at hand, something that might be referred to as considerations of comity: "the mere result of the necessity of getting along with a neighbour nation, or neighbouring states . . . while theoretically, perhaps each nation had the right within its own boundaries to do as it saw fit, there were limits of companionship which required accommodation."[91]

The unratified 1932 Treaty was subsequently re-examined. In particular, an addition was made to its Article 7, expressly recognizing continued U.S. sovereignty over Lake Michigan.[92] Nevertheless, the amended version of 1938 was also not ratified; similar endeavours in 1941 equally failed to be approved by the U.S. Senate.[93] In 1954 and 1956, President Eisenhower, citing the opposition expressed by Canada, vetoed two bills that had been approved by

---

89 Great Lakes-St. Lawrence Deep Waterway Treaty between the United States and Canada, Sen. Ex. C., 72 Cong., 2 Sess.

90 Bédard, *supra* note 7, at 46.

91 Simsarian, *supra* note 60, at 515. The American Department of State solicitor in 1926 in an internal note expressed the same opinion: "It seems obvious that Canada is possessed of rights in the boundary waters, and in Lake Michigan, which are assured by law and by the terms of the Treaty of 1909, and that the diversions from Lake Michigan at Chicago sufficiently affect such rights as to require this Government, upon objection, to effect a remedy . . . Canada has substantial rights in respect of the waters of Lake Michigan which must be respected, and . . . these rights are recognized at least by implication in the second paragraph of Article 2 of the Boundary Waters Treaty of 1909 . . . " (quotation taken from Piper, *supra* note 38, at 99).

92 *Ibid.*, 517. Under the text of the added provision: "Nothing in this article or in any other article shall be construed as infringing or impairing, in any way, the sovereignty of the United States of America over Lake Michigan."

93 Bédard, *supra* note 7, at 46, states: "Toutefois, faute d'approbation par le Sénat des États-Unis, ces mesures ne furent jamais mises en application, pas plus, d'ailleurs que celles, identiques prévues par l'article 8 de l'accord du 19 mars 1941, qui, lui non plus n'a jamais pu obtenir la majorité des voix requises au Sénat des États-Unis."

Congress and authorized an increased diversion.[94] The Water Resources Development Act (Public Law 94-587), passed in 1976 by Congress, which provided for "a study and demonstration program affecting the rate of the Chicago diversion,"[95] was included in the reference to the IJC. The most recent decision by the U.S. Supreme Court on the matter, dated June 12, 1967, restricts diversion rights at Chicago, effective March 1, 1970.[96]

The Chicago diversion has remained a source of irritation between the two countries. It is more than a simple diversion issue, since in fact it entails a net loss to the Great Lakes system. The water diverted is not returned to the latter but is channelled into the Mississippi River drainage basin. Canada has continued to express strong opposition to increased diversions; nevertheless, while the United States has yet to take such action, there have been recent proposals to divert unilaterally the waters of Lake Michigan to relieve the drought-stricken areas of the American Southwest and West.[97]

This issue has finally become the subject of a series of references to the IJC regarding the levels of the Great Lakes, Lake Michigan being included in the Great Lakes system.[98] The 1967 reference was the first Commission docket to encompass Lake Michigan; this docket was "certainly within the spirit if not the letter of Article 9 of the Boundary Waters Treaty."[99]

Where in the past both governments have appeared reticent in referring the Lake Michigan issue to the IJC, the practice now adopted by both is to approach the Great Lakes system as a whole. This practice may provide the Commission with an opportunity to

---

94 IJC, Great Lakes Diversions Report 15.

95 *Ibid.* The program failed to receive adequate funding in the U.S., and new legislation is required before further action can be taken.

96 *Wisconsin* v. *Illinois*, 388 U.S. 426 (1967) (reprinted in IJC, Great Lakes Further Regulation Report, 91-93) limited diversion to 3,200 cubic feet per second, annually, from the earlier high of 10,000 cubic feet (283m^3) per second. A state permit is required for major new or increased consumptive uses.

97 Kalavrouziotis, *supra* note 66, at 658, refers to "Fire and Water," *Economist,* July 23, 1988, at 22-23, in which these diversion proposals (which have never been acted upon) are discussed.

98 See IJC, IJC Activities 1987-1988, at 40-43, docket numbers 82R, 83R, 94R, 95R, 200R, 104R, 106R, and 111R.

99 D. C. Piper, "A Significant Docket for the International Joint Commission," 59 Am. J. Int'l L. 593-97, 594 (1965).

resolve definitively the Chicago diversion question. Although the report of the IJC will not be binding on the two governments, "one can anticipate [that it] will carry considerable weight. . . ."[100]

THE SOURIS RIVER

The Souris River is a small watercourse that rises in Saskatchewan and crosses the border south into North Dakota before turning north (again across the border) through southwestern Manitoba on its way to Lake Winnipeg and Hudson Bay. It was the subject of a joint reference to the IJC in 1940.[101] The Commission was asked, *inter alia*, "what apportionment should be made of the waters of the Souris (Mouse) River and its tributaries. . . ."[102] The matter focused on competing uses for the limited resources of the Souris. Saskatchewan, where human consumptive needs have priority, claimed that Article 2 of the Boundary Waters Treaty entitled it to do with its waters as it pleased (especially in times of shortage). It was also concerned that Manitoba was being deprived of its share of the waters of the basin for human consumption.[103] North Dakota, where huge amounts of water were used for wildlife refuges (thus depleting the flow into Manitoba), claimed rights of prior appropriation.[104]

The IJC responded with a recommendation of interim measures, which the two states agreed to adopt. The measures called for preservation of the status quo, with the added proviso that Manitoba be afforded a regulated flow; new uses would require the permission of the IJC.[105]

In 1957 Saskatchewan advised the government of Canada that it no longer considered itself bound by the interim measures of

---

100 *Ibid.*, 596.

101 Bloomfield and FitzGerald, *supra* note 37, at 154.

102 IJC, Report of Mar. 19, 1958 on the Souris River, with special reference to the interim measures recommended in its report of Oct. 2, 1940, at 1 [hereinafter IJC, Souris River Report].

103 Saskatchewan, under Article 2 of the Boundary Waters Treaty was free to divert as it pleased (i.e. by pipeline to Manitoba). Instead, it continued to pass 50 per cent of the natural flow of the Souris to North Dakota until the matter could be finally resolved: IJC, Souris River Report 5.

104 Bloomfield and FitzGerald, *supra* note 37, at 155.

105 IJC, Souris River Report 2-3.

1940.[106] While the province was willing to allow 50 per cent of the flow of the Souris to pass south of the border pending resolution of the matter, it demanded a "permanent settlement" and claimed increased diversion rights. This led to a reference to the IJC that resulted in an adjustment of the interim measures. The IJC's recommendations confirmed the importance of "making water available for human and livestock consumption and for household use."[107] Additionally, the IJC affirmed the provisions of Article 2 of the 1909 Boundary Waters Treaty, stating: "These measures also recognize that once they are in effect, the use of water within a province or State will be under the exclusive jurisdiction of that political entity and that each province or State may then utilize its share of the water in accordance with its own laws governing the use of water."[108] Canada and the United States approved the recommendations of the IJC, creating a joint board of engineers to ensure compliance with the recommendations.

The issue has recently been resolved by a treaty[109] whereby Canada agreed to construct two dams for storage and flood control.[110] The agreement, following the Columbia River accords,[111] provided for flood control payments,[112] shared operations costs,[113] and required continuing notification and consultation regarding the implementation of the project.[114] Water quality concerns received special attention with the creation of a "Bilateral Water Quality Monitoring Group," which is responsible for ensuring continued

---

[106] Saskatchewan asked for "a permanent settlement" demanding increased diversion; it "always considered that the waters in Saskatchewan belong to Saskatchewan while they are within the boundaries of the province and this view is consistent with the terms of Article II of the 1909 Treaty": IJC, Souris River Report 5.

[107] *Ibid.*, 7.

[108] *Ibid.*, 7-8.

[109] The agreement between the Government of Canada and the Government of the United States of America for Water Supply and Flood Control in the Souris River Basin came into force upon signing, Mar. 24, 1989.

[110] Article 2 refers to the details regarding the construction of the Rafferty and Alameda dams.

[111] See *infra* note 117 and accompanying text.

[112] Article 4.

[113] Article 4(3) provides that construction costs for the dams will be allocated "on the proportionate use of the Rafferty Dam and Alameda Dam for flood control in the U.S.A. and water supply in Canada."

[114] Articles 3(5), 4(4) (5) (6), 5, 8 (1).

monitoring of water quality.[115] Individuals are not given rights of action.[116]

THE COLUMBIA RIVER DISPUTE

The Columbia River Treaty and protocols, which were ratified in 1964,[117] marked the unequivocal demise of the Harmon Doctrine in respect of Canada-United States relations. This treaty also put an end to one of the most heated and extended debates in Canada-United States history.[118]

The Columbia River basin system covers an enormous area in the western parts of Canada and the United States; the river, one of the longest in North America, stretches over nearly 2,000 kilometres.[119] It traverses the Canada–United States border twice before reaching the Pacific Ocean, and drains an area of some 676,000 km^2 in two Canadian provinces and seven U.S. states.[120] Its average runoff is 22 million hectare-metres per year, and its numerous tributaries comprise both boundary and non-boundary waters.[121]

Both Canada and the United States were anxious to develop and control the Columbia basin.[122] In 1944 they jointly requested the

[115] Article 6.

[116] Article 11(2). Article 2 of the Boundary Waters Treaty would still seem to apply.

[117] Treaty Relating to the Co-operative Development of the Water Resources of the Columbia River Basin, Jan. 17, 1961, with related agreements effected by exchange of notes at Washington Jan. 22, 1964, and at Ottawa Sept. 16, 1964, 542 UN Treaty Series 244, C.T.S. 1964/2 [hereinafter Columbia River Treaty].

[118] Yet, in the midst of these debates, "one of the interesting things about the diversion argument was that virtually no one suggested that the 1909 Treaty should be terminated, although Article 14 of the 1909 Treaty provides that it may be terminated on twelve months' written notice": Johnson, *supra* note 73, at 239.

[119] In North America, only the Mississippi, St. Lawrence, and Mackenzie rivers exceed the flow of the Columbia River. See D. G. Lemarquand, *International Rivers: The Politics of Cooperation* 54 (1977).

[120] K. N. Lee, "The Columbia River Basin: Experimenting with Sustainability," 31(6) Environment 7 (July/August 1989).

[121] Johnson, *supra* note 73, at 171.

[122] The United States was especially concerned with flood control on the Columbia River (The Dalles had been devastated by a flood in 1894). The other major issue was the development of hydroelectric power. Eleven applications regarding development of the Kootenay River were put to the IJC between

IJC to investigate and make recommendations regarding the development of the water resources of the Columbia; the reference included tributary waters, a clear exception to Article 2 of the 1909 Treaty. The elaboration of the Commission's report in response to this request took some fifteen years.

The IJC found that the primary uses of the Columbia River basin were the generation of hydroelectric power, flood control, and irrigation. This assessment was based entirely on engineering and economic considerations.[123] The Commission proposed three plans that could accommodate the uses identified.[124] The Columbia River Treaty would embody a combination of two of the plans.[125]

The two major issues in the Columbia River dispute were Canada's diversion rights[126] and the matter of downstream benefits.[127] Regarding the first issue, the United States argued that Article 2 of the Boundary Waters Treaty was subject to the rules of customary law in the field, which provided (at a minimum) that uses be equitably apportioned and (more ideally) that previous existing uses constitute an important factor in the determination of equitable use.[128] Canada's position was that Article 2 permitted unilateral

---

1927 and 1944. IJC, Report on Principles for Determining and Apportioning Benefits from Cooperative Use of Storage of Waters and Electrical Interconnection Within the Columbia River System 26 [hereinafter IJC, Columbia River Apportionment Report].

[123] Johnson, *supra* note 73, at 212.

[124] *Ibid.*, 212-16. See A. G. L. McNaughton, "The Proposed Columbia River Treaty," 18 Int'l J. 148-65 (1963).

[125] A combination of the Non-Diversion and Copper Creek Diversion Plans was adopted. Control of the Columbia would come from three dams to be built in Canada: the Mica (the largest on the main stem of the Columbia), the Arrow Lakes (on the main river), and the Duncan Lake (on the Kootenay system tributary).

[126] Article 2 of the 1909 Boundary Waters Treaty was at the heart of the debate. For a summary of the arguments advanced by both sides, see Johnson, *supra* note 73, at 205-6, and 167-70.

[127] The United States refused to compensate Canada for the downstream benefits (increased flood control and hydroelectric power) that it would receive as a result of the development.

[128] See "Legal Aspects of the Use of Systems of International Waters: With Special Reference to the Columbia-Kootenay River System Under the Treaty of 1909 and Under Customary International Law," Memorandum of the Department of State prepared by Mr. William L. Griffin, April 1958, Sen. Doc. 118, 85th Cong., 2nd Sess., 146 [hereinafter Griffin Memorandum], which states:

diversion of those tributary waters located on its side of the border.[129] The issue of downstream benefits was also polarized: the United States refused to consider that Canada should receive any compensation for the benefits to be received in the United States as a result of development of the river in Canada.[130] Both these hotly debated issues were finally resolved in accordance with the recommendations of the IJC.

In response to a request by the two governments for recommendations regarding the apportionment of the costs and benefits of the project,[131] the IJC proposed an equal sharing of the downstream benefits and costs. In making its recommendations, it "was guided by the basic concept that the principles recommended . . . should result in an equitable sharing of the benefits attributable to their co-operative undertakings and that these should result in advantage to each country as compared with alternatives available to that country."[132] This guideline formed the basis for the three general and thirteen specific principles recommended by the IJC,[133] all of which would be included in the Columbia River Treaty.[134] At the core of the general principles formulated by the

---

"Riparians are entitled to share in the use and benefits of a system of international waters on a just and equitable basis." See also R. W. Johnson, "Effect of Existing Uses on the Equitable Apportionment of International Rivers: An American View," 1 Univ. Brit. Col. L. Rev. 389-98 (1959-1963); D. M. M. Goldie, "Effect of Existing Uses on Equitable Apportionment of International Rivers: A Canadian View," *ibid.*, 399-408.

129 Griffin Memorandum, *ibid.*, 1-5; Johnson, *supra* note 73, at 203.

130 C. E. Martin, "International Water Problems in the West," in Deener, *supra* note 39, at 55, discusses the principles of legal settlement and the positions taken by each of the two states in the Columbia River dispute.

131 The IJC was asked to provide "recommendations concerning the principles to be applied in determining: (a) the benefits which will result from the cooperative use of storage of waters and electrical interconnection within the Columbia River System and (b) the apportionment between the two countries of such benefits more particularly in regard to electrical generation and flood control": IJC, Columbia River Apportionment Report 2.

132 *Ibid.*

133 The recommendations included three general principles, seven "power principles" and six "flood control" principles: *ibid.*, 5-30.

134 The Treaty incorporates the "sharing-of-benefits principle": M. Epstein, "The Columbia River Treaty: A Chronological Study," 5 Columbia J. Transnational L. 167-72, 169 (1966).

IJC was the notion that all factors be considered in the evaluation of the benefits and costs of the project.[135]

The Treaty provides for a scheme ensuring the control and regulation of the flow of the basin's waters. Canada agreed to construct three major storage dams (at Mica Creek, Arrow Lakes, and Duncan Lake) that would be the source of increased production of hydroelectric power and flood control.[136] In return, Canada was to be entitled to half the downstream power benefits[137] and would receive a lump sum ($64.4 million U.S.) for primary flood control[138] plus a share of the excess hydroelectric power generated. Canada further agreed to restrict its right to divert the waters of the Kootenay over a specified period of time,[139] and the United States was given five years from the date of ratification of the Treaty to proceed with the Libby Dam development.[140] Additional provisions of the Treaty and subsequent protocols cover future calls for flood control,[141] the calculation and payment of power benefits (for Canada),[142] the creation of a technical board,[143] and a mechanism for dispute resolution.[144]

The Columbia River Treaty and the subsequent protocols were

---

[135] The IJC stated that, while a benefit-cost ratio approach was an important guideline in apportioning the benefits and costs of the project, "there may be important non-monetary factors, not reflected in the benefit-cost ratio, which may require consideration and which may be of compelling influence in choosing projects for construction. Such factors include the disruption of community and regional economies, scenic, historic or aesthetic considerations, the preservation of fish and wildlife, and similar considerations, which cannot be adequately evaluated in monetary terms": IJC, Columbia River Apportionment Report 6.

[136] Columbia River Treaty, Article 4.

[137] *Ibid.*, Article 5; power benefits as determined under Article 7.

[138] *Ibid.*, Article 6.

[139] *Ibid.*, Article 13 provides for increased rights of diversion; these have not been acted on: N. A. Swainson, "The Columbia River Treaty: Where Do We Go From Here?" 26 Natural Res. J. 243-60, 247 (1986).

[140] *Ibid.*, Article 12. The United States exercised this option: Swainson, *supra* note 139.

[141] *Ibid.*, Article 1, Protocol.

[142] *Ibid.*, Article 8, Protocol and Annex B of the Treaty.

[143] *Ibid.*, Article 15, "Permanent Engineering Board."

[144] *Ibid.*, Article 16.

ratified in 1964[145] with the following joint statement issued by the Canadian prime minister and the president of the United States: "The Treaty, together with the arrangements now being made, represents an important step in achieving optimum development of the water resources of the Columbia River basin as a whole, from which the United States and Canada will each receive benefits materially larger than either could obtain independently."[146] Both governments expressed their satisfaction over their agreement on the apportionment of the uses of the waters of the Columbia River basin system. Provision was made, however, that the Columbia River Treaty not serve as a precedent: Article 2 of the Boundary Waters Treaty is to continue to govern outstanding water disputes.[147]

THE GARRISON DIVERSION UNIT

In 1965 the United States Congress authorized the construction of the Garrison Diversion Unit (GDU), a project in North Dakota involving a diversion from the Missouri (one of the principal rivers of the Mississippi drainage basin) into the Hudson Bay drainage basin via the Souris and Red Rivers which flow into Manitoba. This project also affects the waters of the Assiniboine River and Lakes Manitoba and Winnipeg.[148] When construction commenced in 1967, the governments of Canada and Manitoba complained that the return flows resulting from the scheme would have adverse

---

[145] The Columbia River Treaty was signed by Prime Minister Diefenbaker and President Eisenhower in 1961. The Protocol was finalized in 1964 under the new governments of President Kennedy in the United States and Prime Minister Pearson in Canada. The resolution of the issue was a priority for all of the four national government parties involved over the course of the conflict.

[146] J. G. Castel, *International Law* 416 (1976).

[147] Article 17 of the Columbia River Treaty and para. 12 of the Protocol provide that the Columbia River agreement does not set any precedent. The provisions of Article 2 of the 1909 Boundary Waters Treaty survive for all other international watercourses.

[148] IJC, "Transboundary Implications of the Garrison Diversion Unit," Report to the Governments of Canada and the United States 5 (1977) [hereinafter IJC, Garrison Report]. See *ibid.*, 5-9, for a history of the issue, and 11-18 for more details of the project. See also Lynton K. Caldwell, "Garrison Diversion: Constraints on Conflict Resolution," 24 Natural Res. J. 839-63 (1984); K. R. Nossal, "The International Joint Commission and the Garrison Diversion," International Perspectives 22-25(1978).

transboundary effects, including flooding, degraded water quality, and transfer of foreign biota into the Hudson Bay drainage basin.[149]

In their joint reference to the IJC in 1975, Canada and the United States asked the Commission to report on the transboundary implications of the GDU and to make recommendations that would ensure compliance with Article 4 of the Boundary Waters Treaty. In the event that the IJC made recommendations "concerning measures to avoid or relieve adverse effects in Canada, it was requested to estimate the costs of such measures."[150] The IJC established the International Garrison Diversion Study Board, conducted eight public hearings, and entertained written submissions.

The state of North Dakota argued, *inter alia*, that the Boundary Waters Treaty gave it "the right to use its water as it [saw] fit, provided that it passed the water into Canada in a useable form,"[151] and that in any event Article 2 of the 1909 Treaty provided "for a remedy should injury to health or property in Canada occur since Canadians may claim for damages in United States courts."[152] Canada (and Manitoba and its citizens) maintained that the transboundary impacts would be adverse, numerous, and require increased treatment practices and expenditures.[153] The IJC recommended "that the portion of the Garrison Diversion Unit which affects waters flowing into Canada not be built at this time"[154] on the basis of its conclusion that "the construction and operation of the Garrison Diversion Unit as envisaged would cause injury to health and

149 IJC, Garrison Report, *ibid.*

150 *Ibid.*, 6; complete text of the reference, *ibid.*, 130-32. The reference urged the United States and Canada ascribe particular importance to the views of the Commission on this matter. Accordingly, the Commission is requested to complete its investigation and submit its report in the minimum possible time, consistent with a thorough examination of the subject, but in any case, not later than October 31, 1976": *ibid.*, 132 (the date of the reference was Oct. 22, 1975, and the final report was made on Aug. 12, 1977).

151 *Ibid.*, 88. North Dakota suggested that "its own strict water quality standards would guarantee the utility of return flows passed into Canada."

152 *Ibid.*

153 *Ibid.*, 89-93. The adverse impacts included degraded water quality, inter-basin transfer of foreign biota with subsequent reduction of fish population, decreased waterfowl population, increased blackfly population, and serious injury to the health and property of native peoples in Canada.

154 *Ibid.*, 121.

property in Canada as a result of adverse impacts on the water quality and biological resources in Manitoba."[155]

In arriving at its conclusions, the IJC chose to adopt a broad interpretation of the concept of "transboundary implications" (referred to in the joint reference). It held that the use of this term meant that the reference included matters "which go beyond the traditional concept of pollution."[156] The IJC considered this to be a "forward-looking concept," meaning that uses will not be analyzed from "a narrow pollution sense, but rather advice will be sought as to the general impacts of projects on the natural resources of the adjoining country;" it thus adopted a "total systems concept" in its approach to the issue.[157]

The IJC stated that the approach under Article 4 of the Boundary Waters Treaty "is to simply forbid pollution to the injury of health or property. This requires a frequent determination of 'pollution,' of 'injury,' of 'health,' and of 'property' and thus inevitably invites disputes over law and fact, and provokes acrimony between neighbours."[158] This approach was considered to be *ex post facto*, one "which does not envisage any prior joint planning of a shared transboundary water resource where each partner may be upstream in some cases and, in others, downstream."[159]

The IJC preferred "the other possibility" to water quality management, "which by its very agreement on commonly-shared objectives will prevent disputes and also will likely enhance the possibility of the optimum use of the river without stimulating harassing debates as to who 'owns' what with the right to use or abuse 'his share' of the water."[160] It suggested that "it would be far better to approach the problem of GDU and other basin developments from

155 *Ibid.*, 3.
156 *Ibid.*, 96-97.
157 *Ibid.*, 97.
158 *Ibid.*, 117.
159 *Ibid.*
160 *Ibid.* The IJC stated further: "At present, Canada and the United States are constrained in resource development activities only by Article IV for the upstream neighbour and by local law and policy for the downstream country. In such a situation the downstream state naturally will seek to utilize, to the fullest extent possible, the potential municipal and industrial uses of its share of the river. It also will demand of the upstream state that the waters come to the boundary free from pollution, at least to the extent defined as 'injury.' Such debates tend to provoke procedural and negotiating disputes that are likely to be not only distressing but insoluble": *ibid.*, 118.

the aspect of equitable utilization of the river basin or watercourse on behalf of both countries, through a system of water quality management based on agreed objectives and standards. . . . This is not a requirement of the Boundary Waters Treaty but rather is a conception that goes beyond that Treaty. . . ."[161]

On this note, following its recommendation against the GDU insofar as the latter could affect Canadian waters, the IJC recommended that the two countries negotiate "appropriate water quality agreements for the Souris and Red Rivers."[162] This recommendation appeared to anticipate the possible complete construction of the GDU, which could be envisaged under the conditions set out in the IJC's second recommendation.[163] To date, however, the Garrison Dam Unit has not been built.

POPLAR RIVER BASIN

The IJC made recommendations to the governments of Canada and the United States on the apportionment of the uses of the waters of the Poplar River Basin on April 12, 1978, in response to a reference dating back to 1948.[164] The Poplar River rises in southern Saskatchewan and flows into northeastern Montana, emptying into the Missouri River near Poplar, Montana; it has three main branches that originate in Canada, traversing an "area where water is life."[165] All the basin waters crossing the boundary originate in Saskatchewan, where four major storage facilities have been built to conserve the spring run-off.

The 1948 reference was concerned with apportionment of the waters (quantity issues); questions of air pollution and water quality thus fell outside the scope of the reference, although these issues

---

161 *Ibid.*

162 *Ibid.*, 122 (Recommendation 3). The IJC was not unanimous in its position; Commissioner Beaupré, while in agreement with most of the IJC's conclusions and recommendations, differed on the approach taken to the Water Quality Agreement portion of the Report: *ibid.*, 125-28.

163 *Ibid.*, 122. Recommendation 2 provides that "if and when" the two governments agree that the risk of biota transfer is eliminated or agreed to be no longer a matter of concern, the GDU could be constructed, provided that six conditions were met.

164 IJC, Water Apportionment in the Poplar River Basin, 1978 [hereinafter IJC, Poplar River Report]. The text of the reference is found at 83-84.

165 *Ibid.*, 3. Uses of the basins were largely appropriated: the IJC noted that there were 225 projects in Saskatchewan and 672 projects in Montana: *ibid.*, 15-16; for domestic, irrigation, municipal, industrial, and wildlife purposes: *ibid.*, 19.

were frequently raised as concerns throughout the proceedings. Extreme claims were made by each side in the dispute over apportionment. The Saskatchewan Power Corporation (which, in 1974, announced a development project that included a thermal electric plant, storage reservoir, and lignite coal mine) argued that Article 2 of the Boundary Waters Treaty gave it "the exclusive jurisdiction and control over the use and diversion over all Poplar River waters arising in Saskatchewan"; the Sioux and Assiniboine tribes of the Fort Peck Indian Reservation in Montana claimed an "inchoate right to the use of the waters of the Poplar" rejecting the notion of any apportionment based on "an historic right"; Montana wanted an equitable sharing.[166]

The alternative (and slightly more reasonable) claims advanced by each side focused on equitable apportionment with reference by Montana and Saskatchewan to the ILA's Helsinki Rules. The issue became which factors should be considered and what weight should be given to the factors, especially in view of Articles 4 and 2 of the Boundary Waters Treaty. The IJC "in assessing the apportionment recommended by the Board . . . [gave] due consideration to all the factors identified [in the Helsinki Rules]."[167]

The IJC concluded its 1978 study with a recommendation that "the waters of the Poplar River Basin, which originate in Canada and which, in their natural channels, would cross the International Boundary, be apportioned equally between the United States and Canada with flexibility among individual transboundary streams. . . ."[168] The apportionment agreement (to be worked out

---

166 Saskatchewan held the view that as upstream user it could be entitled to 70 per cent of the natural flow at the Boundary "without detrimental effects to the downstream country. . . .": *ibid.*, 37. The Fort Peck Sioux and Assiniboine tribes claimed a 70 per cent apportionment in favour of the United States on the basis of "existing uses of water and development potential": *ibid.*, 47. Montana urged that the Saskatchewan power plant (already under construction) should not be considered as an existing use: *ibid.*, 46; and while Montana "did not argue for existing use consideration on behalf of the Fort Peck Indians . . . [it] claimed the special nature of their dependence on Poplar flows should be considered": *ibid.*, 40.

167 *Ibid.*, 68.

168 *Ibid.*, 81. This recommendation was subject to the conditions set out by the IJC at 23-25 of the Report, where the particular flows of each river and its tributaries are apportioned so that the net result is an equal division of the aggregate natural flow.

between the two states) would be reviewed upon completion of the IJC's water quality studies of the basin initiated by joint reference of August 2, 1977.

The 1977 reference requested the IJC to report upon the water quality of the Poplar River, "including the transboundary water quality implications of the thermal power station of the Saskatchewan Power Corporation and its ancilliary facilities . . . and make recommendations which would assist Governments in ensuring that the provisions of Article 4 of the [Boundary Waters Treaty] are honoured."[169] In its 1981 Report on the matter, the IJC concluded "that the apportionment recommended in 1978 remains equitable and should be adopted . . . and that Article 4 of the Treaty will not be violated in so doing."[170] In reaching this recommendation, the IJC referred again to the Helsinki Rules and discussed at length the relationship between equitable apportionment and Article 4 of the 1909 Treaty. The Commission decided that, while the use of waters upstream in Saskatchewan would cause some adverse water quality impacts on uses downstream (in Montana), this fact alone would not constitute an automatic violation of Article 4. The IJC stated that "issues of equitable apportionment and the obligations of Article 4 must be examined at the same time" and added that "water quality objectives can equally well be viewed as one of the conditions of an equitable apportionment."[171] The practical import of this approach meant that adverse effects (on water quantity and quality) could be condoned provided that there was an equitable apportionment of water resources; this lifted the constraints on development imposed by Article 4 and made equitable apportionment the governing test.[172]

---

169 IJC, *Water Quality in the Poplar River Basin*, 1981 [hereinafter IJC, 1981 *Poplar Water Quality Report*].

170 IJC, 1981 *Poplar River Water Quality Report*, 199.

171 *Ibid.*, 191, 203.

172 In the Poplar River water quality reference this approach led the IJC to conclude: "Thus, considering the above uncertainties, the small extent of the estimated impacts on downstream users in relation to the basin as a whole, the actions taken and commitments made in Canada to minimize the effects, the proposed division of the transboundary flows, and the course of action hereinafter recommended, the Commission concludes that the apportionment recommended in 1978 remains equitable and should be adopted . . . and that Article 4 of the Treaty will not be violated in so doing": *ibid.*, 198-99.

FLATHEAD RIVER: RECENT RECOMMENDATIONS BY THE IJC

The Flathead River basin, which drains an area of some 18,400 km², is composed of three strands of the Flathead River: the North Fork, which has its source in south-eastern British Columbia, and the Middle and South Forks, which rise in the Bob Marshall Wilderness in the United States.[173] The three watercourses converge and empty into the Flathead, "the largest natural freshwater lake in the continental United States west of the Mississippi."[174] In 1984–1985, pursuant to Article 9 of the Boundary Waters Treaty, the IJC received letters from the United States and Canada requesting that it "examine and report on the water quality and quantity of the Flathead River, relating to the transboundary water quality and quantity implications of a proposed open pit coal mine on Cabin Creek, a tributary of the North Fork of the Flathead River" and that it "make recommendations that would assist the Governments in ensuring that the provisions of Article 4 of the Boundary Waters Treaty of 1909" would be honoured.[175] The IJC established the Flathead River International Study Board to deal with the matter. The Board established a subcommittee, a task force, and four technical committees, and commenced its work in April 1985. Its final report was submitted to the IJC in July 1988.[176]

Following its review of the comprehensive reports of the Study Board, the IJC noted that "nearly all of the Board's conclusions are subject to varying degrees of uncertainty" and emphasized the insufficiency of information in numerous areas.[177] While the Board found that the development would not affect water quantity, water quality concerns were a different matter. The Board suggested that

173 D. Ross, "International Management of the Flathead River Basin," 1 Colorado J. Int'l Environmental L. and Pol. 223-39, 223 (1990).

174 IJC, "Impacts of a Proposed Coal Mine in the Flathead River Basin," Dec. 1988, at 6 [hereinafter IJC, Flathead River Report].

175 Ibid., 3. For the full text of the reference, see ibid., Appendix A, 15-16. Article 4 of the Boundary Waters Treaty provides that waters "shall not be polluted on either side to the injury of health or property on the other."

176 See Ibid., 4, for a list of the reports submitted by the Flathead River International Study Board.

177 The uncertainties included concerns over "groundwater flows between the mines site and the creeks, with concomitant concern about toxic levels of nitrogen components, temperature changes and dissolved oxygen levels [and] potential risk of extreme or unusual events occurring such as the failure of waste dumps and settling ponds"; there were also uncertainties about the impact on various fish populations: ibid., 7.

"there is the strong probability" that at some time reverse ground-water flow would "undoubtedly have the deleterious effect fore-seen for the eggs and fry in the spawning ground and habitat . . . and act as an impediment to the adult fish in reaching and/or using those altered grounds."[178]

The IJC found that the loss of the fishery that could result from the development scheme would "create a negative impact on the associated infrastructure since the affected fish populations migrate for much of their adult lives to the United States waters."[179] It concluded that "the pollution expected to cause these con-sequences to the fishery would clearly constitute a breach of Article 4."[180] The pollution on one side of the border would have an adverse effect on a fishery that migrated across the border, and this, in the IJC's opinion, was contrary to Article 4. The IJC asserted that:

there are far-reaching implications of this Article IV principle. . . . In such cases, there is a mutual obligation to protect a fishery that migrates between the United States and Canada by a range of management practices in both countries which will ensure that the provisions of the Treaty will be honoured jointly. This principle should apply, even though the degree of the risk cannot be measured with certainty, unless and until it is agreed that such an impact . . . or the risk of it occurring is acceptable to both parties.[181]

The coalmine was not approved by the Commission, which believed that:

when any proposed development project has been shown to create an identified risk of a transboundary impact in contravention of the Treaty, existence of that risk should be sufficient to prevent the development from proceeding. Having in mind the risks and the sensitivity of uses downstream (including Glacier National Park) to environmental changes, the Commission considered the mine proposal to be such a case. This, together with the damage to the fishery . . . constitute the basis for the recommendations.[182]

The IJC emphasized that it did not base its conclusion "as to the harmful effects on the fish solely on the anticipated results of the liberation of toxic substances. Rather the conclusion is based on the overwhelming evidence . . . that a significant loss of fish population

178 *Ibid.*, 8.
179 *Ibid.*
180 *Ibid.*, 9.
181 *Ibid.*
182 *Ibid.*

will occur as the result of a combination of the adverse effects of one or more of the predicted changes and not solely because of the increased level of toxic substances."[183] However, while the Commission recommended the rejection of the coal mine proposal, it offered guidelines under which the project might be approved in the future.[184]

IV OTHER ISSUES

Three points should be made here: first, while the IJC has been involved in many watercourse disputes, the two neighbours have not referred all disputes to the Commission;[185] second, the Commission has not always been unanimous in its recommendations;[186]

---

[183] *Ibid.*, 8.

[184] *Ibid.*, 11. The IJC's recommendations were that:

  (1) the mine proposal as presently defined and understood not be approved;

  (2) the mine proposal not receive regulatory approval in the future unless and until it can be demonstrated that:

  (a) the potential transboundary impacts identified in the report of the Flathead River International Study Board have been determined with reasonable certainty and would constitute a level of risk acceptable to both Governments; and,

  (b) the potential impacts on the sports fishery populations and habitat in the Flathead River System would not occur or could be fully mitigated in an effective and assured manner; and,

  (3) the Governments encourage and pursue, with the appropriate jurisdictions, other opportunities for defining and implementing compatible and sustainable development activities and management strategies in the upper Flathead River basin.

[185] The IJC, Great Lakes Diversions Report, Appendix G, 82, lists the following as "Suggested Diversions that Have International Implications": Grand Canal Plan (Kierans); Great Lakes-Pacific Waterways Plan (Decker); North American Water and Power Alliance (NAWAPA); Magnum Plan (Magnusson); Kuiper Plan (Kuiper); Central North America Water Project (CeNAWP); Western States Water Augmentation Concept (Smith); NAWAPA + MUSHEC or Mexican-States Hydroelectric Commission (source quoted Asit K. Biswas, "North American Water Transfers: An Overview," Water Supply and Management, 1978, vol. 2). To date, the IJC has not been involved in any of the foregoing projects.

[186] E.g., in the Belly-Waterton Rivers Reference of Jan. 12, 1948, under which the IJC was asked to make recommendations on the apportionment and uses of the waters of the Belly and Waterton Rivers, the Commission divided on national lines; a joint report was not made to the governments. R. B. Bilder, in "When Neighbours Quarrel: Canada-U.S. Dispute Settlement Experience,"

and, finally, while recent issues have led to an expanded role for the IJC,[187] the Canadian and United States governments have the final say.[188]

Under the Great Lakes Levels References of 1964,[189] 1977,[190] and 1986,[191] and the Great Lakes Water Quality Agreements,[192] the IJC has been involved in the multiple issues relating to the Great Lakes ecosystem. In a news release following the 1986 Great Lakes Water Levels Reference, the IJC stated that "it appreciates and welcomes the fact that this far-reaching Reference will involve new initiatives and that its nature and terms authorize the Commission to undertake new approaches far beyond those authorized in

---

Disputes Processing Research Program, Working Papers, Series 8, 55 (May 1987) notes that out of 110 applications and references considered to that date by the IJC, "in only four cases have there been dissenting opinions; in only two of these were the dissents divided on national lines. Only two reports of any of the Boards of the Commission have divided along national lines. More than three-quarters of the Commission recommendations with respect to its references have been adopted by the two governments, in one form or another."

[187] The 1972 Great Lakes Water Quality Agreement granted the IJC the authority to oversee pollution projects and to establish a Great Lakes regional office.

[188] See D. Munton, "Paradoxes and Prospects," in R. Spencer, J. Kirton, and K. R. Nossal (eds.), *The International Joint Commission Seventy Years On* 60, at 81 (1981). Munton discusses three recent situations (the St. Marys River ice boom, Point Roberts, and the Windsor regional office) in which the IJC attempted unsuccessfully to broaden its reaches; he concludes, at 81: "The Commission nevertheless remains a less than equal match for the sovereign will of the two governments which created it." Munton also notes that where transboundary problems are more controversial (i.e. "where up-stream and down-stream 'stakes' are not similar"), and in view of the emergence of complex ecosystem issues, the task of the IJC will become increasingly more difficult.

[189] For text of the Reference, see *supra* note 81.

[190] *Ibid.*

[191] The 1986 Reference is found in "Living With The Lakes: Challenges and Opportunities: A Progress Report to the International Joint Commission," by the Project Management Team, Apppendix 1, 67-75 (July 1989) [hereinafter IJC, Great Lakes Report, 1989].

[192] Great Lakes Water Quality Agreement, United States-Canada, Apr. 15, 1972, C.T.S. 1972/12, 23 UST 301, 24 UST 2268, TIAS No. 7312, 7747; amended 1978, Great Lakes Water Quality Agreement, United States-Canada, Nov. 22, 1978, C.T.S. 1978/20, 30 UST 1384, TIAS No. 9257.

previous References."[193] The earlier studies of the Great Lakes Levels References culminated in the recognition of the complexity of the issue: "a new paradigm, a new way of thinking . . . a new methodology" is required.[194] An earlier example of the IJC's creative involvement in the resolution of an international watercourse problem occurred in the Skagit-High Ross Dam dispute, in which the IJC provided the impetus for the settlement of a four-decade long controversy.[195]

Canada and the United States have requested the aid of the IJC in resolving numerous problems of watercourse use allocation. While the Boundary Waters Treaty provides guidelines to be considered in the resolution of these problems, history has shown that the IJC has taken a creative and flexible approach to the application of these guidelines. Remarkably, Canada and the United States have, in the majority of cases, concurred in the recommendations made by the Commission.

V ANALYSIS OF THE CASE STUDIES: EQUITABLE UTILIZATION OR NO APPRECIABLE HARM?

Which rule, equitable utilization or no appreciable harm, has governed the resolution of Canada-United States watercourse disputes? The response to this question will be considered in the context of the three propositions that have been advanced in support of the primacy of the no appreciable harm rule.[196]

IT PROTECTS THE WEAKER STATE THAT HAS SUFFERED HARM.

Under the ILC's no appreciable harm rule, a use that causes appreciable harm cannot be justified on the ground that is equita-

---

[193] IJC, Great Lakes, 1989, at 2; for the full text of the news release, see *ibid.*, Appendix 2, 79-80.

[194] *Ibid.*, 2.

[195] The Skagit-High Ross Dam project involved the Skagit River, which rises in British Columbia, and Ross Lake, located in the state of Washington. The IJC's 1942 approval of the Seattle City Light Company's hydroelectric development project was challenged by British Columbia and the bitter controversy was finally resolved by a complex agreement on March 30, 1984, the result of creative intervention by the IJC. For further discussion, see Lemarquand, *supra* note 119, at 79-93, and J. K. Kirn, and M. E. Marts, "The Skagit-High Ross Dam Controversy: Negotiation and Settlement," 26 Natural Res. J. 261-90 (1986); R. D. Hayton, and A. E. Utton, "Transboundary Groundwaters: The Bellagio Draft Treaty," 29 Natural Res. J. 663-722, 711 (1989).

[196] See *supra* note 16.

ble. The state that stands to suffer harm is thus protected: uses that cause appreciable harm are simply not allowed. In Canada-United States relations, each has been the "weaker state." In the Lake of the Woods, St. Mary and Milk rivers, Chicago diversion, and Garrison diversion cases, Canada could be considered to have been the "weaker state"; conversely, the United States was the "victim state" in the Niagara River, the Souris River, the Columbia River, the Poplar River, and the Flathead River disputes. In each of the foregoing, the development of the river basin in one state adversely affected uses in the other state. This fact alone, however, was not the basis for the resolution of the ensuing conflicts. Instead, the allegation of harm acted as a catalyst that caused the matter to be referred to the IJC.

The recommendations of the IJC (almost always adopted by the two states) were not concerned with the identification or protection of the weaker state; they were based on considerations of all the circumstances relevant to each case. In the final analysis, however, the governments of Canada and the United States agreed to balance the equities of each case; each took turns protecting the weaker one.

Canada and the United States have voluntarily protected each other by refusing unilaterally to perform or continue harmful activities, even though the latter were clearly allowed by treaty. The reference of Article 2 cases to the IJC and subsequent adoption of the Commission's recommendations corroborate this point. Thus, in the Chicago diversion, the United States opted to protect Canada by restricting unilateral diversions in Michigan and referring the issue to the IJC. In the Columbia River conflict, Canada saved the United States by agreeing to a development scheme that imposed serious restrictions on Canada's diversion rights and led to the flooding of some sixty-seven kilometres of Canadian territory. In the Souris River dispute, Saskatchewan volunteered 50 per cent of the river's flow throughout the controversy until the matter was finally resolved by agreement. The United States protected Canada's irrigation rights by agreeing to an equal division of the combined waters of the St. Mary and Milk rivers. Similar actions were taken in the Niagara and the Poplar River conflicts. In the Garrison Diversion and Flathead River proposals (dealt with at more length below) the IJC encouraged the two states to work out an acceptable agreement to resolve their dispute. It can be concluded that

Canada-United States practice does not bear out the argument that the no appreciable harm rule is to be preferred on the ground that it protects the weaker state that has suffered harm. As has been demonstrated above, Canada and the United States have not adopted a liability-based approach to the resolution of their international water resource disputes.[197] Legal redress was not sought by the weaker state that suffered harm; Canada and the United States worked out acceptable compromises in each situation.

Is the Canada-United States experience a special case? Does the high level of *bon voisinage* enjoyed by the two states affect their approach to water allocation problems? Can the first argument advanced in favour of the primacy of the no appreciable harm rule be maintained in a situation where states are not friendly neighbours? Even in this context, the proposition suffers several drawbacks. First, there is the absolute character of the alleged rule: uses that cause appreciable harm are automatically prohibited. This grants the state that first uses the waters an effective veto power, for any new use will arguably cause appreciable harm. In this scenario, the weaker state in terms of the no harm rule is often, in economic reality, the stronger state — the state that first developed the watercourse. In short, the so-called weaker state is merely the downstream state. Is this unilateral restraint on upstream development defensible? It is certainly not always equitable.

A second drawback lies in the definition of the term "appreciable"; the ILC has not provided a definition that can be applied easily in practice. Because of this imprecision, the determination of a breach of the rule becomes, in the first instance, one of auto-appreciation, and, failing amicable resolution, one ultimately requiring third party adjudication. International adjudication in the field of natural resource allocation is characterized by nuanced findings and compromise solutions; the very notion of sovereign equality mitigates against flat rulings that one state has harmed another, except in extreme situations. Decisions in this field often amount to a balancing of the equities, a careful building of compromise solutions. In this context, the "protection of the weaker state" argument is simply superfluous. Thus, the first argument falls.

197 R. B. Bilder, "The Settlement of Disputes in the Field of the International Law of the Environment," 144 Recueil des cours 139-240, 178 (1975-I).

IT IS EASIER TO DETERMINE A BREACH OF THE NO APPRECIABLE
HARM RULE.

First, it should be stated that the ease with which a breach of an
international obligation can be ascertained has never been a crite-
rion for proving the existence of a rule. Why should it apply here?

Second, the very imprecision of the concept of appreciable harm,
as noted above, belies the argument. Without a clear definition of
the word "appreciable," breaches of the rules remain difficult to
determine. As pointed out by Griffin, "[t]he concept of injury in
international law is very complex; and it is difficult to set an absolute
limit by which the injury is sufficient to provide legitimate grounds
for opposing action taken by a riparian."[198] The problem becomes
more complex, because the ILC has left open two critical questions:
what is the legal standard for the breach? Will evidence of harm
suffice to engage responsibility or must there be injury?[199] The
ILC's committee on state responsibility has been left to deal with
these important issues.[200]

Examination of the case studies reveals a further problem with
this argument. Definitional problems aside, states appear loath to
force the issue. For example, in the long-standing Chicago diversion dispute, where it appears that the lowering of the Great Lakes
may bring about an appreciable harm, Canada has yet to bring legal
action. A second phenomenon is the issue of competing appreciable harms: which irrigation rights were to prevail in the St. Mary and
Milk River dispute, those south or north of the border? Most current problems of watercourse use allocation will involve conflict of
uses problems, and in that context the relative ease with which
breaches are established is simply irrelevant. Equity and equitable
principles will be appealed to in the settlement of these problems.
Thus the "easier to prove a breach of" argument must also be
discarded.

PRIMACY OF THE NO-HARM RULE IS PREFERABLE IN CASES OF
POLLUTION AND OTHER ENVIRONMENTAL HARM.

Of the three arguments in support of the primacy of the no
appreciable harm rule, this one might be the most persuasive. The

[198] Griffin Memorandum, *supra* note 128, 148-49.

[199] See Bourne, "Principles," *supra* note 8, at 83-88 on the "injury/harm"
debate.

[200] McCaffrey, "Recent Developments," *supra* note 10.

ILC has taken the position that pollution that causes appreciable harm can never qualify as an equitable use.[201] This is entirely defensible, but does it support the primacy of the no appreciable harm rule? The lack of normative clarity of the appreciable harm threshold, coupled with the paramountcy of state sovereignty, militate against adopting no appreciable harm as the governing rule. This is ill strated by the Garrison Dam diversion project and the Flathead River development proposal. In each case, the IJC recommended against the development schemes because they violated the no pollution provision of Article 4 of the Boundary Waters Treaty. However, this finding resulted from an extension of the meaning and scope of the no pollution paragraph, a feat accomplished through recourse to the equitable utilization rule. Thus, it is in cases of pollution harm that the real supremacy of the equitable utilization rule can be shown. The flexibility of the latter allows for consideration of all relevant circumstances, a quality that is of critical importance in the newly emerging international law of the environment.

In the Garrison Diversion project, the IJC adopted a broad interpretation of the question put to it: "transboundary implications" included matters "which go beyond the traditional concept of pollution;" it was a "forward-looking concept," which encouraged a "total systems" approach to the issue at hand. The IJC rejected the limited approach dictated by Article 4, preferring the other possibility of water quality management, that of equitable utilization. While the IJC recommended against the GDU, it left the door open, recommending that the two states negotiate water quality agreements before proceeding with the development. The IJC had recourse to the equitable utilization rule and invited the two states to arrive at some agreement on that basis.

In the Flathead proposal, the IJC's approach can be explained in the same way. Referring to reports filled with uncertainties, the IJC adopted a cautionary approach and recommended against the coal

---

[201] Article 21(2) of the ILC Draft Articles provides: "Watercourse States shall, individually or jointly, prevent, reduce and control pollution of an international watercourse that may cause appreciable harm to other watercourse States or to their environment, including harm to human health or safety, to the use of the waters for any beneficial purpose or to the living resources of the watercourse. Watercourse States shall take steps to harmonize their policies in this connection." The commentary to the article states: "This paragraph is a specific application of the general obligation contained in article 7 not to cause appreciable harm to other watercourse States."

mine development on account of a mere risk of transboundary impact. Reading "a mutual obligation to protect a fishery" into the "far-reaching implications of Article 4," the Commission attempted to substantiate its position by finding that loss of a fishery constituted a violation of the Boundary Waters Treaty. This unprecedented endeavour cannot find explanation within the confines of the no appreciable harm rule, which in its application promotes, as political scientists might refer to it, a "zero-sum game." The rule is absolute: either there is or there is not appreciable harm, and the destiny of the project follows accordingly. Notions such as risk or a "strong possibility" of harm have no place in the no appreciable harm rule. By contrast, they could come within the purview of equitable utilization: risk of harm triggers the procedural rules of that principle and encourages a settlement that takes this factor into account.[202] The equitable utilization rule thus offers broader opportunities for protecting the environment; the practical reconciliation of the competing interests can be undertaken in an approach similar to that adopted by the IJC in the 1981 Poplar River Water Quality Report.[203]

In addition, the equitable utilization rule offers the possibility of "environmentalizing" earlier use-allocation cases. This would be possible in the Columbia River dispute (in which the initial allocation was based primarily on engineering concerns) and has, in fact, occurred in the Chicago diversion question through the recent Great Lakes references to the IJC.

---

[202] Handl, *supra* note 9, at 61-62.

[203] The IJC demonstrated how water quality objectives can be a condition of an equitable apportionment; see IJC, 1981 *Poplar River Water Quality Report*, 203. For a similar approach, see Caflisch, "*Sic Utere*," *supra* note 14, Part 5, "Analyse et conclusions," in which he concludes, *inter alia*, that the equitable utilization rule (with the proviso that a use that causes serious harm should never qualify as equitable) should be the governing rule. Professor Lammers suggests that the "mitigated no substantial harm principle" should be the primary rule in pollution questions, since it offers a less flexible standard than equitable utilization: see J. G. Lammers, "'Balancing the Equities' in International Environmental Law," in *The Future of the International Law of the Environment*, 153-65 (Colloque 1984, Académie de droit international de La Haye, 1985); Lammers, *supra* note 8, at 496-501, 540-43, 580-84, 600; also J. G. Polakiewicz, "La Responsabilité de l'État en matière de pollution des eaux fluviales ou souterraines internationales," 118 Journal du droit international, 283-347 (1991), who argues that the protection of the environment should be the primary rule, and that in no case should appreciable harm caused by pollution qualify as an equitable use.

In conclusion, then, none of the three arguments offered in support of the primacy of the no appreciable harm principle is convincing. In fact, the principle is not supported by international practice. Following a general survey of state practice, Professor McCaffrey concluded that:

State practice, however, does not indicate that there is an absolute no-harm rule with respect to watercourses. It is more supportive of the proposition that where there is intense competition for a watercourse, an accommodation will be worked out that attempts to achieve an equitable and reasonable allocation of the uses and benefits of the watercourse. . . . One can conclude that the "no-harm" doctrine is not supported in state practice. . . .[204]

And, contrary to what may appear to be the policy of an influential international organization, the World Bank, it has in practice operated in accordance with the equitable utilization rule.[205]

VI   CONCLUSION

Two caveats must be made before any definitive conclusions are reached: first, the state practice examined above is limited; second, there is a temptation to take the *lex ferenda* to be the *lex lata*.[206] Therefore, conclusions drawn from case studies must be taken with caution.

In this context, the following conclusion would, however, appear to be safe: the state practice examined does not support the ILC's

204 See S. C. McCaffrey, "The Non-Navigational Uses of International Watercourses," Proceedings of the Eighty-Fourth Annual Meeting of the American Society of International Law 1990, 228-36, 231 [hereinafter McCaffrey, "Non-Navigational Uses"].

205 The comments made by Mr. R. Krishna in McCaffrey, "Non-Navigational Uses," *ibid.*, 234-35, on close examination reveal the primacy of equitable utilization. Also the Indus River settlement between Pakistan and India, in which the World Bank played a central role, was resolved in accordance with the equitable utilization rule.

206 Prosper Weil stated in his article "Towards Relative Normativity in International Law?" 77 Am. J. Int'l L. 413-42, at 415 (1983), that "[t]he acts accomplished by subjects of international law are so diverse in character that it is no simple matter for a jurist to determine what may be called the normativity threshold; i.e. the line of transition between the nonlegal and the legal, between what does not constitute a norm and what does." See also H. Ruiz Fabri, "Règles coutumières générales et droit international fluvial," 36 Annuaire français de droit international 818-42, at 842 (1990): "L'ambiguïté qui imprègne la recherche de règles coutumières générales en droit fluvial n'est dès lors pas près d'être levée."

no appreciable harm rule as the principle governing the settlement of disputes regarding the allocation of non-navigational uses of international water resources. While the concept of harm might draw international attention to a watercourse dispute, the no appreciable harm rule has not governed the resolution of conflicts.

The equitable utilization rule as formulated by the ILA and developed by state practice, which encompasses substantial injury as one of the factors to be considered in defining equitable utilization, is the one adopted by Canada and the United States. Whenever a matter had been referred to the IJC, equitable utilization was resorted to; all relevant circumstances, including the important but not always decisive factor of harm/injury, were considered in the IJC's recommendations. More importantly, Canada and the United States adopted the Commission's report in most cases, thereby embracing the equitable utilization approach to watercourse dispute resolution.

In addition to the inconsistency of the no appreciable harm approach with the state practice examined above, there are fundamental problems with the rule itself. Its imprecise definition prevents ready application in practice; its absoluteness is at odds with the notion of sovereign equality. States and adjudicators are loath to adopt a rule that requires a finding of wrongdoing, especially in matters involving the allocation of natural resources.

The cases examined suggest further that Canada and the United States will adhere to certain guidelines in the resolution of their future disputes: first, all categories of international waters will be treated as boundary waters; second, the development of international watercourses will focus on the optimal use of the basin as a whole, with a maximum of benefit and minimum of detriment to each state; and third, environmental concerns will be considered as important factors in the determination of equitable use. This is especially true in situations that involve pollution harm, in which mere risk of transboundary harm might trigger the procedural rules of equitable utilization.[207] The "reasonable state test"[208] can work: the experience between Canada and the United States attests to this.

---

[207] The prominence of transnational environmental impact assessments appears to be a consequence of this: see Handl, *supra* note 9, at 56-57.

[208] C. B. Bourne, "International Law and Pollution of International Rivers and Lakes," 6 Univ. Brit. L. Rev. 115-36, 121 (1971).

As governments prepare their written submissions to the ILC on its Draft Articles, they may be left with this gentle reminder:

Whatever may be the philosophical basis of the law of nations, it is beyond dispute that its actual rules have in this way been hammered out on the hard anvil of experience. Alike in public and in private law, the rules which govern conduct are worked out to meet the proved needs of mankind, and it is only in experience that the final proof of these needs is to be found.[209]

[209] Smith, *supra* note 33, at 144.

Sommaire

Les utilisations des cours d'eaux internationaux à des fins autres que la navigation

En juillet 1992, la Commission du droit international (CDI) a adopté en première lecture un ensemble de projets d'articles intitulé "Droit relatif aux utilisations des cours d'eaux internationaux à des fins autres que la navigation." Les gouvernements ont été invités à se prononcer sur ce projet d'articles jusqu'à la fin 1992.

La présente étude démontre que la Commission du droit international, l'International Law Association (ILA), et l'Institut de droit international (IDI) ont tous insisté sur l'importance de deux principes, l'"utilisation équitable" et l'"obligation de ne pas causer de dommages appréciables," dans l'élaboration des règles relatives à l'attribution de droits pour les utilisations des cours d'eaux internationaux à des fins autres que la navigation. À l'inverse de l'approche accordant la priorité au principe de l'utilisation équitable, adoptée par l'ILA et l'IDI, la CDI considère que la règle stipulant l'obligation de ne pas causer de dommages appréciables constitue la norme fondamentale.

À cet égard, un examen de la pratique bilatérale du Canada et des États-Unis, entre autres cette relative aux fleuves St-Mary et Milk, Columbia, Flathead et à la déviation de Chicago, révèle que ces deux États ont adopté une approche fondée sur la règle de l'"utilisation équitable." Ainsi le présent article mène à la conclusion que la Commission du droit international devrait revoir sa position relative à la place occupée par la règle de l'obligation de ne pas causer de dommages appréciables.

Visit, Search, Diversion, and Capture in Naval Warfare: Part II, Developments since 1945

WOLFF HEINTSCHEL VON HEINEGG*

SINCE THE SECOND WORLD WAR, international armed conflicts at sea have been limited, and the belligerents have rarely (if at all) made use of the traditional law of prize. Hence, any attempt to assess the current state of customary prize law must look beyond the actual behaviour of states during armed conflicts. The first section of this article deals with armed conflicts in which at least one of the parties involved exercised what seem to be the traditional measures of economic warfare at sea (A-E), and with three of the most recent military manuals (F). The second section is devoted to certain legal developments since 1945 and their possible impact on the legality of prize measures.

I STATE PRACTICE SINCE THE SECOND WORLD WAR

A RELEVANCE OF THE IRAQ-KUWAIT CONFLICT

During the 1990-91 Iraq-Kuwait conflict, the Coalition forces intercepted merchant shipping bound for Iraqi ports as well as merchant shipping departing from these ports. The Coalition interpreted the terms "war material" and "contraband" broadly, and

* Institut für Friedenssicherungsrecht und Humanitares Völkerrecht, Ruhr-Universität Bochum. This article is Part II of a study on Visit, Search, Diversion, and Capture, Part I of which was published in Volume XXIX of this *Yearbook* at pages 283-329.

enemy as well as neutral merchant vessels were shadowed over hundreds of miles by ships and aircraft making use of satellites for communication and surveillance. During the seven months of the conflict, "more than 165 ships from 19 Coalition navies challenged more than 7,500 merchant vessels, boarded 964 ships to inspect manifests and cargo holds, and diverted 51 ships carrying more than one million tons of cargo in violation of the UNSC sanctions."[1] The small proportion of ships boarded or diverted was mainly attributable to the intelligence network,[2] which allowed the Coalition forces to make use of a continuously updated list of suspect shipping. Hence, it is likely that in future conflicts modern technology will enable belligerents with the necessary technical means to exercise ocean-wide control; this will certainly have an impact on the law of visit, search, diversion, and capture.

However, for two reasons the Iraq-Kuwait conflict will not be addressed here. First, it may be premature to try to establish to what extent the traditional law will be — or already is — influenced by modern technology. Second, the Coalition measures that affected Iraq's economy were authorized by the United Nations Security Council. The United States executive orders freezing Iraqi and Kuwaiti assets, for example, did not cite Trading with the Enemy legislation but rather referred to other emergency legislation as well as to Security Council resolutions.[3] The United States interception notices also referred to Security Council resolutions and to the inherent right of collective self-defence under Article 51 of the United Nations Charter.[4] Therefore, the legal nature of this conflict is unique and can hardly be generalized, even though the Coalition — with modifications in the area of capture and adjudication — to a considerable extent adhered to the traditional rules.

---

[1] U.S. Department of Defense, *Conduct of the Persian Gulf War*, Final Report to Congress, at 76 (April 1992).

[2] According to the U.S. Department of Defense, there were not enough helicopters able to insert a full takedown team onto a vessel. Therefore, altogether there occurred only 11 takedowns: *ibid.*, 78.

[3] Exec. Orders No. 12, 724-25, 55 Fed. Reg. 33089-92 (1990), issued Aug. 9, 1990, citing, *inter alia*, S.C. Res. 661, the National Emergencies Act, 50 U.S.C. paras. 1601-51 (1988), the International Emergency Economic Powers Act, *ibid.*, paras. 1701-6 (1988), and the UN Participation Act, 22 *ibid.* paras. 287-87e (1988).

[4] E.g., Special Warning No. 80, Aug. 17, 1990, in Defense Mapping Agency Hydrographic/Topographic Center, Notice to Mariners III-1.15 (No. 36, 1990).

B ARAB-ISRAELI CONFLICTS

During the Arab-Israeli conflicts, Egyptian forces in numerous instances seized Israeli goods or goods bound for Israel, even when these were found on board neutral merchant vessels.[5] Third states frequently protested against the Egyptian measures taken against ships flying their flags.[6]

On February 6, 1950, King Farouk issued a decree,[7] under which manifests and cargoes of ships could be inspected to make sure that no arms, ammunition, war material, or other goods constituting contraband or bound, directly or indirectly, to Israel or Israeli-controlled territories, were on board. Article 10 enumerated *inter alia* the following goods to be seized as prize (contraband): fuel of any kind, chemicals, ships, motor vehicles, money, and gold. According to Article 11, enemy destination was assumed whenever these goods were shipped indirectly to persons or authorities in territories under Israeli control or to consignees whose names were included in a black list. In 1953, foodstuffs and "all other commodities which are likely to strengthen the war potential of the Zionists in Palestine in any way whatsoever" were added to the list of contraband goods.[8]

In 1951, after ships destined to Eilat had been intercepted at the entrance of the Gulf of Aquaba, Israel turned to the United Nations, referring to the armistice of Rhodes of February 24, 1949, and to resolutions of the Security Council prohibiting further hostilities.[9]

---

[5] See *inter alia* E. D. Brown, "World War Prize Law Applied in a Limited War Situation: Egyptian Restrictions on Neutral Shipping with Israel," 50 Minnesota L. Rev. 849 (1965-66); Y. Dinstein, "The Laws of War at Sea," Isr.YBHR, 56 (1980); L. Gross, "Passage through the Suez Canal of Israel-Bound Cargo and Israel Ships," 51 Am. J. Int'l L. 530 (1957).

[6] See *inter alia* Security Council, SCOR, 553rd meeting of Aug. 16, 1951, at 23.

[7] "Réglementant la procédure relative à l'inspection des navires et des avions et la capture des prises de la guerre Palestinienne" (J. O. [France] No. 36 of Apr. 4, 1950), later Loi No. 32 du 1er avril 1950 relative au Conseil de Prises (J. O. [France] No. 64 of June 26, 1950). English translation in UN Doc. S/3179 (Feb. 15, 1954).

[8] See R. Ottmüller, *Die Anwendung von Seekriegsrecht in militärischen Konflikten seit 1945*, at 133, 180 (Hamburg, 1978); J. Trappe, "On the Jurisdiction of the Egyptian Prize Court, 1948-1960," 10 Rev.Egypt.DI 60 (1960).

[9] UN Security Council, 558th meeting, Sept. 1, 1951, SCOR paras. 5, 6; UN Docs. S/2322 and S/1367. See also the statement by the Israeli delegate during the 658th meeting on Feb. 5, 1954.

On the other hand, Egypt asserted national security interests and stated that an armistice did not end a state of war.[10] The Egyptian prize court in Alexandria approved these considerations as legally important in two decisions.[11]

Between 1949 and the end of the 1950s, the Egyptian prize court often referred to the decisions of prize courts made during the two world wars. Whereas in a number of cases neutral cargo was released,[12] the principle that a neutral flag covers enemy cargo was acknowledged only if the neutral did not co-operate with the enemy.[13] Enemy destination was assumed in conformity with, for example, British prize jurisdiction of the two world wars,[14] and black lists played an important role.[15] All goods labelled "Produce of Israel" were considered to be of enemy character.[16] The notion of contraband was broadly interpreted to include items such as tea, coffee, onions, and spices.[17] The judgments of the Egyptian prize court bore a strong resemblance to the prize judgments of the two world wars. It is, however, remarkable that all ships and goods affected had been captured in Egyptian ports. In fact, some of the goods had been unloaded before the outbreak of hostilities in

---

10 Statement of the Egyptian delegate during the 661st meeting of the Security Council on Mar. 12, 1954 (SCOR paras. 4 ff.), and during the 682nd meeting on Oct. 14, 1954 (SCOR para. 113).

11 *The Lea Lott* (Dec. 12, 1959), 28 I.L.R. 652 (1963) and 16 Rev.Egypt.DI 106 (1960); *The Inge Toft* (Apr. 10, 1960), 31 I.L.R. 510 (1966) and 16 Rev.Egypt.DI 118 (1960).

12 *The Zemalek,* 6 Rev.Egypt.DI 212 (1950); *The Triport,* 6 Rev.Egypt.DI 266 (1950); *The Nord Cap,* 5 Rev.Egypt.DI 149 (1949); *The Narrandera,* 5 Rev.Egypt.DI 152 (1949); *The Talthybias,* 6 Rev.Egypt.DI 227 (1950).

13 *The Captain Manoli,* 28 I.L.R. 662 (1963); 15 Rev.Egypt.DI 186 (1959); *The Inge Toft* (Apr. 10, 1960), 31 I.L.R. 510 (1966); 16 Rev.Egypt.DI 118(1960).

14 *The Arsia,* 6 Rev.Egypt.DI 223 (1950); *The Empire Pickwick,* 5 Rev.Egypt.DI 148 (1949); *The Hoegh de Vries,* 6 Rev.Egypt.DI 225 (1950); *The Fedala,* 13 Rev.Egypt.DI 131 (1957).

15 *The Derwenthal,* 6 Rev.Egypt.DI 218 (1950); *The Lea Lott,* 16 Rev.Egypt.DI 106 (1960).

16 *The Marine Cap,* 16 I.L.R. 571 (1949); 5 Rev.Egypt.DI 155 (1949); *The Inge Toft,* 31 I.L.R. 510 (1966); 16 Rev.Egypt.DI 118 (1960).

17 *The Good Hope,* 16 I.L.R. 574 (1949); 6 Rev.Egypt.DI 214 (1950); *The Derwenthal,* 6 Rev.Egypt.DI 218 (1950); *The Hemland,* 16 I.L.R. 597 (1949); 5 Rev.Egypt.DI 155 (1949); *The Hoegh de Vries,* 17 I.L.R. 447 (1950); 6 Rev.Egypt.DI 225 (1950).

1948.[18] In the case of the *Inge Toft,* the court expressly indicated that Egypt did not exercise its rights on the high seas but restricted itself to Egyptian (and Israeli) territorial waters and ports.[19] Even though the Security Council in September 1951 characterized the Egyptian practice as an "abuse of the exercise of the right of visit, search and seizure,"[20] Egypt more or less regularly maintained this practice until the conclusion of the peace treaty of 1979.[21]

During the Arab-Israeli conflict of 1973, international shipping was warned not to enter the region of war, which at first comprised Egyptian and Israeli territorial waters, and later grew to include other parts of the sea as well as ports in Egypt, Syria, and Libya.[22] On October 6, 1973, Syrian naval units captured the Greek passenger ship *Romantica* and diverted it to Tartarus. The following day, after an intervention by the Italian ambassador, the *Romantica* was released.[23] Further incidents of this kind did not take place, because international shipping refrained from entering the danger zones. Until November 1973, however, Egyptian naval forces regularly stopped, visited, and searched neutral merchant vessels.[24] The reaction of third states to the conflict differed considerably. A number of African states unilaterally terminated or suspended diplomatic relations with Israel,[25] Arab states decided on a boycott of oil exports to Israel and the United States,[26] and Great Britain decided on an arms embargo that in practice affected only Israel.[27] Other West European states, with the exception of Portugal, did not

---

18 *The Triport,* 6 Rev.Egypt.DI 266 (1950); *The Nord Cap,* 5 Rev.Egypt.DI 149 (1949); *The Talthybias,* 6 Rev.Egypt.DI 227 (1950).

19 31 I.L.R. 518 (1966); see also D. P. O'Connell, "International Law and Contemporary Naval Operations," 44 BYIL 19, 27 (1970).

20 UN Doc. S/2322.

21 Cf. H. Hecker, "Indien erläßt ein Prisengesetz," Verfassung und Recht in Übersee 455 (1972); see also R. R. Baxter, "The Law of War in the Arab-Israeli Conflict: On Water and on Land," 5 Towson State J. Int'l Aff. 1-17 (1971).

22 Cf. 71 Marine-Rundschau 46 (1974); see also R. Ottmüller, *op. cit. supra* note 8, at 292; W. Jablonsky, "Die Seekriegführung im vierten Nahostkrieg," 71 Marine-Rundschau 645-65 (1974).

23 Cf. 71 Marine-Rundschau 46 (1974).

24 The last neutral merchant ship that was visited and searched by an Egyptian warship in November 1973 was the Japanese *Kijo Maru*; see 71 Marine-Rundschau 115 (1974).

25 Archiv der Gegenwart 1973, 18229 A 6.

26 Ibid., 18315 A 2 B.

27 R. Ottmüller, *op. cit. supra* note 8, at 294.

allow their territories to be used for the supply or assistance of any of the belligerents.[28] Only after the armistice agreement of November 11, 1973, and further agreements in 1975 were merchant ships destined for Israel allowed to pass through the Suez Canal unmolested.

C INDIA–PAKISTAN

During the 1965 conflict between India and Pakistan, commercial intercourse between the respective belligerents and third states was interfered with considerably.[29] By reference to the Import and Export (Control) Act, 1950, Pakistan prohibited all exports to and imports from India.[30] According to the Pakistani Detention of Enemy Ships, Aircraft and Goods Ordinance, "no enemy ships or aircraft, and no enemy goods on board any ship or aircraft or any railway [were] allowed to depart from, or to be taken out of Pakistan, and all such goods [were to] be detained and . . . be taken prize."[31] Pakistan, referring to the conflict as a "war" and considering it necessary "to specify the articles which it is the intention of the Government of Pakistan to treat as contraband of war," issued two "schedules" on absolute and conditional contraband that were annexed to the Proclamation as to Contraband of War of September 9, 1965.[32] Pakistan replaced those two schedules on September

---

[28] Archiv der Gegenwart 1973, 18315 A 5. E.g., the Federal Republic of Germany had assured the Egyptian government that no U.S. war material destined for Israel would be shipped from German territory. Hence, the Israeli merchant vessel *Palmah* had to leave the port of Bremerhaven without cargo; see 70 Marine-Rundschau 47 (1973).

[29] Cf. P. Sharma, *The Indo-Pakistan Maritime Conflict, 1965: A Legal Appraisal* (Bombay, 1970).

[30] *Gazette of Pakistan Extraordinaire* of Sept. 9, 1965.

[31] *The All Pakistan Legal Decisions* 1965, at 575.

[32] *Ibid.*, at 437. Schedule I on absolute contraband comprised:

"(a) All kinds of arms, ammunitions and explosives, and all kinds of materials or appliances suitable for use in chemical, biological or atomic warfare; machines for the manufacture or repair of any of the foregoing; component parts thereof, articles necessary or convenient for their use; materials or ingredients used in their manufacture; articles necessary or convenient for the production or use of such materials or ingredients.

(b) Fuel of all kinds; all contrivances for, or means of, transportation on land, in water or air, and machines used in their manufacture or

1 1, 1965, and, without further distinguishing between absolute and conditional contraband, issued a new list on the following articles of "contraband of war":[33]

(1) all kinds of arms and ammunitions and explosives; their components and ingredients, and radioactive materials;

(2) crude oil and fuel and lubricants of all kinds;

(3) all means of transportation on land, in water or air, and components thereof;

(4) electronics and telecommunication equipment;

(5) optical equipment specially designed for military use;

(6) precious metals and objects made thereof, coin bullion, currency, evidence of debts, debentures, bonds, coupons, stocks, and shares or any negotiable or marketable security; precious or semi-precious stones, jewels.

On September 14, 1965, India also issued a list, referring to those articles that were included in the Pakistani Schedule I as absolute contraband, the transport of which to Pakistan was prohibited "for the maintenance of the security of India."[34]

Neither India nor Pakistan officially published their contraband lists.

---

repair; component parts thereof; instruments, articles and animals necessary or convenient for their use; materials or ingredients used in their manufacture, articles necessary or convenient for the production or use of such materials or ingredients.

(c) All means of communication, tools, implements, instruments, equipment, maps, pictures, papers and other articles, machines, or documents necessary or convenient for carrying on hostile operations; articles necessary or convenient for their manufacture or use.

(d) Precious metals and objects made thereof, coin bullion, currency, evidence of debts, debentures, bonds, coupons, stocks and shares of any negotiable or marketable security; precious or semi-precious stones, jewels; also metal, materials, dies, plates, machinery, or other articles necessary or convenient for their production, manufacture.

Schedule II on conditional contraband comprised "All kinds of food, foodstuffs, feed, forage and clothing and manufactured textile products; tobacco, articles and material necessary or convenient for their production, manufacture or use."

[33] "In Supersession of the Proclamation as to Contraband of War, dated 9th September, 1965," *The All Pakistan Legal Decisions* 1965, at 472.

[34] Published in *Gazette of India Extraordinaire* of Sept. 14, 1965, Part II, Section 3, Subsection (i).

A considerable number of ships and their cargoes were captured by Pakistan and, in its decision of October 28, 1965, the High Court of Dacca condemned 50 ships and their cargoes as "good prize."[35] Most of these cargoes consisted of Indian tea belonging to Indian owners or to British corporations carrying on business in India. Indian measures were less rigorous; in some cases, vessels were allowed to unload cargo destined for India and to leave port even when carrying cargo destined for Pakistan.[36] The Indian government challenged the seizure of Indian cargo on neutral ships by Pakistan before the Security Council, asserting that the laws of prize can be exercised in a formal state of war only.[37] Pakistan maintained that these measures were justified by the right of self-defence. In December 1965 India and Pakistan lifted their respective restrictions on (neutral) commercial shipping.[38]

During the 1971 war with Pakistan, India captured three Pakistani merchant vessels whereas Pakistan apparently was unable to interfere with Indian merchant shipping.[39] However, neutral merchant shipping was affected by measures of both belligerents. In darkness, neutral ships were not allowed to approach to within seventy-five nautical miles of the Pakistani coast, and neutral ships in Pakistani ports were damaged by Indian attacks. When India declared a blockade of eastern Pakistan on December 4, 1971, neutral ships were allowed to leave the blockaded area within a period of twenty-four hours. When it became evident that the markings and names of many ships had been changed, the Indian navy stopped, visited, and diverted them to Calcutta if they carried cargo of military significance.[40] On December 10, 1971, the Indian government announced that neutral ships would be given a period of grace until the morning of December 12 to leave the port of

---

[35] See 46 Int'l Leg. Mat. 472 (1970); 69 RGDIP 182 (1965).

[36] *Ibid.*.

[37] P. Sharma, *op. cit. supra* note 29, at 87.

[38] R. Ottmüller, *op. cit. supra* note 8, at 186.

[39] The correct number of captured Pakistani vessels is not clear; it ranges from three to ten. See D. K. Palit, *The Lightning Campaign*, 150 (Salisbury, 1972); J. Rohwer, "Der indisch-pakistanische Konflikt 1971," 71 Marine-Rundschau 7 (1974); R. Kaul, "The Indo-Pakistani War and the Changing Balance of Power in the Indian Ocean," 99 U.S. Naval Inst. Proc. 172 (May 1973).

[40] D. K. Palit, *supra*, at 150; J. Rohwer, 71 Marine-Rundschau 7 (1974); R. Kaul, 99 U.S. Naval Inst. Proc. 172 (May 1973).

Karachi and Pakistani territorial waters. In all, Pakistan and India boarded and searched about 115 neutral ships.[41]

On December 3, 1971, Pakistan had issued a list of contraband goods but modified it on December 17, 1971. This list was almost identical to the list issued in 1965, but the following articles were added:

(7) implements and apparatus for manufacture or repair of all types of military hardware equipment;

(8) All other types of goods and equipment, and parts and accessories thereof, that can be used or may assist in the conduct of war.[42]

India, on December 5, 1971, in a verbal message transmitted the following contraband list to the diplomatic representatives in New Delhi:[43]

(1) arms of all kinds, including arms for sporting purposes, and their distinctive component parts,

(2) projectiles, charges, and cartridges of all kinds, and their distinctive component parts,

(3) powder and explosives specially prepared for use in war,

(4) gunmountings, limber boxes, limbers, military wagons, file forges, and their distinctive component parts,

(5) clothing and equipment of a distinctively military character,

(6) all kinds of harness of a distinctively military character,

(7) saddle, draught, and pack animals suitable for use in war,

(8) articles of camp equipment, and their distinctive component parts,

(9) armour plates,

---

[41] D. K. Palit, *op. cit. supra* note 39, at 149.

[42] *Gazette of Pakistan, Extraordinary*, Dec. 17, 1971, reprinted in *The All Pakistan Decisions* 5, Vol. XXIV, at 113 (1972).

[43] Printed in R. Ottmüller, *op. cit. supra* note 8, at 275. In the introduction India declared:
   1. Whereas the security of India is threatened by aggression of Pakistan and by the armed conflict initiated by it . . . whereas it is necessary to specify the articles, which are intended to be treated as contraband of war.
   2. Now, therefore, the Government of India declares that during the continuance of this armed conflict or until the Government of India do give further public notice, the articles in schedule hereto shall be treated as contraband of war.
   3. The Government of India reserves the right to add, to delete, to modify the schedule as and when it finds necessary."

(10) warships, including boats, and their distinctive component parts of such nature that they can only be used on a vessel of war,

(11) aeroplanes, airships, balloons, and aircraft of all kinds and their component parts, together with accessories and articles recognizable as intended for use in connection with balloons and aircraft,

(12) implements and apparatus designed exclusively for the manufacture of war, for the manufacture or repair of arms, or war material for use on land and sea,

(13) surface to surface missiles, surface to air missiles, air to surface rockets and guided missiles and warheads for any of the above weapons, mechanical or electronic equipment to support or operate the above items,

(14) any other class of materials or items as may assist the army in the prosecution of the armed conflict against the Union of India.

In a further verbal message of December 8, 1971, the Indian government informed the diplomatic representatives that all ships destined for one of the following ports were liable to control: Okha, Bombay, Goa, Cochin, Madras, Visakhapatnam, Paradip, and Port Blair.

On December 15, 1971, The Bengal Chamber of Commerce and Industry informed neutral shipping that it would run no risk in the Bay of Bengal if the following instructions were obeyed:

(a) No ship should approach Sandheads to a distance less than 40 miles between dusk and dawn.

(b) Masters should be warned that they are liable whilst on passage in the Bay, to be challenged by Units of Indian Navy to establish their bonafides; they should cooperate and they will get courtesy and considerate treatment.

(c) For such ships as have left Calcutta having been detained here on account of their contraband cargo, which they had to discharge in accordance with official instructions, it is strongly suggested that masters should obtain an endorsement from customs to the effect that all contraband cargo has been discharged. In addition, it is further recommended that agent should obtain an endorsement from the Indian Navy to the same effect and the officer to be contacted in this respect is. . . .[44]

On December 16, 1971, the Indian parliament adopted the Naval and Aircraft Prize Act, 1971.[45] It defined "prize" as "anything which . . . may be subjected to adjudication . . . including a

---

[44] Circular Letter No. 59 — Int. of Dec. 15, 1971 concerning "Safety Measures to Be Taken by Neutral Ships in the Bay of Bengal."

[45] Gazette of India, Dec. 16, 1971, Part II, section 1, at 671.

ship or an aircraft and goods carried therein irrespective of whether the ship is captured at sea or seized in port or whether the aircraft is on or over land or sea at the time of capture or seizure." By section 3 (3), the Act applies "during war or as a measure of reprisal during an armed conflict or in the exercise of the right of self-defence" and, by section 4 (3), the Prize Court "shall adjudge and condemn all such ships, vessels, aircraft and goods belonging to any country or state or the nationals, citizens or subjects thereof."

The Naval and Aircraft Prize Act, 1971, had no practical relevance but the Indian navy stopped and searched more than one hundred neutral merchant vessels during the conflict, which lasted only two weeks.[46] On December 21, 1971, India suspended all measures of visit and search of neutral vessels.

Although there was some uncertainty whether the 1965 conflict could be characterized as a war in the traditional legal sense,[47] the parties to the conflict agreed that the measures of economic warfare were more or less in accordance with the traditional law. Certainly, the parties applied these measures extensively.[48] The 1971 conflict, however, was characterized as a "war" in the traditional sense not only by the parties to the conflict but also by third states, such as the United States. Visit, search, and other measures of economic warfare were exercised in accordance with the practice of states during the two world wars. The same is true with regard to the lists of contraband that did not distinguish between absolute and conditional contraband but applied a single notion of "contraband of war."[49]

D ALGERIA AND VIETNAM

Naval forces were engaged in many other conflicts and crisis situations after the Second World War. However, except in the French engagement in Algeria, the Vietnam conflict, and the Gulf war between Iran and Iraq, prize measures or measures that can be

---

[46] D. K. Palit, *op. cit. supra* note 39, at 149; J. Rohwer, 71 Marine-Rundschau 22 (1974).

[47] See *inter alia* Ch. Rousseau, 69 RGDIP 78, at 89 (1965): "il n'est pas facile de qualifier la situation qui a découlée de l'ouverture des hostilités entre les États."

[48] D. Schindler, "Aspects contemporains de la neutralité," 121 Receuil des Cours 223, 282 (1967 II); E. Lauterpacht, "The Legal Irrelevance of the 'State of War'," 62 Am. Soc. Int'l L. Proc. 58, 60 (1968).

[49] R. Ottmüller, *op. cit. supra* note 8, at 283.

labelled as such either did not play an important role or were of such an extraordinary character — as, for example, in the Cuban quarantine[50] — that they have no relevance for the present study.[51]

Algeria

Although the Algerian conflict[52] was not an international armed conflict but rather an "emergency,"[53] it is of some interest, because from 1954 the French navy exercised control over 2,500 ships per annum in its efforts to control the infiltration of arms and munitions. These measures were based on a decree of March 17, 1956, relating to the state of emergency in Algeria.[54] According to Articles 4 and 5, vessels of less than one hundred tons were liable to visit and search in the customs zone that had been extended to fifty kilometers from the Algerian coast. After 1958, vessels of more than one hundred tons were also stopped and visited. Whereas most of the measures were taken within a distance of approximately fifty kilometers off the Algerian coast, a number of ships were visited outside those waters.[55] Diversion orders were given to a ship only where boarding was prevented by bad weather,[56] where the nature

50 See, e.g., C. Q. Christol/C. R. Davies, "Maritime Quarantine: The Naval Interdiction of Offensive Weapons and Associated Material to Cuba," 57 Am. J. Int'l L. 525 (1963); C. G. Fenwick, "The Quarantine Against Cuba, Legal or Illegal?," 57 Am. J. Int'l L. 588 (1963); W. T. Mallison, "Limited Naval Blockade or Quarantine Interdiction: National and Collective Defense Claims Valid Under International Law," George Washington L. Rev. 335 (1962).

51 The Korean conflict involved a formal blockade proclamation, but the primary naval campaign involved fishing boat interception: see M. W. Cagle/F. A. Manson, *The Sea War in Korea* 281, 296 (Annapolis, 1957). The Falklands/Malvinas conflict took place in one of the less travelled sea areas, and all attacks on merchantmen involved ships integrated into the war-fighting or war-sustaining effort except Argentina's attack on the *S.S. Hercules*; see *Amerada Hess Shipping Corp.* v. *Argentine Republic*, 638 F. Supp. 73 (S.D.N.Y., 1986).

52 Cf. L. Lucchini, "Actes de contrainte exercés par la France en Haute Mer au cours des opérations en Algérie," Annuaire Français de Droit International 803-22 (1966).

53 D. P. O'Connell, 44 BYIL 36 (1970).

54 Décret 56/274, Journal Officiel de Mar. 19, 1956 at 2665.

55 E.g., the German vessel *Bilbao* and the Bulgarian *Chipka* in the English Channel, the German *Las Palmas* twenty-two nautical miles south of Cape Vicent, the German *Archsum* fifty-four nautical miles east of Gibraltar.

56 That was the case with regard to the German vessels *Helga Böge, Alcyone, Weissensee,* and *R. C. Rickmers*; see R. Ottmüller, *op. cit. supra* note 8, at 135.

of the cargo did not allow a thorough search,[57] or where the cargo consisted of arms, ammunition, and explosives.[58] In the latter case, the cargo was seized unless it could be proved that it did not constitute any danger for the French army in Algeria.[59] In general, the ships were soon released. Even though the French navy acted very politely and tried to delay the vessels affected as little as possible, French warships made it sufficiently clear that they were prepared to apply force if their orders were disregarded. When the flag states protested sharply against these measures, the French government justified them by referring to the rights of self-defence and self-preservation.[60] However, if detention proved to be unfounded, compensation was paid to the owner.[61]

Vietnam

The Vietnam conflict is of interest for the present subject in two respects. By Operation Market Time, the exercise of the rights of visit, search, and capture was restricted to a belt of twelve nautical miles measured from the baselines of South Vietnam.[62] According to the Decree on Sea Surveillance of the Republic of Vietnam of April 27, 1965,[63] the three-nautical-mile territorial sea of South Vietnam was declared a defensive sea area, and ships that were not clearly engaged in innocent passage were made subject to visit, search, and even capture. Vessels in passage of a contiguous zone of twelve nautical miles were subjected to the control of the Republic of Vietnam. By that decree, "vessels within the contiguous zone suspected of preparing to aid in infringements of the customs, fiscal or immigration regulations . . . [were] subject to visit and search, and [could] be subject to arrest and disposition." Operation Sea Dragon was limited to North-Vietnamese vessels and to the twelve-

---

57 That was the case with regard to the Polish vessel *Monte Cassino* and the Italian vessel *Baizar*; see Annuaire Français de Droit International, 1962, at 921.

58 That was the case with regard to the German vessel *Morsum*, the British *Athos II* and the Dutch *Bjess Bosch*.

59 R. Ottmüller, *op. cit. supra* note 8, at 137.

60 With regard to the Yugoslav vessel *Slovenija*, French Foreign Minister Pineau declared in January 1958: "Il y a aucune commune mesure entre les prejudice subi par la Jugoslavie, de fait de l'arraisonnement d'un navire, et celui qui eût subi la France, si lesdites armes avaient été dirigés contre nos soldats."

61 E.g., in the case of the German vessel *Helga Böge*.

62 D. P. O'Connell, 44 BYIL 30 (1970).

63 Printed in 4 Int'l. Leg. Mat. 461 (1965).

mile territorial sea of North Vietnam.[64] The United States navy did not interfere with Vietnamese vessels used exclusively for fishing along the coast or with small boats employed in local trade, even though Vietnam was not a party to Hague Convention XI.[65] However, after it had become evident that these vessels were used for transport of ammunition and other military goods, they lost their protected status.[66]

E IRAN–IRAQ

During the Iran-Iraq war, both parties to the conflict made numerous attacks on neutral merchant shipping, especially within exclusion zones.[67] Another, although minor feature of the war was the visit, search, diversion, and detention of neutral merchant vessels, and (by Iran), the capture and confiscation of goods found on board these ships.

In a letter dated August 19, 1981,[68] Iraq accused Iran of having captured a Danish ship passing through the Strait of Hormuz and of having forced it to sail to an Iranian port. Iraq considered this act of capture and ordering into port a flagrant violation of established rules of international law concerning freedom of navigation through straits used for international navigation.[69] On September 8, 1985, the commander in chief of the Iranian navy announced that any ship suspected of transporting goods destined for Iraq would be stopped and its cargo confiscated;[70] he added that Iran had already proceeded in this way against two Kuwaiti ships (*Al*

64 For an overview of U.S. measures in North Vietnamese waters, see F. B. Swayze, "Traditional Principles of Blockade in Modern Practice: United States Mining of Internal and Territorial Waters of North Vietnam," 29 JAG Journal 143-73 (1977).

65 D. P. O'Connell, *The Influence of Law on Sea Power* 177 (Manchester, 1975).

66 D. P. O'Connell, 44 BYIL 33 (1970).

67 With regard to exclusion zones in the Gulf, see the study by W. J. Fenrick, "The Exclusion Zone Device in the Law of Naval Warfare," XXIV *Canadian Yearbook of International Law* 91, 116 (1986); also R. Leckow, "The Iran-Iraq Conflict in the Gulf: The Law of War Zones," 37 Int'l & Comp. L. Q. 629-44 (1988).

68 UN Doc. S/14637.

69 Report of the Security Council, June 16, 1981 — June 15, 1982, UN GA Off. Rec.: Thirty-Seventh Session, Supp. No. 2 (A/37/2), at 65, para. 902.

70 On July 23, 1985, Tehran had issued a statement that the Iranian Navy would, in accordance with International Maritime Law, confiscate any cargo destined for the Iraqi regime.

Muharraq, June 1985, and *Al Wattgah*, September 4, 1985). The Italian vessel *Merzario Britannia* had been stopped on September 6, 1985; it was, however, neither captured nor was its cargo confiscated. In a letter to the United Nations Secretary General dated September 20, 1985,[71] Kuwait complained about the search and detention of Kuwaiti as well as of Italian and Chinese ships. Iran replied that it had a right to search because the ships affected had been carrying arms destined for Iraq.[72] Later in 1985 and at the beginning of 1986, ships destined for the United Arab Empirate (UAE) were stopped and some of them were ordered into the port of Bandar Abbas.[73] Altogether, between August 1, 1985, and January 12, 1986, fourteen neutral merchant vessels were stopped and searched by Iranian naval forces. By the end of 1987, the number of neutrals that had been stopped and searched increased considerably.[74] On November 17, 1987, Iran adopted a law under which all goods belonging to states at war with Iran were liable to capture and condemnation. Goods belonging to neutral states or to neutral or enemy nationals were liable to capture if they fell into certain categories. The first of these categories concerned goods the transport of which to enemy territory was prohibited altogether; the second concerned goods destined, directly or indirectly, for enemy territory, if they effectively contributed to sustaining the enemy's war effort.[75] Reaction by the flag states against visit, search, capture,

---

[71] UN Doc. S/17482.

[72] Letter of Sept. 25, 1985, UN Doc. S/17496.

[73] On Oct. 8, 1985, Iran was reported to have detained cargo destined to the UAE consisting *inter alia* of electronic equipment. On Oct. 10, 1985, the German vessel *Ville d'Aurore* was stopped on its journey from Oman to Dubai. In Nov. 1985, again a German and a Kuwaiti vessel were stopped by Iranian forces. In Jan. 1986, the search of a U.S. ship and a British ship was reported.

[74] On Jan. 2, 1986, the Danish vessel *Homeland*, and on Jan. 12, 1986 the U.S. ship *President Tailor* and seven further neutral merchant vessels; cf. Ch. Rousseau, "Chronique," 90 RGDIP 678 (1986). For an overview of Iranian and Iraqi actions taken against neutral merchant vessels, see House of Commons, Third Special Report from the Defence Committee (Session 1986-87) The Protection of British Merchant Shipping in the Persian Gulf (Report and Memoranda, London 1987).

[75] See A. Gioia and N. Ronzitti, "The Law of Neutrality: Third States' Commercial Rights and Duties," in I. F. Dekker and H. H. G. Post (eds.), *The Gulf War of 1980–1988*, at 231 (Dordrecht/Boston/London, 1992).

and detention was not uniform;[76] only in a few cases was a formal protest made.[77]

There are, however, two events that are worth mentioning. First, in October 1985, when an Iranian warship approached the French merchant vessel *Ville d'Angers*, a French warship operating in the area positioned itself between the two ships and warned the Iranian warship that it would not hesitate to resort to the use of force if the Iranian endeavoured to intercept the merchant.[78] Despite this incident and the successful deterrence of the Iranian warship, the Sécretaire d'État français à la Mer announced that French tankers would not be escorted by French warships.[79]

Second, as a result of escalating attacks on Kuwaiti vessels since September 1986, the United States responded in March 1987 to a Kuwaiti request by placing eleven of Kuwait's oil tankers under the American flag.[80] Starting in the spring of 1988, all eleven reflagged tankers were transiting the Persian Gulf escorted by United States warships. Additionally, the United States and other states deployed naval units in the Gulf and in the Strait of Hormuz to protect international shipping and to carry out minesweeping operations. The United States emphasized that its actions were fully consistent with the applicable rules of international law, which clearly recognize the right of a neutral state to escort and protect ships that are flying its flag and not carrying contraband.[81] The United States added that its ships would not be carrying oil from Iraq; neither party would thus have "any basis for taking hostile actions against U.S. naval ships or the vessels they protect."

The United Nations Security Council first dealt with the hos-

76 With regard to the British position that the exercise of the right of visit and search is lawful only if it constitutes an act of self-defence under Art. 51 of the UN Charter, see *infra* notes 147 ff. and accompanying text.

77 E.g., the protest by the USSR with regard to Iranian measures taken against the Soviet tankers *Piotr Yemisov* and *Tutov* on Sept. 2 and 3, 1986; cf. Ch. Rousseau, "Chronique," 91 RGDIP 139 (1987). For further examples of the reactions of flag states, see A. Gioia and N. Ronzitti, *op. cit. supra* note 75, at 226.

78 Ch. Rousseau, "Chronique," 90 RGDIP 233 (1986).

79 Ch. Rousseau, "Chronique," 91 RGDIP 139 (1987).

80 Department of Defense, *A Report to the Congress on Security Arrangements in the Persian Gulf* (June 15, 1987), ii (Report by the Secretary of Defense, C. Weinberger).

81 See, *inter alia*, 87 Dept. of State Bull. 87 (June 1987); *ibid.*, 60 (July 1987); *ibid.*, 78 (Aug. 1987); *ibid.*, 42 (Oct. 1987). See also A. Gioia and N. Ronzitti, *supra* note 75, at 240.

tilities at sea in resolution 540 of October 31, 1983. In paragraph 3, it "[A]ffirms the right of free navigation and commerce in international waters, calls on all States to respect this right. . . ." During a meeting of the Security Council in May 1984, most of the delegates referred to the law of peace. Only the Dutch delegate made it clear that according to the law of war belligerents were entitled to restrict navigation to and from ports belonging to the respective enemy; thus, he added, third parties were necessarily affected by these measures.[82] In resolution 582 of February 24, 1986, as well as in resolution 598 (1987), the Security Council *inter alia* expressed its regret for attacks on neutral shipping in the Gulf.

F RECENT MILITARY MANUALS

The final aspects of state practice after the Second World War that are of significance for this study are the manuals on the law of naval warfare, especially the parts on visit, search, and capture. Although there are several of these manuals, the present article will concentrate on the recently issued United States Commanders' Handbook (NWP 9),[83] Canadian Draft Manual,[84] and German Manual,[85] which set out the respective states' understanding of the present status of the law.

Enemy Character

Of Vessels

According to section 7.5 of the NWP9:

[a]ll vessels operating under an enemy flag, and all aircraft bearing enemy markings, possess enemy character. However, the fact that a merchant ship flies a neutral flag, or that an aircraft bears neutral markings, does not necessarily establish neutral character. Any vessel or aircraft, other than a warship or military aircraft, owned or controlled by a belligerent possesses enemy character, regardless of whether it is operating under a neutral flag or is bearing neutral markings.

[82] SCOR, Doc. S/PV 2546, June 1, 1984.

[83] *The Commander's Handbook on the Law of Naval Operations* (Washington, D.C., 1989) [hereinafter NWP 9].

[84] Canadian Forces, *Law of Armed Conflict Manual (Second Draft)* [hereinafter Canadian Draft Manual].

[85] *Humanitäres Völkerrecht in bewaffneten Konflikten: Handbuch*, ZDv 15/2 (Bonn, Aug. 1992) [hereinafter ZDv 15/2].

In a footnote to this provision the Annotated Supplement to NWP 9 states that:

[A] neutral nation may grant a merchant vessel or aircraft the right to operate under its flag, even though the vessel or aircraft remains substantially owned or controlled by enemy interests. According to the international law of prize, such a vessel or aircraft nevertheless possesses enemy character and may be treated as an enemy by the concerned belligerent.

There is no settled practice among nations regarding the conditions under which the transfer of enemy merchant vessels (and, presumably, aircraft) to a neutral flag legitimately may be made. Despite agreement that such transfers will not be recognized when fraudulently made for the purpose of evading belligerent capture, nations differ in the specific conditions that they require to be met before such transfers can be considered as bona fide. However, it is generally recognized that, at the very least, all such transfers must result in the complete divestiture of enemy ownership and control. The problem of transfer is mainly the proper concern of prize courts rather than of an operating naval commander, and the latter is entitled to seize any vessel transferred from an enemy to a neutral flag when such transfer has been made either immediately prior to, or during, hostilities.

According to an annotation to section 716 of the Canadian Draft Manual[86] and paragraph 1022 of the German Manual,[87] the enemy character of vessels and aircraft is established by the same criteria. Therefore, the three manuals agree that the enemy character of vessels and aircraft is determined *prima facie* by the flag they are flying or by the markings they are bearing. Any vessel or aircraft owned or controlled by a belligerent possesses enemy character, even where it is operating under a neutral flag or is bearing neutral markings. As to the determination of the enemy character of the owners of vessels, however, there are differences. Under section 723 of the Canadian Draft Manual, the enemy character of persons may be determined by their commercial domicile in territory belonging to or occupied by an enemy belligerent. The German Manual, on the other hand, refers to the nationality of the owner or, if the

86 "All vessels operating under an enemy flag and all aircraft bearing enemy markings possess enemy character. However, the fact that a merchant vessel flies a neutral flag or that an aircraft bears neutral markings does not necessarily establish neutral character. Any merchant vessel or aircraft owned or controlled by or for an enemy State, enemy persons, or any enemy corporation possesses enemy character, regardless of whether or not such a vessel or aircraft operates under a neutral flag or bears neutral markings."

87 "In principle, the enemy character of a merchant vessel is determined by the flag the ship is entitled to fly."

owner is a stateless person, to his or her residence; in the case of corporations, their seat is relevant.[88]

Section 7.5.2 of NWP 9 specifies that neutral vessels and aircraft, other than warships and military aircraft, acquire enemy character and may be treated by a belligerent as enemy merchant vessels or aircraft when "operating directly under enemy control, orders, charter, employment, or direction, [or when] resisting an attempt to establish identity, including visit and search."[89]

Of Goods

NWP 9 makes no provision for establishing the enemy character of goods found on board merchant vessels. Under section 723 of the Canadian Draft Manual, goods are of enemy character if the commercial domicile of the owner is in territory belonging to or occupied by an enemy belligerent. All goods found on board enemy vessels or aircraft are presumed to be of enemy character in the absence of proof of their neutral character. Notwithstanding any transfer of title to enemy goods already at sea, these goods retain their enemy character.

Except with regard to transfer of title and the presumption of enemy character of goods found on board enemy merchant vessels, the German Manual adopts a different approach. The enemy or neutral character of cargo is determined "by the nationality of the owner or, if the owner is a stateless person, by his residence. In the case of corporations their seat is relevant."[90] Hence, the determination of the enemy character of goods (as well as of vessels and aircraft) differs considerably. The Canadian Draft Manual and NWP 9 follow the Anglo-American doctrine that had been adopted during the Second World War.[91] The German manual, however, emphasizes the nationality of the owners, as was the case in continental European doctrine before 1945.[92] Since there is still no

---

[88] See ZDv 15/2, para. 1027.

[89] If neutral merchant vessels and aircraft take a direct part in the hostilities on the side of the adversary or if they act in any capacity as a naval or military auxiliary to the enemy's armed forces according to NWP 9, section 7.5.1, they acquire the character of an enemy warship or military aircraft. The same applies according to the Canadian Draft Manual, section 717, para. 4.

[90] ZDv 15/2, para. 1027.

[91] See Part I of this study in XXIX *Canadian Yearbook of International Law*, 288 (1991).

[92] *Ibid.*

settled practice, one must conclude that states are free to lay down
the principles under which they will determine the enemy character of ships, aircraft, and goods. There is, however, agreement that
transfers will not be recognized when fraudulently made for the
purpose of evading belligerent capture.

Visit, Search, Diversion, and "Navicerts"

On the right of belligerents to visit and search all merchant
vessels and aircraft, whether enemy or neutral, the three manuals
are analogous.[93] If visit and search at sea are deemed hazardous or
impracticable, the neutral vessel may be escorted by the summon-
ing warship or aircraft.[94] Since the Canadian Draft Manual is not yet
completed, it lacks provisions on neutral warships, neutral state
ships, and neutral merchant vessels travelling under convoy of
neutral warships of the same nationality. Section 7.6 of NWP 9
exempts all these vessels from visit and search; however, the "convoy commander may be required to provide in writing to the
commanding officer of an intercepting belligerent warship information as to the character of the vessels and of their cargoes which
could otherwise be obtained by visit and search. Should it be determined by the convoy commander that a vessel under his charge
possesses enemy character or carries contraband cargo, he is obliged to withdraw his protection of the offending vessel, making it
liable to visit and search, and possible capture, by the belligerent
warship." A similar rule is laid down in paragraph 1142 of the
German Manual, which provides that "the right of inspection shall
not apply to merchant ships flying neutral flags when they are
escorted by a neutral warship (convoy). In this case, however, a
warship of a party to the conflict may request the commander of the
neutral warship to provide information on the type and destination
of the cargo." NWP 9 as well as the German Manual, however, are
silent on the consequences if the convoy commander does not
comply with this obligation.

The three manuals under scrutiny here do not differ with regard
to the consequences if there is resistance to visit and search or if the
summoned vessel takes to flight. In case of flight, the vessel may be
pursued and stopped, by forcible means if necessary.[95] In case of

93 Canadian Draft Manual, section 720; ZDv 15/2, paras. 1014, 1140; NWP 9,
    section 7.6.

94 *Ibid.*, section 720, para. 2.e.; NWP 9, section 7.6.1, para. 5.

95 *Ibid.*, section 720, para. 2.c.; NWP 9, section 7.6.1, para. 3.

active resistance, enemy merchant ships may be attacked and destroyed,[96] while neutral merchant vessels and aircraft are liable to capture.[97]

There seems to be agreement that, owing to changes in warfare, visit and search at sea have become hazardous or impracticable. Hence, NWP 9,[98] the Canadian Draft Manual,[99] and the German Manual[100] directly or indirectly acknowledge the practice of issuing navicerts or aircerts to control the flow of goods on and over the high seas. Navicerts or aircerts issued by one belligerent have no effect on the visit and search rights of a belligerent of the opposing side.[101]

Capture and Destruction of Enemy Merchant Vessels and Enemy Aircraft and Capture of Goods on Board Such Vehicles

General Rule on Capture and Destruction

According to each of the three manuals, enemy merchant vessels[102] and civil aircraft may be captured outside neutral jurisdiction, unless specially protected.[103] Previous exercise of visit and search is not required, provided that positive determination of enemy status can be made by other means.[104] Leaving aside the special cases in which enemy merchant vessels and aircraft may be considered legitimate military objectives,[105] they may, in case of military necessity, be destroyed only after all possible measures have been taken to provide for the safety of passengers and crew.[106]

---

[96] *Ibid.*, section 716, para. 3.a.; NWP 9, section 8.2.2.2; ZDv 15/2, para. 1025.

[97] *Ibid.*, section 717, para. 1.e.; NWP 9, section 7.9.

[98] Section 7.4.2.

[99] Section 720, para. 2.f. (10).

[100] Para. 1141.

[101] NWP 9, section 7.4.2.

[102] In principle, the term "merchant vessel" also applies to other seagoing private vessels, such as yachts and pleasure boats.

[103] Canadian Draft Manual, section 716, para. 1; NWP 9, section 8.2.2.1; ZDv 15/2, para. 1023. The same applies to enemy warships and military aircraft, since they are "classical" military objectives.

[104] NWP 9, section 8.2.2.1.

[105] Canadian Draft Manual, section 716, paras. 3, 4, and 5; NWP 9, section 8.2.2.2; ZDv 15/2, para. 1025. If they are military objectives, they may be attacked and sunk like enemy warships.

[106] *Ibid.*, section 716, para. 2; NWP 9, section 8.2.2.1; ZDv 15/2, para. 1026.

Documents and papers relating to the prize should be safeguarded and, if practicable, the personal effects of passengers should be saved.[107]

With the exception of specially protected articles, all goods found on board enemy merchant vessels and aircraft may be captured.[108] Subject to a decision of a prize court they may be confiscated, unless — with the exception of contraband — it can be proved that they are of neutral character.[109]

Enemy Vessels and Aircraft Exempt from Capture (and Destruction)

The three manuals do not differ with regard to the classes of enemy vessels and aircraft that are exempt from capture (and destruction).[110] A precondition for their specially protected status is that they are innocently employed in their exempt category.[111] These specially protected vessels and aircraft must not take part in the hostilities, must not hamper the movement of combatants, must submit to identification and inspection procedures, and may be ordered out of harm's way. These specifically exempt vessels and aircraft include:

(1) vessels and aircraft designated for and engaged in the exchange of prisoners (cartel vessels);

(2) Properly designated and marked hospital ships, medical transports, coastal rescue craft, and known medical aircraft;

(3) vessels charged with religious, non-military scientific, or philanthropic missions (vessels engaged in the collection of scientific data of potential military application are not exempt);

(4) vessels and aircraft guaranteed safe conduct by previous arrangement between the belligerents;

(5) small coastal (not deep-sea) fishing vessels and small boats engaged in local coastal trade; these craft, however, are subject to the regulations of a belligerent naval commander operating in the area.

107 *Ibid.*
108 *Ibid.*, section 723, para. 3; ZDv 15/2, para. 1028.
109 *Ibid.*
110 *Ibid.*, section 718; NWP 9, section 8.2.3; ZDv 15/2, paras. 1034 ff. and 1054 ff.
111 *Ibid.*

With regard to the latter category, in a footnote to the respective provision of NWP 9, it is emphasized that "the immunity of small coastal fishing vessels and small boats depends entirely upon their 'innocent employment.' If found to be assisting a belligerent in any manner whatever (e.g., if incorporated within a belligerent's naval intelligence network), they may be captured or destroyed." Refusal by an exempt vessel or aircraft to provide immediate identification is considered to be an act of refusing to stop upon being summoned, particularly in the light of modern communications.[112]

With regard to passenger vessels and civil airliners, there are considerable differences. Whereas the Canadian Draft Manual obviously treats them in the same manner as enemy merchant ships or non-military aircraft, NWP 9 provides:

> Civilian passenger vessels at sea and civil airliners in flight are subject to capture but are exempt from destruction. Although enemy lines of communication are generally legitimate military targets in modern warfare, civilian passenger vessels at sea, and civil airliners in flight, are exempt from destruction, unless at the time of the encounter they are being utilized by the enemy for a military purpose (e.g. transporting troops or military cargo) or refuse to respond to the directions of the intercepting warship or military aircraft. Such passenger vessels in port and airliners on the ground are not protected from destruction.[113]

The German Manual, in paragraph 1034, includes a provision to the same effect. In the second draft of the German Manual "passenger ships used exclusively for the transport of civilians" were not only exempted from destruction but also from capture, provided that they complied with the conditions lawfully imposed on them, did not abuse their mission, and were not engaged in any other activity bringing them under the definition of a military objective. According to paragraph 1036, the same was to apply to civilian airliners. In its final form, however, civilian passenger vessels and civilian aircraft are subject only to the right of capture; civilian aircraft may be ordered to land on the ground or water to be searched.[114]

Another difference between the German Manual and the two other manuals may be found in paragraph 1024, which provides that enemy merchant vessels in port at the outbreak of hostilities and other vessels that fall within the scope of the 1907 Hague

[112] NWP 9, section 8.2.3, footnote 63; ZDv 15/2, para. 1035.

[113] *Ibid*, para. 6.

[114] ZDv 15/2, para. 1036.

Convention VI are to be granted a period of grace to allow them to depart unmolested. In a commentary that is presently under preparation, however, it is made clear that these rules are not likely to be of much practical significance.

Goods Exempt from Capture

The Canadian Draft Manual and NWP 9 exempt certain categories of goods from capture as contraband.[115] According to the Canadian Draft Manual these are:

a. free articles, i.e. goods not susceptible for use in armed conflict;
b. articles intended exclusively for the treatment of wounded and sick members of the armed forces and for the prevention of disease. The particulars concerning the carriage of such articles must be transmitted to the adverse State and approved by it; and
c. articles provided for by a convention (treaty) or by special arrangement as between the belligerents.

NWP 9 includes the same provisions, with the following two additional categories of protected articles:

3. Medical and hospital stores, religious objects, clothing, bedding, essential foodstuffs, and means of shelter for the civilian population in general, and women and children in particular, provided there is not serious reason to believe that such goods will be diverted to other purpose, or that a definite military advantage would accrue to the enemy by their substitution for enemy goods that would thereby become available for military purposes.
4. Items destined for prisoners of war, including individual parcels and collective relief shipments containing food, clothing, medical supplies, religious objects, and educational, cultural, and athletic articles.

Since in these two manuals contraband is being dealt with in the context of neutrality and measures against neutral trade, one might be inclined to restrict these rules to goods found on board neutral merchant vessels (and aircraft). But in view of the purpose of the enumerated articles — with the exception of "free articles" and probably athletic articles — one may conclude that they also are exempt from capture when found on board enemy vessels.

The German Manual in general exempts the following articles from capture, irrespective of the law of contraband:

- objects belonging to the passengers or the crew of a captured ship and intended for their personal use;

115 Canadian Draft Manual, section 721, para. 6; NWP 9, section 7.4.1.2.

- material exclusively intended for the treatment of the wounded and sick, the prevention of disease or for religious purposes, provided that the transport of such material has been approved of by the capturing party;

- instruments and other material belonging to relief societies;

- cultural property;

- postal correspondence of the national Prisoner of War Bureau and the Central Prisoners of War Information Agency;

- postal consignments and relief shipments destined for prisoners of war and civilian internees as well as postal consignments dispatched by these persons;

- relief shipments intended for the population of occupied territory, provided that the conditions attached by the capturing party to the conveyance of such shipments are observed; and

- relief shipments intended for the population of any territory under the control of a party to the conflict other than occupied territory.[116]

Capture and Destruction of Neutral Merchant Vessels and Aircraft and Capture of Goods on Board Such Vehicles

Capture and Destruction of Neutral Merchant Vessels and Aircraft

Although it is acknowledged that in principle neutral merchant vessels and aircraft are exempt from capture,[117] according to the three manuals neutral merchant vessels and aircraft are liable to capture if engaged in any of the following activities:

1. Avoiding an attempt to establish identity

2. Resisting visit and search

3. Carrying contraband

4. Breaking or attempting to break a blockade

5. Presenting irregular or fraudulent papers; lacking necessary papers; or destroying, defacing or concealing papers

6. Violating regulations established by a belligerent within the immediate area of naval operations

116 ZDv 15/2, para. 1031.

117 NWP 9, section 7.4.

114   *Annuaire canadien de Droit international 1992*

7. Carrying personnel in the military or public service of the enemy
8. Communicating information in the interest of the enemy.[118]

In section 717 of the Canadian Draft Manual, neutral merchant vessels and aircraft are also subject to capture when "operating directly under enemy control, orders, charter, employment or direction." In NWP 9 section 7.5.2, such an act as well as resistance to "an attempt to establish identity, including visit and search" renders the neutral vessel or aircraft liable to the same treatment as enemy merchant vessels or aircraft.

Of course, according to the Canadian and United States manuals, neutral merchant vessels and aircraft are liable to destruction if they take a direct part in the hostilities on the side of the enemy or if they act in any capacity as a naval or military auxiliary to the enemy's armed forces.[119] In all other cases neutral vessels and aircraft may be destroyed only after every reasonable effort has been made to avoid destruction. The "capturing officer, therefore, should not order such destruction without being entirely satisfied that the prize can neither be sent into a belligerent port or airfield nor, in his opinion, properly be released. Should it become necessary that the prize be destroyed, the capturing officer must provide for the safety of the passengers and crew. In that event, all documents and papers relating to the prize should be saved. If practicable the personal effects of passengers should also be safeguarded."[120]

Goods on Board Neutral Merchant Vessels and Aircraft
(Contraband)

As already shown, while NWP 9, the Canadian Draft Manual, and the German Manual acknowledge that a neutral is not obliged to forbid its citizens to engage in commerce with belligerent nations,[121] they render neutral merchant vessels and aircraft liable to capture if engaged in the carriage of contraband. These manuals

118 *Ibid.*, section 7.9.

119 Canadian Draft Manual, section 717, para. 4; NWP 9, section 7.5.1. It may be added that, according to the Canadian Draft Manual, the same applies if they "actively resist visit and search or capture; refuse to stop upon being duly summoned; or sail under convoy of enemy warships or military aircraft."

120 NWP 9, section 7.9.1. See also Canadian Draft Manual, section 717, paras. 2 and 3; ZDv 15/2, para. 1148.

121 *Ibid.*, section 7.4; ZDv 15/2, para. 1109.

uphold the traditional distinction between absolute and conditional contraband, but they agree that this distinction is of minor
relevance today.[122] Hence, the "precise nature of a belligerent's
contraband list may vary according to the particular circumstances
of the armed conflict."[123] The doctrine of continuous voyage is
applied to both categories.[124] However, in NWP 9 it is made clear
that "although conditional contraband is liable to capture if
ultimately destined for the use of an enemy government and its
armed forces, enemy destination of conditional contraband must
be factually established and cannot be presumed."[125]

G CONCLUSION

It follows from the practice since 1945 that states are inclined to
follow the traditional law insofar as measures of economic warfare
at sea are concerned. Ships encountered beyond neutral jurisdiction may be stopped, visited, diverted, and searched regardless of
their function or nationality. The only important exceptions relate
to neutral warships and government ships and to neutral merchant
ships travelling under convoy of a neutral warship or military aircraft of the same nationality. Enemy property at sea is still not
exempt from capture. Insofar as certain articles exempt from capture are concerned, the extended scope of Additional Protocol I
seems to have had some influence.[126] Neutral merchant vessels and
aircraft are liable to capture and destruction if they engage in
activities that sustain the enemy's war fighting capability. Cargo on
board neutral merchant vessels may be captured if these vessels
engage in what may still be labelled unneutral service or if the
goods are included in contraband lists. The distinction between
absolute and conditional contraband is upheld only formally. Materially it will depend on the circumstances whether an article will be
included in contraband lists. Finally, at least according to the three
military manuals examined here, states seem to be prepared to

[122] Canadian Draft Manual, section 721, para. 1; NWP 9, section 7.4.1 ; ZDv
15/2, para. 1143.

[123] Canadian Draft Manual, section 721, para. 2.

[124] Canadian Draft Manual, section 721, paras. 3 and 4; NWP 9, section 7.4.1.1.

[125] NWP 9, section 7.4.1.1.

[126] For this reason the German Manual, in para. 1031, exempts certain articles
that are not protected under the provisions of NWP 9 and of the Canadian
Draft Manual.

make use of the navicert and ship's warrant system as known from the two world wars.

II. Legal Developments Since 1945 and Their Possible Impact on Measures of Economic Warfare at Sea

At present, some remarkable efforts are being made to establish further legal restrictions on the conduct of belligerents.[127] Although the majority of belligerent measures, even when affecting nationals of third states, are more or less in accordance with the traditional law developed by state practice, these efforts are not confined to an extensive or restrictive interpretation of existing rules of international law on the topic of armed conflict. Rather, certain principles and rules that up to now have been considered to be legally irrelevant for the understanding of the law of (naval) warfare, or that at least have been considered as being superseded by the law of war and neutrality, are being made use of.

A PROHIBITION OF THE USE OF FORCE AND ARTICLE 51 OF THE UNITED NATIONS CHARTER

General Influence of the Law of the United Nations Charter

In considering the possible effects of the United Nations Charter on the law of naval warfare and the law of neutrality, the question arises whether coercive measures permissible under the traditional law are now legal.[128] First, it should be emphasized that, whether or not the position subscribing to a direct influence of the Charter on the law of naval warfare is correct, the law of the Charter has not

---

127 Ch. Greenwood, "Self-defence and the Conduct of International Armed Conflict," in Y. Dinstein and M. Tabory (eds.), *International Law at a Time of Perplexity* 273 (Dordrecht/Boston/London, 1988); R. Lagoni, "Gewaltverbot, Seekriegsrecht und Schiffahrtsfreiheit im Golfkrieg," in W. Fürst, R. Herzog, and D. C. Umbach (eds.), *Festschrift für Wolfgang Zeidler*, Vol. 2, 1833 (Berlin/ New York, 1987); N. Ronzitti, "The Crisis of the Traditional Law Regulating International Armed Conflicts at Sea and the Need for its Revision," in N. Ronzitti (ed.), *The Law of Naval Warfare* 1 (Dordrecht/Boston/London, 1988).

128 M. Bothe, "Neutrality in Naval Warfare: What is Left of Traditional International Law?" in A. J. M. Delissen and G. J. Tanja (eds.), *Humanitarian Law of Armed Conflict: Challenges Ahead* 392 (Dordrecht/Boston/London, 1991); N. Ronzitti, "The Crisis of the Traditional Law Regulating International Armed Conflicts at Sea and the Need for Its Revision," in N. Ronzitti (ed.), *op. cit.* *supra* note 127, at 1.

superseded or rendered obsolete the laws of war and neutrality.[129] Of course, in view of the recent Gulf war, the position may be taken that any act by an aggressor is illegal, thus rendering its possible legality under the laws of war and neutrality obsolete.[130] However, even if the Security Council has been able to establish who the aggressor is, and even if military enforcement measures under Chapter 7 of the Charter are decided upon, the laws of war still apply, at least insofar as individual single acts are concerned. Neither has the law of the Charter rendered neutrality legally impossible. A duty to assist the victim of an act of aggression exists only where there is a binding decision of the Security Council to that effect.[131] If the Security Council has taken a binding decision under Chapter 7, one may take the position that no member state may claim to be neutral.[132] However, the recent Gulf war has shown that, even where the Security Council takes measures under Chapter 7, some states prefer to consider themselves neutral instead of getting involved.[133]

Even in exceptional cases like the recent Gulf war, therefore, there are two yardsticks: one provides for a legal evaluation of the conflict in question, and the other for a legal evaluation of the use of force.[134] In this context, if the laws of war and neutrality are considered a legal order that applies to armed conflicts exclusively (in the sense of an order of necessity), the law of the United

---

129 That position is taken by C. G. Fenwick, *International Law,* 727 (4th ed., New York, 1965); see also C. G. Fenwick, "The Old Order Changeth, Yielding Place to New," 47 Am. J. Int'l L. 84 (1953); M. v. Gleichenstein, *Das Verhältnis des neutralen Mitgliedstaates zur Organisation der Vereinten Nationen, dargestellt am Beispiel der Schweiz* 63 (Hamburg, 1952). For further references, see R. L. Bindschedler, "Frieden, Krieg und Neutralität im Völkerrecht der Gegenwart," in *Festschrift für W. Wengler,* Vol 1, at 27, 31 (Berlin, 1973).

130 See W. Heintschel v. Heinegg, "Kriegsentschädigung, Reparation oder Schadenersatz?: Die möglichen Forderungen an den Irak nach Beendigung des Golf-Kriegs," 90 Zeitschrift für Vergleichende Rechtswissenschaft 113 (1991); F. Berber, *Lehrbuch des Völkerrechts,* Vol. II, at 238 (Munich, 1969).

131 L. M. Goodrich, E. Hambro, and A. P. Simons, *Charter of the United Nations* 300 (New York/London, 1969); J. A. Frowein, "Commentary on art. 42," in B. Simma (ed.), *Charta der Vereinten Nationen: Kommentar* 588 (Munich, 1991).

132 H. Fischer and W. Heintschel v. Heinegg, "Kein Mitgliedstaat der UN kann im Golfkrieg 'neutral' sein," BO-FAX Nr. 10 (Jan. 31, 1991).

133 E.g., Iran declared its neutrality and decided to observe certain traditional neutral obligations such as retaining Iraqi soldiers and aircraft.

134 This is, e.g., also acknowledged by Ch. Greenwood, *op. cit. supra* note 127, at 274; and by M. Bothe, *op. cit. supra* note 128, at 392.

Nations Charter will have no bearing on the interpretation of belligerent rights and duties.

Charter's Influence on Measures of Economic Warfare

According to an increasing number of international lawyers,[135] belligerent measures will be considered illegal under the United States Charter if they are in excess of what is reasonably necessary and proportionate, even where the states concerned comply with the requirements of the laws of armed conflict.

Leaving aside attacks on, and destruction of, enemy merchant vessels, the influence of the Charter on measures of economic warfare affecting enemy merchant vessels and enemy goods is not dealt with in great depth.[136] Ronzitti, for example, merely states that such measures are not in themselves inconsistent with the right of self-defence as long as they meet the test of necessity and proportionality.[137] Thus, according to him, in a large-scale conflict measures of economic warfare are justified, whereas in a small conflict they are less justified or are not justifiable at all.[138]

At first glance, this position seems to be convincing. When applied to a given situation, however, it involves too many uncertainties. Even if it were possible to clearly establish what a "large-scale conflict" is — and who doubts that at least the parties to an ongoing conflict would claim it to be one if they wanted to apply certain measures — this would not in itself imply that all measures of economic warfare taken within such a conflict are necessary and proportionate and hence legal. The traditional law does not confer upon a belligerent an unrestricted right to take measures of economic warfare against enemy merchant vessels and enemy goods. Visit, search, diversion, and capture must be exercised in accordance with certain well-established rules.[139] Captured enemy vessels

135 Ch. Greenwood *op. cit. supra* note 127; R. Lagoni, *op. cit. supra* note 127; N. Ronzitti, *op. cit. supra* note 127; M. Bothe, *op. cit. supra* note 128.

136 *Ibid.*

137 N. Ronzitti, *op. cit. supra* note 127, at 4.

138 *Ibid.*

139 See Part I of this study in XXIX *Canadian Yearbook of International Law* [hereinafter Yearbook], at 304 (1991). See also Annex AS7-3 to the Annotated Supplement to The Commander's Handbook on the Law of Naval Operations (NWP 9 (REV.A)/FMFM 1-10: "OPNAVINST 3120.328 Standard Organization and Regulations of the U.S. Navy"; Annex AS/-4: "Instructions for Prize

and goods must be taken into port and, what is more important, adjudicated upon; property does not pass to the captor until the prize has been condemned by a prize court.[140] Hence, with regard to measures of economic warfare against enemy ships and goods, there seems to be no necessity to add criteria to the traditional law that neither clarify the law nor improve the protection of vessels and goods. The only question that may be asked is whether the condemnation of enemy vessels and goods is still a legal practice.[141] As has been shown by state practice, including military manuals, states obviously are unwilling to exempt enemy private property from the exercise of prize measures.[142] Accordingly, other international lawyers maintain that "the question of the liability of enemy private property [to] be expropriated by a belligerent is not, at the present time, being annulled and replaced by a rule according immunity to 'unoffending private property'."[143] Thus, it seems, under contemporary international law the capture and condemnation by belligerents of enemy merchant vessels, irrespective of the nature of their cargo and their destination, as well as of enemy goods, still constitute legitimate measures.

Much greater attention is paid to the possible influence of the Charter, especially Article 51, on measures of economic warfare where neutral vessels are concerned.[144] In this regard, the above-mentioned international lawyers take the view that, if the principles of necessity and proportionality apply to the relationship between belligerents, they also apply to the relationship between belligerents and neutrals.[145] According to this point of view, in the light of post-Second World War state practice, measures of economic

---

Masters, Naval Prize Commissioners and Special Naval Prize Commissioners";
and Annex AS/-5: United States Prize Statutes, 10 U.S. Code, Chap. 655
(1982).

[140] See Part I of this study in Vol. XXIX of this Yearbook at 304 ff. (1991).

[141] To this effect, see H. Lauterpacht, "Rules of Warfare in an Unlawful War," in
G. A. Lipsky (ed.), *Law and Politics in the World Community* 89, 104 (Berkeley/
Los Angeles, 1953).

[142] See Part I of this study in Vol. XXIX of this Yearbook at 304 (1991), and *supra*
notes 102 ff. and accompanying text.

[143] L. F. E. Goldie, "Excursus" (unpublished paper); see also Y. Dinstein,
Isr.YBHR 40 (1980).

[144] Ch. Greenwood, *op. cit. supra* note 127, at 283; R. Lagoni, *op. cit. supra* note
127, at 1843; N. Ronzitti, *op. cit. supra* note 127, at 7.

[145] *Ibid.*

warfare against neutral merchant vessels may be lawful provided they are justifiable in terms of necessity and proportionality, since they do not constitute violations of the prohibition of the use of force, nor do they constitute aggression. These authors also seem to agree that it would be completely unreasonable to forbid belligerents to take action against neutral vessels that, for instance, are loaded with a cargo of war material bound for an enemy port.[146]

The latter point seems to reflect the traditional law as developed by the practice of states since 1945. The fact that, for example, in the Vietnam conflict measures of economic warfare were restricted, and that during the Falklands war none of the belligerents exercised the doctrine of contraband, does not justify the position that neutral merchant vessels are entirely exempt from measures of economic warfare. During the Vietnam war, the United States endeavoured to limit the conflict. Because of American naval superiority (or better, because of North Vietnam's naval inferiority), there was no military necessity to involve vessels of third states, if one leaves aside the mining of Haiphong. The theatre of war during the Falklands conflict was so remote that for purely practical reasons the institution of exclusion zones affected the shipping of third states only to a very limited extent. It is questionable, however, whether state practice since 1945 also justifies the conclusion that neutral merchant shipping may only be interfered with if the measures in question are necessary and proportionate in the light of Article 51 of the Charter. Although it may be desirable to limit the exercise of economic warfare measures at sea, a rule of customary international law derived from Article 51 that restricts the exercise of traditional rights of economic warfare at sea may only be in a state of development. Voluntary self-restrictions by some belligerents as well as some statements by state officials that are often motivated by mere political considerations do not justify the conclusion that a rule to that effect already exists. Since a considerable number of states in their manuals or otherwise still adhere to the traditional rules on visit, search, diversion, and capture, these rules have not yet fallen into desuetude. The belligerent right to stop, visit, and search neutral merchant vessels probably is not affected at all. Even if the right of capture may now be limited with regard to these vessels, it still exists. To exercise it properly, a belligerent must

---

[146] N. Ronzitti, *op. cit. supra* note 127, at 10. See also M. Bothe, *op. cit. supra* note 128, at 393.

be entitled to verify whether a ship may be considered enemy or whether the function she serves may be characterized as neutral. The most far reaching position with regard to the possible effects of Article 51 of the Charter on belligerent rights to interfere with vessels flying a neutral flag was taken by Great Britain during the Iran-Iraq war. At that time, the Foreign and Commonwealth Office offered the following advice[147] to British shipping in the event that vessels were intercepted:

(1) British policy rests on the general principle that the freedom of navigation in international waters shall be upheld.

(2) In the case of the conflict between Iran and Iraq, HMG's policy is not to sell, or grant export licences for, arms that would prolong or exacerbate the conflict. There should be no grounds for the Iranians to suspect a British ship proceeding directly from a British port of carrying arms supplies to Iraq.

(3) As regards foreign flag vessels and ones that have been loaded in non-British ports, masters should be aware that cargoes of arms loaded in foreign ports are likely to be regarded by Iran as war material if they are destined for Iraq.

(4) If vessels carrying arms to Iraq are detained by Iranian authorities in their territorial waters, the Iranians may choose to apply their own laws on the matter.

(5) British masters should be aware that a state which is actively engaged in armed conflict may, in exercise of its inherent right of self-defence under Article 51 of the United Nations Charter, stop and search a merchant ship in its territorial sea or on the high seas, provided that there is reasonable ground for suspecting that the ship is taking arms or other war material to the other side for use in that conflict. This is an exceptional right, however, and if the suspicions prove unfounded and the ship has not committed acts calculated to give rise to suspicion, then the ship has a good claim to compensation for loss caused by delay.

(6) Although in many instances Iran will have no legal right to stop and search shipping, our advice is that British merchant ships should not resist or evade attempts to board and search. The master should, however, remind the boarding party that they are causing his ship delay and that his owner may wish to pursue a claim for compensation. The master should present the ship's papers in good order to avoid being asked to enter a port and to keep the delay to a minimum. If a ship is stopped and searched, the master should inform the nearest British government representative as soon as possible.

(7) Recently the Iranians have declared that strategic goods destined for Kuwait will be treated as if they were going to a hostile nation. Masters

---

[147] Printed in House of Commons, Third Special Report from the Defence Committee (Session 1986-87), *supra* note 74 at 91-92.

of vessels carrying goods to Kuwait may find it helpful to show clearly that the final user is genuinely Kuwaiti to avoid misunderstandings with the Iranian authorities.

(8) Local port authorities in the UAE, Saudi Arabia, or Kuwait may wish to screen a searched vessel before allowing her to berth: they too should be informed that the Iranians have searched the vessel.

(9) A merchant ship using the international traffic separation scheme through the Strait of Hormuz would pass through Omani waters. There should be less risk of interference from the Iranian navy when using this separation scheme.

In the statement by the British government following the Iranian interception of the British merchant vessel *Barber Perseus* in 1986, the reference to Article 51 was slightly different: "under Article 51 of the United Nations Charter a State such as Iran, actively engaged in an armed conflict, is entitled in exercise of its inherent right of self-defence, to stop and search a foreign merchant ship on the high seas if there is reasonable ground for suspecting that the ship is taking arms to the other side for use in the conflict."[148] This position implies that capture of neutral merchant vessels is legal only if they are in fact taking arms to the adversary. Goods on board these vessels could be captured only if they are arms or war material. In view of state practice after the Second World War and of the most recent military manuals, it is doubtful whether the British position reflects existing international law. Furthermore, the British approach seems to be too flexible in that it would allow the British government or any other government taking a similar position to establish whether the belligerents in an ongoing conflict are entitled to exercise the traditional rights of visit, search, and capture.[149] Be that as it may, the fact that British official policy was not to sell, or grant export licences for, arms that would prolong or exacerbate the conflict, is of some importance. It may contribute to the development of a rule of customary international law to the effect that neutral merchant ships may not be interfered with if the flag state's official policy is to prohibit the transfer of arms and war material to any of the belligerents. This, however, is more important

148 Statement by the Minister of State, Foreign and Commonwealth Office, Jan. 28, 1986, House of Commons Debates, Vol. 90, col. 426; reprinted in 57 BYIL 583 (1986).

149 Of course, as one author has put it, the effectiveness of the law of neutrality to a great extent depends on the neutrals' abilitities to enforce that law: see P. M. Norton, "Between the Ideology and the Reality: The Shadow of the Law of Neutrality," 17 Harv. Int'l L. J. 249, 276 (1976).

in the context of freedom of navigation and the doctrine of contraband[150] than with regard to the exercise of visit, search, and diversion in the light of Article 51 of the Charter.

B ENFORCEMENT OF FREEDOM OF NAVIGATION AND COMMERCE BY NEUTRAL STATES

It is generally acknowledged that neutral merchant vessels and neutral civil aircraft, in times of peace as in times of war (armed conflict), enjoy the rights of freedom of navigation and of overflight respectively,[151] and thus, in principle, are immune from capture and seizure as prize.[152] The rights of free navigation and overflight have, however, never been considered absolute.[153] According to Article 2, paragraph 1 of the 1958 Geneva Convention on the High Seas[154] and Article 87, paragraph 1 of the 1982 United Nations Convention on the Law of the Sea,[155] which beyond doubt reflect customary international law,[156] these rights are subject to "other rules of international law." Traditionally, these other rules have certainly included visit, search, and seizure of merchant shipping.[157] Hence, under the traditional law, neutral merchant vessels can be seized and captured in four exceptional situations:[158] (1) refusal to stop or to permit visit and search; (2) violation of a blockade; (3) carrying contraband; (4) unneutral service.

If a belligerent interferes with neutral merchant ships to verify whether any of these situations exist, the neutral flag state must acquiesce in an encroachment on the right of freedom of navigation. The same applies with regard to the right of free commerce. It is a sound principle of international law that neutral nationals are

[150] See section B of this article, *infra.*

[151] The position taken here is that freedom of navigation is of importance only with regard to neutral shipping. In the case of enemy shipping, it plays no decisive role.

[152] See *inter alia* Y. Dinstein, Isr.YBHR 40 (1980).

[153] See Part I of this study in Vol. XXIX of this Yearbook at 296 (1991).

[154] UN Doc. A/CONF.13/L.53.

[155] UN Doc. A/CONF.62/122.

[156] See *inter alia* Ch. Gloria, "Internationales öffentliches Seerecht," in K. Ipsen, *Völkerrecht,* § 49 Rn. 4 ff. (3d ed., Munich, 1990).

[157] W. S. Fenrick, "Legal Aspects of the Falklands Naval Conflict," RDPMDG 243 (1985); R. Ottmüller, *op. cit. supra* note 8, at 35; R. Lagoni, *op. cit. supra* note 127, at 1835.

[158] See *inter alia* Y. Dinstein, Isr.YBHR 40 (1980).

entitled to engage in trade with belligerents subject only to certain limitations.[159] Since these limitations date back to the beginning of the twentieth century when the right of states to wage war was undisputed, the question arises whether belligerent measures of economic warfare against neutral merchant shipping still comply with a modern understanding of the freedoms of navigation and commerce during an international armed conflict.

One may then ask whether the distinction between enemy and neutral merchant vessels is still significant, since the number of vessels flying a so-called "flag of convenience"[160] has increased considerably,[161] and made it more difficult to establish which ships are neutral and which are enemy in character. It would, however, go too far to conclude from this fact that belligerents no longer need to respect a neutral flag if it belongs to the category of "flags of convenience." Of course, the fact that a vessel is flying such a flag may give rise to suspicion. If the vessel has no genuine link with the state of the flag, it is permissible to ignore a flag of convenience and to consider the vessel in question and its cargo to be of enemy character.[162] Nevertheless, the flying of a flag of convenience alone is not a sufficient ground for a belligerent to treat the vessel concerned in the same manner as an enemy merchant ship. This position fails to consider that the institution of a blockade is still the only permissible and comprehensive means to interdict commerce with the enemy. Accordingly, none of the military manuals under scrutiny in this article include a provision that vessels flying a flag of convenience are liable to the same treatment as enemy merchant vessels.[163]

The question arises, therefore, whether state practice since 1945 has contributed to the development of further legal restraints on belligerent measures that encroach upon the freedoms of navigation and commerce. In view of the war between Iran and Iraq, some

159 This follows from the 1856 Paris Declaration, Hague Convention XIII, and the 1909 London Declaration.

160 According to B. A. Boczek, *Flags of Convenience: An International Legal Study* 2 (Cambridge, Ma, 1982), "functionally, a 'flag of convenience' can be defined as the flag of any country allowing the registration of foreign-owned and foreign-controlled vessels under conditions which, for whatever reasons, are convenient and opportune for the persons who are registering the vessel."

161 Today about one quarter of the total merchant shipping is flying the flags of Panama and of Liberia.

162 Y. Dinstein, Isr.YBHR 40 (1980).

163 See *supra* notes 86 ff. and accompanying text.

authors seem to believe that these principles are now under attack.[164] Nevertheless, the better view seems to be that the opposite is true. There have, of course, been violations, especially in the numerous attacks on neutral oil tankers.[165] States not parties to the conflict, however, have not acquiesced in them; on the contrary, the vigorous opposition of the international community to these violations proves that states are not willing to accept the exercise of certain traditional or alleged rights when they are aimed at neutral merchant shipping.

What conclusions may be drawn from the attitude of states and from the resolutions of the United Nations Security Council during the Iran-Iraq war? First, it is doubtful whether the resolutions of the Security Council that affirm the right of free navigation and commerce in international waters apply to visit, search, and capture.[166] In the case of the resolutions on the Iran-Iraq war, one may argue that the Security Council was referring only to the numerous attacks on neutral merchant vessels. Still, it is remarkable that the Security Council considered those rights to be of continuing validity and therefore imposed certain restrictions on the belligerents.

With regard to the attitude of states, a short remark should be made concerning the legality of the reflagging of Kuwaiti tankers by the United States under present international law. Because the "genuine link" between the ships and the United States seemed to be lacking, the reflagging of the Kuwaiti tankers was criticized almost immediately as transparent, and the United States was accused of using temporary flags as an excuse to employ the use of force. The State Department's legal adviser responded to the criticism by arguing that the application of American statutory procedures constituted a sufficient genuine link to fulfil the requirements of the 1958 Convention.[167] He noted that the vessels complied with the vessel documentation laws of the United States. Specifically, the vessels in question were subject to United States laws and jurisdiction, met United States requirements for ownership, manning, and safety, were subject to United States tax laws,

[164] E.g., A. Gioia and N. Ronzitti, *op. cit. supra* note 75, at 221.

[165] Cf. R. Danziger, "The Persian Gulf Tanker War," 111 U.S. Naval Inst. Proc. 160 (May, 1985); see also the Conference Report on "The Persian/Arabian Gulf Tanker War: International Law or International Chaos," 19 Ocean Development and Int'l L. 299-321 (1988).

[166] E.g., Res. 540 (1983) of Oct. 31, 1983.

[167] A. D. Sofaer, "Complied with U.S. Laws," *New York Times*, Aug. 16, 1987.

and were available to the government for the Military Sealift Command.

In truth, the vagueness of the genuine link language in multilateral conventions[168] gives nations considerable discretion to apply the concept to suit their policy objectives as long as the domestic implementation meets certain minimum international standards.[169] On the other hand, there are good grounds to doubt whether the reflagging was within the spirit of the law, because a political action of this type has nothing to do with the existence of a genuine link as defined in the merchant shipping industry.[170] Be that as it may, given the exigencies of the situation, the reflagging — as well as the deployment of naval forces in the Persian Gulf — may be considered an "unusual measure to meet an extraordinary situation"[171] and thus an effective state protest against actions by Iran and Iraq that are objectionable under international law. While the reflagging, convoying, and deployment of naval forces have certainly helped clarify the law insofar as the destruction of, and attacks on, neutral merchant vessels are concerned, the question remains whether these activities and other actions taken by third states have also been of significance with regard to the legality of belligerent measures of economic warfare against neutral merchant shipping. Since, in the Iran-Iraq war, states not parties to the conflict more or less acquiesced in the exercise of visit, search, diversion, and capture, one may be inclined to answer that question in the negative. It is asserted here, however, that at least in regard to three of these activities, the attitude of third states has had repercussions on the law of economic warfare at sea.

Great Britain, while referring to the freedom of navigation, officially declared that "in the case of the conflict between Iran and Iraq, HMG's policy is not to sell, or grant export licences for arms which would prolong or exacerbate the conflict.

There should be no grounds for the Iranians to suspect a British ship proceeding directly from a British port of carrying arms sup-

---

168 In this respect, see M. L. McConnell, "Darkening Confusion Mounted Upon Darkening Confusion: The Search for the Elusive Genuine Link," 16 J. of Maritime L. and Com. 365 (1985).

169 M. H. Nordquist and M. G. Wachenfeld, "Legal Aspects of Reflagging Kuwaiti Tankers and Laying of Mines in the Persian Gulf," 31 GYIL 138, 139 (1988).

170 *Ibid.*, 151.

171 U.S. Dept. of State, Current Policy No. 958, International Shipping and the Iran-Iraq War (May 17, 1987), at 2.

plies to Iraq.''[172] The United States, in emphasizing the legality of convoying ships flying its flag, declared that the ships were not carrying contraband and oil from Iraq.[173] These statements can be considered as expressing an *opinio iuris* to the effect that belligerents today are not entitled to interfere with neutral ships where there are no grounds for suspecting that these ships are engaged in what may still be labelled "unneutral service," especially when the flag state has made it clear that it would not grant export licences for merchant vessels of belligerent countries that are flying its flag. A ship may be intercepted only if there is sufficient proof that it is not complying with these limitations. Of course, one cannot yet speak of an established rule of customary international law, because many states still consider the traditional rules to apply. Apparently, however, a trend has emerged towards stronger protection of neutral merchant shipping during a conflict, at least insofar as the conflict remains localized.

Even those who cannot subscribe to this conclusion cannot deny that the reactions of third states during the Gulf war have affected the notion of contraband and the status of neutral convoys. In recent state practice, neutral convoys seem to have been exempted from belligerent measures of economic warfare provided that the neutral flag state has taken a position of strict impartiality. It may be argued that neutral convoys have been effective during the Gulf war only because *inter alia* the United States was involved. For a rule of international law to emerge, however, it does not matter whether the states involved are large or small; it suffices if their interests are specially affected and if they behave in a way that may serve as evidence of a certain legal point of view.[174] But it would be too far reaching to assimilate a convoy to state territory and thus conclude that the exercise of visit and search by a belligerent against a neutral convoy constitutes an illegal use of force under the United Nations Charter.[175] The fact that in the Iran-Iraq war the belligerents refrained from enforcing the rights of visit and search

---

172 Advice by the Foreign and Commonwealth Office to British Shipping, printed in House of Commons, Third Special Report from the Defence Committee (Session 1986-87), *supra* note 74 at 91-92.

173 87 Dept. of State Bull. 60 (July 1987); *ibid.*, 42 (Oct. 1987); 88 Dept. of State Bull. 44 (June 1988); see also A. Gioia and N. Ronzitti, *op. cit. supra* note 75, at 233.

174 *North Sea Continental Shelf Cases*, [1969] I.C.J. Rep. 42, para. 73.

175 Such a position is taken by M. Bothe, "Neutrality at Sea," in I. F. Dekker and H. H. G. Post (eds.), *op. cit. supra* note 75, at 205, 210.

against merchant ships travelling under neutral convoy does not justify the conclusion that "uniting a number of merchant ships under the protection of a warship would make the whole unit a piece of the state itself."[176]

With regard to the notion of contraband, war material and goods capable of directly strengthening the war-sustaining effort of the belligerents may still be considered to fall into that category and thus be liable to capture. Other goods, however, may probably not be captured when on board merchant vessels flying the flag of a state that is not a party to the conflict.

The doctrine of continuous voyage is still valid. It is doubtful, however, whether the same is true with regard to the traditional rule according to which only goods bound for an enemy port or for the enemy's forces may be seized, not those coming from an enemy port. Although there was no explicit declaration to this effect during the first Gulf war, the United States' statement concerning the cargo of vessels protected by its naval units seems indirectly to acknowledge that oil (or other goods important for the economy of a belligerent) being exported by the belligerent may be considered contraband or at least liable to capture, even when on board neutral vessels. If the practice of states during the Iran-Iraq war lacked the uniformity necessary for the development of a rule of customary law, then either the traditional rule is still in force or there is no rule at all.

A final answer to the question whether the practice of states during the Iran-Iraq war has lead to a comprehensive and generally accepted doctrine of contraband cannot yet be given. Other goods than arms and war material — with the latter being interpreted broadly — may thus still be considered contraband. In view of the readiness of states to limit the rights of belligerents to capture and condemn goods found on board neutral merchant vessels, however, it may be useful to examine trade restrictions in general. In this respect, the so-called COCOM-list could be used to support the rule that at least all articles comprised in the list may legitimately be considered contraband and thus liable to capture (and condemnation).

It is suggested, then, that the general status of neutral merchant shipping in an armed conflict *de lege ferenda* is as follows. At the outset, there is a rebuttable presumption for their general exemption from capture. The reasons justifying capture (and probably

176 *Ibid.*

diversion) will depend on the policy of the flag state. If its policy is not to support any of the belligerents with war material, strong reasons will be needed to justify capture. Minor standards will apply if the flag state's policy is otherwise. Where the flag state is neither able nor willing to exercise the necessary control, belligerents will be entitled to exercise all those rights conferred upon them by the traditional law.

C ARMED CONFLICT, WAR, NEUTRALITY, AND NON-BELLIGERENCY

The most important treaties on the status of neutrals date back to 1907. Since then, the laws of neutrality have not been updated. The "double dichotomy"[177] between war and peace and between neutrality and belligerency seems to have been challenged by state practice and by the progressive development of international law.

In many fields the notion of "war" has been replaced by the notion of "(international) armed conflict."[178] The question therefore arises whether the traditional law of neutrality applies in such an armed conflict or whether it applies only in a formal state of war.[179] If the latter position is taken,[180] one may argue that the rights of belligerents to interfere with third states do not exist during an international armed conflict, which is not a war in the formal sense.[181] However, according to the position taken in this article, attempts to define the legal concept of war have proven unsuccessful. It would, for example, be difficult to explain why the unilateral decision of one of the parties to the conflict to treat that conflict as a war should have the effect of imposing duties on third

[177] M. Bothe, *op. cit. supra* note 128, at 389.

[178] K. J. Partsch, "Armed Conflict," in R. Bernhardt (ed.), *Encyclopedia of Public International Law*, Instalment 3, at 27 (1982) [hereafter EPIL].

[179] Proponents of the latter position are: R. W. Tucker, *The Law of War and Neutrality at Sea* 199 (Washington, D.C., 1957); L. Delbez, "La notion juridique de guerre," 57 RGDIP 177-209 (1953); E. Lauterpacht, 62 Am. Soc. Int'l L. Proc. 58 (1968); E. Castrén, *The Present Law of War and Neutrality* 31 (Helsinki, 1954); E. Kussbach, "Neutral Trading," EPIL 4, at 9 (1982); W. Meng, "War," EPIL 4, at 290 (1982).

[180] In numerous instances, parties to a conflict wanted to avoid the conflict being designated "war" in the legal sense in order to avoid certain legal (or political) restraints.

[181] See, e.g., R. L. Bindschedler, "Neutrality, Concept and General Rules," EPIL 4, at 10 (1982); E. Kussbach, "L'évolution de la notion de neutralité dans les conflits armés," 17 Military L. and L. of War Rev. 26 (1979).

states and their merchant shipping. Similar difficulties exist with regard to an objective definition of war.[182]

During the Second World War, certain states described their position as one of non-belligerency — that is, they supported one of the belligerent parties without becoming involved in the military conflict.[183] The same was true for a considerable number of states during the Iran-Iraq war. These or similar examples seem to have had an influence on the drafting of Additional Protocol I, which includes a number of provisions distinguishing between "neutrals" and "states not participating in an armed conflict."[184] Does that imply that there is today an intermediate status between neutrality and non-belligerency? Does that also imply that the traditional law of neutrality indeed applies only in a formal state of war? Is it necessary to establish rules governing non-participation, in addition to those governing neutrality *stricto sensu*? At first glance, state practice after the Second World War seems to justify such a view. However, during the Gulf war, many states not directly participating in the hostilities, even though taking a position of non-belligerency and not of neutrality *stricto sensu* (or better perhaps, a position of benevolent neutrality) seem to have acquiesced in the exercise of visit and search. Additionally, it would be both unrealistic and inappropriate to deny parties to an armed conflict (as distinguished from parties to a war) the right, for example, to control the flow of contraband.[185]

Finally, the question remains whether there is a need to elaborate rules on non-belligerency. It is submitted that acts of states taking a position of non-belligerency may still be evaluated in the light of the traditional rules on neutrality. This is shown by the fact that financial or material assistance to Iraq by a number of countries was not considered to deprive them of their neutral status or to violate their duty of impartiality; they simply were non-belligerents who took a position in favour of one of the belligerents without taking part in the hostilities. There is no need to establish in the law an intermediate status between belligerency and neutrality. Certain

---

182 F. Grob in 1949 had furnished ample proof for the non-existence of a "state of war" in the legal sense: see F. Grob, *The Relativity of War and Peace* 179 (New Haven, 1949).

183 See *inter alia* R. L. Bindschedler, EPIL 4, at 13 (1982).

184 Arts. 2 (c), 9 (2), 19, 31, 39, 64.

185 M. Bothe, *op. cit. supra* note 128, at 390.

acts by a non-belligerent state may constitute violations of the traditional law of neutrality, and may therefore give rise to an appropriate reaction by the belligerent party affected.

Nevertheless, there still is considerable uncertainty on these questions that should be remedied in any revision of the law of naval warfare. Especially it needs to be established in what circumstances acts of non-belligerent states affect their neutral status. It seems that unneutral service performed by a non-belligerent state would not be sufficient to justify the use of force against that state, since unneutral service is not an armed attack. This, however, is not the subject of this study. Unneutral service, performed not by a state but by an individual merchantman, has no impact on the neutral status of the flag state. Thus, the reaction of the belligerent must be evaluated in the light of the traditional law developed by state practice since 1945.

D 1977 ADDITIONAL PROTOCOL I

The question remains to what extent the rules and principles of the 1977 Additional Protocol I to the Geneva Conventions of August 12, 1949 are of relevance for belligerent measures of economic warfare at sea. Although the famous dispute between Meyrowitz[186] and Rauch[187] as to the applicability of Additional Protocol I to naval warfare is no longer considered to be important, it may be recalled that the provisions of Part IV, Section I do not directly apply to ship-to-ship, ship-to-air or air-to-ship attacks, unless they affect the civilian population on land.[188] Belligerent conduct restricted to the sea and the airspace above it remains governed by the rules of customary international law. Insofar as these customary rules are concerned, there is widespread agreement that these comprise, beside the traditional law of naval warfare as developed by state practice, the definition of "military objectives" as set out in Article 52, paragraph 2 as well as in other rules and principles of

---

[186] H. Meyrowitz, "Le protocole additionel I aux Conventions de Genève de 1949 et le droit de la guerre maritime," 89 RGDIP 243 (1985).

[187] E. Rauch, *The Protocol Additional I to the Geneva Conventions for the Protection of Victims of International Armed Conflicts and the United Nations Convention on the Law of the Sea: Repercussions on the Law of Naval Warfare* 57 (Berlin, 1984).

[188] M. Bothe, "Commentary on the 1977 Geneva Protocol I," in N. Ronzitti (ed.), *op. cit. supra* note 127, at 761.

Additional Protocol I.[189] The definition of military objectives, beside destruction and neutralization, also includes capture. This, however, in no way justifies the conclusion that only enemy vessels, enemy aircraft, and enemy goods that fulfil the elements of that definition are liable to capture. The reference to capture in the definition is nothing but a concrete formulation of the principle of proportionality, to the effect that belligerents are obliged to consider that capture can offer a "definite military advantage" over destruction and neutralization. The applicability of the definition of military objectives has not superseded the rules governing economic warfare at sea that remain applicable *qua* customary international law. The definition of military objectives, despite the reference to capture, therefore has no impact on the legality of the exercise of visit, search, diversion, and capture. If ships and goods that qualify as military objectives are captured, they are not captured as prizes and consequently need not be adjudicated upon.

In contrast to the definition of military objectives, the rules of Additional Protocol I on protected vessels, aircraft, and objects are of relevance for the legality of measures of economic warfare. In this context it is suggested that consideration be given to the lists of protected vessels and aircraft and the lists of protected goods and articles that are included in the military manuals quoted above.[190] In this connection it may also be of interest to consider to what extent Article 70, paragraph 1, Additional Protocol I is of importance.[191]

It must be emphasized that the effects of Additional Protocol I and the respective rules of customary international law on measures of economic warfare against neutral merchant ships and goods found on board these vessels are confined to the relationship between the parties to an international armed conflict. Therefore, they can only be used indirectly insofar as neutral ships and goods

189 For an overview, see M. Bothe, *ibid.*, 760. See also the commentaries and preliminary results of the Round-Table of Experts on International Humanitarian Law Applicable to Armed Conflicts at Sea held in Bochum (FRG) in 1989, in W. Heintschel v. von Heinegg (ed.), *The Military Objective and the Principle of Distinction in the Law of Naval Warfare* (Bochum, 1991). The three manuals under scrutiny here also acknowledge the customary character of the definition of military objectives and its validity for the law of naval warfare: see NWP 9, section 8.1.1; Canadian Draft Manual, section 714; ZDv 15/2, para. 1017.

190 *Supra* notes 110 ff. and accompanying text.

191 See M. Bothe, in N. Ronzitti (ed.), *op. cit. supra* note 127, at 763.

are concerned. Of course, if certain enemy vessels and goods are exempt from capture because they belong to specially protected categories, in principle the same exemption must apply to neutral vessels and goods serving the same functions. In these situations the rules of Additional Protocol I need not be interpreted extensively. Nevertheless, it must be kept in mind that the legal status of neutral property at sea does not originate from the laws of war *stricto sensu* but from the laws of neutrality.

III. Conclusions

A ENEMY CHARACTER

Prima facie, the enemy character of a ship is still determined by the flag she flies. If the flag is not conclusive because there remain reasons for suspicion, it is unsettled whether the nationality of the owner or his domicile or other reasons may justify considering the ship to be of enemy character. The same holds true with regard to enemy goods. There is only agreement to the effect that with regard to goods found on board enemy merchant vessels there is a rebuttable presumption of their enemy character.

B VISIT, SEARCH, DIVERSION, AND NAVICERTS

Despite a tendency to restrict the exercise of visit and search as far as neutral merchant vessels are concerned, the traditional law under which all merchant vessels (and civil aircraft), whether enemy or neutral, may be visited and searched anywhere on the sea with the exception of neutral waters has remained unchanged. This follows from the fact that capture is still a legal measure. If under certain conditions belligerents are entitled to capture ships (aircraft) and goods, they must be entitled to verify whether these conditions are fulfilled. The same is true with regard to diversion and ordering into port, because in modern armed conflicts the exercise of the traditional rights of visit and search at sea is even more hazardous than it was, for example, during the Second World War. Certainly, new sensor and weapons technologies will have an impact on measures of economic warfare at sea. In particular, the use of satellites for communication and surveillance will enable belligerents to identify neutral as well as enemy shipping over considerable distances.

The only exception to the rights of visit, search, and diversion relates to neutral merchant vessels travelling under convoy of a warship that flies the same flag. In this situation, visit, search, and diversion must be exercised according to a specific procedure and in such a manner as to avoid undue delays, unnecessary interference, and unnecessary hazards.

In contrast to neutral merchant vessels (and aircraft), enemy vessels (and aircraft) are not obliged to submit to visit, search and diversion. If a vessel (aircraft) forcibly resists, it is liable to capture and, under certain conditions, to destruction. If a ship (aircraft) merely endeavours to escape, she may be stopped by the use of reasonable force.

Navicerts and ship's warrants today seem to be legitimate means of commerce control. In this context, however, the question arises whether the attitude of neutral states toward export controls in their respective territories may render these methods obsolete.

C ENEMY SHIPS (AIRCRAFT) AND GOODS

Private enemy property at sea is liable to capture either because it fulfils the requirements of military objectives or because it may be considered a "good prize." There is no rule of international law under which private enemy property at sea is immune from capture. For all states, trade at sea is of such importance that, when belligerents, they will not renounce a right that enables them to hit the enemy's economy effectively. Only those enemy vessels (aircraft) and goods that serve special functions are exempt from capture under conventional and customary law. In this context, one may consider exempting from capture passenger vessels that are transporting civilians and no contraband articles, because capture always implies certain hazards for the ship concerned. If a belligerent wishes to make use of such a vessel, it can be requisitioned. Enemy merchant vessels in enemy port at the outbreak of hostilities, however, are not, and never have been protected by any binding rule. Today, because it is possible to integrate almost any merchant vessel into naval forces without major technical difficulties, states will be even less willing to agree to such a rule than they were in 1907. Nevertheless, if the direct influence of the United Nations Charter on the law of economic warfare at sea is accepted, the legality of condemning enemy property will probably have to be reconsidered. If all measures have to meet the principles of necessity and proportionality set out in the Charter, it is doubtful whether the acquisition of all enemy property at sea is legally justified.

D NEUTRAL VESSELS (AIRCRAFT) AND GOODS ON BOARD SUCH
VESSELS (AIRCRAFT)

There is, at the outset, a rebuttable presumption that neutral vessels (aircraft) and goods on board these vessels (aircraft) are immune from capture. Neutral vessels (and aircraft) may, however, still be captured if engaged in: (1) resistance to visit, search and diversion; (2) breach of blockade; (3) carriage of contraband; and (4) unneutral service. The reasons justifying capture in these situations will depend on the policy of the flag state. If the flag state's official policy is not to allow the support of any of the belligerents with arms and war material, the reasons justifying capture of its ships proceeding directly from one of its ports will have to be of a serious nature. Minor standards will apply if the flag state is not committed to this policy. In all other situations, goods on board neutral merchant vessels (and civil aircraft) may be captured only if they constitute contraband. There is no general agreement on which articles may legitimately be considered contraband, unless they are arms or war material destined to the enemy. In this respect, existing trade limitations should be observed. Although the doctrine of continuous voyage remains valid, the question remains whether this is also true with regard to the restriction of the doctrine of contraband to goods transported to enemy territory or to the enemy's armed forces.

E INFLUENCE OF CERTAIN PRINCIPLES ON THE LEGALITY OF
MEASURES OF ECONOMIC WARFARE

It is doubtful whether the law of the United Nations Charter has had an impact on measures of economic warfare directed against enemy merchant vessels (aircraft) and goods. With regard to measures directed against neutral vessels (aircraft), the law may be in a state of change. Even so, the Charter would not necessarily affect the substance of the law of naval warfare and the law of neutrality. In the case of an international armed conflict, the influence of the Charter would only restrict the belligerents' right to make immediate use of the whole body of that law.

The freedom of navigation (overflight) and commerce enjoyed by neutral merchant vessels (and aircraft) today plays an increasingly important role. If neutral flag states do not support any of the belligerents with arms or war material and if they have adopted effective national measures of trade control, they are allowed to enforce the freedom of navigation (and overflight) —

for example, by the deployment of armed forces in the region in question.
The impact of Additional Protocol I on the law of economic warfare at sea has been minor. Its rules cannot be applied directly to neutrals; they are directly applicable only to the relationship between the parties to a conflict.

Sommaire

Droit de visite, fouille, déroutement, et capture dans la guerre maritime. Partie II: Développements depuis 1945

Ici la deuxième partie de l'article qui était publié dans le volume XXIX de l'Annuaire. Elle examine la pratique des États depuis 1945.

Bien que les belligérants aient eu tendance depuis 1945 à ne pas recourir à la guerre maritime économique et à opter plutôt pour une politique de torpillage sans restriction, il est encore pertinent d'examiner les mesures relevant de la guerre maritime qui sont acceptables en vertu du droit international traditionnel et de se demander si ces règles s'appliquent à la guerre maritime moderne.

Le traitement des équipages et des passagers ainsi que la réquisition et la légalité ne sont pas abordées.

L'investigation dans le programme nucléaire irakien

INTRODUCTION

S INGULIÈRE, EN CE QU'ELLE REQUIERT L'ACCEPTATION de l'État — l'Irak — à l'encontre duquel elle a été conçue,[1] la résolution 687 adoptée par le Conseil de Sécurité le 3 avril 1991 s'inscrit cependant dans la logique qui a sous-tendu l'action de l'organe "exécutif" de l'ONU au fil de l'affaire du Golfe[2] et visant, entre autres, à restaurer dans cette partie du Proche-Orient un équilibre des forces susceptible de préserver une relative stabilité nécessaire à l'instauration d'un ordre régional dans lequel, selon les termes mêmes de la résolution en question, les armes de destruction massive seraient bannies.[3]

---

* Professeure, Département des Sciences Juridiques, Université du Québec à Montréal.

---

[1] S/Res/687 (1991), 3 avril 1991, § 33.

[2] S. Sur, *La résolution 687 (3 avril 1991) du Conseil de Sécurité dans l'affaire du Golfe: problèmes de rétablissement et de garantie de la paix*, New York Institut des Nations Unies pour la recherche sur le désarmement UNIDIR Travaux de recherche no 12, New York, 1992, aux pp. 8-12, également publié dans (1991) 37-*A.F.D.I.* 25-97 sur lequel nous nous baserons dans la suite de nos références à cette étude.

[3] S/Res/687 (1991), Préambule: "Rappelant l'objectif que constitue la création d'une zone exempte d'armes nucléaires dans la région du Moyen-Orient"; ainsi que le paragraphe 14, dans lequel le Conseil de Sécurité "note que les mesures que doit prendre l'Irak, en application des paragraphes 8 à 13 de la présente résolution s'inscrivent dans une démarche dont les objectifs sont de créer au Moyen-Orient une zone exempte d'armes de destruction massive et de tous missiles vecteurs ainsi que de parvenir à une interdiction générale des armes chimiques."

Singulière, la résolution 687 l'est également par le dispositif qu'elle crée afin de contraindre l'Irak à se conformer aux instruments conventionnels du droit international relatifs à la non-prolifération des armes nucléaires et au désarmement en général.[4] Il en résulte de nombreuses interrogations à cet égard, dont seules nous préoccuperont, ici, celles qui concernent la tentative de l'Irak d'acquérir une capacité militaire nucléaire. La principale question que soulève ce sujet a trait au système de garanties établi en vertu du Traité sur la non-prolifération des armes nucléaires — TNP de 1968,[5] et mis en oeuvre par l'Agence Internationale de l'Énergie Atomique — AIEA: comment l'Irak a pu déjouer les mécanismes de surveillance de l'Agence, et celle-ci a-t-elle failli à sa mission dans ce domaine.

Pour une bonne part, les réponses peuvent être d'ordre juridique: en effet, une comparaison entre les procédures suivies en vertu du TNP et le processus déclenché sur la base de la résolution 687 permet de comprendre de quelle manière l'Irak a violé ses obligations au regard du droit international et les raisons pour lesquelles l'Agence n'était pas en mesure d'identifier de telles contraventions aux dispositions du Traité. Ce sont donc à la fois les fondements et l'étendue de l'action de l'AIEA qui se sont trouvés modifiés aux termes de la décision du Conseil de Sécurité ouvrant la voie à l'investigation que l'on sait en vue de mettre à jour l'ampleur du programme nucléaire irakien et de remédier à un tel état de fait par le démantèlement intégral de tout ce potentiel destiné, selon les preuves rassemblées, à des fins militaires contraires aux engagements juridiques de l'Irak.

I Le tnp et les fondements de l'investigation

Selon l'article II du TNP, les États non dotés d'armes nucléaires (ENDAN) et qui sont parties au traité prennent un engagement général de ne pas fabriquer ni acquérir de quelque manière que ce

---

[4] Rappelons que la résolution 687 ne se préoccupe pas seulement du potentiel militaire irakien, mais énonce, en outre, l'ensemble des conditions du cessez-le-feu mettant fin à la guerre du Golfe, à l'occupation du Koweit par les troupes irakiennes, et devant régir l'Irak quant à sa responsabilité internationale résultant du conflit et de ses conséquences.

[5] *Traité sur la non-prolifération des armes nucléaires*, 1er juillet 1968, signé à Londres, Washington et Moscou, dans G. Fischer, *La non-prolifération des armes nucléaires*, Paris, LGDJ, 1969, aux pp. 215-20.

soit des armes ou autres dispositifs nucléaires explosifs.[6] Cette disposition constitue la pierre angulaire de l'ensemble des obligations qui seront contractées par un ENDAN, tel l'Irak, et qui concourent à assurer que des installations, équipements et matières nucléaires obtenus dans le cadre d'activités civiles ne seront pas détournés vers des objets militaires.

La nature conventionnelle de ce renoncement marque du même volontarisme caractéristique du droit international l'édifice juridique sur lequel reposera la surveillance par l'AIEA du respect d'un tel engagement. Au contraire, la résolution 687 va chercher à dépasser les contraintes d'un tel système pour en combler les lacunes et réaliser pleinement l'objectif du Traité.

A LE CONSENSUALISME DANS LE SYSTÈME DU TNP

En vertu de l'article III du TNP, un ENDAN s'engage à négocier et conclure avec l'AIEA, dans un délai déterminé, un accord relatif au système de garanties de l'Agence par lequel il accepte les garanties ainsi stipulées dans un instrument spécifique. Par cette stipulation le régime statutaire de garanties de l'Agence acquiert à la fois un caractère contraignant et un champ plus large d'application: en effet, le Statut de l'AIEA lui confère des responsabilités et des droits pour les seuls projets de l'Agence elle-même ou lorsque les parties intéressées invitent l'Agence à appliquer des garanties.[7] Il s'agit donc, initialement, d'une option ouverte aux États et non d'une obligation leur incombant; avec le TNP, les États parties au Traité soumettent désormais l'ensemble de leurs activités nucléaires pacifiques à un contrôle obligatoire de l'AIEA.[8]

Ainsi dans cette perspective, l'action de l'AIEA revêt un double fondement juridique consensuel: l'adhésion au TNP qui emporte consentement au système de garanties de l'Agence, et l'accord

---

6 *Traité sur la non-prolifération des armes nucléaires, op. cit.*, l'article II se lit comme suit: "Tout État non doté d'armes nucléaires qui est partie au traité s'engage à n'accepter de qui que ce soit, ni directement, ni indirectement, le transfert d'armes nucléaires ou autres dispositifs explosifs nucléaires ou du contrôle de telles armes ou de tels dispositifs explosifs; à ne fabriquer ni acquérir de quelque autre manière des armes nucléaires ou autres dispositifs nucléaires explosifs; et à ne rechercher ni recevoir une aide quelconque pour la fabrication d'armes nucléaires ou autres dispositifs nucléaires explosifs."

7 Article XIII, *Statut de l'Agence Internationale de l'Énergie Atomique*, 23 octobre 1956, tel qu'amendé au 28 décembre 1984, AIEA, Vienne 1990.

8 D. M. Edwards, "International Legal Aspects of Safeguards and the Non-Proliferation of Nuclear Weapons," (1984) 33 *Int'l & Comp. L.Q.*, 1-21, à la p. 11.

subséquent que l'ENDAN doit,[9] du fait même de son adhésion, conclure avec l'AIEA car "le droit de l'Agence de faire des inspections dans un pays et d'appliquer les garanties n'existe que si un accord entre l'Agence et l'État est entré en vigueur."[10] De ce fait, ledit accord devient la pièce centrale, sur le plan juridique, du système de garanties. Aussi l'AIEA a-t-elle élaboré un schéma de base pour ce type d'accords[11] qu'elle va être amenée à conclure pour être en mesure de remplir les fonctions que lui confie le TNP.

Comme l'Irak devient partie au Traité sur la non-prolifération, le 29 octobre 1969, c'est un semblable accord qu'il signe avec l'Agence et qui entre en vigueur le 29 février 1972. Selon l'énoncé de l'article premier de ce texte,[12] "l'Irak s'engage, en vertu du paragraphe I de l'article III du Traité, à accepter des garanties, conformément aux termes du présent Accord, sur toutes les matières brutes et tous les produits fissiles spéciaux dans toutes les activités nucléaires pacifiques exercées sur son territoire, sous sa juridiction, ou entreprises sous son contrôle en quelque lieu que ce soit, à seule fin de vérifier que ces matières et produits ne sont pas détournés vers des armes nucléaires ou d'autres dispositifs explosifs nucléaires." Parallèlement sont établis le droit et l'obligation de l'Agence de veiller à l'application de telles garanties;[13] de même, est stipulée la coopération entre l'Irak et l'Agence pour faciliter la mise en oeuvre des garanties.[14]

9 Il convient de souligner que les ENDAN non parties au TNP ne seront soumis au système de garanties que si l'État fournisseur de produits fissiles ou matières brutes, ou encore d'équipements permettant leur fabrication est lui-même partie au TNP, ce qui lui impose, en vertu de l'article I et de l'article III de ne rien transférer à un ENDAN pour des fins militaires et d'assurer à cet effet un contrôle par l'AIEA sur les produits matières ou équipements ainsi procurés. Dans ces conditions "le contrôle sera moins étendu sur les États non nucléaires qui n'adhèrent pas au traité"; voir G. Fischer, *op. cit. supra*, note 5, aux pp. 102-3.

10 H. Blix, "Aspects juridiques des garanties de l'Agence Internationale de l'Énergie Atomique," (1983) *A.F.D.I.*, 37-58, à la p. 44.

11 *Structure et contenu des accords à conclure entre l'Agence et les États dans le cadre du Traité sur la Non-Prolifération des armes nucléaires*, INFCIRC/153 (corrigé), Vienne, AIEA, mars 1975.

12 Texte de l'accord entre l'Irak et l'Agence relatif à l'application de garanties dans le cadre du traité sur la non-prolifération des armes nucléaires, INFCIRC/172, Vienne, AIEA, 26 février 1973.

13 *Ibid.*, article 2.

14 *Ibid.*, article 3.

Dans le processus qui se déclenchera sur cette base, l'AIEA n'acquiert pas pour autant une autonomie de mouvement. Tout d'abord, elle doit obtenir le consentement de l'Irak à la désignation des inspecteurs[15] que l'Agence propose d'envoyer et dont les noms, titres, nationalités et autres renseignements utiles sont communiqués par écrit au gouvernement irakien qui fait savoir au directeur général s'il accepte la proposition[16] ou s'il a une objection contre une désignation donnée, auquel cas l'Agence propose une ou plusieurs autres désignations.[17]

D'un autre côté, ce n'est pas l'Agence qui collecte de son propre chef les informations nécessaires à l'application des garanties: la mise en oeuvre effective des garanties dépend des renseignements que l'Irak lui-même fournit à l'AIEA au sujet des matières nucléaires soumises aux garanties et des installations ayant une importance à cet égard; quant à l'Agence, elle demande seulement un minimum de renseignements nécessaires pour exécuter ses obligations.[18]

En outre, les garanties doivent être appliquées de manière à ne pas "gêner indûment les activités nucléaires pacifiques de l'Irak," à demeurer compatibles avec les pratiques de saine gestion permettant une conduite économique et sûre des activités, et sans entraver le progrès technologique de l'Irak.[19] Aussi est-il prévu que l'Agence donne préavis à l'Irak concernant l'arrivée des inspecteurs.[20]

Certes, la possibilité de procéder à des inspections inopinées, sans notification préalable, est également consignée dans le texte de l'Accord entre l'Irak et l'AIEA;[21] néanmoins cette disposition demeure d'une portée limitée dans la pratique, d'autant qu'elle convie l'Agence à aviser périodiquement le gouvernement irakien "de son programme général d'inspections annoncées et inopinées en précisant les périodes générales pendant lesquelles des inspections sont prévues" et qu'elle l'engage à réduire au minimum les difficultés pratiques que de tels contrôles seraient susceptibles de causer au programme d'opérations irakien.

---

15 *Ibid.*, article 9.
16 *Ibid.*, article 85.
17 *Ibid.*, article 9.
18 *Ibid.*, article 8.
19 *Ibid.*, article 4.
20 *Ibid.*, article 83.
21 *Ibid.*, article 84.

Cette dynamique consensuelle, qui non seulement fonde mais préside aux différentes étapes de la mise en oeuvre des garanties, imprime au système des faiblesses évidentes puisque l'engagement de l'Agence — chargée de l'élaboration et de l'application des mesures de vérification de la conformité des États à leurs obligations conventionnelles en vertu du TNP — ne fait que refléter celui de l'État,[22] de sorte que la bonne foi comme règle essentielle du droit des traités acquiert dans ce contexte une dimension tout à fait particulière. À cet égard, d'ailleurs, les responsables de l'AIEA ont souvent souligné que la confiance était à la fois la base et l'objectif du mécanisme des garanties, avançant que dans le contexte de la non-prolifération les États ne cherchent pas à se dissuader eux-mêmes à travers l'inspection mais à fournir une confirmation de leur respect des engagements qu'ils ont contractés à cet effet.[23]

Par ailleurs, l'insuffisance des moyens financiers et en personnel de l'Agence[24] ne pouvait qu'accentuer les défaillances du dispositif. Aussi, les États maîtrisant la technologie nucléaire et constituant le groupe principal de fournisseurs dans l'ensemble du commerce nucléaire international avaient-ils entrepris de se réunir à Londres, en 1975, à l'initiative des États-Unis, afin d'établir une politique concertée et d'arrêter un nombre "de règles communes visant à permettre un développement des exportations nucléaires compatible avec l'objectif de non-prolifération des armes nucléaires."[25] Le "Club de Londres"[26] avait ainsi élaboré une série de Directives et recommandations qui avaient été communiquées à l'AIEA en 1978 et qui prévoyaient notamment un élargissement du rôle de l'Agence dont le contrôle allait s'appliquer désormais à un plus grand nombre d'articles nucléaires, de même qu'à tous les pays

---

[22] H. Blix, *op. cit. supra*, note 10, à la p. 49.

[23] H. Blix, "Pour une plus grande confiance," (1984) 26-3 *AIEA Bulletin*, aux pp. 3-6.

[24] S. Courteix, "Le contrôle de la prolifération des armes nucléaires," (1982-83) 28 *McGill Law Journal* 591-607, à la p. 598.

[25] S. Courteix, *Exportations nucléaires et non-prolifération*, Paris, Economica, 1978, p. 47.

[26] Formé initialement des sept pays fondateurs qui s'étaient réunis en 1975 dans la capitale britannique — la République fédérale d'Allemagne, le Canada, les États-Unis, la France, le Japon, le Royaume-Uni et l'URSS — le "Club de Londres" s'était élargi entre 1976 et 1978 à la République démocratique d'Allemagne, la Belgique, l'Italie, les Pays-Bas, la Pologne, la Suède, la Tchécoslovaquie, la Suisse et l'Australie.

clients, non dotés d'armes nucléaires, y compris ceux qui n'avaient pas signé le TNP.[27]

Malgré ces mesures, il demeurait indéniable que la confiance restait la clef de voûte de la crédibilité du système des garanties. Or, ce paramètre revêt des aspects largement politiques, et le raid de l'aviation israélienne conduit en juin 1981, contre le réacteur de recherche irakien Tamuz I, montrait bien que la perception des situations dans ce domaine peut diverger, comme cela avait été souligné par le directeur général de l'AIEA à l'époque devant le Conseil de Sécurité.[28] D'ailleurs, l'État hébreu n'avait pas été le seul à se préoccuper des accords passés, en 1975, entre la France et le gouvernement Irakien: les États-Unis, en particulier, avaient manifesté de profondes inquiétudes au sujet de la vente d'uranium hautement enrichi et avaient tenté de dissuader les responsables français de procéder à de telles fournitures; mais la proposition française de substituer un combustible plus faiblement enrichi devait être rejetée par l'Irak en tant que modification au contrat initial.[29]

Avec le recul des évènements, il est permis de constater que l'étendue du consensualisme qui sous-tend la mise en oeuvre des inspections dans le cadre du régime de garanties du TNP mine gravement son efficacité; et il semble bien que cette faille originelle et fondamentale du système n'a pas échappé à un État comme l'Irak, lequel a réussi, malgré les mesures supplémentaires convenues par le "Club de Londres," à contourner l'ensemble des dispositifs de non-prolifération, notamment par une diversification de ses sources d'approvisionnement en équipements et en matières

---

[27] S. Courteix, "Le contrôle de la prolifération des armes nucléaires," *op. cit. supra*, note 24, à la p. 599; et, du même auteur, *Exportations nucléaires et non-prolifération*, *op. cit.*, *supra* note 25, aux pp. 54-57; rappelons que cette concertation faisait suite à l'explosion nucléaire réalisée par l'Inde, en 1974, grâce à un réacteur civil expérimental de la filière canadienne (CANDU) et alors que ce pays n'était pas partie au TNP. Le document des "Directives relatives aux transferts d'articles nucléaires" établi en 1977 par le "Club de Londres," est désigné par l'AIEA sous la cote INFCIRC/254.

[28] L. M. Muntzig, "Safeguards and Nuclear Safety: A Personal Perspective," (1982) 24.2 *IAEA Bulletin* 7-10; l'auteur écrit: "In reporting on the raid to the UN Security Council the then IAEA Director General Dr. Sigvard Eklund noted, with ironic understatement, that Israel had 'evidently not felt assured by our findings and by our ability to continue to discharge our safeguarding responsibilities satisfactorily'."

[29] J. E. Birnberg, "The Sun Sets on Tamuz I: The Israeli Raid on Iraq's Nuclear Reactor," (1983) 13 *Cal. Western Int'l L.J.*, 86-115, aux pp. 92-93.

nucléaires. C'est vraisemblablement cette même conclusion qui a présidé à l'adoption de la résolution 687 du Conseil de Sécurité.

B LES BASES RÉSOLUTOIRES DE L'INVESTIGATION

À son dernier alinéa du long préambule introductif aux décisions arrêtées dans la résolution 687, le Conseil de Sécurité estime "qu'il se doit de prendre, en vertu du chapitre VII de la Charte, les mesures énoncées" par la suite.[30] C'est donc sur sa responsabilité primoridale et générale relative au maintien de la paix et de la sécurité internationales que se fondent le dispositif résolutoire et l'action que le Conseil entend entreprendre à l'égard de l'Irak.[31] Et dans le contexte de la fin de la guerre froide, l'organe exécutif de l'instance universelle peut désormais recourir à son pouvoir de contrainte, si cela s'avère nécessaire, afin d'assurer une mise en oeuvre effective de sa résolution;[32] car la référence générale au chapitre VII consolide le caractère obligatoire des décisions que le Conseil de sécurité prendra aux termes de ladite résolution.[33]

D'un autre côté, l'Irak est invité "à réaffirmer inconditionnelle-ment qu'il respectera les obligations que lui impose le Traité du 1er juillet 1968 sur la non-prolifération des armes nucléaires,"[34] ce qui signifie que le Conseil de Sécurité entend également s'appuyer sur les engagements contractés par le gouvernement irakien au regard du droit international et le porter à s'y conformer et les exécuter, non selon les modalités qui lui paraîtraient opportunes comme État souverain mais de la manière que l'instance internationale jugera désormais appropriée. Ce lien ainsi établi entre la résolution 687 et le TNP[35] confère un double fondement au processus d'investiga-

---

[30] S/Res/687 (1991), Préambule.

[31] D'ailleurs, toujours dans le Préambule de la résolution 687, le Conseil de Sécurité affirme avoir "présent à l'esprit l'objectif du rétablissement de la paix et de la sécurité internationales dans la région."

[32] S. Sur, *op. cit. supra*, note 2, à la p. 37; à propos de la résolution 687, l'auteur écrit: "elle obéit d'abord à une logique de rétablissement et de garantie de la paix, et non plus à une gradation coercitive culminant avec le recours à la force. Les mesures qu'elle comporte n'en sont pas moins contraignantes. Leur caractère coercitif à l'encontre de l'Iraq est même nettement plus marqué."

[33] *Ibid.*, p. 39.

[34] S/Res/687 (1991), paragraphe II.

[35] E. Chauvistré, *The Implications of IAEA Inspections under Security Council Resolution 687 UNIDIR* — United Nations Institute for Disarmament Research, Research

tion dans le programme nucléaire irakien et aux moyens que le
Conseil définira à cet effet.

Enfin, un troisième élément sert d'assise à l'ensemble des dispositions de la résolution 687 et des mesures subséquentes résultant de
son application: c'est le consentement de l'Irak, requis par le Conseil de Sécurité comme préalable à la suspension de la contrainte
armée entreprise sur la base de la résolution 678 du 29 novembre
1990.[36] Cette démarche a deux effets majeurs: celui d'emporter,
d'abord, "acquiescement de l'Irak à la validité de la résolution,
dans son principe comme dans son contenu"[37] de manière à
l'empêcher de la remettre en cause, dans sa totalité ou par rapport
à l'un de ses éléments;[38] celui d'offrir une garantie préalable pour

---

Paper No. 11, New York, United Nations, 1992, à la p. 6; il a cependant été
considéré qu'en l'absence d'une compétence du Conseil de Sécurité pour
constater la violation d'un traité — en l'occurence le TNP — auquel il n'est pas
partie, celui-ci ne pouvait s'appuyer que sur ses propres compétences (telles
celles relatives à la paix et la sécurité internationales) pour établir directement
les obligations d'un État Membre, l'Irak, d'une manière, d'ailleurs, qui lui
permet d'aller au-delà des strictes exigences d'un traité donné: "Il en résulte
que les obligations qu'il impose unilatéralement sont indépendantes de tout
traité, existant ou à conclure, que les modifications voire la disparition éventuelle de ce traité, ou simplement un retrait de l'Irak, seraient sans influence
sur des obligations qui ont pour fondement nécessaire et suffisant la résolution
687 elle-même, et elle seule" (Serge Sur, *op. cit. supra*, note 2, aux pp. 59-60).
Sans remettre en cause la pertinence d'un tel constat, il nous semble, cependant, s'agissant du TNP, que l'impact de la résolution 687 ne concerne pas tant
les strictes obligations fondamentales de l'Irak aux termes du traité que les
modalités de contrôle de sa conformité à de telles obligations comme nous le
verrons plus loin; et c'est à ce niveau que se situe le lien entre la résolution et
le TNP.

36 S/Res/687 (1991), Paragraphe 33, selon lequel le Conseil de Sécurité
"déclare que, dès que l'Irak aura notifié officiellement au Secrétaire général et
au Conseil de Sécurité son acceptation des dispositions qui précèdent, un
cessez-le-feu en bonne et due forme entrera en vigueur entre l'Irak et le Koweit
ainsi que les États Membres coopérant avec le Koweit en application de la
résolution 678 (1990)."

37 S. Sur, "La résolution 687 dans l'affaire du Golfe," *op. cit. supra*, note 2, à la
p. 42.

38 *Ibid.*, p. 43; l'auteur considère que le consentement de l'Irak "produit un effet
d'estoppel." Dans cette optique, il va de soi que cette forme particulière de
consensualisme s'inscrit, dans ses effets, à l'inverse de celle qui marque le
système issu du TNP: ici ce n'est plus l'État, en l'occurrence l'Irak, mais
l'organisation internationale qui définit — et a toute latitude désormais pour le
faire — les moyens susceptibles de satisfaire aux objectifs et résultats
recherchés.

la mise en oeuvre pratique de la résolution et son exécution conformément à la seule interprétation que fixera le Conseil de Sécurité,[39] car de cette acceptation résulte une "reconnaissance de la compétence unilatérale de principe du Conseil."[40]

Pour assurer l'application de ses décisions relatives au programme nucléaire irakien, le Conseil de Sécurité aura recours à deux mécanismes institutionnels: La Commission Spéciale, créée en vertu de cette même résolution 687;[41] et l'Agence Internationale de l'Énergie Atomique (AIEA), toutes deux appelées à agir en coopération.[42]

Présidée par l'ancien chef de la délégation suédoise à la Conférence sur le Désarmement, Rolf Ekéus, La Commission Spéciale — UNSCOM a été divisée en différents sous-groupes selon les systèmes d'armements visés par le plan résolutoire de désarmement de l'Irak;[43] l'un de ces sous-groupes était responsable des armes nucléaires, et c'est bien dans ce domaine que la Commission a joué un rôle technique en apportant l'expertise de ses membres spécialistes du nucléaire militaire.[44] Pour l'essentiel, l'UNSCOM est chargée d'apporter son concours à l'AIEA dans la garde et l'enlèvement de tous matériaux que l'Irak avait en sa possession et qui seraient susceptibles de servir à la production d'armes nucléaires;[45] elle est également appelée à procéder à la désignation de sites supplémentaires à inspecter et que le gouvernement irakien n'aurait pas mentionnés dans la déclaration exigée de lui à cet égard.[46]

L'AIEA, pour sa part, va assumer l'inspection sur place des capacités nucléaires de l'Irak;[47] à la demande du Conseil de Sécurité, elle va élaborer et lui soumettre "un plan prévoyant la destruction, l'enlèvement ou la neutralisation, en tant que de besoin,"[48] des matériaux, sous-systèmes, composants, moyens de recherche-déve-

---

[39] *Ibid.*, p. 43.

[40] *Ibid.*, p. 43.

[41] S/Res/687 (1991), article 9, (b), (i).

[42] *Ibid.*, articles 9, (b) (iii), 12 et 13.

[43] S. Sur, *op. cit. supra*, note 2, à la p. 76; E. Chauvistré, *op. cit. supra*, note 35, à la p. 7.

[44] S. Sur, *ibid.*, à la p. 80; *ibid.*, aux pp. 76-77, sur le fonctionnement d'ensemble de l'UNSCOM.

[45] S/Res/687 (1991), article 12.

[46] *Ibid.*, article 13.

[47] *Ibid.*, article 13.

[48] *Ibid.*, article 13.

loppement, d'appui ou de production pouvant servir à la fabrication d'armes nucléaires.[49] La résolution 687 ne prévoit pas un contrôle de l'AIEA sur des armes nucléaires qui seraient découvertes en Irak;[50] une telle perspective eût été malaisée à gérer par une organisation vouée, en vertu de son propre statut, à la promotion de l'utilisation de l'énergie atomique à des fins pacifiques.[51]

Bien que ne faisant pas partie de la famille des institutions spécialisées de l'ONU au sens de l'article 57 de la Charte, l'Agence est liée à l'Organisation Universelle, à la fois par son statut[52] et par un Accord régissant leurs relations, dans lequel est confirmé le caractère autonome de l'AIEA en même temps que son fonctionnement "sous l'égide des Nations Unies."[53] En vertu de cet Accord, l'Agence s'est engagée à coopérer avec le Conseil de Sécurité, et à lui fournir, à sa demande, toute information et assistance qu'il pourrait requérir dans l'exercice de ses responsabilités relatives au maintien et au rétablissement de la paix et de la sécurité internationales.[54] De ce fait, les dispositions de la résolution 687 s'adressant au Directeur Général de l'AIEA s'analysent comme une requête du Conseil de Sécurité fondée sur l'Accord en question.

Toutefois, comme il est demandé à l'Agence, aux termes de la résolution 687, "d'un côté de participer à des opérations d'inspection de caractère militaire, et de l'autre de placer sous supervision

[49] *Ibid.*, articles 12 et 13.

[50] E. Chauvistré, *op. cit. supra*, note 35 à la p. 5; l'auteur en conclut que le Conseil de Sécurité ne s'attendait pas à ce que des armes nucléaires assemblées soient trouvés en Irak, ou alors, le cas échéant, qu'il entendait se réserver le droit de les placer sous sa garde.

[51] *Statut de l'Agence Internationale de l'Énergie Atomique*, articles II et III.

[52] *Ibid.*, article III, B.1, 4 et 5, stipulant que l'AIEA "agit selon les buts et principes adoptés par les Nations Unies en vue de favoriser la paix et la coopération internationales, conformément à la politique suivie par les Nations Unies en vue de réaliser un désarmement universel garanti et conformément à tout accord international conclu en application de cette politique"; que l'Agence adresse des rapports annuels à l'Assemblée Générale et, s'il y a lieu, au Conseil de Sécurité, de même qu'au Conseil Économique et Social et aux autres organes de l'ONU dans les domaines relevant de leurs compétences respectives. Sur l'Agence, voir G. Fischer, l'Agence Internationale de l'Énergie Atomique, (1956) AFDI, 616-34.

[53] *Agreement Governing the Relationship between the United Nations and the International Atomic Energy Agency*, entré en vigueur le 14 novembre 1957, INFCIRC II, Article I. 1 et 2. Voir G. Fischer, "L'Accord entre l'ONU et l'Agence Internationale de l'Énergie Atomique," (1957) AFDI, 375-83.

[54] *Ibid.*, article IX.

des activités civiles, bien au-delà du régime régulier des garanties,"[55] l'ensemble de l'action de l'AIEA conduite dans ce cadre devait sans cesse s'appuyer sur le Conseil de Sécurité, lui-même se fondant sur ladite résolution, pour définir les moyens et modalités permettant d'en réaliser une complète application; pareillement, l'Agence s'adossera sur les compétences dévolues à l'UNSCOM pour pouvoir exécuter un mandat qui dépasse son domaine d'opération statutaire ou conventionnel, en vertu du TNP notamment, à la fois sur le plan de ses capacités juridiques et techniques.[56]

Les différents éléments de cet édifice juridique et institutionnel vont contribuer à façonner un processus sans précédent dans la pratique de l'ONU et de l'AIEA. Pour mesurer le travail accompli dans un tel cadre, nous nous attacherons à analyser les principaux traits du système de garanties et l'impact de la résolution 687 à cet égard.

II Le système des garanties et la portée de l'investigation

Comme il puise sa source dans des obligations juridiques, le système des garanties n'en est pas moins composé d'une série de mesures techniques établies précisément de manière à respecter les frontières des engagements conventionnels des États concernés tout en permettant à l'AIEA de s'acquitter des fonctions de contrôle dont elle est investie à cet égard. Pour bien comprendre les moyens identifiés par les experts de l'Agence dans ce cadre consensuel, il faut avoir présent à l'esprit d'une part, que la fonction de vérification ne concerne que des activités civiles dont il faut s'assurer qu'elles demeurent "uniquement pacifiques,"[57] et d'autre part, que le dispositif ainsi mis en place repose sur une philosophie visant à "accroître la confiance"[58] et pour cela à faire en sorte que le risque de détection à lui seul suffise à dissuader de tout détournement.[59] Ce n'est donc pas un système de désarmement ou de

---

[55] S. Sur, *op. cit. supra*, note 2, à la p. 79.

[56] Dans sa déclaration à la trente-cinquième session de la Conférence Générale, le 16 septembre 1991, le Directeur Général de l'AIEA, Hans Blix, soulignait cet aspect inédit: "In fulfilling the mandate given to it by the Security Council regarding nuclear activities in Iraq, the Agency is in part treading new ground. It is not only verifying peaceful uses of nuclear energy but also looking for any attempts to make a military use of it."

[57] H. Blix, "Pour une plus grande confiance," *op. cit. supra*, note 23, à la p. 3.

[58] *Ibid.*, p. 3.

[59] *Ibid.*, p. 3.

contrôle d'armements habilitant, éventuellement, l'instance responsable à rechercher, de son propre mouvement et par ses moyens des indices ou des sites dont l'inspection lui paraîtrait opportune.[60]

Or l'un des objectifs de la résolution 687 est la maîtrise des armements dans la région du Moyen-Orient;[61] aussi est-elle orientée vers un certain nombre de mesures de désarmement à l'intérieur desquelles s'inscrit l'investigation dans le programme nucléaire irakien. C'est pourquoi le fonctionnement et les opérations de l'AIEA dans l'exécution du mandat qui lui est confié par le Conseil de Sécurité se démarqueront nettement de son rôle habituel de vérification en vertu du système des garanties.

A LES PROCÉDURES DU MÉCANISME DE GARANTIES DU TNP

La pierre angulaire du système des garanties est constituée par un dispositif de comptabilité des matières nucléaires, reposant sur une obligation d'information incombant à l'État concerné,[62] en l'occurrence l'Irak. En effet, l'Accord entre le gouvernement irakien et l'AIEA sur l'application des garanties énonce que pour en assurer une mise en oeuvre effective, "l'Irak fournit à l'Agence . . . des renseignements concernant les matières nucléaires soumises aux garanties . . . et les caractéristiques des installations qui ont une importance du point de vue du contrôle de ces matières."[63] L'aspect essentiel de cette obligation d'information revêt la forme d'un système national de comptabilité et de contrôle desdites matières nucléaires[64] que l'Irak doit établir et appliquer pour toutes celles que l'Accord soumet aux garanties.[65]

L'objectif des modalités d'application des garanties étant de "déceler rapidement le détournement des quantités significatives de matières nucléaires"[66] vers des finalités militaires ou inconnues, la comptabilité-matières, considérée comme une mesure d'impor-

---

[60] D. A. V. Fischer, "Safeguards: A Model for General Arms Control?" (1982) 24-2 *AIEA Bulletin* 45-49, à la p. 45.

[61] S/Res/687 (1991), paragraphe 16 du Préambule et article 14; sur cet aspect, voir S. Sur, *op. cit. supra*, note 2, aux pp. 52-55.

[62] INFCIRC/153 (corrigé), *op. cit. supra*, note 11, paragraphe 8.

[63] INFCIRC/172, *op. cit. supra*, note 12, article 8(a).

[64] *Ibid.*, articles 31 et 32.

[65] *Ibid.*, article 7.

[66] *Ibid.*, article 28.

tance essentielle, est assortie de deux dispositifs complémentaires: le confinement et la surveillance.[67]

Le confinement vise à définir, à l'intérieur de chaque installation nucléaire, des zones de bilan matières (ZBM) où l'on détermine toutes les entrées et sorties de matières à partir de l'identification par l'exploitant d'un stock physique initial qu'il porte dans un registre où il consignera ultérieurement les variations de stock.[68] Des points de mesure principaux sont répartis dans les différentes ZBM et représentent autant d'endroits d'où est mesurée la quantité de matières nucléaires afin d'en déterminer les mouvements ou la quantité en stock.[69] Des inventaires physiques sont périodiquement effectués par l'exploitant: le degré de concordance de leurs résultats avec les inventaires comptables correspondants représente l'élément cardinal de la comptabilité des matières nucléaires. De fait, si une différence d'inventaire dépasse une valeur imputable soit à l'imprécision des mesures soit à d'autres raisons d'ordre technique, la possibilité d'un détournement doit alors être envisagée.[70]

Parallèlement, une surveillance des installations est assurée ''afin de détecter des mouvements non déclarés de matières nucléaires, des fraudes concernant le confinement, de fausses informations ou la violation de dispositifs de garanties.''[71] L'observation, à cet égard, est surtout réalisée par l'utilisation de caméras automatiques prenant des clichés à des intervalles plus courts que le temps nécessaire pour procéder à un détournement de matière nucléaire.[72] Il peut arriver que les tâches de surveillance soient confiées à du personnel affecté de manière permanente ou périodique à des points d'observation stratégique.[73]

Les principales règles et méthodes que doit appliquer l'Irak dans la tenue de la comptabilité-matières sont généralement énoncées dans l'Accord qui le lie vis-à-vis de l'Agence.[74] Différents rapports comptables doivent être présentés par l'Irak à l'AIEA,[75] de telles

---

[67] *Ibid.*, article 29.

[68] *Les garanties de l'AIEA, Présentation*, IAEA/SG/INF/3, Vienne, AIEA, 1982, p. 22.

[69] *Ibid.*, p. 22.

[70] *Ibid.*, pp. 22-23.

[71] *Ibid.*, p. 26.

[72] *Ibid.*, pp. 26-27.

[73] *Ibid.*, p. 26.

[74] INFCIRC/172, *op. cit. supra*, note 12, articles 32 et 51-58.

[75] *Ibid.*, articles 62-69.

exigences s'inscrivant également par ailleurs dans le cadre de l'obligation d'information. Cette dernière porte, en outre, sur un certain nombre de renseignements descriptifs relatifs à chacune des installations existantes comme à toute nouvelle installation, et que l'Irak doit communiquer à l'Agence[76] afin de lui permettre, par une connaissance suffisamment détaillée des caractéristiques des installations et des matières nucléaires, une vérification plus aisée et une détermination utile des zones de bilan matières de même que des modalités comptables et techniques y afférentes.[77]

Quant aux matières assujetties aux garanties, il s'agit de l'uranium et du thorium qui n'ont pas atteint le stade du cycle du combustible, ainsi que des matières nucléaires dont la composition et la pureté sont propres à la fabrication de combustible ou à la séparation des isotopes.[78] À la demande de l'Irak, et dans certaines conditions, une exemption des garanties peut être agréée par l'Agence sous réserve de la nature des matières et de l'importance des quantités en cause.[79]

L'Agence, pour sa part, va appliquer les garanties en tenant pleinement compte des perfectionnements technologiques dans ce domaine et en faisant "son possible pour optimiser le rapport coût/efficacité."[80] C'est d'ailleurs dans cette optique qu'elle a recours au confinement pour définir les zones de bilan matières, mais aussi à des méthodes statistiques et de sondage aléatoire, visant à évaluer le flux des matières nucléaires ainsi qu'à une "concentration des activités de vérification sur les stades du cycle du combustible nucléaire où sont produites, transformées, utilisées ou stockées des matières nucléaires à partir desquelles des armes nucléaires ou des explosifs nucléaires peuvent être facilement fabriqués."[81]

Il importe de souligner que la manière dont l'Agence applique les garanties vise à vérifier les résultats enregistrés par le système irakien en tenant compte dûment de son efficacité technique.[82] De plus, en faisant ainsi usage de ce système irakien de comptabilité et

[76] *Ibid.*, articles 42, 43 et 45.

[77] *Ibid.*, article 46.

[78] *Ibid.*, article 34.

[79] *Ibid.*, articles 36 et 37.

[80] *Ibid.*, article 6 (a).

[81] *Ibid.*, article 6 (b).

[82] *Ibid.*, article 7 (b).

de contrôle, elle doit éviter de répéter inutilement les opérations comptables et les contrôles accomplis par l'Irak.[83] De même, est-ce sur la base du rapport initial établi par les autorités irakiennes que l'AIEA dresse un inventaire unique de toutes les matières nucléaires en Irak quelle que soit leur origine et qui sont soumises au régime des garanties en vertu de l'Accord entre le gouvernement irakien et l'Agence; la tenue à jour de cet inventaire se fonde, pareillement, sur les rapports ultérieurs fournis par l'Irak et sur les résultats des opérations de vérification entreprises par l'AIEA[84] lors de ses inspections.

Dans le cadre du TNP, trois types d'inspections peuvent être déclenchées par l'Agence: les inspections régulières, dont l'objet est d'assurer la conformité des informations consignées dans les rapports soumis par l'État aux données des relevés comptables et des relevés d'opérations de l'exploitant, et cela, principalement, en procédant à une vérification du volume, de l'emplacement et de l'identité des matières nucléaires, de même qu'en enquêtant sur les écarts pouvant apparaître à propos d'un même article entre les notifications reçues de l'expéditeur et les informations fournies par le destinataire; les inspections ad hoc, qui concernent surtout la vérification des renseignements relatifs à la conception de nouvelles installations nucléaires, les changements intervenus entre le rapport initial présenté par l'État après la conclusion de l'accord de garanties et la première inspection régulière, et les matières en provenance ou à destination de l'étranger; enfin des inspections spéciales ont lieu, selon des procédures particulières, en cas de circonstances inhabituelles portées à la connaissance de l'Agence ou lorsque les informations fournies par l'État sont jugées inadéquates.[85]

Au cours de leurs inspections, les agents de l'AIEA examinent les relevés pertinents, mesurent eux-mêmes les quantités de matières nucléaires sous garanties, vérifient le bon fonctionnement des équipements, veillent à ce que les échantillons qu'ils se procurent soient convenablement prélevés, testés, manipulés et expédiés; ils entretiennent leur propre équipement de surveillance et posent, inspectent ou retirent les scellés que l'AIEA fixe dans le cadre du confinement.[86]

[83] Ibid., article 31.
[84] Ibid., article 41.
[85] IAEA/SG/INF/3, op. cit. supra, note 68, aux pp. 27-28.
[86] Ibid., pp. 28-29.

À la lumière de cet ensemble de procédures et mécanismes, les limites du système de garanties sont aisées à identifier: l'initiative et la responsabilité en matière de communication des informations requises demeurent du seul ressort des États tant exportateurs qu'importateurs de matières, équipements et installations nucléaires; de ce fait, l'efficacité du régime des garanties repose sur l'hypothèse de l'improbabilité d'une entente entre deux États pour procéder à un détournement vers des fins autres que civiles et pacifiques.[87] En outre, l'AIEA n'a aucun moyen d'empêcher concrètement un État de violer les accords de garanties; et comme le TNP ne prévoit pas de pénalités en cas de violation de ses dispositions, les seules sanctions dont dispose l'AIEA sont celles prévues dans son Statut et que peut prendre le Conseil des Gouverneurs: après avoir accordé un délai à l'État en cause pour se mettre en conformité avec ses obligations, il s'agira, alors, de réduire ou interrompre l'aide accordée par l'Agence à l'État incriminé, et de demander la restitution des produits et du matériel mis à sa disposition ou encore de le priver de l'exercice des privilèges et droits inhérents à sa qualité de Membre.[88]

Outre le consensualisme et les restrictions qui s'y rattachent à l'endroit de l'Agence et de ses inspecteurs, les limites financières à l'intérieur desquelles opère l'Agence pour mettre en oeuvre les garanties hypothèquent sensiblement leur efficacité: malgré leur progression, les ressources dont bénéficie l'AIEA demeurent insuffisantes pour ses activités en matière de garanties, de sorte que l'Agence selon son propre constat, n'arrive pas à réaliser un niveau adéquat d'inspection, en particulier à assurer un volume satisfaisant de son "activité réelle d'inspection régulière" par installation telle qu'antérieurement définie selon une formule-type agréée entre elle et l'État concerné.[89]

Les insuffisances du contrôle technique du système de garanties[90] et nombre de préoccupations politiques, associées aux différentes critiques émises au sujet des défaillances de ce dispositif de contrôle de la non-prolifération, avaient conduit certains responsa-

---

[87] *Les garanties de l'AIEA: Buts, limites, résultats*, IAEA/SG/INF/4, Vienne, AIEA, 1984, p. 39.

[88] Statut de l'AIEA, *op. cit.*, article XII, paragraphe C; H. Blix, *op. cit. supra*, note 10, aux pp. 55-57.

[89] IAEA/SG/INF/4, *op. cit. supra*, note 87, pp. 40-41.

[90] S. Courteix, "Le contrôle de la prolifération des armes nucléaires," *op. cit. supra*, note 24, à la p. 598.

bles et observateurs à considérer qu'il serait plus approprié de concentrer le processus de vérification sur l'ensemble du cycle du combustible, plutôt que sur les matières et les installations nucléaires.[91] Cependant, une telle distinction n'a pas toujours paru probante comme moyen d'améliorer la performance des garanties en tant qu'outil dissuasif en matière de non-prolifération.[92] D'une part, tel qu'il a été élaboré pour être mis en oeuvre et tel qu'il est appliqué, le système des garanties n'a pas négligé de porter également son attention sur le cycle du combustible nucléaire;[93] mais surtout, il ne semble pas que les lacunes du mécanisme de garanties puissent être comblées par le seul recours à des correctifs d'ordre technique, un accroissement des ressources financières et une augmentation du corps des inspecteurs de l'AIEA: l'examen du cadre juridique présidant à l'application des garanties montre, en effet, que ce sont les modalités de stipulation des droits de l'Agence et des obligations des États qui grèvent le régime des garanties.

D'ailleurs, c'est bien à ce niveau précis que la résolution 687 du Conseil de Sécurité opère une rupture, qui a permis de déployer en Irak une théorie de moyens d'inspection et de modes de sanction (démantèlement, destruction, expropriation) qu'en tout état de cause le TNP et le Statut de l'AIEA considérés en tant que tels n'auraient en aucune manière autorisés.

B ÉTENDUE ET EFFET DE L'INVESTIGATION

Quinze mois après l'adoption de la résolution 687, par le Conseil de Sécurité, l'AIEA avait accompli douze missions d'inspection en Irak et soumis au Conseil de Sécurité les rapports subséquents. Dès la fin de la seconde mission, l'équipe d'inspection devait conclure, sur la base des preuves rassemblées sur place que les autorités irakiennes poursuivaient un programme non déclaré d'enrichissement de l'uranium utilisant une technique électromagnétique de séparation des isotopes (EMIS).[94] Avec cette première découverte d'importance, il apparaissait d'ores et déjà que l'Irak avait violé ses

---

91 P. Gummett, "From NPT to INFCE: Developments in Thinking about Nuclear Non-Proliferation," (1981) 57 *International Legal Affairs*, 549-67; "INFCE" signifie "International Nuclear Fuel Cycle Evaluation."

92 H. Gruemm, "L'application des garanties au cycle du combustible: méthodologies," (1984) 26-3 *AIEA Bulletin* 20-24.

93 INFCIRC/153 (corrigé), *op. cit. supra*, note 12, paragraphe b (c).

94 S/22788, 15 juillet 1991, *Consolidated Report on the First Two IAEA Inspections under Security Council Resolution 687 (1991) of Iraqi Nuclear Capabilities*, paragraphe 5.

obligations en vertu de l'Accord de Garanties conclu avec l'Agence selon les exigences du TNP; aussi, le 18 juillet 1991, le Conseil des Gouverneurs de l'AIEA devait-il constater officiellement ces manquements du gouvernement irakien, condamner les violations qui en résultaient à l'égard de l'Accord en cause et décider de les porter à la connaissance du Conseil de Sécurité et de l'Assemblée Générale des Nations Unies conformément à l'article XII, paragraphe C, du Statut de l'Agence.[95]

Cette démarche du Conseil des Gouverneurs résultait d'un rapport que le directeur général de l'AIEA lui avait soumis[96] précisément dans le cadre et sur la base des activités que l'Agence avait alors commencé à conduire en vertu de la résolution 687 du Conseil de Sécurité. L'on peut donc d'emblée mesurer l'impact du dispositif résolutoire car c'est grâce à ses stipulations que l'AIEA a poursuivi l'investigation sans devoir attendre un "délai raisonnable" qui aurait permis à l'Irak de prendre des "mesures correctives" ainsi que cela aurait été le cas sous l'empire du seul Statut de l'Agence.[97]

Toutefois, le parcours qui permettra à l'AIEA de confirmer de façon concluante l'existence d'un programme irakien d'armement nucléaire aura été semé de divergences avec l'Irak relatives aux modalités d'action des inspecteurs de l'Agence et à leurs prérogatives. De ce fait, le Conseil de Sécurité a dû intervenir à plusieurs reprises pour clarifier à l'intention de l'Irak la portée des termes de sa résolution 687 par rapport à l'investigation dans le programme nucléaire irakien.

Il convient, tout d'abord, de souligner qu'au paragraphe 15 du Préambule de la résolution 687, le Conseil de Sécurité s'était dit "préoccupé par les informations dont disposent des États Membres, selon lesquelles l'Irak a cherché à acquérir des matériaux en vue d'un programme d'armement nucléaire." C'est justement à partir de ce genre de données que la Commission Spéciale va désigner des sites à l'inspection de l'AIEA; plus précisément, l'identification de certaines installations suspectées d'être reliées à un programme clandestin de production d'uranium hautement enrichi procédait de sources du renseignement américain.[98] Sans

95 AIEA, GC(XXXV)/978, 16 septembre 1991, *Manquement de l'Irak à ses obligations en matières de garanties*, Note de couverture, paragraphe 2.

96 *Ibid.*, annexe 1.

97 Statut de l'AIEA, *op. cit. supra*, note 7, article XII, paragraphe C.

98 E. Chauvistré, *op. cit. supra*, note 35, à la p. 10.

l'autorité du Conseil de Sécurité — exercée, en l'espèce, par le canal de la Commission — et l'assujettissement de l'Agence à cette autorité par l'effet conjugué de la résolution 687 et de l'Accord qui la liait à l'ONU, l'AIEA n'aurait pu entreprendre des inspections sur des sites non déclarés par l'Irak,[99] puisque le fonctionnement conventionnel du régime de garanties applicable sur le territoire irakien ne l'aurait pas permis.

En réalité, la résolution 687 avait requis le Gouvernement irakien de remettre au Secrétaire Général de l'ONU et au Directeur général de l'AIEA une déclaration précisant l'emplacement de tous les matériaux pouvant servir à la production d'armes nucléaires avec l'indication des quantités et spécifications[100] des articles visés. Dans une première déclaration, en date du 18 avril 1991, l'Irak remettait à l'Agence une liste sur laquelle figuraient toutes les matières antérieurement déclarées à l'AIEA en vertu de l'Accord de garanties,[101] et affirmait n'avoir "pas d'installations industrielles ou d'appuis associés à une forme quelconque d'utilisation de l'énergie nucléaire qui devaient être déclarées."[102] Une telle position montre que les autorités irakiennes ont pu croire, dans un premier temps, avoir toujours la possibilité de se prévaloir des dispositions de l'Accord de garanties vis-à-vis de l'Agence et lui barrer ainsi l'accès à des sites non déclarés, d'autant que, parallèlement, elles acheminaient une déclaration aux Nations Unies selon laquelle l'Irak ne possède pas d'armement nucléaire et ne détient pas de matières susceptibles de servir à la production d'armes nucléaires, ce qui, dans leur entendement, aurait probablement dû suffire à les mettre en conformité avec la résolution 687 du Conseil de Sécurité.

Toutefois, grâce au mandat qui lui a été confié aux termes de la résolution 687, le Directeur Général de l'AIEA va pouvoir exiger davantage d'informations de la part de l'Irak: dans une lettre en date du 19 août 1991, il rappelle au gouvernement irakien que l'uranium fortement enrichi figure à l'inventaire des matières nucléaires soumises au régime des garanties et devant être déclarées; mais, surtout, il souligne qu'en application de la résolution, "les installations de retraitement du combustible nucléaire ou de séparation du plutonium de l'uranium ou les installations de séparation des isotopes de l'uranium, ou tout programme de recherche

99 Ibid., p. 8.
100 S/Res/687 (1991), paragraphe 12.
101 AIEA, GC (XXXV) 978, Annexe I (Gov/2530, 16 juillet 1991).
102 Ibid., Annexe 8 (Gov/or. 758, 6 septembre 1991), paragraphe 5.

ou toute installation de fabrication en rapport avec ces activités"[103] devaient être déclarés, qu'ils aient ou non été endommagés ou détruits lors des bombardements effectués par la Coalition d'États ayant agi sur la base de la résolution 678 du Conseil de Sécurité.[104]

Plus tard, lorsque les équipes d'inspection auront recueilli les preuves sur l'existence d'activités d'enrichissement, la mission de haut-niveau en visite en Irak[105] demandera expressément à recevoir une déclaration supplémentaire indiquant tous les articles et matières en rapport avec l'enrichissement ou le retraitement, et obtiendra des autorités irakiennes "la promesse que des listes d'articles considérés par l'Iraq comme pouvant contrevenir aux dispositions de la résolution 687 (1991) seraient communiquées."[106] Ainsi, une lettre de l'Irak en date du 7 juillet et à laquelle lesdites listes étaient jointes devait être acheminée au Secrétaire général de l'ONU et au Directeur général de l'AIEA; cette lettre révélait l'existence de trois progammes d'enrichissement de l'uranium selon différents procédés — chimique, électromagnétique et par centrifugation — et dotés d'importants équipements et matières,[107] de même que la production d'un demi-kilogramme environ d'uranium enrichi à 4%. Ces premières étapes du processus d'investigation dans le programme nucléaire irakien montrent bien comme le mécanisme déclenché par la résolution 687 s'écarte du régime conventionnel de garanties: l'AIEA n'est plus limitée par les seules déclarations de l'Irak pour inspecter sites, équipements et matières; qui plus est, elle peut requérir les autorités irakiennes d'établir des déclarations plus conformes aux constats résultant des activités menées par ses inspecteurs sur les sites non-déclarés; corrélativement, les autorités irakiennes sont dépour-

---

[103] *Ibid.*

[104] S/Res/678 (1990), 29 novembre 1990, paragraphe 2.

[105] À la demande du Conseil de Sécurité une mission de haut-niveau composée du directeur général de l'AIEA, Hans Blix, du Président de la Commission Spéciale, Rolf Ekeus, et du secrétaire général adjoint aux affaires de désarmement, Yasushi Akashi, s'était rendue à Bagdad le 30 juin 1991 en vue d'obtenir un accès immédiat et sans entraves pour l'équipe d'inspecteurs qui avait été empêchée d'accomplir sa mission en divers sites désignés et avait pu observer le déménagement par le personnel irakien d'équipement et matériels de ces mêmes localisations vers des destinations inconnues. Cf. *IAEA Inspections and Iraq's Nuclear Capabilities*, IAEA/PI/A35E, April 1992, pp. 5-6.

[106] AIEA, GC (XXXV)/978, Annexe 8 (Gov/or. 758, 6 septembre 1991), paragraphe 8.

[107] *Ibid.*, paragraphe 9.

vues des moyens juridiques de s'opposer aux demandes et actions de l'Agence, sous peine de se trouver en contravention avec les obligations leur incombant désormais en vertu de la résolution 687 du Conseil de Sécurité.

À mesure que les travaux d'inspection progressaient, l'importance du programme nucléaire irakien clandestinement développé apparaissait plus clairement; en particulier, lors de la quatrième mission d'inspection de l'Agence (27 juillet-10 août 1991), les autorités irakiennes remettaient aux inspecteurs de l'AIEA une liste de matières nucléaires sur laquelle figuraient, une fois de plus, des matières qui n'avaient pas été déclarées précédemment et de laquelle il ressortait surtout que l'Irak avait entrepris la production et la séparation non déclarées de plutonium dans des installations auxquelles les inspecteurs de l'Agence en vertu du régime de garanties n'avaient pas eu accès.[108]

L'ensemble des informations ainsi collectées, combiné aux entraves que l'Irak avait pu mettre à certains égards au déroulement des activités d'inspection vont conduire le Conseil de sécurité à compléter le dispositif résolutoire par l'adoption, le 15 août 1991, de la résolution 707 dans laquelle il exige, notamment, que l'Irak "autorise la Commission spéciale, l'AIEA et leurs équipes d'inspection à utiliser des avions et des hélicoptères sur tout le territoire iraquien à toutes fins pertinentes, y compris d'inspection, de surveillance, d'observation aérienne, de transport et de logistique, sans entrave d'aucune sorte et conformément aux dispositions et conditions éventuellement fixées par la Commission spéciale."[109] Par ailleurs, le Conseil de Sécurité devait décider, dans cette même résolution que l'Irak ne conservait aucun droit de propriété sur les matériaux qui, aux termes du paragraphe 12 de la résolution 687, doivent être détruits, enlevés ou neutralisés.[110]

De telles mesures, à l'évidence, revêtent un caractère exceptionnel, inédit, et établissent des "obligations nouvelles et plus étendues que les règles conventionnelles et a fortiori coutumières"[111] du droit international. Concrètement, cela signifie une aliénation de la souveraineté de l'État irakien pour tout ce qui concerne l'investigation dans son programme nucléaire et les besoins s'y

---

108 S/22986, 11 septembre 1991, *Report on the Fourth IAEA On-site Inspection in Iraq under Security Council Resolution 687* (1991), paragraphe 29.

109 S/Res/707 (1991), 15 août 1991, paragraphe 3.v.

110 *Ibid.*, paragraphe 4.

111 S. Sur, *op. cit. supra*, note 2, aux pp. 60-61.

rattachant; à cela s'ajoute l'expropriation qu'opère la résolution
707 par rapport à tous les matériaux, équipements et autres moyens
identifiés par les inspecteurs de la Commission spéciale et de
l'AIEA comme susceptibles de servir à la fabrication d'armes
nucléaires et devant par conséquent être détruits, enlevés ou neutralisés tout en étant placés sous le contrôle exclusif de l'AIEA.[112]

Comme la mission de l'Agence en vertu de la résolution 687 vise
des activités nucléaires pouvant s'avérer de nature militaire, la
plupart des fonctions assumées par l'AIEA dans le cadre de ses
missions à cet égard seront entièrement nouvelles pour cette Organisation. Ainsi, parallèlement à des opérations similaires à ses inspections régulières orientées vers le contrôle d'inventaire et le
prélèvement d'échantillons, l'AIEA aura à identifier des installations de production de matières utilisables dans la fabrication
d'armes nucléaires; elle aura à évaluer les capacités industrielles
irakiennes de construction d'usines d'extraction et d'enrichissement de l'uranium, ce qui implique des inspections dans des secteurs non-nucléaires de l'industrie du pays; l'Agence sera également amenée à repérer des installations potentielles d'armement et
à rechercher les preuves de plans pour un programme d'armes
nucléaires, ce qui comporte l'analyse de documents indiquant
l'existence d'une infrastructure de recherche et de production
reliée à un tel programme; enfin l'AIEA devra procéder à l'enlèvement de tout matériel utilisable pour la mise au point d'armes
nucléaires.[113]

C'est la sixième mission d'inspection de l'AIEA qui mettra la
main sur des documents prouvant l'existence d'un programme
irakien complet de recherche relatif aux armes nucléaires et reposant sur un large réseau international d'approvisionnement.[114]

---

112 Bien qu'aux termes de son Statut (article IX), l'AIEA soit habilitée à avoir en
sa possession, à entreposer et conserver sous sa garde des produits fissiles
spéciaux, l'enlèvement de matériaux est considéré comme constituant une
nouvelle tâche pour l'Agence compte tenu de la pratique de l'AIEA. Étant
donné que l'Agence ne dispose pas de l'installation requise pour entreposer
de tels matériaux, British Nuclear Fuel et la firme française COGEMA se sont
vues confier le mandat de récupérer lesdits matériaux pour le compte de
l'Agence, le combustible irradié devant être retraité et maintenu sous régime
de garanties. Cf. E. Chauvistré, *op. cit. supra*, note 35, aux pp. 16-17.

113 *Ibid.*, pp. 15-18.

114 S/23122, *First Report on the Sixth IAEA On-Site Inspection in Iraq under Security
Council Resolution 687* (1991), 22-30 septembre 1991, paragraphe 3. L'équipe
d'inspecteurs devait ainsi obtenir la preuve que la Commission Irakienne de

Ensuite, avec la septième mission d'inspection, les opérations de destruction des équipements d'enrichissement et de retraitement commenceront.[115] À cette même époque, les autorités irakiennes admettaient que des études et des recherches avaient été entreprises en vue d'un programme d'armement nucléaire.[116] Lors de la huitième mission d'inspection, en novembre 1991, se déroule le premier enlèvement d'uranium hautement enrichi chargé sur un vol cargo des Nations Unies sous la supervision de l'équipe de l'AIEA.[117] Les missions ultérieures poursuivront un même travail d'investigation extensive, de destruction et d'enlèvement selon ce qui est jugé nécessaire.

L'investigation dans les activités nucléaires irakiennes ne se limite pas aux opérations de démantèlement du programme incriminé comme violant les engagements conventionnels, en droit international, souscrits par l'Irak: par sa résolution 687, le Conseil de Sécurité requérait également le Directeur Général de l'AIEA de lui soumettre un plan de contrôle et de vérification continus de l'exécution par l'Irak de ses obligations tant aux termes de la résolution elle-même qu'en vertu du TNP.[118] Dans sa résolution 707, le Conseil de Sécurité, préoccupé par les résultats des premières missions d'inspection indiquant l'existence d'activités nucléaires irakiennes orientées vers des fins militaires, devait aller

---

l'Énergie Atomique, et les Ministères de la Défense et de l'Industrie étaient impliqués dans un programme d'armement nucléaire axé sur l'implosion. La huitième mission d'inspection de l'AIEA devait déterminer que la Commission Irakienne de l'Énergie Atomique, pour appuyer son programme d'enrichissement de l'uranium et ses efforts de mise au point d'armes nucléaires, avait établi avec grand succès et sécurité un réseau d'approvisionnement comprenant d'importantes entreprises occidentales et tirant profit du caractère polyvalent des équipements ainsi obtenus. Voir: S/23283, *Report on the Eight IAEA On-Site Inspections in Iraq under Security Council Resolution 687* (1991), 11-18 novembre 1991, paragraphes 8-17.

115 S/23215, *Report on the Seventh IAEA On-Site Inspection in Iraq under Security Council Resolution 687* (1991), 11-22 octobre 1991, paragraphes 52-54.

116 *Ibid.*, paragraphe 2.

117 S/23283, *op. cit. supra*, note 114, paragraphe 37. Cette opération avait été préparée avec le concours de représentants du Ministère de l'Énergie Atomique et de l'Industrie de l'ancienne Union Soviétique; les matières nucléaires étaient expédiées à Moscou, l'uranium hautement enrichi devant être retraité dans des installations de l'ancienne URSS, et allaient être placées sous le contrôle de l'AIEA.

118 S/Res/687, paragraphe 13.

plus loin en exigeant de l'Irak qu'il "mette un terme à toute activité nucléaire de quelque nature que ce soit, à l'exception de l'usage des isotopes à des fins médicales, agronomiques et industrielles, jusqu'à ce que le Conseil de Sécurité constate que l'Iraq respecte pleinement la présente résolution et les paragraphes 12 et 13 de la résolution 687 (1991), et que l'AIEA constate de son côté que l'Iraq respecte pleinement l'Accord de garanties qu'il a conclu avec elle."[119]

Le plan déposé par le Directeur Général de l'AIEA devait donc tenir compte des obligations supplémentaires imposées à l'Irak en vertu de la résolution 707 du Conseil de Sécurité — agissant, là encore, dans le cadre du Chapitre VII de la Charte — et des obligations qui s'ensuivaient pareillement pour les autres États de respecter les sanctions et prohibitions appliquées à l'endroit de l'Irak jusqu'à leur suspension par le Conseil de Sécurité.[120] Ce plan prévoit une grande liberté de manoeuvre de l'Agence: mener sans entrave des inspections à n'importe quel moment en quelque site, installation, zone, localité ou autre sur désignation de la Commission Spéciale ou même à l'initiative propre de l'AIEA; arrêter et inspecter des véhicules, navires, aéronefs ou autres moyens de transport en Iraq et restreindre ou empêcher les importations et exportations de matériel; établir des modes spéciaux de surveillance et d'inspection, y compris la présence prolongée ou continue d'inspecteurs; mettre en oeuvre toute une suite d'autres mesures comparables à celles auxquelles recourt l'AIEA dans le courant de ses inspections régulières.[121]

Ce plan a été approuvé par la résolution 715 du Conseil de Sécurité,[122] et s'ajoute donc à l'ensemble des autres dispositifs résolutoires régissant désormais, et jusqu'à nouvel ordre, toute activité nucléaire en Irak.

CONCLUSION

Dans la foulée de l'affaire irakienne, le Conseil des Gouverneurs de l'AIEA devait demander au directeur général de préparer une

[119] S/Res/707, paragraphe 3.vi).

[120] S/22872/Rev.1, 20 septembre 1991, Plan for Future Ongoing Monitoring and Verification of Iraq's Compliance with Paragraph 12 of Part C of Security Council Resolution 687 (1991) and with the Requirements of Paragraphs 3 and 5 of Resolution 707 (1991), paragraphe 9.

[121] *Ibid.*, paragraphes 31-32.

[122] S/Res/715 (1991), 11 octobre 1991, paragraphe 1.

proposition pour l'établissement d'un mécanisme et de procédures à l'intérieur de l'Agence à travers lesquels les États Membres pourraient mettre à la disposition d'un secrétariat spécial de l'AIEA des informations dont ils disposent relativement à l'éventuelle existence d'installations nucléaires non déclarées dans des États signataires du TNP;[123] si de telles informations s'avèrent crédibles, le secrétariat pourrait requérir une inspection spéciale pour les vérifier. Mais, comme le soulignait le directeur général de l'Agence dans sa déclaration devant le Conseil de Sécurité, dans le cas où l'État ainsi mis en cause refusait d'autoriser une telle inspection, le Conseil des Gouverneurs n'aurait d'autre choix, compte tenu de la faiblesse de son pouvoir de sanction, que de porter le cas devant le Conseil de Sécurité lequel peut décider des mesures de contraintes si cela est jugé nécessaire.[124]

En d'autres termes, tant que le système de garanties issu du TNP demeure en l'état, et continue par conséquent de limiter la marge d'opération de l'Agence en l'assujettissant à un consensualisme inégal où prédominent les États, il est permis de craindre que le seul moyen par lequel il soit possible de sanctionner un État qui aurait violé ses engagements en vertu du TNP et de l'amener à s'y conformer soit l'exercice, à son encontre, d'une action armée dans le cadre du Chapitre VII, suivi d'un processus de contrôle étendu appliqué sous l'égide du Conseil de Sécurité comme cela s'est produit en Irak.

Il n'est pas certain, dans un monde davantage complexe et qui connaît de nombreux bouleversements et convulsions, qu'une telle perspective ne soit pas aussi dangereuse que la prolifération nucléaire à laquelle, paradoxalement, l'on assiste depuis la fin de la guerre froide entre l'Est et l'Ouest avec le transfert vers des pays en voie de développement d'arsenaux et d'équipements accompagnés parfois de scientifiques contractés par les États acquéreurs pour servir dans des activités nucléaires dont les finalités militaires ne peuvent pas être écartées.

Aussi, il nous semble qu'à moyen terme, c'est une modification fondamentale du régime des garanties qui est requise afin de doter l'AIEA de moyens de contrôle et d'une capacité juridique et effective d'inspection. C'est donc au niveau des Accords de garanties

123 Statement by Dr. H. Blix, Director General of the IAEA, at informal consultations in the Security Council regarding Iraq and resolutions 687 and 707 (1991), 8 October 1991 (Document sans cote).
124 *Ibid.*

qu'un travail de révision doit être opéré à l'intérieur de l'Agence afin de rendre le système plus dissuasif et efficace qu'il n'a pu l'être jusqu'à présent.

Summary

Investigation of the Iraqi Nuclear Program

The legal framework under the NPT safeguards system did not allow the IAEA to discover any infringement of Iraq's obligations pertaining to non-proliferation and non-acquisition of nuclear weapons. Security Council Resolution 687 goes beyond NPT's narrow limits and therefore permits the IAEA and the United Nations to look into a wide range of Iraqi industrial activities and thus find what are considered by experts to be military-oriented undertakings that violate international law and obligations under NPT. The author explores the capacity and work of IAEA within both the NPT safeguards system and Security Council Resolution 687, as well as related legal implications.

International Organizations:
What Makes Them Work?

BRYAN SCHWARTZ*

and

ELLIOT LEVEN†

INTRODUCTION

What makes an international organization work? Why are some international organizations so much more successful than others? Of course, each organization has its own unique background and history, but are any general patterns or trends discernible across the diverse spectrum of organizations?

International organizations are assuming a crucial place in world affairs. The European Community (EC) provides an outstanding example of the overall rise of international organizations. The EC is in the process of taking bold new steps towards economic and political integration, and may soon be expanding its membership.[1] Its 1992 project will significantly promote free trade within the Community.[2] Member states are planning to expand the European

---

* Professor, Faculty of Law, University of Manitoba.

† LL.B., University of Manitoba.

---

[1] See "Altered States," *The Economist*, July 11, 1992, European Community Survey, at 5; "On the Way to the Forum," *ibid.*, 14; and "Essence of Maastricht," *ibid.*, 10.

[2] *Ibid.*

monetary system by creating a central bank and European currency.[3] Many of the longstanding democracies on the periphery of the existing Community may soon be seeking or obtaining membership.[4]

The EC has the potential to be the most productive economic unit in the world. If it continues to deepen and widen its embrace, the achievement will mark a turning point in human history. A novel and thriving form of supranational organization will exist on the site of some of the most vicious and devastating confrontations between peoples and between sovereign states.

Another factor that has moved international organizations to centre stage is the break-up of the Soviet Union. As a result of this break-up, the North Atlantic Treaty Organization (NATO) is in the process of reconsideration and reorganization, and the Warsaw Treaty Organization has dissolved. Russia may eventually join the General Agreement on Tariffs and Trade (GATT) and the International Monetary Fund (IMF), and is already contributing to the revitalization of the UN Security Council by finding more areas of common agreement with the United States.[5] The former satellites of the Soviet Union would like to become members of the EC, and Estonia, Latvia, Lithuania, Poland, Czechoslovakia, Hungary, and Slovenia could all join by the year 2000.[6]

The study of international organizations should go hand-in-hand with the examination of federal forms within states. A number of states are in the process of reorganizing themselves in ways that may draw on international models and experience.[7] The premier of Quebec has recently cited the European Community as a model for the future relationship between what is now the province of Quebec and a federal Canada.[8] In South Africa, federal or confederal structures may have to be devised to secure some balance of equality and security among the different peoples and states.

[3] See "Memo to Maastricht," *The Economist,* Nov. 30, 1991, at 69.

[4] It is anticipated that Austria, Norway, and Sweden will become members of the European Community by 1996. Malta is slated to join by 2000. See "Altered States," *The Economist,* July 11, 1992, European Community Survey, at 5.

[5] See "The Tortoise and the Hare," *Time* (Canadian edition), Sept. 10, 1990, at 20.

[6] See "Altered States," *The Economist,* July 11, 1992, European Community Survey, at 5.

[7] See "On Russia's Rim," *The Economist,* Jan. 20, 1990, at 13.

[8] See the interview with Quebec premier Robert Bourassa in *Time* (Canadian edition), July 9, 1990, at 10.

The primary focus of inquiry in this article is the *effectiveness* of organizations. An "effective" organization for present purposes is one that is able to produce and implement decisions that significantly affect the state of affairs over which it has jurisdiction. This definition enables one to see the moral value of what an organization does as a partially distinct question. The IMF, for example, appears to be an effective organization, but some critics condemn it as being domineering in its conduct with debtor nations and misguided in the economic policies it imposes.[9] Once the issue of effectiveness is identified as the focus of inquiry, it becomes possible to examine the extent to which moral values influence effectiveness. For instance, do organizations tend to be more effective if they are composed of democratic states?

This article will examine thirteen factors that may or may not be important to an organization's effectiveness. In each case, an *a priori* discussion of whether a factor ought to help will be followed by an examination of whether it actually does.

These factors are:

(1) the existence of bureaucracies that maintain an ethic of impartiality;

(2) a high volume of decisions;

(3) a well-defined overall objective, followed up by specific programs to implement it;

(4) confinement of the organization's scope to utilitarian objectives that transcend political differences among members;

(5) guaranteed funding;

(6) a balance of power among members;

(7) the ability to reach decisions quickly;

(8) incremental growth in membership;

(9) the legal authority to impose sanctions;

(10) decision-making processes that do not require unanimity, but require more than a simple majority, and limit "opting-out" by dissident members;

(11) charismatic leadership;

(12) shared values among members;

(13) democratic principles among members.

While the authority to punish states that do not accept decisions might, *a priori*, seem to be a crucial factor, the practical reality is

9 See "The World Bank and the IMF: A Panel," 80 Am. Soc. Int'l L. Proc. 21-42 (1986).

more subtle. Respect for decisions is often better secured by positive incentives, including the long-term benefits that the institution has to offer if a party does not undermine it to avoid short-term pain. Authority to enforce decisions may be considered a significant factor, but it is easy to overestimate its importance.

BUREAUCRACIES WITH AN ETHIC OF IMPARTIALITY

An organization is more likely to be effective if much of its work is done by bureaucratic or judicial agencies staffed by people who are committed to the goals of the organization, rather than by people who are advancing the special interests or ideology of their state of origin.

Impartial bureaucracies contribute to effectiveness in a number of ways. States will often have more confidence in the outputs of impartial bureaucracies than in political votes. The existence of impartial bureaucracies or judicial arms also saves politicians from themselves. Political actors in pursuit of domestic popularity may be bound to assert what appears to be national interest at the expense of the overall good of the members of the organization. In fact, by transferring authority to a credible bureaucracy or judicial agency, politicians may be able to advance the long-term interests of their constituencies without paying the political price. Furthermore, impartial bureaucracies do the hard work of formulating or implementing policies without wasting time on political posturing, or tailoring their actions to satisfy the personal or political needs of politicians.

The EC has benefited greatly from the existence of impartial bureaucratic and administrative arms. For example, the European Court of Justice has produced a steady flow of effective decisions on the interpretation of EC treaties.[10] Also, the European Commission has had a leading role in establishing and implementing the political agenda of the evolving Community.[11]

The EC has adopted a variety of measures to foster impartiality. With respect to the European Court of Justice, only one collective decision is issued; individual judges are given little opportunity to colour their decisions to achieve personal popularity in their home state, or in the EC generally. European Commissioners have fixed terms of office; they cannot be recalled by their home states

10 See "Where the Buck Stops," *The Economist*, May 6, 1989, at 48-50.
11 See "The Locomotive of 1992," *The Economist*, Mar. 25, 1989, at 56-58.

(although the home government may choose not to reappoint them). Overall, the EC can draw on the expertise of public servants whose substantial salaries and security of office encourage them to see themselves as having a long-term, secure commitment to the service of the EC.

Organizations can sometimes draw on various professional ethics. The EC can draw on the spirit of civil service neutrality that applies to most state bureacracies within it. The European Court of Justice and European Court of Human Rights can draw on the ethic of judicial impartiality. In its peacekeeping operations, the United Nations is often able to rely on the principles of professional, nonpolitical soldiering on which many state armies are based. The Universal Postal Union (UPU) requires that all members of its executive council be high officials of national postal administrations, with at least ten years' service.[12] (On one occasion, when a Soviet member was late in arriving, a Soviet diplomat who did not meet the UPU criteria was denied the right to vote in his place.) The International Law Commission is often able to find *rapporteurs* — experts who do the technical work of researching and drafting treaties — whose professional standards of thoroughness, accuracy, and precision can provide a sound framework for working out the final political compromises.[13]

Many of the judicial and administrative arms of the United Nations have suffered from the inability of the organization to ensure impartiality among its staff. Individuals from authoritarian states may be personally vulnerable if they subordinate the interests of their home states to those of the organization. They may be sent in the first place because they are uncritical adherents to the ideology and leadership of their governments.

Bureaucratic impartiality and shared political values are closely related factors. Often, bureaucrats and judges are required to invent or refine the goals of organizations, not merely apply well-defined standards established by political authorities. If the individuals and member states involved share the same political values, impartiality may still be preserved. Intersubjective agreement will, to some extent, compensate for the absence of external standards. But if bureaucrats or judges come from drastically different politi-

---

12 See Evan Luard, *International Agencies: The Emerging Framework of Interdependence*,
    23 (London: Royal Institute of International Affairs, 1977).

13 See "The International Law Commission," 17 Victoria Univ. Wellington L. Rev.
    1-16 (1987).

cal cultures, they may, in all good faith, understand and define the legitimate values of the organization in very different ways.

A quasi-judicial organization that has successfully maintained an ethic of impartiality in dealing with potentially volatile disputes is the International Centre for the Settlement of Investment Disputes (ICSID). An autonomous organization closely linked with the World Bank, ICSID impartially arbitrates disputes between foreign investors and (usually Third World) host governments. Set as they are against the background of north-south tensions and suspicions about colonialist and imperialist motives, these disputes can be bitter and complex.

ICSID has overcome these potential hurdles by establishing a track record of efficiency and impartiality.[14] ICSID uses a tripartite arbitration system complemented by an impartial review (appeal) mechanism. ICSID's success speaks for itself: the ICSID convention was originally ratified by twenty countries in 1966; today it has been ratified by over ninety. The volume of cases dealt with by the ICSID has grown dramatically. ICSID arbitration clauses have become more and more common in international investment contracts.

VOLUME

Do international organizations work better if they produce a relatively high volume of decisions? There is a strong *a priori* argument for believing that they do. A state may be driven to comply with one unpalatable decision because disobedience undermines the organization and, in the long run, the effective functioning of the organization is in the interest of that state. If the organization is active over the long run, there is a reasonable chance that the temporarily unhappy state will have its share of "wins."

An organization's "track record" of decisions also enables states outside the organization to assess the risks of submitting themselves to its jurisdiction. When the organization is bound, or at least influenced, by its precedents, the development of a body of previous decisions adds to the predictability of its future conduct.

The European Court of Justice and the European Court of Human Rights are two examples of courts with a fairly high volume of decisions. They have both probably benefited in credibility from their long record of reasonable and impartial decisions to date, and

14 David Lopina discusses the progress of ICSID through the 1980s in "The International Centre for Settlement Investment Disputes: Investment Arbitration for the 1990s,'" 4 Ohio State J. on Dispute Resolution 107-22 (1988).

the prospect that this situation will continue. By contrast, the credibility of the International Court of Justice (ICJ) has suffered from the sparseness of its workload. On the basis of its sparse corpus of decisions to date, it is difficult to predict, on the basis of precedent and judicial realism, how it would react to many issues. Given the many states that have already opted out of its jurisdiction, and the prospect that others will do so in the future, a state with a substantial risk of losing a particular case has little incentive to absorb the embarrassment and material loss of doing so. When it refused to participate in the Nicaragua case after the ICJ found it had jurisdiction, the United States did not seem concerned about its own stake in undermining the long-term effectiveness of the institution.[15]

It is true that the United States had in the recent past won its case against Iran over the illegality of detaining diplomats.[16] But that case was the only successful action for the United States in modern history, and the losing litigant essentially ignored it. The United States has a much better record of compliance with adjudicatory agencies — such as the GATT — that offer it the prospect for a reasonable number of successes over the long term.

Volume is not a positive factor when the output is consistently ignored or rejected. For many years, the United Nations General Assembly certainly produced a very high volume of resolutions. The Assembly has very little legal authority, however, and the moral suasion of its declarations has been compromised in a number of ways. For one thing, the one state/one vote formula allows resolutions to carry despite the objections of a large group of states, some of which may be vitally interested in the matter. For another, the Assembly has often passed one-sided resolutions that were favourable to the interests (or at least the rhetoric) of Soviet bloc and Third World states.

Another consideration that suggests the positive effect of volume is almost tautological. The more decisions an organization makes, the more impact it has. The more *objectionable* decisions an organization makes, however, the more likely an existing member is to drop out, and the less likely a new state is to enter. Either possibility reduces the effectiveness of the organization. Furthermore, some states will be deterred from participating in an organization by the

15 See "Appraisals of the ICJ's Decision: *Nicaragua v. United States,*" (Jan. 1987) 81 Am. J. Int'l L. 77-183 (1987).

16 See Ted L. Stein, "Contempt, Crisis and the Court: The World Court and the Hostage Rescue Attempt," 76 Am. J. Int'l L. 499-531 (1982).

very fact that it is effective, and therefore may limit their freedom of action.

The GATT is a good example of an organization with both volume and teeth. GATT's *raison d'être* is essentially to remove trade barriers. Every barrier that is eliminated is a step in the right direction. A high volume of decisions has contributed to its practical effectiveness. Furthermore, GATT's "most favoured nation" principle (whereby a trade concession made to one state is effectively made to all GATT states) gives volume a multiplier effect. Each barrier that is eliminated automatically topples scores of adjacent barriers.

WELL-DEFINED OVERALL OBJECTIVE: SPECIFIC PROGRAMS TO ACHIEVE IT

Will an organization with a well-defined *raison d'être* function more effectively than one with a nebulous or undefined program? It should in theory, provided that the program is realistic. An organization dedicated to putting an astronaut on Pluto by 1992 would certainly have a clearly fixed program, but it would hardly be a successful organization.

The North Atlantic Treaty Organization (NATO), the South East Asia Treaty Organization (SEATO), and the Central Treaty Organization (CENTO) all had fixed programs: essentially, to counter and contain the Soviet Union's military influence. SEATO and CENTO were so ill-conceived and intrinsically unrealistic, however, that they never became fully functional and eventually ceased to exist (with no apparent ill effects).

NATO, on the other hand, was realistically conceived and had a concrete, fixed program. Although NATO too will eventually disappear, it did its job well in the Stalin-to-Gorbachev era. Had NATO's program been more nebulous (less focused on the perceived Soviet threat), it would likely have functioned less effectively. For example, NATO never troubled itself about territorial disputes between its own members (Canada and the United States or Greece and Turkey). NATO wisely left the Cyprus imbroglio to the United Nations. By husbanding its resources and focusing them on Moscow, NATO functioned as smoothly as any multinational military alliance in recent history.

One of the most successful international organizations today is the EC. For this reason, the EC will figure prominently in later sections of this paper. Although its eventual destination was not known, the leading individuals and the states in the EC have always understood that a primary purpose of the organization is the promotion of economic integration.[17] Through its vicissitudes, that basic direction has inspired and guided the Community.

In implementing its overall economic ideal, the EC has demonstrated the virtues of specific and well-defined programs of implementation. The EC's bold plan for a unified European market before 1992 is based on the concept of such a fixed program. The first step in implementing the plan was taken when Lord Cockfield, commissioner of the EC's internal market, proposed a list of 300 measures (now 279) that were needed for a unified market. Suddenly, EC members were confronted with an explicit game plan and a deadline of 1992, rather than the usual vaguely defined statement of principles that is so common in the realm of international organizations. To their credit, the EC members rose to the challenge and accepted Cockfield's fixed program and timetable. The pace of change in Europe in the near future may well be breathtaking.[18]

The GATT, with its commitment to world free trade, has also benefited from an overall sense of direction. It has backed up the commitment with a series of rounds from which more specific directives — including specific and practical arrangements on tariff levels — were negotiated.

The International Civil Aviation Organization (ICAO) has had mixed success since its creation in 1947. It has been effective in fostering high technical and safety standards for global air travel, but has had very limited success in freeing air traffic and landing rights from the control of individual states. One of ICAO's handicaps has been its lack of a defined overall program. Although some members of ICAO have pushed for the deregulation of air routes, the organization itself has never actually made deregulation a goal.[19]

LIMITATIONS ON OBJECTIVES

It would seem likely that an organization can achieve a greater percentage of an objective if that objective lies in a specific regula-

---

[17] See *Europe Without Frontiers: Completing the International Market* (Luxemberg: Office for Official Publications of the Communities, 1989).

[18] *The Economist* captures some of the drama of this project in a survey titled "Europe's Internal Market," July 9, 1988.

[19] See Eugene Sochor, "From the DC-3 to Hypersonic Flight: ICAO in a Changing Environment," 55 J. Air L. and Com. 407-40 (1989).

tory area in which states are trying to achieve the same concrete goals, regardless of ideology. In fact, a number of organizations have such limited objectives. For example, the Universal Postal Union's mandate is "to secure the organization and improvement of the postal services and to promote in this sphere the development of international collaboration."[20] On the other hand, some organizations have suffered for not being able to exclude wider political issues from their operation — for example, the United Nations Educational, Scientific, and Cultural Organization (UNESCO).

Even where an organization cannot exclude controversial issues, it may be able to make more headway if it confines its operation to a specialized area, rather than addressing a broader range of issues. The division of regulatory labour should allow the bureaucrats and state representatives involved to build up a store of experience and mutual understanding. Also, the states will have the opportunity to expand co-operation in that area despite their disagreement in others. The countervailing consideration is that, with more issues within an organization's purview, there may be greater opportunity for participating states to find mutually beneficial trade-offs. In practice, wider trade-offs that end up affecting specialized agencies can occur; for example, the United States has used its leading role in the IMF as leverage in higher level negotiations with states, concerning their human rights policies.

The practical record suggests that the advantages of specialization often outweigh whatever opportunities are lost for wider deal-making. Within the United Nations system, several of the specialized agencies, such as the World Health Organization,[21] the International Law Commission, the World Bank,[22] the IMF,[23] and the Commission on Refugees have achieved some of their objectives despite ongoing divisions among the member states on many issues of interest and ideology. Other international organizations, such as the GATT and the EC, illustrate the advantages of leaving some issues off an organization's agenda.

Conversely, apart from their specialized agencies, organizations with unlimited mandates have tended to be ineffective. The general

20 P. J. G. Kapteyn et al., *International Organization and Integration*, IB, 1.7.a. (The Hague: Mortimer Nijhoff Publishers, 1982).

21 See Luard, *supra* note 12, at 153-66.

22 *Ibid.*, 240-63.

23 *Ibid.*, 219-39.

organs of the United Nations, the Organization of American States (OAS), and the Organization of African Unity (OAU) have not been effective in pursuing their open-ended mandates.[24] The purpose of the United Nations, as expressed in the UN Charter, is to "maintain international peace . . . to develop friendly relations among nations . . . to achieve international cooperation in solving international problems of an economic, social, cultural or humanitarian character . . ." and other expansive goals.[25] The charters of the OAS ("to achieve an order of peace and justice . . .")[26] and of the Organization of African Unity (". . . to achieve a better life for the peoples of Africa . . .")[27] are similarly vague and ambitious.

Of course, limited scope is no guarantee of success. The Statute of the Organization of Petroleum Exporting Countries (OPEC) states that the "principle aim of the organization should be the coordination and unification of the petroleum policies of member countries and the determination of the best means for safeguarding their interests, individually and collectively."[28] Although OPEC was extremely successful at fulfilling its mandate for several years during the 1970s, it has had repeated setbacks in the years since. In the light of Iraq's 1990 invasion of Kuwait and the aftermath of the invasion, OPEC's future prospects have certainly become much dimmer. The possible reasons for OPEC's failures will be discussed later, in the sections dealing with shared values and with democracy.

GUARANTEED FUNDING

Is guaranteed funding essential for an international organization's success? It might seem that a guaranteed source of income leaves an organization less vulnerable to self-interested pressure tactics from major financial contributors. On the other hand, the

---

[24] The factor identified here has been the subject of a considerable literature revolving around the term "functionalism." For a brief introduction, see Paul Taylor, "Functionalism: the Theory of David Mitrany," in Paul Taylor and A. J. Groom (eds.), *International Organizations* 236 (London: Francis Pinter Ltd., 1978), and R. J. Harrison "Neofunctionalism," *ibid.*

[25] J. Grenville and B. Wasserstein, *The Major International Treaties Since* 1945: *A History and Guide with Texts* 64 (New York: Methuen, 1987).

[26] *Ibid.*, 92.

[27] *Ibid.*, 338.

[28] Burns, Weston et al., *Basic Documents in International Law and World Order* 43 (St. Paul, Minn.: West Publishing, 1980).

power of the purse has been a crucial factor in the development of parliamentary democracies; the ability of states to withdraw funding from organizations might be a useful and relatively restrained instrument for curbing fiscal irresponsibility or high-handedness by an organization's bureaucrats or political majority.

General tardiness or reluctance to pay assessed dues may do little more than demoralize an organization's staff. Even a deliberate decision to withhold dues in order to stage a symbolic protest may have little effect, if the dues form only a small part of an organization's budget. A dues protest by a major benefactor can have a much more significant effect.

The best case study in this area is the United States' experience with UNESCO. UNESCO's budget for 1984-85 was about $390 million (U.S.). This amount covered the cost of maintaining UNESCO's 2,300-person bureaucracy in Paris, several hundred annual international conferences, and programs in the developing world. The latter category accounted for about 20 per cent of the organization's budget. The United States footed about 25 per cent of UNESCO's annual bill.

American displeasure with UNESCO's fiscal situation (and with its increasingly anti-west political agenda) led to the United States' decision in December 1983 to withdraw its membership at the end of 1984. Subsequently, budgetary reforms were made at UNESCO and the United States eventually rejoined.

A decade earlier, the United States had clashed with UNESCO over what it perceived as an unacceptable incident of "Israel-bashing" within the organization. On November 21, 1974, Israel was excluded from UNESCO's European regional group, thereby becoming the only UNESCO member not in a regional group. This action followed a UNESCO resolution condemning Israel for alleged wrongdoing in carrying out archaeological excavations in Jerusalem.[29]

The American Congress, on December 30, 1974, responded by voting to withhold the United States contribution to the UNESCO budget. The action was effective. In 1976, UNESCO admitted Israel to the European regional group. The United States also clashed with the International Labour Organization and with the International Atomic Energy Association over perceived incidents of Israel-

[29] The saga of Israel and UNESCO is chronicled by Frederic Kirgis, Jr. in *International Organizations in their Legal Setting: Documents, Comments and Questions* 547-53 (St. Paul, Minn.: West Publishing, 1977).

bashing and other political issues. Again, the United States used its financial clout to effect positive change in an organizational setting. The UNESCO experience raises questions about the guaranteed funding of organizations. The most common method of funding international organizations is to levy membership dues, based roughly on ability to pay, upon all members. In theory, this system seems more or less fair. In practice, however, this makes the international organization vulnerable to a withdrawal by the largest, richest member or members.[30] The effect of giving larger members a "weighted vote" in an organization will be explored later.

Furthermore, guaranteed funding does not necessarily secure administrative efficiency. On the one hand, long-range planning can be undertaken and staff morale can be maintained if guaranteed funding is the norm. On the other hand, guaranteed funding can lead to bloated bureaucracies and inefficient spending, as in the case of UNESCO before 1984. The threat of spending cuts may actually be a catalyst for efficiency.

BALANCE AMONG MEMBERS

Does an organization work more effectively if there is a reasonable balance in the power of its members? ("Power" here means the ensemble of a state's underlying economic, military, and political power, and its specific authority and influence within the organization). Or does it facilitate effectiveness for an organization to be led by a single, dominant member or group of members?

There does not appear to be a clear-cut answer to this question. One the one hand, the dominance of a member may enable an organization to overcome administrative and political inertia or even active disagreement among members about objectives and means to achieve them. Leadership by a single state, or small core of states, may be particularly effective in an organization like the IMF or World Bank, in which the leader or leaders wield influence by supplying the benefits that an organization distributes. Attaching strings to a benefit appears to offend the sensibilities of smaller states less than does attempting to directly impose constraints on their freedom. On the other hand, less powerful states may be unwilling to participate in an organization if their interests are not protected against humiliating or materially injurious domination by a powerful member or group of members.

[30] In 1990 the total debt/arrears of the United States to the UN and its agencies was approximately $438 million.

Some of the most successful organizations manage to achieve an equilibrium between dynamic leadership by the few and protection of minority interests. Among the organizations most thoroughly dominated by a single member were the now-dissolving Warsaw Pact and the Council for Mutual Economic Assistance (COMECON). It can be argued, of course, that these were not actually international organizations at all, because true international organizations presuppose voluntary membership. The Warsaw Pact and COMECON, as they were, might be more accurately described as arms of empire — the artificial creations of a single, imperialist member.

Even so, Soviet domination of COMECON had at least some benefits for other members. The economic relationship between the USSR and Cuba, under the auspices of COMECON, certainly did a lot more good for the Cuban economy (in the form of cheap or free petroleum products) than for the Soviet economy. An economic organization less dominated by a single member might have worked less well from a Cuban perspective.

The opposite of this line of thinking is that artificial Soviet support has encouraged the Cuban economy to remain grossly inefficient for several decades. Had Cuba been forced to pay the market price for oil all along, it might have been forced to implement positive economic reforms years ago.

Two international organizations that are characterized by single-member domination and voluntary membership are the World Bank and the IMF. Weighted voting has given the United States effective veto power over all major World Bank and IMF decisions.[31] Unwritten agreements have given American nationals leading positions in the bureaucracies of these organizations. It is possible that the organizations would not have been born or continued to develop without the leading American role. There can be little doubt that these organizations have been effective — again, in the sense of having a significant impact on affairs within their purview. Whether the IMF operates virtuously is an ongoing matter of controversy.

Organizations characterized by a balance among leading members have a mixed record. The OAU, in which the fifty-one members have equal rights and powers, has not distinguished itself for successfully fulfilling the terms of its charter. Nor has it performed

[31] See Douglas Williams, *Specialized Agencies and the U.N.: The System in Crisis* 160 (New York: St. Martin's Press, 1987).

well in comparison with a regional organization like the EC. OAU defenders or apologists might argue that, given the massive problems confronting the nations of Africa, the OAU has actually performed about as well as can be reasonably expected. By articulating (or at least paying lip service to) the goal of a peaceful, united Africa, the OAU has given its members an ideal to which they can strive.

Ironically, the international organization that most resembles the OAU is the OAS. Whereas the OAU is a collection of small, relatively weak members, the OAS is dominated by the United States both in terms of underlying economic and military power, and in terms of its role as dominant financier of the apparatus and programs within the organization itself. But both organizations serve as little more than "talk shops" that discuss regional issues and rarely act decisively to solve major regional problems.[32] The balance-versus-domination question seems almost irrelevant here.

The effects of balance on the EC have been complex. Germany and France have often taken leading roles in developing EC policy. Their individual and joint leadership was, during the initial thirty years of its existence, the driving force behind the expansion of the European Community. An EC dominated solely by Germany would likely have scared other European states in the 1950s.

Maintaining balance between these two leading members, and within Europe generally, has always been an essential reason for the Community's existence. Procedural mechanisms have been designed to protect minority states from domination, whether by granting a veto to each state, giving smaller states a weighted vote that exceeds their share of the population, or using a one state/one representative system.

Furthermore, the original pre-eminence of Germany and France was sometimes an impediment, rather than a spur, to the Community's further development. France's President de Gaulle was able to block the entry of the United Kingdom into the Community in January, 1963 and for many years thereafter. The achievement of greater balance within the Community, brought about by the eventual entry of the United Kingdom and the upsurge in the economic strength of Italy, do not seem to have fundamentally impaired the development of the Community.

[32] See L. Ronald Scheman, "The OAS and the Quest for International Cooperation: American Vision or Mirage," 13 Case Western Reserve J. Int'l L. 83-105 (1981).

If examples of intrastate federalism are examined, it does not appear that leadership by a core group of states is decisive. The United States is a highly integrated form of federalism, but no state or group of states has a dominant voice. The structure of the U.S. Senate, giving equal power to each state, large or small, has served to minimize domination by larger or wealthier states. By contrast, Canadian politics have traditionally been dominated by the residents and governments of the two central provinces. Whatever additional leadership has been provided has been counterbalanced by the sense of alienation and distrust that has emerged in the less populous parts of the country.

The Security Council of the United Nations exemplifies an entrenched form of leadership by five permanent members. The inability of the permanent members over the years to achieve a consensus has seriously impaired the effectiveness of the Council and of the United Nations as a whole. It remains to be seen whether the more co-operative relationship now emerging among the five powers will last, and if so, whether it will provide a major new impetus to the activity and effectiveness of the United Nations as a whole.[33]

For practical purposes, it may be necessary for organizations formally or informally to group states into larger units. The Law of the Sea negotiations, for example, proceeded by lumping states into five different groups; once each group achieved an internal consensus, it was able to negotiate with others. But these aggregation techniques may, if anything, diminish the opportunity and necessity for a few states to play a dominant role. States that have no real clout when going solo may have a real impact when they join their voices. In the din of many voices, someone may choose to shout in order to provide some direction to the discussion.

Focus and direction can be maintained in a balanced organization by the efforts of credible bureaucratic and judicial agencies. In the EC, for example, the Commission has often provided essential initiative and direction.

EXPEDITIOUSNESS

Do organizations that reach decisions expeditiously work better than those that function at a slower pace? To some extent, this is just a matter of common sense — undue delays never enhance any

[33] See "Renaissance on the East River," *The Economist*, Dec. 15, 1990, at 43-44.

organization's performance. This fact has been recognized by a number of organizations in which effectiveness and credibility have been impaired by long delays in making decisions. The GATT and the European Court of Human Rights, for example, have recently taken major steps to expedite their dispute-resolution processes. As the EC's 1992 project illustrates, deadlines can be very useful in promoting political activity. They can also be essential to bringing diplomatic negotiations to a reasonably prompt conclusion. Such processes as GATT's Uruguay round might benefit considerably from agreement upon fixed deadlines for concluding various stages of negotiation.

INCREMENTAL GROWTH IN MEMBERSHIP AND JURISDICTION

Do organizations that begin with few members and grow gradually have an advantage over those that begin with many members? Several successful international organizations have indeed followed the former pattern. The EC grew from six, to nine, to ten, to twelve members, and will likely grow to include twice that number eventually. As the organization grew, its projects became more ambitious and its achievements more conspicuous. (Of course, we have no way of knowing what the EC would be like today if all of today's members had joined back in the 1950s.) Furthermore, the EC has expanded its scope incrementally from its inception as a coal and steel union to embrace other areas of trade and economic coordination. A monetary union is to be the next step. Had the EC attempted to tackle all of these projects in the 1950s, it would not likely have succeeded.

One can also provide examples of organizations that started small and failed abysmally. The little-mourned East African Community (EAC), which included only Tanzania, Kenya, and Uganda, did not last long enough to grow further.[34]

GATT is another organization that has grown incrementally. GATT was born in 1948 with twenty-three members. Today ninety-six members come under the GATT umbrella, not including some who participate in GATT on a *de facto* basis only. The prospect of Russia's joining GATT in the future, given its size and economic potential, is exciting and encouraging for GATT enthusiasts. GATT has by no means been an unqualified success. It has not resolved the issue of agricultural subsidies, nor has it tackled the complex-

[34] See W. Feld and R. Jordan, *International Organizations: A Comparative Approach* 173-78 (New York: Praeger, 1983).

ities of trade in services, intellectual property, discriminatory quality standards, discriminatory public purchasing, obstructive customs procedures, and voluntary restraints. To its credit, however, GATT has made great progress in the area of international trade in goods. During the GATT era, tariffs have been reduced from an industrial country average of 40 per cent in 1947, to less than 5 per cent in 1990. The volume of international trade is ten times greater than it was at GATT's inception.[35]

Of course, some incremental growth was necessary by definition. Although virtually all of the world's major trading states joined GATT early in its existence, many of GATT's current members were not independent states in 1948. Still, the ability of GATT to develop and implement its policies over the long term successfully has enhanced the organization's credibility and encouraged new members to join. Twelve countries are currently waiting to become members.

SANCTIONS

Do organizations function better if they have the legal authority to impose sanctions for non-compliance with organizational policy?

One possible sanction is military force. The Security Council has the authority to resort to it, but has rarely relied upon it. On occasion, forces under United Nations command, or enforcement actions by states acting with the authority of the UN, has helped to implement organizational decisions; among the examples are the actions in Korea and the Congo. The OAS authorized the United States' "quarantine" action against Cuba during the Cuban missile crisis. Armed force is a feasible enforcement measure only in rare cases. Usually, the burden of human and economic cost on the enforcing agency is high, and moral and humanitarian considerations inhibit imposing suffering on others; the prospect of success is uncertain, as are the risks of further escalation. It is also important to recognize that even successful military coercion of a state is likely to produce within it resentment, fear of outsiders, and heightened nationalism.

Economic sanctions have many of the same drawbacks, albeit to a lesser degree, as military coercion. The practical record of their effectiveness is difficult to assess. It has proved very difficult in practice to enforce sanctions (as, for example, those against Rho-

35 See "GATT Brief," *The Economist*, Apr. 21, 1990, at 85-86.

desia and South Africa), and when states have finally reformed themselves after many years of sanctions, it is not entirely clear whether the sanctions were responsible or whether political and military pressure prevailed. Sanctions probably had a significant impact upon the Rhodesian and South African situations. Nevertheless, the difficulty of securing consistent compliance and the many years needed for any impact to occur suggest that embargoes can only be effective in exceptional cases.[36]

The IMF and the World Bank exercise a different sort of sanction power. Since these organizations are in the business of making loans or loan guarantees to members, states that want the money must abide by IMF and World Bank policies. This is not really so much a question of sanctions as of the "he who pays the piper calls the tune" principle. Of course, states are free to ignore IMF policies and forego the loans. Some states do just this. Most states, however, find the IMF's and World Bank's "bribe power" to be very persuasive. Developing states' criticism of the IMF and the World Bank misses the point; just as no one can force developing states to accept IMF and World Bank loans, so no one can force developed states to part with their money against their wills.

It appears that carrots are generally more practical and effective than sticks. The organization holding them out is less inhibited by moral and humanitarian considerations; it is easier to implement a decision to grant or withdraw largesse than it is to coerce the will of another; and there is less chance that the state subjected to inducements will develop resentful and nonco-operative attitudes in the long run.[37]

GATT itself does not impose sanctions, but the agreement does authorize members to impose a limited form of sanctions unilaterally. In a sense, GATT allows members an authorized safety valve — that is, states retain a tightly constrained right to retaliatory action while still remaining under the overall GATT umbrella.

The EC and federal states (like the United States and Canada) do not need sanction power to operate effectively. Their member

---

[36] One economic weapon that seems to be quite practical and effective is freezing the assets of an adversary. For example, it seemed to produce results (eventually) in the U.S.-Iran hostage situation.

[37] While conditions imposed on IMF loans have produced popular resentment, even the occasional riot, it is doubtful that the resentment is comparable to that which would result from measures such as embargoes or military action that are more clearly punitive.

states (or provinces) voluntarily, though not always happily, go along with organizational or federal policy as the price of membership. This might lead us to the conclusion that sanction power is generally overrated. As a rule of thumb, if members genuinely support an organization like the EC, they abide by its decisions without being threatened with sanctions; if members do not support an organization, the threat of sanctions is largely meaningless. (The verdict on the 1990-91 United Nations sanctions against Iraq is unclear. Some argue that these sanctions would have been effective if they had been carried on for a longer period of time.)

DECISION-MAKING RULES

The principle of one-member-one-vote, regardless of ability to pay, has a nice ring of fairness to it. Some organizations that use the system function relatively well (UPU, for example). GATT uses a more informal system of policy-making that is based more on consensus than on voting. Of course, owing to the nature of trade, the large trading states have a somewhat greater role in the formation of GATT consensus than the smaller ones.

Problems arise with one-member-one-vote when the biggest pipers are prevented too often from calling the tunes. The United States experience at UNESCO is instructive. Unable to control UNESCO policy through a weighted vote, the United States was so frustrated that it pulled out completely. Some would argue that the United States has no right to impose its will on poorer states. This may well be morally persuasive. The reality of the matter, though, is that no state will retain membership in an organization when it perceives that it no longer has a vested interest in staying. UNESCO has retained the one-member-one-vote system, but the United States is once again a member. A heightened sense of political realism seemed to suffice at UNESCO, and a change in the voting system was not necessary. Depending on one's overall view of the moral performance of the IMF and the World Bank, weighted voting is either an essential ingredient in the success of these organizations or it is an unfair vehicle that allows rich states to oppress poor ones. Of course, some poor states, (for example, Cuba) have never been IMF or World Bank members. States dissatisfied with these organizations could always have joined Cuba and escaped the "oppression." Again, the focus is not on the morality of the IMF and the World Bank, but on their potency.

In place of the majority voting and weighted voting systems, an organization can require unanimity for some or all decisions. The United Nations Security Council requires Great Power unanimity (each has a veto) on policy decisions. The EC Council of Ministers requires unanimity for decisions on some issues, such as taxes. The Council also needs unanimity to override a European Parliament veto.[38] A system of majority voting is almost always faster at making decisions than a system requiring unanimity.

Motivated by the desire to avoid long delays and by the 1992 deadline for many important issues, EC members have been willing to sacrifice their old veto rights, presumably for the greater good. As the EC grows larger in future years, unanimity will become harder and harder to attain, and majority voting will become even more attractive. Therefore, the general trend in the EC has been away from unanimity and towards majority voting.

An *a priori* analysis indicates that the EC is moving in the appropriate direction — that is, towards requiring super majorities, but not permitting the obstruction of decisions by a very small minority. Super majorities are required because states tend to be fearful of surrendering their authority to supernational entities, and a large zone of comfort is needed to secure their initial participation in a decision-making process. Furthermore, there will be varying perspectives (each skewed in the direction of a state's own interests) on what counts as a legitimate majority. Populous states will want an emphasis on number of people, less populous ones on number of governments. Economically powerful states will consider gross national product or economic activity as worthy of special weight. By requiring a high level of agreement before a decision proceeds, an organization helps to ensure that its decision has moral legitimacy from a variety of different, often competing perspectives. On the other hand, a requirement of unanimity may prevent an organization from making any hard choices in the common interest. It is liable to give potential holdouts a disproportionate ability to extract concessions from the large majority.

Majority rule can be undermined, even practically nullified, by provisions that allow a dissenting state to opt out of the decision. Some organizations that do not provide members with the veto do, indeed, allow members to opt out of their decisions. The International Labour Organization (ILO) functions this way. Labour conventions are debated and voted upon, but members are not forced

---

[38] "The powers that be," *The Economist*, Feb. 25, 1989, at 49-50.

to adopt these conventions. The United States, for example, has ratified only seven of the more than 160 ILO conventions. Certainly, some psychological pressure is exerted to induce members to ratify conventions but, for practical purposes, members have full opt-out rights.[39] As a result, a patchwork of different labour conventions has been ratified in a variety of combinations by different states.

A more recent example of an opting-out provision that has the potential to undermine majority rule can be found in the Maastricht Treaty. Following this provision, Britain was allowed to opt out of the European Currency Union (ECU) provided that it accepted a date for the setting of European Monetary Union (EMU).[40] Some commentators fear that granting the British the right to opt out of the single currency provision of EMU will result in EC *à la carte* in the future as other countries from different backgrounds and economies seek entrance to the EC.[41]

CHARISMATIC LEADERSHIP

Does an organization need a strong or charismatic leader to work well? Little has been written about the roles of individual leaders in creating and shaping an international organization.

Perhaps the most interesting case of one man's influence in an organization is that of United States President Woodrow Wilson and the League of Nations. Without Wilson's personal determination (perhaps obsession), the League would likely not have been created at all. Ignoring his opponents at home and abroad, Wilson persistently used his power and stature to push for the League's creation.

Ironically, Wilson may have inadvertently signed the League's eventual death warrant. By ignoring anti-League voices in the United States Congress, and refusing to discuss possible compromises regarding the League's functions, Wilson may have insured that Congress would block United States membership in the League. Although the League had other problems in its short and

---

[39] See Linda L. Moy, "The U.S. Legal Role in International Labor Organization Conventions and Recommendations," 22 Int'l Lawyer 767-74 (1988).

[40] Treaty of European Union, Protocol on Certain Provision Relating to the United Kingdom of Great Britain and Northern Ireland, 31 Int'l Leg. Mat. 247, 355 (1992).

[41] See "Dreaming Spires," *The Economist*, European Community Survey, July 11, 1992, at 29.

sad history, the absence of the United States was an important factor in its failure.[42]

Strong leaders played important roles in other organizations. Charles De Gaulle left his mark on the EC. Among other things, he almost single-handedly kept the United Kingdom out of the EC. Some would argue that the strong leadership of Jacques Delors has been decisive in reinvigorating the EC and making the 1992 initiative possible.[43]

When all is said and done, it is probably fair to say that a strong leader can hasten or delay organizational achievements. In the long run, however, organizations rise and fall on the basis of other factors. De Gaulle may have delayed the United Kingdom's membership in the EC but he could not prevent it — after all, he was mortal. Also, if European economic co-ordination makes sense, it would have happened sooner or later, with or without Delors.

SHARED VALUES

Do organizations function better if all their members have shared values? It is certainly to be expected that underlying agreement among peoples on broad cultural, religious, and political values would make it more likely that their governments would be able to participate successfully in joint ventures. One of the factors that has contributed to the effectiveness of the EC is the restriction of membership to western European, multi-party democracies. For a while, the United Kingdom was excluded partly because of French perception that its people were not European enough in their outlook.

It is also to be expected that an upward spiral may operate, in which shared values contribute to successful international organizations, and the latter help to mould an ever greater sense of community. The long experience of living in one federal system, with a strong central government, powerful military, and constitutionally guaranteed free movement of ideas and people, has helped to create the strong and distinctive American identity. As the EC creates more opportunity for shared political and economic activity, the people within the Community may acquire an increasingly strong sense of European identity.

[42] George Scott argues that, during most of its history, the League actually functioned better than many people realize, in *The Rise and Fall of the League of Nations* (London: Hutchinson and Co., 1973).

[43] See "General Jacques De Gaulle," *The Economist*, June 16, 1990, at 58.

Broadly shared values do not seem to be necessary for the functioning of organizations with limited scope, such as the UPU or the International Meteorological Organization, or for the technical standards operations of the International Civil Aviation Organization. These organizations are limited to a narrow purpose — such as having mail delivered — that is held in common.

On the other hand, more ambitious functionalist organizations naturally require substantial commonality among members. Membership in GATT presupposes a shared commitment to some of the basic tenets of a market economy. The technical reason for this supposition is best explained in a "GATT Brief" published in *The Economist*:

GATT does not require countries to adopt western style capitalism. It does not care who owns the factories and how they are run. It does assume that businesses can decide how much to buy and sell in response to price signals and that prices broadly reflect costs. Where prices are fixed by bureaucrats and goods are allocated by plan directives, GATT rules cannot operate sensibly. For instance, GATT permits members to levy extra duties if goods are being dumped on their markets at prices below production costs. But if no one knows what production costs are, how can dumping be proved or disproved?[44]

It is now apparent that future membership of the former Soviet republics in GATT will depend on their economic reforms.

The League of Arab States (Arab League) is an international organization that appears to hold some broadly shared values. The peoples within it share a similar linguistic, religious, and cultural heritage. Of course, what appears similar to an outside, casual observer may be highly diverse to an actual participant. Christian Europe has hardly been a model of harmonious unity over the centuries. There are, in fact, broad differences of religious belief, economic activity, and cultural traditions within the Arab world. For example, those Arab League states with large petroleum reserves have very different economic problems and goals from those states with little oil.

It may be, however, that the single biggest obstacle to the effective functioning of the Arab League is that none of its member states is a multi-party democracy. Instead, there is a variety of autocratic systems of government, including monarchies and military dictatorships. These autocratically run governments are unlikely to

---

[44] *The Economist*, Apr. 28, 1990, at 80-81.

co-operate in effective international organizations, because the sense of respect for the rule of law and deference to the will of the majority are not likely to exist among the leadership elite. Also, where the free movement of ideas and people across boundaries does not exist, there will be no interchange to help build up a sense of trust and community at the popular level.

The pact of the Arab League provides that the purpose of the organization is "the strengthening of relations between the member states; the co-ordination of their policies in order to achieve co-operation between them . . . on the following matters: [Economic and financial affairs, communications, cultural affairs, nationality, social affairs, health problems]."[45] The Arab League has been extremely successful in generating a voluminous, consistent, and colourful stream of anti-Zionist rhetoric throughout the years. With the exception of Egypt, its members have also been relatively successful in maintaining an anti-Israel trade embargo. The League's accomplishments in other fields have been less conspicuous. Iraq's 1990 invasion of Kuwait, in particular, demonstrated no consistency with the League's espoused principles. Under article 5 of the League's pact, "any resort to force in order to resolve disputes arising between two or more member states of the League is prohibited."

It might be countered that the United States frequently flouts the will of international organizations — for example, by ignoring the ICJ in the Nicaragua case, or by its actions in Panama and Grenada. The same charge could be levelled against Israel. Do these examples demonstrate that democracies do not necessarily extend respect for the rule of law or majority rule to the larger, world community? Not really. The United States and Israel have often seen international organizations as largely consisting of authoritarian and totalitarian governments, and as such, bodies whose moral legitimacy is grossly compromised.

DEMOCRATIC PRINCIPLES AMONG MEMBERS

Do international organizations work better if all members are democracies? Is democracy the crucial factor that differentiates the EC and the Arab League?

To begin with, nation states are inanimate. Decisions made by members of international organizations are actually made by

45 Kapteyn, *supra* note 20, at II.G.1.a.

national leaders — that is, members of the species *homo sapiens*, who are shaped by real life experiences.

The national leaders of democracies tend to be politicians with ample experience in the fine art of getting elected by large numbers of voters and staying elected — in short, they are men and women familiar with compromise. Even the most doctrinaire of democratic politicians will generally have to make political compromises during the course of their careers.

Leaders of non-democratic nations — dictators or absolute monarchs — are likely to have far less personal experience with the necessity of political compromise. On the contrary, many have attained and retained power specifically because of their inflexibility and unwillingness to tolerate dissent.

If the hallmark of an effective international organization is its ability to bridge gaps among members and achieve a measure of consensus on diverse issues, it is logical to suppose that organizations whose members are all democracies will usually work better.

Politicians from democracies are also usually experienced in losing more or less graciously. The average politician would have spent time in opposition as well as government. Although democratic forms of government (featuring elections every two, four, or six years) are sometimes criticized for engendering short-term thinking, leaders from non-democratic states may be even less prepared to focus on long-term goals. Opposition politicians tend to respect the rules of parliamentary decorum, knowing that the stability of that decorum will serve them well in the future, when they form a government. Dictators and autocrats have less experience in this sort of reasoning.

Organizations with a limited scope, such as UPU, IMO, or ICAO, can function fairly well despite their inclusion of many non-democratic members. For organizations with more complex and ambitious mandates, however, democracy seems to be an enormous asset. It can be argued that too much democracy may actually be counter-productive. Had Woodrow Wilson been a dictator, the United States would have joined the League of Nations and the League would have worked better. Then again, had Wilson been a dictator, he might never have been attracted to the ideal of the League of Nations in the first place.

Furthermore, there are democracies and then there are democracies. Japan has a functioning democracy on paper, but the Liberal Democratic party always forms the majority government in Japan.

India has a functioning democracy, but with a relatively high degree of institutionalized political graft and corruption. Some might even question the nature of American federal democracy, given the extraordinarily high cost of campaigning in recent years. Nevertheless, the bottom line is that an atmosphere of free speech and journalistic freedom prevents politicians (even in Japan, India, and the United States) from behaving like dictators.

There are still some states (although their numbers are rapidly dwindling) that view multi-party democracy as just one among several equally legitimate political systems. It remains to be seen how their views will stand the test of time. Meanwhile, international organizations composed of, or dominated by, democratic members will continue to function more successfully, by and large, than organizations dominated by non-democratic members.

CONCLUSIONS

For the purposes of this analysis, ideas about what makes organizations work have been divided into thirteen discrete categories. In fact, this division is somewhat artificial; in reality, the thirteen factors operate simultaneously and in such complex combinations that it is often impossible to determine which factor predominates. Did the East African Community fail because it did not have limited scope, or because it did not have a fixed program, or because its members did not share enough values, or because the members were not multi-party democracies? Does the EC work because of balance among its members or because it grew gradually and incrementally? It is impossible to answer these questions with precision or certainty. Nevertheless, the general trends identified can be of practical use to existing or future organizations. Lord Cockfield's 300 points can serve as an example of a fixed program inspiring tangible results — an example that can benefit other international organizations.

If, at some future date, the industrialized states of Asia explore the idea of an Asian Economic Community, they may want to consider limiting membership to multi-party democracies. They may want to confine themselves, initially, to an organization of limited scope — for example, a coal and steel community (to steal a page out of the EC's book). They may want to create an Asian Court of Justice to resolve sensitive disputes with an ethic of impartiality. They may or may not seek mechanisms to prevent Japan's domination of the organization. Different voting systems may be explored to strike a balance between Japan's interests and those of smaller states. In any event, the member states will certainly want to examine the track records of other regional organizations, in an attempt to discern what factors influence an organization's successful performance.

To brave a prediction on a more imminent event, the framework of this article predicts excellent prospects for the planned European Monetary Union (EMU), including a common European currency, and a European central bank, now being developed. The common values and democratic nature of EC states will contribute to EMU's success. The monetary union will likely work better if its structure ensures a high level of bureaucratic independence from member governments, and an ethic of impartiality in decision making. A high volume of decisions, a well-defined overall goal, a limited utilitarian objective, and a process of incremental growth can also contribute to EMU's strength.

The governments of the EC's member states will never agree completely upon every detail of a common monetary policy. In particular, there will always be a certain tension between those governments that see a low rate of inflation as the highest economic priority, and those that are willing to tolerate higher inflation rates when monetary policy is used to stimulate the economy and reduce unemployment.

To protect the proposed European central bank from this inevitable tension, the bank could be given a high degree of independence from EC politicians. Central banks in western states all have a certain degree of independence. Central bankers whose terms of office overlap those of national governments and who are allowed to make decisions at arm's length from the politicians can make decisions that are relatively free from party politics and "hometown" favouritism. In fact, the closer the European central bank comes to an apolitical, judicial model, the easier it will be for the bankers to make decisions with the impartiality and effectiveness of European Court judges.

The European central bank will have to make regular and important decisions about a variety of monetary issues, including interest rates and money supply. The high volume of significant decisions should, over the long term, give the bank the opportunity to demonstrate its even-handedness and reliability, and thus foster confidence in its decisions and support for its ongoing operations.

The bank may be given a broad mandate to manage monetary

affairs, but no specific direction on the low inflation versus low unemployment issue. As a result, the bank may be more vulnerable to criticism from states or groups of states that favour a direction other than the one the bank is pursuing at any given moment. If the bank's priorities are established from the beginning and spelled out in the bank's constituting documents, some of this potential criticism can be avoided. If more flexibility is needed, it should be possible to have the bank's specific objectives revised by interstate agreement every five or ten years; developing each new consensus will be difficult, but it will be done at the political level, and once established, will leave the bank less vulnerable to criticism from dissatisfied customers.

The proposed bank will be more effective by virtue of its limited, utilitarian objective. Confined to setting monetary policy, the bank will not be sidetracked or bogged down in other EC issues. While the bank is making its monetary decisions, other EC organs will be debating agricultural, defence, foreign trade, and regional development policies. None of these areas is completely discrete, and decisions made in one arena will affect all other arenas to a greater or lesser degree. The central bankers, however, will be authorized to concentrate on one specific field of operations, and thus, to a considerable extent, will be able to sidestep many complicated or emotional controversies.

European Monetary Union (EMU), like the EC itself, is a product of incremental growth. The European monetary system was created in 1979. During the 1980s, the system's exchange rate mechanism evolved and more member states brought their national currencies into the mechanism. The movement to a central bank and a single currency will involve further transitional steps. Although it was rejected at Maastricht, one proposal (aimed primarily at the United Kingdom, which is the EC state least enthusiastic about EMU) involved an opt in system, which would have allowed EC states to abandon their national currencies and adopt the new European currency in their own time. Reluctant states could then wait for several years before taking the EMU plunge. Such an incremental approach would have prevented further delays in moving EMU ahead. Instead, the EC agreed at Maastricht that the United Kingdom alone would have the right to opt out of the ECU.

EMU states share many important common values. All EMU states are market economies and all have strong trading links. Some tensions, particularly on the inflation versus employment question, will emerge from the fact that some EMU states are wealthier and more industrialized than others. Other EC initiatives, such as regional development plans, will reduce this difference over time. In general, EMU will be strengthened by the common economic goals of its members.

The democratic element will also foster the success of EMU. Because states will be allowed to join EMU only after their national parliaments have approved the decision, the voters of EMU member states will feel a certain stake in the venture's success. In Denmark and Ireland, national referenda have already been held. While the Danes rejected the Maastricht Treaty, the Irish, who derive 5 per cent of their national budget from the EC, embraced the treaty. In the United Kingdom, the decision was hotly debated in at least one general election. Because the democratic process has been followed, unpopular decisions by the central bank will be somewhat more palatable. A monetary union foisted on a helpless populace by an authoritarian junta would certainly enjoy less popular support.

Central bank decisions will also be more palatable to EC leaders because they are all democratic politicians. These leaders, particularly those with some experience in coalition goverments, are accustomed to winning some political battles and losing others; they may dislike some central bank decisions, but will likely take them in their stride as inevitable facts of democratic life.

Although EC states must still surmount several obstacles on their march towards EMU and though, once established, EMU will still face numerous hurdles, the prospects for eventual success are very bright. By drawing upon the experiences and lessons of other international organizations, EMU can improve its prospects even further.

Sommaire

Les organisations internationales: Les facteurs d'efficacité

Les auteurs soulignent et analysent les facteurs qui favorisent l'efficacité d'un organisme international. Selon les auteurs, les organisations les plus réussies sont celles dont le rôle est précis et utilitaire. Elles ont notamment pour tâche de mettre en oeuvre des programmes très spécifiques. Ce sont aussi des organisations gérées par une bureaucratie qui se veut impartiale.

Au départ modeste, leur champ d'activité et leurs membres croissent lente-ment, en fonction de l'évolution des besoins et de la situation internatio-nale. Elles adoptent également de nombreuses décisions en suivant un processus décisionnel rapide qui préfère la règle du consensus à celle de l'unanimité. De plus, elles se composent d'États démocratiques. Finalement, les auteurs notent que le pouvoir de sanctionner ne représente pas une condition importante et essentielle à l'efficacité d'un organisme international.

Les cadres juridiques de la capitalisation des dettes commerciales des États

VILAYSOUN LOUNGNARATH, JR.*

L E RALENTISSEMENT ÉCONOMIQUE sévère qui a frappé l'économie mondiale au début des années quatre-vingt a mis en relief l'acuité et l'ampleur de l'endettement extérieur des pays en voie de développement. Si l'incapacité de plusieurs pays du tiers-monde d'assurer le service de leur dette a sérieusement ébranlé le système bancaire, il reste que la débâcle a été évitée. L'infléchissement de la crise tient en partie à la convergence d'efforts vers le déploiement de techniques innovatrices de réduction de la dette. La capitalisation des dettes commerciales[1] est l'une d'entre elles et fait l'objet de cette étude.

---

* Professeur, Faculté de droit de l'Université de Montréal; membre du Barreau de Québec et du Barreau de l'État de New York; ce texte a été préparé dans le cadre de la session 1992 du *Centre d'étude et de recherche de droit international et de relations internationales de l'Académie de droit international* (La Haye, Pays-Bas). Le thème de cette session était *La dette extérieure des États*. L'auteur tient à remercier le Professeur Dominique Carreau, de l'Université Paris-I, Maître Daniel Desjardins de l'Étude Hudon, Gendron, Harris, Thomas et Maître François Bourassa de la Banque Nationale du Canada pour leurs commentaires judicieux, de même que Catherine Bohémier et Philippe Labelle pour leur assistance. Les opinions émises dans cette étude n'engagent que l'auteur.

---

[1] Bien connu sous sa désignation anglaise de "debt-equity swap." Pour une description de quelques-unes de ces techniques innovatrices de réduction de la dette, voir L. C. BUCHHEIT, "The Changing Tactics of Sovereign Debt Restructuring," *International Financial Law Review*, novembre 1987, à la p. 35.

La capitalisation des dettes désigne ces transactions dont l'objet est la conversion de la dette extérieure d'un pays en voie de développement en prises de participation étrangères dans une entreprise du pays-débiteur. La transaction peut s'organiser de diverses façons, dépendant des objectifs recherchés et des contraintes de l'espèce. Dans le schéma de base, on retrouve les acteurs suivants: (1) la banque créancière; (2) l'investisseur étranger, qui peut être la banque créancière, une autre institution financière ou plus souvent une entreprise industrielle ou commerciale; (3) le débiteur, soit une entité publique ou privée d'un pays en voie de développement; (4) la Banque centrale de l'État-débiteur; (5) le régulateur de l'État-débiteur, la régulation des opérations de capitalisation des dettes étant très souvent effectuée par la Banque centrale; (6) l'entreprise locale bénéficiant de l'injection de capital; (7) divers intermédiaires.

L'opération typique se décompose en plusieurs étapes. La banque créancière désire se départir d'une créance qu'elle détient à l'endroit d'un pays-débiteur. Ce prêt est libellé en devises étrangères. La créance se transige sur le marché secondaire à une valeur inférieure à sa valeur nominale. Une société étrangère est désireuse d'investir dans le pays-débiteur. Via un intermédiaire, elle achète la créance de la banque sur le marché secondaire à sa valeur marchande. Sur remise du titre de la créance, la Banque centrale du pays-débiteur fournira des crédits libellés en monnaie nationale. La somme versée par la Banque centrale ne sera jamais inférieure au prix du marché secondaire, mais le pays-débiteur cherchera en règle générale à s'approprier une partie de la décote en rachetant la créance à un prix inférieur à l'équivalent de sa valeur nominale en monnaie nationale. Ces crédits seront injectés dans une entreprise locale qui émettra en contrepartie des actions au bénéfice de l'investisseur étranger. L'entreprise locale utilisera ces crédits pour financer des projets d'investissement préalablement autorisés par les autorités compétentes du pays-débiteur. Ces crédits peuvent être fournis directement à l'investisseur étranger, qui les dirigera par la suite vers l'entreprise locale. Suivant un autre scénario, la Banque centrale ouvre un compte en monnaie locale au bénéfice de l'entreprise locale désignée.[2] Enfin, ces crédits peuvent aussi provenir du

---

2 C'est notamment le cas du programme mexicain de capitalisation des dettes de 1986-87. Voir à ce sujet COMISION NATIONAL DE INVERSIONES EXTRANJERAS Y SECRETARIA DE HACIENDA Y CRÉDITO PUBLICO, *Manual Oper-*

produit de la vente sur les marchés des capitaux intérieurs de titres de dette libellés en monnaie locale et émis au bénéfice de l'investisseur étranger par la Banque centrale en contrepartie de la remise de la créance.[3]

Un certain degré de concomitance existe entre ces diverses démarches. Ainsi, dans la pratique, l'investisseur étranger ne procédera pas à l'achat d'une créance ou d'un bloc de créances sur le marché secondaire sans avoir obtenu au préalable le feu vert pour ses projets d'investissement de la Banque centrale du pays-débiteur ou des autorités gouvernementales mandatées pour administrer le programme de capitalisation des dettes.

Comme on peut le constater, une opération de capitalisation de dettes s'insère dans une pluralité de cadres juridiques. La réglementation nationale de la banque créancière encouragera ou dissuadera cette dernière de participer à des opérations de capitalisation de dettes. Il faut aussi tenir compte du cadre juridique des transactions effectuées sur le marché secondaire, de la compatibilité d'une opération de capitalisation des dettes avec le prêt syndiqué ou le contrat de rééchelonnement, de même que de l'environnement réglementaire installé par l'État-débiteur, ce dernier cadre s'imposant comme le principal déterminant d'une opération de capitalisation des dettes. L'emploi optimal de la technique de la capitalisation de la dette commerciale pose donc comme préalable que les autorités compétentes et acteurs concernés gérant ces

---

ativo para la capitalizacion de Pasivos y Substitucion de Deuda Publica por Inversion, 1986 au chapitre VI; le programme philippin employait aussi ce genre de technique: L. C. BUCHHEIT, *Debt Reduction Techniques: The Capitalization of Sovereign Debt: An Introduction,* dans *Latin American Sovereign Debt Management: Legal and Regulatory Aspects,* 98-111, 101 (Washington, D.C., 1990).

[3] La technique a été utilisée dans le programme chilien de capitalisation des dettes. Voir L. C. BUCHHEIT, *supra* note 1, à la p. 101. Pour une description sommaire de certaines transactions articulées autour de la capitalisation des dettes, voir J. CAREY, F. D. LEVENTHAL et I. M. IRVINE, Chile's Debt-for-Equity Programme: Hotter Than Most? (1990) *IFL Rev.* 9, 28-32, où l'on décrit notamment la transaction se rapportant au financement de la construction d'un moulin de pâte à papier dans le sud du Chili. Voir aussi UNITED NATIONS CENTRE ON TRANSNATIONAL CORPORATIONS, *Debt Equity Conversions: A Guide for Decision Makers,* Nations Unies, 6 (New York, 1990) [ci-après Debt-Equity Conversions], où est décrit le financement d'un investissement de Chrysler au Mexique. Plus près de nous, la Société des Alcools du Québec serait sur le point d'acheter un vignoble au Chili au moyen de la technique de la capitalisation des dettes: voir *La SAQ s'apprête à acheter un vignoble au Chili,* La Presse, Montréal, 4 mai 1992, à la p. A-3.

cadres juridiques les aménagent de manière à permettre, sinon favoriser, le recours à cette technique.

Il est proposé dans cette étude de décrire les principaux cadres juridiques que traverse une opération de capitalisation de la dette. Par cette description, on cherchera à faire ressortir que l'emploi optimal de la technique de la capitalisation de la dette dans une stratégie visant la réduction de la dette et le développement économique de l'État-débiteur passe par un arrimage entre ces cadres et le déploiement d'efforts convergents des gouvernements des pays industrialisés, des institutions créancières et des États-débiteurs en vue d'aménager les cadres juridiques qu'ils assument de manière à faciliter la mise-en-oeuvre d'opérations de capitalisation de dettes.

I   LES CADRES JURIDIQUES EXTÉRIEURS AU PAYS-DÉBITEUR

A   LE MARCHÉ SECONDAIRE

Depuis sa création, en 1982, le marché secondaire de la dette des pays en voie de développement a connu un essor considérable. Le volume des transactions est ainsi passé de quelques 6 milliards de dollars U.S. en 1985 à plus de 60 milliards en 1989.[4] À l'origine, les banques commerciales se livraient essentiellement sur ce marché à des échanges de créances afin de diversifier leur portefeuille ou bénéficier de certains avantages fiscaux. Avec le développement des programmes de capitalisation des dettes, le marché secondaire s'est vu attribuer une vocation additionnelle puisque c'est sur ce marché que l'investisseur se procure les créances à capitaliser. La mise en place des programmes de capitalisation des dettes n'a donc pas été sans contribuer à l'augmentation du nombre de transactions sur le marché secondaire.[5]

Sur le marché secondaire, les créances sont négociées avec une décote qui est supposée refléter leur valeur réelle. Les cours y

[4] P. GAJDECZKA et M. STONE, "Le marché secondaire de la dette des pays en développement," *Finances et développement*, décembre 1990, à la p. 22.

[5] Selon une étude des Nations Unies, quatre facteurs auraient contribué à l'expansion du marché secondaire: (1) un nombre croissant de banques souhaitaient vendre ou convertir leurs créances à une valeur inférieure à la valeur nominale; (2) l'uniformisation progressive des instruments financiers utilisés comme vecteurs de la dette extérieure des pays en voie de développement, ce processus rendant le marché secondaire plus fluide et plus facile à gérer; (3) une simplification graduelle des procédures de transfert de créances; (4) la mise en place de programmes de conversion de la dette dans plusieurs pays-débiteurs. Voir à ce sujet DEBT-EQUITY CONVERSIONS, *supra* note 3, à la p. 18.

seraient principalement déterminés par le jugement que portent les opérateurs sur la situation économique et financière du pays-débiteur, le risque politique encouru et, plus fondamentalement, sur la probabilité de remboursement de la dette conformément aux termes contractuels.[6] Des analystes n'ont cependant pas manqué de soulever des doutes sérieux sur l'efficience de ce marché et sa capacité d'évaluer avec justesse la valeur réelle des créances transigées, soulignant notamment son fonctionnement informel, l'absence de centralisation institutionnelle et l'inexistence d'un cadre réglementaire.[7] On a aussi relevé qu'il existe un écart entre les cours officiels et les prix réellement pratiqués dans les transactions.[8]

1 Fonctions économiques du marché secondaire dans une opération de capitalisation des dettes: un aperçu

La décote sur le marché secondaire est en quelque sorte la locomotive de l'opération de capitalisation des dettes. L'intérêt financier de l'investisseur tient, en effet, à l'existence d'un écart entre la valeur de rachat de la créance et son cours sur le marché secondaire. Cet écart n'existe que si, au préalable, la créance est soumise à une décote sur le marché secondaire.

Par ailleurs, un marché secondaire développé facilite la tâche des intermédiaires financiers et réduit ainsi les frais de transaction assumés par l'investisseur à raison du recours à la capitalisation des dettes comme véhicule d'investissement.[9] L'État-débiteur peut, d'ailleurs, chercher à accroître la fluidité du marché secondaire

---

6 Pour une évaluation et une présentation des facteurs susceptibles d'influencer le cours du marché secondaire de la dette des pays en voie de développement, voir GUJDECZKA et STONE, *supra* note 4, à la p. 24.

7 DEBT-EQUITY CONVERSIONS, *supra* note 3, aux pp. 18-19; l'inefficience du marché secondaire est aussi soulignée par M. BLACKWELL et S. NOCERA, *Debt-Equity Swaps*, 12 février 1988, *FMI*, 13-20 (Document de travail, F.M.I., manuscrit non publié).

8 GUZDECZKA et STONE, *supra* note 4, à la p. 25.

9 Le Marché secondaire réduit les coûts de transaction de quatre façons: (1) il est plus facile et plus économique d'assembler la dette requise pour l'opération de capitalisation; (2) le marché secondaire fournit un "réservoir" de créances facilement accessibles, réduisant d'autant le besoin de maintenir des inventaires; (3) les intermédiaires ne sont pas limités à une fonction de mandataire et peuvent agir comme preneurs fermes; (4) le marché secondaire fournit un mécanisme économique pour déterminer la valeur réelle des créances. Voir à ce sujet DEBT-EQUITY CONVERSIONS, *supra* note 3, aux pp. 19-20.

dans la perspective d'inciter les investisseurs à se prévaloir de son programme de capitalisation des dettes. C'est ce qu'ont fait les autorités Philippines en lançant en 1987 le programme des "Philippines Investment Notes" (mieux connu sous l'acronyme de PINS).[10] Ces titres de créance étaient libellés en devises étrangères et avaient une échéance de six ans. Ils ne portaient pas intérêt et étaient vendus à escompte. Le PIN pouvait cependant être racheté avant échéance dans le cadre d'une opération de capitalisation, la banque centrale versant alors au détenteur l'équivalent en monnaie locale de la valeur nominale du titre. Celui-ci avait donc intérêt à se prévaloir de l'option de rachat le plus tôt possible. Le PIN ne faisait pas l'objet de restriction de cessibilité, ce qui facilitait sa manipulation sur le marché secondaire. Les émissions de PINS étaient synchronisées avec les remboursements d'intérêts de sa dette extérieure de manière à minimiser l'impact du paiement de ces derniers sur les réserves nationales de devises étrangères. Lorsque le programme a débuté, en 1987, la faiblesse du marché secondaire nuisait aux opérations de capitalisation des dettes philippines. Les émissions de PINS avaient donc aussi pour but de rendre disponible sur le marché secondaire des instruments financiers adéquats pour les opérations de capitalisation des dettes et ainsi encourager ce type de transaction.[11]

2   Le marché secondaire: aspects juridiques

Le transfert de la créance sur le marché secondaire est ordinairement effectué au moyen d'un arrangement contractuel établissant une cession de créance (*assignment*)[12] ou une participation dans la créance.[13]

---

10 Le programme philippin de capitalisation des dettes a cependant été suspendu en 1988: *Les banques transnationales et les conversions de la dette en prise de participation*, Rapport du secrétaire général, New York, Organisation des Nations Unies 1991, 11; le programme philippin de capitalisation des dettes se trouve présenté à CENTRAL BANK OF THE PHILIPPINES, *Program for the Conversion of Philippines External Debt into Equity Investments*, circulaire numéro 1111, 1986.

11 Sur le programme philippin des PINS, voir "Philippines: Explanatory Memorandum on Philippine Investment," (1987) 26 *I.L.M.* 808 et L. C. BUCHHEIT, *supra* note 1, à la p. 39.

12 L'*assignment* est un concept de *common law* tandis que la cession de créance est une institution du droit civil. Bien que ces deux véhicules juridiques présentent des similarités, ils ne sont pas rigoureusement identiques.

13 Participation en droit new-yorkais, sous-participation en droit anglais.

Les principaux paramètres du régime juridique du transfert de la créance organisé sous forme de cession de créance (*assignment*) se retrouvent essentiellement dans deux documents contractuels, soit le contrat de prêt (ou l'accord de rééchelonnement) et le contrat documentant le transfert de la créance. Une problématique de droit international privé est posée lorsque ces contrats obéissent à des droits substantifs différents. Pour les fins de résoudre des questions de conflit de lois, l'auteur Wood suggère une approche analytique.[14] Afin de déterminer si les droits et obligations sont transférables, on appliquerait la loi gouvernant le contrat de prêt ou l'accord de rééchelonnement.[15] Par contre, la validité du transfert, tant au plan des conditions de forme que des conditions substantives dépendra de la loi applicable au contrat par lequel le transfert s'effectue.[16]

D'ordinaire, le contrat de prêt (ou l'accord de rééchelonnement) contient une clause précisant la mesure dans laquelle les droits et obligations sont transférables. Cette clause, qui place en point de mire le consentement du débiteur, peut se présenter suivant diverses configurations. Ainsi une version prévoit qu'il n'est pas nécessaire d'obtenir l'assentiment de l'État-débiteur pour réaliser le transfert de la créance.[17] Une variante plus restrictive n'autorisera le transfert que si l'emprunteur y consent, l'assentiment ne pouvant cependant pas être déraisonnablement refusé et étant réputé avoir été donné en l'absence de formulation d'objection à l'intérieur d'un certain délai.[18] Même si l'obtention du consentement du débiteur n'est pas strictement nécessaire aux termes du contrat de prêt ou de l'Accord de rééchelonnement, il est quand même d'usage de rechercher son assentiment au transfert de la créance.[19]

---

[14] P. WOOD, *Law and Practice of International Finance* 340-41 (Sweet & Maxwell, Londres, 1980).

[15] *Ibid.*

[16] *Ibid.*

[17] Une telle clause est reproduite dans D. DESJARDINS, "Assignment and Sub-Participation Agreements: A Basic Overview" [1986] 65 R.B. Can. 224, 231; voir aussi R. H. RYAN, JR., "Participation in Loans under New York Law," *International Financial Law Review*, octobre 1984, 40.

[18] Une telle clause se trouve à l'art. 12.10(b) de l'*Accord de rééchelonnement des Philippines*, 10 avril 1986.

[19] D. DESJARDINS, *supra* note 17, à la p. 227.

De manière générale, le contrat constatant le transfert de la créance stipulera que le transfert porte autant sur les droits que sur les obligations du créancier initial. Il prévoira aussi que l'exécution du transfert de la créance est subordonnée à la délivrance d'un avis au débiteur et à la banque agissant à titre de coordonnatrice du prêt syndiqué (agent bank) ou de l'Accord de rééchelonnement (servicing bank).[20] L'avis contriendra de l'information sur l'étendue des droits et obligations transférés et précisera le montant en cause.[21] En outre, le contrat de transfert typique assujettira l'effectivité du transfert de la créance à la délivrance au débiteur et à l'institution coordonnatrice d'un engagement écrit de la part de l'acquéreur de la créance, engagement par lequel ce dernier s'engage à être lié par les termes et conditions du contrat de prêt ou de l'accord de rééchelonnement. Ces deux types de conditions se retrouveront aussi dans la clause du contrat de prêt ou de l'accord de rééchelonnement relative à la transférabilité des créances.[22]

La délivrance de ces avis et engagements produit plusieurs effets aux termes du contrat constatant le transfert de la créance et du contrat de prêt ou de l'accord de rééchelonnement. Sur délivrance de ces avis et engagements, les paiements en capital et intérêts seront dûs directement à l'acquéreur de la créance. À partir de ce moment, celui-ci assumera entièrement le risque associé à la créance, et le lien de droit entre le créancier initial et le débiteur sera définitivement rompu.

La documentation contractuelle typique emploie la terminologie de l'*assignment*. Mais le transfert de la créance d'une institution bancaire sur un pays en voie de développement constitue-t-il vraiment une cession de créance ou un *assignment*? Ne devrait-on pas plutôt y voir une novation par changement de créancier? Dans un transfert de créance organisé sous forme de novation par changement de créancier, il y a rupture du lien de droit entre le créancier initial et le débiteur, et établissement d'un lien de droit similaire ou identique entre le débiteur et l'acquéreur de la créance. Le couplage de l'extinction du lien de droit initial avec la création d'une

20 Dans le système de la *common law*, on parle de *conditions precedent*: ces conditions doivent être remplies pour que le contrat crée des obligations exécutoires. Voir J. D. CALAMARI et J. M. PERILLO, *Contracts* 439-40 (West Publishing Co., St-Paul, 1987, 3e édition) (pour la *common law* américaine).

21 D. DESJARDINS, *supra* note 17, à la p. 231.

22 À titre d'exemple, voir l'art. 12.10 (b) de l'*Accord de rééchelonnement des Philippines*, *supra* note 18.

toute nouvelle relation juridique est le propre de la novation, qu'elle soit régie par le droit civil ou la *common law*.[23] Alors que la novation entraîne la disparition du lien de droit initial entre le créancier et le débiteur, et son remplacement par une relation juridique inédite, la cession de créance et l'*assignment* n'ont qu'un effet translatif, en ce que le lien de droit initial subsiste et est dirigé, en partie ou en totalité, vers un autre créancier.[24] Par ailleurs, la novation sera invalide sans l'assentiment de toutes les parties au contrat initial, ce qui inclut au premier chef le débiteur de la créance transférée. Il y a cependant moyen d'obtenir préalablement du débiteur et des autres créanciers qu'ils consentent au transfert de la créance organisé sous forme de novation par changement de créancier en prévoyant dans le contrat de prêt ou l'accord de rééchelonnement que les consentements du débiteur et des autres créanciers sont réputés avoir été donnés si certaines conditions sont remplies.[25] Par contre, dans la cession de créance ou l'*assignment*, la validité du transfert de la créance n'est pas assujettie à l'obtention du consentement du débiteur; tout au plus, ce dernier doit-il recevoir une notification du transfert pour que celui-ci lui soit opposable et que le cessionnaire puisse obtenir un droit prioritaire.[26]

[23] Sur la novation en *common law*, voir J. CHITTY, *Chitty on Contracts* 902 et 1002 (Sweet & Maxwell, Londres, 1989) (pour le droit britannique), G. H. L. FRIEDMAN, *The Law of Contract in Canada* 430 et 471 (Carswell, Toronto, 1976) (pour le droit anglo-canadien) et A. L. CORBIN, *Corbin on Contracts*, tome VI, 185-232 (West Publishing Co., St-Paul, 1962) (pour le droit américain); sur la novation en droit civil, voir J. L. BAUDOIN, *Les obligations* 494-502 (Les Editions Yvon Blais Inc., Cowansville, 1989) (pour le droit québécois), J. CHEVALIER et L. BACH, *Droit civil*, tome 1, 441-43 (Les Éditions Sirey, 1989), *Juris-Classeur civil*, arts. 1271 à 1281 du code civil français, Fasc. 1, H. MAZEAUD, L. MAZEAUD, J. MAZEAUD et F. CHABAS, *Leçons de droit civil*, tome II, 1245-56 (Mont-Chrestien, Paris, 1991) (pour le droit civil français).

[24] J. CHITTY, *id.*, 902-3 (pour la *common law* britannique); G. H. L. FRIEDMAN, *id.*, 429-30 (pour la *common law* anglo-canadienne); CALAMARI et PERILLO, *supra* note 20, aux pp. 724-26 (pour la *common law* américaine); J. L. BAUDOIN, *id.*, 556 (pour le droit civil québécois); *Juris-Classeur civil*, art. 1689 à 1695 du code civil français, Fasc. 1, 3 (pour le droit civil français).

[25] R. H. RYAN, JR., *supra* note 17, à la p. 40.

[26] Dans le cas de figure général de *common law*, l'avis écrit informant le débiteur du transfert de la créance est suffisant et n'est soumis à aucune exigence quant à la forme. Voir CHITTY, *supra* note 23, à la p. 872 et FRIEDMAN, *supra* note 23, à la p. 437. Le droit civil est plus formaliste; ainsi l'art. 1571 C.c.B.C. stipule que "l'acheteur n'a pas de possession utile à l'encontre des tiers, tant que l'acte

Le transfert de la créance d'une institution bancaire sur un pays en voie de développement, tel qu'il a été décrit et tel qu'il est organisé dans la pratique, nous semble plus proche de la novation par changement de créancier que de la cession de créance ou de *l'assignment* et ce, malgré la terminologie utilisée dans les documents contractuels. En effet, les mécanismes de la cession de créance et de l'*assignment* portent sur des droits; ils ne peuvent transférer des obligations.[27] Or la créance d'une institution financière sur un pays en voie de développement telle que défini par le contrat de prêt syndiqué ou l'accord de rééchelonnement se présente comme un faisceau complexe de droits et obligations dirigés non seulement vers le débiteur mais aussi vers les autres créanciers parties au contrat de prêt. Pour cette raison, le détachement du créancier initial du cadre contractuel délimité par le contrat de prêt ou l'Accord de rééchelonnement peut difficilement s'effectuer autrement que par une opération de novation, l'institution de la cession de la créance ou de l'*assignment* apparaissant inadéquate au plan théorique pour caractériser le transfert de la créance.[28]

Le contrat de prêt syndiqué ou le contrat de rééchelonnement vient parfois interdire le transfert des créances à des entités autres que des banques et des institutions financières.[29] Cela pose un problème lorsque l'acquéreur est une entreprise industrielle ou commerciale et si le contrat de prêt syndiqué ou le contrat de rééchelonnement n'exempte pas les opérations de capitalisation des dettes de l'application de cette limite à la transférabilité. On contournera alors la difficulté en organisant la transaction sous forme de sous-participation dans le prêt. Le contrat de prêt ou le contrat de rééchelonnement peut reconnaître expressément le droit de la banque créancière de céder des participations dans ses

---

de vente n'a pas été signifié et qu'il n'en a pas délivré copie au débiteur." L'art. 1690 du code civil français pose un principe similaire. L'auteur Wood souligne, quant à lui, que le droit français est plus sévère que le droit anglais pour ce qui concerne le formalisme entourant l'avis au débiteur de la cession de créance: Wood, *supra* note 14, aux pp. 341-42.

27 En *common law*, voir CHITTY, *supra* note 23, à la p. 897, FRIEDMAN, *supra* note 23, aux pp. 445-46, CORBIN, *supra* note 23, aux pp. 452-59, *Lounsbury Co. c. Duthie* [1957] R.C.S. 590, 9 D.L.R. (2d) 225, *Simpson and Ors c. Cousins* [1923] 1 D.L.R. 106 (C.A.I.P.E.); en droit civil, voir BAUDOIN, *supra* note 23, à la p. 555.

28 C'est d'ailleurs la position exprimée par RYAN, *supra* note 17, à la p. 40.

29 C'est le cas de l'*Accord de rééchelonnement des Philippines*, *supra* note 18, tel qu'il en ressort du libellé de l'art. 12.10 (b).

créances.[30] Le lien de droit initial entre le pays-débiteur et la banque subsiste intégralement, et cette dernière demeure le créancier nominal jusqu'à ce que la créance soit rachetée par la Banque centrale de l'État-débiteur.

L'acquéreur de la créance n'a pas de rapport de droit direct avec le débiteur. Le contrat de participation a toutefois pour effet de donner à l'acquéreur de la créance un droit opposable au créancier nominal quant aux paiements en intérêts et capital, bien qu'en matière d'intérêt, le taux prévu peut être différent du taux stipulé dans le contrat de prêt initial ou le contrat de rééchelonnement. Le contrat de participation transférera aussi à l'acquéreur de la créance les risques associés au prêt, ou à tout le moins une partie des risques qui y sont associés.[31]

B L'INCIDENCE DE LA RÉGLEMENTATION BANCAIRE SUR LES OPÉRATIONS DE CAPITALISATION DE DETTES COMMERCIALES

La réglementation bancaire nationale peut encourager ou dissuader une banque créancière de participer à une opération de capitalisation de dettes. Le rôle de la réglementation bancaire se situe à plusieurs niveaux, que l'on va présenter en se servant de l'exemple spécifique de la réglementation canadienne.[32]

I La réglementation bancaire et l'engagement de la banque à titre d'investisseur

Bien que cela ne soit pas le cas le plus fréquent, la banque créancière peut décider d'acquérir elle-même des prises de partici-

---

30 *Id.*, art. 12.10 (b) (IV).

31 Sur le contrat de sous-participation, voir RYAN, JR, *supra* note 17, C. CHANCE, "Developing a Secondary Market in Loan Assets," *International Financial Law Review*, octobre 1984, 22, DESJARDINS, *supra* note 17; une décision américaine, *Yale Express System Inc.* 245 F. Supp. 790 (NY Dist. Ct. 1965), et une décision française, *Bellat* c. *B.N.P.*, Gazette du Palais, 1975-2-727, sont venus confirmer qu'il n'y a pas de relation contractuelle s'établissant entre l'emprunteur et le sous-participant.

32 Au cours des dernières années les banques à charte canadiennes ont réduit sensiblement leur portefeuille de prêts aux pays en développement, notamment en vendant un volume important de ces prêts sur le marché secondaire et en ayant recours à la capitalisation de la dette. Voir BANQUE NATIONALE DU CANADA, *Rapport annuel*, 1991, 22, BANQUE SCOTIA, *Rapport annuel*, 1991, 40-41, BANQUE DE MONTRÉAL, *Rapport annuel*, 1991, 50-52, BANQUE CANADIENNE IMPÉRIALE DE COMMERCE, *Rapport annuel*, 1991, 35, BANQUE ROYALE DU CANADA, *Rapport annuel*, 1991, 13-14.

pation à l'étranger. Se pose alors la question de savoir si la réglementation nationale autorise une institution bancaire à faire de
telles acquisitions. Au Canada, l'article 472(4) de la nouvelle *Loi sur
les banques*[33] autorise explicitement les banques à charte canadiennes à acquérir des prises de participation dans les entreprises
étrangères si tant est que cela soit effectué dans le cadre d'un
programme de réaménagement de la dette extérieure. C'est là une
dérogation au principe général voulant qu'une banque canadienne
ne puisse acquérir des prises de participation dans une entreprise
industrielle ou commerciale.[34] C'est aussi une innovation par rapport à l'ancienne *Loi sur les banques*:[35] pour fonder la légalité d'une
opération de capitalisation des dettes engageant une banque à
charte canadienne à titre d'investisseur, on avait rien trouvé de
mieux que de s'en remettre à une interprétation *a contrario* de
l'ancien article 193(4) qui interdisait à une banque de "posséder
des actions conférant plus de dix pour cent de l'ensemble des votes
attachés aux actions en circulation d'une société canadienne." Il
était ainsi soutenu que la prohibition de l'ancien article 193(4) ne
visait que les prises de participation dans les entreprises canadiennes et ne couvrait pas les prises de participation dans les
sociétés étrangères.[36]

La participation d'une banque à titre d'investisseur est-elle
encouragée par les règles comptables et le cadre réglementaire
auxquels elle est soumise? Une récente ligne directrice du *Bureau
du surintendant des institutions financières du Canada*[37] demande aux
banques d'évaluer à leur juste valeur les prises de participation
acquises dans le cadre d'une opération de capitalisation des dettes,
et ce au jour où la transaction est conclue. La singularité de chaque

33 *Loi sur les banques et les opérations bancaires*, projet de loi C-19, adopté le 9
décembre 1991. 3ᵉ session, 34ᵉ législature (Canada), entrée en vigueur le 1er
juin 1992.

34 Ce principe général est caractérisé par une certaine dose de relativité puisque
les arts 10 (1) et 466 (1) de la *Loi sur les banques et les opérations bancaires*, *ibid.*,
autorisent une institution bancaire à détenir une prise de participation dans
une personne morale représentant 10 pour cent au moins des droits de votes
attachés à l'ensemble des actions en circulation de celle-ci et 25 pour cent ou
moins de l'avoir des actionnaires.

35 *Loi sur les banques*, L.R.C. (1985) c. B-1.

36 Entretien avec Maître François Bourassa, premier conseiller juridique, international et financement, Banque nationale du Canada, 17 juillet 1992.

37 Ligne directrice C-4 sur les prêts aux pays désignés, octobre 1990, révisée en
mars 1991 [ci-après *ligne directrice C-4*].

opération de capitalisation et surtout les doutes quant à la robustesse du marché secondaire ont amené le régulateur à ne pas retenir une évaluation fondée sur le cours du marché secondaire de la créance.[38] Dans son bulletin de mai 1988, l'*American Institute of Certified Public Accountants* propose notamment quatre facteurs pour déterminer la juste valeur des titres de participation:[39] (1) les transactions similaires entraînant le versement de sommes d'argent; (2) l'estimé des flux monétaires provenant des actions acquises ou des actifs reçus; (3) la valeur marchande de prises de participation similaires; (4) l'existence de restrictions de change affectant les dividendes, la vente des prises de participation ou le rapatriement du capital. Une banque à charte aurait donc une incitation comptable à participer à titre d'investisseur dans une opération de capitalisation de dettes si la juste valeur des actions acquises est supérieure au cours de la créance sur le marché secondaire ou à sa valeur comptable nette.

Finalement, il est à noter que la ligne directrice c-4 stipule que suite à un échange de dettes contre des participations entraînant une perte comptable pour la banque, celle-ci pourrait devoir reconsidérer "la suffisance du solde des provisions à l'égard des risque-pays."[40] Cet énoncé porte un effet dissuasif: la crainte de devoir réviser à la hausse les provisions à l'égard des risque-pays[41] pourrait, en effet, inciter une banque à renoncer à une opération de capitalisation des dettes entraînant l'inscription d'une perte comptable sur son bilan.

2   *La réglementation bancaire encourage-t-elle les banques à vendre leurs créances sur le marché secondaire?*

Comme on l'a déjà souligné, il est relativement peu fréquent qu'une banque s'engage à titre d'investisseur dans une opération

---

[38] Voir à ce sujet le Bulletin de l'AMERICAN INSTITUTE OF CERTIFIED PUBLIC ACCOUNTANTS, "Accounting for Foreign Debt Equity Swaps," Practice Bulletin 4, *I.C.P.A.*, (mai 1988) 4.

[39] *Id.*, 5.

[40] *Id.*, 6; on reprend ici la suggestion de l'ICPA: "Recognition of a Debt-Equity Swap Loss Should Be among the Factors to be Considered by Management in Its Periodic Assessment of the Adequacy of the Allowance for Loan Losses with Respect to Its Remaining Portfolio of Loans to Debtors in Financially Troubled Countries."

[41] D. CARREAU et J. Y. MARTIN, "La capitalisation des dettes commerciales: un moyen de réduction de l'endettement extérieur des États," (1990) 11 *Banque et Droit* 127, 134.

de capitalisation de dettes. La réglementation nationale n'y est pas toujours favorable et, surtout, les institutions financières n'ont pas toujours l'expertise dans la gestion d'entreprises industrielles et commerciales. Les banques jouent néanmoins un rôle capital dans le cas de figure où l'investisseur étranger est une entreprise commerciale ou industrielle indépendante puisqu'elles alimentent le marché secondaire à même leur portefeuille de créances sur les pays en voie de développement. Or les opérations de capitalisation des dettes seraient difficiles à organiser en l'absence d'un marché secondaire fonctionnel. La réglementation bancaire favorise donc la réalisation d'operations de capitalisation de dettes dans la mesure où elle encourage les banques à se départir de leurs créances sur le marché secondaire, ou à tout le moins si elle ne les dissuade pas d'agir de la sorte.

À ce titre, il faut examiner deux aspects de la réglementation bancaire: les exigences en matière de provisionnement et le traitement fiscal.

Le surintendant des institutions financières impose aux banques canadiennes de maintenir un niveau minimal de provisions représentant 35 pour cent des risques encourus dans quarante-cinq pays, considérés à risque par les autorités administratives canadiennes.[42] Toutes les banques canadiennes ont provisionné à des niveaux excédant ce seuil minimal de 35 pour cent.[43] Cette exigence réglementaire encourage les banques à liquider leurs titres de créance sur le marché secondaire. En effet, ces provisions étant exclues du capital réglementaire, le coût de financement associé aux créances sur les pays en difficulté est élevé du fait qu'on se trouve à immobiliser du capital en sus du capital réglementaire; la banque a donc intérêt à remplacer ces actifs par des liquidités ou des actifs plus sûrs. Par contre, le traitement fiscal n'encouragerait pas les banques à vendre leurs créances sur le marché secondaire. En effet, au moment où elle inscrit sa provision au bilan, la banque obtient une déduction fiscale pouvant aller jusqu'à 45 pour cent de la valeur nominale de la créance provisionnée.[44] La plus grande part du

---

[42] *Ligne directrice C-4*, *supra* note 37.

[43] J. HAY et N. PAUL, "Regulation and Taxation of Commercial Banks during the International Debt Crisis," *Bank Technical Paper* 158 (octobre 1991), 83.

[44] *Id.*, 85; art. 8000, *Règlement de l'impôt sur le revenu*, reproduit dans CCH Canadienne limitée, *Loi de l'impôt sur le revenu du Canada et règlements*, 21e édition, 1992 (Codification des règlements du Canada, 1978, c. 945, tels que modi-

bénéfice fiscal est donc obtenue au moment de l'inscription de la provision au bilan et non pas au moment où la créance est vendue sur le marché secondaire. On se retrouve aussi dans une situation où il y a une incitation fiscale significative à provisionner, mais peu d'incitation fiscale à se départir des créances sur le marché secondaire.

C LE CONTRAT DE RÉÉCHELONNEMENT

Les opérations de capitalisation des dettes doivent être conformes aux contrats de prêt syndiqué et aux contrats de rééchelonnement. Le principe du traitement égal des créanciers s'est notamment traduit par l'élaboration dans ces instruments de clauses dont l'application stricte ferait obstacle à la capitalisation des dettes. Une autre difficulté est posée par les restrictions contractuelles à la cessibilité des créances prévues dans la plupart des contrats de rééchelonnement. Dans cette partie, on examinera comment se déploient ces problèmes et les techniques employées pour les contourner.

1 *La capitalisation des dettes et le principe du traitement égal des créanciers*

Même si elle évolue dans la dynamique collective d'un prêt syndiqué ou d'un contrat de rééchelonnement, une institution prêteuse cherche tout naturellement à promouvoir ses intérêts propres. Afin de réduire la tentation du resquillage et de dissuader les créanciers de se livrer une concurrence contreproductive et stérile pour l'ensemble d'entre eux, le prêt syndiqué ou le contrat de rééchelonnement typique contient une série de dispositions dont l'objet est d'assurer un traitement égal des créanciers. Le principe du traitement égal des créanciers appartient à la charpente des prêts syndiqués et des contrats de rééchelonnement de la dette extérieure. Le plan Brady,[45] axé autour d'une stratégie de

---

fiés); voir aussi art. 20(1) (l) (ii) A, *Loi de l'impôt sur le revenu*, reproduite dans *Loi de l'impôt sur le revenu du Canada et règlements, id.* (chap. 63, S.C. 1970-71-72 telle que modifiée).

[45] Le plan Brady, du nom du secrétaire au trésor américain, met l'accent sur la réduction du fardeau de la dette des pays en développement et sur le déploiement de mesures visant la stimulation de leur croissance; les grands axiomes du plan Brady furent annoncés dans un discours prononcé le 10 mars 1989. Sur le plan Brady, voir L. C. BUCHHEIT, *The Background to Brady's Initiative* (avril

réduction de l'endettement, n'altère pas l'essence de ce principe même s'il en atténue parfois la rigueur ou le subordonne au déploiement d'initiatives innovatrices visant la réduction de la dette. Ebenroth et Woggan[46] dénombrent quatre types de clauses contractuelles mettant en oeuvre le principe du traitement égal des créanciers. Il s'agit de la clause négative (*negative pledge clause*), de la clause *pari passu* (*pari passu clause*), de la clause de remboursements anticipés obligatoires (*mandatory prepayment clause*) et de la clause de partage (*sharing clause*). Les tribunaux ne se sont jamais prononcés sur la compatibilité de ces clauses avec les programmes de capitalisation des dettes. Il reste que des aspects d'une opération typique heurtent, ne serait-ce qu'au plan théorique, certaines valeurs enchassées dans ces clauses. La prudence la plus élémentaire commandait d'insérer la possibilité de recourir à ce type d'opération dans la logique interne du contrat de rééchelonnement, ce qui a d'ailleurs été fait dans la plupart des accords de rééchelonnement négociés au courant des années quatre-vingt. On examinera maintenant les clauses mettant en oeuvre le principe du traitement égal des créanciers, le rapport que chacune d'entre elles entretient avec la capitalisation des dettes et les mécanismes élaborés dans les accords de rééchelonnement en vue de se prémunir contre toute attaque quant à la légalité d'opérations de capitalisation des dettes.

(a)   La clause négative

La clause négative est insérée dans les contrats de rééchelonnements.[47] Elle interdit au débiteur de créer des sûretés tant que subsiste sa dette. Une variante consiste à n'autoriser la constitution

---

1990) *International Financial Law Review* 29. L'Accord de rééchelonnement du Mexique du 4 février 1990 a été le premier accord de rééchelonnement conclu sous l'égide du Plan Brady; voir à ce sujet H. SCHMIEGELOW, "The Mexican Debt Agreement: A Model for Solving the International Debt Problem?", *Aussenpolitik* III/90, 291-96; d'autres pays comme les Philippines et le Vénézuéla ont emboîté le pas et conclu des accords de rééchelonnement de type Brady.

46 EBENROTH, C. T. et R. WOGGON, "The Development of the Equal Treatment Principle in the International Debt Crisis," (1991) 12 *Michigan Journal of International Law* 690, 695-709.

47 *Id.*, 700-1; sur la clause négative, voir L. C. BUCHHEIT, "Negative Pledge Clauses: The Games People Play," (juin 1990) *International Financial Law Review* 10; pour un exemple de clause négative, voir les arts 8.03 et 8.04 de *l'Accord de rééchelonnement des Philippines, supra* note 18.

de sûretés au bénéfice d'autres créanciers que dans la mesure où les banques participant au rééchelonnement obtiennent les mêmes sûretés. Le contrat de rééchelonnement typique contient cependant une liste limitative d'exceptions, car soumettre l'État-débiteur à une prohibition absolue de constituer des sûretés pourrait empêcher ou compliquer la conclusion de transactions commerciales pourtant bénéfiques à son économie.

Puisque la capitalisation des dettes n'a pas pour conséquence de constituer une sûreté au bénéfice du détenteur de la créance convertie, il n'y a pas lieu de se préoccuper de l'arrimage entre la clause négative et le mécanisme de capitalisation des dettes.

(b) La clause *pari passu*

La clause *pari passu* marque le principe du traitement égal des créanciers dans le champ des créances non garanties puisqu'elle protège les banques prêteuses contre un traitement défavorable de leurs créances par rapport aux autres créances non-garanties. L'objectif est d'éviter que les créances des banques prêteuses soient subordonnées aux autres créances non-garanties. La clause *pari passu* typique,[48] présente tant dans le contrat de prêt syndiqué que dans le contrat de rééchelonnement, empêchera un état-débiteur d'attribuer de manière formelle des priorités différentes aux créances non-garanties libellées en devise étrangères, ou encore d'assigner des sources de revenu en devises étrangères au service de dettes spécifiques.

L'égalité de traitement prescrite par la clause *pari passu* ne serait pas absolue. Ebenroth et Woggon relèvent ainsi quatre types de traitement différentiel qui ne transgresseraient pas la clause *pari passu*. D'abord, un état débiteur pourrait rendre inadmissible à son programme de capitalisation des dettes des créanciers ayant refusé de participer à un rééchelonnement de la dette[49] ou d'avancer de nouveaux crédits. Un traitement différentiel découle aussi de l'octroi par des tierces parties de sûretés au bénéfice de créanciers individuels, un tel type de sureté se situant, par ailleurs hors de la portée de la clause négative. En troisième lieu, l'état débiteur

---

48 Sur la clause *pari passu*, voir L. C. BUCHHEIT, "The Pari Passu Clause *Sub Specie Aeternitatis*," (décembre 1991) *International Financial Law Review* 11; pour un exemple de clause *pari passu*, voir l'art. 7, 01 (f) de l'*Accord de rééchelonnement des philippines*, *supra* note 18.

49 Le Mexique a fait de telles menaces, en 1987, M. J. TUCKER, "Debt-for-Equity Swaps in Mexico," (1988) 23 *Texas International Law Journal* 443, 452.

pourra accorder la priorité au remboursement des créanciers exerçant une option de sortie, dans le cadre d'un accord de rééchelonnement.

Finalement, toute entreprise de rééchelonnement introduira une différentiation de traitement entre les créances soumises à l'accord de rééchelonnement et celles dont les modalités de remboursement demeurent gouvernés par les conventions de prêts originales.

La clause *pari passu* affecte-t-elle la capacité d'un État-débiteur de mettre en place un programme de capitalisation des dettes? Certains estiment que la portée de cette clause est limitée et que son effet se limite à empêcher l'État-débiteur d'instituer un système de priorités formelles entre les créances non garanties libellées en devises étrangères. Des commentateurs notent ainsi que "the clause has not achieved any practical significance in the management of restructurings to date."[50] Suivant cette interprétation, la clause *pari passu* n'introduirait donc pas de contrainte significative vis-à-vis la capitalisation des dettes. Par contre, une interprétation large de la clause *pari passu* empêcherait un État-débiteur de capitaliser les dettes d'un créancier non garanti n'ayant pas adhéré au contrat de rééchelonnement ou ne faisant pas partie du syndicat bancaire. Pour évacuer ces hésitations sur la portée réelle de la clause *pari passu*, certains accords de rééchelonnement exempteront de l'application de la clause les capitalisations de dettes.

(c)   La clause de partage

Avec la clause de remboursements anticipés obligatoires, la clause de partage est l'élément du prêt syndiqué ou du contrat de rééchelonnement qui a l'incidence la plus significative sur le mécanisme de la capitalisation des dettes. Toutes deux justifient l'élaboration d'un régime particulier pour la capitalisation des dettes dans l'accord de rééchelonnement.

La clause de partage se retrouve autant dans le contrat de prêt syndiqué que dans l'accord de rééchelonnement. En vertu de cette disposition, les remboursements en intérêts et capital sont distribués aux institutions participantes au prorata de leur créance. La clause s'est déployée sous plusieurs géométries. Suivant un modèle que l'on retrouve surtout dans la première vague de prêts syndiqués, une des banques prêteuses agit à titre d'agent collecteur et

50 EBENROTH et WOGGON, *supra* note 46, à la p. 709.

distribue les sommes reçues du débiteur aux membres du syndicat bancaire. Tout excédent reçu directement par l'un d'entre eux est remis à l'agent collecteur, qui s'occupe ensuite d'en faire une distribution proportionnelle. Une autre formulation de la clause de partage prévoit que le partage de l'excédent s'effectue directement entre les institutions prêteuses sans le concours d'un agent collecteur; la banque ayant reçu un remboursement excédant sa part rééquilibre la situation en achetant des participations aux créances détenues par les autres membres du syndicat bancaire.[51] Les versions plus récentes de la clause de partage couvrent non seulement les paiements volontaires de l'État-débiteur en devises étrangères mais aussi d'autres méthodes de remboursement comme la compensation, le paiement résultant d'une poursuite judiciaire ou l'exécution d'une sûreté.[52] Enfin, lorsque la clause de partage fait partie d'un accord de rééchelonnement consolidant plusieurs prêts syndiqués et prêts uniques, les pouvoirs et fonctions des agents collecteurs sont centralisés et transférés à une seule institution financière.[53]

La capitalisation des dettes déclenche-t-elle le mécanisme de partage incorporé dans un prêt syndiqué ou un contrat de rééchelonnement? La question est controversée.[54] Comme l'écrivent Ebenroth et Woggon, "there is disagreement among the banks about the significance of a sharing clause when the debtor does not make payment in the agreed currency, but secures the acquiescence of single creditor banks in payment in the local currency, for example, in connection with debt-equity swaps, debt-for-products swaps or debt-for-bonds swaps."[55] La capitalisation des dettes suppose, en effet, que la banque centrale rachète en monnaie locale la créance. Or il est possible que la clause de partage force le partage proportionnel du versement d'une somme en monnaie locale au bénéfice d'un seul créancier. Par ailleurs, le fait que la créance ait été cédée à une tierce partie à la convention de prêt syndiqué ou à l'accord de rééchelonnement ne met pas en échec la clause de partage puisque, en règle générale, le mécanisme de transfert de créance qui y

---

[51] C'est le mécanisme qui a été retenu dans l'*Accord de rééchelonnement des Philippines, supra* note 18, art. 5.03.

[52] *Ibid.*

[53] Dans le contrat de rééchelonnement, cette institution est identifiée comme la "servicing bank."

[54] CARREAU, MARTIN, *supra* note 41, à la p. 132.

[55] EBENROTH et WOGGON, *supra* note 46, à la p. 697.

est prévu impose au cessionnaire les obligations assumées par le cédant tant vis-à-vis le débiteur qu'à l'égard des autres créanciers.[56]

Afin d'éviter l'incertitude juridique, l'usage est d'insérer dans l'Accord de rééchelonnement des dispositions prévoyant expressément la possibilité pour l'État-débiteur de capitaliser ses dettes et soustrayant ce type d'opération de l'application de la clause de partage.[57]

(d) La clause de remboursement anticipé obligatoire

La clause de remboursement anticipé obligatoire (*mandatory prepayment clause*) a été élaborée à la faveur des entreprises de rééchelonnement de la dette et a été incorporée dans la plupart de ces accords.[58] En vertu de cette clause, le débiteur remboursant prématurément des créances soustraites à l'application de l'accord de rééchelonnement se verra imposer l'obligation d'étendre le remboursement par anticipation aux créanciers participant au rééchelonnement. Ce remboursement anticipé et celui ayant été effectué au bénéfice des créanciers évoluant à l'extérieur de l'accord de rééchelonnement devront être dans la même proportion du principal de la créance.

La clause de remboursement anticipé obligatoire se situe ainsi dans le prolongement de la clause de partage, toutes deux convergeant vers l'objectif d'un partage équitable des paiements en principal et intérêts entre les créanciers. Mais elle présente aussi des similitudes avec la clause *pari passu* du fait qu'elle produit indirectement des effets juridiques sur le créancier extérieur à l'accord de rééchelonnement, en contraignant le comportement du débiteur à son égard.

---

56 À titre d'exemple, voir l'art. 12.10(b) de l'*Accord de rééchelonnement des Philippines, supra* note 18; on note cependant qu'en vertu de cette clause, le créancier ne peut transférer ses droits et obligations découlant du contrat de rééchelonnement qu'à une autre banque ou institution financière.

57 L. C. BUCHHEIT, "Debt Reduction Techniques: The Capitalization of Sovereign Debt, An Introduction," dans *Latin American Sovereign Debt Management: Legal and Regulatory Aspects* 98-111, 101 (Washington, D.C., 1990); à titre d'exemple, voir art. 5.11(f) de l'*Accord de rééchelonnement du Mexique*, 19 août 1985, reproduit en annexe dans EBENROTH et WOGGON, *supra* note 46; voir aussi *Accord de rééchelonnement des philippines, supra* note 18, aux arts 5.03(1) et 5.11; dans l'accord philippin, la technique utilisée a consisté à exclure du champ de la clause de partage les paiements effectués en devise locale.

58 À titre d'exemple, voir art. 4.02 de l'*Accord de rééchelonnement des philippines, supra* note 18.

Dans la plupart des cas, l'État-debiteur et les institutions financières participant au rééchelonnement voudront favoriser la capitalisation de dettes qui en sont exclues. Il importe alors d'aménager la clause de remboursements anticipés obligatoires de manière à ce qu'elle ne soit pas déclenchée par une opération de capitalisation portant sur des dettes non rééchelonnées. Une technique efficace et largement répandue consiste à restreindre la portée de la clause aux remboursements anticipés effectués en devise étrangère; la capitalisation des dettes jouit alors d'une immunité, l'opération étant centrée autour d'un rachat de la créance en monnaie locale.[59]

(e)   Les restrictions sur le rapatriement des dividendes et du capital

On constate donc que la mise en place d'un mécanisme de capitalisation des dettes nécessite une relativisation du principe du traitement égal des créanciers. Celle-ci se formule d'abord en termes d'un régime d'exception à l'application de la clause de partage, de la clause des remboursements anticipés obligatoires et de la clause *pari passu*, clauses présentes dans l'accord de rééchelonnement typique. L'affirmation de la primauté du principe du traitement égal des créanciers amènera, toutefois, les parties à l'accord de rééchelonnement à imposer des restrictions sur le transfert du capital-actions issu de la conversion des dettes de même que sur le rapatriement des profits découlant de l'investissement.[60] Ces restrictions couvriront un terme ayant un rapport direct avec l'échéance prévue pour la créance échangée. L'idée générale est d'assurer une certaine égalité entre l'investisseur étranger et le créancier en ne faisant pas bénéficier ce dernier d'une séquence de flux en devises étrangères systématiquement plus avantageuse que celle qui aurait été produite par la créance, n'eut été de sa conversion.

---

59 BUCHHEIT, *supra* note 57, aux pp. 104-5; à titre d'exemple, voir l'art. 4.02 (b) de l'*Accord de rééchelonnement des Philippines*, *supra* note 18; une autre technique est utilisée dans l'*Accord de rééchelonnement du Mexique*, 19 août 1985: en effet, l'art. 5.11 (f) prévoit expressément que la clause de remboursements anticipés ne s'applique pas à la capitalisation des dettes.

60 D. ASIEDU-AKROFI, ''A Comparative Analysis of Debt Equity Swap Programs in Five Major Debtor Countries'' (1988-89) 12 *Hastings Int'l & Comp. L. Rev.* 537, 541; CARREAU et MARTIN, *supra* note 41, à la p. 131.

2 La cessibilité des créances

Comme on l'a mentionné plus haut, certains contrats de prêt syndiqués et certains accords de rééchelonnement empêchent en termes formels une banque participante de faire une cession de créance à une entité autre qu'une banque ou une institution financière. L'État-débiteur accorde de l'importance à cette restriction du fait que l'entrée en scène de créanciers non bancaires est susceptible de compliquer la conclusion d'un accord de rééchelonnement couplé à l'octroi de nouveaux crédits. Un créancier non bancaire ponctuel aura, en effet, davantage de réticences à avancer de nouveaux fonds qu'une institution financière lourdement impliquée dans le financement de la dette d'un État, cette dernière risquant gros dans l'éventualité où l'insuffisance de fonds provoquerait un effondrement financier et économique de l'État-débiteur.

La clause limitant la cessibilité des créances produit cependant un effet pervers: elle réduit considérablement la gamme des opérations de capitalisation des dettes pouvant être réalisées puisque le plus souvent, c'est une entreprise industrielle ou commerciale qui achètera une créance sur le marché secondaire afin de la convertir en prise de participation. On corrigera la situation en prévoyant dans l'accord de rééchelonnement un régime d'exception pour la cession de créances à des entités non-financières pour des fins de capitalisation de dettes.[61] Alternativement, l'institution financière pourra céder à l'investisseur une participation dans sa créance. Rappelons que ce contrat crée exclusivement des obligations pour la banque et l'investisseur; il est inopposable à l'État-débiteur et la banque demeure le créancier nominal jusqu'à ce que la créance soit rachetée par la Banque centrale de l'État-débiteur.[62]

II LE CADRE RÉGLEMENTAIRE DE L'ÉTAT-DÉBITEUR

Le droit interne de l'État-débiteur gouvernera deux volets importants d'une opération de capitalisation des dettes, soit le rachat de la créance et l'investissement dans la compagnie locale. Ces transactions sont documentées dans un contrat d'échange. Y sont parties l'entreprise locale, le régulateur chargé d'administrer le programme de capitalisation des dettes dans l'État-débiteur et le créan-

[61] M. CHAMBERLIN, M. GRUSSON et P. WELTCHEK, "Debt Reduction Techniques: Sovereign Debt Exchanges," dans *Latin American Sovereign Debt Management: Legal and Regulatory Aspects* 111-73, 128 (Washington, D.C., 1990).
[62] *Supra*, à la section I-A-2.

cier nominal.[63] Les paramètres de ce contrat d'échange dépendront autant des caractéristiques du cadre réglementaire de l'État-débiteur que de la volonté des parties. Il convient donc d'examiner les principaux déterminants de ce cadre réglementaire, soit les objectifs que se donnent le concepteur du cadre et les contraintes auxquelles il est soumis.

A LES OBJECTIFS DU CADRE RÉGLEMENTAIRE NATIONAL

La capitalisation des dettes se distingue des autres techniques de rééchelonnement et de réduction de l'endettement en ce qu'elle est non seulement un mode de gestion de la dette mais aussi un outil de politique économique. Ainsi, l'aménagement du cadre réglementaire mis en place par l'État-débiteur reflétera des arbitrages entre de multiples objectifs, parfois divergents: réduction du fardeau de la dette, certes, mais aussi apport d'investissements étrangers directs, appropriation d'une partie de la décote du marché secondaire, soutien aux programmes de privatisation d'entreprises d'État, incitation au rapatriement des capitaux fugitifs.

1 Les objectifs primaires

(a) La réduction de l'endettement

Au premier chef, l'État-débiteur installe un programme de capitalisation des dettes pour réduire son endettement extérieur. L'assertion mérite cependant une nuance. Bien que la capitalisation des dettes atténue la pression du service de la dette sur les finances publiques, elle n'en modifie pas pour autant la balance des paiements au bénéfice de l'État-débiteur. En effet, la capitalisation des dettes s'articule autour de l'échange d'une dette assortie d'un service fixe d'obligations de remboursement à échoir contre un titre dont la valeur marchande et le rendement dépendent de la rentabilité de l'investissement qu'il sert à financer. Abstraction faite des rentrées de devises que peut amener un investissement dans des activités d'exportation ou de substitution des importation, la

63 Le créancier nominal sera la banque créancière si la transaction sur le marché secondaire a été organisée sous forme de participation; ce sera l'investisseur étranger s'il y a eu transfert de créance et novation. Sur le contrat d'échange, voir CHAMBERLIN, GRUSON et WELTCHEK, *supra* note 61, aux pp. 132-33 et sur le cas spécifique du programme mexicain de 1986-87, voir O. ESTRELLA, "Making the Most of Mexican Debt/Equity Swaps," (octobre 1987) *International Financial Law Review* 35, 36.

capitalisation des dettes pourrait, au moins en théorie, aggraver la position débitrice nette du pays si les versements à l'étranger de dividendes ou de capitaux associés aux prises de participation dépassent les remboursements d'intérêts et de principal relatifs à la dette convertie.[64] Si la capitalisation des dettes n'entraîne pas automatiquement et obligatoirement un redressement de la balance des paiements, il demeure néanmoins difficile d'évaluer si globalement la capitalisation des dettes a un effet positif ou négatif sur la balance des paiements.[65] Aussi serait-il plus juste d'affirmer que la capitalisation de la dette n'entraîne pas tant une réduction de la charge que doit supporter le pays-débiteur qu'un transfert sur l'investisseur étranger du risque que l'emprunteur n'honore pas ses obligations internationales.[66]

(b)   La promotion d'investissements étrangers

Le deuxième objectif d'importance sous-jacent à un programme de capitalisation des dettes est la promotion d'investissements étrangers s'inscrivant dans le cadre de la politique industrielle de l'État-débiteur. D'une part, l'offre de capital étranger est stimulée par la subvention qu'accorde indirectement l'État-débiteur à l'investisseur étranger lorsqu'il lui rachète la créance pour une somme d'argent plus élevée que le prix d'acquisition de cette dernière sur le marché secondaire. D'autre part, la demande de capital étranger fait l'objet d'un renforcement dans le pays-débiteur. Dans le cas de figure typique, la dette extérieure élevée conduit le gouvernement à se tourner vers le marché des capitaux locaux pour financer son déficit. Il s'ensuit une raréfaction du capital disponible pour financer les investissements du secteur

64 Il est vrai, cependant, que dans sa réglementation des opérations de capitalisation des dettes, l'État-débiteur impose normalement des restrictions sur le rapatriement des dividendes et du capital; il se dote ainsi d'un levier significatif pour gérer l'impact de la capitalisation des dettes sur la balance des paiements. *Supra* à la section I-C-1-(e).

65 *Les banques transnationales et les conversions de la dette en prises de participations*, Rapport du Secrétaire général, New York, 1991. E/C.10/1991/5, 22.

66 M. BLACKWELL et S. NOCERA, "Les effets de la conversion de la dette en prises de participation: qu'entend-on par conversion de dettes en prises de participation, quels en sont les bénéficiaires, en quoi l'économie du pays emprunteur en est-elle affectée?" (1988, n° 2) 25 *Fin. & Dev.* 15, 16; pour une démonstration plus étoffée sur ce point, voir BLACKWELL et NOCERA, *supra* note 7, aux pp. 23-27.

privé local, une augmentation des taux d'intérêt et un accroissement de ses coûts de financement. Dans ce contexte, le capital
étranger issu d'une opération de capitalisation des dettes apparaî-
tra pour l'entreprise locale comme une source de financement
intéressante.

Les programmes de capitalisation des dettes attirent-ils de nouveaux investissements? Ou au contraire, ne font-ils que subventionner des investissements qui de toute façon auraient été effectués?
C'est toute la controverse de la complémentarité des investissements suscités par la capitalisation des dettes. Une récente analyse
de la *Commission des sociétés transnationales du Conseil économique et
social des Nations-Unies* établit une corrélation entre le niveau des
investissements étrangers directs et la mise en place de programmes
de capitalisation des dettes au Chili, au Mexique, en Argentine et
aux Philippines.[67] La Commission est d'avis que "les programmes
d'échanges de créances contre des actifs ont déterminé certains
apports d'investissements étrangers directs qui n'auraient pas été
effectués en leur absence."[68] On ajoute cependant que cet apport
est difficile à chiffrer avec précision.

L'État-débiteur conçoit le cadre réglementaire en fonction de
l'objectif primaire à placer en priorité. Ce choix est politique. C'est
ainsi que la réduction de la dette extérieure était l'objectif prioritaire du programme chilien de capitalisation des dettes.[69] En revan-

---

67 *Supra* note 65, à la p. 15; sur cette controverse de la complémentarité des
investissements effectués via le mécanisme de la capitalisation des dettes, voir J.
BERGSMAN et W. EDISIS, *Debt-Equity Swaps and Foreign Direct Investment in Latin
America*, International Finance Corporation, Discussion Paper 2, Washington,
1988, 7-11.

68 *Id.*, 16.

69 Le programme chilien prévoit trois mécanismes de capitalisation des dettes: le
mécanisme prévu au chapitre XVIII du *Compendio de Cambios Internationales,
Banco Central de Chile, Compendio de Cambios Internationales*, Acuerdo n°
1-647-01-850514, D.O. (15 mai 1985), [ci-après le chapitre XVIII]; le
mécanisme prévu au chapitre XIX du *Compendio de Cambios Internationales,
Banco Central de Chile, Compendio de Cambios Internationales*, Acuerdo N°
1-647-02-850514, D.O. (15 mai 1985), [ci-après le chapitre XIX]; le
mécanisme prévu dans le *Decreto Ley [D.L.] 600*, tel que modifié à D.L. 1.748,
art. 1(e), D.O. (18 mars 1977), [ci-après le Décret 600]. Ces textes sont
reproduits et commentés dans *World Bank: Report on Chilean Debt Conversion with
Chilean Rules on Investment with Foreign Debt Instruments and Provision in a Debt
Restructuring Agreement for Such Investments*, 24 septembre 1986, (1987) 26
I.L.M. 819; voir aussi M. L. WILLIAMSON, *Chile's Debt Conversion Program: Its
Promises and Limitations*, (1991) 27 *Stanford Journal of International Law* 437.

che des déclarations de haut-fonctionnaires mexicains laissent croire que le programme mis en oeuvre dans la foulée des accords de rééchelonnement de 1985 privilégiait plutôt l'objectif de la promotion des investissements étrangers complémentaires.[70]

2 *Les objectifs secondaires*

Il se trouve un certain nombre d'objectifs accessoires aux objectifs primaires de la réduction du fardeau de la dette et de la stimulation des investissements étrangers.

Via le cadre réglementaire, l'État-débiteur peut chercher à profiter de la décote dont ses créances font l'objet sur le marché secondaire. Il s'agira pour la Banque centrale de l'État-débiteur de racheter la créance pour un montant inférieur à sa valeur nominale. Il importe que les concepteurs du cadre réglementaire déterminent soigneusement le rapport qu'ils cherchent à établir entre l'objectif de promouvoir les investissements étrangers et celui de l'appropriation de la décote par l'État-débiteur. En effet, cette dernière amenuise l'écart entre le prix de la créance sur le marché secondaire et sa valeur de rachat en devise locale, réduisant d'autant l'intérêt pour l'investisseur étranger. La récupération par l'État-débiteur d'un segment important de la décote pourrait donc se réaliser au détriment de la complémentarité des investissements étrangers.

Plusieurs techniques sont utilisées pour atteindre cet objectif d'appropriation de la décote. D'abord, le partage de la décote peut faire l'objet de négociations entre les autorités de l'État-debiteur et l'investisseur étranger.[71] Une alternative consiste à laisser l'autorité administrative fixer préalablement le taux de la décote récupérée, ce dernier étant fixé en fonction de la nature de l'investissement. La gamme des décotes est alors employée pour orienter les investissements et le mécanisme d'appropriation de la décote s'insère ainsi

---

[70] F. C. B. BRACHER, A. MENDES, L. A. FONCERRADA PASCAL et A. R. SANCHEZ GONZALER, "Debt Reduction Techniques: Debt to Equity Programs in Brazil and Mexico," dans *Latin American Sovereign Debt Management: Legal and Regulatory Aspects* 173-86, 182 (Washington, D.C. 1990). M. J. TUCKER, "Debt-for-Equity Swaps in Mexico" (1988) 23 *Texas International Law Journal* 443, 460.

[71] Le cas typique est le chapitre XIX du programme chilien: F. LARRAIN et A. VELACO, "Can Swaps Solve the Debt Crisis?: Lessons from the Chilian Experience," *Princeton Studies in International Finance* (N° 69, novembre 1990).

dans le cadre de la politique industrielle de l'État.[72] Le gouvernement peut aussi utiliser la fiscalité et taxer la différence entre le prix d'achat et le prix de rachat de sa dette.[73] Mais c'est la technique de la vente aux enchères qui au fil de l'expérience semble produire les meilleurs résultats, du moins en regard de l'objectif d'appropriation de la décote.[74] Cette technique subordonne au jeu des forces du marché le découpage de la décote. Des quotas périodiques de créances à capitaliser sont soumis à un système de ventes aux enchères. En théorie, ce système devrait retenir les projets d'investissements présentant les rendements les plus élevés; il devrait aussi procurer à l'État une portion raisonnable de la décote, l'hypothèse étant qu'un investisseur pressentant un rendement élevé sur son investissement sera disposé à offrir davantage pour obtenir sa part du quota. Il présente cependant l'inconvénient de peu contribuer à la complémentarité des investissements. Un État-débiteur pour qui l'objectif d'accroître les investissements étrangers dans des secteurs jugés clés prime sur l'objectif d'augmenter ses revenus par l'appropriation de la décote va sans doute privilégier un processus décisionnel administratif plutôt qu'un mécanisme d'enchères en ce qui a trait à l'octroi des créances capitalisables.

La capitalisation des dettes a aussi été utilisée pour faciliter la privatisation des entreprises publiques.[75] Évidemment, il doit y avoir au préalable une volonté politique de mettre en chantier une entreprise de privatisation. L'échange de la dette contre des prises de participation dans des entreprises publiques présente l'avantage

---

[72] Le cas typique est le programme mexicain de 1986-87 où la décote récupérée variait entre 0% et 25% de la valeur nominale de la créance, dépendant du type d'investissement effectué. Voir à ce sujet D. H. BRILL, ''Debt-Equity Swaps as a New Mode of Debt Restructuring,'' *Internationale Verschulden und wirtschaftliche Entwicklung aus rechtlicher Sicht*, Baden-Baden, 1988, 23, 30.

[73] BERGSMAN et EDISIS, *supra* note 67, à la p. 23.

[74] C'est là l'opinion exprimée par BERGSMAN et EDISIS, *id.*, 20; les programmes argentin, brésilien (suspendu en 1989), vénézuélien (depuis 1990) de même que le programme mexicain de 1990 et le chapitre XVIII du programme chilien attribuent les quotas par l'entremise d'un système d'enchères. Voir à ce sujet *Les banques transnationales et les conversions de la dette en prises de participation*, *supra* note 65, à la p. 11.

[75] Ainsi le programme mexicain de 1990 limite le mécanisme de la capitalisation des dettes aux investissements dans les projets d'infrastructure et aux prises de participation dans les entreprises privatisées: R. J. F. TORTES-LANDA, ''Report on the New Rules for the Operation of Debt-Equity Swaps in Mexico,'' (1991) 25 International Lawyer 733, 735.

de ne pas attiser l'inflation, aucune liquidité n'étant introduite dans le système monétaire local.

Finalement, en prévoyant la participation de ses ressortissants au programme de capitalisation des dettes, l'État-débiteur encourage-rait ces derniers à rapatrier leurs capitaux et contribuerait ainsi à freiner ou inverser les dynamiques de fuite des capitaux.[76]

B   LES CONTRAINTES À CONSIDÉRER DANS L'ÉLABORATION DU
     CADRE RÉGLEMENTAIRE

I   *Le potentiel inflationniste de la capitalisation des dettes*

Le financement du rachat des créances extérieures via l'émission de monnaie locale par la banque centrale se solde par une augmen-tation de la masse monétaire et des pressions inflationnistes. Un effet similaire résulte d'opérations de capitalisation de dettes d'entreprises du secteur public ou privé financées au moyen des prêts en monnaie locale consentis par la banque centrale. Blackwell et Wocera[77] estimaient qu'à la fin de 1986, la capitalisation de 5 pour cent de l'encours de la dette commerciale aurait entraîné une augmentation potentielle de la masse monétaire de 35.8 pour cent en Argentine, 32.8 pour cent au Brésil, 58.5 pour cent au Mexique et 33.6 pour cent aux Philippines. Le caractère inflationniste du mécanisme de la capitalisation des dettes pose donc une limite structurelle à son emploi dans une entreprise de réduction de l'endettement extérieur, limite dont on doit particulièrement tenir compte dans la conception du cadre réglementaire lorsque des objectifs quantitatifs ont été fixés dans le cadre de programmes de stabilisation du *Fonds monétaire international* eu égard au taux d'inflation et à la masse monétaire.[78]

On comprendra aisément la sensibilité des États-débiteur au risque que la capitalisation des dettes accentue la spirale inflation-niste, plusieurs d'entre eux étant déjà aux prises avec des taux

---

[76] On estime à environ 385 millions de dollars U.S. le capital privé à l'étranger qui a été rapatrié au Chili entre 1985 et 1987 par le biais des programmes de capitalisation de la dette. Voir D. ASIEDU-AKROFI, "A Comparative Analysis of Debt Equity Swap Programs in Five Major Debtor Countries," (1988-89) 12 *Hastings Int'l & Comp. L. Rev.* 537, 569. Par ailleurs, le FMI estimait à 250 milliards de dollars U.S. la fuite des capitaux dont auraient été victimes les pays en voie de développement de 1979 à 1985: *DEBT-EQUITY CONVERSIONS*, *supra* note 3, à la p. 37.

[77] BLACKWELL et NOCERA, *supra* note 66, à la p. 16.

[78] CARREAU et MARTIN, *supra* note 41, à la p. 129.

d'inflation très élevés. Les répercussions négatives de la capitalisation des dettes sur la masse monétaire ont d'ailleurs été invoquées par le Mexique pour justifier la suspension de son programme en novembre 1987.[79] Au Brésil, le programme de capitalisation des dettes a été interrompu en 1989, notamment par crainte qu'il exacerbe le climat hyperinflationniste existant.[80]

Ce ne sont cependant pas toutes les opérations de capitalisation des dettes qui engendrent des pressions inflationnistes. La masse monétaire ne sera pas affectée par un échange de la dette extérieure d'une entreprise privée contre une prise de participation. De même, la conversion de créances extérieures effectuées dans le cadre d'un plan de privatisation d'un entreprise d'État n'introduit pas de liquidité dans le système monétaire domestique et, par conséquent, n'entraîne pas un contrecoup inflationniste.

Diverses techniques sont employées pour réduire, voire neutraliser l'effet inflationniste de la capitalisation des dettes. Au Chili, par exemple, les chapitres XVIII et XIX du *Compendio de Cambios Internationales* prévoient que les créances extérieures de la Banque centrale sont échangées contre des obligations à long terme de l'État. L'investisseur peut capitaliser directement l'entreprise locale avec ces titres; plus fréquemment, il finance sa prise de participation en liquidant les titres sur les marchés secondaires locaux. Le procédé ne gonfle pas la masse monétaire et n'engendre pas d'inflation. Il présuppose, toutefois, que le marché financier intérieur soit assez développé pour absorber les émissions d'obligations publiques à long terme. La technique n'est pas sans comporter des inconvénients: les titres gouvernementaux font concurrence avec les besoins d'emprunt à long terme du secteur privé, ce qui se traduit par une éviction de l'investissement privé et une hausse des taux d'intérêt; de plus, le budget de l'État est grevé par les intérêts à payer sur les obligations.[81]

La technique la plus répandue pour contenir le risque inflationniste demeure l'imposition de quotas sur la valeur des créances à capitaliser. L'efficacité de la protection contre l'inflation est alors

---

[79] TUCKER, *supra* note 49, à la p. 452.

[80] *Les banques transnationales et les conversions de la dette en prises de participation*, *supra* note 65, aux pp. 18-19.

[81] WILLIAMSON, *supra* note 69, aux pp. 478-79; voir aussi F. LARRAIN et A. VELASCO, ''Can Swaps Solve the Debt Crisis?: Lessons from the Chilean Experience,'' (novembre 1990) 69 *Princeton Studies in International Finance*, 41-42.

en relation inverse avec la complémentarité des investissements étrangers et, bien sûr, le volume de la dette réduite.

Finalement, le danger d'inflation est réduit si la réglementation répartit dans le temps l'introduction des liquidités dans le système monétaire local. Le Mexique et les Philippines ont mis en oeuvre une réglementation allant dans ce sens: le produit du rachat de la créance est déposé dans un compte auprès des autorités publiques et ce dernier sera débité, à mesure qu'avance le projet auquel le capital est affecté.[82]

2 *La contrainte politique*

De par son essence, la capitalisation de dette a pour conséquence un accroissement du contrôle étranger sur l'économie nationale. Certes, la venue du capital étranger peut s'inscrire dans un dessein politique: le gouvernement souhaite rendre plus dynamique l'économie en la libéralisant et en privatisant certaines entreprises d'État; ou plus simplement, il calcule que l'investisseur étranger implantera des méthodes de gestion plus efficaces ou procédera à des transferts de technologie porteurs de retombées. Toutefois, la mainmise de leviers économiques significatifs par des étrangers peut heurter le sentiment nationaliste. Dans le cas spécifique de la capitalisation des dettes, le ressentiment sera amplifié par deux facteurs: d'une part, le mécanisme fait bénéficier l'investisseur étranger d'une subvention indirecte à l'acquisition d'éléments d'actif; d'autre part, certains États-débiteurs[83] empêchent leurs nationaux de participer aux programmes de capitalisation des dettes, de crainte que ces derniers se lancent dans des "opérations d'aller et retour."[84]

La capitalisation de la dette extérieure effectuée sur une grande échelle suppose donc un risque politique. La gestion de celui-ci

---

[82] BUCHHEIT, *supra* note 57, à la p. 101.

[83] C'était notamment le cas du Brésil, dont le programme de capitalisation des dettes a cependant été suspendu en janvier 1989: *Les banques transnationales et les conversions de la dette en prises de participation, supra* note 65, à la p. 11.

[84] *Id.*, 7; La commission des sociétés transnationales du Conseil économique et social des Nations Unies décrit le processus d'aller-retour, mieux connu sous le vocable anglais de "round-tripping," comme suit: "opération dans laquelle des devises étrangères sont introduites de l'extérieur ou achetées sur le marché parallèle en vue d'acquérir avec une décote des titres de créance sur l'extérieur, qui sont ensuite rachetés en monnaie nationale, puis reconvertis en devises étrangères et exportés."

dépend davantage de la capacité du gouvernement de susciter une dynamique politique favorable à l'investissement étranger que des paramètres juridiques de son programme de capitalisation de la dette extérieure. À toutes fins utiles, le concepteur du cadre réglementaire dispose d'un seul levier susceptible d'atténuer le risque politique, soit l'aménagement de l'admissibilité et de la participation des nationaux au programme de capitalisation des dettes. Il faudra alors chercher à limiter ou dissuader les "opérations d'aller et retour" par l'emploi de diverses techniques tels des quotas sur les créances extérieures que les nationaux peuvent capitaliser, le monitorage de l'écart entre le taux de change officiel et le taux de change parallèle ou le resserrement du contrôle des changes et des mouvements transnationaux des capitaux, étant entendu que ces techniques ont une portée limitée ou une efficacité relative.[85]

En aménageant son cadre réglementaire de la capitalisation des dettes, l'État-débiteur va au-delà du déploiement d'un mécanisme de réduction de sa dette extérieure; il cherchera aussi à se prémunir contre le risque inflationniste, à minimiser le danger de désaveu politique et, surtout, à exploiter la rente théoriquement disponible, constituée par l'écart entre le prix payé par l'investisseur pour acquérir la créance sur le marché secondaire et le minimum de la valeur nominale de la créance ou de la valeur actualisée de l'investissement. Cette rente, l'État-débiteur peut s'en approprier une partie sous forme de revenu; alternativement ou concurremment, il peut s'en servir pour subventionner indirectement l'investissement et orienter ainsi ce dernier dans le sens de la politique économique étatique.

C   LES TECHNIQUES

Pour atteindre les objectifs ci-haut décrits, une série de techniques sont utilisées, le dosage et la combinaison variant d'un cadre réglementaire à l'autre.

1   La sélectivité des investissements

Dans la plupart des programmes de capitalisation des dettes, les investissements étrangers sont uniquement autorisés dans des secteurs jugés prioritaires, pour des fins spécifiques ou encore doivent

---

[85] *DEBT-EQUITY CONVERSIONS, supra* note 3, à la p. 42.

être localisés dans des régions déterminées.[86] Une approche moins coercitive consiste à canaliser les investissements vers les secteurs d'intérêt par la modulation, en fonction de la nature de l'investissement, de l'écart entre la valeur nominale de la créance et sa valeur de rachat.[87] On peut aussi prévoir une échelle de taux pour les frais administratifs ou encore pour l'apport obligatoire d'argent frais.[88]

L'accent est d'ordinaire mis sur les investissements susceptibles d'améliorer la balance des paiements, c'est-à-dire ceux qui accroissent la capacité productive du secteur de l'exportation ou ont pour objet la substitution des importations. Les investissements dans les secteurs des services sont peu encouragés. Les contraintes inflationniste et politique limitant structurellement le volume des créances convertibles en prises de participation, l'État-débiteur tente légitimement d'obtenir des investissements de qualité, complémentaires et compatibles avec les objectifs de sa politique économique.

2   L'apport d'argent frais

Des réglementations nationales stipulent que l'investissement ne peut être financé en totalité par des fonds issus de l'opération de capitalisation, un pourcentage déterminé du coût de l'investissement devant être financé minimalement par "l'apport d'argent frais."[89] Comme il a déjà été mentionné, il est possible de moduler

[86] Les banques transnationales et les conversions de la dette en prises de participation, *supra* note 65, à la p. 11.

[87] Un écart minime caractérisera les investissements prioritaires tandis qu'un écart élevé sera associé à l'investissement dans un secteur de moindre importance stratégique. Le Mexique a utilisé ce genre de modulation dans son programme de 1986-87. Voir à ce sujet D. H. BRILL, "Debt-Equity Swaps as a New Mode of Debt Restructuring," dans *International Debts and Economics*, K. M. Meesen, éditeur, 23-32 (Nomos-Verlagsgesellschaft, Baden-Baden, janvier 1987.

[88] C'était le cas du programme philippin avant qu'il ne soit suspendu. L'apport obligatoire d'argent frais représentait de 0 à 60% du coût d'un projet, le taux dépendant du degré de priorité attribué à l'investissement et du montant de la commission due à la Banque centrale. Voir *Les banques transnationales et les conversions de la dette en prises de participations, supra* note 65, à la p. 10.

[89] Le programme mexicain de 1990 prévoit que les fonds provenant d'une opération de capitalisation des dettes ne peuvent financer plus de 50% d'une prise de participation dans une entreprise privatisée, le reste devant être financée à même un apport d'"argent frais"; voir à ce sujet R. J. F. TORTES-LANDA, "Report on the New Rules for the Operation of Debt-Equity Swaps in Mexico," (1991) 25 International Lawyer, 733, 735-36. On a déjà

les exigences d'apport obligatoire d'argent frais de manière à orienter les investissements vers les secteurs stratégiques.

Ce type de mesure a essentiellement pour but d'accroître la complémentarité des investissements. D'aucuns doutent que l'exigence d'apport d'argent frais ait des incidences positives sur la complémentarité des investissements et font plutôt ressortir l'effet dissuasif d'une telle mesure sur les investissements.[90] Ils ajoutent que dans le cadre d'un système où les créances à capitaliser sont soumises à des quotas périodiques et attribuées aux enchères, l'exigence d'apport d'argent frais se traduit, du moins au plan théorique, par une réduction de la participation des investisseurs et par conséquent un prix de rachat moins avantageux pour l'État-débiteur.

Il n'en demeure pas moins qu'au plan politique, l'exigence d'apport d'argent frais tempérera la réaction nationaliste en donnant à tout le moins une impression que le pays n'est pas en train de brader son potentiel de développement économique à des intérêts étrangers.

3   Les quotas périodiques sur les créances convertibles en prise de participation

Dans tous les programmes de capitalisation, les créances convertibles sont soumises à des limites quantitatives. La répartition des créances convertibles est alors effectuée au moyen d'enchères ou est assujettie à un processus à l'intérieur duquel l'autorité administrative exerce un pouvoir discrétionnaire.

L'établissement de quotas périodiques fournit une protection contre l'inflation et réduit sans doute le risque politique. En outre, dans un système d'attribution des créances capitalisables par enchères, l'État-débiteur s'approprie une décote dont l'importance croît avec le caractère restrictif du quota.

4   Les techniques d'appropriation de la décote par l'État-débiteur

Celles-ci ont été décrites dans la section II-A-2.

---

mentionné le cas du programme philippin. Au Vénézuéla, l'apport obligatoire d'argent frais représente 70% du coût du projet sauf dans le secteur du tourisme où le produit de la capitalisation des dettes peut servir à financer un maximum de 50% du coût du projet; voir à ce sujet, *Les banques transnationales et les conversions de la dette en prises de participation, supra* note 65, à la p. 10.

90 BERGSMAN et EDISIS, *supra* note 67, à la p. 22.

5 *Les restrictions sur le rapatriement des dividendes, des profits et du capital*

Le cadre réglementaire typique interdit à l'investisseur étranger de rapatrier les dividendes, les profits et le capital à l'intérieur d'une période donnée et fixe aussi des restrictions sur la cession du capital.[91] Ces restrictions découlent parfois des clauses du contrat de rééchelonnement visant à établir une parité de traitement entre le créancier bancaire et l'investisseur étranger participant à l'opération de capitalisation des dettes. Elles procèdent aussi de l'intérêt de l'État-débiteur dans la régulation de l'incidence des opérations de capitalisation sur sa balance des paiements.

CONCLUSION

En parcourant cette étude, on s'est probablement convaincu que la capitalisation des dettes commerciales se présente comme une transaction complexe, mettant en relation plusieurs cadres juridiques et plusieurs juridictions nationales. Peut-on compter exclusivement sur la convergence des intérêts des acteurs pour arrimer de manière optimale les divers cadres juridiques sur lesquels une opération de capitalisation des dettes se construit? Il est permis d'en douter. La capitalisation des dettes va au-delà de la technique juridique; elle emporte un certain degré de mobilisation des décideurs politiques et des intervenants. Aux autorités politiques et administratives des pays industrialisés, il incombe d'aménager la réglementation bancaire de manière à aplanir les obstacles que rencontrerait la banque désireuse de s'engager dans une opération de capitalisation des dettes. Aux créanciers placés sous le parapluie d'un contrat de prêt syndiqué ou d'un accord de rééchelonnement, il est demandé de relativiser le principe du traitement égal des créanciers. Mais surtout, les arbitrages délicats que doit effectuer l'État-débiteur dans l'élaboration de son cadre réglementaire présupposent l'adhésion à un discours politique valorisant la libéralisation de l'économie nationale et l'ouverture au capital étranger.

En bout de piste, le succès d'un programme de capitalisation des dettes dépend de l'attrait que représente le pays-débiteur pour l'investisseur étranger. Ce dernier se verra, certes, influencé par la stratégie corporative poursuivie mais aussi par des considérations

---

91 Pour les principaux programmes de capitalisation des dettes, ces limites sont résumées dans *Les banques transnationales et les conversions de la dette en prises de participation, supra* note 65, à la p. 11.

liées à la stabilité politique du pays-débiteur, son potentiel de développement, la qualité des infra-structures, la disponibilité d'une main d'oeuvre bien formée et compétente, et de façon générale, la politique économique menée par l'administration. C'est donc, nous semble-t'il, à l'intérieur d'un stratégie globale de développement que devrait s'insérer le mécanisme de la capitalisation des dettes comme technique de réduction du fardeau de la dette.[92] En façonnant des principes généreux axés sur la nécessaire coopération internationale et le droit au développement, le droit international public peut sans doute appuyer le dialogue des décideurs politiques et des parties directement intéressées au problème de la dette extérieure, ce dialogue s'imposant comme le vecteur principal de la convergence des cadres juridiques sous-jacents au mécanisme de la capitalisation des dettes commerciales.[93]

[92] On notera que la capitalisation des dettes fait partie des stratégies de réaménagement de la dette prônées par le Club de Paris; voir à titre d'exemple, MINISTÈRE DE L'ÉCONOMIE, DES FINANCES ET DU BUDGET (FRANCE), "Le réaménagement de la dette extérieure du Sénégal," dans *Les notes bleues*, 15 juillet 1991, no 549 (référence: communiqué du 24 juin 1991, DICOM no 1722); MINISTÈRE DE L'ÉCONOMIE, DES FINANCES ET DU BUDGET (FRANCE), "Le réaménagement de la dette extérieure de l'Égypte," dans *Les notes bleues*, 10 juin 1991, no 544 (référence: communiqué du 27 mai 1991, DICOM no 1670); MINISTÈRE DE L'ÉCONOMIE, DES FINANCES ET DU BUDGET (FRANCE), "Le réaménagement de la dette extérieure de la Pologne," dans *Les notes bleues*, 6 mai 1991, no 539 (référence: communiqué du 21 avril 1991, DICOM no 1628); MINISTÈRE DE L'ÉCONOMIE, DES FINANCES ET DU BUDGET (FRANCE), "Le réaménagement de la dette du Nicaragua et du Bénin," dans *Les notes bleues*, 13 janvier 1992, no 575 (référence: communiqués des 18 et 19 décembre 1991, DICOM, no 2004 et 2007).

[93] Sur le rapport entre le rééchelonnement de la dette et le droit international public, plus spécifiquement le droit au développement et l'obligation de coopération internationale, voir J. N. MEETARBHAN, *Vers un droit international de la dette extérieure?*, Rapport présenté dans le cadre du Centre d'étude et de recherche de droit international et de relations internationales, session 1992, La Haye (non publié).

Summary

Methods of Capitalizing Sovereign Commercial Debt

Debt-equity swaps have been a technique used to cope with developing countries' debt crisis. This type of operation involves various legal techniques. Thus, the national regulation of the creditor institution has an impact on the degree and nature of its participation in debt-equity swaps. These operations should not conflict with the provisions of the syndicated loan or the debt-restructuring agreement. As well, the financial transaction should reflect the constraints inherent in the legal rules governing secondary markets as well as those related to the regulatory scheme set up by the debtor country. This article describes the various legal techniques and shows that international co-operation is necessary to optimize use of debt-equity swaps in a strategy aimed at reduction of developing countries' debt and at their economic growth.

The American Convention on Human Rights: Canada's Present Law and the Effect of Ratification

INTRODUCTION

O N NOVEMBER 13, 1989, Canada signed the Charter of the Organization of the American States and became a member of the Inter-American system upon depositing its instrument of ratification on January 8, 1990. Though Canada held observer status since 1972, until recently it played a passive role with respect to the Organization of American States (OAS).[1] With the growing significance of regional systems in such matters as free trade, economic and ecosystem interdependence, and human rights, however, Canada has decided to become more involved in the Inter-American system.[2]

---

* BA, LL.B. (Queen's), LL.M. (Columbia), Counsel, Crown Law Office – Criminal, Ministry of the Attorney General of Ontario. The views expressed herein are those of the writer and do not necessarily reflect the views of the government of Ontario.

---

1 Although not participating in the OAS, Canada was an active member of six hemispheric organizations, such as the Pan-American Health Organization.

2 Address by Prime Minister Mulroney, Meeting of Hemispheric Leaders, San Jose, Costa Rica, Oct. 27, 1989; Remarks of the Secretary of State for External Affairs at the Meeting of the Council of the Organization of American States, Washington, DC, Nov. 13, 1989; Canada's First Year in the Organization of the American States: Implementing the Strategy for Latin America, Jan. 1991.

The government of Canada is presently giving consideration to ratifying the American Convention on Human Rights.[3] Consultations are being carried out with the provincial and territorial governments. In the light of Canada's long-standing efforts to comply with other international human rights treaties such as the International Covenant on Civil and Political Rights (ICCPR),[4] ratification of the American Convention should be a mere formality.[5] There are however, certain enumerated rights in the American Convention that are of considerable significance to the criminal justice system in Canada and call for closer scrutiny; not the least of these are the scope of the right to life[6] and the restrictive approach to capital punishment.[7]

This article analyzes the particular substantive rights set out in the American Convention that apply to the criminal process to determine whether existing law in Canada conforms with the obligations created by the Convention. It compares the particular substantive human rights obligations of the American Convention that relate to the criminal process with the corresponding rights and protections guaranteed by Canadian law. Where these differ, it considers whether Canada would be required either to alter its present laws or to enter a reservation, understanding, or declaration with respect to certain articles of the Convention.

Upon joining the Organization of American States, Canada became subject to the human rights regime that has its constitutional basis in the OAS Charter. As a member state, Canada is bound by the American Declaration of the Rights and Duties of

---

[3] American Convention on Human Rights, adopted Nov. 22, 1969, OAS Doc. A/ser. K/XVI/I.1, doc. 65 rev. 1 corr. 1 (1970), OAS Treaty Series 36 (entered into force July 18, 1978 upon deposit of eleventh instrument of ratification).

[4] International Covenant on Civil and Political Rights, adopted Dec. 16, 1966, 993 UNTS 3 (in force for Canada Aug. 19, 1976).

[5] Although it refers to the American Declaration on the Rights and Duties of Man, not the American Convention, see the memorandum of the Legal Bureau, Department of External Affairs, Dec. 14, 1989, in 28 Canadian Yearbook of International Law 496 (1990), which states:

> Canadian compliance with the human rights provisions of the OAS Charter and the 1948 American Declaration should not pose any major difficulties since these provisions largely correspond to rights enshrined in the Canadian Charter of Rights and Freedoms and to Canada's existing international obligations.

[6] American Convention on Human Rights, *supra* note 3, Art. 4(1).

[7] *Ibid.*, Art. 4(2)–(6).

Man,[8] and automatically accepts the jurisdiction of the Inter-American Commission on Human Rights to receive petitions from individuals who allege violations of the American Declaration.[9]

For those countries ratifying the American Convention, there is a dual regime, or two-staged process, established for the protection of human rights. The Convention establishes the Inter-American Court on Human Rights and delineates the power and function of the Inter-American Commission on Human Rights with respect to state parties to the Convention. As a result of ratification, Canada would automatically accept the jurisdiction of the Inter-American Commission to deal with private complaints from "any person or group of persons, or any nongovernmental entity legally recognized in one or more member states in the Organization."[10] Ratification does not automatically grant the Commission jurisdiction to deal with complaints filed by one state party against another unless both states, in addition to ratifying the Convention, make a declaration recognizing the interstate complaint jurisdiction of the Commission.[11] In both individual and interstate complaint proceedings, the Commission is the first body to deal with a communication and attempts to encourage a friendly settlement. If such a settlement is not reached, either the Commission or the state party may refer the matter to the Inter-American Court. If the matter is not forwarded to the Court, the Commission may in certain circumstances issue a report.

The Inter-American Court is vested with the power to perform two distinct judicial functions; it exercises both adjudicatory and advisory jurisdiction. Its adjudicatory or contentious jurisdiction allows it to decide disputes involving charges that a state party has

8 Inter-American Court of Human Rights, Advisory Opinion OC-10/89, Interpretation of the American Declaration of the Rights and Duties of Man Within the Framework of Article 64 of the American Convention on Human Rights, OAS Doc. OAS/Ser.L/V/III.21 doc. 14 (1989).

9 For an explanation of the human rights obligations of OAS member states that are not party to the American Convention, see Thomas Buergenthal, "The Inter-American System for the Protection of Human Rights," in Theodor Meron (ed.), *Human Rights in International Law: Legal and Policy Issues* 439 (1984); in relation to Canada, see William A. Schabas, "Substantive and Procedural Hurdles to Canada's Ratification of the American Convention on Human Rights," 12 H.R.L.J. 405 (1991).

10 American Convention on Human Rights, *supra* note 3, Art. 44.

11 *Ibid.*, Art. 45.

violated the human rights guarantees of the Convention.[12] Upon ratifying the Convention, a state does not automatically subject itself to the contentious jurisdiction of the Inter-American Court; the Court acquires jurisdiction only when a declaration is filed by the state to that effect.[13] The Court's advisory jurisdiction empowers it to interpret the Convention and other human rights instruments at the request of OAS members and various OAS organs.[14] There are distinct differences between the two jurisdictions:

> Resort to the advisory jurisdiction of the Court, whether it be by the Inter-American Commission, the other O.A.S. organs, or the member states, has a number of advantages that its contentious jurisdiction does not provide. The latter can only be invoked by and against states that have recognized the Court's jurisdiction; no such requirement applies to its advisory jurisdiction. Although the Court's decision in a contentious case is binding, which of course is not true of an advisory opinion, that distinction may not be of great practical significance. Compliance and non-compliance by states with their international obligations depend less on the formal status of a judgement and its abstract enforceability. Much more important is its impact as a force capable of legitimating governmental conduct and the perception of governments about the political cost of non-compliance. States may find it as difficult in some cases to disregard an advisory opinion as a binding decision.[15]

Although few cases have been decided by the Inter-American Court pursuant to its contentious jurisdiction, its advisory opinions[16] and the decisions of the Inter-American Commission have begun to establish the content of rights enumerated in the Convention.

SUBSTANTIVE HUMAN RIGHTS UNDER THE AMERICAN
CONVENTION AND CANADIAN CRIMINAL LAW: A COMPARISON

ARTICLE 1(2): THE DEFINITION OF "PERSON"

Article 1(2) of the American Convention defines "person" as "every human being," indicating that corporations and other legal persons are not protected. But if an injury to a corporation or association does give rise to a violation of an individual's rights

12 *Ibid.*, Art. 62.

13 *Ibid.*, Art. 62(1), (2).

14 *Ibid.*, Art. 64.

15 Buergenthal, *supra* note 9, at 470.

16 As of December 1991, there were eleven advisory opinions by the Inter-American Court on Human Rights.

under the Convention, to that extent "it can be assumed to give rise to a cause of action."[17] This definition is significant in Canadian law in that the Supreme Court of Canada has, in interpreting the scope of certain legal rights in the Canadian Charter of Rights and Freedoms, limited their applicability with respect to corporations. Owing to the wording of section 7 of the Charter[18] and the nature of the rights guaranteed, the Supreme Court in *Irwin Toy Ltd. v. A.G. Quebec* held that "a corporation cannot avail itself of the protection offered by s. 7 of the Charter."[19] Further, certain legal rights guaranteed by section 11 of the Charter, being accorded to any "person" charged with an offence, appear by their very nature to be inapplicable to corporations. For example, because a corporation cannot physically be imprisoned, it makes little sense to suggest that a corporation has a right "not to be denied reasonable bail without just cause" under section 11(e). Similarly, in *R. v. Amway Corp.*,[20] the Supreme Court of Canada held that, since a corporation could not be a witness in any proceedings, corporations had no protection under that section.[21] To the extent that corporations have limited rights under the Charter, Canadian law is consistent with the obligations under the American Convention.

The Supreme Court of Canada has, however, granted corporations certain constitutional rights in the criminal process, thereby guaranteeing rights not protected in the American Convention. Although it determined that section 11(c) of the Charter does not apply to corporations, the Court recently held that section 11(b), which guarantees the "right to be tried within a reasonable time," can be invoked by a corporation.[22] Since, by definition, Article 8 of the American Convention (the right to a hearing within a reasonable time) applies to human persons, the American Convention

---

[17] T. Buergenthal, R. Norris, D. Shelton, *Protecting Human Rights in the Americas, Selected Problems* 3rd ed., 9 (N. D. Engel, 1990).

[18] The Canadian Charter of Rights and Freedoms, set forth in the Constitution Act, 1982, s. 7 states: "Everyone has the right to life, liberty and security of the person and the right not to be deprived therof except in accordance with the principles of fundamental justice."

[19] *Irwin Toy Ltd. v. A.G. Quebec*, [1989] 1 S.C.R. 927, 1001.

[20] [1989] 1 S.C.R. 21, 37.

[21] The Canadian Charter of Rights and Freedoms, *supra* note 18, s.11 states: "Any person charged with an offence has the right . . . (c) not to be compelled to be a witness in proceedings against that person in respect of the offence; . . . (e) not to be denied reasonable bail without just cause."

[22] *R. v. C.I.P. Inc.*, [1992] 1 S.C.R. 843.

does not grant a parallel right to corporations. This distinction would not create a problem for Canada, since Canadian law would exceed the obligations imposed by the Convention.

ARTICLE 4: THE RIGHT TO LIFE

The right to life provision in Article 4 of the American Convention will cause the greatest concern as the Canadian government contemplates ratification. This provision is more specific with respect to the content of the right to life than the similar provisions in the American Declaration on the Rights and Duties of Man,[23] the European Convention,[24] and the ICCPR.[25]

Right to Life "in General from the Moment of Conception"

Article 4.1 states that "Every person has the right to have his life respected. This right shall be protected by law and, in general, from the moment of conception. No one shall be arbitrarily deprived of his life." Besides the reference to the right to life "in general, from the moment of conception," Article 4 lists restrictions and prohibitions on the use of the death penalty. Although existing Canadian law is not far from meeting its obligations under Article 4 regarding the use of the death penalty, the same cannot be said with respect to the guarantee of the right to life "in general from the moment of conception."

It is far from clear what specific protection or guarantees are included in the phrase "in general from the moment of conception." Since this phrase is not found in other major international human rights instruments, its meaning has not been examined by other human rights bodies. Neither the Human Rights Committee established under the ICCPR,[26] nor the European Court of Human Rights established pursuant to the European Convention,[27] have yet been required to consider whether the more general phrase "right to life" used in each respective instrument requires restric-

23 OAS Off. Rec. OEA/Ser.L/V/II.23 doc. 21. rev. 6 (1948), Art. 1.
24 Convention for the Protection of Human Rights and Fundamental Freedoms (European Convention), Nov. 4, 1950, 213 UN Treaty Series 221, Art. 2.
25 *Supra* note 4, Art. 6.
26 *Ibid.*, Art. 28.
27 *Supra* note 24, Art. 19(2).

tions on abortion.[28] The issue did, however, come before the European Commission of Human Rights in *Paton* v. *United Kingdom*.[29] In that case, the Commission held, based on the context of the provision and the object and purpose of the Convention, that the right to life guaranteed by Article 2 did not recognize an absolute right to life of the fetus; it did not decide whether the provision had some application to the fetus, or whether it mandated certain limitations on abortion.

The scope of the right to life was recently considered in the drafting of the Convention on the Rights of the Child;[30] in the final two sessions in 1988, the question of the rights of the child before birth was raised in the working group. Before this, there had been no discussion that specifically addressed the protection of the child before birth. In the November-December session of the working group, several countries strongly advocated a reference in the preamble to the protection of the child before birth, similar to that in the 1959 United Nations Declaration on the Rights of the Child.[31] Eventually a compromise was reached, with the preamble making reference to protection of the child "before and after birth." On behalf of the working group, the chairman read into the record the statement that the addition of these words in the preamble was not intended to prejudice the interpretation of Article 1 or other articles of the Convention.[32] A memorandum from the legal bureau of the Department of External Affairs, Canada, indicated the Canadian delegation's position on the compromise reached in the working group:

> The compromise solution did not satisfy the concerns of all states that participated in the WG [working group]. However, there was a recognition that the Convention must retain a degree of flexibility in order to

28 Although the European Court of Human Rights has yet to deal with abortion under Art. 2, right to life, it is faced with issues concerning restrictions on abortion. Presently pending before the European Court is an application concerning the legality of restrictions in Ireland on the counselling of pregnant women on the availability of abortions in foreign clinics, see "Open Door Counselling Ltd. and Dublin Well Woman Centre Ltd. and Others v. Ireland," 12 H.R.L.J. 479 (1991).

29 App. No. 8416/78, 19 Eur. Comm'n H.R. Dec. & Rep. 244 (1980).

30 Nov. 20, 1989, UN Doc. A/RES/44/25.

31 G.A. Res. 1386, UN Doc. A/4354 (1959).

32 Department of External Affairs, Memorandum of the Legal Bureau, Mar. 30, 1989, in 27 Canadian Yearbook of International Law 376, 377 (1989).

allow states enough latitude to address this sensitive issue in accordance
with their national legislation. The Canadian delegation to the WG
sessions supported the need for a flexible approach. . . .[33]

In the light of this drafting history, the decision of the Inter-
American Commission on Human Rights[34] on the right to life
contained in the American Declaration on the Rights and Duties of
Man must be considered. The issue brought before the Commission from the United States was whether the protection of the right
to life, guaranteed in the American Declaration on the Rights and
Duties of Man, extended to the unborn. Since the United States is
not a party to the American Convention, the petition alleged a
violation by the United States pursuant to its obligations under the
American Declaration, as a member state of the OAS. The American Declaration guarantees the "right to life, liberty and security of
the person"[35] but makes no reference to the qualifying phrase, "in
general, from the moment of conception," which is found in the
American Convention. The Inter-American Commission considered the difference in wording in the two documents as well as the
framers' intention in drafting Article 1 of the American Declaration. It concluded that the guarantee in the American Declaration
did not prohibit the decisions of the courts in the United States that
permitted abortion.

In dealing with the petition, the Inter-American Court was confronted with an argument resulting from the use of the Convention
as an aid to interpreting the Declaration. The petitioners claimed
that the phrase "in general" in Article 4(1) of the Convention did
not qualify the words "from the moment of conception" but
applied to all aspects of the provision. The Inter-American Commission, after reviewing the adoption of the right to life provision in
the Convention, disagreed, holding that:

In the light of this history, it is clear that the petitioners' interpretation of
the definition given by the American Convention on the right to life is
incorrect. The addition of the phrase, "in general, from the moment of
conception" does not mean that the drafters of the Convention intended
to modify the concept of the right to life that prevailed in Bogota, when
they approved the American Declaration. The legal implications of the

[33] *Ibid.*, 377.
[34] Protection of Life Prior to Birth, Resolution No. 23/81, Case 2141 (United
States of America), IACHR Annual Report, 1980-81, OAS Doc. OEA/Ser.L/V/
II.54, doc. 9 rev. 1, 2 H.R.L.J. 110 (1981).
[35] American Declaration on the Rights and Duties of Man, *supra* note 23, Art. 1.

clause "in general, from the moment of conception" are substantially
different from the shorter clause "from the moment of conception" as
appears repeatedly in the petitioner's briefs.[36]

As was indicated in this decision, the legislative history of Article
4.1 in the American Convention is not without controversy.[37] The
first draft by the Inter-American Council of Jurists included the
phrase "from the moment of conception." In redrafting the Convention, the Inter-American Commission, in the light of objections,
introduced the words "in general." Despite proposals on the one
hand to delete the phrase completely and on the other to remove
the words "in general," in the end the present text was adopted.
Based on the wording of Article 4 of the Convention, the history of
the provision, and the inference to be drawn from the Commission's decision, it appears safe to conclude that the right does not
establish an absolute prohibition on the practice of abortion. The
question remains, however, whether the words "in general" leave it
to the individual member states to determine whether pre-natal life
will be protected at all. On the one hand, it is conceivable that the
wording leaves it open to each state to decide whether it will protect
human life from conception or birth.[38] On the other, it is arguable
that the wording requires at least minimum regulation of or limitations on the practice of abortion. If the right requires no limitations
on the practice of abortion, the words "in general, from the
moment of conception" will be irrelevant, and presumably would
not have been included.

If the right to life is construed as an absolute prohibition, or as
requiring restrictions on abortion, in the light of the Supreme
Court of Canada's decision in *R. v. Morgentaler, Smoling and Scott,*[39]
Canada would be open upon ratification to claims of being in
violation of Article 4. In that case, the Court struck down the

---

[36] 2 H.R.L.J. 110, 117 (1981).

[37] For a more thorough review of the history of the drafting of the right to life in
the American Convention, see Schabas, *supra* note 9; J. Colon-Collazo, "A
Legislative History of the Right to Life in the Inter-American System," in B. G.
Ramcharan (ed.), *The Right to Life in International Law* (1985).

[38] See Francisco Jose Aguilar-Urbina, "An Overview of the Main Differences
between the Systems Established by the Optional Protocol to the ICCPR and
the ACHR As Regards Individual Communications," [1991-1992] Can.
H.R.Y.B. 127, 134, n. 26, in which Prof. Aguilar-Urbina, a member of the UN
Human Rights Committee, puts forward this position.

[39] [1988] 1 S.C.R. 30.

legislation that criminalized the act of procuring an abortion except in certain permitted circumstances as being contrary to the Canadian Charter of Rights and Freedoms.[40] As a result, Canada presently has no law regulating abortion.

Considering the uncertainty of the content of the right to life in the American Convention and the present state of the law in Canada, the Canadian government must give serious consideration to entering a reservation when ratifying the Convention. Although Canada's intention in entering a reservation presumably would be to exclude or vary the legal effect of this one particular aspect of the right to life, it would have to be careful in setting out its reservation. If it is incompatible with the object or purpose of the treaty, it is impermissible pursuant to Article 75 of the American Convention.[41] Because the right to life under Article 4 is non-derogable, meaning that it cannot be suspended even in times of "war, public danger or other emergency that threatens the independence or security" of the state,[42] the nature and extent of the reservation becomes even more significant.

A general reservation to Article 4, enabling the Canadian government to suspend the right to life, may very well be incompatible with the object and purpose of the Convention. Conversely, a reservation that is carefully worded and specifically limited, not depriving the right to life as a whole of its basic purpose, presumably would not be incompatible with the Convention. The Inter-American Court in an Advisory Opinion[43] concerning the extension of the death penalty in Guatemala noted this distinction. Guatemala, having entered a reservation to Article 4(4) at the time of ratification, subsequently relied on it as a justification for the extension of the death penalty to crimes to which it did not apply at the time of ratification, contrary to Article 4(2) of the Convention. In interpreting the scope of the reservation, the Inter-American Court stated:

[40] S. 287 (previously s. 251)of the Criminal Code of Canada, R.S.C. 1985, c. C-46 (as amended), was struck down by reason of its violation of s. 7 of the Charter.

[41] Art. 75 states: "This Convention shall be subject to reservations only in conformity with the provisions of the Vienna Convention on the Law of Treaties signed on May 23, 1969." The Vienna Convention on the Law of Treaties, Art. 19, prohibits reservations where they would be incompatible with the object and purpose of the Convention.

[42] American Convention on Human Rights, *supra* note 3, Art. 27.

[43] Restrictions to the Death Penalty (Art. 4(2), (4) American Convention on Human Rights), Advisory Opinion OC-3/83, Sept. 8, 1983, Series A, No. 3.

Consequently, the first question which arises when interpreting a reservation is whether it is compatible with the object and purpose of the treaty. Article 27 allows the State Parties to suspend, in the time of war, public danger, or other emergency that threatens their independence or security, the obligations they assumed by ratifying the Convention, provided that in doing so they do not suspend or derogate from certain basic or essential rights, among them the right to life guaranteed by Article 4. It would follow therefrom that a reservation which was designed to enable a State to suspend any of the non-derogable fundamental rights must be deemed to be incompatible with the object and purpose of the Convention and, consequently, not permitted by it. The situation would be different *if the reservation sought merely to restrict aspects of a non-derogable right without depriving the right as a whole of its basic purpose.*[44]

In considering the form and content of a possible reservation, Canada may take note of the "interpretative declaration" entered by Mexico with respect to the right to life upon its accession to the American Convention. It is worded as follows: "With respect to paragraph 1 of Article 4 it considers that the expression 'in general', used in said paragraph, does not constitute an obligation to adopt or maintain in force legislation that protects life 'from the moment of conception' inasmuch as this matter belongs to the domain reserved to the States."[45] This "interpretative declaration" may be read in two ways. As a declaration, it simply states Mexico's understanding or interpretation to be given Article 4(1). But to the extent that it attempts to exclude the application of the article since, according to Mexico, "the matter belongs to the domain reserved to the States," it is more akin to a reservation. It appears from the context of the "interpretative declaration" that Mexico did not intend to enter a reservation with respect to the broader right to life; rather, by entering a declaration as to the interpretation of the words "in general" in Article 4(1), Mexico interpreted this phrase as permitting each state party to determine domestically the extent of the obligation to protect life "from the moment of conception."

The potential obligations created by the wording of Article 4.1 may force the Continuing Federal-Provincial-Territorial Committee of Officials Responsible for Human Rights and the Canadian parliament to determine Canada's position on this sensitive issue. At the least it will require a carefully worded reservation. As a narrowly construed reservation appears acceptable, this should not be a barrier to the ratification of the American Convention.

44 *Ibid.*, 63 (emphasis added).

45 OAS Doc. OEA/Ser.Lv/II.71, Doc. 6 rev. 1, at 62.

Restrictions on the Death Penalty

No executions have taken place in Canada since December 1962. Since the coming into force of the Criminal Law Amendment Act (No. 2), 1976[46] on July 16, 1976, the death penalty has officially been abolished for all crimes except certain offences under the National Defence Act.[47] Although the retention of the death penalty for certain military offences has had no practical effect, its presence in federal legislation places Canada in violation of its obligations under the International Covenant on Civil and Political Rights.[48] Potentially, the consequence will be the same upon Canada's ratification of the American Convention.

The restrictions on the use of capital punishment set out in Article 4(2)-(6) would have implications for both present and future legislation. Article 4(5) prohibits the imposition of the death penalty upon persons who, at the time of the offence, were under eighteen years of age or over seventy years of age, or upon pregnant women. In Canada the Code of Service Discipline, encompassing Parts IV–IX of the National Defence Act, imposes mandatory death sentences in certain circumstances, regardless of the age or status of the convicted. Thus, this legislation would be in violation of Article 4(5) of the Convention.

Similar limitations on the use of capital punishment based on age and pregnancy are set out in the ICCPR, Article 6(5), to which Canada is a party. Without establishing a maximum age for the imposition of the death penalty, the ICCPR also prohibits the imposition of capital punishment on those who commit an offence while under eighteen years of age, and on pregnant women. In Canada's first Report[49] to the Human Rights Committee in 1979 on the implementation of the provisions of the Covenant, it was acknowledged that the Code of Service Discipline placed Canada in a precarious position:

As regards persons subject to the Code of Service Discipline (*National Defence Act*, R.S.C. 1970, ch. N-4, s. 55; *Geneva Conventions Act*, R.S.C. 1970,

46 S.C. 1974-75-76, c. 105.

47 R.S.C. 1985, c. N-5, Parts IV–IX "Code of Service Discipline."

48 *Supra* note 4, Art. 6(5).

49 International Covenant on Civil and Political Rights: Report of Canada on Implementation of the Provisions of the Covenant, Mar. 1979, No. S2-83-1979 (Ottawa: Supply and Services Canada, 1979).

ch. G-3, s.7) and condemned to death thereunder, there is no provision in the *National Defence Act*, or in the regulations adopted under this Act, which prohibits the execution of a person under eighteen years of age or a pregnant woman. However, under s. 178(1) of the *National Defence Act*, 'a punishment of death imposed by a court martial is subject to approval by the Governor in Council' and cannot be carried out without his consent. Since the Governor in Council is fully aware of the obligations which Canada has contracted under this Covenant, it is unlikely that a person under eighteen years of age, or a pregnant woman would be executed for an offence against the Code of Service Discipline.[50]

Although the Report does not expressly state it, the obligation under both the ICCPR and the American Convention is not to execute anyone who is under the age of eighteen years at the time of the commission of the offence, not simply that the guarantee prohibits the execution of "a person under eighteen years of age."

In March 1983, to supplement answers given to the Human Rights Committee at the time of its review of Canada's first Report, the Department of the Secretary of State filed a Supplementary Report,[51] which responded to two questions pertaining to the retention of the death penalty in Canada for military offences. The second question by the Human Rights Committee focused on the comments in Canada's first Report that it was unlikely that Canada would violate its international obligations, since the Governor in Council was fully aware of them. The question was directed at whether the law was, in fact, in conformity with the Covenant on this point.[52] After quoting from Canada's first Report, the Supplemental Report concluded:

The federal government is thus aware of the difficulties raised by the existence of the death penalty for certain offences against the *Code of Service Discipline* in relation to Article 6(5) of the Covenant. This question was raised in a report prepared by the Interdepartmental Committee on Human Rights, and is now being considered by this Committee."[53]

---

[50] *Ibid.*, 22.

[51] Supplementary Report of Canada on the Application of the Provisions of the International Covenant on Civil and Political Rights in Response to Questions Posed by the Human Rights Committee in March 1980, Mar. 1983 (Ottawa: Secretary of State, Canada, 1983).

[52] *Ibid.*, 29.

[53] *Ibid.*, 30.

Six years later, in Canada's Second Report to the Human Rights Committee[54] submitted in July 1989, it was once again acknowledged that "The death penalty still exists, however, under the *Code of Service Discipline* in the *National Defence Act.* The death penalty provisions of this Act are currently under review, and specific attention is being given to article 6 of the Covenant."[55] In Canada's Third Report, submitted in August 1990, Article 6 of the ICCPR is not mentioned and Canada's compliance regarding the death penalty is not addressed.

The review of Canadian legislation in contemplation of ratification of the American Convention will once again bring this issue to the forefront. The Canadian government should take this opportunity to bring the law into line with its international obligations, obligations that it has acknowledged since ratifying the ICCPR. Apart from Canada's obligation under the ICCPR, it is arguable that Canada is in violation of customary international law by maintaining laws that permit the execution of individuals who are under eighteen years of age when the offence is committed.[56] There is even authority for the proposition that there is recognized a norm of *jus cogens* that prohibits the state execution of children.[57] To meet this obligation, Canada would have to repeal the offending legislation that permits the execution of offenders under the Code of Service Discipline regardless of age or status. The Continuing Committee responsible for human rights matters should also review this archaic legislation in the light of evolving standards of interna-

54 Second and Third Reports of Canada, International Covenant on Civil and Political Rights, No. Ci96-54/1990E (Ottawa: Human Rights Directorate, Multiculturalism and Citizenship, Canada, 1990).

55 *Ibid.*, 5.

56 See Application of the Death Penalty on Juveniles in the United States, Res. No. 3/87, Case 9647 (United States), Mar. 27, 1987, 8 H.R.L.J. 345 (1987). At present there are only six countries that impose the death penalty for criminal offences on individuals who were under the age of eighteen years old at the time of the offence: Bangladesh, Pakistan, Iran, Iraq, Nigeria, and the United States. Assuming there is a rule of customary international law, Canada would not be in a position to claim persistent objector status.

57 *Ibid.*, 345. The Inter-American Commission drew two conclusions regarding the characterization of this rule as a peremptory norm: first, that it was a peremptory norm of the member states of the OAS (which may be questioned on the basis that it is not derived from the international community as a whole), and second, that the age of this prohibition had not been conclusively determined.

tional human rights law,[58] in contemplation of abolishing the death penalty altogether.

The implications of Article 4 for future legislation in Canada are evident in the text of subsections (2), (3), and (4). Article 4(4) places limitations on the type of offences to which the death penalty, if in existence, can apply. More significant are portions of subsections (2) and (3), which read: "In countries that have not abolished the death penalty . . . the application of such punishment shall not be extended to crimes to which it does not presently apply"; and "The death penalty shall not be reestablished in states that have abolished it." The effects of these provisions are obvious. If Canada retains capital punishment for certain military offences, this punishment cannot be extended to any other offences, and if it abolishes capital punishment for the remaining military offences, it cannot be reinstated. In the light of Canada's rejection of the death penalty for criminal offences,[59] its position on capital punishment in the international sphere,[60] its present obligations under the ICCPR, and evolving standards of decency,[61] the government should ratify Article 4 without any reservations to its provisions on capital punishment. Since Article 4 as a whole "reveals a clear

[58] Second Optional Protocol to the International Covenant on Civil and Political Rights Aimed at Abolition of Death Penalty, Off. Doc. G.A., 44th Sess., A/Res/44/128; Protocol 6 to the Convention for the Protection of Human Rights and Fundamental Freedoms concerning the Abolition of the Death Penalty (European Convention), E.T.S. 114; Additional Protocol to the American Convention on Human Rights to Abolish the Death Penalty, 29 I.L.M. 1447 (1990).

[59] There have been two free votes in the Canadian House of Commons on the issue of capital punishment. The first was in 1976 when capital punishment was abolished for criminal offences, and the second on June 30, 1987, when a motion for the reinstatement of capital punishment was defeated.

[60] In the UN Economic and Social Council in December 1971, Canada voted in favour of a resolution affirming the goal of abolishing capital punishment. Canada also voted in the UN General Assembly in favour of the Second Optional Protocol to the International Covenant on Civil and Political Rights, which called for measures to abolish the death penalty: G.A. Res. 44/128 adopted Dec. 15, 1989. See also *Kindler* v. *Canada (Minister of Justice)* (1991), 67 C.C.C. (3d) 1, 29-30 *per* Cory, J.(dissenting) (discussion of Canada's international commitments).

[61] See comments by Justices of the Supreme Court of Canada on the appropriateness of capital punishment in Canadian society, in *Kindler* v. *Canada (Minister of Justice)*, *supra* note 60 *per* La Forest, J. at 10-11; *per* Sopinka, J.(dissenting) at 16-17; *per* Cory, J. (dissenting) at 27-38. See also recent developments in international human rights law, *supra* note 58.

tendency to restrict the scope of this penalty both as far as its imposition and its application are concerned",[62] reservations to Article 4(2) and (3) may be seen, in any event, as being incompatible with the object and purpose of the Convention.

ARTICLE 7: THE RIGHT TO PERSONAL LIBERTY — RELEASE PENDING TRIAL

Article 7 of the Convention encompasses the right to personal liberty and security. Article 7(5) sets out multiple safeguards for individuals detained, as follows:

7(5) Any person detained shall be brought promptly before a judge or other officer authorized by law to exercise judicial power and shall be entitled to trial within a reasonable time or to be released without prejudice to the continuation of the proceedings. His release may be subject to guarantees to assure his appearance for trial.

Similar wording appears in Article 9 of the Civil and Political Rights Covenant, which states that "release may be subject to guarantees to appear for trial." If the maxim *inclusio unius est exclusio alterius* is applied in interpreting this section, conditions cannot be imposed other than those related to ensuring the appearance of the accused.

The Criminal Code of Canada establishes a regime whereby an accused person may be released by the arresting officer or the officer in charge, or, if detained, must be taken before a justice without unreasonable delay and within twenty-four hours where a justice is available.[63] When release is granted, the justice may direct that an accused abide by certain conditions, including that the accused: "abstain from communicating with any witness or other person expressly named in the order except in accordance with such conditions specified in the order as the justice deems necessary [and] comply with such other reasonable conditions specified in the order as the justice considers desirable."[64]

To the extent that conditions imposed pursuant to section

---

[62] 4 H.R.L.J. 339, 353 (1983).

[63] Criminal Code of Canada, R.S.C. 1985, c. C-46, s. 503. Pursuant to s. 515 of the Criminal Code, a justice cannot grant release to an accused charged with an offence (e.g., murder) that is listed in s. 469 of the Criminal Code; such an accused is subject to a different release procedure.

[64] *Ibid.*, s. 515(4). See e.g. *R. v. Bielefeld*, (1981), 64 C.C.C.(2d) 216 (B.C.S.C.), in which it was held that a condition related to the prevention of the commisssion of further offences was validly imposed.

515 (4) of the Criminal Code are unrelated to guaranteeing an accused's appearance for trial, Canadian law appears inconsistent with the American Convention. If Article 7(5) of the Convention is not interpreted as excluding other considerations in imposing conditions, then the inconsistency does not exist. Considering that Canada's present obligation under the ICCPR in this respect is almost identical, a reservation to this article in the American Convention would be of limited effect.

ARTICLE 8: THE RIGHT TO A FAIR TRIAL — RIGHT TO COUNSEL

The right to a fair trial is protected by Article 8 of the Convention. Article 8(2) enumerates the minimum guarantees to which every person accused of a criminal offence is entitled. For the most part, the Canadian Charter of Rights and Freedoms and the Criminal Code of Canada provide this protection. Of the guarantees listed, that in Article 8(2)(e) pertaining to the right to be assisted by counsel is noteworthy for two reasons: first, it is somewhat unclear from the article itself what the content of the right to be assisted by counsel is for an indigent accused; and, second, since the administration of justice in Canada falls within the jurisdiction of the provincial governments, the provision of legal assistance is a provincial rather than a federal obligation.

Both the International Covenant on Civil and Political Rights[65] and the European Convention[66] explicitly guarantee free legal assistance when an accused has insufficient means to pay, and the interests of justice require it. Article 8(2)(e) of the American Convention states:

8(2) Every person accused of a criminal offence has the right to be presumed innocent so long as his guilt has not been proven according to law. During the proceedings, every person is entitled, with full equality, to the following minimum guarantees:
. . .
(e) the inalienable right to be assisted by counsel provided by the state, paid or not as the domestic law provides, if the accused does not defend himself personally or engage his own counsel within the time period established by law.

Counsel provided by the state will be paid only if the domestic law so provides. It appears that the state is required to provide the "inalienable right to be assisted by counsel" but is not required to

[65] *Supra* note 4, Art. 14(3)(d).
[66] *Supra* note 24, Art. 6(3)(c).

pay for it. Unless the state is able to compel *pro bono* assistance of counsel, this right guarantees little for the indigent accused.

The Inter-American Court confronted the issue of an indigent's right to counsel in a recent Advisory Opinion. Although dealing with it in terms of whether the lack of counsel justified the failure to exhaust domestic legal remedies, the Court held, with respect to Article 8(2)(e), that:

> In cases where the accused neither defends himself nor engages his own counsel within the time period established by law, he has the right to be assisted by counsel provided by the state, paid or not as the domestic law provides. To that extent the Convention guarantees the right to counsel in criminal proceedings. But since it does not stipulate that legal counsel be provided free of charge when required, an indigent would suffer discrimination for reasons of his "economic status" if, when in need of legal counsel, the state were not to provide it to him free of charge.
> Article 8 must, then, be read to require legal counsel only when that is necessary for a fair hearing.[67]

To the extent that "when the interests of justice so require" can be equated with "when necessary for a fair hearing," the obligations to be fulfilled by the Canadian provincial governments under the American Convention would be similar to those under the ICCPR.

In Canada, the practice of the provinces has been to provide free legal assistance to those who meet certain financial requirements. This practice has been recognized by the Supreme Court of Canada as part of the constitutional right to retain and instruct counsel pursuant to section 10(b) of the Canadian Charter of Rights and Freedoms. In *R. v. Brydges*,[68] Lamer, J.(as he then was) on behalf of the majority, after citing Article 14(3)(d) of the ICCPR, concluded:

> All of this is to reinforce the view that the right to retain and instruct counsel, in modern Canadian society, has come to mean more than the right to retain a lawyer privately. It now also means the right to have access to counsel free of charge where the accused meets certain financial criteria set up by the provincial Legal Aid plan, and the right to have access to immediate, though temporary, advice from duty counsel irrespective of financial status.[69]

The Ontario Court of Appeal has held that, when an accused is ineligible for assistance from the provincial legal aid programs, certain circumstances may merit appointment of counsel. It stated

---

67 Exceptions to the Exhaustion of Domestic Remedies, Advisory Opinion OC-11/90, Aug. 10, 1990, Series A, No. 11, 12 H.R.L.J. 20, 22 (1991).

68 [1990] 1 S.C.R. 190.

69 *Ibid.*, 214-15.

that sections 7 and 11(d) of the Charter require counsel to be paid for where the accused wishes counsel, cannot pay for one, and representation by counsel is essential to a fair trial.[70]

The Inter-American Court has interpreted Article 8 to include the right to legal assistance paid for by the state, when necessary to ensure a fair trial. Although the Charter has not expressly guaranteed the right of an indigent accused to be provided with counsel,[71] the courts have substantially recognized this right in related Charter provisions.

ARTICLE 9: THE IMPOSITION OF A LIGHTER PUNISHMENT

The American Convention, in common with the International Covenant on Civil and Political Rights, establishes the right of an accused to benefit from a subsequent reduction of penalty following conviction for a criminal offence.[72] The last sentence of Article 9, which deals with the freedom from *ex post facto* laws, states , "If subsequent to the commission of the offense the law provides for the imposition of a lighter punishment, the guilty person shall benefit therefrom."[73] Canadian law, however, recognizes no such right. The Charter provision that addresses a reduction in penalty following conviction is clearly inconsistent with Article 9, and has been held in one court decision[74] to be directly in conflict with the similar provision in the ICCPR. The relevant provision in section 11 of the Charter guarantees that "[a]ny person charged with an offence has the right . . . (i) if found guilty of the offence and if the punishment for the offence has been varied between the time of commission and the time of sentencing, to the benefit of the lesser punishment."

Canada's international obligation under the comparable provision in the ICCPR came before the Supreme Court of Canada in 1987 in *R. v. Milne*.[75] In that case, the appellant had been convicted of gross indecency and on the basis of this substantive offence was

---

70 *R. v. Rowbotham* (1988), 41 C.C.C. (3d) 1 (Ont. C.A.).

71 See *Deutsch v. Law Society of Upper Canada Legal Aid Fund* (1985), 11 O.A.C. 30 (Ont. Div. Ct.) (reference to the Hays Joyal Committee Minutes in which Justice Minister Jean Chrétien argued that free legal assistance was adequately covered by provincial legal aid plans and that the right to free legal assistance should not be entrenched in the Charter).

72 American Convention on Human Rights, *supra* note 3, Art. 15(1).

73 *Ibid.*, Art. 9.

74 *Re Mitchell and R.* (1984), 6 C.C.C. (3d) 193 (Ont. H.C.).

75 [1987] 2 S.C.R. 512.

classified as a dangerous offender and given an indeterminate sentence. Subsequent amendments to the Criminal Code removed the offence of gross indecency from the list of offences for which an indeterminate sentence could be imposed. The Supreme Court of Canada dismissed the appeal, finding that there had been no violation of the Charter. In doing so, the Court addressed the application of Article 15 of the ICCPR to the case. La Forest, J. for the majority stated:

Counsel concedes that it [Article 15] has not been adopted as part of the law, but he submits that the Court should use the provision as an aid in interpreting ss. 9 (arbitrary detention) and 12 (cruel and unusual punishment) of the *Charter* in a way that invalidates at least a penalty of the magnitude of an indeterminate sentence at a time when that penalty could no longer be imposed. But even assuming the present situation can be said to fall within the ambit of the Article in the Covenant (which is by no means clear) . . . [i]t is difficult to see how such an approach could be taken in light of the fact that specific attention was given to this matter in s. 11(i) of the *Charter,* which limits the rights of an accused in this regard to the benefit of a reduction in sentencing made between the time of the commission of the offence and the time of sentencing.[76]

The Supreme Court of Canada's decision in *R. v. Milne* makes three things clear. First, there is no comparable protection in Canadian law to that guaranteed by Article 15 of the ICCPR and Article 9 of the American Convention. Second, in the light of the Canadian government's practice not to incorporate human rights treaties expressly through implementing legislation, the appellant in *R. v. Milne* could not invoke the rights guaranteed in the ICCPR as part of the domestic law. And, third, since there is no ambiguity in the wording of section 11(i) of the Charter, the relevant provisions in international human rights treaties will have no interpretative value.

Although Canadian courts have recognized the inconsistency between Canada's international obligations and its domestic guarantees, the two most recent reports by Canada to the Human Rights Committee have failed to address this issue.[77] In the Second Report, submitted in July 1989, the portion of the Report dealing with Canada's obligations under Article 15 insofar as the change in the

---

76 *Ibid.,* 527.

77 In responding to two communications submitted to the Human Rights Committee concerning the right to retroactivity of a lighter penalty in Canada, the Committee essentially held that Art. 15 of the ICCPR was inapplicable in the circumstances of each case. See *Van Duzen* v. *Canada No. 50/1979,* Apr. 7, 1982, 3 H.R.L.J. 181 (1982); *MacIsaac* v. *Canada No. 55/1979,* Oct. 14, 1982, 3 H.R.L.J. 218 (1982).

penalty provision is concerned, simply stated that "Section 11(i) of the Charter provides that 'if the punishment for the offence has been varied between the time of the commission and the time of sentencing, [the offender is entitled] to the benefit of the lesser punishment'."[78] In the Third Report, submitted in August 1990, no mention was made of Article 15.

If Article 9 of the American Convention were incorporated into domestic law through implementing legislation, it could have a significant effect. Recently, the Supreme Court of Canada in *R. v. Martineau*,[79] following an earlier decision in *R. v. Vaillancourt*,[80] struck down two constructive homicide provisions in the Criminal Code[81] as being unconstitutional. The two provisions permitted the conviction and sentencing of an accused for murder although the intention to murder (*mens rea*) was absent. The detention of those previously convicted under what has now been held to be an unconstitutional provision has been held to be valid under Canadian law.[82] On the one hand, it could be argued that, because the striking down of this unconstitutional provision does not result in the imposition of a lighter punishment on those convicted of murder, Article 9 has not been violated. On the other hand, because the Court has struck down the very basis of the conviction, those detained are legally liable only for the lesser underlying offence; therefore, they should only be liable for the penalty of the lesser underlying offence. In this sense, the convicted persons are deprived of the benefit of the subsequent change in the validity of legislation and the resultant lighter punishment imposed on those who presently commit the same offence.

If, by ratifying the American Convention and remaining a party to the ICCPR, Canada recognizes the repugnancy of upholding a penalty that the courts or a Canadian legislative body subsequently deem invalid, it should also recognize that the offence is no longer valid under law. Meeting Canada's obligations in this respect may have serious implications for the criminal law whenever the

---

78 Second and Third Reports of Canada, International Covenant on Civil and Political Rights, *supra* note 54, at 14.

79 [1990] 2 S.C.R. 633.

80 [1987] 2 S.C.R. 636.

81 *Supra* note 63, ss. 229(c), 230.

82 See *R. v. Sarson* (1992), 73 C.C.C. (3d) 1 (Ont. Ct. Gen. Div.); *André Chartrand v. Director of Leclerc Detention Centre* (Quebec Court of Appeal, unreported, July 29, 1992; leave to apply to S.C.C. filed Oct. 6, 1992).

Supreme Court strikes down a provision of the Criminal Code that had either created a substantive offence or established a minimum sentence.[83] In the light of Canada's existing obligation under the ICCPR, a reservation or declaration aimed at excluding or modifying the legal effect of Article 9 of the American Convention would be of limited relevance.

ARTICLES 27 AND 30: SUSPENSION OF AND LIMITATIONS ON RIGHTS

The American Convention establishes a different statutory regime for the limitation and suspension of rights from that found in the Canadian Charter of Rights and Freedoms. Rights are set forth in a similar fashion in both documents, with each right enunciated in a separate section or article. When considering permissible limitations on rights, the Charter, unlike the Convention, has one limiting provision that applies to all rights;[84] rights acknowledged in the Charter are not absolute, but are subject "only to such reasonable limits prescribed by law as can be demonstrably justified in a free and democratic society."[85] In the American Convention, on the other hand, acceptable circumstances for the limitation of particular rights are set out within the article recognizing the right.[86] Any restriction must be in accordance with "laws enacted for reasons of general interest and in accordance with the purpose for which such restrictions have been established."[87] If there is no stated restriction, it seems that no limitation can be placed on the exercise of that right. In this sense, limitations on certain rights justifiable under the Charter may be unacceptable under the Convention.

This difference may be more imagined than real. First, the determination of what is demonstrably justifiable in a free and demo-

---

[83] E.g., *Smith* v. *The Queen*, [1987] 1 S.C.R. 1045.

[84] See the Charter, *supra* note 18, s. 1. Although s. 1 of the Charter applies to all rights, its application is limited with respect to certain rights. For example, it is hard to imagine a punishment found to be cruel and unusual being demonstrably justified in a free and democratic society.

[85] *Ibid.*

[86] American Convention on Human Rights, *supra* note 3, Arts. 8(5), 12(3), 13(2), (5), 15, 16(2), 21(2), 22(3), (4).

[87] *Ibid.*, Art. 30. For the Inter-American Court's interpretation of "in accordance with laws" in Art. 30 of the American Convention, see "The Word 'Laws' in Article 30 of the American Convention on Human Rights," Advisory Opinion OC-6/86, Series A, No. 6, in 7 H.R.L.J. 231 (1986).

cratic society will be informed by the practice of other "free and democratic" states in the international community. It will also be based on general pronouncements on what is considered justifiable in instruments such as the American Convention itself. Second, although the general schemes of the Charter and the Convention are different, Article 32(2) of the Convention could be used to accomplish the same ends as section 1 of the Canadian Charter, since it states that "The rights of each person are limited by the rights of others, by the security of all, and by the just demands of the general welfare, in a democratic society."

The circumstances that permit derogation or suspension of rights, and those rights that are considered non-derogable differ in the Canadian Charter and the American Convention. Article 27 of the latter states that only in time of war, public danger, or other emergency that threatens the independence or security of a state party, may measures be employed that derogate from obligations under the Convention. Furthermore, derogation may take place only to the extent and for the time required by the exigencies of the situation; it may not involve discrimination on grounds of race, colour, sex, language, religion, or social origin. Most importantly, Article 27 prohibits the suspension, under any circumstances, of specific articles in the Convention, including Article 4 (right to life), Article 5 (right to humane treatment), and Article 9 (freedom of conscience and religion). In addition, the Inter-American Court of Human Rights has identified the right of *habeas corpus* as a non-derogable right.[88]

In Canada, pursuant to section 33 of the Charter, both the federal and provincial legislatures are given the authority to override or opt out of the application of a Charter provision. This section permits the operation of federal or provincial legislation notwithstanding that it may be inconsistent with sections 2 or 7 to 15 of the Charter. The only requirement for invoking the notwithstanding clause is that the particular legislative body expressly declares such to be the case in an act of the legislature. The only restriction on the declaration is that it will cease to have effect, unless re-enacted, five years after it comes into force. Section 33 lays down only requirements of form for the exercise of this power, and there is no basis for interpreting this section as providing for

88 Habeas Corpus in Emergency Situations (Non Derogable Guarantee), Advisory Opinion OC-8/87, Series A, No. 8, in 9 H.R.L.J. 94 (1988).

substantive review of the legislative policy in exercising that power.[89]

Under section 33 of the Charter, no legal requirement or justification, such as war, public danger, or emergency is needed to invoke the notwithstanding clause. Further, the section 33 override applies to certain rights that under the American Convention are non-derogable — for example, Charter sections 7 (right to life), 9 (right not to be arbitrarily detained or imprisoned), and 12 (freedom from cruel and unusual treatment or punishment). This override has been invoked on occasion,[90] most recently in 1988 when the province of Quebec passed legislation derogating from sections 2(b) and 15 of the Charter in order to preserve its sign language law.[91] Since Canada's derogation clause is entrenched in the constitution and is the result of "political compromises of the federal system and the complexities of repatriation of the constitution,"[92] it is inconceivable that it will be altered in any way in contemplation of ratifying the Convention. This conclusion is supported by the fact that the drafters of the Canadian Charter (although influenced considerably by the ICCPR, which has a derogation provision similar to that in the American Convention) still included section 33.

The federal parliament has, under the Emergencies Act,[93] provided that derogations of rights may be permitted in times of "national emergency," "public welfare emergency," or a "war emergency." This Act, which repeals the War Measures Act, recognizes Canada's international obligations with respect to the suspension of rights in its preamble, which states:

AND WHEREAS the Governor in Council, in taking such special temporary measures, would be subject to the *Canadian Charter of Rights and Freedoms* and the *Canadian Bill of Rights* and must have regard to the *International Covenant on Civil and Political Rights*, particularly with respect

---

89 See *Ford* v. *Quebec (Attorney General)*, [1988] 2 S.C.R. 712.

90 An Act Respecting the Constitution Act, 1982, S.Q. 1982, c. 21; S.G.E.U. Dispute Settlement Act, S.S. 1984-85-86, c. 111; An Act to Amend the Act to Promote the Development of Agricultural Operations, S.Q. 1986, c. 54; An Act to Again Amend the Education Act and the Act Respecting the Conseil Supérieur de l'Éducation and to Amend the Act Respecting the Ministère de l'Éducation, S.Q. 1986, c. 101; An Act to Amend Various Legislation Respecting the Pension Plans of the Public and Parapublic Sectors, S.Q. 1987, c. 47.

91 An Act to Amend the Charter of the French Language, S.Q. 1988, c. 54.

92 William A. Schabas, *International Human Rights Law and the Canadian Charter* 9 (Carswell, 1991).

93 S.C. 1988, c. 29.

to those fundamental rights that are not to be limited or abridged even in a national emergency . . .

This preamble suggests that, in a time of emergency, those rights protected as non-derogable under the ICCPR are to be recognized as not being subject to suspension.

CONCLUSION

Canada, for the most part, should have little difficulty in meeting its obligations under the American Convention. In those few cases in which the substantive content of the right is inconsistent with Canadian law, Canada will need either to enter some form of reservation or introduce new legislation to meet its obligation. As is Canada's practice, if legislation is passed it is unlikely to be in the form of implementing legislation.[94]

If existing Canadian laws conform with those obligations that Canada has taken on, implementing legislation will be unnecessary. But it is evident that certain obligations under the American Convention — for example, Article 9: the right to subsequent change in penalty; Article 4(5): restriction on capital punishment based on age or status — are not compatible with domestic legislation; and where there is no ambiguity in domestic law, the provisions of the American Convention imposing these obligations would have neither binding nor interpretative effect.

In considering ratification, Canada has the option under Article 28 of the Convention to invoke the "federal clause" by declaration at the time of ratification, thus limiting the application of the Convention to matters within the competence of the federal authority. To the extent that the provincial governments adopted appropriate provisions for the fulfilment of the Convention, Canada may declare its application to be extended to the provinces. Since Canada has already ratified human rights treaties that do not contain a "federal clause," and generally human rights treaties are intended to be universal in their application, Canada should not invoke the federal clause in the American Convention.

Canada has traditionally taken the position with respect to non-human-rights treaties that federal-state clauses in treaties are desirable. As stated by the Head of the Treaty Section, Legal Division, Department of External Affairs in 1964,

94 For a comprehensive analysis of domestic law as implementing legislation, see *Anne F. Bayefsky, International Human Rights Law: Use in Canadian Charter of Rights and Freedoms Litigation* 23-105 (Toronto: Butterworths, 1992).

Reservations are important for Canada with regard to the implementation of treaties. Canada frequently strives to have a *federal-state clause* inserted in a multilateral convention or she may enter a reservation, both of which have the effect of reserving Canada's obligations at international law with regard to matters within the legislative jurisdiction of the Provinces.[95]

The Department of the Secretary of State, in the case of non-human-rights treaties, appears to have generally maintained this position.[96]

Time has demonstrated that federal-state clauses are unnecessary for Canada in the area of human rights treaties. When Canada acceded to the Convention on the Political Rights of Women in 1957, it entered a reservation on the grounds of the federal nature of the legislative system.[97] Significantly, Canada's subsequent inability to insert a federal-state clause in many human rights treaties has not prevented Canada from becoming a party to these treaties. Despite initially opposing the exclusion of a federal-state clause from the International Covenant on Civil and Political Rights,[98] Canada became a party to it. On March 25, 1980, Canada's Ambassador to the United Nations, in relation to Canada's implementation of the Covenant, said: "Thus, while it required an extensive process of consultation, the constitutional division of powers in no way affected the international responsibility of Canada."[99] Canada also assumed obligations under treaties such as the International Convention on the Elimination of All Forms of Racial Discrimination[100] and the Convention on the Elimination of All Forms of Discrimination Against Women[101] despite the absence of federal-state clauses.

[95] 3 Canadian Yearbook of International Law 336, 340 (1965).

[96] See the Department of the Secretary of State, Memorandum of Legal Bureau, Oct. 26, 1980, *ibid.*, vol. 19, 335, 335-37 (1981); Department of the Secretary of State, Memorandum of Legal Bureau, Jan. 19, 1988, *ibid.*, vol. 26, 328, 328-29 (1988); Department of the Secretary of State, Memorandum of Legal Bureau, Apr. 4, 1989, *ibid.*, vol. 27, 389, 389-390 (1989).

[97] *Ibid.*, vol. 7, 324, 325 (1969).

[98] Department of the Secretary of State, Letter of Legal Bureau, Mar. 17, 1982, *ibid.*, vol. 21, 319, 320 (1983).

[99] Statement of Canada's Ambassador to the United Nations, Geneva, Mar. 25, 1980, *ibid.*, vol. 19, 338 (1981).

[100] Adopted Dec. 21, 1965, 660 UN Treaty Series 195.

[101] Adopted Dec. 18, 1979, [1982] Can. T.S. 31.

According to Thomas Buergenthal, former Justice of the Inter-American Court, Article 28 of the American Convention is "an anachronism which harks back to the days of the League of Nations."[102] Canada has been able to participate actively in the international community as a party to most human rights treaties whose obligations extend to all parts of the federal state. Canada has even been cited as an example of a federal state that has been able to adhere to these instruments without federal-state reservations.[103] There is, then, no apparent reason for Canada to make a declaration under Article 28 of the American Convention.

Upon becoming a member of the Organization of American States, Canada became actively involved in an effort to be a "full and constructive citizen."[104] In February 1990, Canadian experts participated in an OAS electoral observer mission for elections in Nicaragua, and in June 1990 Canada's proposal to establish a Unit for Democratic Development was accepted unanimously by the General Assembly.[105] Canada's entrance into the OAS was welcomed by all member states and was seen as a positive force for renewal. As recalled by Jean-Paul Hubert, Canada's First Ambassador and Permanent Representative to the OAS, "I would even go so far as to say that not only were we welcomed, but our presence was awaited as a potential catalyst for a much needed exercise in renewal and adaptation to changing realities with the hemisphere. I have heard many expressions of such sentiment."[106]

Canada's ratification of the American Convention would demonstrate its intention to become a "full and constructive citizen" and its commitment to the transition of the Inter-American system. It would reaffirm Canada's commitment to those human rights it has previously recognized and would widen the scope of human rights protection, specifically in the area of limitations on the use of the death penalty. Since most western industrialized nations are moving away from the death penalty, Canada's adoption of these restric-

---

[102] Buergenthal, *supra* note 9, at 445.

[103] *Ibid.*, 446.

[104] Canada's First Year in the Organization of American States: Implementing the Strategy for Latin America, Jan. 1991.

[105] Report of Canada's First Year in the Organization of American States, Jan. 1991, at 6,13.

[106] Jean-Paul Hubert, "Canada's Initial Experience as a New Member of the OAS," *Canada in the Americas: Agenda for the 90s, A Report of a Conference On Canada's Foreign Policy by the Group of 78*, at 18, (Ottawa, 1991).

tions would be welcome. Ratification would bring to the forefront the necessity for entering a reservation, or at least an understanding, to the right to life "in general, from the moment of conception." Although as a general principle Canada should discourage reservations to human rights conventions, a reservation would seem to be necessary in the light of Canada's present law.

Canada's ratification of the American Convention would enhance Canada's reputation in the international community and the OAS as a country that respects human rights. The Convention's real impact on domestic law would depend on the reservations entered, the extent to which it is implemented as federal, provincial, or territorial law, and the relevance it is given in the interpretation of the Canadian Charter of Rights and Freedoms.

Notes and Comments

The International Court as Emerging Constitutional Court and the Co-ordinate UN Institutions (Especially the Security Council): Implications of the *Aerial Incident at Lockerbie*

INTRODUCTION

T HE DECISION OF THE INTERNATIONAL COURT OF JUSTICE IN THE *Aerial Incident at Lockerbie (Provisional Measures)*[1] in April 1992 has implications for the future constitutional relations of the main, co-ordinate United Nations institutions, and especially for relations between the Court and the Security Council. With the ending of the Cold War and the collapse of the Soviet (Communist) regimes in Russia itself and in eastern Europe, the political basic premise (Grundnorm) on which Security Council and General Assembly practice had been predicated — that is, the established Soviet-western bipolar model of world public order, and the resultant political balance of power between the Soviet bloc countries and western and western-leaning states — also disappeared.[2] Since the Second World War, throughout the Cold War, peaceful co-existence, and *détente* between the two blocs, the ever-present possibility of a veto in the Security Council by any one of the five permanent members had compelled consensus, or at least accommodation on

---

[1] *Questions of Interpretation and Application of the 1971 Montreal Convention arising from the Aerial Incident at Lockerbie (Provisional Measures) (Libya v. U.K.)*, [1992] ICJ Rep. 3; (*Libya v. U.S.*), [1992], ICJ Rep. 114.

[2] See, generally, *From Coexistence to Cooperation: International Law and Organisation in the post-Cold War Era*, McWhinney, Ross, Tunkin, Vereshchetin (eds.) (1991). On the preceding Cold War era, see McWhinney, *The International Law of Détente* (1978).

a basis of reciprocal self-interest, as a precondition of legal action. Only on rare occasions had this not occurred. In the Korean crisis of 1950, the Soviet Union had chosen to absent itself from the Security Council; again, during the Korean crisis, the General Assembly, under western initiative, had chosen to assert its legal competence to take measures to maintain international peace and security in default of Security Council action, thereby setting a rarely-followed precedent in its "Uniting for Peace Resolution."[3]

In the post-Cold War era, the much trumpeted "New World Order" has yet to emerge, and in the United Nations no new political equilibrium has arisen to replace the old Soviet-western bipolar system of checks and balances. In the past few years, with the disappearance of Soviet (and then Russian) effective power, and the muting of the Chinese voice in the aftermath of the 1990 student-led troubles, the largely unchallenged leadership role for the United States has been seriously weakened by the latter's economic decline. Some observers, rather fancifully, have suggested that, with the disappearance of the former Soviet counterweight to the United States in the Security Council, the International Court may be tempted to fill the gap in effective law-making power within the United Nations system by interposing itself as a new form of constitutional check-and-balance against the politically unbridled power of the Security Council. This interpretation, insofar as it purports to be based on the International Court's judgment in *Aerial Incident at Lockerbie (Provisional Measures)*, reflects a lack of acquaintance with the historical development of the Court's jurisprudence over the past several decades.

The Court, to be sure, has been evolving into the role of a special constitutional court similar to those in European constitutions. But no sudden development has occurred that compares with *Marbury v. Madison*,[4] which asserted a new power of judicial review for the fledgling U.S. Supreme Court at the beginning of the nineteenth century. Nevertheless, the International Court, starting with the Advisory Opinion in *Namibia*, 1971,[5] has practised the skills of judicial activism and judicial self-restraint and, at the same time,

---

[3] UN G.A. Res. 377 A(V), Nov. 3, 1950 (adopted by a vote of 52 to 5, with 2 abstentions.)

[4] 1 Cranch 137 (1803).

[5] *Legal Consequences for States of the Continued Presence of South Africa in Namibia (South West Africa) Notwithstanding Security Council Resolution 276 (1970), Advisory Opinion,* [1971] ICJ Rep. 16.

explored the issues of constitutional separation of powers and the proper balance to be observed between the Court and the Security Council and General Assembly. Considerations of inter-institutional comity and of mutual deference and co-operation in problem-solving have become paramount in this judicial elaboration of constitutional competence.[6]

Aerial Incident at Lockerbie (Provisional Measures)[7] resulted from the destruction by international terrorist action of a United States Pan American civil passenger commercial aircraft in British airspace over Scotland on December 21, 1988 with resultant loss of life of the passengers and air crew. "Aerial Incident" is the euphemistic designation applied by the International Court to a whole series of such cases, beginning in the early 1950s with Soviet-United States early Cold War confrontations. The aerial incident at Lockerbie followed the shooting down by a United States Navy warship in Iranian airspace over Iranian territorial waters on July 3, 1988 of an Iranian civil passenger commercial aircraft on a regularly scheduled international flight, again with resultant loss of life of all passengers and air crew. An Iranian suit against the United States was pending in the International Court. The Court had already made one preliminary procedural ruling on that suit[8] when it was called upon to decide in *Aerial Incident at Lockerbie (Provisional Measures)*.

The case was brought before the Court by the government of Libya, which requested that the Court urgently invoke provisional measures under Article 41 of its statute to enjoin the two respondent states, the United Kingdom and the United States, "from taking against Libya measures calculated to exert coercion on it or to compel it to surrender . . . to any jurisdiction outside of Libya" two Libyan nationals who were alleged by the two respondent states to be responsible for the destruction of the U.S. airplane in British airspace. The Montreal Convention of 1971 (Convention for the Suppression of Unlawful Acts against the Safety of Civil Aviation), which necessarily would be interpreted and applied in the Court's eventual ruling on the substantive legal issues in the case, expressly incorporates (at the urging of the principal western states, which

6 See generally McWhinney, *Judicial Settlement of International Disputes* 142-47, 157-58.(1991).

7 *Libya v. U.K.*, [1992] ICJ Rep. 3; *Libya v. U.S.*, [1992] ICJ Rep. 114.

8 *Aerial Incident of 3 July 1988 (Islamic Republic of Iran v. U.S.A.), Order of 13 December 1989*, [1989] ICJ Rep. 132.

drafted and negotiated the Convention) the principle *aut dedere, aut judicare.* That principle allows the state of nationality of an alleged offender against the Convention's provisions the choice either to extradite the alleged offender for trial in a foreign jurisdiction, or, if it so chooses, to "submit the case to its competent authorities for the purpose of prosecution."[9]

For the purposes of the adjudication of *Aerial Incident at Lockerbie,* the President of the Court, Judge Jennings, as a national of one of the parties to the case (the United Kingdom) was disabled, under Article 32(1) of the Rules of Court, from exercising the functions of President in respect of the case. Vice-President Oda therefore automatically became Acting President of the Court for the purposes of the case. Since the plaintiff state, Libya, was not already represented on the bench of the full Court, it was enabled to name an *ad hoc* judge (as it happened, a national of Egypt), under Article 31(2) of the Court's statute.

The decisions of the International Court in what were two separate but conjoined cases (*Libya* v. *United Kingdom* and *Libya* v. *United States*) were rendered by an eleven-to-five vote. Acting President Oda signed the official opinion of the Court; each of the five-member minority, comprising Judges Bedjaoui (Algeria), Weeramantry (Sri Lanka), Ranjeva (Malagasy), Ajibola (Nigeria), and Judge *ad hoc* El-Kosheri filed an individual dissenting opinion. In addition to the official opinion of the Court, there were, from among the majority judges, individual Declarations by Acting President Oda and Judge Ni; a joint Declaration signed by Judges Evensen, Tarassov, Guillaume, and Aquilar Mawdsley; and separate opinions filed by Judges Lachs and Shahabuddeen, respectively. In summary, the cases resulted in an eleven-opinion judgment, of which six were majority (including Declarations and separate opinions), and five minority.

This proliferation of judicial opinion-writing reflects the rather novel international and constitutional law aspects of these cases. The Court, concentrating on the rôle and powers of the United Nations Security Council in the post-Cold War era, and noting the disappearance of the erstwhile east-west political balance and equilibrium of forces, apparently felt the need to define (or redefine) the constitutional relationship between the International Court

9 Montreal Convention, 1971, Article 7. See, generally McWhinney, *Aerial Piracy and International Terrorism: The Illegal Diversion of Aircraft and International Law* 45 *et seq.* (2nd rev. ed., 1987).

and the Security Council as co-ordinate institutions. The proliferation of judicial opinions in *Aerial Incident at Lockerbie* may also reflect some questions that arose about the facts on which the Security Council decisions were based; already, a widely-circulated U.S. weekly, in a study re-published and cited in Europe,[10] had cast some doubt on the issue of Libyan responsibility for the Lockerbie aerial disaster.

The opinion of the Court in *Aerial Incident at Lockerbie*[11] cites United Nations Security Council Resolution 731 of January 21, 1992. This Resolution recited, in its preamble, the "world-wide persistence of acts of international terrorism in all its forms" and "illegal activities directed against international civil aviation," and went on to affirm what it characterized as the "right of all States, in accordance with the Charter of the United Nations and relevant principles of International Law, to protect their nationals from acts of international terrorism that constitute threats to international peace and security." The Resolution proceeded to stigmatize the Libyan government for its non-compliance with the demands of the British and U.S. governments for the surrender for trial in Britain and the United States of Libyan nationals and for payment of "appropriate compensation." It pointed out that the Security Council was "deeply concerned over the results of investigations, which implicate officials of the Libyan government"; further, it "strongly deplore(d) the fact that the Libyan government has not yet responded effectively" to the British, U.S., and French demands; and, finally, it "urge(d) the Libyan government immediately to provide a full and effective response."

On March 31, 1992, three days after the close of the legal hearings before the International Court on the request by Libya for the indication by the Court of provisional measures, the Security Council chose to adopt a further resolution, Resolution 748, which involved a preambular recital followed by two decisions under Chapter 7 of the UN Charter. The preambular recital was formulated as follows:

Determining . . . that the failure of the Libyan government to demonstrate by concrete actions its renunciation of terrorism and in particular its continued failure to respond fully and effectively to the requests in

10 *Time*, Apr. 19, 1992; quoted in *Le Monde* (Paris), Apr. 17, 1992; republished in *Die Zeit* (Hamburg), May 1, 1992.

11 *Libya v. U.K.*,[1992] ICJ Rep. 3, at 3-16 (the detailed citations that follow are from this case); *Libya v. U.S.*, [1992] ICJ Rep. 114, at 114-28.

resolution 731 (1992) constitute a threat to international peace and security.

The decisions under Chapter 7 were pronounced as follows: "that the Libyan government must now comply without any further delay" with Resolution 731 (1992); and "that the Libyan government must commit itself definitively to cease all forms of terrorist action and all assistance to terrorist groups and that it must promptly, by concrete actions, demonstrate its renunciation of terrorism."

The *ratio* of the International Court majority decision on the Libyan government's application for provisional measures under Article 41 of the Court statute is set out in one short paragraph of the Court's opinion.[12] This paragraph states, first, that Libya and the two respondent states, "as Members of the United Nations, are obliged to accept and carry out the decisions of the Security Council in accordance with Article 25 of the Charter;" second, that this obligation of the parties under Article 25 of the UN Charter *prima facie* extended to the Security Council decision in Resolution 748 of March 31, 1992; and third, that, in accordance with Article 103 of the UN Charter, the obligations of the parties that derive from Resolution 748 must "prevail over their obligations under any other international agreement including the Montreal Convention." From all that, the Court concluded, first, that "whatever the situation previous to the adoption of [Security Council Resolution 748 (1992)] the rights claimed by Libya under the Montreal Convention cannot now be regarded as appropriate for protection by the indication of provisional measures"[13] and, second, that "an indication of the measures requested by Libya would be likely to impair the rights which appear *prima facie* to be enjoyed by the [two respondent states] by virtue of Security Council Resolution 748 (1992)."[14]

Acting President Oda's declaration,[15] which accompanied the opinion of the Court, is a very short, three-page statement focused on one point — that he is "not in agreement with the Court's taking United Nations Security Council Resolution 748 (1992) as

12 [1992] ICJ Rep. 3, 15 (para. 39).
13 *Ibid.*, 15 (para. 40).
14 *Ibid.*, 15 (para. 41).
15 *Ibid.*, 17-19.

its sole ground."[16] Before suggesting alternative grounds to Resolution 748 upon which the Court might have based its decision, Judge Oda nevertheless rallied himself firmly and categorically in support of the constitutional principle on which the opinion of Court was postulated — namely, the supremacy of Security Council Resolutions in terms of United Nations law:

I do not deny that under the positive law of the United Nations Charter a resolution of the Security Council may have binding force, irrespective of the question whether it is consonant with international law derived from other sources. There is certainly nothing to oblige the Security Council, acting within its terms of reference, to carry out a full evaluation of the possibly relevant rules and circumstances before proceeding to the decisions it deems necessary. . . . Since, as I understand the matter, a decision of the Security Council, properly taken in the exercise of its competence, cannot be summarily reopened, and since it is apparent that Resolution 748 (1992) embodies such a decision, the Court has at present no choice but to acknowledge the pre-eminence of that resolution.[17]

An alternative (and in Judge Oda's view, presumably better) *ratio* for the rejection of Libya's application would have been what he saw as a "mismatch between the object of the [Libyan] application and the rights sought to be protected."[18] In explaining this point, he suggested:

although a State which has jurisdiction in respect of criminal proceedings against any person who happens to be in a foreign territory is free to request the territorial sovereign to extradite that person (a principle admittedly supported by the Montreal Convention), the immediate question put by Libya is whether or not the coercive reinforcement of that request could be deemed contrary to international law. This, to repeat, relates to protection of sovereign rights under general international law but not to the interpretation and application of the Montreal Convention which is the subject matter of the present case. The claim on the ground of the violation of sovereign rights would have instituted a totally different litigation, and whether or not the Court has jurisdiction to deal with that issue is certainly a different matter.

This analysis may seem over-technical, but is not so in relation to the apparent object of Libya's application, which is to seek a declaratory judgment concerning the application and interpretation of the Montreal Convention.[19]

[16] *Ibid.*, 17.
[17] *Ibid.*
[18] *Ibid.*, 19.
[19] *Ibid.*

The doctrine here invoked by Judge Oda is one of judicial self-restraint; of avoiding "higher," constitutional issues, and of deciding instead on "lesser," non-constitutional grounds where these are available. It is an aspect of that positivist, technical approach to the judicial process and judicial reasoning that was inherent in the late nineteenth century German civil law teachings "received" in Japanese law in the Meiji era, and that continued to influence Japanese legal education in Judge Oda's earlier formative years as jurist. The doctrine was well evidenced, six years before *Aerial Incident at Lockerbie*, in the *Nicaragua Merits*[20] decision of the International Court, in which Judge Oda joined with the British member of the Court, Judge Jennings, in dissenting on essentially technical, non-substantive grounds from the majority's holdings. (In *Nicaragua Merits*, Judges Oda and Jennings had joined in dissent the U.S. member of the Court, Judge Schwebel, who disagreed with the Court majority on other grounds.)

Among the other opinions of the Court majority in *Aerial Incident at Lockerbie*, that of Judge Lachs stands out. Judge Lachs, probably to a greater degree than other judges, had over the years rejected any notion of an abstract, artificial constitutional separation of powers between the Court on the one hand and the Security Council and General Assembly on the other. He had argued instead for a full complementarity of powers that should sensibly be exercised with inter-institutional comity and co-operation.[21] While re-affirming this point of view in *Aerial Incident at Lockerbie*[22] Judge Lachs expressly recognized that the Security Council "by moving on to the terrain of Chapter VII of the Charter, decided certain issues pertaining to the Lockerbie disaster with binding force. . . . While the Court has the vocation of applying international law as a universal law, operating both within and outside the United Nations, it is bound to respect, as part of that law, the binding decisions of the Security Council."[23]

Judge Lachs's position demonstrates judicial self-restraint exercised within the larger intellectual dimension of a conscious policy-making role for the Court. It echoes the doctrine of self-restraint that was applied by the Court much earlier in the *Nuclear*

[20] *Nicaragua* v. *U.S.., Merits, Judgment*, [1986] ICJ Rep. 14.
[21] McWhinney, *supra* note 6 at 9, 142-47, 157-58.
[22] [1992] ICJ Rep. 3, 26.
[23] *Ibid.*

Tests case.[24] In that action, in which Judge Lachs signed the official opinion of the Court, a judicial majority supported a result that effectively advanced international environmental protections forms that were legally *avant-garde*, but only through the legal indirection of an essentially adjectival law-based ruling.[25]

Although the Court in *Aerial Incident at Lockerbie* deferred to the Security Council in the exercise of a styled "concurrent jurisdiction,"[26] it indicated that the exercise of this jurisdiction should be limited to the particular (Chapter 7 of the UN Charter) decisions involved, and that the Court reserves its own full legal competences in other respects.

Among the dissenting judges, Judge Shahabuddeen's extended *obiter dictum* comment on the "serious implications for an impartial trial" of the alleged offenders if, as demanded by the United Kingdom, they should be extradited from Libya for trial before British courts,[27] stands as a veiled caution to the particular respondent state, the United Kingdom, as to its past and future conduct in the affair.

CONCLUSIONS

(1) In *Aerial Incident at Lockerbie (Provisional Measures)*, the Court majority's decision denying Libya's request for provisional measures was rooted in the conceived paramountcy of the United Nations Charter, *qua* legal instrument, over a subsequent international treaty, the Montreal Convention of 1971, in spite of the stipulation in the Montreal Convention that clearly and unequivocally reserves the right of the state of nationality of an alleged offender to prosecute that offender before its own courts, as an alternative to granting extradition. The decision, therefore, seemed by inference to dispose of one of the issues much debated between Soviet and western jurists during the Cold War era — that is, whether the United Nations Charter is (as argued, then, by Soviet jurists) a simple treaty, which may be amended by any subsequent inconsistent treaty, or whether it may represent a "higher" constitutional law or *jus cogens*.

24 *Nuclear Tests (Australia v. France), Judgment of 20 December 1974*, [1974] ICJ Rep. 253.

25 *Ibid.*

26 [1992] ICJ Rep. 3, 26.

27 *Ibid.*, 29-32, especially at 31.

(2) The Court in *Aerial Incident at Lockerbie* did not assert judicial competence to determine whether purported legislative acts or actions of the Security Council complied with the constitutional law of the United Nations Charter; nor did it undertake a judicial review of constitutionality *stricto sensu* or of international law in general. The dissenting five judges clearly offered joinder of issue with the majority of eleven judges on these issues.

(3) The determinations set out in the preambular recital to Security Council Resolution 748 of March 31, 1992, upon which the decisions in the same Resolution are predicated, clearly constitute judicial findings. Some well-known jurists have recently suggested that, on grounds of natural justice and procedural due process, some institutionally-based constitutional checks and balances should be installed to correct these Security Council judicial determinations and maintain the inner harmony of the United Nations as a constitutional system.[28]

(4) The Security Council's action in adopting Resolution 748, with its purportedly legally binding and preemptive determinations and decisions on March 31, 1992, a mere three days after the close of the legal hearings before the International Court on the same general issues, displays, on the face of it, a legal insensitivity to the obligations of constitutional comity and mutual deference and co-operation that are enjoined upon co-ordinate institutions in the same constitutional system.

(5) The public doubt cast by Judge Shahabuddeen in his dissenting opinion upon the possibilities of an impartial trial for the alleged offenders if they should indeed be extradited for trial before British courts, because it was not expressly rejected or disowned by the majority judges either in the official opinion of the Court or in the individual majority opinions, stands on record as a form of legal vindication of the plaintiff states' claim and as a caution in respect to the future conduct of the designated respondent state.

---

[28] See, e.g., Wengler, "International Law and the Concept of a New World Order," in *Federalism-in-the-Making: Contemporary Canadian and German Constitutionalism, National and Transnational*, McWhinney, Zaslove, Wolf (eds.) 122-27 (1992); Lauterpacht, *Aspects of the Administration of International Justice* 37-48 (1991).

(6) While the past history and practice of the International Court would suggest that the plethora of opinions — majority and minority — in *Aerial Incident at Lockerbie* amount (in Justice Felix Frankfurter's celebrated *bon mot*) to a series of solo performances that were not planned and orchestrated in advance, in the *ensemble* the judgment and opinions offer a fully co-ordinated judicial response to a new political-legal situation — that is, the role and responsibilities of the Security Council in the post-Cold War era. The majority and minority judicial opinions, in sum, all contribute to the unfolding of the legal dialectic and to the making of new constitutional law of the United Nations.

(7) In terms of the judicial activism–judicial self-restraint continuum, as demonstrated empirically in the jurisprudence of the new national special constitutional courts, *Aerial Incident at Lockerbie* apparently retreats from the course to judicial activism to which the International Court has been effectively committed since the ruling in *Namibia* in 1971. It is one thing, however, to reject (as the Court has done over the past two decades) the classical, absolutist, "watertight compartments" conceptions of a constitutional separation of powers within the United Nations system that would prevent more than one UN organ from dealing with a particular problem at the same time. It is quite another matter to jump from that earlier, pragmatic constitutional proposition to a further conclusion that the International Court should have plenary constitutional powers to review, and if need be to strike down, the decisions and determinations of the Security Council on the basis of their alleged incompatibility with the UN Charter or with international law in general. In the Court majority view, that might simply have been one constitutional bridge too far to be reached in the confines of a single case. Although the constitutional problem of the proper role and restraints on the Security Council in the post-Cold War era still remains, the minority opinions in the *Aerial Incident at Lockerbie (Provisional Measures)* at least offer an alternative option that may lead to a legal solution.

Edward McWhinney
Simon Fraser University

Sommaire

L'émergence de la Cour Internationale de Justice en tant que Cour Constitutionnelle et les organes principaux des Nations Unies, tel le Conseil de Sécurité: les répercussions juridiques de l'affaire de *L'incident aérien de Lockerbie (la Libye c. le Royaume-Uni)*

La fin de la guerre froide accompagnée de la disparition du système de l'après-guerre fondé sur un équilibre politico-juridique, est-ouest, au sein du Conseil de Sécurité et de l'Assemblée Générale de l'ONU, a des conséquences importantes, bien qu'encore imprécises, pour la Cour Internationale de Justice. Dans sa jurisprudence des dernières deux décennies, la Cour, sous l'impulsion surtout du juge Lachs, a, d'une manière constante, nié l'existence d'une séparation des pouvoirs constitutionnels (telle qu'elle existe dans les systèmes nationaux occidentaux) au niveau des institutions internationales. Au contraire, la Cour a souligné qu'il existe une complémentarité de pouvoirs entre les organes principaux de l'ONU, y inclus la Cour elle-même.

Ainsi, il serait inopportun d'écarter entièrement cette conception hautement pragmatiste pour conclure que la Cour détient aujourd'hui le droit constitutionnel de contrôler, de limiter et de restreindre au nom de la Charte de l'ONU les organes internationaux d'un rang égal à la Cour, tel le Conseil de Sécurité. En effet, la Cour Internationale n'est pas encore une cour constitutionnelle spéciale comme la Cour Suprême des États-Unis ou celle de l'Allemagne, et ce, même si certains des juges de la Haye le laissent sous-entendre actuellement. La controverse susmentionnée est à la base de la divergence intellectuelle entre les onze juges majoritaires et les cinq juges dissidents dans l'affaire de l'incident aérien de Lockerbie (la Libye c. le Royaume-Uni), dont le jugement a été rendu par la Cour Internationale en avril 1992. Cette décision comporte d'importantes conséquences pour la Cour elle-même ainsi que pour l'ONU toute entière.

Consultation Procedures under UN Rules
for the Control of Restrictive Business Practices

INTRODUCTION

D URING THE 1970s, as part of the United Nations' èffort to
promote a new "economic order,"[1] several major undertakings
relating to international trade and development were begun.[2]
These efforts invariably centred around two issues: the need to
assist the less developed countries (LDCs) in their quest for economic and social development, and the need to harness the powers

[1] Declaration on the Establishment of a New International Economic Order, G.A.
Res. 3201 (S-VI), UN GAOR *Ad Hoc* Comm., 6th Spec. Sess., Agenda Item 7, UN
Doc. A/RES/3201 (S-VI) (1974), reprinted in 13 Int'l. Leg. Mat. 715 (1974).
The Declaration was based upon the concepts of equity, sovereign equality,
interdependence, common interest, and co-operation, and was aimed at elim-
inating the widening gap between developed and developing countries. The
Declaration was adopted by the General Assembly on a voice vote. Reservations
were entered by the United States, the United Kingdom, the Federal Republic of
Germany, France, and Japan; Canada did not enter a reservation.

[2] Charter of Economic Rights and Duties of States, G.A. Res. 3281 (XXIX), UN
GAOR 2d Comm., 29th Sess., Agenda Item 48, UN Doc. A/RES/3281 (XXIX)
(1974), reprinted in 14 Int'l. Legal Mat. 251 (1975). For a timely analysis of the
Charter holding the view that it ushered in a new era in international law, see
R. White, "A New International Economic Order," 24 Int'l. & Comp. L.Q. 542
(1975). Compare White with I. Brownlie, *Principles of Public International Law*
541-43 (4th ed. 1990) (maintaining that while certain provisions of the Charter
seem to be evidence of new customary international law, it does not bind the
United States and its associates since they have been "persistent objectors" to
the Charter). The Charter was adopted by the General Assembly on a vote of
120 to 6, with 10 abstentions. Canada abstained and, thus, is not a "persistent
objector" in the strict sense. For other examples of UN undertakings, see Draft
Code of Conduct on Transnational Corporations, UN Doc. E/1990/94 (1990),
UN Doc. ST/CTC/SER. A/4 (1986); Draft International Code of Conduct on
the Transfer of Technology, UN Doc. TD/CODE TOT/25 (1980), reprinted in
19 Int'l. Legal Mat. 773 (1980).

of transnational corporate enterprises to aid in that quest.[3] The Set of Multilaterally Agreed Equitable Principles and Rules for the Control of Restrictive Business Practices[4] is one of those efforts.

As the United Nations nears the end of twenty years of work on these various undertakings, the Set can claim a measure of success. For example, unlike the proposed UN Code of Conduct on Transnational Corporations on which work began in 1975[5] and which has not yet been adopted by the General Assembly,[6] the Set has just celebrated its tenth anniversary.[7] The reasons for its early adoption and implementation seem to rest upon two significant factors.

First, the Set takes the form of recommendations and not a legal code.[8] Because it is always more acceptable to states to be asked to co-operate rather than be told that they must co-operate, the Set is replete with the word "should" and avoids the "shall" language of juristic command. Exemplifying this precatory thrust in the docu-

---

[3] For a discussion of this proposition by the UN Centre on Transnational Corporations, see Draft Code of Conduct on Transnational Corporations, UN Doc. ST/CTC/SER. A/4 (1986), at 1-3. Cf. Muma, "TNC's and Economic Development," 31 CTC Rep. 25 (1991) (which maintains that industrialization and transnational corporations are seen as the engines of growth for LDCs, but create problems as well).

[4] UN Doc. TD/RBP/CONF. 10/Rev. 1, approved G.A. Res. 35/63, 48 UN GAOR-Supp. (No. 61c); UN Doc. A/RES/35/63 (1980), reprinted in 19 Int'l. Legal Mat. 813 (1980) [hereinafter Set].

[5] Information Paper on the Negotiations to Complete The Code of Conduct on Transnational Corporations, UN Doc. E/C. 10/1983/S/2 (1983), para. 9.

[6] As 1991 approached, the General Assembly called for intensive consultations aimed at the adoption of a code for transnational corporations, but adoption has not yet happened: G.A. Res. 45/186, UN GAOR 2d Comm., 45th Sess., Agenda Item 12, UN Doc. A/RES/45/186 (1991).

[7] Report of the Second United Nations Conference to Review all Aspects of the Multilaterally Agreed Equitable Principles and Rules for the Control of Restrictive Business Practices, UN Doc. TD/RBP/CONF. 3/9 (1991) [hereinafter Second Conference Report], para. 3.

[8] Set, *supra* note 4, pream. Since adoption of the Set, several nations have argued that the voluntary nature of the Set is not very effective in controlling RBPs: see Second Conference Report, *supra* note 7, para. 90 (India), para. 164 (China). The market-economy countries and eastern European countries have generally rejected any suggestions that the Set should become a legally binding code, however. See Report of the Intergovernmental Group of Experts on Restrictive Business Practices on its Ninth Session, UN Doc. TD/B/1261 (1990) [hereinafter Ninth Session Report], para. 34 (German Democratic Republic), para. 65 (USSR); Proposals for the Improvement of the Set of Principles and Rules, UN Doc. TD/B/RBP/73 (1990), para. 5 (The Netherlands for Group B).

ment, the concluding section of the Set reads in part as follows: "States which have accepted the Set of Principles and Rules *should take appropriate steps* at the national or regional levels to meet their commitment to the Set of Principles and Rules."[9] Further, the Set establishes an Intergovernmental Group of Experts (IGE) as its institutional machinery. In so doing, it specifically proscribes the Group from acting as a tribunal or in any way passing judgment on the activities of governments and enterprises.[10]

Second, the Set provides benefits both for LDCs and for developed market-economy countries. For LDCs, it promises help in controlling the restrictive business practices (RBPs) of transnational business enterprises, which can result in their obtaining immense international market power and impairing the trade and economic development of the LDCs.[11] For developed market-economy countries, the Set advances the free-market proposition that economic benefits flow from an international marketplace that is open, robust, and free from RBPs.[12] RBPs, sometimes referred to as anti-competitive behaviour, are activities by business enterprises

---

[9] Set, *supra* note 4, Section G.2 [emphasis added].

[10] *Ibid.*, Section G.4: "In the performance of its functions, neither the Intergovernmental Group nor its subsidiary organs shall act like a tribunal or otherwise pass judgement on the activities or conduct of individual Governments or of individual enterprises in connexion with a specific business transaction. The Intergovernmental Group or its subsidiary organs should avoid becoming involved when enterprises to a specific business transaction are in dispute."

[11] Restrictive Business Practices Affecting International Trade, Particularly That of Developing Countries, and the Economic Development of These Countries, UN Doc. TD/RBP/CONF/2 (1979), paras. 1-5; Restrictive Business Practices Information, UN Doc. TD/B/RBP/INF. 19 (1987), para. 27. The Philippines, speaking for the Group of 77 at the Second Review Conference on the Set, called for a solemn commitment from all countries to implement the Set in view of the dominant role played by transnational corporations in the world economy and, in particular, in the economies of the LDCs: Second Conference Report, *supra* note 7, para. 15.

[12] Restrictive Business Practices Information, *supra* note 11, para. 26. The Netherlands, speaking for Group B at the Second Conference on the Set, noted that the Set had an important part to play in controlling anti-competitive practices: Second Conference Report, *supra* note 7, para. 30.

"which aim at gaining a dominant position of market power."[13] A business enterprise can gain such a position either by becoming the sole enterprise engaged in a certain business endeavour or by entering into agreements with competitors to fix prices and allocate markets.[14] The latter types of RBPs are also called cartel agreements.[15]

The control of RBPs may be approached in several ways.[16] National legislation targeted at RBPs is quite common in the developed market-economy countries. It is well known that the United States, for instance, has a significant arsenal of anti-trust law "aimed at preserving free and unfettered competition as the rule of trade."[17] There are limits, however, to the effectiveness of such national legislation at the international level. Even in those coun-

[13] Restrictive Business Practices Information, *supra* note 11, para. 1. In the Set, *supra* note 4, Section B.1, RBPs are defined as follows: " 'Restrictive business practices' means acts or behaviour of enterprises which, through an abuse or acquisition and abuse of a dominant position of market power, limit access to markets or otherwise unduly restrain competition, having or being likely to have adverse effects on international trade, particularly that of developing countries, and on the economic development of these countries, or which through formal, informal, written or unwritten agreements or arrangements among enterprises have the same impact."

[14] Restrictive Business Practices Information, *supra* note 11, para. 2. In the Set, *supra* note 4, Section B.2, dominant market power is defined as follows: " 'Dominant position of market power' refers to a situation where an enterprise, either by itself or acting together with a few other enterprises, is in a position to control the relevant market, for a particular good or service or group of goods or services."

[15] The main types of cartels include: "domestic cartels," which act to keep outsiders from selling in a particular market and can, therefore, seriously hamper imports; "import cartels," which act as centralized buying organizations of the foreign supply of certain products; "export cartels," which act as centralized selling organizations for the sale in foreign places of certain products; and "international cartels," which enterprises from different countries join to control restrictively certain markets. For a review of these main types of cartels and the types of activities in which they engage, see Restrictive Business Practices Information, *supra* note 11, paras. 3-8.

[16] For a general discussion of the various approaches to RBP control, see Moschel, "International Restraints of Competition: A Regulatory Outline," 10 Nw. J. Int'l. L. & Bus. 76 (1989).

[17] See *Northern Pacific Railway* v. *United States*, 356 U.S. 1, 4 (1958) (holding that preferential routing agreements compelling the grantees and lessees of land owned by the railroad to ship over the railroad's lines were unreasonable restraints of trade under s. 1 of the Sherman Act).

tries that subscribe to an "effects doctrine,"[18] problems relating to conflicts of law and international comity work against effective RBP control in the international arena.[19]

In addition to national legislation, bilateral investment and co-operation treaties are also available to control RBPs at the international level; that they may do it more effectively than national legislation is balanced against the fact that they apply their controls

---

[18] The "effects doctrine" adopted by U.S. courts stands for the proposition that a court may exercise jurisdiction in anti-trust matters whenever activity abroad has consequences or effects within the forum state. See *U.S.* v. *Aluminum Company of America*, 148 F.2d 416 (2d Cir. 1945); *Timberlane Lumber Company* v. *Bank of America*, 549 F.2d 597 (9th Cir. 1976); *Laker Airways* v. *Sabena Belgium World Airways*, 731 F.2d 909 (D.C. Cir. 1984). Compare *A. Ahlstrom Osakeyhtio et al.* v. *EEC Commission*, [1987-88 Transfer Binder] Common Mkt. Rep. (CCH) para. 14,491, at 18,595 (1988) (the Court of Justice of the European Communities has not specifically adopted the "effects doctrine," favouring instead the principle of territoriality as the underpinning for jurisdiction; a fair reading of this decision, however, allows for the conclusion that the Court has also not specifically rejected the effects doctrine and therefore has preserved for itself some leeway for the future). For a review of this European Court decision, see Franklyn P. Salimbene, *"The 'Effects Doctrine' and Extraterritorial Jurisdiction in EC Competition Law: The Wood Pulp Case,"* 23 N. Atl. Reg'l. Bus. L. Rev. 201 (1990).

[19] E.g., Canada through the Competition Act (June 1986), the Federal Republic of Germany through the Act Against Restraints of Competition (July 27, 1957), and Finland through the Act on Restrictive Business Practices (1988) have addressed the issue of the jurisdictional reach of competition legislation. Under the Canadian legislation (s. 83), the Competition Tribunal, which deals with civil law matters under the Competition Act, may prohibit the implementation of a decision that is made by a person in Canada as a result of directives from persons outside Canada for the purpose of giving effect to a conspiracy entered into outside Canada that, if entered into in Canada, would have constituted a conspiracy to lessen competition. For the Canadian government's comments on this issue, see Preparations for a Handbook on Restrictive Business Practices Legislation, UN Doc. TD/B/RBP/58 (1989) at 8. The Competition Act, with commentary by the Canadian government, is also set out in this document. Under the German legislation (s. 98(2)), the effects doctrine was adopted, but is viewed as somewhat restrained in its application, owing to considerations of international law and administrative practice. The Finnish legislation does not apply outside Finnish territory insofar as Finnish customers are not affected, although its application may be extended if a treaty between Finland and another country allows for it, or if it is in the interest of Finland's foreign trade. For an analysis of the German and Finnish legislation, see Preparations for a Handbook on Restrictive Business Practices Legislation, UN Doc. TD/B/RBP/71 (1990) at 19, 31.

only in circumstances affecting the signatories.[20] Multilateral approaches may also be used to liberalize trade and protect against barriers to free competition; these take their cue from the General Agreement on Tariffs and Trade (GATT)[21] and from the Organization of Economic Co-operation and Development (OECD).[22] It is into this category of multilateral approaches that the Set falls.

OVERVIEW OF THE SET

While it is not a treaty, the Set carries the force of a General Assembly Resolution.[23] Its aim is to control restrictive business practices that "can adversely affect international trade."[24] In so controlling RBPs, the Set seeks to promote the liberalization of tariff and non-tariff barriers,[25] to nurture competition,[26] to control the concentration of capital and economic power,[27] to protect the interests of consumers,[28] and to maximize benefits to international trade.[29]

---

[20] For examples of such treaties, see the Memorandum of Understanding as to Notification, Consultation, and Co-operation with respect to the Application of National Antitrust Laws, Mar. 9, 1984, Canada-U.S., reprinted in 23 Int'l. Legal Mat. 275 (1984); Agreement Relating to Co-operation on Antitrust Matters, June 29, 1982, U.S.-Austl., reprinted in 21 Int'l. Legal Mat. 702 (1982); Agreement Relating to Mutual Co-operation Regarding Restrictive Business Practices, June 23, 1976, U.S.-G.F.R., reprinted in 15 Int'l. Legal Mat. 1282 (1976).

[21] Opened for signature Oct. 30, 1947, 61 Stat. A3, T.I.A.S. No. 1700, 55 UN Treaty Series 187 (effective Jan. 1, 1948). See also Jackson, *World Trade and the Law of GATT* (1969).

[22] Revised Recommendation of the Council Concerning Co-operation between Member Countries on Restrictive Business Practices Affecting International Trade, OECD Doc. C (86) 44 (1986), reprinted in 25 Int'l. Legal Mat. 1629 (1986).

[23] For a review of the significance in international law of General Assembly resolutions, see I. Brownlie, *supra* note 2, at 14; M. Akehurst, *A Modern Introduction to International Law* 27 (5th ed. 1984).

[24] Set, *supra* note 4, pream.

[25] *Ibid.*, s. A.1.

[26] *Ibid.*, s. A.2(a).

[27] *Ibid.*, s. A.2(b).

[28] *Ibid.*, s. A.3.

[29] *Ibid.*, s. A.4.

Following the statement of objectives, definitions, and scope, the Set is divided into five main sections. Section C lists the equitable principles that are to be applied generally for the control of restrictive business practices. These principles call upon States to take appropriate national, regional, and international action of a mutually reinforcing nature to deal with RBPs.[30] The equitable nature of these principles is highlighted by the implication that states act in good faith through collaboration, the dissemination of information regarding RBPs, a willingness to enter into consultations with other states, and the reminder that developed countries in their control of RBPs ought to be aware of the development needs of LDCs.[31]

Section D is addressed to business enterprises. It calls upon these enterprises to conform with the RBP law of the countries in which they operate, to consult with the governments of those countries in matters relating to RBPs, and to provide information for the control of RBPs to governments within whose jurisdiction they operate.[32] Further, this section sets out the specific types of RBPs from which business enterprises should refrain; these include price-fixing, collusive tendering, market or customer allocation arrangements, allocation by quota as to sales and production, and collective action in the forms of concerted refusals to deal, concerted refusals of supplies to potential importers, and collective denials of access to arrangements or associations that are crucial to competition.[33]

---

[30] *Ibid.*, s. C.

[31] Equity has been associated with several United Nations undertakings that call for co-operation among nations. These requests often encourage collaboration: see, e.g. the Final Act of the Havana Conference on Trade and Employment, UN Doc. E/CONF. 2/78, UN Sales No. 1948. II. D. 4 (1948), art. 11. For the sharing of information, see the *Draft Code of Conduct on Transnational Corporations* (1990), *supra* note 2, paras. 51, 61, and 66(c). For the need for preferential treatment for the developing countries, see the *Declaration on the Establishment of a New International Economic Order*, *supra* note 1, para. 4(n).

[32] Set, *supra* note 4, ss. D.1, D.2.

[33] *Ibid.*, s. D.3. This section of the Set has been criticized for excluding from its purview the dealings between parent enterprises and their subsidiaries. Thus, the Group of 77 has proposed that the exemption for these dealings be deleted (Ninth Session Report, *supra* note 8, Annex III, para 2(a)). S.D.3, however, needs to be read in conjunction with s. D.4, which covers intra-firm transactions where they constitute an abuse or an acquisition and abuse of a dominant position of market power, as follows:

> Enterprises should refrain from the following acts or behavior in a relevant market when, through an abuse or acquisition and abuse of a dominant

Section E focuses on the principles and rules to which states ought to adhere in dealing with RBPs. States are encouraged to adopt and enforce RBP legislation[34] and to take remedial action against the use of RBPs that adversely affect international trade.[35] In their relations with business enterprises, states are called upon to improve their procedures for obtaining information necessary for the control of RBPs[36] while according this business information

---

position of market power, they limit access to markets or otherwise unduly restrain competition, having or being likely to have adverse effects on international trade, particularly that of developing countries, and on the economic development of these countries:

(a) predatory behavior towards competitors, such as using below cost pricing to eliminate competitors;

(b) discriminatory (i.e., unjustifiably differentiated) pricing or terms or conditions in the supply or purchase of goods or services, including by means of the use of pricing policies in transactions *between affiliated enterprises* which overcharge or undercharge for goods or services purchased or supplied . . .

(d) fixing the prices at which goods exported can be resold in importing countries;

(e) restrictions on the importation of goods which have been legitimately marked abroad with a trademark identical or similar to the trademark protected as to identical or similar goods in the importing country where the trademarks in question are of the same origin, i.e., belong to the same owner or are used by *enterprises, between which there is economic, organizational, managerial or legal interdependence* and where the purpose of such restrictions is to maintain artificially high prices [emphasis added].

34 Set, *supra* note 4, s. E.1. The developed market-economy countries have consistently favoured the vigorous implementation of this section. In comments at the Second Review Conference on the Set, the representative for Group B noted that the best defence for international business competition was the enactment and enforcement of national legislation aimed at restrictive business practices. He commented, "Experience with regulatory reform — or deregulation — showed that, once government regulations were removed in a particular sector, the existence of effective competition legislation was of paramount importance": Second Conference Report, *supra* note 7, paras. 26-30.

35 Set, *supra* note 4, s. E.4. The developed market-economy countries, however, have opposed an interpretation of this section that would encourage action by a state, even if there is no effect on its own territory: see Preparations for the United Nations Conference to Review All Aspects of the Set of Multilaterally Agreed Equitable Principles and Rules for the Control of Restrictive Business Practices, UN Doc. TD/B/RBP/69 (1990) [hereinafter Preparations] para. 51.

36 Set, *supra* note 4, s. E.6.

those "reasonable safeguards normally applicable" to protect confidentiality.[37] As a general proposition, states are asked to ensure that treatment of enterprises is "fair, equitable, on the same basis to all . . . and in accordance with established procedures of law."[38] In their dealings with each other, states are invited to establish regional and subregional mechanisms for assisting one another in RBP control[39] and to share their information[40] and expertise[41] with other states that wish to develop and improve their tools for the control of RBPs.

International measures are the focus of Section F. The long-term objective noted in this section is the achievement of "a common approach" by states, consistent with the Set, in their control of RBPs.[42] To assist in this control, the United Nations Conference on Trade and Development (UNCTAD) is to act as a facilitator in the dissemination of information. The Set, therefore, calls upon UNCTAD to provide experts, conduct seminars, prepare handbooks, and sponsor international conferences.[43]

States are encouraged to share in this international effort by agreeing to consult with other states on issues related to the control

[37] *Ibid.*, s. E.5.

[38] *Ibid.*, s. E.3. This standard of treatment is echoed in the *Draft Code of Conduct on Transnational Corporations* (1990), *supra* note 2, paras. 49-50, and in the Final Act of the Havana Conference on Trade and Employment, *supra* note 31, art. 11(2)(a)(i).

[39] Set, *supra* note 4, s. E.7. The LDCs have proposed the establishment of a centralized registry within UNCTAD for reporting RBPs. This registry would be open for consultation by any state on request: see Preparations, *supra* note 35, para. 66.

[40] Set, *supra* note 4, s. E.9.

[41] *Ibid.*, s. E.8. In its effort to assist states in sharing expertise on RBPs, UNCTAD is preparing a handbook on RBP legislation pursuant to s. F.6(c) of the Set. The compilation of the handbook is an ongoing process to which states contribute as legislation is enacted. Recent contributions were offered by Brazil and Norway in anticipation of the Tenth Session of the IGE: Preparations for a Handbook on Restrictive Business Practices Legislation, UN Doc. TD/B/RBP/82 (1991) [hereinafter Handbook].

[42] Set, *supra* note 4, s. F.1.

[43] *Ibid.*, s. F.6. Pursuant to this section, UNCTAD has established a program for technical assistance to LDCs. The assistance takes the form of advisory missions, regional and national seminars, and information collection and dissemination: Restrictive Business Practices Information, *supra* note 11, paras. 35-38. See also Technical Assistance Advisory and Training Programmes on Restrictive Business Practices, UN Doc. TD/RBP/CONF. 3/4 (1990).

of RBPs.[44] The issue of consultations, which is discussed at length in the following section of this article, was raised both at the Second United Nations Conference to Review All Aspects of the Set (Second Conference) held in Geneva during November and December 1990,[45] and at the tenth session of the Intergovernmental Group of Experts (IGE) held also in Geneva during October 1991.[46]

The Set concludes in Section G with the establishment of the IGE as the institutional machinery for UNCTAD's efforts in the control of RBPs.[47] As already noted, the IGE does not act as an enforcement agency,[48] but rather co-ordinates UNCTAD's efforts as facilitator in RBP control.[49] In this regard, the IGE meets annually and issues reports on those discussions and on other subjects germane to implementing the Set.

THE SET AND CONSULTATION PROCEDURES

In considering proposals for the improvement and further development of the Set, the Second Conference addressed three issues: namely, technical assistance, improving transparency, and defining consultation procedures.[50] Subsequently, the UNCTAD secretariat prepared a detailed report with specific proposals in each of the above areas.[51] While the three issues are related, the focus in this article is on consultation procedures.

At the outset, several points should be made regarding the issue of consultation procedures. First, the control of RBPs in a global marketplace with reduced governmental barriers to trade requires some co-ordination among states of their respective competition

---

44 Set, *supra* note 4, s. F.4.

45 *Second Conference Report, supra* note 7, para. 8.

46 Information and Consultation Procedures on Restrictive Business Practices, UN Doc. TD/B/RBP/78 (1991) [hereinafter Information 1991] paras. 11-26.

47 Set, *supra* note 4, s. G.1. The Group of 77 has called for the IGE to be upgraded to the status of a committee within UNCTAD: Ninth Session Report, *supra* note 8, Annex III, para. 2(a).

48 *Supra* note 10.

49 Set, *supra* note 4, s. G.3.

50 Second Conference Report, *supra* note 7, para. 8.

51 Proposals on Transparency and Consultation Procedures in the Field of Restrictive Business Practices, UN Doc. TD/RBP/CONF. 3/3 (1990) [hereinafter Proposals].

policies.[52] This co-ordination seems all the more urgent as many former centrally-planned economies reform their systems and begin to develop market economies, often with little experience in free-market mechanisms.[53]

Second, consultation under the Set provides a convenient vehicle for this co-ordination of national RBP policies.[54] Nevertheless, despite the need for co-ordination, the consultation procedures under the Set have never been followed.[55] The reasons given for this lack of application vary. Speaking for the Group of 77 (the developing countries), at the Second Conference, the Philippines held that the absence of a "more detailed application procedure for . . . consultations" was the reason.[56] India, speaking for itself, was rather blunt in its assessment of the issue, maintaining that the consultation procedures had not been employed because the developing countries had little bargaining power with either the developed market-economy countries or their transnational business enterprises.[57] In its own evaluation of the failure of states to follow the Set's consultation procedures, the IGE provided a welcomed perspective. Noting that other international mechanisms in place for the control of RBPs also had not successfully implemented

---

52 Following the Report of the Second Conference and the call for effective competition legislation at the national level (*supra* note 34), UNCTAD, in its preparations for the tenth session of the IGE noted, "While markets irresistibly lead towards globalization, national jurisdictions are irremediably limited at the national borders. This means that States . . . will have to resort to multilateral efforts to resolve issues in the area of restrictive business practices": Information 1991, *supra* note 46, para. 23.

53 Bulgaria reported that it was undergoing a comprehensive reform of its economic system aiming at the establishment of an open-market economy, and that efforts to improve consultations under the Set were welcome: *Second Conference Report, supra* note 7, paras. 116-119.

54 Restrictive Business Practices Information, *supra* note 11, paras. 30-32.

55 Proposals, *supra* note 51, para. 71. In an assessment of the lack of success in implementing the consultation procedure under the Set, s. F.4, the UNCTAD Secretariat noted that there was no concrete evidence of why the procedure had not been used and proposed, therefore, that measures be adopted to facilitate the use of consultation procedures: Preparations, *supra* note 35, paras. 73-76.

56 Second Conference Report, *supra* note 7, para. 22.

57 *Ibid.*, para. 90.

consultation procedures,[58] it concluded: "at the present time there would seem to be no perfect model for a well-functioning international consultation procedure in the field of RBPs." [59]

Third, while this disappointment with the lack of a working consultation procedure was evident, there was no call at the Second Conference for a change in the language of section F.4 of the Set, which is the consultation clause.[60] Rather, the general thrust of the remarks seemed to be that the process for consultations needed to be clarified.[61] To this end, the UNCTAD secretariat prepared a note for the tenth session of the IGE regarding the consultation procedures.[62] In it, the secretariat emphasized that the provisions of section F.4 provided "a good basis for consultations" and went on

---

[58] Where consultation procedures had been used, as with the OECD procedure, the Secretariat noted that they were followed largely on an informal basis and agreed upon in an *ad hoc* manner: Preparations, *supra* note 35, para. 72. The Revised OECD Recommendation of the Council and the accompanying Appendix, which set out the OECD consultation procedure, were adopted by the Council at its 643d meeting on May 21, 1986: Proposals, *supra* note 51, Annex.

[59] Preparations, *supra* note 35, para. 72.

[60] Section F.4 reads as follows:

(a) Where a State, particularly of a developing country, believes that a consultation with another State or States is appropriate in regard to an issue concerning control of restrictive business practices, it may request a consultation with those States with a view to finding a mutually acceptable solution. When a consultation is to be held, the States involved may request the Secretary-General of UNCTAD to provide mutually agreed conference facilities for such a consultation;

(b) States should accord full consideration to requests for consultations and upon agreement as to the subject of and the procedures for such a consultation, the consultation should take place at an appropriate time;

(c) If the States involved so agree, a joint report on the consultations and their results should be prepared by the States involved and, if they so wish with the assistance of the UNCTAD secretariat, be made available to the Secretary-General of UNCTAD for inclusion in the annual report on restrictive business practices.

[61] See the comments by the representative for the Group of 77 in Second Conference Report, *supra* note 7, para. 22; also comments by the representative for Group D calling for a study for improving consultation procedures in Ninth Session Report, *supra* note 8, para. 36; also comments by the representative for the Group B countries suggesting efforts at identifying elements that would assist states in holding consultations in Second Conference Report, *supra* note 7, para. 34.

[62] Information 1991, *supra* note 46.

to offer "a checklist of possible steps which countries might wish to follow in . . . their request for consultation."[63]

Several scenarios for consultations are envisaged in the secretariat's checklist. Part A addresses the restraints imposed by private companies located in other countries on competition within the country seeking consultations.[64] Under this scenario, an affected state might wish, first, to consult with the state in which the company is located to identify the type of RBP involved; second, to obtain information or evidence regarding the RBP; third, to discuss any difficulties the requesting state might have concerning the service of documents or enforcement of measures; and fourth, to review any unilateral or bilateral enforcement measures that might be undertaken to avoid any adverse effect on the interests of either state.[65]

Part B of the checklist relates to a state's governmental policies regarding RBPs and the effect of those policies at the international level. The requesting state may be either a state affected by the policies of another government or a state whose governmental policies may affect another state. Policies considered here may be in the form of legislation, regulations, and trends in court practice.[66]

Part C addresses the suggested procedures for consultations. It sets forth two approaches, one labeled "informal" and the other "formal."[67] In the commentary on this part, however, the UNCTAD secretariat advises that experience has demonstrated a preference among states for informality in consultations. Therefore, regardless of the label, the checklist offers "only different degrees of informality."[68]

This checklist has been drafted against a backdrop of divergent views regarding consultation procedures in general. These differences seem to centre around two major issues: first, whether the consultation procedure is to be viewed as mandatory; second, whether information can be gathered without disclosing information that ought to remain confidential.

Regarding the first issue, the Group B (developed) countries have always opposed a mandatory consultation procedure. At the ninth session of the IGE in 1990, The Netherlands argued for

[63] *Ibid.*, para. 12.
[64] *Ibid.*, para. 21.
[65] *Ibid.*, para. 21, A(2).
[66] *Ibid.*, para. 16.
[67] *Ibid.*, paras. 21, C (2), (3).
[68] *Ibid.*, para. 19.

Group B that there was no justification "for replacing the Set's consultation procedures with the complex and mandatory consultation regime proposed by the Group of 77."[69] Pointing to the voluntary nature of the OECD consultation process, the representative for Group B maintained that making consultations mandatory was not the way to get countries to engage in consultations. He argued that more countries would engage in consultations if more countries adopted and applied RBP legislation; the solution, therefore, in his view, was for countries to enact the needed legislation.[70] Further, he argued that the rejection of compulsory procedure should also apply to the gathering of information in anticipation of any consultation. On this point, in the report of the Second Conference, The Netherlands "stressed the importance of the voluntary nature of the procedure for requesting information."[71]

In its proposal on consultation procedures written for the Second Conference, the secretariat did not argue for a mandatory procedure. It did, however, suggest that the Set's consultation procedure needed to be facilitated in several ways.[72] It proposed, first, the maintenance of a regularly updated list of the authorities in each country that were empowered to lodge and receive requests for consultations;[73] second, the drafting of a request form for consultations;[74] third, the publication of the results of any consulta-

---

69 Ninth Session Report, *supra* note 8, para. 52. The Group B countries generally have maintained the view that the most effective approach to controlling RBPs is through consultations that are bilateral, informal, and voluntary. There is a rejection of any revision in the language of s. F.4, especially a change that would turn consultations into "arbitrational investigations": Second Conference Report, *supra* note 7, para. 81.

70 Ninth Session Report, *supra* note 8, para. 52.

71 Second Conference Report, *supra* note 7, para. 110.

72 The Secretariat offered the view that the support on the part of Group B for an informal and voluntary consultation procedure under s. F.4 seems to emanate from their experience in the OECD. The Secretariat noted, without criticizing Group B's position, that it was perhaps easier for countries with well-established relationships to forego the support that would be provided by a more formal process: Proposals, *supra* note 51, paras. 74-75.

73 Proposals, *supra* note 51, para. 75.

74 *Ibid.*, para. 76. The Secretariat emphasized that this proposal did not seek to burden the process with formality or obligation and that it left parties full freedom in regard to consultation. The request form has been incorporated into the proposed checklist already discussed, *supra* notes 63-65 and accompanying text.

tions held;[75] and fourth, the implementation of a further procedure for conciliation in cases in which agreements were not
reached in the consultation process.[76] Group B seemed generally to
accept the first two suggestions.[77] The fourth suggestion was
deemed premature.[78] Indeed, there is no reference in the Set to
conciliation. Regarding the third suggestion, the answer is not
clear. Group B has proposed that consultations be held within the
framework of the annual IGE sessions; under these circumstances,
there appears to be no objection to publication of the results.[79]
There is, however, no mention by Group B of whether the results of
consultations outside the IGE sessions ought to be published. In
those situations, the issue of publication seems to be intertwined
with issues relating to the sensitive nature of relations between
states, law enforcement concerns, and the confidentiality of the
information discussed during the consultations.[80]

The second issue over which views diverge relates to this sharing
of information. Recognizing that information is necessary for the
proper development, application, and enforcement of RBP legislation, the Group B countries as well as the Set itself identify two types
of information.[81] They are "publicly available information" and
"other information."[82] The sharing and publication of publicly
available information in the consultation process is accepted.[83] The
sharing of "other information," however, is more problematic, in
the view of Group B. According to the Set, information of this type
must be "necessary to the receiving State" for the effective control
of restrictive business practices, and the sharing of this information
must be consistent with the providing state's established law and

75 *Ibid.*, para. 77.

76 *Ibid.*, para. 78.

77 Second Conference Report, *supra* note 7, para. 109.

78 *Ibid.*, para. 114.

79 *Ibid.*

80 *Ibid.*, para. 112.

81 *Ibid.*, para. 33.

82 Set, s. E.9, reads as follows: "States should, on request, or at their own initiative
when the need comes to their attention, supply to other States, particularly of
developing countries, publicly available information, and, to the extent consistent with their laws and established public policy, other information necessary
to the receiving interested State for its effective control of restrictive business
practices."

83 Second Conference Report, *supra* note 7, para. 110.

public policy. Group B countries approach the issue of sharing "other information" with caution, since the information requested may have been acquired in the course of a governmental investigation,[84] may be commercially confidential,[85] or may for other reasons be illegal to divulge.[86] In this regard, the former centrally-planned Group D countries agree that legal problems might arise "if information which was designed for a specific purpose was also utilized for other purposes."[87]

To some LDCs, this hesitancy on the part of Group B countries concerning the sharing of information seems self-serving. While not speaking as the representative of the Group of 77, India claimed that there had been little evidence of the political will of the developed countries to enforce the Set.[88] In fact, India argued that "there was no justification for RBP control being sacrificed at the altar of global trade competitiveness and of governments deliberately turning a blind eye or even encouraging or colluding with national enterprises in their use of RBPs in international trade."[89] With feelings running as strongly as this among the members of the Group of 77, a few LDCs at the ninth session of the IGE suggested revisions to the Set on the issue of information.[90] Nevertheless, in the Resolution adopted at the close of the Second Conference, rather than changing any language in the Set, the member states simply requested that members provide the secretariat annually with information on new RBP legislation, reports of activities engaged in to control RBPs, and any relevant guidelines and reports that may have been published regarding RBPs.[91]

[84] *Ibid.*

[85] *Ibid.*, para. 33.

[86] *Ibid.*, para. 110.

[87] Ninth Session Report, *supra* note 8, para. 36.

[88] Second Conference Report, *supra* note 7, para. 90.

[89] *Ibid.*, para. 86.

[90] Sri Lanka suggested that s. E.6 should be amended to urge governments of the home states in which business enterprises are located to obtain information from those enterprises if requested to do so by agencies of developing countries: Proposals for the Improvement of the Set of Principles and Rules, *supra* note 8, para. 2. See also Ninth Session Report, *supra* note 8, Annex III (suggested amendments by Algeria on behalf of the Group of 77).

[91] Second Conference Report, *supra* note 7, Annex.

CONCLUSION

The Report of the Intergovernmental Group of Experts on its tenth session has not yet been published.[92] Nevertheless, in view of the results of the Second Conference and the various notes and reports prepared by the UNCTAD secretariat for the tenth session,[93] two observations can be made. First, the language in the Set regarding consultation procedures seems reasonably likely to remain unchanged.[94] Second, while there is the feeling that the Set has not been adequately implemented,[95] there has been some movement on the issue of consultation procedures. Group B for its part has encouraged multilateral consultations[96] and has agreed to the drafting of a checklist for consultation information,[97] and the Group of 77 for its part has registered support for the preliminary steps taken toward the definition of consultation procedures, while accepting that a state's compliance with consultation procedures ought to be voluntary and in consideration of its own legitimate interests.[98] While steps toward agreement may have been taken grudgingly and may appear inconsequential, they bear upon the dual nature of contemporary international economic relations.

[92] A telephone call to the UNCTAD office revealed that, owing to the work being generated by preparations for UNCTAD VIII, the tenth session report had not yet been prepared for publication.

[93] Information 1991, *supra* note 46; Replies by States and Regional Groupings on Steps Taken to Meet Their Commitments to the Set, UN Doc. TD/B/RBP/79 (1991) and TD/B/RBP/79/Add. 1 (1991); Concentration of Market Power, Through Mergers, Take-Overs, Joint Ventures and Other Acquisitions of Control, UN Doc. TD/B/RBP/80 (1991); Revised Draft of Possible Elements for Articles of a Model Law, UN Doc. TD/B/RBP/81 (1991); Handbook, *supra* note 41; Review of Technical Assistance Activities, UN Doc. TD/B/RBP/83 (1991).

[94] See Ninth Session Report, *supra* note 8, para. 34 (Group D opposed textual changes); para. 39 (Group B opposed changes); para. 65 (USSR opposed changes).

[95] Second Conference Report, *supra* note 7, para. 17 (Philippines for the Group of 77); para. 162 (China).

[96] *Ibid.*, paras. 160-161.

[97] *Ibid.*, para. 156.

[98] In their closing statement, the Group of 77 noted their support for the Resolution adopted by the Second Conference, which, *inter alia*, reiterated the voluntary nature of consultations in consideration of legitimate interests: Second Conference Report, *supra* note 7, paras. 155-58, and Annex 8.

While states work to protect their own interests, they do so in the knowledge that all interests are interdependent.

FRANKLYN P. SALIMBENE

Center for Business Ethics, Bentley College, Waltham, MA

Sommaire

Procédures de consultation prévues par les Règles des Nations Unies concernant le contrôle des pratiques commerciales restrictives

Adopté en 1980 par une résolution de l'Assemblée générale, l'Ensemble de principes et de règles équitables convenus au niveau multilatéral pour le contrôle des pratiques commerciales restrictives (Ensemble de principes) énonce bon nombre de règles équitables qui visent à orienter les activités internationales des États et des entreprises commerciales en matière de contrôle des pratiques commerciales restrictives (PCR). L'un de ces principes a été l'objet d'un intérêt particulier lors de la Deuxième conférence de révision sur l'Ensemble de principes tenue en 1990 ainsi que lors de la dixième réunion du Groupe intergouvernemental d'experts en octobre 1991. Il s'agit du principe de consultation.

Jusqu'à la tenue de la dixième réunion, la clause de consultation de l'Ensemble de principes n'avait jamais été invoquée. Bien qu'on ait alors tenté d'expliquer les raisons possibles de cet état de choses, chacun a convenu de l'importance d'encourager les consultations internationales pour le contrôle des PCR. En effet, le besoin de consultation se fait plus pressant pour assurer la coordination internationale des politiques de concurrence étant donné l'importance croissante du marché global pour les économies nationales et la difficile restructuration amorcée par un grand nombre d'anciennes économies à planification centrale.

Les États participant à la Deuxième conférence de révision et à la dixième réunion ont abordé les discussions sur ce besoin de consultation dans le cadre de l'Ensemble de principes par l'intermédiaire de leurs blocs de négociation traditionnels: le Groupe de 77 pour les pays en développement, le Groupe B pour les pays à économie de marché et le Groupe D pour les anciennes économies à planification centrale de l'Europe de l'est. Bien que certains des anciens discours propres aux débats des années 1970 aient été repris, les groupes sont parvenus à s'entendre sur la nécessité de préciser la procédure de consultation prévue par l'Ensemble de principes. Ils ont donné leur appui au projet de rédaction d'une "liste de contrôle" normalisée des consultations, par laquelle un État donné pourrait demander à un autre de participer à des consultations et de fournir des renseignements concernant le contrôle des PCR. En outre, ils ont convenu d'appuyer un processus de consultation qui serait à la fois volontaire, informel et d'accès facile, qu'on procède de façon multilatérale lors des réunions annuelles du Groupe intergouvernemental d'experts ou de façon bilatérale par cas d'espèce.

Récents développements dans
le domaine des services

INTRODUCTION

D ES DÉVELOPPEMENTS IMPORTANTS SONT survenus dans le
domaine des services depuis l'entrée en vigueur de l'Accord
canado-américain de libre-échange (ALÉ).[1] Ce secteur-clé de l'économie canadienne est très vaste et englobe des activités commerciales diversifiées qui vont des services financiers aux services de
transport, en passant par l'informatique et les télécommunications.
De plus, il couvre des aspects variés de la vie économique et sociale
canadienne, la dimension commerce allant aussi de pair, en
matière de services, avec la dimension investissement et mobilité
des travailleurs.

En fil de ligne, il y a l'importante dé-réglementation au niveau
fédéral des institutions financières canadiennes qui a résulté, au
mois de juin 1992, en l'adoption de quatre nouvelles lois sur les
institutions financières. Il s'agit de la *Loi sur les banques*,[2] la *Loi sur les
sociétés d'assurance*,[3] la *Loi sur les associations coopératives de crédit*[4] et la
Loi sur les sociétés de fiducie et de prêt.[5] Une masse de règlements a aussi
été adoptée dans la même foulée.[6] Dans ce secteur, les provinces se
sont aussi montrées très actives. Par exemple, on a observé au

---

[1] Publié comme une annexe à la *Loi de Mise en oeuvre de l'Accord de libre-échange
Canada-États-Unis*, L.C. *1988, c.65.*

[2] 1991, c.46.

[3] 1991, c.47.

[4] 1991, c.48.

[5] 1991, c.45.

[6] Pour une description générale des règlements, voir Gaz. C. 1992, Part I. 423.
Un nombre considérable de règlements ont été abrogés par le *Décret général
d'abrogation de 1992*, DORS 92-329, Gaz. C. 1992, Part.II. 2271. La plupart ont
été remplacés à la même époque ou peu après, ceux qui restent le seront
incessamment.

Québec l'adoption en 1989 de la *Loi sur les intermédiaires de marché*[7] et, sous l'égide de celle-ci, de quelques règlements importants,[8] de singulières modifications aux règles de propriété de la *Loi sur les assurances*,[9] et l'adoption, en 1991, de la nouvelle *Loi sur le courtage immobilier*.[10]

Dans les autres secteurs de services, nous avons assisté, dans le domaine du transport, à l'adoption, au mois de juin 1992, de la *Loi sur le cabotage* qui réserve, de façon générale, le transport par voie maritime de marchandises ou de personnes à l'intérieur des eaux canadiennes aux seuls navires canadiens.[11]

Dans le secteur des communications, le gouvernement canadien, qui avait adopté en 1989 deux règlements sur les droits de retransmission,[12] a jugé nécessaire en 1991 de préciser à la Commission

[7] L.R.Q., c.I-15.1. Elle s'applique aux agents et courtiers en assurance de dommages ou de personnes, aux experts en sinistres, aux planificateurs financiers, aux courtiers et conseillers en valeurs mobilières et à leurs représentants. À ce jour, elle est entrée partiellement en vigueur. Voir le plus récent décret du gouvernement du Québec. Décret 1012-91, Gaz. Q. 1991, Part.II. 4387.

[8] Le *Règlement de l'institut québécois de planification financière*, Décret 1013-91, Gaz. Q. 1991, Part.II. 4400; le *Règlement du Conseil des assurances de personnes sur les intermédiaires de marché en assurance de personnes*, Décret 1014-91, Gaz. Q. 1991, Part.II. 4404; le *Règlement du Conseil des assurances de dommages sur les intermédiaires de marché en assurance de dommages*, Décret 1015-91, Gaz. Q. 1991, Part.II. 4434; le *Règlement de l'Association des intermédiaires en assurance de personnes du Québec*, Décret 1016-91, Gaz. Q. 1991, Part.II. 4466; le *Règlement de l'Association des courtiers d'assurances du Québec*, Décret 1017-91, Gaz. Q. 1991, Part.II. 4472; le *Règlement sur les planificateurs financiers*, Décret 1018-91, Gaz. Q. 1991, Part.II. 4480; le *Règlement sur les titres similaires à celui de planificateurs financiers*, Décret 1019-91, Gaz. Q. 1991, Part.II. 4491; le *Règlement sur les cabinets multidisciplinaires*, Décret 1020-91, Gaz. Q. 1991, Part.II. 4492.

[9] L.R.Q., c.A-32, mod. par la *Loi modifiant la Loi sur les assurances et d'autres dispositions législatives*, 1990, c.86. Les dispositions de cette loi sont entrées en vigueur en deux temps, soit le 15 mars et le 1er juillet 1991. Décret 285-91, Gaz. Q. 1992, Part.II. 1455. Les non-résidents peuvent désormais détenir collectivement jusqu'à 30% des actions des compagnies d'assurance québécoises et peuvent demander à être soustraits, comme les résidents, de l'application des règles sur la propriété.

[10] 1991, c.37. Elle est aujourd'hui partiellement en vigueur. Décret 1255-91, Gaz. Q. 1991, Part.II. 5189.

[11] 1992, c.31. Elle n'était pas encore entrée en vigueur à la date du présent article.

[12] Le *Règlement sur la définition de signal local et signal éloigné*, DORS/89-254, Gaz. C. 1989, Part.II; Le *Règlement sur la définition de petit système de retransmission*, DORS/89-255, Gaz. C. 1989, Part.II.

sur le droit d'auteur les critères qu'elle doit prendre en considération lorsqu'elle établit les tarifs pour la retransmission des signaux éloignés de radio et de télévision.[13]

Dans le domaine des télécommunications et des services informatiques, le projet de loi tant attendu sur les télécommunications a finalement été déposé au mois de février 1992 devant la Chambre des communes.[14] Le Conseil de la radiodiffusion et des télécommunications canadiennes (CRTC) a aussi rendu une importante décision concernant l'introduction de la concurrence dans le service téléphonique interurbain.[15] Quant à elle, la Commission de révision des marchés publics a examiné un nombre considérable de plaintes concernant la fourniture de matériels et logiciels informatiques.[16]

Finalement, dans le secteur des services professionnels, le processus de consultation entre les architectes des deux pays concer-

[13] *Règlement sur les critères applicables aux droits à payer pour la retransmission,* DORS/91/690, Gaz. C. 1991, Part.II. 4647. Ce règlement a été adopté en vertu de la Loi sur le droit d'auteur, L.R.C. C.42, art. 70.63. Notons que les tarifs établis en 1990 par la Commission du droit d'auteur, *Tarifs des droits à payer pour la retransmission de signaux éloignés de radio et de télévision au Canada,* Gaz. C. 1990, Part.I (supp.), continuent provisoirement de s'appliquer en 1992 en attendant que la Commission fixe les tarifs définitifs. Commission du droit d'auteur, *Décision provisoire portant sur les droits à payer pour la retransmission de signaux éloignés de radio et de télévision au Canada en 1992,* Gaz. C. 1991, Part.I. 3777.

[14] P.L. C-62, *Loi concernant les télécommunications,* 3ème sess., 34e Lég. Can., 1991-1992. Notons que le gouvernement entend seulement permettre une participation étrangère limitée dans les entreprises canadiennes de télécommunications. En effet, les entreprises, qui demanderont des licences afin d'exploiter des entreprises de télécommunications au Canada, devront être détenues et contrôlées par des canadiens dans une proportion de 80%. *Ibid.,* arts. 17 et 18 para(3).

[15] Décision Telecom-CRTC 92-12.

[16] Voir notamment les décisions rendues dans les affaires concernant LANs PLUS INC. et le Ministère des Affaires extérieures (micro-ordinateurs et périphériques), Gaz. C. 1989, Part.I. 5102 (avis de plainte); Gaz. C. 1990, Part.I. 466 (décision); 99M Corporation et le Ministère du Revenu national (cartes d'extension), Gaz. C. 1991, Part.I. 1300 (avis de plainte); Gaz. C. 1991, Part.I. 1955 (décision); ENCORE Computer limitée et le Conseil national de recherches du Canada (système d'acquisition de données), Gaz. C. 1992, Part.I. 189 (avis de plainte); Gaz. C. 1992, Part.I. 660 (décision); Network Support Inc. et le Ministère de l'Industrie, des Sciences et de la Technologie (logiciel), Gaz. C. 1992, Part.I. 583 (avis de plainte); Gaz. C. 1992, Part.I. 929 (retrait de la plainte).

nant la reconnaissance professionnelle et l'autorisation d'exercer bat son plein. Des progrès importants ont aussi été réalisés concernant la mobilité des professionnels entre les deux pays.[17]

Suite à ce rapide tour d'horizon, nous examinerons dans les prochaines pages deux de ces développements qui sont d'un grand intérêt pour l'ALÉ. D'abord, nous nous tournerons du côté de la réforme fédérale des institutions financières et commenterons la conformité de la nouvelle *Loi sur les assurances* avec l'ALÉ. Nous glisserons ensuite quelques mots sur l'important processus de consultation en architecture, un processus destiné à servir de modèle pour tous les autres secteurs professionnels sur le plan de la reconnaissance professionnelle et de l'autorisation d'exercer.

LA NOUVELLE *LOI SUR LES ASSURANCES*

La nouvelle *Loi sur les assurances* s'inscrit dans le cadre de la récente dé-réglementation fédérale des institutions financières qui, de façon générale, poursuit un double objectif: assurer une plus grande protection des consommateurs et permettre une plus grande compétition dans le secteur financier au Canada.[18]

D'abord, assurer une meilleure protection des consommateurs au moyen d'une plus grande supervision des institutions financières fédérales, de nouvelles règles sur les conflits d'intérêts et les transactions entre initiés. Ensuite, autoriser une plus grande concurrence en retirant certaines des restrictions entourant la prestation des services financiers au Canada, avec de nouvelles règles sur les pouvoirs commerciaux des institutions financières, sur les investissements ou la propriété des institutions financières. L'introduc-

---

[17] Depuis l'entrée en vigueur de l'ALÉ, deux groupes de modifications ont en effet été apportées au chapitre 15 sur l'autorisation de séjour temporaire pour gens d'affaires qui ont concerné principalement les professionnels. Les modifications finales sont contenues dans les deux avis suivants: Ministère des Affaires extérieures, *Avis*, *Gaz. C.* 1991, Part.I. 463; Ministère des Affaires extérieures, *Avis*, *Gaz. C.* 1992, Part.I. 2571. Les deux pays ont modifié la liste des professions apparaissant à l'annexe 1502.1 de l'ALÉ qui énumère les "professionnels" qui peuvent obtenir une autorisation de séjour temporaire au Canada ou aux États-Unis en ajoutant certains professionnels à cette liste et en en retirant d'autres. Ils ont aussi fixé à l'appendice 2 de l'annexe 1502.1 les exigences minimales ou les équivalences en termes d'études que doivent rencontrer les professionnels qui désirent se prévaloir des dispositions du chapitre 15.

[18] Pour avoir un bref aperçu des objectifs des législations fédérales, consulter *Gaz. C.* 1992, Part.I. 423.

tion d'une plus grande concurrence se joue à un double niveau: à un niveau interne, permettre une plus grande concurrence entre les divers types d'institutions financières canadiennes et aussi, à un niveau externe, permettre une plus grande concurrence des institutions financières étrangères.

Cette ouverture du marché financier canadien aux firmes étrangères ne se fera cependant pas à n'importe quel prix. Le gouvernement entend continuer à protéger l'intégrité du système financier canadien. Il a aussi l'intention d'obtenir, en retour, un meilleur accès aux marchés étrangers pour les institutions financières canadiennes; en d'autres mots, il tentera d'arracher la réciprocité aux gouvernements étrangers.

Par exemple, dans la nouvelle *Loi sur les assurances*, l'établissement de nouvelles sociétés étrangères d'assurance au Canada ou l'acquisition de sociétés canadiennes par des sociétés étrangères sont ainsi sujets à l'autorisation du ministre qui sera donnée sur la base de la réciprocité ou en fonction d'un traitement aussi favorable pour les sociétés canadiennes dans ces pays.[19] Une telle autorisation doit aussi être donnée par le ministre avant qu'une société étrangère ne puisse commencer à garantir des risques au Canada.[20]

À ce titre, la nouvelle *Loi sur les assurances* est particulièrement intéressante. Contrairement aux autres services financiers faisant l'objet de la réforme fédérale, les services rendus par les sociétés d'assurance,[21] à l'exception des sociétés d'assurance-dépôt,[22] sont couverts non seulement par les dispositions de l'ALÉ sur les services financiers mais aussi par celles du chapitre général sur les services et celles du chapitre sur les investissements.[23] Comme il s'agit d'une nouvelle loi, elle ne bénéficie pas de la protection de la clause dite grand-père et doit respecter entièrement les dispositions de l'Accord.[24]

---

19 *Loi sur les sociétés d'assurance*, art. 24, para. (1) et 420(2).

20 *Ibid.*, art. 574, para. (2).

21 Statistiques Canada, *Classification type des industries de 1980*, Approvisionnements et services Canada, Ottawa, 1980, nos 7311, 7331 et 7339.

22 *Ibid.*, no. 7321.

23 Les dispositions du chapitre 16 sur les investissements s'appliquent à la fourniture de services d'assurance dans les aspects non-couverts par le chapitre sur les services financiers. ALÉ, art. 1601, para. (2)(a).

24 ALÉ, arts 1402 et 1607.

La nouvelle *Loi sur les assurances* se conforme-t-elle, pour les américains, aux dispositions de l'ALÉ? En partie. Elle respecte entièrement les engagements souscrits par le Canada dans le chapitre sur les services financiers. Elle reprend en effet les modifications législatives occasionnées par l'ALÉ qui ont trait aux règles de propriété dans les sociétés d'assurance-vie.[25] Par contre, les dispositions de la *Loi sur les sociétés d'assurance* qui rendent l'approbation des investissements américains ou des activités des sociétés américaines d'assurance au Canada sujet à la réciprocité aux États-Unis apparaissent clairement incompatibles avec l'obligation de traitement national du chapitre sur les services et les investissements.[26]

Le Canada s'est en effet engagé dans l'ALÉ à accorder sans réserve le traitement national aux américains lors de l'adoption d'une nouvelle loi touchant l'un des secteurs de services visés par l'Accord. Il ne peut rendre l'octroi du traitement national aux institutions américaines conditionnel à l'octroi d'un traitement similaire aux institutions canadiennes opérant aux États-Unis. L'objectif de réciprocité qu'il poursuit ne peut être atteint simultanément mais sera plutôt réalisé lors de modifications futures aux lois américaines sur les assurances.

Au ministère des finances,[27] on soutient que ces dispositions de la *Loi sur les assurances* ne sont pas incompatibles avec l'ALÉ et qu'elles ne le deviendront que si on en fait usage contre les américains. Et l'on ne voit pas pourquoi le ministre refuserait de donner son approbation aux investissements américains ou aux activités des sociétés américaines d'assurance au Canada. On souligne qu'il dispose à cet égard d'un pouvoir discrétionnaire et que, de toute façon, les sociétés canadiennes bénéficient actuellement du traitement national dans la plupart des États américains. Cette position ambiguë surprend un peu. On peut en effet douter de l'utilité de brandir l'exigence de réciprocité contre les américains si on ne compte pas réellement l'utiliser. On peut aussi s'interroger sur les vaines réticences du Canada à reconnaître de façon inéquivoque dans la loi les concessions octroyées aux américains dans l'ALÉ.

---

[25] *Loi sur les sociétés d'assurance*, arts 427 à 431.

[26] ALÉ, arts 1402.1 et 1602.1.

[27] Conversations privées avec des fonctionnaires du Ministère des finances du Canada.

LES ARCHITECTES

Quelques commentaires s'imposent aussi sur le processus de consultation actuel en matière d'architecture.[28] Il est important non seulement pour les architectes mais aussi pour tous les autres professionnels qui pourraient éventuellement s'en inspirer.

Lors de l'adoption de l'ALÉ, on a fait, jusqu'à un certain point, des architectes les cobayes pour ce qui est de la question de l'autorisation d'exercer et la reconnaissance professionnelle. On disait la partie gagnée d'avance. Les pourparlers avaient déjà débuté entre l'Institut royal d'architecture du Canada et l'*American Institute of Architects*,[29] les résultats ne devaient pas trop se faire attendre.

Les consultations entre les architectes ne se déroulèrent cependant pas comme on l'avait prévu dans les offices gouvernementaux. Au délai convenu dans l'Accord, soit le 31 décembre 1989, les associations professionnelles des deux pays soumettaient uniquement aux deux pays un rapport intérimaire sur l'état des négociations.[30] Une nouvelle échéance était fixée, le 31 décembre 1991.

Depuis, les négociations sur la reconnaissance professionnelle des architectes se sont plutôt déroulées entre le Comité des conseils d'architecture du Canada (CCAC) et le *National Council of Architectural Registration Boards* (NCARB). Ces deux organismes, qui représentent respectivement les associations professionnelles des provinces et les *licensing boards* des États et coordonnent les questions de réglementation, sont beaucoup mieux placés pour agir que l'Institut royal d'architecture du Canada et l'*American Institute of Architects*, qui ne sont ni plus ni moins que des groupes de pression. Notons qu'ils n'ont toutefois aucun pouvoir direct dans l'émission

---

[28] De façon générale, voir à ce sujet Industrie, sciences et technologie Canada, *Architectes: Profil de l'industrie*, Approvisionnements et services Canada, Ottawa, 1992, aux pp. 4-6.

[29] L'Institut royal d'architecture du Canada et l'*American Institute of Architects* avaient en effet conclu en 1987 un accord sur le professionnalisme et les échanges de services architecturaux. *The American Institute of Architects and the Royal Architectural Institute of Canada Accord on Professionalism*, 11 août 1987. De plus, ils s'étaient entendus sur un programme de travail concernant l'autorisation d'exercer et la reconnaissance professionnelle, *Enhanced Canada/United States Trade in Architectural Services RAIC/AIA Work Plan*, 11 août 1987.

[30] *Progress Report to the Department of External Affairs of Canada and the Office of the U.S. Trade Representative on Activities of the American Institute of Architects and the Royal Architectural Institute of Canada to Fulfill Obligations Set Forth in Sectoral Annex 1404 of the Canada-U.S. Free Trade Agreement and the RAIC-AIA Accord on Professionalism*, décembre 1989.

de permis. Celle-ci demeure la prérogative absolue des associations professionnelles des provinces ou des *licensing boards* des États.

À ce jour, les négociations entre les organismes d'architectes canadiens et américains ne sont toujours pas achevées. Des progrès considérables ont toutefois été réalisés sur le plan de la reconnaissance professionnelle et l'autorisation d'exercer. Ils seront entérinés sous peu dans un protocole d'inter-reconnaissance entre le CCAC et le NCARB. Celui-ci est présentement sous étude et devrait être signé au cours de l'année 1993, aux alentours du mois de juin.[31] En voici les points saillants.

Les architectes canadiens qui rencontreront les normes de qualification ayant trait à l'éducation, à l'expérience professionnelle et aux examens, qui ont déjà été définies par le NCARB et adoptées au mois de juillet 1991 dans un document connu sous le nom de l'Annexe C,[32] pourront recevoir le certificat du NCARB. Ce certificat leur permettra ensuite d'obtenir un permis d'exercice dans la majorité des États américains.

Le certificat du NCARB servira aussi à la reconnaissance des architectes américains au Canada. Ceci pourra en surprendre plusieurs. Il faut toutefois dire que le CCAC ne délivre pas de certificat comme le NCARB. On a donc accepté le certificat du NCARB comme document de référence du côté canadien. Ainsi, les diverses associations provinciales, parties au protocole, accorderont des permis aux architectes américains qui seront titulaires du certificat du NCARB et se qualifieront professionnellement au Canada.[33]

Le processus d'émission de permis, qui sera ainsi largement simplifié, sera aussi libéré des entraves usuelles concernant la nationalité ou la résidence. Pour pouvoir obtenir un permis dans un État ou une province, les architectes canadiens et américains n'auront

---

[31] *Interrecognition Agreement between the National Council of Architectural Registration Boards and the Committee of Canadian Architectural Councils*, version présentement sous étude.

[32] NCARB, *Appendix C to Circular of Information No. 1: Education, Training and Practice Standards and Examination Requirements for NCARB Certification of Canadian Architects*, juillet 1991. L'Annexe C vient reconnaître, selon certains critères précis, l'équivalence de la formation académique et professionnelle acquise par les architectes canadiens. Concrètement, un architecte québécois qui aura obtenu un diplôme d'une université reconnue, qui aura réussi les examens de l'Ordre des architectes du Québec et exercera sa profession depuis trois ans aura droit à ce certificat. Voir à ce sujet, "Unanimous Vote for Resolution 13 Paves the Way for U.S./Canadian Reciprocity" *The Reporter*, juillet 1991.

[33] Le pendant canadien de l'Annexe C est l'annexe A.

plus à obtenir la citoyenneté de l'autre pays ou à s'y établir. De plus, ils n'auront plus à exercer leur profession en co-entreprise ou en association avec des architectes locaux.

Un travail considérable a donc été accompli par les deux organismes d'architecture. Ils ne sont cependant pas au bout de leurs peines. Dans les prochains mois, ils devront déployer auprès de leurs membres des efforts considérables de persuasion afin d'en assurer la mise en oeuvre, qui dépendra ultimement de la volonté des associations professionnelles provinciales et des *licensing boards* des États.

Est-ce dire que tous les obstacles à la mobilité des architectes canadiens et américains seront alors supprimés? Ce ne sera malheureusement pas encore le cas. Par exemple, les architectes canadiens ne pourront pas obtenir automatiquement un permis de travail dans tous les États, sur la base du certificat émis par le NCARB. Même s'ils pourront l'avoir automatiquement dans une quarantaine d'États, certains États beaucoup plus protectionnistes, comme la Floride, continueront à exiger, à la fois des américains et des étrangers, des normes plus élevées pour leur émettre des permis. Il reste aussi à revoir les questions d'éthique et à harmoniser les règles qui ont trait aux entités juridiques autorisées à exercer la pratique de l'architecture dans les provinces et États.

En dépit des obstacles subsistant à la libre-prestation des services architecturaux au Canada et aux États-Unis, les opportunités d'affaires seront néanmoins excellentes pour les architectes des deux pays au cours des prochaines années. Elles seront encore meilleures avec l'ouverture future de l'ensemble du marché nord-américain, suite à la signature de l'Accord de libre-échange nord-américain (ALÉNA).[34] Celle-ci ne peut toutefois être envisagée dans un avenir immédiat. Les trois pays chercheront surtout, les premières années, à mieux se connaître; on peut envisager par la suite l'octroi de permis d'exercice sur une base temporaire mais une véritable libéralisation ne peut être escomptée véritablement avant une dizaine d'années.

Soulignons finalement, de façon plus générale, que le couronnement du processus actuel de consultation en matière d'architecture pourrait aussi susciter une plus grande libéralisation de l'ensemble

[34] Le Canada, les États-Unis et le Mexique ont signé, le 8 octobre 1992, un accord de libre-échange nord américain (ALÉNA). Pour plus d'information, voir CANADA, *Accord de libre-échange nord-américain: Vue d'ensemble et description*, Ottawa, Approvisionnements et services Canada, 1992.

des services professionnels en servant de modèle ou de prototype pour les autres professionnels intéressés.Il n'est cependant pas, non plus, sans indiquer les nombreuses difficultés les guettant dans des négociations à deux avec les États-Unis, et, encore plus, à trois avec le Mexique: multiplicité des intervenants, disparité des interlocuteurs, diversités des intérêts des provinces et des États, dissemblances des régimes juridiques. La tâche qui attend les ingénieurs, notaires, comptables et autres professionnels désireux de capitaliser sur l'ALÉ ou le futur ALÉNA est donc considérable.

CONCLUSION

L'impact de ALÉ dans le secteur des services a été jusqu'à présent assez limité. Ceci ne surprend guère vu que les deux pays ont préféré donner en ce domaine aux obligations de l'ALÉ une application limitée, partielle et prospective ou ont choisi, dans le secteur professionnel, de laisser les groupes intéressés s'entendre entre eux. Les deux développements examinés dans ce bref commentaire doivent cependant être vus comme des signes avant-coureurs des développements à venir. De plus en plus de lois et règlements, comme la *Loi sur les assurances,* ne pourront plus échapper à l'application des obligations de l'Accord. La libéralisation des services professionnels, déclenchée par les architectes, est aussi appelée à s'accentuer dans les années à venir et est appelée à prendre, avec l'ALÉNA, une dimension nord-américaine.

CHRISTIAN JOLIVET*
L.L.B.,LL.M. Chercheur au groupe de recherche informatique et droit de l'Université du Québec à Montréal

* Les travaux dont le présent article rend compte ont bénéficié de l'appui financier du Conseil de recherches en sciences humaines du Canada.

State Immunity. *Re Canada Labour Code:*
A Common Sense Solution to the
Commercial Activity Exception*

INTRODUCTION

IN *Re Canada Labour Code*, the Supreme Court of Canada has for the first time considered the State Immunity Act of Canada.[1] The case arose when the United States challenged the jurisdiction of the Canada Labour Relations Board over an application for certification by the Public Service Alliance of Canada on behalf of locally engaged staff at the United States naval base in Argentia, Newfoundland. It is important because it has afforded the Court the opportunity to give direction on the "commercial activity" exception to the rule of immunity set out in the Act.

Parliament enacted the State Immunity Act in 1982 to give effect to the customary international law principle of restrictive immunity. The Act cleared up the doubt that had been lingering in the case law over the continued application of the old common law rule of absolute immunity.[2] But the new law did not represent a radical break with the past. Under section 3, the general rule is still that

---

* The views expressed in this comment are not necessarily those of the Department of Justice or the Government of Canada.

---

[1] *United States of America v. Public Service Alliance of Canada* (indexed as *Re Canada Labour Code*), [1992] 2 S.C.R. 3.

[2] State Immunity Act, S.C. 1980-81-82, c. 95 (now R.S.C. 1985, c. S-18). For the legislative history of the Act, and a comparative analysis of the British State Immunity Act, 1978, c. 33 and the United States Foreign Sovereign Immunities Act, 28 U.S.C. § 1603 *et seq.*, see H. L. Molot and M. L. Jewett, "The State Immunity Act of Canada" (1982) 20 Canadian Yearbook of International Law 79.

foreign states are immune from the jurisdiction of Canadian courts. However, in sections 4-8, five exceptions to immunity are set out, of which two are relevant here: waiver of immunity (section 4) and the commercial activity exception (section 5).

The commercial activity exception is the cornerstone of the scheme of restrictive immunity established under the Act.[3] It codifies the distinction that was emerging in the common law between conduct that relates to public or sovereign activities (*acta jure imperii*) and conduct that relates to commercial acts (*acta jure gestionis*).[4] The foreign state retains immunity with respect to the former but is subject to the jurisdiction of the courts of the host state with respect to the latter. However, the Act provides little guidance on how a court is to determine whether an activity is commercial. Unlike the British State Immunity Act, the Canadian statute does not provide a detailed definition of a commercial transaction; in this respect, it is similar to the Foreign Sovereign Immunities Act of the United States.[5] In *Re Canada Labour Code*, the Supreme Court of Canada has now given direction on the scope of

[3] S. 2 of the State Immunity Act defines "commercial activity" as "any particular transaction, act or conduct or any regular course of conduct that by reason of its nature is of a commercial character." There are two components to this definition. On the one hand, it refers to a "regular course of conduct" that is commercial in nature. This envisages situations in which the foreign government conducts a business, such as a trading company, a commercial bank, or a shipping line. The other part of the definition refers to "any particular transaction, act or conduct" that "by reason of its nature" is commercial in character. It is this latter, transactional focus that is relevant here.

[4] In *Gouvernement de la République démocratique du Congo v. Venne*, [1971] S.C.R. 997, a majority of the Supreme Court of Canada held that a foreign state could claim immunity from the courts of Quebec in relation to a dispute over the fees of an architect for its pavilion at Expo 67. In his dissenting judgment, Laskin, J. (as he then was) attacked the continued validity of an absolute rule of immunity. In *Lorac Transport Ltd. v. The Atra*, [1987] 1 F.C. 108, a case arising before the entry into force of the State Immunity Act, the Federal Court of Appeal held that the common law had evolved since *Venne* to endorse a restrictive scheme of immunity similar to that codified in the Act.

[5] Under s. 3 of the United Kingdom State Immunity Act, 1978, contracts of employment are specifically excluded in the definition of "commercial transaction," with the result that foreign states retain immunity with respect to such matters. However, in draft articles on the jurisdictional immunities of states and their property, the International Law Commission has considered treating *individual* contracts of employment as a separate category from commercial transactions, but with respect to which a foreign state will not enjoy immunity. See, e.g., *Yearbook of the International Law Commission*, vol. 1 in A/CN.4/SER.A/1984.

the exception and has provided an indication of the circumstances
in which it may be invoked.

THE FACTS

In May 1987, the Public Service Alliance of Canada (PSAC) filed
an application with the Canada Labour Relations Board for certification as a bargaining agent on behalf of the Canadian civilian
employees at the United States naval base located at Argentia,
Newfoundland.[6] The naval base was established during the Second
World War pursuant to a 1941 treaty between the United Kingdom
and the United States known as the Leased Bases Agreement.[7]
When Newfoundland entered Confederation in 1949, Canada
became the successor state to the United Kingdom with respect to
the Agreement.

Under the terms of the lease, the base is controlled by the United
States, which, until recently, operated a high security communications centre there, employing about five hundred American and
seventy Canadian military personnel. In addition, the United States
employed sixty Canadian civilians who performed most of the maintenance operations at the base. These locally-engaged workers had
no military functions and no access to the secure facilities of the
base without a special pass and military escort.

In 1982, the Canadian workers entered into a memorandum of
understanding with the base commander through the Union of
National Defence Employees, now a component of PSAC, under
which they agreed that the union and the base commander would
jointly determine whether a majority of employees wanted a collective agreement, and, if so, that they would begin negotiations with a
view to concluding such an agreement. However, this never
occurred because of a dispute between the base commander and
the union over the applicable law. Originally, both parties had
mistakenly believed that United States law would apply.[8] Upon
learning that it would not apply to non-American citizens employed
outside the United States, the base commander appears to have

6 Canada Labour Code, R.S.C. 1985, c. L-2.
7 [1952] C.T.S. No. 14, Mar. 27, 1941. The Agreement established a lease for a
period of 99 years. This lease was incorporated into the laws of Newfoundland
by the American Bases Act, S.N. 1941, c. 12 and continued under the Terms of
Union between Canada and Newfoundland in 1949 (Newfoundland Act, R.S.C.
1985, Appendix II, No. 32, Schedule, s. 18).
8 Federal Service Labor-Management Relations Act, 5 U.S.C. § 7103(a)(2)(i).

been unwilling to proceed under the laws of Canada. Nevertheless, the union began to sign up members and in 1987 it filed an application for certification with the Canada Labour Relations Board.

THE DECISIONS

Canada Labour Relations Board

When the union filed an application for certification with the Board, the United States Department of the Navy objected to the proceedings and claimed the benefits of state immunity under section 3 of the State Immunity Act. On November 12, 1987 the Board held a hearing on the question of jurisdiction, at which the United States did not appear. The Attorney General of Canada, however, who was given status as a *mise-en-cause*, argued that the Board lacked jurisdiction.

The Board found that it had jurisdiction on the grounds that, in entering the local labour market and hiring civilian employees, the United States had engaged in a commercial activity within the meaning of section 5 of the State Immunity Act. However, in view of the "exceptional and complex character of this case," the Board invoked section 28(4) of the Federal Court Act to refer three questions to the Federal Court of Appeal. One of these questions concerned its finding that the United States could not claim state immunity as provided in section 3 of the State Immunity Act, and the other two concerned its finding that Parliament as opposed to the provincial legislature has jurisdiction over labour relations on the base.

Federal Court of Appeal

At the Federal Court of Appeal, the jurisdiction of the Canada Labour Relations Board to entertain the application for certification was unanimously upheld by Mahoney, J. A., who wrote the principal reasons, and by Iacobucci, C. J. (as he then was), who added a separate concurring opinion. Stone, J. A. concurred with both.[9] The United States, supported by the Attorney General of Canada, appeared before the Court for the purpose of invoking immunity. The union and the Board defended the initial finding of

9 See *Re Canada Labour Code*, [1990] 1 F.C. 332.

the Board. As a preliminary matter, it had been conceded that the Board is a "court" for the purposes of the State Immunity Act.

Although the Federal Court of Appeal upheld the jurisdiction of the Board, both Mahoney, J. A. and Iacobucci, C. J. affirmed the Board's decision that the United States had not waived immunity within the meaning of section 4(2)(a) of the State Immunity Act. Under that section, a foreign state submits to the jurisdiction of the court where it "explicitly submits to the jurisdiction of the court by written agreement or otherwise either before or after the proceedings commence."

The union argued that the United States had waived immunity under Article 9 of the 1951 North Atlantic Treaty Status of Forces Agreement, which provides that the conditions of employment and work — in particular wages, supplementary payments, and conditions for the protection of workers — shall be those laid down by the legislation of the receiving state.[10] The Status of Forces Agreement has been implemented in part in Canada through the Visiting Forces Act.[11]

Iacobucci, C. J. found that at most the Status of Forces Agreement amounted to an "implicit" waiver, but that the State Immunity Act required "explicit" submission to the jurisdiction of the court. He could find nothing in the Agreement that constituted explicit submission to "judicial or adjudicative jurisdiction." Mahoney, J. A. also agreed with the Board that the NATO agreement did not meet the test of explicit waiver in the Act. Consequently, at the next stage of the proceedings, the union abandoned its argument that the United States had waived immunity by virtue of the Status of Forces Agreement, and the issue was not argued.

Although the Supreme Court of Canada has not considered the issue of waiver, the decision of the Federal Court of Appeal provides reasonable guidance on the circumstances in which it may be invoked. In the future, to establish waiver, it would appear to be necessary to show that the foreign state has specifically turned its mind to the possibility of "judicial or adjudicative proceedings." In other words, there needs to be some evidence that the foreign state has voluntarily agreed to submit itself, either generally or with respect to a class of matters, to the jurisdiction of the courts of Canada. As a result, it is doubtful that a finding of waiver will be possible where it is asserted merely as the consequence of some

[10] [1953] C.T.S. No. 13.
[11] R.S.C. 1985, c. V-2.

ulterior act; that would not satisfy the requirement of explicitness in the legislation.

On the more important issue of the applicability of the commercial activity exception set out in section 5, the Federal Court of Appeal upheld the finding of the Board that the contracts of employment of the Canadian civilian employees constituted commercial activity within the meaning of section 2 of the State Immunity Act. In so doing, the Court relied upon the "close relationship" between the Canadian Act and the Foreign Sovereign Immunity Act of the United States as justification for drawing inspiration from American authorities to define the extent of the commercial activity exception.[12] In particular, Mahoney, J. A. adopted the "private person" test from the United States Court of Appeals decision in *Texas Trading and Mill Corp.* v. *Federal Republic of Nigeria:* "if the activity is one in which a private person could engage, it [the foreign state] is not entitled to immunity."[13]

The *Texas Trading* case involved a breach of contract for the sale of goods and related letters of credit. However, Mahoney, J. A. said that he could see "no rational basis" for distinguishing between contracts for the purchase of goods or services and contracts of employment for the purposes of the State Immunity Act.[14] He allowed that the exercise by the Board of its jurisdiction to certify "goes a good deal further than the enforcement of employees' rights and employers' obligations under employment contracts," and that he was "disturbed" by this result.[15] Nevertheless, he came to the conclusion that certification proceedings "relate" to the employment of persons under contracts of service, "entry into which is, in my view, plainly, 'conduct . . . of a commercial character' on the part of the U.S."[16] Only where one looks beyond the nature of the contracts of employment to consider their broad purpose — the defence requirements of the United States — could Mahoney, J. A. find a rationalization for state immunity. Nevertheless, in his opinion the statute specifically prohibited any consideration of the "purpose" of a transaction in characterizing it as commercial or not, since a purposive approach would be inimical to the restrictive scheme of immunity established under the Act.

[12] [1990] 1 F.C. 332 at 339.
[13] 647 F.2d 300 (2d Cir., 1981) at 309.
[14] *Supra* note 9, at 347.
[15] *Ibid.*, at 347-48, 349.
[16] *Ibid.*, at 349.

Iacobucci, C. J., although agreeing with the result, expressed a word of caution over the use of the "private person" test.[17] But he came to the same conclusion as Mahoney, J. A. that the employment contracts were the "heart of the matter" and that they constituted a transaction or activity that was commercial in nature.[18] He granted that the purpose of the employment was to further state objects, but he believed that the Canadian Act, like the United States Foreign Sovereign Immunities Act, requires a court to focus exclusively on the nature of the activity rather than on its purpose.[19] For the Chief Justice of the Federal Court, the fact that the Canadian statute, unlike the American legislation, does not specifically proscribe any consideration of purpose was not significant. He held:

I believe the SIA and, in particular, the provisions of section 5 and the definition of commercial activity in section 2, do not countenance the purpose or object of the state's activity but rather compel us to focus on the nature of the alleged commercial activity in issue.[20]

Indeed, Iacobucci, C. J. suggested that a consideration of purpose would introduce a wider net of immunity, such as that which existed under the traditional common law rule of absolute immunity, "which could lead to defeating the statutory objective of adopting a restrictive approach to immunity as reflected in the SIA."[21]

Supreme Court of Canada

The United States appealed the decision of the Federal Court of Appeal to the Supreme Court of Canada. The Attorney General of Canada intervened as a respondent along with the union and the Board, but supported the appellant in arguing that the United States was immune from the jurisdiction of the Board. The Court, in a three–two decision, allowed the appeal, with La Forest, J. delivering the opinion of the majority that the commercial activity exception was inapplicable in the case (L'Heureux-Dubé and

17 *Ibid.*, at 340.

18 *Ibid.*, at 339.

19 The U.S. Foreign Sovereign Immunities Act, *supra* note 2, stipulates that "the commercial character of an activity shall be determined by reference to the nature of the course of conduct or particular transaction or act, rather than by reference to its purpose."

20 *Supra* note 9, at 339.

21 *Ibid.*, at 338-39.

Gonthier, JJ. concurring). Cory, J. wrote the dissenting opinion (Sopinka, J. concurring).

The Majority Opinion

The majority had no difficulty agreeing with the Federal Court of Appeal and the Board that the contracts of employment at the base were the product of a commercial activity on the part of the United States: that is, the act of entering the local labour market and hiring maintenance personnel. Consequently, the Court held that the locally-engaged staff would generally be entitled to enforce their contracts in Canadian courts. However, La Forest, J. found that employment at the base had a double aspect, that it was at once commercial and sovereign in nature, and that the proceedings before the Canada Labour Relations Board related to the sovereign or immune aspects of employment rather than to its commercial elements.

The majority was clearly concerned over the intrusiveness of the collective bargaining regime under the Canada Labour Code into labour-management relations at the base and its potential to disrupt military operations. It found that, under collective bargaining, the United States would be powerless to compel the Argentia employees to end a strike, and that the Board would be able to inquire in a variety of ways into the internal affairs of the base, including such matters as dismissal for security reasons, terms of a collective agreement, and information on operations. In the opinion of the Court, "these would be unacceptable intrusions into the sovereign realm of the Argentia base."[22]

On the other hand, the majority did not want to divest Canadian employees of all recourse to the courts under the common law of contract. Its solution to balancing the interests of the foreign state with those of the workers was to divide matters that strike at the authority of the foreign government to "manage and control" its sovereign activities from those that do not.[23] In other words, the majority distinguished between the individual contracts of employment entered into between the base and the employees and labour relations at the base in general. Further, it assessed the impact of upholding the jurisdiction of the courts on both aspects of employment at the base.[24] La Forest, J. agreed with the finding of the

[22] [1992] 2 S.C.R. 3 at 83.

[23] *Ibid.*, at 78.

[24] *Ibid.*, at 76.

Federal Court of Appeal that the Canada Labour Code conferred powers on a domestic tribunal to force a foreign state to bargain over conditions of employment and ultimately to impose those conditions where the parties could not agree.[25] This result is clearly very different from that obtained when a domestic tribunal enforces the terms of a contract of employment into which the foreign state has freely entered.

The Federal Court of Appeal had disregarded the distinction between contracts of employment and collective bargaining, because it thought that an analysis of the impact of upholding the Board's jurisdiction over labour-management relations in general amounted to straying into a consideration of the purpose of employment at the base rather than into its nature. The Supreme Court of Canada, on the other hand, held that nothing in the Act forbids a court from taking into account the purpose or context of an activity with a view to its characterization, including assessing the impact of upholding jurisdiction on the operations of the foreign state. Relying on the decision of the House of Lords in *I Congreso del Partido*,[26] La Forest, J. held that the court must consider the whole context in which the claim against the state is made. "The entire context," he wrote, "includes both the nature and purpose of the act."[27] The majority found it significant that the Act omitted the explicit requirement in the American statute to characterize an activity by reference to its nature and *not* to its purpose (disagreeing with the Federal Court of Appeal that the requirement is implicit). La Forest, J. said that "by excluding the qualifying language found in the American model, Parliament, it seems to me, must have intended that purpose was to have some place in determining the character of the relevant activity."[28]

---

[25] For the Federal Court of Appeal statement on this point, see *supra* note 12, at 348.

[26] [1983] A.C. 244.

[27] *Supra* note 22, at 73.

[28] *Ibid.*, at 74. Indeed, La Forest, J. questioned whether under U.S. law the courts are truly barred from considering the purpose of an activity. He cited *De Sanchez* v. *Banco Central de Nicaragua*, 770 F.2d 1385 (1985), *Rush Presbyterian-St. Luke's Medical Center* v. *Hellenic Republic*, 877 F.2d 574 (1989), and *Joseph* v. *Office of Consulate General of Nigeria*, 830 F.2d 1018 (1987) for the proposition that American courts continue to consider the purpose of an activity, despite "legislation that would seem to invite the contrary position."

La Forest, J. recognized that purpose should not predominate, since that would convert virtually every commercial activity into an immune sovereign activity. He said, however, that the converse is also true. Rigid adherence to the nature of an act — "an antiseptic distillation of a 'once-and-for-all' characterization of the activity in question" — would render innumerable governmental activities commercial in character.[29] Holding that "nature and purpose are interrelated," he wrote:

if consideration of purpose is helpful in determining the nature of an activity, then such considerations should be and are allowed under the Act. Further, when an activity is multi-faceted in nature (as in the instant case) consideration of its purpose will assist in determining which facets are truly "related" to the proceedings in issue.[30]

The majority, therefore, considered that, taken in context, the proceedings before the Board did not relate to the commercial nature of the contracts of employment, but to the imposition of non-consensual labour-management relations under the Canada Labour Code. Relying on previous decisions of the Court that held that labour relations tribunals impinge upon powers that have traditionally been considered to be management prerogatives,[31] the Court held that "there is too tenuous a connection" between the individual contracts of employment and the collective bargaining regime.[32] Whereas the former may relate to a commercial activity of the United States, the latter would affect the vital management and control of the base.

In arriving at its solution, the majority declined to follow the American case of *Goethe House New York, German Cultural Center* v. *N.I.R.B.*,[33] which had figured largely in the decisions of the Board and the Federal Court of Appeal and in the arguments of the respondents before the Supreme Court of Canada. In that case, a majority of the United States Court of Appeals, in *obiter*, had failed to see how the presence of a union would interfere with Goethe House's implementation of German cultural policy. The Court had

[29] *Ibid.*, at 73.

[30] *Ibid.*, at 70.

[31] *Bell Canada* v. *Quebec (Commission de la Santé et de la Sécurité du Travail,* [1988] 1 S.C.R. 749 at 825 per Beetz, J. (part of a trilogy of cases including *Canadian National Railway Co.* v. *Courtois,* [1988] 1 S.C.R. 868, and *Alltrans Express Ltd.* v. *British Columbia (Workers' Compensation Board),* [1988] 1 S.C.R. 897).

[32] *Supra* note 22, at 81.

[33] 869 F.2d 75 (2d Cir. 1989).

overturned a district court injunction that had been granted on the basis that the German government could claim sovereign immunity from the jurisdiction of the National Labor Relations Board. In *Re Canada Labour Code*, the union and the Board argued that *Goethe House* was directly applicable, since the unionizing of maintenance workers would not affect the military mission of the United States base.

La Forest, J. distinguished the case on the grounds that a military base and a cultural centre involve state activities of a "completely different order."[34] He said that if collective bargaining would be the only effect of certification, he would agree with the majority decision in *Goethe House*. However, in the light of the finding that the Canada Labour Code would permit the Board to intrude into the core management functions of the base, he concluded that the impact of certification would extend beyond unionization or collective bargaining.

Finally, the majority adopted the reservations of Iacobucci, C. J. in the court below with respect to the "private persons" test as a means of distinguishing between acts *jure imperii* and acts *jure gestionis*. It referred to conflicting American authorities to demonstrate the difficulty in applying the test.[35] Specifically, La Forest, J. confined the test to the class of "trading cases" identified by Lord Wilberforce in *I Congreso del Partido*, and indicated the Court's reluctance to see it extended beyond that context.[36]

The Minority Opinion

Although the dissenting opinion of Cory, J. would have upheld the jurisdiction of the Canada Labour Relations Board and denied immunity to the United States, its analysis of the legislative history of the State Immunity Act and the framework for its interpretation is similar to that of the majority. Thus, the Court was unanimous on the difficulty inherent in the "private persons" test that was set out in the American case *Texas Trading*.[37] More important, the dissent agreed with the majority that there should be no necessary dichotomy between the nature and the purpose of an activity, such as that which appeared to prevail under the United States legislation. On this point, Cory, J. wrote: "Sometimes, the nature of the act itself

[34] *Supra* note 22, at 87.

[35] *Ibid.*, at 75.

[36] *Ibid.*, at 89.

[37] *Supra*, note 13.

may only become evident when it is viewed in light of the purpose for which it was undertaken."[38]

Similarly, the dissenting opinion endorsed the contextual approach of the majority in distinguishing between the governmental and commercial activities of a foreign state. In this, Cory, J. approved the dictum of Lord Wilberforce in *I Congreso del Partido*, which states that it is the "whole context" of an activity that must be taken into consideration.[39] In this way, the dissenting opinion agreed that the Canadian statute requires that commercial activity be characterized on a case-by-case basis and does not require an approach that would unduly narrow the scope of the inquiry.

But, although he agreed with the majority on general principles, Cory, J. came to the opposite conclusion from that of the majority, and, it is respectfully submitted, engaged in an analysis that is not on all fours with the principles that the dissent itself endorsed. Thus, the dissent did not really inquire into the purpose or context of employment at the base, despite its endorsement of the possibility of doing so. And notwithstanding the reservations that Cory, J. expressed over the "private persons" text, he for all intents and purposes applied it in saying that "whether or not the United States is entitled to immunity depends . . . on the answer to two questions: (1) what is the task for which the workers were hired? (2) Is the activity of hiring a person to perform that task one in which a private party could engage?"[40]

In his minority judgment, Cory, J. placed great stock in the fact that the employees at the base were not engaged in military functions, but served "merely as support staff."[41] He argued that it made no sense to characterize direct employment of workers by a state as a public act, when the same work performed by private subcontractors would be without question a commercial activity. He then went on to find that:

the employment of maintenance workers with very restricted access to a secure site is certainly an activity in which private parties could engage. The hiring of these workers, therefore, must fall into the category of a private act which by its nature is a commercial activity.[42]

For the minority, the argument that there is a distinction between a

[38] *Supra*, note 22, at 100.
[39] *Ibid.*, at 102-3.
[40] *Supra*, note 22, at 107.
[41] *Ibid.*, at 108.
[42] *Ibid.*

contract of employment that could be considered to be a commercial activity, and a collective bargaining relationship, did not determine the issue. Cory, J. argued that the view that collective bargaining differs in some substantial way from an individual contract of employment arises not so much from a concern over the legal distinction between the two situations but from a concern that, once the Board certifies a union, it would have broad authority to supervise labour-management relations at the base, and from the fear that military operations would be disrupted in the event of a strike by the unionized employees.

For Cory, J., neither the threat of strike action nor the powers of the Board were significant concerns. First, he noted that under the Canada Labour Code there is no bar to the hiring of replacement workers: "it can be, I think, readily assumed that the vast military organization of the United States has easy access to replacement employees."[43] This statement raises the question whether the minority would have come to a different conclusion on immunity if parliament had enacted an "anti-scab" law similar to those that exist in several provinces. Second, Cory, J. recalled that the United States Navy had been prepared to accept an American collective bargaining regime, demonstrating that it was not adverse to the certification of a union in general. Thus, he concluded that there was "no valid reason why Canadians working in Canada should not have the benefit and protection of Canadian law." "Particularly this is so," continued Cory, J., "when it is apparent that Americans working in the United States for a foreign state would, in similar circumstances, have the benefit of American law."[44]

These two statements are open to question, to say the least. The majority specifically rejected the argument that the Canadian workers should have no recourse to the courts and came up with a solution that struck a reasonable balance. As for the minority's view of the situation under United States law, it is speculative at best and hardly the basis for deciding what the law should be in Canada. Indeed, La Forest, J. formally disagreed with the minority's assessment of what the result would be in a similar case under United States law.[45]

[43] *Ibid.*, at 109.

[44] *Ibid.*, at 110-11.

[45] *Ibid.*, at 87. La Forest, J. said that it was not his view that the courts of the United States would consider labour relations at a Canadian embassy or at a foreign military base to constitute a mere commercial activity.

In sum, the minority represents an attempt to give great breadth to the commercial activity exception, although ultimately more on the basis of its view that the Canada Labour Code would have limited impact on the operations of the base and out of its concern for reciprocity flowing from a presumption as to the likely result under United States law than on the basis of any theoretical dispute with the majority. It is true the minority could not accept the idea that there exists a viable distinction between the imposition of a collective bargaining regime and the application of a labour regime agreed to by the parties. But, as mentioned, this amounts to a difference over the impact of collective bargaining and not over whether a court should be engaging in impact analysis in the first place. In this respect, the approach of the minority to the commercial activity exception is closer to that of the majority than it is to that of the Federal Court of Appeal (which believed the Act required a narrower transactional focus).

CONCLUSION

The decision of the Supreme Court of Canada in *Re Canada Labour Code* represents a solid first step in the interpretation of the State Immunity Act. It strikes a reasonable balance between the privileges of foreign states under international law and the public interest in asserting the jurisdiction of the courts and tribunals of Canada when a foreign sovereign engages in a commercial activity in this country. Rejecting any precise method for differentiating between immune and non-immune activities, the Court has adopted a case-by-case or "contextual" approach to the commercial activity exception to immunity, in which both the nature and the purpose of an activity are relevant considerations.

Although both the majority and the minority opinions noted the similarity between the Canadian statute and the Foreign Sovereign Immunities Act of the United States, and amply cited American authorities, the Court has established a distinctively Canadian approach to the application of the commercial activity exception. Both opinions pointed out that the Canadian Act does not enjoin the courts from considering the purpose of an activity in deciding whether it is sovereign or commercial in nature. Indeed, the Court should be commended for moving beyond the rather sterile debate in the American cases on "nature" and "purpose" and engaging in a more realistic assessment of the impact of upholding jurisdiction on the sovereign activities of the foreign state. What the Court has done is to weigh and balance competing interests in a manner similar to its approach to questions of constitutional law. It is not surprising, therefore, that both the majority and the dissent were wary of formalistic techniques such as the "private party" test set out in some of the American cases (although the minority, in view of its subsequent application of the test, appears to have judged the concern as minimal).

Significantly, the majority established a two-stage approach to the question of immunity: first, the judges examined the entire context to determine the nature of the activity, including the purpose of the foreign government in undertaking the activity if that sheds any light on the problem, and second, they assessed the impact of the proceedings on the activity as a whole. They decided that employment at the base had a double aspect, both commercial and sovereign, and that the certification proceedings related to the latter, sovereign aspects of employment at the military base. What is essential is the Court's view that the case concerned collective bargaining under the supervision of a Canadian tribunal with inquisitorial powers, not contracts of employment taken in isolation. If the latter had been the case, the Court made it clear that it would have upheld the jurisdiction of Canadian courts.

So the case cannot be said to be a return to any absolute theory of immunity for a military base, embassy, or other foreign governmental operation in Canada, something the respondents feared. Indeed, although the Court endorsed purposive analysis, it is evident that characterization of an activity as commercial is to be made primarily by reference to its nature. The Court clearly understood that the object of the 1982 legislation was to put in place a scheme of restrictive immunity that unrestrained consideration of purpose would unravel. However, by rejecting simplistic or rigid formulas, and by endorsing a moderate approach to determining whether the proceedings relate to a commercial or sovereign aspect of a state activity, the Court has followed common sense in interpreting the State Immunity Act. In this respect, the Act is off to a good start.

Ross Hornby
Department of Justice, Ottawa

Sommaire

L'immunité des États. *Re Code canadien du travail:* La solution à bon sens de l'exception de l'activité commerciale.

Dans l'affaire Re Code canadien du travail, *[1992] 2 R.C.S. 3, la Cour suprême du Canada interprétait pour la première fois la Loi sur l'immunité des États, L.R.C. 1985, ch. S-18. Cette loi fédérale, adoptée en 1982, codifie la théorie restrictive de l'immunité de juridiction des tribunaux du droit international coutumier. Elle établit une règle générale de l'immunité, à laquelle s'applique cependant un certain nombre d'exceptions, notamment l'exception de l'activité commerciale.*

L'affaire opposait les États-Unis d'Amérique et l'Alliance de la fonction publique du Canada. Ce syndicat demandait l'accréditation à titre d'agent négociateur des civils canadiens travaillant comme personnes de métier pour la marine américaine à la base d'Argentia, à Terre-Neuve. En donnant raison aux États-Unis, la Cour a toutefois évité d'interpréter de façon trop étroite l'exception de l'activité commerciale comme le réclamait l'appelant (les États-Unis).

Rejetant toute "distillation antiseptique afin de qualifier une fois pour toute l'activité en question, quel qu'en soit l'objet," la Cour dans l'arrêt majoritaire a opté pour une méthode contextuelle, faisant de la "nature" d'un acte, ainsi que son "objet" des facteurs pertinents dans l'application de l'exception de l'activité commerciale. Soucieuse d'aller au-delà de ce débat souvent stérile sur la "nature" et l'"objet" d'une activité, la Cour a évalué l'impact de la non-immunité sur l'État étranger, essayant de concilier l'intérêt de ce dernier avec l'intérêt du public dans la juridiction de nos tribunaux.

La majorité a insisté sur la complexité des relations de travail des employés canadiens de la base faisant d'abord ressortir le fait qu'il s'agissait à la fois d'activités commerciales et d'activités souveraines de l'État. Elle a jugé que le fait pour les États-Unis de recruter localement du personnel d'entretien constituait une activité commerciale, et que par conséquent, les employés canadiens avaient le droit de demander aux tribunaux de faire respecter leur contrat de travail. Reconnaissant que l'application des dispositions du Code canadien du travail risqueraient de perturber les opérations militaire de la base, la majorité a toutefois reconnu l'immunité des États-Unis à l'égard de la gestion et du contrôle de l'emploi à la base.

Les dissidents ont mis en doute l'incidence du Code canadien du travail sur les activités militaires de la base et se seraient opposés à ce qu'on fasse droit à la demande d'immunité du gouvernement américain. Ils ont cependant convenu avec la majorité que la façon dont la loi définit l'exception de l'activité commerciale ne s'opposait pas à l'examen de l'objet d'une activité et que le tribunal devait donc tenir compte de l'ensemble du contexte dans lequel elle s'est déroulée.

Chronique de Droit international économique en 1991 / Digest of International Economic Law in 1991

I Commerce

préparé par
MARTIN ST-AMANT*

L'ANNÉE 1991 MARQUE une pause notable dans l'action juridique du Canada au GATT. Les conflits auxquels il fut partie ainsi que l'activité qu'il a déployée cette année là, ont été en effet peu nombreux. Le Canada, en cette période d'incertitude, relativement à la conclusion des négociations commerciales multilatérales de l'Uruguay Round, a ainsi semblé s'en remettre davantage à une mise en oeuvre effective de l'Accord de libre-échange Canada-États-Unis, que ce soit pour accroître l'accès de ses produits et services sur le marché américain ou pour gérer efficacement les différends commerciaux avec son principal partenaire économique.

I CONFLITS ET ACTIVITÉS DANS LE CADRE DU GATT

Dans le cadre du GATT, les principaux conflits impliquant le Canada se rapportaient aux pratiques d'importation de bière et de certaines boissons alcooliques. Ainsi, à la suite de demandes insistantes de la part des États-Unis,[1] le Conseil du GATT instituait le 6

---

* Avocat, Leduc, Lebel (Montréal); candidat au Doctorat en droit commercial international (Université de Paris I).

---

[1] Voir à ce sujet M. ST-AMANT, "Chronique de droit économique international," (1991) 29 *A.C.D.I.*, 418.

317

février, un Groupe spécial chargé d'examiner les pratiques canadiennes d'importation, de distribution et de vente de bière.[2] Le Groupe a présenté son rapport au Conseil du GATT le 16 octobre.[3] Il a conclu que certaines pratiques des organismes provinciaux canadiens qui ont le monopole de commercialisation de la bière, contrevenaient aux dispositions de l'Accord général.[4] Les pratiques visées, lesquelles s'avéraient incompatibles avec les articles II:4, III:4 et XI:1 de l'Accord, concernaient certaines mesures relatives à l'inscription au catalogue, des prescriptions d'emballage, des restrictions concernant l'accès aux points de vente ou la livraison par des circuits privés de la bière importée, des différentiels de majoration, et l'établissement de prix minimaux. Le Groupe spécial recommandait donc au Canada de prendre toutes les mesures raisonnables en son pouvoir afin que les organismes provinciaux se conforment aux dispositions de l'Accord général. Il lui enjoignait en outre, de rendre compte aux Parties Contractantes dès la fin de mars 1992 ou de juillet 1992 des mesures prises pour se plier à ses conclusions. Suite à cette décision, les autorités américaines ont immédiatement indiqué leur intention de recourir à des mesures de représailles sur la base de la section 301 de la législation commerciale américaine si une solution négociée n'était pas trouvée avant la fin de l'année.[5] Le Canada a toutefois fait valoir qu'il était inopportun de prendre de telles mesures alors que le Conseil du GATT n'avait pas encore étudié ce rapport.[6] Il a en outre prétendu qu'en optant pour le règlement du litige par le GATT, les États-Unis avaient accepté de respecter les échéanciers fixés par le Groupe spécial.[7] Du reste, le Canada a souligné qu'il ne s'opposerait pas à l'adoption du rapport à la première réunion du Conseil en 1992.[8]

D'autre part, le Canada a demandé au titre de l'article XXIII:1 l'ouverture de consultations avec les États-Unis au sujet de diverses

---

[2] GATT: C/M/247 (1991), p. 15.

[3] Voir *Focus: Bulletin d'information du GATT*, no 87, 1991, p. 5.

[4] Voir le texte du rapport du Groupe spécial dans le document du GATT: DS17/R (1991).

[5] 56 Fed. Reg. 49747. Une suspension de consolidation de droits et un relèvement des droits sur la bière et autres boissons alcooliques, figurent parmi les mesures de rétorsions envisagées.

[6] Voir Ministre de l'Industrie, des Sciences et de la Technologie et ministre du Commerce extérieur, *Communiqué de presse*, no 273, 28 novembre 1991.

[7] *Ibid.*

[8] Voir *Focus: Bulletin d'information du GATT*, no 87, 1991, p. 5.

mesures appliquées au niveau fédéral et au niveau des États, lesquelles selon ses dires, opéraient une discrimination à l'égard des
exportations canadiennes de bière, de vin et de cidre.[9] Plus précisément, il a fait valoir que l'instauration d'un nouveau crédit d'impôt
dont ne pouvait bénéfier que les producteurs américains de ces
produits, contrevenait à l'article III:4 de l'Accord général.[10] Il a de
plus fait observer que plusieurs pratiques de commercialisation de
boissons alcooliques des États américains, dont notamment les prescriptions de distribution et de disponibilité pour la vente ainsi que
les taxes à l'importation et les crédits d'impôt pour les produits
locaux, s'avéraient non conformes aux dispositions de l'Accord
général et plus particulièrement aux articles III:2 et III:4.[11] Les
consultations n'ayant pas abouti à une solution mutuellement
acceptable, le Canada requéra donc le 12 avril l'établissement d'un
Groupe spécial pour examiner la question.[12] Le Conseil, le 29 mai,
accéda à la requête du Canada.[13]

D'autres événements survenus dans le cadre du GATT ont retenu
notre attention en 1991. Soulignons en premier lieu que le Conseil
du GATT a finalement décidé d'adopter, suite à des demandes
répétées du Canada,[14] le rapport du Groupe spécial sur la viande de
porc frais, réfrigérée et congelée, lequel concluait, on s'en souvien-

9 Voir Ministre du Commerce extérieur, *Communiqué de presse*, no 28, 6 février
1991; *Focus: Bulletin d'information du GATT*, no 78, 1991, p. 2; no 81, 1991, p. 14.

10 Voir *Focus: Bulletin d'information du GATT*, no 81, 1991, p. 14. Cette mesure
américaine en vigueur le 1er janvier 1991 est incorporée dans *l'Omnibus Budget
Reconciliation Act* de 1990.

11 *Ibid.*

12 GATT: DS23/2 (1991).

13 GATT: C/M/250 (1991). Le Conseil, à la demande du Canada, institua un
autre Groupe spécial le 20 décembre afin d'examiner la prétention canadienne, voulant que l'ouverture de l'enquête décrétée par le Département du
Commerce américain et par l'International Trade Commission des États-Unis à
l'égard du magnésium en provenance du Canada ne soit pas justifiable selon
les règles du Code sur les subventions et les droits compensateurs puisque le
plaignant américain ne représentait que 22% de la branche de production
nationale. GATT: C/M/275 (1991).

14 Voir *Focus: Bulletin d'information du GATT*, no 78, 1991, p. 4; no 80, 1991, p. 10;
no 82, 1991, p. 4. Les États-Unis alléguaient, afin de ne pas accepter le rapport,
le fait qu'un groupe spécial binational au terme de l'Accord de libre-échange
Canada-États-Unis devait statuer prochainement sur les droits compensateurs
en question. Le Canada, soutenu par plusieurs autres délégations, prétendait
quant à lui, que les procédures engagées dans le cadre d'arrangements bilatéraux ne sauraient entraver le processus de règlement des différends au GATT.

dra, que les droits compensateurs institués par les États-Unis à l'encontre des importations de viande de porc en provenance du Canada, étaient incompatibles avec l'Accord général.[15] Les États-Unis, pour une deuxième année consécutive, se sont de leur côté déclaré préoccupés par le refus du Canada de mettre en oeuvre les conclusions du rapport adopté par le Conseil en 1989 et condamnant les restrictions canadiennes à l'importation de crème glacée et de yoghourt.[16] Le Canada a cependant réitéré que la mise en oeuvre de ce rapport était conditionnelle au résultat final de l'Uruguay Round,[17] ce qui ne l'a cependant pas empêché d'exiger de la CEE qu'elle donne suite au rapport sur les primes et subventions versées aux transformateurs et aux producteurs d'oléagineux,[18] bien que celle-ci invoquait un argument semblable pour refuser de mettre en oeuvre les conclusions de ce rapport.[19]

II   Mise en oeuvre de l'Accord de libre-échange
     Canada-États-Unis

La troisième année de mise en oeuvre de l'Accord de libre-échange Canada-États-Unis[20] s'est poursuivie harmonieusement. L'Accord, aux dires des gouvernements canadiens et américains, "contribue à réaliser les objectifs commerciaux et économiques des deux pays."[21] Le commerce des biens et des services entre le Canada et les États-Unis se chiffrait d'ailleurs à 203 milliards de

---

[15] GATT: DS7/R (1991), reproduit dans I.B.D.D., Suppl. no 38, p. 32. Sur ce rapport voir par ailleurs, M. ST-AMANT, *loc. cit. supra* note 1, à la p. 417.

[16] Voir *Focus: Bulletin d'information du GATT*, no 78, 1991, p. 4; no 81, 1991, p. 13. Au sujet de ce rapport, voir M. ST-AMANT, "Chronique de droit économique international," (1990) 28 *A.C.D.I.*, p. 434. On se rappellera que le Groupe spécial a conclu que ces restrictions étaient incompatibles avec l'article XI:1 de l'Accord général et ne pouvaient se justifier au titre de l'article XI:2 (c) (i).

[17] *Ibid.*

[18] États-Unis/CEE: Primes et subventions versées aux transformateurs et aux producteurs d'oléagineux et de protéines apparentés destinés à l'alimentation des animaux. GATT: L/6627 (1990), reproduit dans I.B.D.D., Suppl. no 37, p. 91.

[19] Voir *Focus: Bulletin d'information du GATT*, no 81, 1991, p. 12.

[20] *Accord de libre-échange entre le Gouvernement du Canada et le Gouvernement des États-Unis d'Amérique*, signé le 2 janvier 1988, en vigueur le 1er janvier 1989. Reproduit dans (1988) 27 I.L.M. 281 (ci-après dénommé l'Accord de libre-échange).

[21] Voir Ministre de l'Industrie, des Sciences et de la Technologie et ministre du Commerce extérieur, *Communiqué de presse*, no 178, 18 août 1991.

dollars en 1990, soit une augmentation de 3% par rapport à l'année 1989. Quant à l'excédent commercial canadien, il atteignait, cette année-là, 17,3 milliards de dollars; ce qui représentait une hausse par rapport à l'année qui a immédiatement précédé l'entrée en vigueur de l'Accord.[22]

Le Conseil du GATT a par ailleurs adopté en 1991 le rapport du Groupe de travail chargé d'examiner la compatibilité de l'Accord de libre-échange avec l'article XXIV de l'Accord général.[23] Sans remettre en cause la conformité de l'Accord avec le GATT, le rapport fait toutefois état de certaines préoccupations des pays tiers. Celles-ci concernent notamment le maintien d'exceptions au commerce de certains produits agricoles, les effets de détournement de trafic que risque de provoquer l'application des règles d'origine, la suppression des "drawbacks" et des redevances pour opérations douanières, la non-application sélective des mesures d'urgence globales, la question de la priorité de l'Accord sur les règles de l'Accord général, les répercussions que pourraient avoir sur le GATT, les différents mécanismes de règlement des différends prévus par l'Accord et la compatibilité de ce dernier avec les développements futurs du GATT.[24] Alors que les négociations sur un éventuel accord de libre-échange tripartite ont officiellement débuté le 12 juin avec la première réunion des ministres du commerce extérieur du Canada, des États-Unis et du Mexique,[25] il serait maintenant judicieux de décrire de quelle façon la mise en oeuvre législative et jurisprudentielle de l'Accord de libre-échange Canada-États-Unis s'est, dans les faits, réalisée en 1991.

A   MISE EN OEUVRE LÉGISLATIVE

Mise à part la troisième réduction graduelle des droits de douanes, laquelle s'est opérée conformément à l'Accord de libre-

22 Voir *Statistiques Canada*, 1989-90.
23 Voir le texte du rapport dans le document du GATT: L/6927 (1991), reproduit dans I.B.D.D., Suppl. no 38, p. 52.
24 Pour une étude sérieuse du rapport du Groupe de travail, voir I. BERNIER, "Le GATT et les arrangements économiques régionaux: le rapport du Groupe de travail sur l'Accord de libre-échange entre le Canada et les États-Unis," (1992) 33 *C. de D.*, 313-44.
25 Voir Ministre de l'Industrie, des Sciences et de la Technologie et ministre du Commerce extérieur, *Communiqué de presse*, no 171, 30 juillet 1991, annexe.

échange,[26] il y a lieu de souligner la mise en oeuvre provisoire à compter du 1er juillet de la seconde série de réductions accélérées de droits applicables à certains produits.[27] Une troisième et dernière série de consultations pour devancer l'échéance prévue pour l'abolition des droits de douanes a été en outre lancée le 14 novembre 1991.[28] Elle ne portera toutefois que sur les produits pour lesquels l'élimination des droits se devait d'être effective après une période de 10 ans.[29] Dans le secteur de l'agriculture, conformément à l'article 705 de l'Accord de libre-échange, le Canada continuera d'exiger des permis d'importation pour l'orge américain mais devra les éliminer pour les produits du blé et ce, dès que la réglementation de la Commission canadienne du blé sera modifiée.[30] D'autre part, en application de la clause de sauvegarde pour

[26] Tel que le dispose l'Accord, une troisième réduction tarifaire de 20% et de 10% fut effectuée le 1er janvier 1991 sur la catégorie d'échelonnement B et C respectivement. *Accord de libre-échange, supra* note 20, art. 401 (2)(b) et 401 (2)(c). Mentionnons, en outre, la réduction de l'écart de majoration des prix du vin supérieur, qui, le 1er janvier 1991, ne devait plus dépasser 40% de l'écart de base entre l'écart de majoration appliqué en 1987 et l'écart des frais de services réels. *Id.*, art. 803 (c), ainsi que l'élimination progressive des restrictions à l'importation des automobiles d'occasion, qui permet maintenant l'admission en franchise de ces automobiles si elles sont vieilles de quatre ans et plus. *Id.*, art. 1003 (c). D'autre part, s'est opérée la seconde étape de l'élimination des redevances pour opérations douanières qui s'appliquent aux importations en provenance du Canada. *Id.*, art. 403 (b).

[27] Voir Ministre du Commerce extérieur, *Communiqué de presse*, no 154, 3 juillet 1991. Négociée en vertu de l'art. 401 (5) de l'Accord de libre-échange, cette entente couvre plus de 250 numéros tarifaires représentant environ 250 milliards de dollars d'échanges bilatéraux. À titre d'exemple, les moules pour matières plastiques, le styrène, le boeuf et les abrasifs appliqués doivent être admis en franchise. Pour la mise en oeuvre en droit canadien, voir par ailleurs, *Décret no 5 de réduction accélérée des droits de douanes*, (1991) 125 Gaz. Can. II 3222.

[28] Voir Gouvernement du Canada, *Communiqué de presse*, (1991) no 253, 14 novembre 1991. À cet égard, la date limite de la réception des demandes du secteur privé a été fixée au 17 janvier 1992, après quoi il est prévu des discussions entre les deux gouvernements et des consultations avec les industries.

[29] *Ibid.*

[30] Voir Ministre du Commerce extérieur, *Communiqué de presse*, (1991) no 109, 3 mai 1991. Sur cette disposition de l'Accord de libre-échange, voir par ailleurs, ST-AMANT, *loc. cit. supra* note 1, à la p. 424. Soulignons que les deux gouvernements se sont en outre entendus sur la méthodologie à appliquer pour le calcul du niveau de soutien accordé pour le programme américain *Disaster Assistance*

les fruits et légumes frais, prévue à l'article 702 de l'Accord, le
Canada a imposé pour une certaine période, un droit temporaire
additionnel sur les importations de pêches à l'état frais et sur les
tomates à l'état frais ou réfrigéré.[31] Notons également une modification des règles d'origine relatives aux produits oléagineux[32] et la
mise en place d'un régime d'inspection des viandes qui, bien que
calqué sur celui des États-Unis, n'en est pas moins contraire à
l'heure actuelle à l'article 704 de l'Accord de libre-échange.[33]

Plusieurs Groupes de travail, créés en vertu de l'Accord, poursui-
vent par ailleurs leurs travaux. Les Groupes techniques sur l'agriculture chargés d'examiner les règlements et les normes qui affectent
le commerce des produits agricoles, enregistrent peu de progrès
réels.[34] Le Comité sélect de l'automobile, a quant à lui, complété la
première phase de son étude sur la capacité concurrentielle de
l'industrie et on s'attend à ce que son rapport final soit déposé au
début de l'année 1992.[35] En ce qui concerne l'important Groupe
de travail sur les subventions et les recours commerciaux, il est en
attente des résultats des négociations commerciales de l'Uruguay
Round avant d'entreprendre de nouvelles activités.[36] Enfin, le

---

Act. Voir *Echange de Lettres constituant un Accord entre le gouvernement du Canada et
le gouvernement des États-Unis d'Amérique modifiant l'appendice I de l'annexe 705.4 de
l'Accord de libre-échange,* (1991) R.T. Can., no 13.

[31] *Arrêté visant le droit temporaire imposé sur les pêches à l'état frais,* (1991) 125 Gaz.
Can. II 2983; *Arrêté visant le droit temporaire imposé sur les tomates à l'état frais ou
réfrigéré,* (1991) 125 Gaz. Can. II 2488; *Arrêté visant le droit temporaire imposé sur
les tomates à l'état fais ou réfrigéré — Modification,* (1991) Gaz. Can. II 3019. Ces
droits additionnels sont égaux à la différence entre le tarif des États-Unis et le
tarif de la nation la plus favorisée.

[32] *Règlement sur les règles d'origine des marchandises bénéficiant du Tarif des États-Unis
— Modification,* (1991) Gaz. Can. II 3977. Cette modification a été effectuée
selon les termes de l'art. 303 de l'Accord de libre-échange et sa date prévue de
mise en oeuvre est le 1er janvier 1992.

[33] *Règlement de 1990 sur l'inspection des viandes,* (1991) Gaz. Can. II 2362.

[34] Ceci est particulièrement le cas pour le Groupe de travail sur l'inspection des
produits laitiers qui s'est réuni à la demande du Canada afin d'établir des
équivalences entre les normes applicables à la production du lait UHT dans la
province de Québec et les normes sanitaires contenues dans la réglementation
américaine. Rappelons que ces groupes de travail sont, d'autre part, formés en
vertu de l'article 708 de l'Accord de libre-échange.

[35] Ce Groupe de travail est chargé, selon l'article 1004 de l'Accord de libre-
échange, de conseiller les deux gouvernements sur la façon d'améliorer la
compétitivité de l'industrie automobile en Amérique du Nord.

[36] Voir Ministre de l'Industrie, des Sciences et de la Technologie et ministre du
Commerce extérieur, *Communiqué de presse,* no 178, 18 août 1991.

Groupe consultatif sur l'autorisation de séjour temporaire a présenté son rapport à la Commission mixte du commerce canado-américain, laquelle a noté que les procédures nationales d'examen étaient maintenant complétées et que les modifications au chapitre 15 de l'Accord, approuvées par la Commission le 11 octobre 1990, pouvaient s'appliquées dès leur publication par les deux gouvernements.[37]

B   MISE EN OEUVRE JURISPRUDENTIELLE

Les deux principaux mécanismes de règlement des différends prévus par l'Accord de libre-échange ont, depuis l'entrée en vigueur de ce dernier, démontré leur utilité et leur efficacité. L'année 1991 ne fait pas exception à la règle. Des consultations bilatérales fondées sur le chapitre 18 ont ainsi été tenues sur des questions concernant certaines pratiques de la Commission canadienne du blé,[38] sur la commercialisation et la distribution des vins et spiritueux au Canada[39] ainsi qu'à l'égard des livraisons de lait UHT à Porto Rico.[40] Un Groupe spécial fut en outre institué à la demande du Canada pour examiner le traitement des intérêts comme coût direct d'assemblage dans l'interprétation des règles d'origine prévue par l'Accord de libre-échange.[41] Par ailleurs, divers Groupes spéciaux créés en vertu du chapitre 19 pour examiner la compatibilité des décisions finales en matière de droits antidumping et compensateurs au regard du droit national auront rendu leurs décisions. C'est ainsi que le 22 janvier, suite à l'examen après renvoi d'une décision de l'International Trade Commission des États-Unis (ITC), un Groupe spécial concluait que l'omission

---

[37] *Ibid.*

[38] Cette demande de consultation présentée par les États-Unis a pour objet de préciser les obligations du Canada au regard de l'art. 701.3 de l'Accord de libre-échange.

[39] Cette demande de consultation origine des États-Unis et vise à ce que la province de Québec se conforme au chapitre 8 de l'Accord de libre-échange et plus spécifiquement aux dispositions portant sur l'inscription au catalogue, la fixation des prix et la distribution des vins et spiritueux.

[40] Cette demande de consultation à l'initiative du Canada a pour objectif d'éliminer les restrictions de distribution du lait UHT à Porto Rico. Voir Gouvernement du Canada, *Communiqué de presse*, no 287, 13 décembre 1991.

[41] *Traitement des intérêts selon le chapitre 3*, dossier USA-92-1807-01.

de cette dernière à se conformer à la précédente décision du Groupe du 24 août 1990 constituait une erreur de droit.[42] Le Groupe jugeait alors également, que la conclusion de l'ITC à l'effet qu'il existe une menace de préjudice n'était pas appuyée par des preuves substantielles au dossier.[43] Conformément à cette décision, l'ITC annulait par la suite sa conclusion de menace de préjudice.[44] Toutefois, le 29 mars, les États-Unis demandaient, pour la première fois depuis l'entrée en vigueur de l'Accord de libre-échange, la constitution d'un Comité pour contestation extraordinaire afin d'examiner la décision du Groupe spécial rendue le 22 janvier.[45] Le Comité, le 14 juin, dans une décision unanime rejetait les prétentions des États-Unis et confirmait donc la décision du Groupe spécial.[46] Après s'être interrogé sur le rôle que lui a confié les deux parties dans l'Accord,[47] le Comité, dans un second temps, s'est

[42] *Dans l'affaire du porc frais, frigorifié ou congelé du Canada*, Dossier USA-89-1904-11. On se rappelera qu'en 1990, le Groupe spécial, en rendant sa décision dans l'affaire du porc, avait renvoyé le dossier à l'ITC afin qu'elle réexamine de nouveau la preuve. Sur cette décision voir M. ST-AMANT, *loc. cit. supra* note 1, à la p. 428. C'est donc cette décision de l'ITC qui est ici examinée.

[43] Plus spécifiquement, le Groupe en vient à la conclusion que l'ITC, en ouvrant le dossier suite au renvoi pour y inclure de nouvelles preuves, n'a pas respecté les règles de justice naturelle reconnues par la Cour suprême des États-Unis. Il est de plus d'avis que la preuve n'accrédite pas le fait que des subventions plus élevées sur le porc vivant entraineraient une augmentation des importations de viande de porc et une diminution des importations de porc vivant, ni n'établiraient une présomption à l'effet que les importations canadiennes accapareraient une plus large part de marché. Au plan de la procédure, le Groupe admet d'autre part que son pouvoir se limite à confirmer ou à renvoyer les décisions nationales. Dans ces circonstances, il décide de renvoyer de nouveau le dossier à l'ITC afin que cette dernière prenne une décision qui ne soit pas contraire à celle du Groupe spécial.

[44] Voir United States International Trade Commission, *News*, no 91-010, 13 février 1991.

[45] Voir 14 *Int'l Trade Rep.* (BNA) 496 (1991). Le Comité pour contestation extraordinaire est formé selon la procédure décrite à l'annexe 1904.13 de l'Accord de libre-échange et ne peut être institué que dans les cas mentionnés à l'article 1904 (13).

[46] *Dans l'affaire du porc frais, frigorifié ou congelé du Canada*, Dossier EEC-91-1904-01 USA.

[47] Selon le Comité, la procédure pour contestation extraordinaire n'est pas une simple procédure d'appel des décisions des Groupes spéciaux. De telles décisions ne pourront au contraire être contestées que dans des circonstances exceptionnelles, définies expréssement à l'article 1904 (3) de l'Accord de

prononcé sur les allégations américaines à l'effet que le Groupe spécial aurait, sur cinq points, manifestement outrepassé les pouvoirs, l'autorité ou les compétences qui lui ont été conférés par l'Accord.[48] Rejetant toutes ses allégations, le Comité en vient à la conclusion qu'aucune conduite énoncée au paragraphe 13 de l'article 1904 n'a été établie et ainsi confirme-t-il la décision originelle rendue le 22 janvier par le Groupe spécial.[49] D'autre part, un autre Groupe spécial, après renvoi pour décision au Département du commerce américain,[50] décidait que la décision sur renvoi à l'effet que tous les programmes de subventions examinés s'avéraient compensables car restreints à un groupe précis d'industries, n'était pas appuyée pour au moins deux des programmes par une

---

libre-échange. Le Comité prend d'ailleurs soin de souligner qu'à la lumière de sa composition (le Comité est formé de trois juges ou anciens juges d'une Cour fédérale américaine ou d'une Cour de juridiction canadienne) et du délai dans lequel il doit rendre sa décision (30 jours), il n'est pas de son ressort de conduire un appel traditionnel sur le mérite de la décision du Groupe spécial, Groupe dont les membres doivent posséder une expertise en droit commercial international et dont les décisions doivent être rendues 315 jours après la formation du Groupe.

[48] Sur le premier point, en réponse à l'allégation du gouvernement américain selon laquelle le Groupe aurait créé une règle de justice naturelle non prévue en droit américain, le Comité conclut que le Groupe a reconnu et discuté plusieurs précédents américains et qu'ainsi cette première prétention ne remplit pas les conditions énoncées à l'article 1904 (13) de l'Accord. Concernant la seconde allégation à l'effet que le Groupe aurait pris en considération des preuves non versées au dossier, le Comité constate que le Groupe s'est appuyé presque exclusivement sur des preuves colligées au dossier et qu'à cet égard sa conduite n'a pas influé sur sa décision ni menacé l'intégrité du processus d'examen. En réponse au troisième point, le Comité soutient que le Groupe était justifié de demander à l'ITC qu'une décision définitive compatible avec la décision du Groupe soit finalement rendue. Le Comité rejette également la quatrième allégation américaine selon laquelle le Groupe n'aurait pas appliqué l'unique critère d'examen prévu par le droit américain pour tout appel (i.e., si la décision contestée est fondée ou non sur des preuves substantielles au dossier). Enfin, la dernière allégation à l'effet que le Groupe aurait considéré un critère non prévu par le droit américain pour conclure à une menace de préjudice n'est pas non plus fondée selon le Comité puisque ce critère fut mis en oeuvre par l'ITC.

[49] Les droits compensateurs d'un montant de 70 millions $ (CAN) antérieurement imposés devront donc être remboursés aux producteurs canadiens de porc.

[50] Sur ce renvoi, voir M. ST-AMANT, *loc. cit. supra* note 1, à la p. 428.

preuve substantielle au dossier, ni confirmée en droit.[51] Le Groupe a dû par conséquent renvoyer pour une seconde fois la question à l'étude du Département du commerce.[52] Les Groupe spéciaux auront finalement rendu deux autres décisions en 1991: l'une concerne les pièce de rechange pour les épandeuses automotrices[53] et l'autre concerne certains moteurs à induction intégrale.[54]

[51] *Dans l'affaire du porc frais, frigorifié et congelé du Canada*, Dossier USA-89-1904-06. Les deux programmes visés sont le programme de compensation des subventions du Nid-de-Corbeau de l'Alberta et le programme d'assurance-stabilisation des revenus agricoles du Québec.

[52] *Ibid.* Dans une décision datée du 11 avril, le Département du commerce américain se conformait à la décision du Groupe spécial en concluant qu'il n'avait pas suffisamment de preuves au dossier pour affirmer que le programme québécois en cause pouvait donner lieu à l'imposition de mesures compensatoires tout en ordonnant un réexamen des méthodes de calcul des subventions pour le programme albertain. Voir 54 Fed. Reg. 23346. Mentionnons qu'à la suite de la décision du Comité pour contestation extraordinaire, les droits compensateurs furent néanmoins abolis pour tous les programmes en cause en raison du défaut de constatation d'une menace de préjudice.

[53] *Affaire intéressant les pièces de rechange pour les épandeuses automotrices de revêtement bitumineux du Canada*, Dossier USA-90-1904-01. Il s'agissait notamment dans ce dossier de déterminer si la décision du Département du commerce américain d'utiliser les meilleurs renseignements disponibles était justifiée par une preuve substantielle au dossier et était conforme à la législation américaine. En outre, le Groupe devait se prononcer sur la question de savoir si la marge de dumping constatée comme marge correspondant aux meilleurs renseignements disponibles, était justifiée par des preuves au dossier. Le Groupe confirme et renvoie en partie la décision du Département.

[54] *Certains moteurs à induction intégrale sous-évalués, d'un horse-power à deux cents horse-power inclusivement avec exception, originaires ou exportés des États-Unis d'Amérique*, Dossier CDA-90-1904-01. Les questions à décider, eu égard au critère d'examen prévu à la *Loi sur la Cour fédérale*, portaient notamment sur les pouvoirs du Tribunal canadien du commerce extérieur au terme des réexamens à effectuer en vertu de la *Loi sur les mesures spéciales d'importation* et quant aux considérations à donner aux décisions de Revenu Canada, sur des violations possibles par ledit Tribunal des règles de justice naturelle et sur les définitions des expressions "industrie nationale" et "branche de production nationale" insérées dans ladite loi. Sur toutes ces questions, le Groupe spécial confirme la décision du Tribunal canadien du commerce extérieur.

II   Le Canada et le système monétaire international en 1991

préparé par
BERNARD COLAS*

L E DÉMANTELLEMENT DES ÉCHANGES commerciaux du CAEM[1] et la dissolution de l'URSS en 1991 auront souligné l'importance du processus de réforme engagé par ces pays[2] et de l'appui qui doit lui être accordé (partie I). Au niveau interne, l'année 1991 marque l'adoption de nouvelles lois destinées à moderniser les institutions financières canadiennes (partie II).

I   SYSTÈME MONÉTAIRE INTERNATIONAL

En 1991, le Canada a continué à soutenir les programmes de réforme politique et économique des pays de l'ex-URSS, d'Europe centrale et orientale. Il est également resté attaché au problème de la réduction de la dette des pays en développement.

A   TRANSITION DES PAYS D'EUROPE DE L'EST

Les mesures prises par le Canada pour appuyer l'instauration d'économies de marché et la démocratisation de ces pays sont

---

* Avocat au Barreau du Québec. Consultant auprès de L'OCDE. Vice-président à la recherche de la Société de droit international économique. Les opinions exprimées n'engagent que l'auteur.

---

[1] Créé en 1949, le Conseil d'assistance économique mutuelle (CAEM) regroupait l'URSS, six pays d'Europe de l'est, la Mongolie, le Vietnam et Cuba. Il a été officiellement dissous le 28 juin 1991.

[2] *Rapport annuel de la Banque des règlements internationaux*, (1992), pp. 92-102.

329

orchestrées par le Groupe de travail sur l'Europe centrale et l'Europe de l'est, mis sur pied en juillet 1990. Ce Groupe administre un programme d'aide technique[3] d'une valeur d'environ 200 millions CAD (1990-94), coordonne des projets lancés par les secteurs privés et publics et facilite la mise en place de liens politiques et économiques globaux avec cette région.[4] Il participe à l'action concertée avec les autres pays industrialisés du G-24[5] dans le cadre duquel le Canada a convenu en 1991 d'accorder, sur la base des besoins projetés par le Fonds monétaire international (FMI), une aide exceptionnelle de 10 millions USD à la Bulgarie au titre de la balance des paiements, de 12,5 millions USD à la Hongrie, de 25 millions USD à la République fédérative tchèque et slovaque et de 25 millions USD à la Roumanie. Par ailleurs, le gouvernement canadien offre des garanties sur prêt pour permettre aux institutions financières canadiennes de prêter à des taux concessionnels et à plus long terme.[6]

Au plan multilatéral, le Canada a appuyé les demandes d'admission[7] aux institutions de Bretton Woods de l'URSS et des nouvelles républiques indépendantes issues de son démantellement. Avant leur adhésion, la Banque mondiale[8] et le Fonds monétaire international (FMI)[9] leur ont accordé une aide technique et non financière. Enfin, le Canada a versé 180 000 CAD[10] au Centre pour la coopération avec les économies en transition de l'OCDE et a participé à l'inauguration officielle, tenue à Londres du 15 au 17 avril 1991, de la Banque européenne pour la reconstruction et le développement (BERD).

---

[3] Soulignons qu'à la suite de l'assassinat de civils par les militaires soviétiques en Lituanie et en Lettonie, en janvier 1991, le Canada a suspendu son offre d'aide technique à l'URSS, offre qu'il a rétablie au cours de l'été 1991.

[4] *Rapport annuel du Ministère des affaires extérieures du Canada* 1990-1991, (1991), p. 49.

[5] Composé des 24 pays Membres de l'Organisation de coopération et de développement économiques (OCDE).

[6] *Op. cit.*, à la p. 13.

[7] L'Albanie est devenue membre en 1991 de la BIRD, de l'AID et du FMI.

[8] Programme de coopération technique approuvé en août 1991. *Rapport annuel de la Banque mondiale* (1992), p. 143.

[9] Accord spécial conclu avec l'ancienne URSS, à l'exclusion des Pays Baltes, en octobre 1991. *International Monetary Fund Annual Report* (1992), p. 28.

[10] *Op. cit. supra*, note 4, à la p. 50.

B RÉDUCTION DE LA DETTE PUBLIQUE DES PAYS EN DÉVELOPPEMENT

En 1991, les pays-créanciers du Club de Paris ont mené une série de négociations sur la dette publique avec seize pays en développement qui ont débouché, pour la plupart, sur de nouvelles opérations de rééchelonnement.[11] D'autre part, ces pays-créanciers ont reconnu la nécessité d'élargir la portée des mesures d'allégement en faveur des pays à faible revenu. Suite à l'appel lancé par le Groupe des sept pays les plus industrialisés (G-7) lors du Sommet de Londres de juillet 1991, ces pays-créanciers ont convenu en décembre 1991 d'offrir de nouvelles possibilités pour réduire le fardeau de plusieurs pays à faible revenu surendettés qui mènent des politiques d'ajustement appropriées. De ce fait, ils élargissaient la politique adoptée en septembre 1988 dans le cadre des "Conditions de Toronto," tout en conservant les mêmes critères d'admissibilité,[12] et y incluaient certaines idées formulées en septembre 1990 par John Major, alors Chancellier de l'Échiquier du Royaume-Uni.[13]

Ces mesures portent sur le rééchelonnement des arriérés et des montants arrivant à échéance sur les périodes de 12 à 18 mois. Un système de menu à options s'applique aux dettes hors APD (aide publique au développement) en vertu duquel les créanciers peuvent: (1) passer 50 pour cent de la dette consolidée par pertes et profits et rééchelonner le reste aux taux du marché, avec un calendrier de remboursements couvrant vingt-trois ans, dont un différé d'amortissement de six ans, ou (2) rééchelonner la dette à des taux d'intérêts concessionnels, de manière à réduire de 50 pour cent la valeur actualisée nette des montants dus sur une période de remboursement de 23 ans, mais sans différé d'amortissement. Pour les pays-créanciers qui ne peuvent accorder un allégement à des conditions concessionnelles, cet ensemble de mesures prévoit une troisième option qui permet de consolider la dette aux taux du marché et d'étaler le remboursement sur vingt-cinq ans, dont un différé d'amortissement de quatorze ans. Le Bénin et le Nicaragua, sur les échéances intervenant au cours de périodes de quinze à trente mois et sur les arriérés, ont été les premiers à bénéficier de ces mesures.

---

[11] *Financement et dette extérieure des pays en développement, étude 1991,* OCDE, (1992), p. 50. L'Égypte et la Pologne ont également vu une partie de leur dette publique annulée.

[12] Lire la chronique 1988 dans cet Annuaire.

[13] Les "Conditions de Trinidad" sont exposées dans Bank of England, *Quarterly Bulletin,* Nov. 91, p. 505.

C   RÉAMÉNAGEMENT DE LA DETTE COMMERCIALE DES PAYS EN
     DÉVELOPPEMENT

En ce qui concerne la dette commerciale des pays à revenu
intermédiaire, le rythme des opérations de réaménagement s'est
ralenti en 1991[14] et les banques se sont montrées plus prudentes
quant à l'octroi de nouveaux prêts. Les prêts bancaires internationaux qui s'étaient constamment accrus depuis 1988 pour
atteindre 15 milliards USD pour 1990, ont chuté à 7 milliards USD
en 1991. Toutefois, cette chute a été compensée par la forte expansion des emprunts obligataires qui ont fait un bond à 9 milliards
USD en 1991.[15]

Ce désengagement des banques s'est traduit au Canada par une
augmentation des provisions pour pertes sur prêts, entraînant une
baisse de leurs revenus, et par un accroissement de leurs avoirs[16]
dans les limites définies par l'Accord de Bâle sur les fonds propres
de juillet 1988 auquel le Canada a souscrit. Cet accord de Bâle a fait
l'objet, le 6 novembre 1991, d'un amendement destiné à rendre
plus homogènes les critères régissant l'inclusion dans les fonds
propres des provisions générales pour créances douteuses et
l'exclusion des éléments conçus pour faire face à une détérioration
identifiée de la valeur d'actifs particuliers. Sont ainsi exclus du
calcul des fonds propres, les éléments qui reflètent une déprécia-
tion constatée d'actifs soumis au risque-pays, au risque immobilier
ou à tout autre risque sectoriel.

En revanche, l'amendement prend en compte le fait que certaines banques détiennent des réserves dont la qualité est exacte-
ment la même que celle des bénéfices non-distribués et autorise
leur inclusion dans la première catégorie des fonds propres, sous
réserve du respect de critères rigoureux qui les rendent indissocia-
bles des bénéfices non-distribués. Les éléments qui demeurent dans
les provisions générales ou réserves générales pour créances douteuses continuent d'être admis dans les fonds propres de seconde
catégorie, à condition de ne pas représenter plus de 1,25 point des
actifs à risque. Il est peu probable que le Surintendant des institu-

---

[14] Des accords ont été conclus en 1991 avec l'Uruguay, le Nigéria et les
    Philippines.

[15] *Op. cit. supra*, note 8, à la p. 9.

[16] *Rapport annuel du Bureau du Surintendant des institutions financières* (1991),
    pp. 11-12.

tions financières autorise de telles inclusions[17] compte tenu de la suffisance des fonds propres des banques canadiennes.[18]

II Système financier canadien

En 1991, le Canada s'est surtout attaché à réduire les obstacles au marché nord-américain des valeurs mobilières et à autoriser les institutions financières canadiennes à élargir leurs champs d'activités. Ces réformes ont été accompagnées du renforcement des mesures prudentielles dont l'importance, tant au niveau national qu'international, a été soulignée par la liquidation de la Compagnie Trust Standard, de la Compagnie de prêts Standard[19] et de la Banque crédit et commerce Canada (BCCC).

A Déréglementation et mesures prudentielles

Le 1er juillet 1991, les autorités canadiennes et américaines en valeurs mobilières ont adopté un régime d'information multinational (RIM) afin de supprimer certains obstacles à l'égard de divers types d'opérations de valeurs mobilières au Canada et aux États-Unis. Le RIM vise à faciliter l'exécution au Canada et aux États-Unis de certaines émissions de titres, offres publiques de rachat et offres publiques d'achat. Il limite également le nombre des cas pour lesquels il est nécessaire de satisfaire à des exigences réglementaires similaires dans les deux pays relativement aux regroupements d'entreprises, à l'information continue et à d'autres types de dépôts. Ainsi, les émetteurs canadiens qui satisfont à certains critères d'admissibilité peuvent se servir des documents d'information en vigueur au Canada pour les dépôts effectués aux États-Unis et réciproquement certains émetteurs américains peuvent faire des placements au Canada en utilisant des documents d'information établis conformément aux lois américaines.[20]

---

17 Le Surintendant devrait continuer à exiger des banques qu'elles déduisent de leurs actifs les réserves pour créances irrécouvrables. Voir *Ligne directrice C-3: Établissement de provisions pour pertes sur prêts*, octobre 1990.

18 *Op. cit. supra*, note 16, à la p. 11. Au 30 avril 1991, les grandes banques canadiennes affichaient un ratio moyen supérieur au niveau de 8% fixé par l'Accord de Bâle de 1988.

19 Le 2 mai 1991, la Cour Suprême de l'Ontario a émis, pour la première fois depuis que le Bureau du Surintendant existe (1987), une ordonnance de liquidation à l'égard de ces deux institutions de dépôts. Cette crise est attribuable aux problèmes liés à l'immobilier.

20 Quelques informations supplémentaires sont exigées au Canada. Voir *Instructions générales canadiennes*, no. C-45.

Par ailleurs, la réforme canadienne des institutions financières[21] s'est achevée par l'adoption de lois destinées notamment à décloisonner leurs activités. Les banques, les sociétés de fiducie et de prêt et les compagnies d'assurance peuvent dorénavant, sous réserve de l'autorisation du Ministre des finances, acquérir par l'entremise de filiales, des services financiers hors de leurs sphères traditionnelles d'activité.

Le Surintendant des institutions financières se voit octroyer un nouveau pouvoir: celui d'obliger les propriétaires et les sociétés qui contrôlent les institutions financières fédérales, ou leurs filiales, à lui fournir des renseignements.[22] Ceci devrait permettre au Surintendant de mieux comprendre la situation globale des opérations d'une institution financière à capital fermé ou qui fait parti d'un conglomérat financier.

En 1991, le Bureau du Surintendant des institutions financières a poursuivi l'émission de lignes directrices à l'intention des banques qu'il a, pour la première fois, regroupé en deux volumes.[23] Parmi les changements adoptés, citons[24] la "Ligne directrice B-2" qui, codifiant une pratique existante, détermine les limites relatives aux engagements de crédit important assumés par les banques et vise à prévenir la concentration des engagements auprès d'un même créancier et les risques liés à une telle opération. Les engagements d'une banque à l'égard d'une entité (nationale ou internationale) ou d'entités associées ne peuvent, en vertu de cette Ligne directrice, excéder 25 pour cent l'ensemble des fonds propres de la banque. Les engagements d'une filiale de banque étrangère auprès de toute entité ou d'entités associées ne peuvent excéder 100 pour cent de l'ensemble des fonds propres de la filiale. Cette dernière limite peut être réduite, à la discrétion du Surintendant, selon des conditions qui laissent croire au soutien de la banque-mère à sa

---

[21] *Loi sur les sociétés de fiducie et de prêt, Loi sur les banques, loi sur les sociétés d'assurances* et *Loi sur les associations coopératives de crédit* sanctionnées le 13 décembre 1991, S.C. 1991, c. 45 à 48.

[22] Ces lois ont également eu pour effet d'accroître les responsabilités des dirigeants, des vérificateurs et de toute autre personne s'occupant de l'administration des activités d'une institution financière.

[23] Disponible au Bureau du Surintendant: Tél. (613) 990-7655.

[24] Citons également la *Ligne directrice B-4: Prêts de titre*, émise en décembre 1991, laquelle énonce les considérations de prudence relativement aux prêts de titres consentis par les prêteurs.

filiale en cas de pertes et qui garantissent leur surveillance adéquate en vertu du Concordat de Bâle de mai 1983.[25]

B LE CAS DE LA BANQUE CRÉDIT ET COMMERCE CANADA (BCCC)

La mise en liquidation de la BCCC constitue un bon exemple de l'importance que revêt la surveillance des conglomérats financiers dans leur ensemble et de la capacité de soutien d'une banque-mère à l'égard de banques affiliées. Dans ce cas, la défaillance de la maison-mère, la BCCI SA, a déclenché la mise en liquidation de la BCCC.

Au début de l'année 1991, l'exercice de l'activité au Canada de la BCCC avait été limité par le Bureau du Surintendant en raison de la mauvaise qualité de son portefeuille de prêts. Le 5 juillet 1991, des mesures réglementaires prises contre la BCCI SA au Luxembourg,[26] lieu du siège juridique, au Royaume-Uni et dans les Îles Caïmans ont mis un terme à la viabilité économique du groupe BCCI. Afin de protéger les intérêts des créanciers et déposants, le Surintendant a dû, ce même jour, prendre le contrôle des éléments d'actif de la BCCC.[27]

Après étude, le Ministre des finances a ordonné au Surintendant, le 25 juillet, de prendre le contrôle de la BCCC.[28] Par jugement, un liquidateur provisoire a été nommé le 15 août 1991[29] et une ordonnance de mise en liquidation de la BCCC a été rendue le 23 septembre 1991.[30]

Il est à noter que la condamnation prononcée un an plus tôt aux États-Unis à l'encontre de la BCCI pour avoir été reconnue coupable de blanchiment de capitaux avait attiré le regard suspect des autorités bancaires internationales.

---

[25] B. COLAS (éd.) *Accords économiques internationaux: répertoire des accords et des institutions* 238 (1990).

[26] Le Tribunal d'arrondissement de Luxembourg siégeant en matière commerciale a prononcé le sursis à tout paiement de la part de l'établissement de crédit BCCI sur la base que la BCCI avait perdu au-delà de la totalité de son capital social. Voir *Jugement commercial no. 279/91.*

[27] *Loi sur les banques*, S.R.C. 1985, c. B-1, art. 278-1-c.

[28] *Id.*, art. 279-2-c.

[29] C.S. Montréal. 500-05-012334-916.

[30] *Ibid.*

C   BLANCHIMENT DES CAPITAUX

Le Canada avec les pays de l'OCDE et de grands centres financiers[31] combattent ce type d'activités illicites dans le cadre du
Groupe d'action financière sur le blanchiment des capitaux
(GAFI). Créé par le G-7 en 1989, le GAFI a émis quarante recommandations en 1989 dont une partie de celles-ci a été appliquée
par le Canada lors de l'adoption, le 21 juin 1991, de la Loi visant à
faciliter la répression du recyclage financier des produits de la
criminalité.[32] Cette loi, dont le détail se trouve dans le règlement
d'application,[33] a pour objet d'assurer la conservation, par les institutions financières, de dossiers adéquats pour aider les instances
judiciaires à enquêter sur les cas de blanchiment de fonds. Aux
termes du règlement, les personnes qui, dans le cours des affaires,
reçoivent un montant en espèces de plus de 10 000 CAD qu'elles
doivent payer ou transférer à un tiers pour le compte d'autrui, ont
l'obligation de tenir des relevés de ces opérations et de conserver
ces documents pendant une période minimale de cinq ans. Cette
loi s'applique à l'ensemble des institutions financières: des banques
et sociétés de fiducie aux cambistes, courtiers en valeur mobilière et
assureurs-vie.

En conclusion, la mondialisation et le décloisonnement du secteur financier fait apparaître de nouveaux problèmes. Pour éviter
les risques de contagion, les pouvoirs publics nationaux doivent
ainsi continuer à adopter des règles qui garantissent la stabilité de
l'ensemble des institutions financières et à multiplier les initiatives
visant à assurer une meilleure coordination de leurs activités.

[31] Le GAFI, créé par le G-7 en 1989, regroupait en 1991 les 24 pays membres de
l'OCDE, Hong-Kong, Singapour, la Commission des Communautés euro-
péennes et le Conseil de coopération du Golfe. Il a établi son secrétariat à
l'OCDE à sa réunion de septembre 1991.

[32] S.C. 1991, c. 26, sanctionnée le 21 juin 1991.

[33] *Règlement sur le recyclage des produits de la criminalité*, (1992) Gaz. Can. I 1742.

III   Investissement

préparé par
PIERRE RATELLE*

I   CONJONCTURE POLITIQUE ET ÉCONOMIQUE CANADIENNE

E N 1991, LA CONJONCTURE POLITIQUE et économique canadienne a été à l'image de celle que les investisseurs canadiens et
étrangers avaient connue en 1990. Au niveau politique, l'incertitude constitutionnelle a persisté à un point tel que personne ne
pouvait plus affirmer avec certitude que le Canada allait continuer
d'exister dans l'avenir.[1] Au niveau économique, la récession a continué de faire rage, provoquant la faillite de milliers d'entreprises et
la mise à pied de dizaines de milliers de personnes.[2]

---

* Avocat au Barreau de Montréal; Docteur en droit de l'Université Panthéon-
Sorbonne (Paris 1); Chargé de cours au Département des Sciences juridiques
de l'Université du Québec à Montréal; DEA de droit international économique
de l'Université Panthéon-Sorbonne (Paris 1); DEA de droit international public
de l'Université Panthéon-Assas (Paris 2); LL.B. de l'Université Laval.

---

1 Suite à l'échec de l'Accord du Lac Meech en juin 1990, lequel devait ramener le
Québec dans le "giron constitutionnel canadien," l'Assemblée nationale du
Québec a voté une loi qui prévoit la tenue d'un référendum sur la souveraineté
du Québec pour juin ou octobre 1992. Voir *Loi sur le processus de détermination de
l'avenir politique et constitutionnel du Québec*, L.Q. 1991, c. 34; voir aussi P. R.
Hayden, J. H. Burns et al., "The Dangers of Constitutional Uncertainty," in
CCH, *Foreign Investment in Canada: A Guide to the Law* (1991), vol. 1, Feature
Article #2,136.

2 Voir P. C. Newman, "The Recession Does Not a Depression Make," in *Maclean's*,
vol. 103, no. 53, December 31, 1991, p. 45; M. Tessier, "Le dépôt du budget
fédéral," dans *Chronique des relations extérieures du Canada*, janvier-mars 1991, p.
8; "Deficit to Set Record," in *Canadian News Facts*, vol. 25, no. 23, p. 4485.

Cette conjoncture défavorable a eu un impact réel sur la confiance des Canadiens d'investir à l'étranger puisqu'ils y ont investi près de 4.7 milliards de dollars canadiens en 1991, soit 800 millions de moins que l'année précédente.[3] La confiance des investisseurs étrangers à l'égard du Canada a aussi été ébranlée car ils ont investi sur son territoire 8.9 milliards de dollars canadiens en 1991, soit 15% de moins qu'en 1990.[4]

II   Actions unilatérales

A   Mise en oeuvre de l'accord de libre-échange avec les États-Unis

Le 1er janvier 1991 marquait à la fois le second anniversaire de l'Accord de libre-échange entre le Canada et les États-Unis (ALÉ) et le commencement de sa troisième période de transition devant conduire à sa pleine réalisation en matière d'investissement.[5] Pour ce faire, la *Loi sur Investissement Canada* (LIC)[6] a été amendée de manière à ce que le seuil d'examen de l'acquisition directe d'une entreprise canadienne par un Américain passe de 50 millions à 100 millions de dollars canadiens.[7] Quant au seuil d'examen de l'acquisition indirecte d'une entreprise canadienne par un Américain, il est passé de 250 millions à 500 millions de dollars canadiens.[8] Il est intéressant de noter que ces seuils sont respectivement vingt et dix fois plus élevés que les seuils que connaissent les autres investisseurs étrangers.[9] En pratique, cela signifie, qu'à partir de 1991, la plupart des acquisitions d'entreprises canadiennes d'importance effectuées par des Américains ne feront l'objet d'aucun examen par Investissement Canada; par contre celles qui seront effectuées par des non Américains se verront encore soumises fréquemment à cet examen.

[3] Voir Statistique Canada, *Balance des paiements internationaux du Canada; premier trimestre de 1992* (juillet 1992), p. 142.

[4] *Id.*, à la p. 148.

[5] Les versions françaises et anglaises de l'ALÉ font partie de la *Loi de mise en oeuvre de l'Accord de libre-échange entre le Gouvernement du Canada et le Gouvernement des États-Unis d'Amérique*, S.C. 1988, c. 65; une version en langue anglaise est reproduite dans *United States-Canada Free Trade Agreement Implementation Act of 1988*, Pub. L. 100-4449, 102 Stat. 1851 (1988) ainsi que dans (1988) 27 *I.L.M.* 281.

[6] Voir S.C. 1985, c. 20.

[7] Voir ALE, *supra*, note 5, Annexe 1607.3, art. 2 (a) (i) (C).

[8] *Id.*, art. 2 (a) (ii) (C).

[9] Voir LIC, *supra* note 6, arts 11 et 14.

B ASSOUPLISSEMENT À L'ÉGARD DE LA PROPRIÉTÉ ÉTRANGÈRE
DANS L'INDUSTRIE PÉTROLIÈRE ET GAZIÈRE CANADIENNE

Depuis plusiers années, le Canada fait face à un urgent besoin de capitaux étrangers pour financer les projets d'exploration et d'extraction dans son industrie pétrolière et gazière.[10]

Afin d'aider à satisfaire à ce besoin, le ministre de l'Énergie, des mines et des Ressources, a indiqué, lors d'un symposium tenu en 1991, que le Canada avait l'intention d'apporter des assouplissements à sa réglementation limitant la participation maximale que les investisseurs étrangers peuvent détenir dans les entreprises canadiennes opérant dans cette industrie.[11] Ces assouplissements prendront probablement la forme d'amendements apportés à la LIC[12] et aux lois sectorielles restreignant la propriété étrangère dans cette industrie.[13]

C L'AFFAIRE DE HAVILLAND

En 1991, le ministre responsable de l'application de la LIC a rejeté pour la deuxième fois seulement en six ans, sur plus de mille propositions d'acquisition examinées, une proposition d'acquisi-

---

[10] Voir notamment "Oil and Gas Drilling into New Downturn," in *Calgary Herald*, July 16, 1991, à la p. B5.

[11] Voir "Climat des futurs investissements étrangers dans l'industrie pétrolière et gazière canadienne," dans *12ᵉ symposium annuel sur le pétrole et le gaz canadiens parrainé par l'American Stock Exchange*, Toronto, 2 octobre 1991, 6 p.

[12] Nous avons vu que la LIC impose à tout investisseur étranger, y compris américain, qui veut acquérir directement pour cinq millions de dollars ou indirectement pour 50 millions de dollars une entreprise canadienne oeuvrant dans l'industrie pétrolière et gazière, qu'il soumette une proposition d'acquisition à Investissement Canada pour examen. Voir *supra* note 9; ALÉ, *supra* note 5, Annexe 1607.3, art. 4 (exclut l'industrie pétrolière et gazière des assouplissements apportés par l'ALÉ à la LIC en faveur des investisseurs américains).

[13] L'art. 44 de la *Loi sur les hydrocarbures*, S.R.C. 1985, c. 36 (2ième Suppl.), notamment, pose que les concessions de pétrole et de gaz naturel dans le Yukon et dans les Territoires du nord-ouest canadien ne peuvent être accordées qu'à des citoyens canadiens ou à des compagnies admissibles. Pour être admissible, au sens de cette loi, une compagnie doit être constituée au Canada et au moins 50% des actions émises par elle doivent appartenir à des citoyens canadiens. Dans le même sens, voir aussi *Loi de mise en oeuvre de l'Accord Canada — Nouvelle-Écosse sur les hydrocarbures extracôtiers*, L.C. 1988, c. 28.

tion d'une entreprise canadienne par un investisseur étranger.[14] En l'occurrence, il s'agissait de l'acquisition de la compagnie De Havilland Ltd.[15] par le consortium européen Avions de Transport Régional (ATR).[16] La proposition d'ATR a été rejetée au motif qu'elle ne procurait pas, au sens de la LIC, un "bénéfice net" au Canada.[17] Comme le permet la LIC, ATR a fait une seconde proposition au mois de juillet qui n'a pas été formellement acceptée par le ministre.[18] Au mois de septembre suivant, cependant, le ministre a déclaré qu'il se donnait un délai additionnel pour l'examiner.[19] C'est à partir de là que les choses se sont compliquées pour le Canada et ATR. Suite à des pressions faites par Netherlands NV Fokker et British Aerospace PLC, des constructeurs européens d'avions, la Commission de la Communauté européenne économique (CCEÉ) a voulu examiner cette acquisition au motif qu'elle permettrait à ATR de De Havilland de détenir conjointement une part élevée du marché des avions à turbo-propulseurs affectés aux dessertes régionales (50% du marché mondial et 67% du marché européen).[20]

[14] Au sujet du rejet de l'OPA de l'Institut Mérieux SA de France sur la compagnie pharmaceutique Connaught BioSciences Inc., voir P. Ratelle, "Investissement," (1990) 28 A.C.D.I. 451-53.

[15] La compagnie De Havilland, de Downsview, en banlieue de Toronto, est un important constructeur canadien d'avions à turbo-propulseurs affectés aux dessertes régionales qui employait, en 1991, près de cinq mille personnes. Elle a été une société d'État fédérale jusqu'en 1986, année où elle fut vendue au mégaconstructeur d'avions, Boeing Co., de Seattle, aux États-Unis.

[16] Ce consortium ou joint venture était formé d'Alenia SpA d'Italie et d'Aérospatiale SA de France. Ces deux sociétés sont sous le contrôle de leur gouvernement respectif.

[17] Selon le ministre, la proposition d'ATR devait rencontrer les critères suivants: "the new alliance would strengthen the overall Canadian aerospace industry and involve Canadians in a major way; there is a good prospect for De Havilland to become a self-sustainable, commercially viable company within a reasonable period of time; De Havilland's aircraft systems integration capabilities would be maintained and developed and key linkages to the high-tech end of supplier base would be strengthened." Voir Investissement Canada, Release, June 10, 1991.

[18] Id., July 19, 1991.

[19] Id., September 9, 1991.

[20] Voir "Règlement sur les concentrations: la Commission annonce une enquête approfondie dans l'affaire Aérospatiale-Alenia/De Havilland," dans Commission de la Communauté européenne, Information à la Presse, Bruxelles, 12 juin 1991, IP(91) 554. Aux termes du règlement sur les fusions de la CEÉ du 21 décembre

Suite à l'argumentation du commissaire européen à la concurrence, Sir Leon Brittan, la CCEE a annoncé, au mois d'octobre 1991, qu'elle bloquait cette acquisition parce que, selon elle, "it would create a powerful and unassailable dominant position in the world market," lequel aurait "an unacceptable impact on customers and the balance of competition in the European Community market."[21] C'était la première fois que la CCEÉ prenait une telle décision selon le nouveau règlement sur les fusions. À la fin de 1991, le Canada était donc placé devant ce fait accompli: même s'il acceptait qu'ATR achète De Havilland, ATR ne pourrait aller de l'avant parce que la CCEÉ l'en empêchait.[22] Le Canada a bien tenté de s'insurger contre cette décision auprès de la CCEÉ en prétendant qu'elle ne devait pas interférer avec la décision qu'il avait prise, mais sans grand succès.[23] Tout n'était pas cependant perdu pour le Canada puisque le Président de la CCEÉ, Jacques Delors, acceptait à la fin de 1991, de rencontrer ATR afin de trouver des moyens de reformuler leur OPA et la rendre ainsi acceptable aux yeux de la CCEÉ.[24]

III ACTIONS BILATÉRALES

A CONVENTIONS DE PROMOTION ET DE PROTECTION

Le réseau canadien d'accords bilatéraux sur la promotion et la protection des investissements s'est encore étendu en 1991. D'abord, le Canada a conclu trois accords avec, dans l'ordre chro-

---

1989 (No. 4064/89), la CCEÉ doit donner son avis sur les fusions entre entreprises originaires de pays membres qui ont ensemble un chiffre d'affaires cumulé qui atteint cinq milliards d'écus (unité de compte européenne) (6.75 milliards de dollars canadiens). Voir "La politique de concurrence dans un marché unique; objectif 92," dans *Documentation européenne*, no. 1/89.

[21] Voir *Résolution sur l'affaire "De Havilland,"* dans JO No. C280/140 du 10 octobre 1991; "Commission prohibits acquisition by Aerospatiale/Alenia of De Havilland," dans *European Community News*, October 2, 1991 NR(91) 27; "La Commission européenne bloque le rachat de De Havilland par l'Aérospatiale," dans *Le Monde*, 3 octobre 1991, à la p. 40.

[22] Voir "L'Europe et ses pouvoirs," dans *Le Monde*, 7 octobre 1991, à la p. 1.

[23] Voir "Hands Off De Havilland, EC Told," in *Financial Post*, November 27, 1991, à la p. 3.

[24] Voir "EC to Discuss Proposals to Save De Havilland Bid," in *The Citizen*, December 13, 1991, à la p. 3.

nologique, l'Uruguay,[25] la Hongrie[26] et l'Argentine.[27] À l'instar des accords précédents, ces accords prévoient des règles en matière de promotion, d'admission, de traitement, de protection, de transferts, de règlement des différends et de liquidation des investissements entre les pays signataires.[28] Ensuite, le Canada a ratifié l'accord sur les investissements avec la défunte URSS, le premier du genre jamais conclu par le Canada.[29]

B CONVENTIONS FISCALES

Le maillage conventionnel canadien en matière fiscale s'est resserré en 1991.[30] Le Canada a d'abord conclu une convention avec le Mexique.[31] Cette convention sera, il va de soi, fort utile si un accord de libre-échange nord-américain entre éventuellement en vigueur. Le Canada a ensuite ratifié les conventions conclues avec la Papouasie-Nouvelle-Guinée,[32] la Zambie[33] et le Luxem-

---

25 Voir *Accord entre le gouvernement du Canada et le gouvernement de la République orientale de l'Uruguay sur l'encouragement et la protection des investissements*, Ottawa, signé le 16 mai 1991.

26 Voir *Accord entre le gouvernement du Canada et le gouvernement de la République de Hongrie sur l'encouragement et la protection des investissements*, Ottawa, signé le 3 octobre 1991.

27 Voir *Accord entre le gouvernement du Canada et le gouvernement de la République d'Argentine sur l'encouragement et la protection des investissements*, Toronto, signé le 5 novembre 1991.

28 Au sujet des accords précédents, voir P. Ratelle, "Investissement," (1990) 28 *A.C.D.I.* 453-54 et (1991) 29 *A.C.D.I.* 446-47.

29 Voir *Accord entre le gouvernement du Canada et le gouvernement de l'Union des Républiques socialistes soviétiques sur l'encouragement et la protection réciproque des investissements*, [1991] R.T. Can., no. 31.

30 Selon des données fournies par le ministère des Affaires extérieures du Canada, plus de 50 conventions sont actuellement en vigueur. Voir *Liste des traités bilatéraux et multilatéraux du Canada en vigueur au 1er janvier 1988* (1989), pp. 1-1 et ss.; et du même ministère, *Bilateral Treaty Actions Taken by Canada 1989-91* (1992), pp. 1-1 et ss.

31 Voir *Convention entre le gouvernement du Canada et le gouvernement des États-Unis mexicains en vue d'éviter les doubles impositions et de prévenir l'évasion fiscale en matière d'impôts sur le revenu*, Ottawa, signée le 8 avril 1991.

32 Voir *Décret avisant que la Convention en matière d'impôts entre le Canada et la Papouasie-Nouvelle-Guinée est entrée en vigueur le 8 juillet 1991*. TR/91-108. 123 Gaz. Can. II 2992.

33 Voir *Proclamation avisant l'entrée en vigueur de la Convention Canada-République de Zambie à l'égard de l'impôt sur le revenu*, TR/91-35, 125 Gaz. Can. II 1176.

bourg.[34] Ces accords ressemblent *mutatis mutandis* aux accords antérieurs, lesquels ont pour modèle celui de l'OCDE.[35]

IV ACTIONS MULTILATÉRALES

A ACCORD DE LIBRE-ÉCHANGE NORD-AMÉRICAIN

Le 5 février 1991, le Premier ministre du Canada, le Président
des États-Unis, et le Président du Mexique ont annoncé que leurs
pays avaient l'intention d'entreprendre des négociations formelles
au cours de l'été suivant en vue de conclure un accord de libre-
échange nord-américain (ALÉNA).[36]

C'est ainsi que le ministre canadien du Commerce extérieur, a
reçu à Toronto, le 12 juin, ses homologues américain et mexicain,
et leurs équipes de négociation.[37] Une seconde rencontre a eu lieu
les 19 et 20 août suivants à Seattle,[38] et une troisième et dernière
rencontre s'est déroulée, du 26 au 28 octobre, à Zacateras, au
Mexique.[39] Après cette dernière rencontre, les ministres du Commerce extérieur des trois pays ont donné des instructions à leurs
négociateurs en chef pour produire une version préliminaire de
l'ALÉNA avant la fin de janvier 1992.[40]

B L'URUGUAY ROUND DU GATT

Les négociations commerciales multilatérales du l'Uruguay
Round du GATT, qui avaient été interrompues en décembre 1990,
ont repris le 26 février 1991.[41] Après l'intermède de l'été, les pays

---

[34] Voir *Décret avisant que la Convention en matière d'impôts entre le Canada et le Grand-Duché de Luxembourg est entrée en vigueur le 8 juillet 1991*, TR/91-108, 125 Gaz. Can. II 2992.

[35] Le texte de ce modèle est reproduit dans OCDE, *Modèle de convention de double imposition concernant le revenu et la fortune* (septembre 1977), 226 p.

[36] Voir M. Jacot, "Les États-Unis, le Canada et le Mexique vont négocier la création d'une vaste zone de libre-échange," dans *Le Monde*, 7 février 1991, à la p. 28.

[37] Voir notamment M. Tessier, "Les politiques économiques et commerciales," dans *Chronique des relations extérieures du Canada*, juin-septembre 1991, aux pp. 8-9.

[38] Voir Ministre de l'Industrie, des Sciences et de la Technologie et ministre du Commerce extérieur, *Communiqué*, no. 176, 15 août 1991.

[39] Voir *Les Grands dossiers de Washington*, novembre 1991, vol. 2, no. 7, p. 1 et janvier 1992, vol. 2, no. 9, p. 1.

[40] *Ibid.*

[41] Voir *Nouvelles de l'Uruguay Round*, NUR 046, 4 mars 1991.

membres du GATT ont tenté de mettre un terme définitif à ces
négociations commerciales multilatérales, mais sans succès. Le
Secrétaire général du GATT, Arthur Dunkel, a proposé, le 20
décembre 1991, un texte provisoire d'Accord final et a fixé au 13
janvier 1992 la reprise des discussions.[42] Dans le domaine des
TRIM,[43] on ne disposait toujours pas d'un texte de négociations
commun.[44] Il restait plusieurs questions à résoudre: la spécification
des TRIM incompatibles avec les articles III et XI du GATT; l'établissement de disciplines pour les prescriptions de résultat à
l'exportation; la mise en place de dispositions transitoires nécessaires pour les TRIM qui devront être éliminées;[45] le règlement des
différends et les questions institutionnelles. Un diplomate canadien, Germain Denis, a accédé à la présidence du comité de négociation sur les produits.

C   CODE DE LA LIBÉRATION DES MOUVEMENTS DE CAPITAUX DE
    L'OCDE

Le ministre du Commerce extérieur, a annoncé, en mars 1991,[46]
que le Canada avait élargi son engagement envers le Code de
libération des mouvements de capitaux de l'OCDE.[47] L'actuelle
réserve générale du Canada sur l'investissement étranger direct a
été remplacée par des réserves spécifiques touchant des secteurs

---

[42] Voir *Focus: Bulletin d'information du GATT*, no. 87, janvier-février 1992, à la p. 2.

[43] Il s'agit de l'abréviation anglaise pour les *Trade-Related Investment Measures*. Les
TRIM sont en gros, des conditions imposées aux investisseurs étrangers par les
États d'accueil qui modifient artificiellement les flux des échanges. Ce peut
être, par exemple, des prescriptions relatives à la teneur en produits nationaux.
À ce sujet, voir A. Kleitz, "Les entraves à l'investissement et distorsions commer-
ciales," (1990) 162 *l'Observateur de l'OCDE* 23-27.

[44] Voir *Focus: Bulletin d'information du GATT*, no. 83, août 1991, p. 11; Ministre de
l'Industrie, des Sciences et de la Technologie et ministre du Commerce extérieur, *Communiqué*, no. 294, 20 décembre 1991.

[45] Voir *Nouvelles de l'Uruguay Round*, NUR 050, 11 novembre 1991, à la p. 6.

[46] Voir Ministre du Commerce extérieur, *Communiqué*, no. 62, 14 mars 1991.

[47] Ce code vient compléter et renforcer un certain nombre d'instruments visant
la libéralisation de la vie économique internationale, tels que le Code de
l'OCDE portant sur la libération des opérations invisibles courantes, le GATT
et les Statuts du Fonds monétaire international. En simplifiant, on peut dire
que ce code a pour objectif final d'obtenir que les résidents des différents pays
membres puissent opérer entre eux des transactions aussi librement que les
résidents d'un seul et même pays membre. Le texte de ce code est reproduit
dans OCDE, *Code sur la libération des mouvements de capitaux* (décembre 1990)
144 p.

qui continuent de nécessiter une protection spéciale.[48] Des réserves sectorielles ont été inscrites pour les industries suivantes: services financiers, télécommunications, culture, transport aérien et maritime, capture du poisson et énergie.[49] Le processus d'examen actuellement suivi par Investissement Canada a aussi été protégé au moyen d'une réserve.[50]

D   BANQUE EUROPÉENNE POUR LA RECONSTRUCTION ET LE
     DÉVELOPPEMENT (BERD)

Finalement, le Canada a signé, le 25 février 1991, et puis ratifié, le 28 mars suivant, l'*Accord portant création de la Banque Européenne pour la reconstruction et le Développement.*[51] Rappelons que la Banque européenne pour la reconstruction et le développement (BERD), qui a son siège social à Londres, a pour mission de faciliter la transition des pays d'Europe centrale et orientale vers l'économie de marché et la démocratie.[52] Les investissements étrangers sont considérés dans l'Accord comme constituant un moyen pour y parvenir.[53] Après les États-Unis et le Japon, le Canada est le souscripteur non européen le plus important au capital autorisé de la BERD.[54] La part du Canada dans la BERD lui assure un siège au conseil d'administration.[55]

[48] Voir *supra* note 51.

[49] *Ibid.*

[50] *Ibid.*

[51] Voir *Accord portant création de la Banque Européenne pour la reconstruction et le Développement,* [1991] R.T. Can., no. 16.

[52] *Id.,* Préambule.

[53] *Id.,* art. 2 (1).

[54] *Id.,* Annexe A: "Souscriptions initiales au capital autorisé pour les membres potentiels susceptibles de devenir membres conformément aux dispositions de l'article 61."

[55] Voir Ministère des Affaires extérieures et ministère du Commerce extérieur, *Rapport annuel 1990-1991* (mars 1992), à la p. 11.

Canadian Practice in International Law / La pratique canadienne en matière de droit international public

At the Department of External Affairs in 1991-92 / Au ministère des Affaires extérieures en 1991-92

compiled by / préparé par
BARRY MAWHINNEY*

ARMED CONFLICT

Armed Conflict and the Environment

In a memorandum dated July 12, 1991, the Legal Bureau wrote:

1. The customary laws of war, in reflecting the dictates of public conscience, now include a requirement to avoid unnecessary damage to the environment. This includes consideration of environmental effects in the planning of military operations.

2. Such provisions bind all states, whether or not they have ratified various treaties. . . .

---

* Barry Mawhinney, Legal Adviser, Department of External Affairs, Ottawa. The extracts from official correspondence contained in this survey have been made available by courtesy of the Department of External Affairs. Material appearing in the House of Commons Debates is not included. Some of the correspondence from which extracts are given was provided for the general guidance of the inquirer in relation to specific facts which are often not described in full in the extracts contained in this compilation. The statements of law and practice should not necessarily be regarded as a definitive statement by the Department of External Affairs of that law or practice.

On October 22, 1991, the Deputy Permanent Representative of Canada to the United Nations stated:

> In effect, the practice of States, accepted environmental principles, and the public consciousness about the environment have combined with the traditional armed conflict rules on the protection of civilians and their property to produce a customary rule of armed conflict prohibiting unnecessary damage to the environment in wartime.

CLAIMS

Procédure de réclamation contre l'Iraq

Dans un document préparé le 5 juillet 1991, la Direction générale des affaires juridiques écrivait:

> La procédure qui sera suivie par les Nations Unies dans l'attribution des indemnités est la suivante. Le Conseil de sécurité a créé le Fonds de compensation des Nations Unies ("le Fonds") devant servir à compenser les pertes subies suite à l'invasion du Koweit par l'Iraq. Une part des revenus pétroliers de ce pays alimenteront le Fonds, qui sera administré par la Commission de compensation des Nations Unies ("la Commission") en fonction des orientations fixées par un Conseil d'administration ("le Conseil"). . . .
>
> Les États déposeront des réclamations au nom de leurs citoyens devant cette Commission . . . . Suite à la décision finale et au paiement aux États réclamants, ceux-ci seront responsables de la distribution des fonds à leurs citoyens. . . .
>
> Responsabilité: Les personnes qui nous ont fait parvenir des données sur leurs pertes (les "répondants") indiquent en général que leurs pertes sont dûes aux actes de l'armée irakienne, rendant par le fait même le gouvernement de l'Iraq responsable de ces pertes.
>
> Admissibilité: Plus de la moitié des répondants ne possèdent pas la nationalité canadienne. Dans ces conditions, si la règle de droit international de la "nationalité continue" (avoir été citoyen canadien au moment de la perte et en tout temps jusqu'au jugement sur la réclamation) est appliquée sans réserves, le Canada n'endossera pas les réclamations de ces personnes. Celles-ci devront s'adresser à l'État de leur nationalité au moment de la perte (Libye, Jourdain, Inde, Égypte . . .) pour que celui-ci endosse leur réclamation devant les Nations Unies. Les Palestiniens n'auront pas de recours.
>
> Preuve: Une petite minorité des répondants a pu produire des documents pouvant éventuellement faire preuve de leur propriété. Souvent les circonstances dans lesquelles les répondants ont quitté le Koweit ne leur permettaient pas de les apporter, ou ces documents ont été détruits. La pratique du Canada avant d'endosser des réclamations internationales est de s'assurer que celles-ci sont suffisamment documentées. Le Canada pourrait rejeter plus de la moitié des dossiers ouverts à ce jour uniquement sur la base du manque de documentation.

Les réclamations pour dettes contractées par l'Iraq avant ou après la guerre du Golfe ne sont pas du ressort de la Commission.

Compagnies: Selon la pratique canadienne dans ce domaine, les réclamations des compagnies seront endossées si les actifs de celles-ci appartiennent en majorité à des Canadiens. Nous avons reçu un petit nombre de répondants remplissant cette condition, le tout pour moins de deux millions de dollars.

Recours: Le Canada pourrait épouser des réclamations en dommages et intérêts pour pertes matérielles et probablement pour dommages moraux. . . .

JURISDICTION

Extraterritorialité

Dans un document préparé le 29 avril 1992, la Direction générale des affaires juridiques écrivait:

La *Loi sur les mesures économic spéciales* proposée, permettrait, mais sans l'exiger, que le gouvernement prenne des décrets et reglements regissant les activités des Canadiens à l'extérieur du Canada. Le gouvernement pourrait juger si, dans certaines situations, il serait dans l'intérêt du Canada d'appliquer des mesures extraterritoriales.

L'un des principaux objectifs de la *Loi sur les mesures économiques spéciales* proposée est de permettre au Canada de mettre en oeuvre les décisions d'une organisation internationale ou d'une association d'états, dont le Canada est un membre, appelant les états membres à prendre des sanctions économiques. Lorsque le Conseil de sécurité de l'ONU a adopté des résolutions imposant des sanctions obligatoires contre la Rhodésie du Sud (1966), l'Iraq (1990) et la Libye (1992), les états membres se sont vus obligés d'exercer leur compétence sur les activités de leurs ressortissants en dehors de leurs frontières. Le Canada peut faire appliquer les résolutions *obligatoires* du Conseil de sécurité en vertu de la *Loi sur les Nations Unies.* Cependant, lorsqu'une résolution du Conseil de sécurité n'est pas obligatoire, ou si d'autres organisations internationales et associations d'États suivaient l'exemple du Conseil de sécurité et adoptaient des mesures appelant leurs membres à controler les activités de leurs ressortissants, les dispositions du projet de loi C-53 qui autorise la réglementation des activités extraterritoriales s'avéreront nécessaires pour permettre au Canada de mettre en oeuvre la résolution ou les mesures. La *Loi sur les mesures économiques spéciales* permettrait au gouvernement de prendre des mesures visant à dissuader des Canadiens de mener des activités commerciales assujetties à des restrictions dans l'état étranger qui fait l'objet de sanctions ou à décourager des Canadiens de se servir de tiers états hostiles au Canada ou aux valeurs canadiennes pour mener des activités assujetties à des restrictions.

L'adoption d'une loi spéciale qui permettrait d'appliquer des mesures extraterritoriales dans un cas particulier n'est pas une option valable, car le gouvernement ne disposera pas toujours du temps nécessaire pour préparer et faire adopter une telle loi.

En principe, l'application extraterritoriale des lois est acceptable, à condition que l'état qui applique une loi de cette façon puisse prouver qu'il a intérêt à réglementer la conduite de des ressortissants en dehors de ces frontières et faire reconnaître qu'il s'agit d'un intérêt légitime conformément aux principes du droit international. Le principe de nationalité est bien établi dans le droit international et la jurisprudence pour affirmer la juridiction extraterritoriale. Le Canada l'invoque dans certaines dispositions du Code criminel, de la *Loi sur l'enrôlement à l'étranger*, de la Loi sur les secrets officiels et d'autres lois encore. D'autres pays membres de l'OCDE l'invoque dans diverses lois. Le *Emergency Law (Re-enactments and Repeals) Act 1964* du Royaume-Uni, invoquées pour appliquer les sanctions, contiennent des dispositions habilitantes semblables à celles que l'on trouve dans le projet de loi C-53 autorisant l'application de mesures extraterritoriales. Il convient de le noter, étant donné la similitude devues du Canada et du Royaume-Uni relativement à l'application extraterritoriale des lois.

La courtoisie internationale exige que la jurisdiction extraterritoriale sur la base de la nationalité ne soit pas exercée de façon à entraver les intérêts légitimes d'autres ni à exiger des ressortissants d'un état qu'ils agissent de contraire aux 1018 de l'état étranger dans lequel ils se trouvent.

Lorsque le Canada s'est élevé contre les mesures extraterritoriales d'autres pays, c'était soit parce que ces états n'avaient pas agi conformément aux principes de la courtoisie internationale ou que ces mesures reposaient sur de présumées bases juridiques qui ne sont pas généralement reconnues en droit international. Il faut souligner, dans le contexte des relations entre le Canada et les États-Unis, la tendance de ce dernier pays à considérer comme étant américaines les fillales étrangères de sociétés américaines. Aucun pays membre de l'OCDE, mis à part les États-Unis, n'accepte que la nationalité d'une fillale étrangère, constituée dans un pays, soit déterminée par la nationalité de sa société-mère, constituée dans un autre pays. De plus, dans les occasions où le Canada s'est élevé contre l'application extraterritoriale des lois américaines, la mesure en question constituant souvent une application unilatérale de la politique étrangère des États-Unis, et non la mise en oeuvre d'une décision multilatérale d'états partageant les mêmes idées.

Le fait que la *Loi sur les mesures économiques spéciales* permettrait au gouvernement de prendre des mesures extraterritoriales ne signifie pas que le Canada déroge aux positions sur l'extraterritorialité qu'il a défendues auparavant. On ne pourra pertinemment se demander si le Canada déroge à ses politiques de longue date que lorsque le gouvernement aura effectivement adopté des mesures précises d'application extraterritoriale. Les politiques de longue date du Canada semblent indiquer que les gouvernements exerceront une grande circonspection en invoquant la *Loi sur les mesures économiques spéciales* proposée pour adopter des mesures d'application extraterritoriale.

Transborder Abduction

In an *amicus curiae* brief filed with the Supreme Court of the United States in the *Alvarez Machain* in March 1992, the Canadian Government wrote:

The issues presented in this case could have a profound effect on Canada-USA extradition relations. Canada files this brief out of concern for the practice of transborder abductions of fugitives contrary to law. Such abductions contravene fundamental principles of justice that Canada has sought to uphold. They conflict with Canada's sense of the way the return of fugitives with its great neighbour ought to be conducted. Abductions offend against Canada's view of the law in international affairs. Canada is concerned that the United States Government considers it permissible for a law enforcement agency, sworn to uphold the law, to violate a treaty relationship, the sovereignty and laws of a treaty partner and the rights of a fugitive resident of a treaty partner.

Canada has a long tradition of international cooperation through extradition treaties with the United States beginning with the Jay Treaty of November 19, 1794 between Great Britain and the United States. Since 1842, rendition has been governed by a series of agreements of which the extant Treaty of Extradition of December 3, 1971, 27 U.S.T. 985, T.I.A.S. No. 8237 ("Treaty") came into force on March 12, 1976. A Protocol to this Treaty, significantly broadening the types of offenses for which extradition could be granted, came into force on November 26, 1991.

The Treaty, on a reciprocal basis, establishes a comprehensive system for rendition of fugitives, describes the nature of offenses for which extradition may be sought, and guarantees every fugitive access to the courts of the requested nation in order to test the validity of a rendition request.

The Treaty is part of the law of Canada and was negotiated with the understanding by Canada that the agreement would provide the exclusive means whereby Canada and her constituent provinces, and the United States and its constituent states would seek to obtain custody of fugitives from each other. Because this case affects the construction of all petitioners' extradition treaties it raises doubt concerning the correctness of Canada's perception of the mutually agreed upon manifest scope and purpose of the Treaty. Moreover, in this case, the United States seeks the imprimatur of the Court to abrogate if necessary the right of Canadian citizens and others to access Canadian courts, contrary to its solemn undertaking in the Treaty to respect that right.

Canada and the United States enjoy an undefended border more than 3000 miles in length. The ease with which this border may be crossed accounts for the fact that approximately 50% of all American requests for extradition are made to Canada. In 1991, the United States made 74 requests for extradition to Canada and Canada made 47 requests to the United States. Many of these requests emanate from state and local authorities. Transborder incidents, involving bounty hunters, resulted in an exchange of notes in 1988 between Secretary of State George P. Shultz and Secretary of State for External Affairs Joe Clark in an attempt to partially resolve the problem. The position adopted by the petitioner in this case, however, raises a potentially far more serious problem; the spectre not only of federal, but more likely of official state and local incursions to abduct fugitives, where extradition is seen as too costly, too slow or unavailable, in violation of Canada's territorial integrity. This unlawful conduct would in effect be sanctioned in United States law by a decision favouring petitioner. Canada has an interest in ensuring that its treaties are given that construction and application which their express terms, nature, scope and purpose require. Moreover, Canada has an interest, indeed an obligation to its citizens, in taking all steps necessary to protect the rights of its inhabitants and its sovereign interest in its territorial integrity, guaranteed by the Treaty and international law. . . .

Canada submits that the current position of the United States departs from established practice in the relations between the United States and Canada, and among other nations, on which many extradition treaties have been built. Ultimately it departs as well from common sense underpinnings of all such treaties, which is to substitute the rule of law for force in such matters as national sovereignty, the right to give asylum, and the orderly cooperation in the enforcement of criminal laws.

Canada views transborder abductions from Canada to the United States as breaches of the Canada-United States Extradition Treaty and breaches of Canada's sovereignty. Other civilized nations, as well, would not agree with the position of petitioner in this case; they would insist that unless a nation otherwise consents to a removal of a person from its territory, an extradition treaty is the exclusive means for a requesting government to obtain such a removal and that it is the policy of nations to request return of abducted persons. Canada and its component governments do not hold to a policy of abductions from American territory, and if abductions occur, they could not reasonably expect the United States to acquiesce in Canadian courts' disrespect of U.S. sovereignty through exercise of jurisdiction over abducted individuals. The Government of Canada would, upon protest, cooperate to obtain the return of an abducted fugitive.

INTERNATIONAL ECONOMIC LAW

Legal Implications of Tariffication for the FTA (and NAFTA)

In a memorandum dated September 24, 1991 the Legal Bureau wrote:

the following questions are addressed: how Canada's FTA rights and obligations would be affected if there were a decision of the GATT that: (a) all NTB's will be converted to tariff equivalents; (b) Article XI:2(c)(i) rights will be waived; (c) all country specific waivers (e.g., the USA waiver) will be eliminated. You also inquired whether FTA Article 710 overrides Article 401 for agricultural goods. . . .

1. Our general conclusion is that any legally binding agreement in the Uruguay Round or NAFTA to which both Canada and the USA subscribe

will supersede any prior incompatible right or obligation of the FTA by operation of international law, unless there is an express provision in the NAFTA or relevant Uruguay Round agreement to the contrary. An amendment to the FTA would not be essential to accomplish this result, but it would provide greater certainty and would remove the issue from possible Chapter 18 dispute. There are several caveats to this opinion, based on the form that the agreement takes and the exact nature of the proposed measure which we discuss in greater detail in this memorandum. . . .

2. . . . The general rule of FTA precedence in Article 104 applies only to rights and obligations as they existed when the FTA entered into force on January 1, 1989. It does not establish FTA priority with respect to subsequent agreements, such as those that may arise from the Uruguay Round or NAFTA.

3. The relation between the FTA and subsequent agreements between Canada and the U.S. is governed by the principles of hierarchy of treaties under international law. The principle most relevant to your inquiry is contained in the *Vienna Convention on the Law of Treaties* article 30 (3) which provides:

When all the parties to the earlier treaty are parties also to the later treaty but the earlier treaty is not terminated or suspended in operation under article 59, the earlier treaty applies only to the extent that its provisions are compatible with those of the later treaty.

4. Therefore, in the absence of an express treaty provision regarding priority, as between parties to a treaty who become parties to a later, inconsistent, treaty, the earlier treaty will apply only where its provisions are not incompatible with the later treaty. Whether the subsequent treaty relates to the same subject matter and whether there is an inconsistency between the provisions will normally be construed strictly. If it is possible to interpret both the earlier and later treaties in a consistent fashion, there will be a tendency to do so.

5. In addition, there is a principle that specific obligations take precedence over more general ones. This would tend to support precedence to tariffication obligations. Further, the rules of interpretation of international agreements contained in the Vienna Convention on the Law of Treaties stipulate that a subsequent agreement between the parties regarding the interpretation or application of the provisions of an agreement shall be taken into account in interpreting the agreement.

6. All of these principles lead to the conclusion that unless Canada and the U.S. expressly provide otherwise, a *legally binding agreement* reached in the Uruguay Round or in the NAFTA which provides for rights or obligations that conflict with those in the FTA, will prevail over the FTA.

7. In legal terms, the form that the agreement to implement the proposals in (a) to (c) takes can have an impact on whether a formal amendment to the FTA would be required to ensure that the newly agreed obligations in the Uruguay Round prevail over those in the FTA. Our FTA rights and obligations would be superseded by operation of the hierarchy of treaties under international law and an amendment to the FTA would not be required if the measures proposed in (a) through (c)

above are expressed in the form of a treaty (be it a stand alone code or an amendment to the GATT).

8. The legal result if the proposals are implemented through a decision of the CONTRACTING PARTIES under Article XXV of the GATT is not as clear. We would refer you to our memorandum JLET-6173 of July 6, 1990 on the legal status of GATT Article XXV decisions, a copy of which is attached. To summarize, Article XXV decisions are not automatically legally binding as is an agreement in the form of a treaty. However, Article XXV decisions can acquire a legally binding character as an expression of state practice provided there is general acceptance of the measure proposed in the decision. They can also be used to interpret obligations under the GATT by virtue of Article 31 of the Vienna Convention on the Law of Treaties which includes subsequent practice or subsequent agreement regarding the interpretation or application of the treaty as matters to be taken into account in interpreting treaties. . . .

9. Since a subsequent treaty obligation prevails only to the extent of *incompatibility* with a prior treaty obligation, it may be useful to consider each proposal in turn.

10. With respect to proposal (a), it could be argued that tariffication is not incompatible with FTA Articles 401 or 710. Although the expression "tariffication" applies the same label as that which applies to customs duties, it is in some ways a completely different concept, i.e., an attempt to quantify the effect of non-tariff barriers by making them more transparent. It could be argued that it is a completely separate concept that falls outside the regular customs tariff and hence is not affected by the obligations in FTA Article 401 which apply only to customs duties as they were understood at the time the FTA was negotiated. If the domestic implementing legislation were to differentiate between pre-existing customs duties and the new NTB tariff equivalent, this distinction would be easier to sustain. Under this scenario, an agreement on tariffication would not be incompatible with, but rather would co-exist with and supplement the existing obligations in the FTA. Given the scope of tariffication which goes far beyond existing GATT rights and obligations, we would encourage you to ensure that the agreement on tariffication takes the form of a treaty and not merely a decision of the CONTRACTING PARTIES pursuant to Article XXV of the GATT.

11. With respect to (b), a waiver of GATT article XI:2 (c) rights appears to be in direct conflict with Article 407 (reaffirmation of GATT rights with respect to prohibitions or restrictions on trade in goods which the Parties agreed in the Salmon and Herring panel incorporates GATT Article XI) and 710 of the FTA in which it is stated that the parties retain their GATT rights, "including their rights and obligations under GATT Article XI." A waiver of Article XI:2 (c) rights constitutes an amendment to the GATT and should take the legal form either of an amendment to the GATT pursuant to Article XXX or form part of a new agreement. In either case it would constitute an agreement subsequent in time that would prevail over the GATT.

12. With respect to (c), waivers are granted by decision of the CONTRACTING PARTIES and a decision of the CONTRACTING PARTIES to remove them would be the correct legal form to bring this measure into

force. FTA Article 710 provides that the parties retain their rights and obligations under GATT Article XI. The current USA rights and obligations are those under Article XI as limited by the agricultural waiver. A decision to remove the waiver is not directly in conflict with Article 710 — it merely clarifies the nature of the rights and obligations preserved vis-à-vis the United States. Thus, in our view, there is no incompatibility between FTA Article 710 and measure (c). Whether the broader USA obligations under Article XI continue to apply will depend on whether measure (b) enters into force. . . .

13. You also sought views specifically on whether Article 710 overrides Article 401 for agricultural goods. Article 710 provides: Unless otherwise specifically provided in this Chapter, the Parties retain their rights and obligations with respect to agricultural, food, beverage and certain related goods under the General Agreement on Tariffs and Trade (GATT) and agreements negotiated under the GATT, including their rights and obligations under GATT Article XI.

14. In our view, the only sensible interpretation of Article 710 is that it reaffirms any existing GATT and related Code obligations with respect to the matters covered by Chapter 7, i.e., non-tariff measures. To interpret it in a very literal fashion as retaining all GATT rights, including those covered by other Chapters of the FTA, such as tariffs (FTA Article 401) was clearly not the intended result. For example, agricultural products are included in the staging categories of each country's tariff schedule for tariff elimination under the FTA.

15. In any event, given the discussion above of the priority accorded to a subsequent agreements between the same parties, the question of whether Article 710 overrides Article 401 would not be determinative. . . .

16. These are the international legal principles that apply to answer your question. The easy, practical answer to your question is that if both Canada and the USA agree to these measures in the Uruguay Round, it would most clearly express the will of the parties if the FTA were amended accordingly. This can be accomplished relatively simply by an exchange of notes that could record the parties' intention that specific measures agreed to in the Uruguay Round prevail over the FTA.

17. This form of amendment would not make the tariffication/waiver provisions part of the FTA for purposes of any Chapter 18 dispute, but should prevent any dispute that might arise over the fulfilment of FTA rights and obligations that conflict with the proposed measures. Any necessary changes to the domestic FTA implementing legislation could be part of a legislative package to implement the MTN.

Trade and Environment

On April 2, 1992, a representative of the Legal Bureau stated:

It is fair to say that the GATT favours multilateral trade measures over unilateral measures to deal with regional or global environmental problems. The legal compatibility of some multilateral trade measures with the GATT, particularly against non-parties, is still uncertain, however, since none has been subjected to adjudication by a GATT panel. This uncertainty puts countries party to both GATT and IEAs (International Environmental Agreements) in a legal dilemma: in fulfilling their obligations under an environmental convention they don't know whether they are failing their GATT obligations. This dilemma may be resolved partly by generally applicable rules of treaty interpretation. Thus, to the extent that there is an irreconcilable conflict between the GATT and a treaty norm of environmental protection, the rules of the "later treaty" or of the "more specific law" may prevail. However, this solution is useful only if the parties to the conflict are parties to both the environmental convention and the GATT. . . .

Whether it would be possible to negotiate such amendments, supplementary agreements or waivers [to the GATT] is an issue in itself. From a trade perspective, these proposals represent potential trade losses through legitimized discrimination against countries that may have different approaches to common environmental problems; they might also set an unwelcome precedent. Such countries may be reluctant to lose the protection provided by present GATT rules. How, under these circumstances, does one bring about the desired negotiations? Some form of "package negotiation" would presumably be required to take into account the growing "North/South divide" on trade and environment issues, evident at UNCED; developing countries are concerned that environment/trade measures might act as impediments to their development. In the Climate Change Convention negotiations, for example, India has attempted to rule out possible trade measures unless agreed by consensus and compatible with GATT. Future negotiations on these issues will undoubtedly involve, like Montreal Protocol negotiations, questions of funding and transfers of technology. . . .

PRIVILEGES AND IMMUNITIES

Privileges and Immunities under the "Open Skies" Treaty

In a memorandum dated April 30, 1992, the Legal Bureau wrote:

There may be legal problems with the granting of privileges to representatives of foreign states coming to Canada to carry out their responsibilities under the "Open Skies" Treaty. Section 5(1)(c) of the Foreign Missions and International Organizations Act (attached) provides for representatives of the member states of an international organization to have the immunities set out in the Article IV of the Convention on the Privileges and Immunities of the United Nations (attached).

The *first problem* is that although section 5(1)(c) of the legislation grants privileges to representatives of foreign states, it limits this to foreign states that are members of an international organization. This problem may be manageable: an "Open Skies Consultative Commission" has been established pursuant to Article X of the Treaty. . . . The Commission, acting by consensus, has the responsibility for allocating quotas, considering disputes and proposing amendments to the Treaty, so we believe it can properly be described as an organization.

The *second problem* is that Article IV of the Convention on the Privileges and Immunities of the United Nations only provides for privileges and immunities for "representatives of Members to the principal and subsidiary organs of the United Nations and to conferences convened by the United Nations." It may be that s. 5(1)(c) should therefore be read as extending privileges and immunities only to representatives *to an international organization.* "Open Skies" inspectors are not representatives to an international organization. Their rights and duties arise not because of the functions of an international organization but because of a treaty.

We will be seeking the views of the Department of Justice on this issue. If the Department of Justice were to conclude that the present legislation does not cover representatives of States who are coming to Canada to implement "Open Skies," then Canada would not be in a position to implement fully its "Open Skies" commitments.

In respect of privileges: i.e., matters that only involve money, any problems could be addressed either by administrative means or by reimbursing representatives for any costs incurred which would otherwise be covered by a privilege. The question of immunities, although less of a day-to-day concern, would be harder to fix in principle, although in practice, given the limited time in Canada and the types of activities such representatives would be engaged in, these problems too might be manageable.

Pending resolution of the legal issue, we will proceed to prepare a submission to Council which will recommend that Canada ratify the Treaty with an appropriate reservation in respect of privileges and immunities, if necessary. At this stage we would propose a reservation along the following lines:

The Government of Canada declares, with respect to Article XIII, Section II, that it will initially implement the required privileges and immunities to the extent permitted by Canadian law, and that it is reviewing the question of whether any legislative changes will be necessary for Canada to implement fully the required privileges and immunities.

TREATIES

Compatibility of Treaties

In a memorandum dated December 3, 1992, the Legal Bureau wrote:

The basic rule is that in the event of incompatibility of treaty obligations, the later in time prevails unless express provision to the contrary has been made in one of the treaties in question. This basic rule is subject to certain variables. As a result, it would enhance legal certainty for Canada and the United States to review our obligations arising in the Uruguay Round in light of our mutual obligations under the FTA. This would avoid the need to resort to legal construction of the interaction of complicated treaty instruments and set the stage for an agreed understanding of our mutual obligations which would also clarify negotiations of the NAFTA.

To illustrate the legal principles involved in determining priority of treaty obligations, we have prepared the following summary based on the Vienna Convention on the Law of Treaties and customary international law. . . .

1. Express Statement

A treaty can specify its relation to prior or subsequent treaties thereby overriding all but the hierarchical principle noted below.

2. Absence of Express Statement

The general presumption is that a later treaty prevails over an earlier treaty on the same subject matter. This general rule can be countered by any of the following principles:

Hierarchical Principle — obligations of member states under the UN Charter prevail over any inconsistent treaties between them.

Lex Specialis — a specific obligation will take precedence over a more general one.

Principle of Autonomous Operation — applies primarily to international organizations and provides that each international organization must regard itself as bound in the first instance by its own constitution and will naturally apply instruments which it is itself responsible for administering rather than other instruments with which its own instruments may be in conflict.

Principle of Legislative Intent — this is primarily a rule of interpretation under which one may consider the *travaux préparatoires* to a treaty as relevant in determining what its relation to other treaties should be.

Doesn't the FTA prevail over all other treaties?

With respect to *prior* bilateral and multilateral treaties, the FTA is an example of an agreement that expressly provides for its priority (Article 104). However, with respect to *subsequent* bilateral and multilateral treaties, the FTA is generally silent. Therefore, the FTA will only prevail over a subsequent agreement if the subsequent agreement expressly provides for this, or does not conflict with the FTA. For example, if Canada and the United States were to agree in the Uruguay Round to treat something differently than how it was treated in the FTA, that FTA provision would be eclipsed by the subsequent obligation to the extent of any incompatibility. To provide a simple example, if Canada were to agree in the Uruguay Round to a zero tariff on an item that was still subject to a tariff (albeit declining) under the FTA, the MTN obligation would apply. An MTN tariff agreement that was higher than the FTA tariff would not be incompatible with the FTA obligation. Hence the later would continue as between Canada and the United States.

What if a later "agreement" is a resolution of an organisation or an understanding or interpretation of a prior treaty?

A treaty is defined as any international agreement in written form concluded between states whether in a single instrument or in two or more related instruments, whatever its designation. Therefore, the first step is to determine whether the resolution, understanding or interpretation may actually constitute a legally binding agreement notwithstanding its title.

In many cases this is a simple matter. However, in the trade area, the GATT has developed its own practice of interpretations and understandings that officially are not amendments to the GATT (thereby avoiding the cumbersome amending procedure) but which seem to be more than an interpretation of a given text. This practice creates uncertainty in the application of the rules of priority. If those agreed "interpretations" constitute legally binding obligations, they would be considered under the above rules. If, however, they do not constitute legally binding agreements, they fall outside the scope of the rules noted above, i.e. they could not override prior treaty obligations.

How do you determine what is general and what is particular in applying the principle of *lex specialis*?

This is primarily a question of interpretation in each individual case for which there is no general answer. It could be applicable as an argument in determining whether a general prohibition against subsidies in one agreement prevailed over a permitted subsidy with respect to a particular product.

How do you determine whether a later obligation is incompatible?

This is a matter of interpretation based on the specifics of each case. Generally, international jurists and scholars will interpret incompatibility quite narrowly, in an attempt to give full effect to all treaty obligations. A difference of obligation does not automatically result in incompatibility.

The *travaux préparatoires* of the Vienna Convention provides the following example. If a small number of states concluded a consular convention granting wide privileges and immunities and those same States later concluded with other States a consular convention having a much larger number of parties but providing for a more restricted regime, the earlier convention would continue to govern relations between the States parties thereto if the circumstances or the intention of the parties justified its maintenance in force. To take an example closer to home, this would mean that a more restrictive MTN services agreement would not be incompatible with more liberal FTA provisions. In such circumstances the provisions of the FTA would continue in force between Canada and the United States.

What if a later general treaty is incompatible with one provision of an earlier treaty?

The Vienna Convention rules refer to the application of successive treaties *on the same subject matter*. If only one provision of a subsequent treaty conflicts with a previous treaty, it will be a question of interpretation — applying principles such as intent of the parties and *lex specialis* to determine the result.

Thus, where a general treaty impinges indirectly on the content of a particular provision of an earlier treaty the later treaty does not automatically prevail as the treaties as a whole do not relate to the same subject matter. The example given in the *travaux préparatoires* to the Vienna Convention is that a general treaty on the reciprocal enforcement of judgments will not affect the continued applicability of particular provisions concerning the enforcement of judgments contained in an earlier treaty dealing with third party liability in the field of nuclear energy.

Does the hierarchical principle only apply to the UN Charter?

No. This principle may be used by an international organization to support the superiority of the provisions of its constitution over incompatible provisions of treaties adopted within the framework of the organization. This should be borne in mind in the drafting of the proposed Multilateral Trade Organization. Also, *jus cogens* (principles of international law so fundamental that no treaty can erode them) would also prevail over an inconsistent treaty.

What date is relevant in determining the later in time?

The relevant date is the date of the adoption of the text and not that of its entry into force.

Interpretation — Boundary Waters Treaty

In a memorandum dated May 25, 1992, the Legal Bureau wrote:

In the memorandum under reference, you asked whether the Strait of Georgia is a boundary water subject to the provisions of the *Boundary Waters Treaty of 1909* (the "Treaty"). In my opinion, both the ordinary meaning of the term "boundary waters," as defined in the Preliminary Article of the Treaty, and the intent of this definition that such waters be restricted to fresh waters exclude the Strait of Georgia from the provisions of the Treaty dealing with boundary waters. This Article states as follows:

For the purposes of this treaty boundary waters are defined as the waters from main shore to shore of the *lakes and rivers and connecting waterways* [in the French version "et cours d'eau qui les relient," the word "les" referring to lakes and rivers], or the portions thereof, along which the international boundary between the United States and the Dominion of Canada passes, including all bays, arms, and inlets thereof, but not including tributary waters which in their natural channels would flow into such lakes, rivers and waterways, or waters flowing from such lakes, rivers and waterways, or the waters or rivers flowing across the boundary.

The ordinary meaning of the words alone supports the view that the waters of the Strait of Georgia are not boundary waters as defined in the Preliminary Article. The Strait is neither a lake, a river or a waterway connecting a lake or a river nor is it a bay, an arm or an inlet of a lake, river or connecting waterway.

Moreover, in a 1928 article by Robert A. MacKay in the *American Journal of International Law* [22 A.J.I.L. 292 1928)] which was quoted by Bloomfield and Fitzgerald in their 1958 study *Boundary Waters Problems of Canada and the United States*, the term "boundary waters" was said to include "only *fresh* waters along the course of which or through which the international line runs." This view was shared in a November 1978 legal opinion from this Division. . . .

Interpretation — Treaty on Conveyance of Prisoners, and Wrecking and Salvage

In a memorandum dated January 29, 1992 the Legal Bureau wrote:

You asked us for our views on the meaning of the Agreement between Canada and the United States on Extradition, Wrecking and Salvage signed at Washington on May 18, 1908. The Treaty was concluded by the United Kingdom in respect of Canada and provides in Article II for reciprocal wrecking and salvage privileges in, inter alia, the waters of Lake Erie, for vessels from the United States on the Canadian side of the lake. The article goes on to provide,

It is further agreed that such reciprocal wrecking and salvage privileges shall include all necessary towing incident thereto, and that nothing in the Customs, Coasting or other laws or regulations of either country shall restrict in any manner the salvage operations of such vessels or wrecking appliances. . . .

We have been unable to find any negotiating history for the Treaty which would assist us in interpreting Article II, which deals with salvage.

There has, however, been a subsequent agreement between Canada and the United States touching upon matters dealt with in the Convention. Canada and the United States are parties to the Convention for the Protection of the World Cultural and Natural Heritage done at Paris on November 16, 1972 (CTS 1976/45). That Convention notes that deterioration or disappearance of any item of the cultural or natural heritage constitutes a harmful impoverishment of all the nations of the world. Although that Convention only provides collective protection for outstanding sites which have been designated by the state in which the site is located, its expression of the principle that cultural heritage ought to be protected should be taken into account in interpreting the 1908 Treaty.

In considering whether the Treaty applies to the salvage of a historic wreck, the general rule of interpretation, set out in Article 31 of the Vienna Convention on the Law of Treaties, is that a "treaty shall be interpreted in *good faith* in accordance with the *ordinary meaning* to be given to the terms of the treaty in their *context* and in light of its *object and purpose*." We will examine each aspect underlined, in turn, to see its application to the case.

(I) *Good faith*

We do not think it would be acting in bad faith to interpret the treaty as not applying to historic wrecks. Canada and the United States share the goal of respecting cultural heritage, and both countries' laws are evolving in the same direction in this respect. The question before us is a technical one and not one which is of such a nature that either country would allege bad faith in respect of a decision going either way.

(II) *Ordinary Meaning*

On the face of it, the "ordinary meaning" test favours the interpretation that "any property wrecked" includes "historic wrecks."

(III) *Context*

(a)*"such* . . . privileges":

The second paragraph of Article II speaks of *"such* reciprocal . . . salvage privileges." The first paragraph of Article II provides that vessels and wrecking appliances from the other country "may salve any property wrecked and may render aid and assistance to any vessels wrecked, disabled or in distress. . . ."

Thus, the salvage privilege is linked to rendering aid and assistance to wrecked vessels. This is a very different matter than the salving of a vessel which sank more than a century ago. Although ordinary salving is often not contemporaneous with the wrecking of a vessel, the wording suggests that the Treaty contemplated a kind of salvage, which like the rendering of aid and assistance, would be addressing a contemporary occurrence. Even if the meaning of "contemporary" is ill-defined, a 120-year-old wreck would not fit the definition.

(b) "shall not restrict . . . operations":

The Treaty provides that nothing in the laws of the country "shall restrict in any manner the salving operations . . . ." The prohibition appears to emphasize restrictions on operations, re how the salvaging is being done, rather than limitations on which sites could be salved.

(c) "all necessary towing incident thereto":

The first sentence of the paragraph provides that reciprocal wrecking and salvage privileges "shall include all necessary towing incident thereto." The reference to towing reinforces the comment made above: it indicates the intention to prohibit laws that might render salvage impractical by placing restrictions on vessel operations.

(IV) *Object and purpose*

The article's purpose is to grant reciprocal rights of salvage, and to ensure that this grant is not undermined by restrictions. However, it does not prohibit application to salvage vessels of the other country of laws of general application. For example, environmental laws, laws regarding the use of explosives and the Shipping Act, would all be applicable even though they might affect the salving operations. What then of a law of general application, which protects historic underwater artifacts, including historic wrecks? The Treaty's requirement for reciprocal treatment is not affected by such laws. Moreover, the salvage companies of both countries have had 50 years in which to exercise their right. Thus, the restriction is only a very minor one. Indeed, over the 50 years, the "property wrecked" has been converted to a "historic cultural artifact." In this respect, the "restriction" is not a restriction at all.

Implementation of Treaties

In a memorandum of February 4, 1992, the Legal Bureau wrote:

In Canada, treaties are not self-executing. Therefore, Canada's international obligations do not have the direct force of law in domestic law. An international obligation may require domestic legislation, either federally or provincially, or both, for its implementation. The division of powers between the federal and provincial governments is unaffected by the fact that the Royal Prerogative to conclude treaties is exercised exclusively in the name of the Crown in the right of Canada, i.e. by the federal government.

Sucession of Russia to Canada-USSR Double Taxation and Foreign Investment Protection Agreements

In a memorandum dated February 19, 1992, the Legal Bureau wrote:

As we understand it, corporate legal advisors are having difficulty with the lack of a specific document which demonstrates that Russia is bound by the agreements of the former Soviet Union with Canada.

In response, we should note that Mr. Yeltsin specifically acknowledged both the Double Taxation Agreement and the Foreign Investment Protection Agreement between Canada and Russia in paragraph three of the Declaration signed with Prime Minister Mulroney on February 1. An extract from that Declaration is attached, with the reference to the DTA and the FIPA highlighted.

We might also note that both at the United Nations and the meetings in respect of Conventional Forces in Europe (CFE), Russia has consistently maintained, since the end of the Soviet Union as we knew it, that Russia was the continuation of the Soviet Union. No state has disagreed with this position. Canada fully agrees with it.

Parliamentary Declarations in 1991-92 / Déclarations parlementaires en 1991-92

compiled by / préparé par
MAUREEN IRISH*

1. Les droits de la personne/Human Rights

(a) La Chine — China

Hon. Lloyd Axworthy (Winnipeg South Centre): . . . Following the Tiananmen Square massacre, the then Secretary of State for External Affairs stated, and I quote directly: "Programs which benefit or lend prestige to the current hard line policies of the Chinese government should be avoided." Yet, the Minister for International Trade in his visit to China last week endorsed or supported China's membership in GATT, clearly a contradiction of that policy.

Considering that human rights groups have evidence that China uses prison slave labour in producing export products, how can the Secretary of State for External Affairs reconcile the Minister for International Trade's business as usual approach in endorsing China's membership in the GATT with her government's so-called human rights policy? . . .

Hon. Michael Wilson (Minister of Industry, Science and Technology and Minister for International Trade): Mr. Speaker, let me make it very clear that in my discussions with ministers I met in China last week, I discussed and put forward the position of the Government of Canada very forcefully as it relates to human rights.

With regard to the question on the GATT, it is in the interests of Canada, of Canadian traders who are trying to export into China and create jobs here in Canada, to have clear trade policies from the Chinese, a more transparent entry into that market, a more transparent understanding of what their trade policies are and what their industrial policies are so that we can trade more effectively into that market.

On the question of sales of products that are being made in prisons, we have checked very carefully with the Chinese. We have been told that none of the products they have sold to us are made in prisons and we are monitoring that question very, very closely.

(House of Commons Debates, April 27, 1992, pp. 9711-12)
(Débats de la Chambre des Communes, le 27 avril 1992, pp. 9711-12)

---

* Faculty of Law, University of Windsor.

(b) Haïti — Haiti

M. Svend J. Robinson (Burnaby–Kingsway): Monsieur le Président, au mois de février dernier, les Canadiens et Canadiennes ont applaudi l'investiture du gouvernement démocratique de Jean-Bertrand Aristide. Après le coup violent à Haïti, est-ce que la ministre des Affaires extérieures va nous assurer que notre gouvernement ne va pas reconnaître le gouvernement qui est responsable pour ce régime de terreur à Haïti, qu'il va les isoler dans tous les forums internationaux et qu'il va imposer les sanctions économiques contre ces duvalieristes qui tirent sur les enfants et sur les gens dans la rue? . . .

Le très hon. Brian Mulroney (premier ministre): Monsieur le Président, compte tenu de l'importance justement des questions soulevées par mon ami, je peux lui dire que nous avons effectivement l'intention d'agir dans ce sens-là.

Nous n'avons nullement l'intention de reconnaître un groupe de voyous qui se sont emparés du contrôle à Haïti en évinçant un président et un gouvernement démocratiquement élus. Nous allons tout faire pour nous assurer que, dans la mesure du possible, la démocratie trouve un regain de vie en Haïti et que le président Aristide soit de nouveau dans ses fonctions démocratiques à Port-au-Prince.

(House of Commons Debates, October 1, 1991, p. 3052)
(Débats de la Chambre des Communes, le 1 octobre 1991, p. 3052)

(c) Le Timor Oriental-East Timor

Mr. Dan Heap (Trinity–Spadina): . . . I want to ask the minister, whether in spite of Canada's substantial bilateral aid and billion dollar private investment in Indonesia, will Canada now act to support United Nations initiatives to free East Timor from Indonesia?

Hon. Barbara McDougall (Secretary of State for External Affairs): Mr. Speaker, Canada considers that Indonesian sovereignty over East Timor is a fact, recognizing that there has never been any history of independence or self-determination or self-government in that territory.

We do not condone the manner of incorporation and we deplore and condemn the loss of life that occurred, but we very much support the UN-sponsored dialogue between Portugal and Indonesia as the most promising means to reach an understanding in that very unfortunate and unhappy circumstance.

(House of Commons Debates, September 18, 1991, p. 2310)
(Débats de la Chambre des Communes, le 18 septembre 1991, p. 2310)

Mrs. Beryl Gaffney (Nepean): . . . (T)he Secretary of State for External Affairs . . . recently announced the suspension of $30 million in aid to Indonesia because of the November 12 massacre at Dili. In addition, all other aid projects were subject to review. . . . When will this government finally support United Nations Security Council resolutions 384 and 389 which call for the withdrawal of Indonesian troops from East Timor?

Mr. Ross Belsher (Parliamentary Secretary to Minister of Fisheries and Oceans and Minister for the Atlantic Canada Opportunities Agency): . . . (T)he Secretary of State for External Affairs conveyed Canada's dismay of the shootings during meetings with the Indonesian Foreign Minister in Seoul on November 13, 1991 a few hours after the news of the killing of the East Timorese had come to light.

Canadian concerns were also expressed to the Indonesian authorities by the Canadian ambassador in Djakarta and to the Indonesian ambassador in Canada. These Canadian concerns were also raised during the session of the third committee of the current United Nations General Assembly.

On December 9, 1991, the Secretary of State for External Affairs announced:

1. Canada has suspended the approval of new development projects for Indonesia in the order of $30 million.

2. Canada had decided to give an immediate grant of $150,000 to the International Committee of the Red Cross for humanitarian assistance in East Timor.

3. Canada will take into account the results of the Indonesian commission of inquiry set up to investigate the shootings and the action of the Indonesian government in the context of the current broader aid review.

(House of Commons Debates, February 6, 1992, pp. 6533-34) (Débats de la Chambre des Communes, le 6 février 1992, pp. 6533-34)

2. Les différends internationaux et le maintien de la paix/International Disputes and Peacekeeping

La Yougoslavie — Yugoslavia

Hon. Barbara McDougall (Secretary of State for External Affairs): . . . Yugoslavia was in a state of uneasy peace for many years but harmony has eluded it . . . In the past few months the world has witnessed in horror the deterioration of this fragile situation into a state of all-out war. . . .

Nous appuyons sans réserve la déclaration de la CSCE selon laquelle les rivalités que connaît la Yougoslavie doivent être aplanies au moyen de négociations pacifiques, comme le prévoient les principes d'Helsinki de la CSCE, et la déclaration selon laquelle toutes modifications forcées des frontières à l'intérieur de la Yougoslavie sont inacceptables.

However, the CSCE was unable to act effectively in the spring because a number of countries, among them at that time the USSR, were loath to see it move on a conflict within the borders of a member state. The member state of Yugoslavia was a member and is a member of the CSCE.

It was also uncertain. So the torch was passed to the European community to try and settle this conflict.

Nous nous sommes assurés que cette initiative s'inscrivait dans le contexte des plus vastes responsabilités de la CSCE et, à l'instar de la Tchécoslovaquie, de la Pologne et de la Suède, nous avons placé des Canadiens dans les équipes d'observateurs envoyées en Yougoslavie par la Communauté européenne. . . .

Canada was the first country to request a meeting of the United Nations Security Council on the Yugoslav situation. . . . Our view is that the Yugoslav crisis poses not only a human tragedy of enormous proportions but also a direct threat to international peace and security in the area. The collapse of an effective governing authority exacerbates the potential for civil strife and further endangers the peace and security of neighbouring countries. This call for action on the part of the Security Council has been resisted by some of its members who believe that the tragedy of that country remains an internal matter and that Security Council action would constitute interference in its internal affairs. Unfortunately, despite our own pleading, despite our own lobbying, despite our own work with each and every member of the Security Council, including the permanent five and the rotating members, that view has been held by one permanent member that has a veto: China. . . .

The situation also poses a direct challenge to the principles enshrined in the charter of Paris and the aspirations of all participating countries in the Conference on Security and Co-operation in Europe for the peaceful settlement of disputes. We have called for the establishment of a peace-keeping mission and have indicated that we are ready to contribute resources to such a mission. . . .

As in other areas of conflict Canada has sought to use economic and political levers for peace in an even-handed way while at the same time provide humanitarian assistance to the victims of the violence.

When the crisis began I instructed my department to refuse systematically to issue any permits for the export of arms or other military goods to Yugoslavia. Canada has not only supported UN resolution 713 but has moved in advance of it. . . .

Our government continues to receive calls for recognition of those republics which have unilaterally declared independence. I know this is a sensitive point. We shall continue to resist such pressure. First, we believe along with members of the European community and after much soul searching and discussion that recognition of republics that wish to leave Yugoslavia should only be given within the framework of a general agreement. This was discussed with members of the European community, the Conference on Security and Co-operation in Europe and NATO, and I have discussed this personally with Cyrus Vance and with Peter Carrington.

Recognition of Croatia and Slovenia at this time would signal the end of the negotiation process and would leave force and violence to settle the issue.

It would also jeopardize the fate of other republics and minorities who have called for other kinds of arrangements for Yugoslavia. . . .

Canada has fully supported peace efforts by the European community. The EC has played a leading role in this crisis because it has more influence than anyone else on the Yugoslav republics, several of which are seeking membership or have at least expressed the hope of membership in the community. So the community, it is believed, has some leverage.

Earlier this month we joined the European community in announcing a package of sanctions designed to apply pressure to the various factions in Yugoslavia. Specifically, we suspended Canada's general preferential tariff treatment to Yugoslavia. We put Yugoslavia on the area control list, which means that any export to Yugoslavia now requires an export permit.

Nous avons annoncé que toutes les demandes concernant la Yougoslavie et faites aux termes du Programme de développement des marchés d'exportation et aux termes du Programme Renaissance de l'Europe de l'Est seraient refusées et nous avons suspendu, en ce qui concerne la Yougoslavie, les mesures de promotion commerciale et de soutien des échanges. . . .

We have moved early ourselves to provide assistance to victims. Our first step was to provide the international committee of the Red Cross with a contribution of $250,000 in support of its programs in all regions affected by the crisis.

On November 8, we went well beyond this. The Prime Minister announced from Rome that Canada would make an additional $1 million available for humanitarian relief. Funds will be provided for the Canadian Red Cross to purchase emergency relief and medical supplies for the International Committee of the Red Cross to use in Yugoslavia, and the Canadian forces will provide air transport to move those supplies into place.

(House of Commons Debates, November 18, 1991, pp. 4962-65) (Débats de la Chambre des Communes, le 18 novembre 1991, pp. 4962-65)

3. Les relations diplomatiques — Diplomatic Relations

(a) La protection diplomatique/Diplomatic Immunities

Hon. Marcel Danis (for the Secretary of State for External Affairs): . . . Madam Speaker, this bill combines and abates two existing acts dealing with privileges and immunities, the Diplomatic and Consular Privileges and Immunities Act and the Privileges and Immunities International Organizations Act. It will also assist the Canadian Government in its efforts to obtain favourable treatment for the overseas offices of Canada's provinces by permitting, for the first time, the granting of limited privileges and immunities to offices of sub-units of foreign states which, on a reciprocal basis, grant the same treatment to offices of Canadian provinces. . . .

Le statut juridique spécial des missions diplomatiques et consulaires a été intégré à la *Convention de Vienne sur les relations diplomatiques* et à la

Convention de Vienne sur les relations consulaires. Le Canada, à l'instar de la grande majorité des nations, est partie à ces conventions.

At present, the articles of these international conventions that relate directly to the legal status of foreign missions and their personnel are given the force of law in Canada by the Diplomatic and Consular Privileges and Immunities Act. The new act would continue to give force of law to these articles. . . .

International law also grants a special status to international organizations. Membership in the UN, the OECD, and other organizations of states, carries with it the obligation to grant those organizations and their officers certain privileges and immunities. Without legislation permitting the grant of such privileges and immunities, Canada could not be a member of those organizations. Nor could we act as host for such organizations as the International Civil Aviation Organization in Montreal or the Commonwealth of Learning in Vancouver.

At present, such organizations are granted privileges and immunities by Order in Council under the Privileges and Immunities (International Organizations) Act. The level of treatment which Canada can grant international organizations has not changed since the predecessor to that act, the Privileges and Immunities (United Nations) Act, was passed in 1947. But international standards of treatment for such organizations have changed significantly, and the restrictions of the existing legislation have created difficulties for Canada's relations with international organizations, including the largest international organization with headquarters in Canada.

L'Organisation de l'aviation civile internationale a son siège à Montréal. . . .

L'OACI et ses États membres font valoir depuis des années que l'Accord de siège conclu avec le Canada est périmé et mal adapté aux nouveux besoins de l'Organisation. En 1951, par exemple, lorsque Lester Pearson a signé l'Accord de siège existant avec l'OACI, on prévoyait que les représentants des États membres de l'Organisation ne seraient au Canada que pour de courtes périodes chaque année. La pratique de l'Organisation a évolué au cours des années, et il y a aujourd'hui 33 missions permanentes auprès de l'OACI qui résident en permanence à Montréal.

En réponse à ces préoccupations, le Canada a négocié un nouvel Accord de siège avec l'OACI l'an dernier, mais cet accord ne peut être encore en vigueur. Il me fait plaisir de dire que ce nouveau projet de loi permettrait la mise en application du nouvel Accord de siège avec l'OACI, ce qui éliminerait les problèmes qui ont compliqué notre relation toute spéciale avec cette Organisation . . .

A number of Canadian provinces maintain offices abroad. This is a practice that is almost as old as Confederation. As a rule there is a close and co-operative working relationship between Canada's diplomatic missions and these provincial offices. Canada makes every effort to assist them in furthering provincial interests.

When local conditions so require, provincial representatives have even been given the status of Canadian diplomats to ensure they can fulfil the provincial function effectively.

It has also been an established practice for many years that when requested to do so by the provinces, Canada requests foreign states to grant privileges and immunities to provincial officers in those states. A number of countries have agreed to grant such status to Canadian provincial offices. We have always been conscious when seeking such treatment on behalf of the provinces that we had no legal basis to reciprocate.

With this act the government will be able to grant in Canada the status it seeks for Canadian provincial offices abroad. I should note that the bill limits the privileges and immunities that can be granted to such offices to that which is granted to a consular mission.

It is important to understand that this is a limited level of privilege and immunity compared to that of a diplomat. The representative of a sub-unit, such as a consul, would have immunities from Canadian law only in respect to acts performed in the exercise of official functions. It would be up to Canadian courts to decide what is or is not an exercise of official functions.

(House of Commons Debates, October 4, 1991, pp. 3332-34) (Débats de la Chambre des Communes, le 4 octobre 1991, pp. 3332-34)

(b) La reconnaissance/Ukraine/Recognition

Hon. Lloyd Axworthy (Winnipeg South Centre): . . . We are pleased to recognize that the Prime Minister took the step this morning of recognizing the independence of Ukraine. . . . What further conditions, what further assurances is the Prime Minister requiring before full embassy status is given to Kiev and the full diplomatic power of immigration and other negotiations are transferred to that post in Kiev? . . .

Right Hon. Brian Mulroney (Prime Minister): Mr. Speaker, when we saw the results of the vote in Ukraine, the government decided to recognize Ukraine as an independent state. That we have done and we have announced.

It is not unusual, pursuant to such a decision, for a country to open negotiations with regard to the establishment of diplomatic relations. In this case which is quite unusual Canada will wish to be satisfied with respect, for example, to the question of nuclear weapons that will remain under secure control until they are disposed of.

(House of Commons Debates, December 2, 1991, pp. 5635-36) (Débats de la Chambre des Communes, le 2 décembre 1991, pp. 5635-36)

Mr. Alex Kindy (Calgary Northeast): . . . Canada acted very quickly in recognizing Ukraine as an independent state. However, since that time the government has been dragging its feet. As yet we have no ambassador, our mission is temporary, and Ukrainians wishing to visit Canada are still facing bureaucratic road-blocks. . . .

I would like to ask the parliamentary secretary to address as well the issue of Canada's position on the liabilities and assets of the former U.S.S.R.

M. Pierre H. Vincent (secrétaire parlementaire du vice-premier ministre et ministre des Finances):

Monsieur le Président, j'aimerais d'abord souligner l'importance de l'appui que le gouvernement du Canada a accordé à l'Ukraine depuis son accession à l'indépendance. Parmi les premiers à reconnaître ce nouvel État, le Canada a accru sa représentation en établissant une ambassade à Kiev, et est au premier rang des pays occidentaux à établir des programmes en vue d'aider le passage de l'Ukraine à une économie de marché. . . .(L)es dirigeants de l'Ukraine ont rencontré, à plusieurs reprises, des représentants d'autres républiques et de pays de l'Ouest pour discuter du traitement de la dette à l'égard de l'ancienne Union soviétique. Il s'agit d'un dossier d'une certaine importance pour le Canada, qui est l'un des principaux créanciers de l'URSS. Le service des prêts consentis de bonne foi à l'Union soviétique sera assuré, et ce malgré les modifications qu'ont subies les structures politiques. Cette garantie est importante non seulement pour les créanciers concernés mais aussi pour les anciennes républiques, qui ont tout intérêt à ce que soit conservée leur solvabilité afin d'avoir toujours accès au financement provenant du secteur privé et du secteur public de l'Ouest. À la suite de vastes consultations et de discussions menées l'automne dernier auprès des représentants des sept principaux pays industrialisés, la plupart des républiques de l'ancienne Union soviétique se sont accordées pour reconnaître officiellement, en signant un protocole d'entente, leurs responsabilités à l'égard des dettes contractées par l'Union soviétique. Elles se sont aussi entendues pour nommer un agent qui traitera avec les créanciers occidentaux afin d'assurer le service des dettes. L'Ukraine a récemment consenti elle aussi à signer le protocole, et probablement que ce geste constitue une étape importante en vue de la participation intégrale de l'Ukraine aux marchés provinciaux et financiers sur le plan international.

(House of Commons Debates, March 16, 1992, pp. 8319-20)
(Débats de la Chambre des Communes, le 16 mars 1992, pp. 8319-20)

4. *L'extradition — Extradition*

(a) *La Loi sur l'extradition/Extradition Act*

Ms. Campbell (Vancouver Centre): Mr. Speaker, it is my pleasure to submit to the House for second reading Bill C-31, an act to amend the Extradition Act respecting appeals. . . .

Monsieur le Président, en vertu du droit en vigueur, un état avec lequel nous avons conclu un traité d'extradition peut demander au Canada de lui livrer un inculpé ou un délinquent ressortissant de cet état qui se trouve actuellement au Canada.

Cette personne est alors arrêtée et il y a instruction judiciaire sur les fondements de l'inculpation ou sur les raisons qui portent à penser qu'elle s'est enfuie après avoir été condamnée pour avoir commis une infraction sur le territoire de l'état requérant.

Lors de cette instruction, le juge, membre d'une Cour supérieure ou de comté provincial ou territorial, examine les preuves avancées et décide de l'envoi ou non en détention de la personne réclamée, en attendant qu'elle soit remise à l'État requérant.

Si l'on ordonne à l'inculpé ou au délinquent d'attendre son extradition, celui-ci peut requérir un bref d'*habeas corpus* contestant la décision du juge d'extradition. À ce stade, il peut faire valoir tous les droits et libertés que lui garantit la Charte, et en saisir les tribunaux. Il peut également être formé appel de la décision du juge qui a statué sur l'*habeas corpus* à la Cour d'appel provinciale ou territoriale et il peut y avoir pourvoi de l'arrêt de cette dernière en Cour suprême du Canada, si elle autorise le pourvoi.

Si le juge d'extradition n'ordonne pas la remise de la personne à l'État requérant, ce dernier peut se pourvoir directement en Cour suprême du Canada, si elle autorise le pourvoi.

Once this part of the procedure is completed, the minister considers any submissions made by the person sought with respect to humanitarian grounds, questions of fairness and such issues as whether the person would be facing the death penalty in the foreign state.

When the minister considers that the person should be extradited, a surrender warrant will be issued by the minister. The minister's decision with respect to surrender can also be judicially reviewed. That decision can in turn be appealed to the Federal Court of Appeal and with leave of the court to the Supreme Court of Canada. . . .

The bill allows the fugitive or the requesting state to appeal the decision of the extradition judge directly to the provincial or territorial court of appeal on grounds similar to those available to parties to criminal proceedings under the Criminal Code of Canada. The court of appeal is obliged under the bill to schedule the appeal hearing at an early date. In most cases, the minister will be obliged to make a decision whether to surrender the fugitive within 90 days of the committal of the fugitive at the extradition hearing.

Where there is an appeal by the fugitive from the committal the court of appeal can defer the appeal proceedings until the minister has made a decision on surrender. In cases where the legal issues are particularly complex, the minister can postpone the decision on surrender until the court of appeal has made its decision. However, in most cases the minister will make the decision on surrender before any appeal concerning the extradition judge's committal order is heard by the court of appeal.

Since the bill provides that judicial reviews from the minister are to go to the provincial and territorial courts of appeal, appeals from the extradition judge and judicial reviews from the minister's decision will usually be heard together. This will ensure that appeals and reviews will be conducted as expeditiously as possible since all issues will be dealt with together before a single court. Further, it will ensure that in extradition matters there will usually be only one subsequent avenue of recourse, the Supreme Court of Canada.

(House of Commons Debates, November 7, 1991, pp. 4776-78) (Débats de la Chambre des Communes, le 7 novembre 1991, pp. 4776-78)

(b) Alvarez Machain

Mr. Svend J. Robinson (Burnaby–Kingsway): Mr. Speaker, my question is for the Secretary of State for External Affairs. It concerns yesterday's decision of the U.S. Supreme Court that makes a mockery of extradition treaties which have been signed by the United States. . . .

Will she immediately seek an exclusionary amendment to the Canada-U.S. extradition treaty to ensure the United States agents can never get away with this in Canada?

Hon. Barbara McDougall (Secretary of State for External Affairs): Mr. Speaker, as the hon. member knows, Canada was an intervener in the case that led to this decision as it came before the court.

We continue to believe that the appropriate way for U.S. authorities to obtain custody of a criminal suspect is through a request to authorities of other countries, to Canadian authorities for example, under the extradition treaty that exists between our two countries.

Any attempt to abduct someone from Canadian territory we would continue to regard, as we have in the past, as a criminal act.

(House of Commons Debates, June 16, 1992, p. 12152) (Débats de la Chambre des Communes, le 16 juin 1992, p. 12152)

5. Le droit de la mer/Law of the Sea

Les pêches/Fisheries

Hon. Barbara McDougall (Secretary of State for External Affairs): . . . The severe depletion of the northern cod biomass is only the most recent example, although it is certainly the most critical, of the precarious balance of nature, in this case in the northwest Atlantic, and the serious consequences when international management measures are disregarded. . . .

Nous réalisons notre stratégie dans le cadre d'un schéma international. Les dispositions de la Convention sur le droit de la mer constituent le droit coutumier pour ce qui est de la conservation des ressources marines vivantes. L'Organisation des pêches de l'Atlantique Nord-Ouest, qui découle du droit de la mer, est l'organisme régional responsable de la gestion des pêches. L'Organisation des Nations Unies, qui est à l'origine de l'institution de la Conférence sur l'environnement et le développement, est une tribune multilatérale clé pour le règlement pacifique de problèmes internationaux. . . .

Most of the fishing by foreign fleets and all of the overfishing is taking place outside 200 miles in international waters where Canada has no jurisdiction except in relation to Canadian vessels.

Under the Law of the Sea, states have the duty to take such measures for their respective nationals as may be necessary for the conservation of the living resources of the high seas. They also have the duty to co-operate with other states or with regional organizations. But flag states alone have the legal authority to enforce against their own vessels.

The problem of overfishing is centred on the activities of vessels from the European Community, principally Spain and Portugal, and to a lesser extent from a few countries that are not members of NAFO, notably Panama and Korea.

Je tiens à souligner que la plupart des pays qui pêchent dans la zone de l'OPANO, notamment le Japon, la Russie, les Iles Féroé, la Norvège, le Danemark, Cuba, appuient la conservation des pêcheries, respectent les contingents qui leur sont imposés par l'OPANO et collaborent avec le Canada. . . .

Since 1986 the EC and those other countries that do not co-operate with Canada by respecting the conservation decisions of NAFO have not been eligible for benefits in the Canadian zone. Their fishing vessels are barred from Canadian ports except in emergencies. They are not accorded allocations of surplus fish from under-utilized species in the Canadian zone. They are not eligible to take part in commercial ventures involving any fishing by their vessels in Canadian waters.

These restrictions however have failed to induce the co-operation that we sought and vigorously pursued. The cumulative impact had begun to take its severe toll and in 1989 this government initiated a comprehensive campaign bilaterally and multilaterally aimed at ending foreign overfishing in the northwest Atlantic outside the 200-mile limit. . . .

Un grand objectif du Canada dans cette initiative d'ordre juridique est la reconnaissance internationale de l'intérêt spécial d'États côtiers comme le Canada dans la conservation et la gestion des stocks de poisson qui sont récoltés à intérieur et à l'extérieur des zones de pêche nationales.

Le Canada soumettra ses propositions sur la conservation des stocks de poisson de haute-mer à la conférence des Nations Unies sur l'environnement et le développement — le Sommet de la Terre, de Rio de Janeiro — pour amener la Communauté internationale à accepter des améliorations à la conservation des pêcheries de haute-mer. . . .

(House of Commons Debates, March 12, 1992, pp. 8147-49)
(Débats de la Chambre des Communes, le 12 mars 1992, pp. 8147-49)

Hon. Roger C. Simmons (Burin–St. George's): . . . Last week's decision at the earth summit to hold a conference on high seas fishing may help to address the problem in the long term. The real question of course is whether there is a long term and whether there will be any fish left to save a year or two from now. . . .

Hon. John C. Crosbie (Minister of Fisheries and Oceans and Minister for the Atlantic Canada Opportunities Agency):

Mr. Speaker, it was very significant that at the summit meeting in Rio a week ago, for the first time as far as I know, the organized world community of 180 countries recognized that overfishing and the failure to apply principles of sustainable development in the fishery was a major world environmental problem.

The 180 nations there adopted a resolution which was an initiative of Canada together with 39 other countries. This will be a great help to us in the longer term with reference to future fish stocks. . . .

Hon. Roger C. Simmons (Burin–St. George's): . . . The straddling stocks are as vulnerable as ever. . . . I want to know how far the minister is prepared to go to protect that resource? . . . Why is he ruling out taking over custodial management despite the fact that last week at Rio he was strongly urged by an expert in international law to do exactly that?

Hon. John C. Crosby (Minister of Fisheries and Oceans and Minister for the Atlantic Canada Opportunities Agency): . . .

How far am I prepared to go? I am prepared to go as far as is necessary to overcome the issue of overfishing in the northwest Atlantic as well as in the rest of the world.

What is the best way of achieving that? The best way is by getting 180 nations on your side, not having 180 nations oppose you because you want to adopt some premature cowboy tactics and unilaterally extend management controls in an area.

(House of Commons Debates, June 15, 1992, pp. 12020-21)
(Débats de la Chambre des Communes, le 15 juin 1992, pp. 12020-21)

6. *Le droit de l'environnement/Environmental Law*

(a) *CNUED — UNCED*

L'hon. Jean J. Charest (ministre de l'Environnement) propose: "Que la Chambre prenne note de la position canadienne à la Conférence des Nations Unies sur l'environnement et le développement." . . .

L'objectif premier du Sommet Planète Terre et des négociations qui y mènent est de donner le coup d'envoi à une initiative de coopération planétaire au service de ce concept de développement durable. À l'heure actuelle, les nations du monde dérivent, il faut le dire, vers des eaux dangereuses. La Conférence des Nations Unies sur l'environnement, il faut bien le dire aussi — et je vais m'arrêter quelques secondes pour le préciser — parle d'environnement et de développement. . . .

The government is committed to sustainable development and we are acting on that commitment. Canada is one of only three countries in the world to have adopted a comprehensive long-term approach to sustainable development, our green plan.

Over a period of six years the Canadian government, along with the Canadian people and all members of this House, will dedicate its energies to this effort of sustainable development. Canada's green plan is very much at the centre of implementing and articulating this concept of sustainable development in Canada.

The green plan itself is based on that principle and adopts that vision, and also commands and obliges the government to change its ways of making decisions. As well, through a commitment of $3 billion, it enables us to put forward an action plan over this six-year period to put forward a very important number of initiatives. . . .

There are many links between the green plan and the global plan that will be considered in Rio. For example, agenda 21 is a detailed proposal for global action developed in pre-summit negotiations. In chapter after chapter one finds proposals for action that extend and complement action under the green plan.

For example, one chapter of agenda 21 deals with toxic chemicals. It calls for measures to expand our knowledge of the risks associated with the use of these substances and it proposes measures to strengthen information exchange networks on a global scale.

These proposals mirror closely what is happening here in Canada. Last February we announced a $14 million allocation under the green plan for the creation of a national toxicology network. It will link four universities in co-operative research on toxic chemical risks.

We are also making a large investment under the green plan, $85 million, in scientific studies to reduce uncertainties about climate change. That will complement research in agenda 21 with exactly that end in mind, because there is still a lot of uncertainty.

The nations of the world hope to agree on a convention on biodiversity. . . . Biodiversity is about saving plant and animal species, which ties in with our green plan goal of completing a national parks system in this country by the year 2000 to protect examples of all of Canada's natural regions. . . . (T)he goals we pursue in Canada are linked to the goals that we are pursuing in Rio. The headway we make in this country will contribute to the environmental well-being of other countries. Their efforts will contribute to our own. The green plan is also very much part of the global plan.

(House of Commons Debates, May 7, 1992, pp. 10331-34)
(Débats de la Chambre des Communes, le 7 mai 1992, pp. 10331-34)

(b) La biodiversité — Biodiversity

M. Paul Martin (LaSalle–Émard): . . . Il y a deux semaines, lors d'une conférence internationale sur l'environnement, à Nairobi, les pays du monde devaient approuver la Convention sur la biodiversité. À la fin de la conférence, les États–Unis avaient fait vider le texte de sa substance. En dépit de cela, il y a à peine quelques jours, les Américains ont annoncé qu'ils ne signeraient même pas le texte qu'ils avaient pourtant déjà dilué. . . .(L)e Canada va-t-il initier immédiatement une campagne pour retourner au texte original de la convention afin de mieux protéger les espèces animales et végétales dans le monde?

Le très hon. Brian Mulroney (premier ministre): Monsieur le Président, j'ai indiqué plus tôt dans la journée que nous avions l'intention de signer la convention internationale sur la biodiversité et que nous allions également travailler d'arrache-pied avec les pays alliés afin de provoquer des améliorations progressives à ce texte.

(House of Commons Debates, June 1, 1992, p. 11155)

(Débats de la Chambre des Communes, le 1 juin 1992, p. 11155)

(c) Les changements climatiques — Climate Change

Mr. Jim Fulton (Skeena): Mr. Speaker, my question is for the Prime Minister who signed on behalf of Canada the convention for climate change at the earth summit. It regrettably contains no targets or timetables for reductions.

Since Canada publicly committed to stabilize all greenhouse gas emissions at 1990 levels by the year 2000 in Geneva almost two years ago, would the Prime Minister tell this House what Canada's emissions were in 1990 so that Canadians can know what that means by the year 2000?

Hon. Jean J. Charest (Minister of the Environment): Mr. Speaker, I think the hon. member knows that work has been undertaken to make a determination on the baseline level of information . . . I should also point out to the hon. member that the Prime Minister indicated not only would Canada sign the treaty but we would also ratify it within the year. We would also encourage other countries to enter into a prompt start process by which we could go out there and apply the dispositions of the treaty.

(House of Commons Debates, June 16, 1992, p. 12156)

(Débats de la Chambre des Communes, le 16 juin 1992, p. 12156)

7. Le commerce/Trade

(a) Le GATT — Article XI

Hon. Bill McKnight (Minister of Agriculture): . . . As we know, the Director General of GATT, Mr. Dunkel, on December 20 issued a text. He had worked with the countries of the world, some 108 members of GATT, to attempt to come to a conclusion at the negotiating table. He was unable to do that. He then took the debate and the proposals of governments, bound them in a text, and said: "This is as close as I can come to a conclusion. I put it out for nations of the world to look at and to then respond to it."

The GATT members assembled in Geneva on January 13 to make that response to the Dunkel text and to give their reaction. It is interesting to note that not one country of the 108 rejected the text as a basis to continue the negotiations to a successful conclusion. No one has rejected it. All GATT members have remained at the table to put their position. Canada has remained at the table to continue to put our position.

The next important milestone or step will be March 1 . . . [when] countries will be expected to table their revised offers on market access for agricultural products. They are still looking at the impact naturally at that time when all countries will put their market access proposals. Our trading partners, as will Canada, will have to put proposals forward. In general we are optimistic about some parts of the Dunkel text. On other points, particularly in regard to article XI and the strengthening and clarifying, we have grave reservations. . . .

Having expressed what we object to in the Dunkel text, there are areas of considerable promise for establishing a freer, more stable and less distorted agriculture trading community. The draft agreement would indeed provide an improved and more secure access into foreign markets. As well the U.S. section 22 import waiver which has been a temporary waiver in place for almost 40 years, as I understand it, and the EC variable import levies would be removed. They would be as the text is written today converted to tariffs.

There is no doubt that the Dunkel proposals would allow for a better and more secure access for Canadian exports to foreign markets but the multilateral trade rules under which we in Canada benefit would be strengthened and would apply equally to all countries. That is an important point. . . .

Over the past years, there has been an erosion of the ability of article XI as it is interpreted today by GATT to protect our supply managed industries. I can only draw to the attention of the House that processed products, such as ice cream and yogurt, had a GATT ruling against our import controls. It is still an outstanding ruling.

(House of Commons Debates, February 12, 1992, pp. 6868-70)
(Débats de la Chambre des Communes, le 12 février 1992, pp. 6868−70)

Mr. Vic Althouse (Mackenzie): . . . Since the Dunkel report does not mention anything about article XI(2)(c)(i), how is supply management protected with the government's position?

Hon. Bill McKnight (Minister of Agriculture): . . .We had informed the supply management farm leaders, we had informed the SAGIT which advises the government, what Canada would be tabling when we tabled our access along with other countries, that we would be following the Dunkel text with the exception of those industries which were supply managed.

We informed them that in fact we would be tabling no tariff equivalents for supply management but that we would in turn be tabling Canada's position which is to have supply management recognized, article XI recognized and operational or clarified and strengthened. We tabled that as Canada's position.

We have followed the Dunkel text with that exception. . . .

(House of Commons Debates, March 19, 1992, p. 8514)
(Débats de la Chambre des Communes, le 19 mars 1992, p. 8514)

(b) Le bois d'oeuvre (ALE) — Softwood Lumber (FTA)

M. André Plourde (secrétaire parlementaire du ministre du Commerce extérieur):

Madame la Présidente, le mémorandum d'entente entre le Canada et les États–Unis sur le bois d'oeuvre résineux a été négocié pour éviter l'imposition d'un droit compensateur sur les exportations de bois d'oeuvre canadien aux États–Unis. Le mémorandum visait, première-ment, à régler un différend bilatéral amer et hautement politisé sur nos exportations de bois d'oeuvre résineux aux États–Unis et, deuxième-ment, à donner le ton aux provinces d'appliquer les changements pro-posés à leurs politiques forestières qui comprenaient des relèvements des droits de coupe et des autres frais imposés à l'industrie canadienne.

Madame la Présidente, la situation a considérablement changé depuis la signature du mémorandum. Une bonne partie de nos exportations de bois d'oeuvre aux États–Unis n'est plus assujettie au droit à l'exportation. Le droit a été remplacé entièrement en Colombie-Britannique et par-tiellement au Québec et les provinces de l'Atlantique en sont exemptées. Dans l'ensemble, les changements d'application des dispositions du mémorandum ont permis de réduire d'environ 40 millions de dollars les recettes tirées du droit à l'exportation. En 1987, la première année d'application du mémorandum, le droit perçu totalisait 400 millions.

Madame la Présidente, les conditions du marché ont aussi évolué depuis la signature du mémorandum en 1986. Notre part du marché américain a été réduite, passant d'un sommet de 32,8 p. 100 en 1985 à 26,8 p. 100 en 1990, soit son niveau le plus bas en treize ans. L'accroisse-ment de la valeur du dollar canadien et l'augmentation du coût des billes récoltés par l'industrie canadienne ont sensiblement amélioré la com-pétitivité des producteurs américains par rapport à leurs concurrents canadiens.

Le mémorandum a donc servi son objectif et le Canada a, le 4 octobre dernier, exercé son droit de dénoncer l'entente. Le commerce Canada–États–Unis du bois d'oeuvre peut maintenant reprendre dans des condi-tions normales sous réserve des règles de l'Accord de libre-échange et de l'Accord général sur les tarifs douaniers et le commerce.

Madame la Présidente, sous l'effet de pressions, l'administration amér-icaine a décidé d'engager une nouvelle procédure compensatrice contre nos exportations de bois d'oeuvre résineux et a aussi imposé une mesure provisoire à la frontière, obligeant les importateurs à déposer des cau-tions sur les expéditions de bois d'oeuvre reçues de producteurs cana-diens assujettis au droit à l'exportation.

Le gouvernement s'est vivement objecté à cette action américaine et il tente d'obtenir l'établissement immédiat d'un groupe spécial du GATT chargé de décider, premièrement, si le prix qu'un gouvernement exige pour le droit de couper du bois constitue une subvention pouvant don-ner matière à compensation, et si l'exigence de cautionnement imposé en vertu de la section 301 est conforme aux obligations des États–Unis aux termes de l'Accord général du GATT.

(House of Commons Debates, October 21, 1991, p. 3760)
(Débats de la Chambre des Communes, le 21 octobre 1991, p. 3760)

Mr. Brian L. Gardiner (Prince George–Bulkley Valley): . . . Last Friday's decision by the Bush administration to impose a tariff on Canadian softwood exports is in reality a grab for Canada's raw logs. . . .
Mr. Speaker, our staff has just spoken with commerce department officials who say that the decision as to whether the dispute settlement mechanism applies to this dispute is still under review. . . .
Hon. Frank Oberle (Minister of Forestry): . . . I can tell my hon. friend that the MOU is a part of the free trade agreement and we have launched an appeal to the bi-national panel which will eventually resolve this problem for us under the free trade deal.

(House of Commons Debates, May 19, 1992, p. 10884)
(Débats de la Chambre des Communes, le 19 mai 1992, p. 10884)

(c) Les règles d'origine — Rules of Origin

Mr. Jim Peterson (Willowdale): . . . Has the United States consented to binding arbitration of the Honda dispute? Yes or No?
Hon. Michael Wilson (Minister of Industry, Science and Technology and Minister for International Trade): . . . The matter is subject to discussion between the United States and Canada. It might become a matter of chapter 18 consultation between the federal government and the American government, as is the case with the rules of origin question as it relates to non-mortgage interest with the CAMI operation. If that is the case, then that would be subject to negotiation but it would not be binding.

(House of Commons Debates, March 23, 1992, p. 8625)
(Débats de la Chambre des Communes, le 23 mars 1992, p. 8625)

(d) ALENA — NAFTA

L'hon. Jean Chrétien (chef de l'opposition): . . . Comme tout le monde le sait, la Communauté européenne a établi des normes minimales dans le domaine des politiques sociales, agricoles et économiques, de même qu'au niveau des politiques environnementales.
Hier, le ministre a déclaré en cette Chambre que les questions de conditions de travail et d'environnement ne sont pas négociées à la même table que l'Accord de libre-échange entre le Canada, les États–Unis et le Mexique. Je voudrais donc demander au ministre s'il peut donner l'assurance à cette Chambre que si l'on signe l'accord de libre-échange entre le Canada, les États–Unis et le Mexique, on ne le fera que

lorsque les normes minimales concernant les conditions de travail et aussi les conditions de préservation de l'environnement comporteront les mêmes critères pour les Canadiens que pour les Mexicains.

Hon. Michael Wilson (Minister of Industry, Science and Technology and Minister for International Trade): Mr. Speaker, I think my hon. friend has raised an interesting point here because he is comparing the European Community and what they are seeking to achieve and the free trade area between Canada, the United States and possibly Mexico.

In Europe, they are seeking a common market which results in a considerably greater degree of political integration. They want to have the same monetary policy, the same currency as well as these other standards which my friend has referred to.

We are not seeking that with the United States nor with Mexico because we do not want to see the political integration that comes with the common market in the arrangements that we would have with the United States or Mexico.

If my hon. friend wants to pursue that sort of line, I ask him if he would want to have the same health care system in Canada as they have in the United States. Does he want to have the same environmental standards in Canada as they have in the United States, the same labour standards? I do not think he would want to do that. It is for that reason that we want to keep those separate and just limit our discussions to trade. . . .

The Mexicans have invested a considerably greater amount of resources in the enforcement of their environmental standards. They have shut down a major refinery in Mexico City because of the pollution there.

Their standards are comparable to the standards that we have in Canada and that they have in the United States. . . . Check the facts, and hon. members opposite will find that the standards are the same but the enforcement is not.

It is for that reason that we are seeking better enforcement of the rules through the parallel discussions that we are having and the agreements that we are entering into.

I should just make one other point in that for new investment, if a new plant wants to go into Mexico, it is governed by the standards. It is the enforcement of the standards on existing plants which, if they did it too rigorously, would cause great job losses there.

Hon. Jean Chrétien (Leader of the Opposition): Mr. Speaker, that is a terrible admission on the part of the minister to tell us that the standards are accepted but not respected. What we want to know from this government is what it will do if the standards are not respected by Mexicans at the expense of Canadian workers.

Hon. Jean J. Charest (Minister of the Environment): Mr. Speaker, the question of the Leader of the Opposition, interestingly enough, is based on a few assumptions.

Among them is the assumption that Mexicans for some odd reason care less about their environment than Canadians do. That is false. They care as much about their environment as we do. . . .

I think if he were to look at the facts he v ould find that no later than February 25 last, the governments of the Jnited States and Mexico announced a joint border plan to deal with environmental issues, a $450 million initiative.

The Government of Mexico itself has committed its government to increasing the amount of funds very substantially. The Government of Canada will contribute to this effort through a joint agreement signed by Prime Minister Mulroney and President Salinas in March 1990 under which we are going to assist the Mexican government in the enforcement of its environmental laws.

(House of Commons Debates, March 25, 1992, pp. 8763-64)

(Débats de la Chambre des Communes, le 25 mars 1992, pp. 8763-64)

Treaty Action Taken by Canada in 1991 / Mesures prises par le Canada en matière de traités en 1991

prepared by/préparé par
CÉLINE BLAIS*

* Treaty Registrar, Legal Advisory Division, Department of External Affairs/Greffier des Traités, Direction des consultations juridiques, Ministère des Affaires extérieures.

I: BILATERAL

Argentina

Agreement between the Government of Canada and the Government of the Republic of Argentina for the Promotion and Protection of Investments. Toronto, November 5, 1991.

Exchange of Letters between the Government of Canada and the Government of Argentina constituting an Agreement on Reciprocal Employment. Buenos Aires, February 20, 1991. *Entered into force* February 20, 1991. CTS 1991/39.

Bahrain

Memorandum of Agreement between the Government of Canada and the Government of the State of Bahrain concerning the Deployment of Canadian Forces. Manama, January 16, 1991. *Entered into force* January 16, 1991. CTS 1991/9.

Chile

Exchange of Notes constituting an Agreement between the Government of Canada and the Government of Chile concerning the Employment of Dependents of Employees of each Government Assigned to Official Missions in the Other Country. Santiago, January 21, 1991.

Cyprus

Agreement on Social Security between the Government of Canada and the Government of the Republic of Cyprus. Ottawa, January 24, 1990. *Entered into force* May 1, 1991. CTS 1991/25.

Denmark

Exchange of Notes between the Government of Canada and the Government of the Kingdom of Denmark constituting an Agreement to amend Annex B of the 1983 Agreement relating to the Marine Environment. Ottawa, October 7, 1991. *Entered into force* October 7, 1991. CTS 1991/35.

European Atomic Energy Community (Euratom)
Exchange of Letters between the Government of Canada and the European Atomic Energy Community (Euratom) amending the Agreement for Co-operation in the Peaceful Uses of Atomic Energy signed October 6, 1959. Brussels, July 15, 1991. *Entered into force* July 15, 1991. CTS 1991/23.

Finland
Exchange of Notes between the Government of Canada and the Government of Finland regarding the Retransfer of Specified Nuclear Material and constituting an Agreement on the Application of the March 5, 1976 Canada-Finland Agreement concerning the Uses of Nuclear Material, as amended. Helsinki, November 22, 1991. *Entered into force* November 22, 1991. CTS 1991/52.

France
Agreement between the Government of Canada and the Government of the Republic of France regarding Co-operation and Exchanges in the Museums Field. Paris, November 26, 1990. *Entered into force* April 1, 1991. CTS 1991/4.
Treaty between the Government of Canada and the Government of the Republic of France on Mutual Assistance in Penal Matters. Paris, December 15, 1989. *Entered into force* May 1, 1991. CTS 1991/34.

Hong Kong
Agreement between the Government of Canada and the Government of Hong Kong concerning the Investigation of Drug Trafficking and Confiscation of the Proceeds of Drug Trafficking. Hong Kong, November 14, 1990. *Entered into force* February 17, 1991. CTS 1991/18.

Hungary
Agreement between the Government of Canada and the Government of the

Republic of Hungary for the Promotion and Reciprocal Protection of Investments. Ottawa, October 3, 1991.

India
Exchange of Notes between the Government of Canada and the Government of India constituting an Agreement amending the Agreement on Air Services signed at New Delhi on July 20, 1982, as amended (with attachment). New Delhi, May 30, 1991. *Entered into force* May 30, 1991. CTS 1991/41.

Indonesia
General Agreement on Development Cooperation between the Government of Canada and the Government of the Republic of Indonesia (with Annexes). Ottawa, May 21, 1991.

Italy
Agreement on Airworthiness between the Government of Canada and the Government of Italy. Ottawa, February 18, 1991. *Entered into force* February 18, 1991. CTS 1991/7.

Luxembourg
Convention between the Government of Canada and the Government of the Grand Duchy of Luxembourg for the Avoidance of Double Taxation and the Prevention of Fiscal Evasion with Respect to Taxes on Income and on Capital. Luxembourg, January 17, 1989. *Entered into force* July 8, 1991. CTS 1991/21.

Malta
Agreement on Social Security between the Government of Canada and the Government of the Republic of Malta. Toronto, April 4, 1991. *Entered into force* March 1, 1992. CTS 1992/5.

Mexico
Agreement on Film and Television Co-Production between the Government of Canada and the Government of the United Mexican States (with Annex). Ottawa, April 8, 1991. *Entered into force* November 26, 1991. CTS 1991/42.
Agreement between the Government of Canada and the Government of the United States of Mexico concerning

Co-operation in the Fields of Museums and Archaeology. Mexico, November 25, 1991.

Convention between the Government of Canada and the Government of the United Mexican States for the Avoidance of Double Taxation and the Prevention of Fiscal Evasion with Respect to Taxes on Income. Ottawa, April 8, 1991. *Entered into force* May 11, 1992. CTS 1992/15.

Namibia

Agreement between the Government of Canada and the Government of the Republic of Namibia for the Training in Canada of Personnel of the Armed Forces of the Republic of Namibia. Windhoek, September 19, 1991. *Entered into force* September 19, 1991. CTS 1991/48.

Netherlands, The

Exchange of Letters between the Government of Canada and the Government of the Kingdom of The Netherlands constituting an Agreement relating to the Employment of Dependents. The Hague, May 1, 1991. *Entered into force* December 18, 1991. CTS 1991/43.

Treaty between the United Kingdom and The Netherlands for the Mutual Surrender of Fugitive Criminals. London, September 26, 1898. *Entered into force* March 14, 1899. BTS 1899/1. NOTE: Terminated upon the entry into force of the October 13, 1989 Extradition Treaty.

Treaty between the Government of Canada and the Government of the Kingdom of The Netherlands on Extradition. Montreal, October 13, 1989. *Entered into force* December 1, 1991. CTS 1991/32.

Treaty between Canada and the Kingdom of The Netherlands on Mutual Assistance in Criminal Matters. The Hague, May 1, 1991. *Entered into force* May 1, 1992. CTS 1992/9.

Saudi Arabia

Air Transport Agreement between the Government of Canada and the Government of the Kingdom of Saudi Arabia (with Annex). Riyadh, November 14, 1990. *Entered into force* June 9, 1991. CTS 1991/20. NOTE: Not yet published.

Sweden

Exchange of Letters between the Government of Canada and the Government of Sweden regarding the Retransfer of Specified Nuclear Material and constituting an Agreement on the Application of the September 27, 1977 Canada-Sweden Agreement, as amended. Stockholm, November 27, 1991. *Entered into force* November 27, 1991. CTS 1991/46.

Thailand

Exchange of Notes between the Government of Canada and the Government of the Kingdom of Thailand constituting an Agreement amending the Agreement on Air Services signed May 24, 1989. Bangkok, December 25, 1991. *Entered into force* December 25, 1991. CTS 1991/40.

United Kingdom

Protocol between the Government of Canada and the Government of the United Kingdom of Great Britain and Northern Ireland amending the Films Co-Production Agreement done at London on September 12, 1975, as amended on July 9, 1985. Ottawa, July 5, 1991.

Exchange of Notes between the Government of Canada and the Government of the United Kingdom of Great Britain and Northern Ireland constituting an Agreement concerning a Training Scheme for Armed Forces of the United Kingdom of Great Britain and Northern Ireland in Canada. Ottawa, August 20, 1971. *Entered into force* August 20, 1971. NOTE: Replaced by the September 4, 1991 Agreement. (CTS 1991/33). TERMINATED: September 4, 1991.

Exchange of Notes between the Government of Canada and the Government of the United Kingdom of Great Britain and Northern Ireland constituting an Agreement amending and extending the 1971 Agreement concerning a Training Scheme for Armed Forces of the United Kingdom in Canada. Ottawa, November 26, 1979. *Entered into force* November 26, 1979. CTS 1979/23. NOTE: Replaced by September 4, 1991 Agreement (CTS 1991/33). TERMINATED: September 4, 1991.

Exchange of Notes between the Government of Canada and the Government of the United Kingdom of Great Britain and Northern Ireland constituting an Agreement on British Armed Forces Training in Canada. London, September 4, 1991. *Entered into force* September 4, 1991. CTS 1991/33. NOTE: Will remain in force until August 19, 2006.

United States of America (USA)
Exchange of Notes between the Government of Canada and the Government of the United States of America to further amend the Air Transport Agreement signed January 17, 1966 as amended by an Exchange of Notes signed May 8, 1974. Ottawa, May 28, 1991. *Entered into force* May 28, 1991. CTS 1991/14.

Exchange of Notes between the Government of Canada and the Government of the United States of America constituting an Agreement amending the Agreement concerning the Application of Tolls on the St. Lawrence Seaway (with Memorandum of Agreement). Washington, January 17, 1991. *Entered into force* January 25, 1991. CTS 1991/6.

Exchange of Notes between the Government of Canada and the Government of the United States of America constituting an Agreement amending the Agreement concerning the Application of Tolls on the St. Lawrence Seaway (with Memorandum of Agreement). Washington, May 1, 1991. *Entered into force* May 1, 1991. CTS 1991/11. NOTE: Canadian Note April 26, 1991, American Note May 1, 1991.

Exchange of Notes between the Government of Canada and the Government of the United States of America

constituting an Agreement further amending the Agreement concerning the Application of Tolls on the St. Lawrence Seaway. Washington, December 20, 1991. *Entered into force* December 20, 1991. CTS 1991/38.

Exchange of Letters constituting an Agreement between the Government of Canada and the Government of the United States of America amending Schedule I of Annex 705.4 of the Free Trade Agreement. Washington, May 1, 1991. *Entered into force* May 1, 1991. CTS 1991/13.

Exchange of Letters between the Government of Canada and the Government of the United States of America constituting an Agreement to amend the Tariff Schedules contained in Annex 401.5 and to delete Rules 2, 3 and 4 of Section III of Annex 301.2 of Chapter 3 of the Free Trade Agreement. Washington, August 16, 1991. *Entered into force* August 16, 1991. CTS 1991/46.

Exchange of Notes between the Government of Canada and the Government of the United States of America constituting an Agreement to Extend the North American Aerospace Defence Command (NORAD) Agreement for a further five-year period. Washington, April 30, 1991. *Entered into force* April 30, 1991. CTS 1991/19. NOTE: In force April 30, 1991 with effect from May 12, 1991.

Agreement between the Government of Canada and the Government of the United States of America on Air Quality (with Annexes). Ottawa, March 13, 1991. *Entered into force* March 13, 1991. CTS 1991/3.

Protocol amending the Treaty on Extradition between the Government of Canada and the Government of the United States of America signed at Washington on December 3, 1971, as amended by an Exchange of Notes on June 28 and July 9, 1974. Ottawa, January 11, 1988. *Entered into force* November 26, 1991. CTS 1991/37.

Agreement between the Government of Canada and the Government of the

United States of America on Fisheries Enforcement. Ottawa, September 26, 1990. *Entered into force* December 16, 1991. CTS 1991/36.

Exchange of Notes between the Government of Canada and the Government of the United States of America constituting an Agreement to Amend the Memorandum of Arrangements Concerning the Operation of Pilotage Services on the Great Lakes. Washington, February 12, 1991. *Entered into force* February 12, 1991. CTS 1991/15.

Exchange of Notes between the Government of Canada and the Government of the United States of America constituting an Agreement amending the Agreement of June 3, 1976 relating to the Construction, Operation and Maintenance of a Loran-C Station in the Vicinity of Williams Lake, B.C. (with Annex). Washington, May 8, 1991. *Entered into force* May 8, 1991. CTS 1991/12.

Exchange of Notes (January 8 and October 15, 1947) between Canada and the United States of America constituting an Agreement on the Allocation of Channels for Radio Broadcasting. Washington, October 15, 1947. *Entered into force* October 15, 1947. CTS 1947/30. NOTE: Superseded by the February 25, 1991 Agreement. TERMINATED: February 25, 1991.

Exchange of Notes between the Government of Canada and the Government of the United States of America concerning the Use of the 88 to 108 Megahertz Band for Frequency Modulation Broadcasting (FM). Washington, February 25, 1991. *Entered into force* February 25, 1991. CTS 1991/10.

Exchange of Notes between the Government of Canada and the Government of the United States of America

constituting an Agreement for Cooperation in the Radarsat Programme (with Attachment). Washington, November 12, 1991. *Entered into force* November 12, 1991. CTS 1991/50.

Uruguay
Agreement between the Government of Canada and the Government of the Oriental Republic of Uruguay for the Promotion and Protection of Investments. Ottawa, May 16, 1991.

USSR
Protocol to further extend the Trade Agreement between the Government of Canada and the Government of the Union of Soviet Socialist Republics signed at Ottawa on February 29, 1956. Moscow, April 17, 1991. *Entered into force* April 17, 1991. CTS 1991/8.

Agreement between the Government of Canada and the Government of the Union of Soviet Socialist Republics on the Prevention of Dangerous Military Activities (with Annexes). Ottawa, May 10, 1991. *Entered into force* November 10, 1991. CTS 1991/26.

Agreement between the Government of Canada and the Government of the Union of Soviet Socialist Republics for the Promotion and Reciprocal Protection of Investments. Moscow, November 20, 1989. *Entered into force* June 27, 1991. CTS 1991/31.

Venezuela
Exchange of Notes between the Government of Canada and the Government of the Republic of Venezuela concerning Visa Requirements for Non-Immigrant Travellers of the Two Countries. Ottawa, October 8, 1959. *Entered into force* November 1, 1959. CTS 1959/20. TERMINATED: March 11, 1991.

II: MULTILATERAL

Agriculture
International Convention for the Protection of New Varieties of Plants of December 2, 1961 as revised at Geneva

on November 10, 1972, and on October 23, 1978. Done at Paris, December 2, 1961. Signed by Canada October 31, 1979. Ratified by Canada February 4,

1991. *Entered into force* for Canada March 4, 1991. CTS 1991/5.

Agreement on C.A.B International. Done at London, July 8, 1986. Signed by Canada July 29, 1991. Ratified by Canada July 29, 1991. *Entered into force* for Canada July 29, 1991. CTS 1991/47.

Air

Protocol relating to an Amendment to the Convention on International Civil Aviation (Article 50(a)). Done at Montreal, October 26, 1990. *Ratified* by Canada April 19, 1991.

Convention on the Marking of Plastic Explosives for the Purpose of Detection. Done at Montreal, March 1, 1991. *Signed* by Canada March 1, 1991.

Conservation

Convention for the Conservation of Anadromous Stocks in the North Pacific (with Annex). Done at Ottawa, September 20, 1991. Signed by Canada February 11, 1992. *Ratified* by Canada November 6, 1992.

Protocol on Environmental Protection to the Antarctic Treaty. Done at Madrid, October 4, 1991. *Signed* by Canada October 4, 1991.

Customs

Protocol of Amendment to the International Convention on Mutual Administrative Assistance for the Prevention, Investigation and Repression of Customs Offences done at Nairobi on June 9, 1977. Done at Brussels, June 22, 1988. *Ratified* by Canada December 18, 1991.

Defence

Exchange of Notes Constituting an Arrangement between the Governments of Canada, Belgium and The Netherlands and the Government of the Federal Republic of Germany concerning the Status and Access of their Forces in Berlin. Done at Bonn, September 23, 1991. *Signed* by Canada September 23, 1991.

Disarmament

Treaty on Conventional Forces in Europe (with Protocols). Done at

Paris, November 19, 1990. Signed by Canada November 19, 1990. *Ratified* by Canada November 22, 1991.

Environment

Convention on Environmental Impact Assessment in a Transboundary Context. Done at Espoo, February 25, 1991. *Signed* by Canada February 26, 1991.

Finance

Agreement establishing the European Bank for Reconstruction and Development. Done at Paris, May 29, 1990. Signed by Canada May 29, 1990. Ratified by Canada February 25, 1991. *Entered into force* for Canada March 28, 1991. CTS 1991/16.

Fisheries

Protocol II to the Convention on the Prohibition of Fishing with Long Driftnets in the South Pacific. Done at Noumea, October 20, 1990. *Signed* by Canada September 24, 1991.

Amendment to the Annex (as amended in 1986 and 1990) to the International Convention for the High Seas Fisheries of the North Pacific Ocean, as amended by the Protocol signed at Tokyo April 25, 1978. Done at Tokyo, April 25, 1991. Ratified by Canada May 23, 1991. *Entered into force* for Canada May 23, 1991. CTS 1991/53.

Human Rights

Convention on the Rights of the Child. Done at New York, November 20, 1989. Signed by Canada May 28, 1990. Ratified by Canada December 13, 1991. *Entered into force* for Canada January 12, 1992. CTS 1992/3.

Law

United Nations Convention on Contracts for the International Sale of Goods. Done at Vienna, April 11, 1980. Acceded to by Canada April 23, 1991. *Entered into force* for Canada May 1, 1992. CTS 1992/2.

Law of the Sea

Memorandum of Understanding between Canada, Belgium, Germany, Italy, The Netherlands, the United

Kingdom and the United States of America, on the one hand, and China on the other hand, on the Avoidance of Overlaps and Conflicts Relating to Deep Seabed Areas (with Annexes). Done at New York, February 22, 1991. Signed by Canada February 22, 1991. Ratified by Canada February 25, 1991. *Entered into force* for Canada February 22, 1991. CTS 1991/22.

Memorandum of Understanding on the Avoidance of Overlaps ad Conflicts Relating to Deep Sea-Bed Areas between Canada, Belgium, Germany, Italy, The Netherlands, the United Kingdom, the United States of America, on the one hand, and Bulgaria, Czechoslovakia, Poland and the U.S.S.R., as the Certifying States of the Interoceanmetal Joint Organization, on the other hand (with Annexes). Done at New York, August 20, 1991. Signed by Canada August 20, 1991. *Entered into force* for Canada August 28, 1991, with effect from August 20, 1991. CTS 1991/44.

Memorandum of Understanding on the Avoidance of Overlaps and Conflicts Relating to Deep Sea-Bed Areas between Canada, Belgium, Germany, Italy, The Netherlands and the United Kingdom, on the one hand, and Bulgaria, Cuba, Czechoslovakia, Poland and the U.S.S.R., as the Certifying States of the Interoceanmetal Joint Organization, on the other hand (with Annexes). Done at New York, August 20, 1991. Signed by Canada August 20, 1991. *Entered into force* for Canada August 28, 1991, with effect from August 20, 1991. CTS 1991/45.

Marine Science
Convention for a North Pacific Marine Science Organization (PICES). Done at Ottawa, December 12, 1990. Signed by Canada October 22, 1991. Ratified by Canada October 22, 1991. *Entered into force* for Canada March 24, 1992. CTS 1992/8.

Navigation
Proposed Amendment to Article X(2) of the Convention on the International Hydrographic Organization done at Monaco on May 3, 1967, which was approved at the XIIIth International Hydrographic Conference of 1987. Done at Monaco, May 15, 1987. *Ratified* by Canada August 2, 1991.

Peace
Agreement on a Comprehensive Political Settlement of the Cambodia Conflict (with Annexes). Done at Paris, October 23, 1991. Signed by Canada October 23, 1991. *Entered into force* for Canada October 23, 1991. CTS 1991/27.

Agreement concerning the Sovereignty, Independence, Territorial Integrity and Inviolability, Neutrality and National Unity of Cambodia. Done at Paris, October 23, 1991. Signed by Canada October 23, 1991. *Entered into force* for Canada October 23, 1991. CTS 1991/27.

Pollution, Environment
Protocol to the 1979 Convention on Long-Range Transboundary Air Pollution concerning the Control of Emissions of Nitrogen Oxides or their Transboundary Fluxes. Done at Sofia, October 31, 1988. Signed by Canada November 1, 1988. Ratified by Canada January 25, 1991. *Entered into force* for Canada April 25, 1991. CTS 1991/17.

Protocol to the 1979 Convention on Long-Range Transboundary Air Pollution concerning the Control of Emissions of Volatile Organic Compounds. Done at Geneva, November 19, 1991. *Signed* by Canada November 19, 1991.

Postal Matters
General Regulations of the Universal Postal Union (UPU). Done at Washington, December 14, 1989. Signed by Canada December 14, 1989. Acceded to by Canada March 20, 1991. *Entered into force* for Canada March 20, 1991.

Convention and Final Protocol of the Universal Postal Union (UPU). Done at Washington, December 14, 1989. Signed by Canada December 14, 1989. Acceded to by Canada March 20, 1991. *Entered into force* for Canada March 20, 1991.

Fourth Additional Protocol to the Constitution of the Universal Postal Union (UPU). Done at Washington, December 14, 1989. Signed by Canada December 14, 1989. Ratified by Canada March 20, 1991. *Entered into force* for Canada March 20, 1991.
Postal Parcels Arrangement and Final Protocol (UPU). Done at Washington, December 14, 1989. Signed by Canada December 14, 1989. Acceded to by Canada March 20, 1991. *Entered into force* for Canada March 20, 1991.

Telecommunications
Final Acts of the World Administrative Radio Conference for the Mobile Services, (MOB-83), Geneva, 1983. Done at Geneva, March 18, 1983. Ratified by Canada February 20, 1991. *Entered into force* for Canada February 20, 1991. NOTE: Applied with effect from January 15, 1985. Available for reference purposes from the Library, Communications Canada.
Final Acts of the World Administrative Radio Conference for the Planning of the HF Bands Allocated to the Broadcasting Service (HFBC-87), Geneva, 1987. Done at Geneva, March 8, 1987. Ratified by Canada February 20, 1991. *Entered into force* for Canada February 20, 1991.
Final Acts of the World Administrative Radio Conference for the Mobile Services (MOB-87), Geneva, 1987. Done at Geneva, October 17, 1987. Ratified by Canada February 20, 1991. *Entered into force* for Canada February 20, 1991. NOTE: Applied with effect from October 3, 1989 with reservations. Availabe for reference purposes from the Library, Communications Canada.
Final Acts of the Regional Administrative Radio Conference to Establish a Plan for the Broadcasting Service in the Band 1 605-1 705 kHz in Region 2, Rio de Janeiro, 1988. Done at Rio de Janeiro, June 8, 1988. Ratified by Canada February 20, 1991. *Entered into force* for Canada February 20, 1991. NOTE: Applied with effect from July 1, 1990. Available for reference purposes from

the Library, Communications Canada.
Final Acts of the World Administrative Radio Conference on the Use of the Geostationary-Satellite Orbit and the Planning of Space Services Utilizing It (ORB-88), Geneva, 1988. Done at Geneva, October 6, 1988. Ratified by Canada February 20, 1991. *Entered into force* for Canada February 20, 1991. NOTE: Applied with effect from March 16, 1990 subject to a declaration. Available for reference purposes from the Library, Communications Canada.
Final Acts of the World Administrative Telegraph and Telephone Conference (WATTC-88), Melbourne, 1988. Done at Melbourne, December 9, 1988. Ratified by Canada February 20, 1991. *Entered into force* for Canada February 20, 1991. NOTE: Applied with effect from July 4, 1990. Available for reference purposes from the Library, Communications Canada.
Constitution and Convention of the International Telecommunication Union, Nice, 1989. Done at Nice, June 30, 1989. Signed by Canada June 30, 1989. *Ratified* by Canada February 20, 1991. NOTE: Subject to a declaration. Available for reference purposes from the Library, Communications Canada.
Optional Protocol on the Compulsory Settlement of Disputes Relating to the Constitution of the ITU, to the Convention of the ITU and to the Administrative Regulations, Nice, 1989. Done at Nice, June 30, 1989. *Ratified* by Canada February 20, 1991. Available for reference purposes from the Library, Communications Canada.

Textiles
Protocol Maintaining in Force the Arrangement Regarding International Trade in Textiles. Done at Geneva, July 31, 1991. Signed by Canada August 7, 1991. Ratified by Canada December 4, 1991. *Entered into force* for Canada December 4, 1991. CTS 1991/49.

United Nations
Resolutions adopted by the United Nations Security Council acting under Chapter VII of the Charter of the

United Nations. (a) on the Situation in the Persian Gulf and (b) on the Embargo on All Deliveries of Weapons and Military Equipment to Yugoslavia. Done at New York, beginning March 2, 1991. *Entered into force* for Canada when passed by the Security Council. CTS 1991/51. NOTE: Decisions of the Security Council taken under Chapter VII of the United Nations Charter are binding on all members of the United Nations when passed.

War — Rules of Warfare
Modification of Canada's reservations to the Protocol for the Prohibition of the Use in War of Asphyxiating, Poisonous or Other Gases, and of Bacteriological Methods of Warfare done at Geneva June 17, 1925. Done at Geneva, September 6, 1991. *Entered into force* for Canada September 6, 1991. NOTE: Modification to Canada's reservations to the Protocol insofar as they relate to bacteriological methods of warfare.

Protocol Additional to the Geneva Conventions of August 12, 1949, and relating to the protection of Victims of International Armed Conflicts (Protocol I) (with Annexes). Done at Geneva, June 8, 1977. Signed by Canada December 12, 1977. Ratified by Canada November 20, 1990. *Entered into force* for Canada May 20, 1991. CTS 1991/2.

Protocol Additional to the Geneva Conventions of August 12, 1949, relating to the Protection of Victims of Non-International Armed Conflicts (Protocol II). Done at Geneva, June 8, 1977. Signed by Canada December 12, 1977. Ratified by Canada November 20, 1990. *Entered into force* for Canada May 20, 1991. CTS 1991/2.

War Graves
Agreement between the Governments of Canada, the United Kingdom, Australia, New Zealand and India, and the Government of the Tunisian Republic concerning Commonwealth War Cemeteries, Graves, and Memorials in Tunisia. Done at Tunis, May 2, 1990. Signed by Canada May 2, 1990. *Entered into force* for Canada October 1, 1991. CTS 1991/24.

Women, Status of
Inter-American Convention on the Nationality of Women. Done at Montevideo, December 26, 1933. Signed by Canada October 23, 1991. Acceded to by Canada October 23, 1991. *Entered into force* for Canada October 23, 1991. CTS 1991/28.

Inter-American Convention on the Granting of Political Rights to Women. Done at Bogota, May 2, 1948. Signed by Canada October 23, 1991. Ratified by Canada October 23, 1991. *Entered into force* for Canada October 23, 1991. CTS 1991/29.

Inter-American Convention on the Granting of Civil Rights to Women. Done at Bogota, May 2, 1948. Signed by Canada October 23, 1991. Ratified by Canada October 23, 1991. *Entered into force* for Canada October 23, 1991. CTS 1991/30.

I: BILATÉRAUX

Arabie Saoudite
Accord sur le transport aérien entre le gouvernement du Canada et le gouvernement du Royaume d'Arabie saoudite (avec Annexe). Riyadh, le 14 novembre 1990. *En vigueur* le 9 juin 1991. RTC 1991/20. NOTE: Pas encore publié.

Argentine
Échange de Lettres entre le gouvernement du Canada et le gouvernement de l'Argentine constituant un Accord concernant l'emploi de personnes à charge. Buenos Aires, le 20 février 1991. *En vigueur* le 20 février 1991. RTC 1991/39.

Accord entre le gouvernement du Canada et le gouvernement de la République d'Argentine sur l'encouragement et la protection des investissements. Toronto, le 5 novembre 1991.

Bahreïn
Protocole d'Entente entre le gouvernement du Canada et le gouvernement de l'État de Bahreïn. Manama, le 16 janvier 1991. *En vigueur* le 16 janvier 1991. RTC 1991/9.

Chili
Échange de Notes entre le gouvernement du Canada et le gouvernement du Chili constituant un Accord relatif à l'emploi de personnes à la charge des employés de chaque gouvernement en poste dans des missions officielles dans l'autre pays. Santiago, le 21 janvier 1991.

Chypre
Accord sur la sécurité sociale entre le gouvernement du Canada et le gouvernement de la République de Chypre. Ottawa, le 24 janvier 1990. *En vigueur* le 1er mai 1991. RTC 1991/25.

Communauté européenne de l'énergie atomique (Euratom)
Échange de Lettres entre le gouvernement du Canada et la Communauté européenne de l'énergie atomique (Euratom) modifiant l'accord concernant les utilisations pacifiques de l'énergie atomique du 6 octobre 1959. Bruxelles, le 15 juillet 1991. *En vigueur* le 15 juillet 1991. RTC 1991/23.

Danemark
Échange de Notes entre le gouvernement du Canada et le gouvernement du Royaume du Danemark constituant un Accord modifiant l'Annexe B de l'Accord de 1983 concernant le milieu marin. Ottawa, le 7 octobre 1991. *En vigueur* le 7 octobre 1991. RTC 1991/35.

États-Unis d'Amérique
Échange de Notes entre le gouvernement du Canada et le gouvernement des États-Unis d'Amérique constituant un Accord modifiant de nouveau l'Accord relatif aux transports aériens

signé le 17 janvier 1966 tel que modifié par un Échange de Notes signé le 8 mai 1974. Ottawa, le 28 mai 1991. *En vigueur* le 28 mai 1991. RTC 1991/14.
Échange de Lettres constituant un Accord entre le gouvernement du Canada et le gouvernement des États-Unis d'Amérique modifiant l'appendice 1 de l'annexe 705.4 de l'Accord de libre-échange. Washington, le 1er mai 1991. *En vigueur* le 1er mai 1991. RTC 1991/13.
Échange de Lettres entre le gouvernement du Canada et le gouvernement des États-Unis d'Amérique constituant un Accord modifiant les Listes tarifaires contenues à l'Annexe 401.5 et rayant les Règles 2, 3 et 4 de la Section III de l'Annexe 301.2 au Chapitre 3 de l'Accord de libre-échange. Washington, le 16 août 1991. *En vigueur* le 16 août 1991. RTC 1991/46.
Échange de Notes entre le gouvernement du Canada et le gouvernement des États-Unis d'Amérique constituant un Accord prolongeant l'Accord du Commandement de la Défense aérospatiale de l'Amérique du Nord (NORAD) pour une période de cinq ans. Washington, le 30 avril 1991. *En vigueur* le 30 avril 1991. RTC 1991/19 avec effet à partir du 12 mai 1991.
Échange de Notes entre le gouvernement du Canada et le gouvernement des États-Unis d'Amérique constituant un Accord concernant l'application des taux de péage sur la Voie maritime du Saint-Laurent (avec Mémorandum d'Accord). Washington, le 1er mai 1991. *En vigueur* le 1er mai 1991. RTC 1991/11. NOTE: Note canadienne le 26 avril 1991, Note américaine le 1er mai 1991.
Échange de Notes entre le gouvernement du Canada et le gouvernement des États-Unis d'Amérique constituant un Accord modifiant l'Accord concernant l'application des taux de péage sur la Voie maritime du Saint-Laurent (avec Mémorandum d'Accord). Washington, le 17 janvier 1991.
En vigueur le 25 janvier 1991. RTC 1991/6.

Échange de Notes constituant un Accord entre le gouvernement du Canada et le gouvernement des États-Unis d'Amérique modifiant l'Accord concernant l'application des taux de péage sur la Voie maritime du Saint-Laurent. Washington, le 20 décembre 1991. *En vigueur* le 20 décembre 1991. RTC 1991/38.

Accord entre le gouvernement du Canada et le gouvernement des États-Unis d'Amérique sur la qualité de l'air (avec Annexes). Ottawa, le 13 mars 1991. *En vigueur* le 13 mars 1991. RTC 1991/3.

Protocole modifiant le Traité d'extradition entre le gouvernement du Canada et le gouvernement des États-Unis d'Amérique signé à Washington le 3 décembre 1971, en sa version modifiée par Échange de Notes le 28 juin et le 9 juillet 1974. Ottawa, le 11 janvier 1988. *En vigueur* le 26 novembre 1991. RTC 1991/37.

Échange de Notes entre le gouvernement du Canada et le gouvernement des États-Unis d'Amérique constituant un Accord modifiant l'Accord du 3 juin 1976 concernant la construction, l'exploitation et l'entretien de la station Loran-C située près de Williams Lake, C.-B. (avec Annexe). Washington, le 8 mai 1991. *En vigueur* le 8 mai 1991. RTC 1991/12.

Échange de Notes entre le gouvernement du Canada et le gouvernement des États-Unis d'Amérique constituant un Accord modifiant le Mémoire d'accord sur les services de pilotage dans les Grands Lacs. Washington, le 12 février 1991. *En vigueur* le 12 février 1991. RTC 1991/15.

Accord entre le gouvernement du Canada et le gouvernement des États-Unis d'Amérique concernant l'application de la législation sur les pêches. Ottawa, le 26 septembre 1990. *En vigueur* le 16 décembre 1991. RTC 1991/36.

Échange de Notes entre le gouvernement du Canada et le gouvernement des États-Unis d'Amérique concernant l'utilisation de la bande de fréquences de 88 à 108 mégahertz pour la radio-diffusion en modulation de fréquence (FM). Washington, le 25 février 1991. *En vigueur* le 25 février 1991. RTC 1991/10.

Échange de Notes (8 janvier et 15 octobre 1947) entre le Canada et les États-Unis d'Amérique portant Accord sur l'attribution de voies de radiodiffusion. Washington, le 15 octobre 1947. *En vigueur* le 15 octobre 1947. RTC 1947/30. NOTE: Substitué par l'Accord du 25 février 1991. TERMINÉ: le 25 février 1991.

Échange de Notes entre le gouvernement du Canada et le gouvernement des États-Unis d'Amérique constituant un Accord en matière de coopération dans le cadre du programme Radarsat (avec Annexe). Washington, le 12 novembre 1991. *En vigueur* le 12 novembre 1991. RTC 1991/50.

Finlande

Échange de Lettres entre le gouvernement du Canada et le gouvernement de la Finlande relatif aux transferts de matières nucléaires spécifiées et constituant un Accord concernant l'application de l'Accord Canada-Finlande du 5 mars 1976, tel que modifié. Helsinki, le 22 novembre 1991. *En vigueur* le 22 novembre 1991. RTC 1991/52.

France

Accord entre le gouvernement du Canada et le gouvernement de la République française concernant la coopération et les échanges dans le domaine des musées. Paris, le 26 novembre 1990. *En vigueur* le 1ᵉʳ avril 1991. RTC 1991/4.

Convention d'entraide judiciaire en matière pénale entre le gouvernement du Canada et le gouvernement de la République française. Paris, le 15 décembre 1989. *En vigueur* le 1ᵉʳ mai 1991. RTC 1991/34.

Grande-Bretagne

Protocole entre le gouvernement du Canada et le gouvernement du Royaume-Uni de Grande-Bretagne et d'Irlande du Nord modifiant l'Accord de coproduction cinématographique fait à Londres le 12 septembre 1975, et modifié le 9 juillet 1985. Ottawa, le 5 juillet 1991.

Hong Kong
Accord entre le gouvernement du Canada et le gouvernement de Hong Kong concernant les enquêtes sur le trafic des drogues et la confiscation du produit du trafic des drogues. Hong Kong, le 14 novembre 1990. *En vigueur* le 17 février 1991. RTC 1991/18.

Hongrie
Accord entre le gouvernement du Canada et le gouvernement de la République de Hongrie sur l'encouragement et la protection réciproque des investissements. Ottawa, le 3 octobre 1991.

Inde
Échange de Notes entre le gouvernement du Canada et le gouvernement de l'Inde constituant un Accord modifiant l'Accord signé à New Delhi le 20 juillet 1982 tel que modifié (document en annexe). New Delhi, le 30 mai 1991. *En vigueur* le 30 mai 1991. RTC 1991/41.

Indonésie
Accord général sur la coopération au développement entre le gouvernement du Canada et le gouvernement de la République d'Indonésie (avec Annexes). Ottawa, le 21 mai 1991.

Italie
Accord de navigabilité entre le gouvernement du Canada et le gouvernement de l'Italie. Ottawa, le 18 février 1991. *En vigueur* le 18 février 1991. RTC 1991/7.

Luxembourg
Convention entre le gouvernement du Canada et le gouvernement du Grand-Duché de Luxembourg en vue d'éviter les doubles impositions et de prévenir l'évasion fiscale en matière d'impôts sur le revenu et sur la fortune. Luxembourg, le 17 janvier 1989. *En vigueur* le 8 juillet 1991. RTC 1991/21.

Malte
Accord sur la sécurité sociale entre le gouvernement du Canada et le gouver-

nement de la République de Malte. Toronto, le 4 avril 1991. *En vigueur* le 1er mars 1992. RTC 1992/5.

Mexique
Accord de coproduction d'oeuvres cinématographiques et audiovisuelles entre le gouvernement du Canada et le gouvernement des États-Unis Mexicains (avec Annexe). Ottawa, le 8 avril 1991. *En vigueur* le 26 novembre 1991. RTC 1991/42.
Accord entre le gouvernement du Canada et le gouvernement des États-Unis Mexicains concernant la coopération dans les domaines des musées et de l'archéologie. Mexico, le 25 novembre 1991.
Convention entre le gouvernement du Canada et le gouvernement des États-Unis Mexicains en vue d'éviter les doubles impositions et de prévenir l'évasion fiscale en matière d'impôts sur le revenu. Ottawa, le 8 avril 1991. *En vigueur* le 11 mai 1992. RTC 1992/15.

Namibie
Accord entre le gouvernement du Canada et le gouvernement de la République de Namibie concernant la formation au Canada de personnel des forces armées de la République de Namibie. Windhoek, le 19 septembre 1991. *En vigueur* le 19 septembre 1991. RTC 1991/48.

Pays-Bas
Échange de Lettres entre le gouvernement du Canada et le gouvernement des Pays-Bas constituant un Accord relatif à l'emploi des personnes à charge. La Haye, le 1er mai 1991. *En vigueur* le 18 décembre 1991. RTC 1991/43.
Traité d'entraide judiciaire en matière pénale entre le Canada et le Royaume des Pays-Bas. La Haye, le 1er mai 1991. *En vigueur* le 1er mai 1992. RTC 1992/9.
Traité entre le Royaume-Uni et les Pays-Bas pour l'extradition mutuelle de criminels fugitifs. Londres, le 26 septembre 1898. *En vigueur* le 14 mars 1899. BTS 1899/1. NOTE: Terminé le 1er décembre 1991 dès l'entrée en vig-

ueur de la Convention du 13 octobre 1989.

Convention entre le gouvernement du Canada et le gouvernement du Royaume des Pays-Bas en matière d'extradition. Montréal, le 13 octobre 1989. *En vigueur* le 1er décembre 1991. RTC 1991/32.

Royaume-Uni
Échange de Notes entre le gouvernement du Canada et le gouvernement du Royaume-Uni de Grande-Bretagne et d'Irlande du Nord constituant un Accord relatif à l'entraînement des Forces armées britanniques au Canada. Londres, le 4 septembre 1991. *En vigueur* le 4 septembre 1991. RTC 1991/33. NOTE: Restera en vigueur jusqu'au 19 août 2006.

Échange de Notes entre le gouvernement du Canada et le gouvernement du Royaume-Uni de Grande Bretagne et d'Irlande du Nord constituant un Accord modifiant et prolongeant l'Accord de 1971 relatif à l'entraînement des Forces armées britanniques au Canada. Ottawa, le 26 novembre 1979. *En vigueur* le 26 novembre 1979. RTC 1979/23. NOTE: Remplacée par l'Accord du 4 septembre 1991. RTC 1991/33. TERMINÉ: le 4 septembre 1991.

Échange de Notes entre le gouvernement du Canada et le gouvernement du Royaume-Uni de Grande-Bretagne et d'Irlande du Nord constituant un Accord relatif à l'entraînement des Forces armées britanniques au Canada. Ottawa, le 20 août 1971. *En vigueur* le 20 août 1971.

NOTE: Remplacé par l'Accord du 4 septembre 1991. RTC 1991/33. TERMINÉ: le 4 septembre 1991.

Suède
Échange de Lettres entre le gouvernement du Canada et le gouvernement de la Suède relatif aux transferts de matières nucléaires spécifiées et constituant un Accord concernant l'application de l'Accord Canada-Suède du 27 septembre 1977 tel que modifié. Stockholm, le 27 novembre 1991. *En vigueur* le 27 novembre 1991. RTC 1991/46.

Thaïlande
Échange de Notes entre le gouvernement du Canada et le gouvernement du Royaume de Thaïlande constituant un Accord modifiant l'Accord sur les services aériens signé le 24 mai 1989. Bangkok, le 25 décembre 1991. *En vigueur* le 25 décembre 1991. RTC 1991/40.

URSS
Protocole prolongeant l'Accord commercial conclu entre le gouvernement du Canada et le gouvernement de l'Union des Républiques socialistes soviétiques signé à Ottawa le 26 février 1956. Ottawa, le 17 avril 1991. *En vigueur* le 17 avril 1991. RTC 1991/8.

Accord entre le gouvernement du Canada et le gouvernement de l'Union des Républiques socialistes soviétiques relatif à la prévention des activités militaires dangereuses (avec Annexes). Ottawa, le 10 mai 1991. *En vigueur* le 10 novembre 1991. RTC 1991/26.

Accord entre le gouvernement du Canada et le gouvernement de l'Union des Républiques socialistes soviétiques sur l'encouragement et la protection reciproque des investissements. Moscou, le 20 novembre 1989. *En vigueur* le 27 juin 1991. RTC 1991/31.

Uruguay
Accord entre le gouvernement du Canada et le gouvernement de la République orientale de l'Uruguay sur l'encouragement et la protection des investissements. Ottawa, le 16 mai 1991.

Venezuela
Échange de Notes entre le gouvernement du Canada et le gouvernement de la République du Venezuela constituant un Accord sur les conditions à remplir par les voyageurs non immigrants des deux pays pour l'obtention de visas. Ottawa, le 8 octobre 1959. *En vigueur* le 1er novembre 1959. RTC 1959/20. TERMINÉ: le 11 mars 1991.

II: TRAITÉS MULTILATÉRAUX

Agriculture

Convention Internationale pour la protection des obtentions végétales du 2 décembre 1961, telle que revisée à Genève le 10 novembre 1972 et le 23 octobre 1978. Paris, le 2 décembre 1961. Signée par le Canada le 31 octobre 1979. Ratifiée par le Canada le 4 février 1991. *En vigueur* pour le Canada le 4 mars 1991. RTC 1991/5.

Accord relatif au CAB International. Londres, le 8 juillet 1986. Signé par le Canada le 29 juillet 1991. Ratifié par le Canada le 29 juillet 1991. *En vigueur* pour le Canada le 29 juillet 1991. RTC 1991/47.

Air

Convention sur le marquage des explosifs plastiques et en feuilles aux fins de détection. Montréal, le 1er mars 1991. *Signée* par le Canada le 1er mars 1991. Protocole portant amendement de la Convention relative à l'aviation civile internationale (article 50(a)). Montréal, le 26 octobre 1990. *Ratifié* par le Canada le 19 avril 1991.

Cimetières de guerre

Accord entre les gouvernements du Canada, du Royaume-Uni de Grande-Bretagne et d'Irlande du Nord, de l'Australie, de la Nouvelle-Zélande et de l'Inde et le gouvernement de la République Tunisienne concernant les cimetières, sépultures et monuments militaires en Tunisie. Tunis, le 2 mai 1990. Signé par le Canada le 2 mai 1990. *En vigueur* pour le Canada le 1er octobre 1991. RTC 1991/24.

Conservation

Protocole au Traité sur l'Antarctique relatif à la protection de l'environnement. Madrid, le 4 octobre 1991. *Signé* par le Canada le 4 octobre 1991 Convention concernant la conservation des espèces anadromes dans l'océan Pacifique Nord (avec Annexe). Ottawa, le 20 septembre 1991. Signée par le Canada le 11 février 1992. *Ratifiée* par le Canada le 6 novembre 1992.

Défense

Échange de Notes constituant un Arrangement entre les gouvernements du Canada, de la Belgique et des Pays-Bas et le gouvernment de la République fédérale d'Allemagne concernant le statut et l'accès des Forces canadiennes, belges et néerlandaises à Berlin. Bonn, le 23 septembre 1991. *Signé* par le Canada le 23 septembre 1991.

Désarmement

Traité sur les forces armées conventionnelles en Europe (avec Protocoles). Paris, le 19 novembre 1990. Signé par le Canada le 19 novembre 1990. *Ratifié* par le Canada le 22 novembre 1991. NOTE: Traité appliqué provisoirement à partir du 17 juillet 1992.

Douanes

Protocole d'amendement de la Convention internationale d'assistance mutuelle administrative en vue de prévenir, de rechercher et de réprimer les infractions douanières faite à Nairobi le 9 juin 1977. Bruxelles, le 22 juin 1988. *Ratifié* par le Canada le 18 décembre 1991.

Droit de la mer

Mémoire d'entente ente le Canada, la Belgique, l'Allemagne, l'Italie, les Pays-Bas, le Royaume-Uni, et les États-Unis d'Amérique, d'une part, et la Chine, d'autre part, visant à éviter les chevauchements et les conflits relatifs aux zones des grands fonds marins (avec Annexes). New York, le 22 février 1991. Signé par le Canada le 22 février 1991. Ratifié par le Canada le 22 février 1991. *En vigueur* pour le Canada le 22 février 1991. RTC 1991/22.
Mémoire d'entente visant à éviter les chevauchements et les conflits relatifs aux sites miniers des grands fonds marins entre le Canada, l'Allemagne, la Belgique, les États-Unis d'Amérique, l'Italie, les Pays-Bas et le Royaume-Uni, d'une part, et la Bulgarie, Cuba, la Pologne, la Tchécoslovaquie, et l'U.R.S.S. en qualité d'États certificateurs de l'orga-

nisation conjointe "Interoceanmetal" d'autre part (avec Annexes). New York, le 20 août 1991. Signé par le Canada le 20 août 1991. *En vigueur* pour le Canada le 28 août 1991. RTC 1991/44. NOTE: *En vigueur* le 28 août 1991 avec effet à compter du 20 août 1991.

Mémoire d'Entente visant a éviter les chevauchements et les conflits relatifs aux zones des grands fonds marins entre le Canada, l'Allemagne, la Belgique, l'Italie, les Pays-Bas, et le Royaume Uni d'une part, et la Bulgarie, Cuba, la Pologne, la Tchécoslovaquie et l'U.R.S.S. en qualité d'États certificateurs de l'organisation conjointe "Interoceanmetal" d'autre part (avec Annexes). New York, le 20 août 1991. Signé par le Canada le 20 août 1991. *En vigueur* pour le Canada le 28 août 1991. RTC 1991/45. NOTE: *En vigueur* le 28 août 1991 avec effet à compter du 20 août 1991.

Droit de la guerre

Protocole additionnel aux Conventions de Genève du 12 août 1949 relatif à la protection des victimes des conflits armés internationaux (Protocole I) (avec Annexes). Genève, le 8 juin 1977. Signé par le Canada le 12 décembre 1977. Ratifié par le Canada le 20 novembre 1990. *En vigueur* pour le Canada le 20 mai 1991. RTC 1991/2.

Protocole additionnel aux Conventions de Genève du 12 août 1949 relatif à la protection des victimes des conflits armés non internationaux (Protocole II). Genève, le 8 juin 1977. Signé par le Canada le 12 décembre 1977. Ratifié par le Canada le 20 novembre 1990. *En vigueur* pour le Canada le 20 mai 1991. RTC 1991/2.

Droit

Convention des Nations Unies sur les contrats de vente internationale de marchandises. Vienne, le 11 avril 1980. Adhésion par le Canada le 23 avril 1991. *En vigueur* pour le Canada le 1ᵉʳ mai 1992. RTC 1992/2. NOTE: Adhésion accompagnée d'une déclaration.

Droits de la personne

Convention relative aux droits de l'enfant. New York, le 20 novembre 1989. Signée par le Canada le 28 mai 1990. Ratifiée par le Canada le 13 décembre 1991. *En vigueur* pour le Canada le 12 janvier 1992. RTC 1992/3.

Environnement

Convention sur l'évaluation de l'impact sur l'environnement dans un contexte transfrontière. Espoo, le 25 février 1991. *Signée* par le Canada le 26 février 1991.

Femme, condition de la

Convention interaméricaine sur la nationalité de la femme. Montevideo, le 26 décembre 1933. Signée par le Canada le 23 octobre 1991. Adhésion par le Canada le 23 octobre 1991. *En vigueur* pour le Canada le 23 octobre 1991. RTC 1991/28.

Convention interaméricaine sur la concession des droits politiques à la femme. Bogota, le 2 mai 1948. Signée par le Canada le 23 octobre 1991. Ratifiée par le Canada le 23 octobre 1991. *En vigueur* pour le Canada le 23 octobre 1991. RTC 1991/29.

Convention interaméricaine sur la concession des droits civils à la femme. Bogota, le 2 mai 1948. Signée par le Canada le 23 octobre 1991. Ratifiée par le Canada le 23 octobre 1991. *En vigueur* pour le Canada le 23 octobre 1991. RTC 1991/30.

Finance

Accord portant création de la Banque Européenne pour la reconstruction et le développement. Paris, le 29 mai 1990. Signé par le Canada le 29 mai 1990. Ratifié par le Canada le 25 février 1991. *En vigueur* pour le Canada le 28 mars 1991. RTC 1991/16.

Guerre

Modification des réserves faites par le Canada relativement au Protocole du 17 juin 1925 concernant la prohibition d'emploi à la guerre de gaz asphyxiants, toxiques ou similaires et de moyens bactériologiques. Genève, le 6 septembre 1991. *En vigueur* pour le Canada le 6 septembre 1991. NOTE: Modification des réserves faites par le Canada relativement au Protocole en ce qui a trait aux moyens bactériologiques.

Nations Unies
Résolutions adoptées par le Conseil de Sécurité des Nations Unies, agissant en vertu du Chapitre VII de la Charte des Nations Unies concernant a) la situation dans le Golfe persique, et b) un embargo général et complet sur toutes les livraisons d'armements et d'équipements militaires à la Yougoslavie. New York, à compter du 2 mars 1991. *En vigueur* pour le Canada à la date d'adoption. RTC 1991/51. NOTE: Les décisions du Conseil de sécurité, prises en vertu du chapitre VII de la charte des Nations Unies, sont obligatoires pour tous les membres des Nations Unies avec effet immédiat.

Navigation
Proposition de modification de l'Article X (2) de la Convention relative à l'Organisation hydrographique internationale faite à Monaco le 3 mai 1967, qui a été approuvée par la XIIIᵉ conférence hydrographique internationale de 1987. Monaco, le 15 mai 1987. *Ratifiée* par le Canada le 2 août 1991.

Paix
Accord pour un Règlement politique global du conflit du Cambodge (avec Annexes). Paris, le 23 octobre 1991. Signé par le Canada le 23 octobre 1991. *En vigueur* pour le Canada le 23 octobre 1991. RTC 1991/27.
Accord relatif à la souveraineté, l'indépendance, l'intégrité et l'inviolabilité territoriale, la neutralité et l'unité nationale du Cambodge. Paris, le 23 octobre 1991. Signé par le Canada le 23 octobre 1991. *En vigueur* pour le Canada le 23 octobre 1991. RTC 1991/27.

Pêche
Modification à l'Annexe de la Convention internationale concernant les pêcheries hauturières de l'océan Paci-

fique Nord, telle que modifiée par le protocole signé à Tokyo le 25 avril 1978. Tokyo, le 25 avril 1991. Ratifiée par le Canada le 23 mai 1991. *En vigueur* pour le Canada le 23 mai 1991. RTC 1991.
Protocole II à la Convention pour l'interdiction de la pêche au filet maillant dérivant de grande dimension dans le Pacifique du Sud, Protocole II. Noumea, le 20 octobre 1990. *Signé* par le Canada le 24 septembre 1991.

Pollution, Environnement
Protocole à la Convention sur la pollution atmosphérique transfrontière à longue distance de 1979, relatif à la lutte contre les émissions des composés volatiles ou leurs flux transfrontières. Genève, le 19 novembre 1991. *Signé* par le Canada le 19 novembre 1991.
Protocole à la Convention de 1979 sur la pollution atmosphérique transfrontière à longue distance de 1979, relatif à la lutte contre les émissions d'oxydes d'azote ou leurs flux transfrontières. Sofia, le 31 octobre 1988. Signé par le Canada le 1ᵉʳ novembre 1988. Ratifié par le Canada le 25 janvier 1991. *En vigueur* pour le Canada le 25 avril 1991. RTC 1991/17.

Questions postales
Convention postale universelle et Protocole final (UPU). Washington, le 14 décembre 1989. Signés par le Canada le 14 décembre 1989. Adhésion par le Canada le 20 mars 1991. *En vigueur* pour le Canada le 20 mars 1991. NOTE: *En vigueur* le 20 mars avec effet à partir du 1er janvier 1991.
Quatrième Protocole additionnel à la Constitution de l'Union postale universelle (UPU). Washington, le 14 décembre 1989. Signé par le Canada le 14 décembre 1989. Ratifié par le Canada le 20 mars 1991. *En vigueur* pour le Canada le 20 mars 1991. NOTE: *En vigueur* le 20 mars avec effet à partir du 1er janvier 1991.
Règlement général de l'Union postale universelle (UPU). Washington, le 14 décembre 1989. Signé par le Canada le 14 décembre 1989. Adhésion par le

Canada le 20 mars 1991. *En vigueur* pour le Canada le 20 mars 1991. NOTE: *En vigueur* le 20 mars avec effet à partier du 1er janvier 1991.

Arrangement concernant les colis postaux et Protocole final (UPU). Washington, le 14 décembre 1989. Signés par le Canada le 14 décembre 1989. Adhésion par le Canada le 20 mars 1991. *En vigueur* pour le Canada le 20 mars 1991. NOTE: *En vigueur* le 20 mars avec effet à partir du 1er janvier 1991.

Sciences marines
Convention portant création d'une organisation pour les sciences marines dans le Pacifique Nord (PICES). Ottawa, le 12 décembre 1990. Signée par le Canada le 22 octobre 1991. Ratifiée par le Canada le 22 octobre 1991. *En vigueur* pour le Canada le 24 mars 1992. RTC 1992/8. NOTE: *Entre en vigueur* le 24 mars 1992.

Télécommunications
Actes finals de la Conférence administrative mondiale des radiocommunications pour les services mobiles (MOB-87), Genève 1987. Genève, le 17 octobre 1987. Ratifiés par le Canada le 20 février 1991. *En vigueur* pour le Canada le 20 février 1991. NOTE: Appliqués avec effet à partir du 3 octobre 1989 avec réserves. Documents de renseignements disponibles à la Bibliothèque, Communications Canada.

Actes finals de la Conférence administrative mondiale des radiocommunications pour la planification des bandes d'ondes décamétriques attribuées au service de radiodiffusion (HFBC-87), Genève 1987. Genève, le 8 mars 1987. Ratifiés par le Canada le 20 février 1991. *En vigueur* pour le Canada le 20 février 1991. NOTE: Appliqués avec effet à partir du 1er Septembre 1988, compte tenu d'une déclaration. Documents de renseignements disponibles à la Bibliothèque, Communications Canada.

Actes finals de la Conférence administrative mondiale des radiocommunications pour les services mobiles

(MOB-83), Genève 1983. Genève, le 18 mars 1983. Ratifiés par le Canada le 20 février 1991. *En vigueur* pour le Canada le 20 février 1991. NOTE: Appliqués avec effet à partir du 15 janvier 1985. Documents de renseignements disponibles à la Bibliothèque, Communications Canada.

Actes finals de la Conférence administrative régionale des radiocommunications chargée d'établir un Plan pour le service de radiodiffusion dans la bande 1605-1705 kHz dans la Région 2, Rio de Janeiro 1988. Rio de Janeiro, le 8 juin 1988. Ratifiés par le Canada le 20 février 1991. *En vigueur* pour le Canada le 20 février 1991. NOTE: Appliqués avec effet à partir du 1er juillet 1990. Documents de renseignements disponibles à la Bibliothèque, Communications Canada.

Actes finals de la Conférence administrative mondiale des radiocommunications sur l'utilisation de l'orbite des satellites géostationnaires et la planification des services spatiaux utilisant cette orbite (ORB-88), Genève 1988. Genève, le 6 octobre 1988. Ratifiés par le Canada le 20 février 1991. *En vigueur* pour le Canada le 20 février 1991. NOTE: Appliqués avec effet à partir du 16 mars 1990, compte tenu d'une déclaration. Documents de renseignements disponibles à la Bibliothèque, Communications Canada.

Constitution et Convention de l'Union internationale des télécommunications, Nice 1989. Nice, le 30 juin 1989. Signées par le Canada le 30 juin 1989. *Ratifiées* par le Canada le 20 février 1991. NOTE: compte tenu d'une déclaration.

Actes finals de la Conférence administrative mondiale télégraphique et téléphonique (CAMTT-88), Melbourne 1988. Melbourne, le 9 décembre 1988. Ratifiés par le Canada le 20 février 1991. *En vigueur* pour le Canada le 20 février 1991. NOTE: Appliqués avec effet à partir du 4 juillet 1990. Documents de renseignements disponibles à la Bibliothèque, Communications Canada.

Annuaire canadien de Droit international 1992

Protocole facultatif concernant le
règlement obligatoire des différends
relatifs à la Constitution de l'Union
internationale des télécommunications, à la Convention de l'Union internationale des télécommunications et
aux Règlements administratifs, Nice
1989. Nice, le 30 juin 1989. *Ratifié* par
le Canada le 20 février 1991.

Textiles
Protocole portant maintien en vigueur
de l'Arrangement concernant le com-
merce international des textiles.
Genève, le 31 juillet 1991. Signé par le
Canada le 7 août 1991. Ratifié par le
Canada le 4 décembre 1991. *En vigueur*
pour le Canada le 4 décembre 1991.
RTC 1991/49.

ADDENDUM: TREATY ACTIONS
TAKEN BY CANADA, 1990/MES-
URES PRISES PAR LE CANADA EN
MATIÈRE DE TRAITÉS, 1990

I   BILATERAL

United States of America
Agreement on Bilateral Defence Consultations. Ottawa, August 21, 1990. *In
force* August 21, 1990.

II   MULTILATERAL

Law
Amendment to Article 6 (1) of the
Statute for the International Institute
for the Unification of Private Law,
Rome May 3, 1990. Canada's Instrument of accession deposited May 3,
1990. Will enter into force when
approved by a majority of two-thirds of
the participating governments.

Fisheries
Amendment to the Annex (as
amended in 1866) to the International
Convention for the High Seas Fisheries
of the North Pacific Ocean as amended
by the Protocol signed at Tokyo, April
25, 1978. Tokyo April 24, 1990. Canada's Instrument of Ratification deposited May 17, 1990. *In force* May 17,
1990; *in force* for Canada May 17, 1990.

I   BILATÉRAUX

États-Unis d'Amérique
Accord relatif aux consultations inter-
gouvernementales concernant la
défense. Ottawa, le 21 août 1990. *En
vigueur* le 21 août 1990.

II   MULTILATÉRAUX

Droit
Amendement au paragraphe 1 de
l'Article 6 du Statut organique de l'Institut international pour l'unification du
droit privé. Rome le 3 mai 1990. Adhésion du Canada le 3 mai 1990. Entrera
en vigueur dès l'approbation par la
majorité des deux tiers des gouvernements participants.

Pêche
Modification à l'Annexe (telle que
modifiée en 1986) de la Convention
internationale concernant les pêcheries hauturières de l'Océan Pacifique
Nord, telle que modifiée par le Protocole signé à Tokyo le 25 avril 1978.
Tokyo le 24 avril 1990. En vigueur le
17 mai 1990; *en vigueur* pour le Canada
le 17 mai 1990.

---

* The items in this addendum are additions to the Treaty Action section in
Volume XXIX (1991), at 529. Mesures en matière de traités à ajouter au
Volume XXIX (1991), à la p. 529.

Canadian Cases in International Law in 1991-92 / La jurisprudence canadienne en matière de droit international en 1991-92

compiled by / préparé par
JOOST BLOM*

I. PUBLIC INTERNATIONAL LAW/DROIT INTERNATIONAL PUBLIC

Jurisdiction — criminal offences — territorial scope

R. v. Finta (1992), 92 D.L.R. (4th) 1. Ontario Court of Appeal. (Leave to appeal granted, Dec. 10, 1992 (S.C.C.).)

This was an appeal by the Crown from the accused's acquittal on charges relating to the unlawful confinement and robbery of Jews in Hungary in 1944. The charges were brought under section 7(3.71) of the Criminal Code, R.S.C. 1985, c. C-46 (as amended by R.S.C. 1985, c. 30 (3rd Supp.), section 1(1)), dealing with war crimes and crimes against humanity committed outside Canada. The accused's unsuccessful challenge to the constitutional validity of these offences was noted in 28 *Canadian Yearbook of International Law* 589 (1990). That decision turned in part on the finding, which was the subject of the note, that war crimes and crimes against humanity were already recognized as such under international law in 1944. The present appeal turned in part on the Crown's argument that the trial judge had erred in leaving to the jury the question whether the accused's actions had constituted, in fact, war crimes or crimes against humanity. It was, the argument ran, a question of the court's jurisdiction and thus a question for the judge.

---

* Professor of Law, University of British Columbia.

The majority concluded that the issue was properly left to the jury. The issue did not go to the jurisdiction of the court, but to the territorial scope of the offences. A finding that the act or omission in question constituted a war crime or crime against humanity was one of the conditions to be satisfied if the act or omission was to be deemed committed in Canada under section 7(3.71). Under section 6(2) of the Criminal Code, unless a statutory provision indicates otherwise, the fact that an act was committed in Canada is a constituent element of any offence under the Code. The issue therefore went to the question of guilt or innocence and, as such, was a question for the jury.

Seas — territorial sea and economic zones

Note. R. v. *Alegria* (1992), 96 Nfld. & P.E.I. R. 128 (Nfld. C.A.) affirmed the decision noted in 26 *Canadian Yearbook of International Law* 402 (1988), that the regulation defining the 200-mile Canadian fishing zone had been validly enacted pursuant to the Territorial Sea and Fishing Zones Act, R.S.C. 1985, c. T-8, section 4.

Sovereign immunity

Re Canada Labour Code, [1992] 2 S.C.R. 50, 91 D.L.R. (4th) 449. Supreme Court of Canada.

The question in this case was whether the Canada Labour Relations Board had the power to hold a certification hearing with respect to the Canadian civilian support staff at the United States naval base at Argentia, Newfoundland. The United States claimed sovereign immunity from the Board's jurisdiction. The union maintained that such immunity was denied by section 5 of the State Immunity Act, now R.S.C. 1985, c. S-18, which says that a foreign state "is not immune from the jurisdiction of a court in any proceedings that relate to any commercial activity of the foreign state." As a subsidiary argument, the union relied on Article 9(4) of the North Atlantic Treaty Status of Forces Agreement (SOFA), under which "[t]he conditions of employment and work . . . shall be those laid down by the legislation of the receiving state."

The Federal Court of Appeal, whose decision is noted in 28 *Canadian Yearbook of International Law* 592 (1990), held that the contracts of employment in question were by their nature "commercial activity," notwithstanding that their ultimate purpose was public or governmental. The Supreme Court of Canada reversed that decision by a majority of three to two. All the judges agreed that the definition of "commercial activity" in section 2 of the Act ("any particular transaction, act or conduct . . . that by reason of its nature is of a commercial character") allowed the purpose of the activity, as well as its nature, to be taken into account. Although the drafters of the definition had modelled it on the equivalent United States legislation (Foreign Sovereign Immunities Act of 1976, 28 U.S.C.S. 1603(d)), they had omitted the express statement in the American version that the issue was to be resolved according to the nature of the activity "rather than by reference to its purpose." That omission had been deliberate. The proper approach was to view the activity in its entire context.

The majority distinguished between a bare contract of employment at the base, which was of itself generally a commercial activity, and the management and operation of the base, which was a sovereign activity. The objective of the certification proceedings was the imposition of collective bargaining by the Canadian state and under the control of a Canadian court. That objective was so closely connected to the management of the base that it constituted an unacceptable interference with American sovereignty. The possibility of a legal strike, and the loss of the services of some sixty full-time employees, would interfere seriously with the operation of the base. The use of replacement workers was currently legal but might not be so in the future. Under the Labour Code, the Board would have far-reaching powers to inquire into employment decisions and make orders with respect to various management decisions on the base. All of these amounted to unacceptable intrusions into the sovereign realm.

As for Article 9(4) of SOFA, it had not been the subject of implementing legislation and so had no legal effect in Canada. Insofar as it might influence the interpretation of the State Immunity Act, it was superseded by Article 29 of the 1941 agreement between Canada (originally the United Kingdom, for Newfoundland) and the United States relating to the lease of the base, which provided that "no laws of [Canada] which would derogate from or prejudice any of the rights conferred on the United States by the Lease or by this Agreement shall be applicable within the Leased Area, save with the concurrence of the United States."

The dissenting judges thought that the certification proceedings related to commercial activity. They applied a test that was specifically rejected by the majority: namely, whether the activity in question — hiring a person to perform the various tasks that the workers in question were assigned to do — was one in which a private party could engage. The answer was yes. The workers served no purpose that was critical to the operation of the communications centre that was the core of the sovereign activity at the base. Indeed, the same work was occasionally performed by workers hired by, and working for, a private contractor called in by the base to perform the task. No valid distinction could be drawn between the contracts of employment and collective bargaining by the employees. The Board's exercise of its powers would not significantly inhibit the United States from exercising its sovereign powers at the base. There was no good reason why the support workers should be denied the benefit and protection of Canadian labour law.

Note. See also *D. & J. Coustas Shipping Co. S.A.* v. *Cia. de Navegaçao Lloyd Brasileiro* (1990), 48 F.T.R. 161 (F.C.T.D.), which held that the State Immunity Act did not apply to a Brazilian company merely because the Brazilian state had originally created the company and was still a majority shareholder. Because the company had not been shown to be an organ of the state, it could not invoke section 10(4) of the Act, which gives a state or agency of a state sixty days to challenge the registration in Canada of a judgment against it.

II. CONFLICT OF LAWS/DROIT INTERNATIONAL PRIVÉ

A. *Jurisdiction/Compétence des tribunaux*

1. *Common law and federal*

(a) *Service* ex juris

Service ex juris — *claim in respect of trust* — *location of trust property*

*Columbia Trust Co.*v. *Skalbania*, [1992] 5 W.W.R. 216, 68 B.C.L.R. (2d) 353. British Columbia Supreme Court.

In this action, the plaintiffs, an individual and his corporate vehicle, claimed that one of the defendants, a numbered company, held on trust for the plaintiffs its shares in two federally incorporated companies, or was obliged by contract to transfer those shares to the corporate plaintiff. The plaintiffs had obtained an injunction against the corporate defendant, its principal shareholder, and a British Columbia trust company with which the shares had been pledged, not to transfer or deal with the shares in question. The numbered company probably did not carry on business in British Columbia, and its principal shareholder did not reside there. The two companies whose shares were the subject of the action did not carry on business in the province. The share certificates in question were in the province, but under the federal companies legislation they were not negotiable instruments. The share registries for both companies were outside the province. Under these circumstances, Newbury, J. held that the injunction should be set aside because the court had no jurisdiction.

The plaintiffs' claim did not fall under any of the heads in Rule 13(1) of the British Columbia Supreme Court Rules, defining when service *ex juris* is authorized without leave. In particular, it was very problematical whether the alleged breach of contract was "committed in British Columbia" (Rule 13(1)(g)), because the obligation to transfer the shares would have had to be carried out in the provinces where the two share registries were situated. The injunction sought was not one "as to anything to be done in British Columbia" (Rule 13(1)(i)), because a dealing with the share certificates currently held by the trust company was legally insignificant; a change in the share registry was necessary for the shares to be dealt with effectively. Similarly, the claim for the execution of a trust was not "as to property in British Columbia" (Rule 13(1)(f)), because trust property was to be considered located where it could effectively be dealt with. In this case, that meant the place of the share registry or the place where the trustee carries on business or resides, neither of which was in British Columbia.

Service ex juris — *necessary or proper party to an action properly brought against another person served in the province*

Note. See *Suncor Inc.* v. *Canada Wire & Cable Ltd.* (1990), 114 A.R. 341 (Q.B.).

Service ex juris — *claim for injunction*

Note. See *McCulloch* v. *JPW Invts. Inc.*, [1992] 5 W.W.R. 650, 68 B.C.L.R. (2d) 382 (S.C.).

(b) *Declining jurisdiction* — *agreed choice of forum*

Note. See *Mithras Management Ltd.* v. *New Visions Entertainment Corp.* (1992), 90 D.L.R. (4th) 726 (Ont. Gen. Div.), in which the proceedings were stayed on two grounds: a contractual choice of a Californian forum, and the need to give effect, for reasons of comity, to a stay of all actions against the defendant by a United States bankruptcy court.

(c) *Declining jurisdiction* — forum non conveniens

Defendant served in the jurisdiction

Note. A stay of proceedings on the ground of *forum non conveniens* was granted in *693663 Ontario Inc.* v. *Deloitte & Touche Inc.* (1991), 109 N.S.R. (2d) 295 (C.A.), affirming (1990), 102 N.S.R. (2d) 376 (T.D.); and in *Garson Holdings Ltd.* v. *Norman Wade Co.* (1991), 111 N.S.R. (2d) 32 (T.D.). It was refused in *Paterson* v. *Hamilton* (1991), 115 A.R. 73 (C.A.); *Northland Properties Ltd.* v. *Equitable Trust Co.* (1991), 9 W.A.C. 293 (B.C.C.A.); and *Marfleet* v. *First City Trust Co.* (1991), 11 W.A.C. 299 (B.C.C.A.). A stay was refused in *May* v. *Greenwood* (1991), 85 D.L.R. (4th) 683, 4 C.P.C. (2d) 273 (Ont. Gen. Div.), because the plaintiff was claiming damages in Ontario for a statutory cause of action of which he might not be able to avail himself in Manitoba, the alternative forum. But the denial of the stay was on terms that the plaintiff not proceed further with a parallel action he had begun in Manitoba. In *Canastrand Industries Ltd.* v. The *"Lara S,"* [1992] 3 F.C. 398, 54 F.T.R. 145 (T.D.), an action was allowed to continue despite a parallel action brought by the same plaintiff in Greece; the latter was not a duplicitous proceeding because its purpose was to obtain security for payment of the eventual Canadian judgment.

Defendant served ex juris

Bushell v. *T & N plc* (1992), 92 D.L.R. (4th) 288, 67 B.C.L.R. (2d) 330. British Columbia Court of Appeal.

Three asbestos producers in Quebec were defendants in fifty-six actions brought by individuals for personal injuries suffered as a result of exposure to the defendants' products in British Columbia. Three corporations had also brought actions against the defendants for property damage allegedly caused in British Columbia by the use of the defendants' products. The defendants applied to have the service *ex juris* on them set aside or, alternatively, for a declaration that the court had no jurisdiction or would decline jurisdiction. The defendants admitted that service *ex juris* without leave was authorized by British Columbia Supreme Court Rule 13(1)(h) ("the proceeding is founded on a tort committed in British Columbia") or Rule 13(1)(o) ("the claim arises out of goods or merchandise sold or delivered in British Columbia"). They also conceded that British Columbia was as natural a forum for the actions against them as Quebec. They argued, however, that in an application to set the service aside, the burden to justify service *ex juris* was on the plaintiffs. In order to do so, the plaintiffs had to show that justice could better be done in British Columbia. In deciding that question, the court should take into consideration not only any legitimate advantage that the plaintiffs might have in a British Columbia court, but also any legitimate advantage that the defendants would have in a Quebec court of which they would be deprived if the actions proceeded in British Columbia. In this case, according to the defendants, the plaintiffs' actions would be statute-barred in Quebec. That was an advantage for the plaintiffs in British Columbia, but the obverse was that the defendants would be deprived of their right to invoke the applicable limitation period in Quebec. Thus the advantages and disadvantages were evenly balanced, and the court should find that the plaintiffs had not met the burden of demonstrating that the actions could better be heard in British Columbia.

The Court of Appeal agreed with the defendants' version of the criteria to be applied in exercising the court's discretion in relation to sustaining service *ex juris*. In cases where the defendant was served in the province, the defendant had the burden of showing that the court was *forum non conveniens*, and a plaintiff would not lightly be denied its choice of situs. In cases of service *ex juris*, the onus was on the plaintiff not just to satisfy the *forum conveniens* test, but also to persuade the court that a reasonable measure of fairness and justice sufficient to meet the reasonable expectations of the national and international legal communities would be preserved if the court exercised jurisdiction.

Nevertheless, it was held that the plaintiffs had satisfied the burden on them. The expiry of the limitation period in Quebec was not a strong factor in the defendants' favour. This was "mass tort" litigation. The reason that the writs had not been served on the defendants until after the Quebec limitation period had expired was that service had been delayed while a test case on various preliminary issues had worked its way through the British Columbia courts. A master of the British Columbia Supreme Court had renewed the writs, and they were eventually served on the defendants an average of eighteen months after they were issued. Although they had not expressly consented to the actions against them being held in abeyance, the defendants were certainly aware of the situation, and themselves benefited from the settlement of various preliminary issues in the test case. A second factor in favour of continuing the actions against the defendants was that the plaintiffs were alleging that the defendants had conspired with other asbestos producers, who were also defendants in the British Columbia litigation, to conceal the dangerous nature of their products. For that reason, it was highly desirable that the defendants should be parties along with the other principal players in the asbestos business.

Note. This case is significant, not just as a decision on jurisdiction in "mass tort" litigation, but also as the first decision to hold squarely that the burden of justifying service *ex juris* is on the plaintiff, even in a case where the rules of court permit such service without leave. Since the introduction of these rules in most provinces in the 1970s, the courts have generally tended to assume that the shift from requiring leave for service *ex juris* to permitting it without leave (in most provinces, only in roughly the same categories of claim as those in which leave could formerly have been sought) also shifted the burden on the issue of declining jurisdiction. (For an example, decided just before this case, see *Tang* v. *Cheng,* [1992] 5 W.W.R. 228, 68 B.C.L.R. (2d) 365 (S.C.).) The *Bushell* case makes it clear that the procedural shift does not mean a shift in the burden of showing the court is *forum conveniens* where service *ex juris* is challenged. The burden rests on the plaintiff, whether service is effected with or without leave. It remains to be seen whether the same reasoning will prevail in Ontario, where Civil Procedure Rule 17.06(2)(c) is worded so as to suggest that a defendant has the burden of showing that Ontario is not a convenient forum.

Other cases this year on the discretionary element in service *ex juris* were *Pandalus Nordique Ltée* v. *Ulstein Propeller A/S* (1991), 105 N.S.R. (2d) 52 (T.D.) (product liability of Norwegian manufacturer, jurisdiction taken); *Ronald A. Chisholm Ltd.* v. *Agro & Diverses Souscriptions Internationales — ADSI — S.A.* (1991), 4 O.R. (3d) 537, 2 C.P.C. (3d) 120 (Ont. Gen. Div.) (liability of French insurer, jurisdiction taken); *Furlong* v. *Station Mont Tremblay Lodge Inc.* (1991), 83 D.L.R. (4th) 750, 4 O.R. (3d) 693 (Gen. Div.) (liability of Quebec ski lodge operator for skiing accident, jurisdiction not taken); *Newgrade Energy Inc.* v. *Kubota America Corp.* (1991), 95 Sask. R. 304 (Q.B.), leave to appeal refused (1991), 97 Sask. R. 32 (C.A.) (product liability of American distributor and Japanese manufacturer, jurisdiction taken); and *Aanestad* v. *Saskatchewan* (1991), 101 Sask. R. 103 (Q.B.) (action by Saskatchewan investors against the Saskatchewan government for its role in a bank collapse in Alberta, jurisdiction taken over third party claims against Alberta residents).

(d) *Actions concerning property*

Matrimonial property

Note. See *Forsythe* v. *Forsythe* (1991), 33 R.F.L. (3d) 359 (B.C.S.C.).

Succession and administration

Note. See *Smallman* v. *Smallman Estate* (1991), 41 E.T.R. 86 (Ont. Gen. Div.), which applies the rule that a court has jurisdiction to order testator's family maintenance out of the testator's movables, wherever situated, if the testator died while domiciled in the province.

(e) *Matrimonial actions*

Divorce — transfer of proceedings to another province

Note. On the discretion to transfer corollary proceedings for custody under the Divorce Act, R.S.C. 1985, c. 3 (2nd Supp.), section 6(1), to another province, see *Palshnuk* v. *Palshnuk* (1991), 33 R.F.L. (3d) 194 (Man. C.A.); *Mohrbutter* v. *Mohrbutter* (1991), 34 R.F.L. (3d) 357 (Sask. Q.B.); and *Rempel* v. *Reynolds* (1991), 94 Sask. R. 299 (Q.B.).

Support for spouse or child

Note. The Divorce Act, R.S.C. 1985, c. 3 (2nd Supp.), gives jurisdiction to award support only where the divorce is granted by the same court: see *Lietz* v. *Lietz* (1990), 111 N.B.R. (2d) 128 (Q.B.). For jurisdiction under provincial statutes relating to support, see *Abbott* v. *Squires* (1991), 34 R.F.L. (3d) 303, 105 N.S.R. (2d) 218 (Fam. Ct.) (support ordered for child resident in the province); and *Trotter* v. *Trotter* (1992), 90 D.L.R. (4th) 554 (Ont. Gen. Div.) (no jurisdiction to vary unregistered foreign support order).

The Canadian Yearbook of International Law 1992

(f) *Infants and children*

Adoption

Note. Where a child was proposed to be adopted by residents of British Columbia, only that province's court was the *forum conveniens* for deciding on the merits of the adoption: *S.(S.M.)* v. *A.(J.)* (1992), 89 D.L.R. (4th) 204, 64 B.C.L.R. (2d) 344 (C.A.). An Alaskan Native Indian tribe, which under a United States statute had a prior right to the placement of the child, was not an entity that, under British Columbia law, could assert custody rights in opposition to the adoption.

Custody — no extraprovincial order

Note. Jurisdiction in custody was declined in favour of proceedings pending in a court in Connecticut, where the children had previously lived, in *Franford* v. *Franford* (1991), 75 Man. R. 75 (C.A.). On a court's power to vary its own custody order after the children have moved out of the province, see *Chadda* v. *Nolin* (1990), 110 N.B.R. (2d) 281 (C.A.); and *Kingwell* v. *Kingwell* (1991), 35 R.F.L. (3d) 373 (Ont. Gen. Div.).

Custody — local order — removal from province — Hague Convention on Child Abduction

Note. The use of the Hague Convention to force return of a child to Canada was discussed in *Bagnell* v. *Bagnell* (1991), 33 R.F.L. (3d) 165, 108 N.S.R. (2d) 482 (Fam. Ct.).

Extraprovincial custody orders — enforcement and variation

Note. The following cases all considered the enforceability of extraprovincial custody orders under provincial enforcement statutes: *Merasty* v. *Merasty* (1991), 33 R.F.L. (3d) 437 (Alta. C.A.); *MacKay* v. *Hough* (1991), 33 R.F.L. (3d) 218, 72 Man. R. 312 (Q.B.); *Sharpe* v. *Sharpe* (1991), 71 Man. R. (2d) 64 (Q.B.); and *de Medeiros* v. *de Medeiros* (1992), 39 R.F.L. (3d) 274 (Ont. Gen. Div.). See also *Terry* v. *Terry* (1991), 91 Sask. R. 101 (Q.B.).

Extraprovincial custody orders — enforcement — Hague Convention on Child Abduction

Note. The "serious risk of harm" exception in the Convention was applied in *H.(E.A.)* v. *H.(R.F.)* (1991), 37 R.F.L. (3d) 446 (N.S. Fam. Ct.).

(g) *Admiralty*

High seas — drilling platform

Note. See *Bow Valley Husky (Bermuda) Ltd.* v. *Saint John Shipbuilding Ltd.* (1992), 91 D.L.R. (4th) 621, 97 Nfld. & P.E.I. R. 217 (Nfld. C.A.).

(h) *Injunctions against carrying on legal proceedings in another jurisdiction*

Note. In an Alberta action, the defendants pleaded as a defence a consent judgment in a class action in United States federal court. They also applied for a stay of proceedings on the ground of *forum non conveniens*, which the court refused. They then brought contempt proceedings in the United States in respect of the Alberta plaintiffs' attempt to sue in spite of the judgment. The Alberta judge enjoined the defendant from prosecuting the American proceedings, on the ground that it was an oppressive move to keep the plaintiff from bringing the issue before the Alberta court, which had expressly decided that it should hear it: *Southern Mills Invts. Ltd.* v. *Hamilton* (1991), 83 Alta. L.R. (2d) 368, 3 C.P.C. (3d) 125 (Q.B.).

2. *Québec*

Obligations

Toute la cause d'action a pris naissance au Québec (Art. 68(2) C.P.)

Daly c. *Lalonde*, [1991] A.J.Q. 787, No 2159. Cour d'appel du Québec.

L'intimé a intenté une action en dommages-intérêts au motif d'atteinte à sa réputation personnelle et professionelle contre la défenderesse et l'appelant solidairement. La défenderesse n'avait ni domicile, ni résidence, ni bien au Québec. La Cour a rejeté la requête en exception déclinatoire de la défenderesse. Selon les faits allégués dans la déclaration, il s'agissait d'une faute délictuelle: par leur conduite illégale et malicieuse, l'appelant et la défenderesse ont miné la compétence et la crédibilité de l'intimé lors de rencontres à Montréal et à Toronto. La faute reprochée serait survenue au Québec, de même que les dommages subis par l'intimé. Le lien entre la faute et les dommages existait et les trois éléments de la cause d'action d'un recours délictuel ou quasi délictuel ont été ainsi établis. Les allégations concernant les rencontres à Montréal étaient suffisantes en elles-mêmes pour conférer compétence aux tribunaux du Québec.

Défendeur possède des biens au Québec (Art. 68(3) C.P.)

Caisse populaire Notre-Dame-de-Québec c. *de Leeuw* (1991), 43 Q.A.C. 237. Cour d'appel du Québec.

L'appelant, domicilié en Ontario, était l'actionnaire de Joaillerie Blanc d'Ivoire Inc. à qui l'intimée consentit une ouverture de crédit de 39 000 $. Dans un contrat séparé, signé en Ontario, l'appelant se porta caution de l'emprunt de Joaillerie. Joaillerie fit faillite. L'intimée poursuivit l'appelant au Québec en vertu du contrat de cautionnement. La Cour d'appel a accueilli le moyen déclinatoire de l'appelant. L'action était purement contractuelle; or, la cause d'action avait pris naissance au lieu de la formation du contrat en Ontario (articles 68(2) et (3) C.P.). Les actions de l'appelant dans la compagnie n'étaient pas des biens au Québec au sens de l'article 68(1) C.P. Le capital-action dont les actions étaient partie était inexistant en raison de l'absence de tout actif et de l'accumulation d'un important passif impayé malgré la liquidation, puisque la faillite de la société commerciale ne la libère pas de ses dettes.

Note. Veuillez voir aussi *Narni Establishment Vaduz* c. *Brooks Design Ltd.,* [1991] A.J.Q. 787, No 2159 (C.S.).

B. *Procedure/Procédure*

Common law and federal

Pretrial procedure

Discovery — reliance on foreign nondisclosure laws

Note. See *Comaplex Resources Int'l Ltd.* v. *Schaffhauser Kantonalbank* (1991), 84 D.L.R. (4th) 343, 5 C.P.C. (3d) 180 (Ont. Gen. Div.).

C. *Foreign judgments/Jugements étrangers*

1. *Common law and federal*

(a) *Conditions for enforcement by action or registration*

Jurisdiction of original court — submission by the defendant to its jurisdiction

> *Note.* See *Gourmet Resources Int'l Inc.* v. *Paramount Capital Corp.* (1991), 5 C.P.C. (3d) 140 (Ont. Gen. Div.) (submission by arguing the merits); and *Bridal Fair Inc.* v. *A.D. & D. Promotions Inc.* (1991), 85 Alta. L.R. (2d) 318, 5 C.P.C. (3d) 152 (Q.B. (M.C.)) (submission by contract).

Jurisdiction of original court — real and substantial connection

Federal Deposit Ins. Corp. v. *Vanstone* (1992), 88 D.L.R. (4th) 448, [1992] 2 W.W.R. 407. British Columbia Supreme Court.

The defendant, who at the time lived in Oklahoma, borrowed funds from two Oklahoma banks in 1985 and 1986 to finance the acquisition, together with others, of a controlling interest in certain Oklahoma banks. The lending banks later became insolvent. In 1988, the plaintiff, as liquidating agent for one bank and receiver of the other, brought actions in United States District Court in Oklahoma on the promissory notes that the defendant had given to the banks. The defendant now lived in British Columbia. He was served with process in the actions but did not appear. Judgments were given against him in default for $896,084.76 and $299,902.19 (U.S.), the principal and accrued interest, as well as for post-judgment interest accruing at the contractual rate. The plaintiff brought an action on these judgments in British Columbia.

Gow, J. held that the judgments should be enforced under the principle in *Morguard Investments Ltd.* v. *De Savoye*, [1990] 3 S.C.R. 1077, 76 D.L.R. (4th) 256 (noted in 29 *Canadian Yearbook of International Law* 556 (1991)). Although the defendant had neither been served in Oklahoma nor submitted to the jurisdiction of its courts, there was a real and substantial connection between the foreign court's jurisdiction, the transaction in respect of which it had granted judgment, and the defaulting defendant, so as to make it inherently reasonable for the foreign court to exercise the jurisdiction that it did. It was true that the *Morguard* case expressly limited its decision to judgments from elsewhere in Canada, but other first instance judges in British Columbia had already extended the new recognition rule to judgments from the United States, and Gow, J. followed them most willingly.

The defendant argued that one judgment should not be enforced because, it was said, bank documentation indicated that the bank had received $150,000 on one of the notes, which was not taken into consideration when the default judgment was obtained. The judge decided that this could not be brought within the doctrine of "manifest error" as a defence to enforcement of a foreign default judgment, even if that doctrine was still good law (it had not been applied outside British Columbia and had been expressly rejected in Ontario). A manifest error could only be relied on if it appeared on the face of the judgment. Otherwise, the rule prevailed that an enforcing court could not inquire into the merits of a foreign judgment that was entitled to recognition under the rules of the conflict of laws.

Note. The extension of the *Morguard* rule to default judgments from truly foreign courts is still controversial. The nub of the debate is whether it is reasonable to expect that defendants should defend actions against them anywhere in the world, so long as there is a real and substantial connection between the litigation and the foreign court. For, if the *Morguard* rule applies, a defendant who chooses not to defend such an action may find that the default judgment is enforceable in Canada with no opportunity to present a defence on the merits. Despite this debatable premise, the British Columbia courts were quick to treat judgments from the United States as identical to Canadian judgments for the purposes of the *Morguard* rule. The earlier cases that Gow, J. referred to were *Clarke v. Lo Bianco* (1991), 84 D.L.R. (4th) 244, 59 B.C.L.R. (2d) 334 (S.C.), and *Minckler & Kirschbaum v. Sheppard* (1991), 60 B.C.L.R. (2d) 360, 3 C.P.C. (3d) 104 (S.C.). After his judgment, two more cases held likewise: *McMickle v. Van Straaten* (1992), 93 D.L.R. (4th) 74 (B.C.S.C.), and *Moses v. Shore Boat Builders Ltd.*, [1992] 5 W.W.R. 282, 68 B.C.L.R. (2d) 394 (S.C.). The latter was under appeal at the time of writing.

The *Morguard* decision means that the common law rules for enforcement of a foreign default judgment are now much more liberal than those in the uniform Canadian reciprocal enforcement legislation, which typically reflect the pre-*Morguard* view of jurisdiction. Some judges have been persuaded, wrongly, that *Morguard* has somehow amended the reciprocal enforcement legislation: see *Fabrelle Wallcoverings & Textiles Ltd.* v. *North American Decorative Prod-*

ucts Inc. (1992), 6 C.P.C. (3d) 170 (Ont. Gen. Div.); and *Acme Video Inc. v. Hedges* (1992), 10 O.R. (3d) 503 (Gen. Div.).

(b) *Defences to enforcement by action or registration*

Public policy

Boardwalk Regency Corp. v. Maalouf (1992), 88 D.L.R. (4th) 612, 6 O.R. (3d) 737. Ontario Court of Appeal.

The defendant was sued in New Jersey on a $43,000 (U.S.) cheque he had given to an Atlantic City, New Jersey, gambling casino in repayment of its loans to him for the purposes of gambling. Judgment was given against him in default. The casino sued on the judgment in Ontario. The defendant argued that enforcement of the judgment would be contrary either to the Gaming Act, R.S.O. 1980, c. 183, or to the public policy of Ontario. By a majority, the Ontario Court of Appeal, reversing the trial judge, held the judgment enforceable. The Ontario statute could not apply as such to litigation in New Jersey, which concerned a contract whose proper law was the law of New Jersey. The only question was whether the statutory language reflected a public policy against enforcing a judgment given for a debt on such a contract. In order to impose itself on obligations otherwise subject to foreign law, public policy must run through the fabric of society to the extent that the right claimed is not consonant with Ontario's system of justice and general moral outlook. Since 1969, the prohibition of gambling in Canadian criminal law had been subject to the exception of lottery schemes conducted by a federal or provincial government. This showed that the prohibition did not reflect a public perception that gambling was immoral. Activities conducted by an enterprise licensed by the state of New Jersey could not be regarded as carrying a different colour of morality from those sanctioned by a Canadian government. The dissenting judge thought that the Criminal Code prohibition of gambling did reflect a general public policy that applied to a case like this, in which the casino's activity could not have been licensed under the law of Ontario. Judgment was given for the principal amount of the debt, plus prejudgment and postjudgment interest at the rate prevailing in New Jersey, converted from United States into Canadian currency at the exchange rate prevailing on the date of the Ontario judgment.

Note. See also *Auerbach c. Resorts International Hotel Inc.*, below, under 2. Québec, (a) *Exemplification — conditions de fond.*

(c) Enforcement by registration under reciprocal enforcement of judgements legislation

Note. See *Fabrelle Wallcoverings & Textiles Ltd.* v. *North American Decorative Products Inc.*, above, under (a) *Conditions for enforcement by action or registration.*

(d) Enforcement by registration under reciprocal enforcement of maintenance orders legislation

Note. On the enforcement of final maintenance orders made corollary to divorce proceedings in another province, see *British Columbia (Director of Maintenance Enforcement)* v. *Fults* (1991), 63 B.C.L.R. (2d) 169 (S.C.); and *Whalley* v. *Barsalou* (1990), 114 N.B.R. (2d) 384 (Q.B.). On the confirmation of provisional orders made in another province, see *B.(K.J.)* v. *P.(E.G.)* (1992), 90 D.L.R. (4th) 364 (Man. C.A.), which held that the confirmation could include a finding of paternity on which the original court had made a preliminary finding; and *Jordanov* v. *Filon* (1991), 33 R.F.L. (3d) 306, 96 Sask. R. 152 (Q.B.).

(e) Arbitral awards

Enforcement — New York Convention

Note. See *Compania Maritima Villa Nova S.A.* v. *Northern Sales Co.*, [1992] 1 F.C. 550 (C.A.), in which an English arbitral award was enforced under the United Nations Foreign Arbitral Award Act, R.S.C. 1985, c. 16 (2nd Supp.). The limitation period for enforcing the award was held to be the period fixed by Canadian law, not English law.

Enforcement — UNCITRAL Model Law

Note. See *Schreter* v. *Gasmac Inc.* (1992), 89 D.L.R. (4th) 365, 41 C.P.R. (3d) 494 (Ont. Gen. Div.), which enforced an American arbitration award under Article 35 of the UNCITRAL Model Law, enacted by the International Commercial Arbitration Act, R.S.O. 1990, c. I.9, and considered several defences under Article 36.

2. *Québec*

(a) *Exemplification — conditions de fond*

Ordre public

Auerbach c. *Resorts International Hotel Inc.*, [1992] R.J.Q. 302, 89 D.L.R. (4th) 688. Cour d'appel du Québec.

L'appelant régla une dette de jeu dans un hôtel du New Jersey à l'aide d'un chèque personnel de 10 000 $ (U.S.) que sa banque refusa d'honorer, faute de provision suffisante. Le 1er avril 1985, le tribunal compétent du New Jersey rendit jugement pour cette somme contre l'appelant. Cette action lui avait été signifié à son domicile au Québec, mais il ne la contesta pas. Il était admis que le jeu est légal au New Jersey et qu'une dette de jeu peut faire l'objet de procédures en recouvrement devant les tribunaux. L'appelant a prétendu que les tribunaux québécois ne devraient pas accorder l'exemplification du jugement, et ce, pour des raisons d'ordre public liées au fait que l'article 1927 C.C., dénie le droit d'action pour recouvrement de dettes de jeu.

La Cour d'appel a affirmé la décision de la Cour provinciale (notée dans le tome 1987 de cet *Annuaire* à la page 515) d'accueillir l'action en exemplification du jugement. Lorsque l'authenticité d'un jugement étranger n'est pas contestée, l'article 1220 C.C. permet d'inférer l'existence d'une présomption suivant laquelle un droit a été régulièrement acquis à l'étranger. C'est la partie contestant ce droit qui doit prouver que le jugement étranger est erroné. Les seules défenses qui peuvent être soulevées sont celles que le défendeur aurait pu soulever devant le tribunal étranger.

L'appelant n'aurait pas pu invoquer une défense comme celle prévue à l'article 1927 C.C. au New Jersey. Tous les contrats de jeu ne sont pas illégaux ou immoraux au Québec. L'article 1927 C.C., puisqu'il dénie un droit d'action, doit être strictement interprété. Il ne s'applique pas à un contrat soumis à une juridiction étrangère lorsque le jugement rendu ne viole pas les principes d'ordre public du Québec. En matière d'exemplification de jugement, l'ordre public est moins exigeant. Les tribunaux québécois agissent avec plus de retenue devant ce concept évolutif quand il s'agit de l'appliquer à la reconnaissance de droits valablement acquis à l'étranger. Vu le nombre grandissant de loteries et de jeux divers ici et ailleurs, on ne peut pas être surpris que les contrats de jeu soient permis et qu'ils soient susceptibles d'action devant les tribunaux étrangers. Il serait plutôt contraire à l'ordre public que le Québec devienne un refuge pour les joueurs, qui pourraient ainsi conserver le fruit tiré d'une activité de jeu et de pari tout en refusant de s'acquitter de dettes préalablement contractées.

(b) *Exemplification — révision*

Turbide c. *Chevarie*, [1992] R.J.Q. 745. Cour supérieure du Québec.

The plaintiff and her late husband, domiciled in Quebec, were staying at a trailer park in Florida. There her husband stopped to watch the defendants, also domiciled in Quebec, trying to start the mobile home that belonged to one of the defendants. They were trying to start it by pouring gasoline into the carburetor. As a result of the defendants' negligence, the plaintiff's husband was severely burned when he was struck by a quantity of gasoline that had ignited. After an unsuccessful application for compensation to the Régie de l'assurance automobile du Québec, and an action in the Quebec Superior Court that was abandoned, the plaintiff and her husband brought an action in Florida against the defendants, who were personally served there and defended the action. The plaintiff's husband obtained judgment for $250,000 (U.S.), the plaintiff a judgment for $10,000 (U.S.), and a third judgment was given for costs. The plaintiff and her husband brought the present proceedings in Quebec for exemplification of the Florida judgments under Article 178 C.P. The claim of the husband, who died during the proceedings, was continued by the plaintiff as his universal legatee and executrix of his estate.

Halperin, J. exemplified the judgments. The plaintiff had shown that the Florida court had international jurisdiction. The grounds of international jurisdiction paralleled those in article 68 C.P. for the jurisdiction of the courts of Quebec. Here, the whole cause of action arose in Florida (by analogy with Article 68(2) C.P.), both defendants were personally served there, and both submitted to the court's jurisdiction.

The judge rejected arguments of bad faith and public policy, which were based on the fact that the plaintiff and her husband had brought their action in Florida. Their failure to appeal the rejection of their claim by the Régie was not by itself evidence of bad faith. They had the choice of seeking compensation by commencing litigation either in Quebec or in Florida. They were entitled to sue in the jurisdiction that best suited their legitimate interests.

Under article 178 C.P., the defendants could raise defences that would have been available in the original jurisdiction. The defendants argued that the plaintiff's civil action was barred by the Loi sur l'assurance automobile, L.R.Q., c. A-25, and Article 1056d C.C., which restrict a person injured in an accident arising from the use of an automobile to the remedies in the automobile insurance legislation. The court held that, even if the accident arose from the use of an automobile, which on the facts it did not, it was doubtful whether it could take away a right of action for an accident that took place outside Quebec. In any event, it was certain that it could not apply to the exemplification of a foreign judgment on a claim arising out of a foreign accident. Nor could the defendants invoke the prescription of the original claims under Article 2190(2) C.C. before the actions were brought in Florida, since the prescription rules of the *lex loci delicti* were obviously applicable in the Florida proceedings. The amounts of the Florida judgments were converted into Canadian currency at the rate of exchange on the dates of the original judgments; it made little difference whether that date was used or the date on which the action in exemplification was commenced.

D. *Choice of law (including status of persons)/Conflits de lois (y compris statut personnel)*

1. *Common law and federal*

(a) *Characterization*

Procedure or substance

Note. See *Furlong* v. *Station Mont Tremblay Lodge Inc.* (1991), 83 D.L.R. (4th) 750, 4 O.R. (3d) 693 (Gen. Div.) (Quebec limitation period for delictual claim held substantive); and *Cardel Leasing Ltd.* v. *Maxmenko* (1991), 2 P.P.S.A.C. (2d) 302 (Ont. Gen. Div.) (British Columbia "seize or sue" rule for enforcement of rights under equipment lease held substantive, but applicable anyway to an Ontario lease by virtue of an express clause in the contract).

Procedure or substance — right to maritime lien

Note. Shibamoto & Co. v. *Western Fish Producers Inc. Estate*, [1991] 3 F.C. 214 (T.D.) applied the Canadian rule that whether a claim gives rise to a maritime lien is a question of substantive rights, governed by the law of the place where the lien is said to have arisen.

(b) *Contract*

Proper law — agreed choice — implied agreement

Note. Ontario Bus Industries Inc. v. *The Federal Calumet*, [1992] 1 F.C. 245 (T.D.), held that notwithstanding an express choice of forum in the bill of lading in favour of the courts of Canada, a contract of carriage from Belgium to Canada was governed by Belgian law, as indicated by an express reference to the Hague-Visby Rules, which were compulsorily applicable under Belgian law.

(c) *Torts*

Tort outside the province

Tolofson v. *Jensen* (1992), 89 D.L.R. (4th) 129, [1992] 3 W.W.R. 743. British Columbia Court of Appeal (Leave to appeal granted, Oct. 1, 1992 (S.C.C.)).

The plaintiff, then twelve years old, was injured in 1979 in an accident when he was a passenger in his father's automobile in Saskatchewan. He and his father, then as now, lived in British Columbia; the car was registered and insured in that province. In 1987, after reaching his majority, he began an action against his father, as the driver of the car in which he was injured, and against the Saskatchewan resident who drove the other car involved in the accident. In British Columbia, the applicable limitation period was postponed owing to the plaintiff's having been a minor at the time of the accident. In Saskatchewan, the limitation period was not postponed on that account, and had expired in 1980. Moreover, at the time of the accident, Saskatchewan law did not permit a passenger to sue his driver unless he could prove wanton or wilful misconduct. British Columbia law gave recovery for simple negligence.

A motion that the action against the father be stayed on the ground of *forum non conveniens* was dismissed on the ground that the plaintiff had legitimate juridical advantages if he sued in British Columbia — namely, the differences in the applicable limitation period and the standard of care. On appeal, it was conceded that the *forum non conveniens* argument could not succeed, but the defendant father argued for a declaration that the law to be applied to the issues of the limitation period and the standard of care was the law of Saskatchewan. The Court of Appeal held that the case was covered by *McLean* v. *Pettigrew*, [1945] S.C.R. 62, which held that a plaintiff can recover for a tort committed outside the province on the basis of the tort law of the forum, so long as the defendant's act was a civil or criminal wrong by the law of the place where the tort was committed. The court refused to distinguish *McLean* v. *Pettigrew* in order to apply the Saskatchewan rules as to civil liability. A number of Ontario cases involving accidents in Quebec had distinguished *McLean* and applied the Quebec law of delict, including its statutory bar to any civil action arising out of an automobile accident. In each of those cases, however, the basis of the distinction was that the defendant had been a resident of Quebec and had no reason to expect that any law other than that of Quebec might apply. Here the defendant was a resident of British Columbia, and applying British Columbia law in respect of the present suit would not seem inappropriate. The fact that another defendant was a resident of Saskatchewan did not alter this conclusion. The court also noted that both the Saskatchewan rules in question, relating to the limitation period and the standard of care, had been repealed since the accident.

Note. See also *Kim* v. *Yun* (1991), 4 O.R. (3d) 455, 6 C.C.L.I. (2d) 263 (Ont. Gen. Div.), which applied Ontario law to an action by one Quebec resident against another for injuries suffered in an accident in Ontario; and *Furlong* v. *Station Mont Tremblay Lodge Inc.* (1991), 83 D.L.R. (4th) 750, 4 O.R. (3d) 693 (Ont. Gen. Div.).

(d) *Property*

Movables — tangible — personal property security

Note. See *Re Searcy*, [1992] 1 W.W.R. 573, 8 C.B.R. (3d) 11 (B.C.S.C.), on when a creditor "has knowledge" that goods have been brought into a province, so as to begin the period within which the creditor's security interest must be registered in order to "continue perfected" in the province; and *Advance Diamond Drilling Ltd.* v. *National Bank Leasing Inc.* (1992), 3 P.P.S.A.C. (2d) 154 (B.C.S.C.), which held that the priorities between two security interests had to be decided according to Ontario law, which governed the validity of both interests. See also *Mithras Management Ltd.* v. *New Visions Entertainment Corp.* (1992), 90 D.L.R. (4th) 726 (Ont. Gen. Div.).

Matrimonial property

Tezcan v. *Tezcan* (1992), 87 D.L.R. (4th) 503, 62 B.C.L.R. (2d)
344. British Columbia Court of Appeal.

The plaintiff brought an action in British Columbia against her
former husband, resident in Turkey, claiming a share of her husband's interests in certain immovable property in Vancouver, British
Columbia, on the basis that these were family assets under Part 3 of
the Family Relations Act, R.S.B.C. 1979, c. 121. The parties were
originally from Turkey but had lived in Vancouver from 1961, soon
after their marriage, until 1968. In that year they returned perma-
nently to Turkey, where they lived for the remainder of their
marriage. They were divorced in 1983 in Turkey. The divorce
decree did not deal with the parties' property. Under Turkish law, as
found at trial, a husband and wife are separate as to property unless
they expressly agree to adopt another regime, which the parties in
this case had not done. The Family Relations Act includes no
provision on choice of law.

The court upheld the decision of Harvey, J. in a decision noted in
28 *Canadian Yearbook of International Law* 627 (1990) that the
British Columbia statute applied. According to both Turkish law, as
proved, and British Columbia law the wife's claim was to be characterized as one for an interest in immovable property, and was thus
governed by the *lex situs* of the property. The fact that a court could
vary the extent of a spouse's interest depending on the equities
between the parties did not make it a personal claim that might be
considered to be movable property. It was an interest in the asset
itself. The right created by the statute was described in section
43(2) as "an undivided half interest in the family asset as a tenant
in common." This definition of the wife's right as an interest in
property distinguished the British Columbia regime from those in
the other common law provinces, which gave only a personal right
to a share in the value of the matrimonial assets.

The husband also argued that the Turkish system of separate
property should be applied, on the ground that it was an implied
contract imposed upon the parties by law in the absence of a
contrary agreement. On the authority of *De Nicols* v. *Curlier*, [1900]
A.C. 21 (H.L.), this implied contract would extend to the parties'
rights to immovable property outside Turkey. The court held that
the existence and validity of such an implied contract had to be
determined according to the law of Turkey. The trial judge had

found, on the basis of the expert evidence, that Turkish law did not regard the regime of separate property as an implied contract. Moreover, even if there was an implied contract, the expert evidence tended to show that Turkish law would not regard it as extending to immovables outside Turkey.

The court rejected a further argument that the *lex situs* rule for determining rights in immovable property should be rejected, in the context of matrimonial property disputes, in favour of a reference to the law of the country with the most real and substantial connection with the division of property.

Finally, it was held that the judge had made no error in taking into account the value of the immovable family assets in Turkey when he decided on the apportionment of the immovable property in British Columbia. His order was varied, however, from one awarding the wife an actual share of the property to one awarding her $709,800, representing the value of that share. This would enable the husband, if he wished, to satisfy his obligations to the wife without selling the properties, which might be disadvantageous to him because of capital gains taxes and other considerations.

Note. The Court of Appeal was unimpressed with the argument that applying the *lex situs* to the wife's claim for a share of immovable family assets would open up the possibility that the family assets as a whole could be subject to different matrimonial property regimes. It was always open, the court said, for the parties to avoid this result by agreement. That is true, but there is a good deal to be said for applying a single regime in the first place. This is the solution adopted by the matrimonial property statutes in most other common law provinces. Typically, they refer questions of the division of matrimonial assets, irrespective of the location or nature of those assets, to the law of the spouses' last common habitual residence. See, for example, the Family Law Act, R.S.O. 1990, c. F.3, section 15, applied in *Bosch* v. *Bosch* (1991), 36 R.F.L. (3d) 302, 49 O.A.C. 346 (Ont. C.A.).

2. *Québec*

Propriété

Régime matrimonial

Note. Veuillez voir *A.(E.)* c. *D.(M.H.)* (1991), 42 Q.A.C. 144 (C.A. Qué.).

Book Reviews / Recensions de livres

From Coexistence to Cooperation: International Law and Organization in the Post-Cold War Era. Edited by Edward McWhinney, Douglas Ross, Gregory Tunkin, Vladlen Vereshchetin. Dordrecht/ Boston/London: Martinus Nijhoff, 1991. Pp. xiv, 297 (US $95.00).

What a contrast emerges from a comparison of Soviet legal writing of the Stalin era and scholarship after 1990! No one now holds to the "class warfare" theme. Of course, academicians of earlier years enjoyed a certain latitude in expressing views on fundamentals of international law, and none more so than Gregory Tunkin, now in his 85th year, to whom this volume is dedicated; nevertheless, before 1990 western analysts of Soviet authors believed that Soviet scholarship was dictated in the main by the communist party. Soviet authors were studied in the west not for originality of thought but as harbingers of what might be expected from Soviet diplomats at the next General Assembly.

All of this changed when Foreign Minister Eduard A. Shevarnadze, in his celebrated Siberian speech in 1989, (presumably with Secretary General M. I. Gorbachev's approval), rejected class struggle as the motivation for Soviet policy. Following this speech, the shackles placed on Soviet scholars were broken, and they dared say what they thought — or almost so. The caveat needs to be added, because Gorbachev's call for "new thinking" unleashed an element of Marxist scholasticism that emerged particularly in printed material. Conflicting views among scholars remained, but there was general agreement that, as a result of "new thinking," co-existence had made room for co-operation. Edward McWhinney called for change with the title of this volume; he did not need to add that there were no dissenting voices to argue that no change had occurred.

427

The idea of co-existence originated with Lenin. He hoped for a transition to world communism through class warfare, but, as a realist, he anticipated that neighbouring states would be hostile to that concept. Co-existence was therefore necessary for survival. During Stalin's era, Lenin's compromise was ended, and the New Economic Policy of the 1920s was wiped away and class warfare resumed. Not until Stalin's death in 1953 was there revival of the concept of co-existence by a resolution of the communist party of 1956 in the general area of foreign policy. Gregory Tunkin took up the slogan for his new concept of international law: it was to be an international law of "peaceful co-existence." His colleagues in Belgrade put the phrase upon the agenda for the Dubrovnik Conference of the International Law Association, but they replaced an adjective; it was to be a law of peaceful co-existence, but it was to be renamed as "active co-existence."

So much for history: today all Soviet authors have abandoned class warfare as an instrument of international law. Gregory Tunkin sets the goal of the new aim with a newly minted policy. In his words: "National interest must be subordinate or at least reconciled with the common interest of mankind." He envisages a law of humanity as a whole, not a class law to stimulate change.

McWhinney in his paper finds Soviet policy making the same five points today that are enunciated by western scholars. He concludes that very little in the operational definition of the "New Thinking" program for reconstruction of international law and organization could or should surprise or upset Canadian jurists.

Within this volume, a reader can explore a wide variety of ideas that advance the search for peace, propounded by authors from both east and west. For example, V. S. Vereshchetin, who is frequently said to have inherited Tunkin's mantle, discusses former President Eisenhower's proposal for "open skies." He senses that mutual surveillance of this type would heighten confidence, but he thinks the policy gives too little attention to outer space. In his view, the increasing militarization of space is alarming, and he would support France's proposal for an International Space Agency.

John J. Noble of Canada lauds the Draft Committee on Open Skies, but he says that Canada still wants a more accommodating partner. He senses that the Soviet side still fears that the west will try to undermine it, and that significant bastions of old thinking remain within the bureaucracies of both superpowers.

Douglas Ross continues in this vein. He commends what has been done to clear the way for new thinking on the nuclear disarmament process, but finds many obstacles remaining. Control, in his view, must be broadened.

Sergei Federenko, in reviewing the achievements and failures of SALT, sees a still-surviving legacy of superpower conflict that is likely to persist for the foreseeable future. He finds faults in the negotiating process, and proposes that the existing negotiating teams of military officers be replaced by mixed teams in both Moscow and Washington. He proposes a permanent bilateral forum of military, political, and technical experts to exchange information on strategic stability and the arms control process.

Serge April, in his paper on the environment, points out that no place, even the Arctic, is safe from environmental damage, and expresses the hope that new laws will be enacted to address this problem. He believes that this issue requires not solely the attention of lawyers but a multidisciplinary approach.

Charles B. Bourne is concerned with the protection of fresh water resources. He notes the emergence of new law, but urges that attention also be paid to procedures, such as consultation and negotiation that have already been used successfully by the international community in making new laws.

The paper by A. Movchan discusses the issues raised by navigation on the north coasts of Canada and the Soviet Union. Applying the rules of maritime law, he argues that espionage on the coasts is an issue that can be met only by continuing to apply the rule of innocent passage. He hails the United Nations Law of the Sea of 1982 as a long step forward, and lauds the Soviet-Canadian Conference of International Law and Arms Control Specialists.

Returning to the topic of transnational co-operation, Jason Reiskind reviews the remarkable case of COSMOS 954, which dropped radioactive debris on Canada when controls failed. He argues that low earth orbits of this type must be prohibited. Nicholas Mateesco Matte, in his survey of the 1964 Outer Space Treaty, concludes that, although communication satellites have opened up the world, their use carries an element of risk. He argues that satellites should be controlled, for they are not all benevolent.

The papers devoted to economics will hold the interest of the commercially minded, and those on human rights — an area of the law that has become especially important in recent years — will be thought-provoking for all readers. Perhaps the most elusive problem is terrorism, especially in times of emergency. Daniel Turp urges transformation of the Human Rights Committee into an expert body whose role will be to codify and develop the law. He also envisages the establishment of an international court of human rights.

McWhinney and Ross add a postscript to this volume. In their view, the end of Cold War public order has forced the Soviet Union to transcend its original ethno-cultural Russian sources and enter into the general language of discourse of contemporary international law and organization throughout the world community. Certainly this volume testifies to the accuracy of this conclusion. It now leaves to the new era the resolution of disputes that are stimulated not by the Cold War but by simple greed and by endless revanchist efforts to cleanse ethnic communities. There is much yet to be done to advance the cause of peace.

JOHN N. HAZARD
Columbia University

International Law in Theory and Practice. By Oscar Schachter. Dordrecht: Martinus Nijhoff, 1991. Pp. xi, 431. (Dfl 250).

Oscar Schachter is that rarest of persons — one who has combined a lifetime of service as an active international legal practitioner with years of dedicated scholarship within the academic community. His lucid commentaries and analytic essays have been received over the years with the utmost of respect, and have been awarded some of the most eminent citations available within the discipline, among them the Manley Hudson Gold Medal.

The treatise reviewed here originated in the materials presented by the author to the 1982 General Course at the Hague Academy of International Law. Its format is accordingly as sweeping as may be expected in those circumstances, ranging from observations on the nature of principles of international law through a careful analysis of the prohibition, uses, and responses to force, and on to discussions of jurisdiction and enforcement of awards. The original lectures (published earlier in the Recueil des Cours series) have been revised and extended in the light of changing practices in the intervening decade. Written for this volume, for example, are chapters on the environment and on collective security. Also, the volume includes a balanced and useful commentary on the United Nations Law of the Sea Convention and a discussion of the novel treatment accorded the sea-bed beyond national jurisdiction. A particularly attractive chapter is dedicated to the dynamics engendered by the tensions between sovereign rights and international business.

Professor Schachter has not missed the opportunity to express his own deeply-felt convictions. As did Judge Manfred Lachs in his similar volume a few years ago,[1] this author dedicates considerable attention to the challenging, evolving, and often controversial field of international human rights. He states forcefully his view that economic and social rights and obligations are inextricably linked, as are the relationships between countries north and south. "There is an obvious failure of the developed world to meet the most pressing needs of the needy and disadvantaged States. . . . [W]e are all in the same boat and must act to overcome the tragic imbalance that now exists."

In his preface, Professor Schachter reveals his own experience as well as the high level of his convictions when he writes that international law is not simply a reflection of political power but has "its distinctive character and relative autonomy." In theory and in practice, from broad overviews to specific examples, the meticulously disciplined and coherent mind of this eminent and persuasive jurist is throughout clearly revealed. This treatise deserves to be an enduring and oft-referred volume in public and personal libraries throughout the international community.

IVAN L. HEAD
University of British Columbia

---

[1] *The Development and General Trends of International Law in Our Time* (Dordrecht: Martinus Nijhoff, 1984).

International Human Rights: Problems of Law, Policy and Practice. By Richard B. Lillich. 2d ed. Boston: Little Brown, 1991. Pp. 1062. ISBN 0-316-52616-9.

Like its predecessor, edited jointly by Professor Lillich and Justice Newman, the second edition of *International Human Rights*, edited this time by Lillich alone, is intended as a teaching guide for use in American law schools. The difference between it and the first edition is that the problems chosen for discussion have been selected to deal with issues that have arisen in the twelve years that have elapsed between editions.

Following the first edition, the twelve problems have been divided into three groups. The first group is devoted to the substantive law found in or flowing from the Charter. The first problem is concerned with Idi Amin's expulsion of Asians. This is followed by an account of the extent to which national courts are bound by the Charter, in the light of *Sei Fujii* v. *California* (217 P.2d 481 (1950), 242 P.2d 617 (1952)), *Filartiga* v. *Pena-Irala* (630 F.2d 876 (1980)), *Fernandez* v. *Wilkinson* (505 F.Supp. 787 (1980), and *Forti* v. *Suarez Mason* (694 F.Supp. 707 (1988), which showed a slight retreat from *Filartiga* in holding that there had been a failure to "establish that there is anything approaching universal consensus as to what constitutes 'cruel, inhuman or degrading treatment'." The third problem in this group investigates the obligations that states have assumed under UN human rights treaties, examining from this point of view the question of Surinam and the Covenant on Civil and Political Rights. The first group closes with an examination of the extent to which the UN can create human rights norms other than by treaty or resolution, using as an example the Standard Minimum Rules for the Treatment of Prisoners.

The second group of problems deals with the procedural methods by which human rights law is "enforced" by the United Nations or by other international or national action. The most significant problems faced by the United Nations, as may now be seen in connection with the allegations of war crimes and crimes against humanity in Bosnia-Hercegovina, is that of fact-finding. Some sixty pages of the text are devoted to this issue, culminating in two pages from the judgment of the Inter-American Court of Human Rights in the *Velásquez Rodriguez* case, 1988. This is followed by a section that deals with the right of petition by individuals and non-governmental organizations. The issue of sanctions against South Africa is used to exemplify the effectiveness of coercive measures in securing compliance with human rights standards. This part of the volume closes with the problem of Bangladesh as an example of the use of force by the United Nations or by member states in the name of human rights. It is to be anticipated that a third edition would substitute the problems arising in Bosnia or Somalia for, or in addition to, this example.

The final group is devoted to four unrelated matters. First, there is a discussion of the activities of the European Court of Human Rights as seen in *Ireland* v. *United Kingdom* (1977) and the *Soering* case (1989); the latter is a most important case with regard to extradition when the death penalty is involved. The work of the Inter-American Court brings further comment on *Velásquez Rodriguez*. Second, there is comment on the problem of human rights during armed conflict and states of emergency, looking at My Lai and Calley, *Yamashita*, Protocol I, 1977, and the *Nicaragua* case before the International Court of Justice, together with Protocol II, 1977, and states of emergency. Surprisingly, *Ireland* v. *U.K.* is not mentioned in this regard. The third section is concerned with international criminal law — war-crimes, genocide, *apartheid*, terrorism, and torture — as a means of enforcing respect for human rights; while the final section is devoted to a problem that has become increasingly significant since the Carter regime — namely, the use of human rights as a weapon of foreign policy.

Lillich's collection, in addition to examining the issues mentioned, provides a selection of doctrinal material and a number of questions concerning each. This textbook is a useful addition to the increasing volume of material now available to students in the field of human rights law.

L. C. GREEN
University of Alberta, Edmonton

International Human Rights Law. By Anne F. Bayefsky. Toronto: Butterworths, 1992. Pp. lxvi, 756. ISBN 0-409-90372-8.

Since the adoption of the Charter of Rights and Freedoms, there has been a plethora of writings on its significance, while the number of judicial decisions relating to its application is constantly increasing. Often, however, both writers and judges appear to have little interest in, or awareness of, the extent to which the Charter reflects the philosophies of the Universal Declaration of Human Rights or the International Covenants to which Canada is a party. Frequently, they also seem to ignore the fact that the Charter sometimes uses the language of the European Convention, even though the interpretations of the European Court might be helpful in interpreting the Canadian Charter. Moreover, now that Canada is a member of the Organization of American States, Canadian lawyers and judges might do well to make themselves aware of the terms of the American Convention and the activities of the American Court and Commission.

Professor Bayefsky's *International Human Rights Law* helps to fill the lacuna, emphasizing the connection between Canadian law and the international law of human rights. In fact, the subtitle of her book is "Use in Canadian Charter of Rights and Freedoms Litigation." Readers may be surprised to find that, regardless of the cynicism often shown by Canadian lawyers towards international law, Professor Bayefsky is able to cite in a mere 143 pages no less than 205 cases between 1982 and the end of 1990 in which there was reference to one or other of the international instruments dealing with human rights, starting with *Canada (A.G.)* v. *Stuart*(1982), 137 D.L.R. (3d) 740, when the Federal Court of Appeal refused to consider the Convention on the Elimination of All Forms of Discrimination Against Women in interpreting the 1971 Unemployment Insurance Act (p. 72), and finishing with *R.*v. *Keegstra* (1990) 1 C.R. (4th) 129, when Dickson, C. J. referred to both the Convention on the Elimination of Racial Discrimination and the International Covenant on Civil and Political Rights (pp. 80-91).

The bulk of the book is taken up by a variety of appendices, reproducing the relevant articles of the various international documents as well as citing the decisions of international organs that may be relevant to the various provisions in the Canadian Charter. Professor Bayefsky's most useful appendix is that in which she compares the Charter with international human rights law on a section-by-section basis.

The author's method of comparing cases in showing both the positive and negative attitude of the Supreme Court towards international law is interesting. Thus, in *Smith* v. *R.*, [1987] S.C.R. 1045, concerning the minimum term of imprisonment for importing narcotics, the Chief Justice stated that "experience in other countries regarding the Covenant and the Optional Protocol, to which Canada acceded in 1976, may on occasion be of assistance in attempting to give meaning to relevant provisions of the Charter. However, I am not aware of any international jurisprudence on the interpretation of Article 7 [of the Covenant] that would be of assistance to us in the present appeal" (p. 81) In contrast, in *R.* v. *Milne*, [1987] 2 S.C.R. 512, when the problem concerned a reduction in the statutory sentence subsequent to the commission of the offence and the application of the Covenant, the Supreme Court was not prepared to give the same consideration to the Covenant and Canada's international obligations thereunder "where the Charter contained clear words to the contrary" (p. 83).

While readers will be most interested in examining the extent to which Canadian courts have applied — or failed to apply — conventions to which Canada is a party, it is also worth being reminded that some judges are prepared to go further, looking to the European Convention, as was done by the Ontario Court of Appeal in *R.* v. *Kopyto* (1987), 61 C.R. (3d) 209, leading Professor Bayefsky to comment that such decisions "indicate (1) that such law, including the European Convention of Human Rights and its jurisprudence, is relevant in the same sense as United States law — it is informative, but not binding; and (2) that the informative value of such law is increased by the language of the Charter, in particular s.1's reference to limitations demonstrably justified in a 'free and democratic society.' The jurisprudence of the European Convention, *inter alia*, is relevant in determining the requirements of a free and democratic society" (p. 128).

One value of Professor Bayefsky's *International Human Rights Law* lies in the material it offers to practitioners in the field to enable them to use, whenever relevant, the provisions of international instruments, particularly those to which Canada is a party, when arguing cases relating to the Charter. "There is now what might be identified as a Charter era in the relationship between domestic law and international convention law in Canada. In unprecedented degrees conventional law, both binding and non-binding, has been cited in Canadian courts. The Supreme Court of Canada has indicated that such references are legitimate, and even required in the case of binding obligations. This legal development is consistent with the representations of Canadian officials both abroad and at home. Both federal and provincial governments have made it clear that it is appropriate for Canadian courts to refer to international law in the course of interpreting domestic law. These views have primarily been expressed in the context of the Charter" (p. 129). One might hope that this willingness to refer and even use international law would spread to other areas, such as prosecutions of war criminals.

L. C. GREEN
University of Alberta

The Nuremberg Trial and International Law. Edited by George
Ginsburgs and V. N. Kudriavtsev. Dordrecht: Martinus Nijhoff,
1990. Pp. xvi, 288 (U.S. $125.00). ISBN 0-7923-0798-4.

The decision of the Security Council in 1992 to establish a
Commission to investigate allegations of war crimes and crimes
against humanity in the former Yugoslavia revived interest in the
precedent set by the International Military Tribunal at Nuremberg.
The value of this collection of essays by American and Soviet
scholars, edited by Professors Ginsburgs of Rutgers and Kudriavtsev
of the Soviet Academy of Sciences, is reduced somewhat by the
chauvinism and prejudices of some of the contributors. Too often
they appear to be involved in a contest to prove that the United
States or the Soviet Union played a major role in agitation for the
prosecution of war criminals, or for introducing this or that part of
the London Charter establishing the Tribunal, or for particular
charges in the indictment.

Moreover, some of the Soviet contributors seem to have been
more concerned with serving party ideology — which they may now
be regretting — than contributing to academic study. This may be
seen, for example, in the paper by Professor Lukashuk on "International Illegality and Criminality of Aggression," in which he
states that "a historic benchmark in the creation of conditions for
the prohibition of aggression and resort to force in general was the
Great October socialist revolution, the revolution of peace and
justice" (p. 124). He goes on to praise the "decree of peace"
prepared by Lenin and affirmed by the Congress of Soviets in 1917,
which condemned "the seizure of foreign lands and the forcible
annexation of foreign peoples" (*ibid.*), and refers to the non-
aggression treaties entered by the Soviet Union, including that with
Lithuania (p. 128), but makes no mention, critical or otherwise, of
the absorption of that and other Baltic states. Perhaps the worst
offender is Mme Lediakh, whose contribution to the final chapter
on "The Influence of the Nuremberg Trial on the Development of
International Law" is concerned with "the application of the
Nuremberg principles by other military tribunals and national
courts." Her main purpose, however, appears to be to fight the
Cold War. She compares the record of the western allies and the
German Federal Republic regarding war crimes trials unfavourably
with that of the Soviet Union (pp. 265, 272-76), and consistently
beats the party drum. This is made clear when, in citing the *Krupp*
trial, she states "the organic link between the activities of the

monopolies and the Hitlerite state apparatus was fully laid bare, [and] the decisive role of the German monopolies in Hitler's seizure with the aim of employing the Nazi regime as a weapon in the fight against and the repression of the workers' movement and its vanguard — the Communist Party of Germany — was brought to light" (p. 273).

Nearly every one of the contributors refers to the atrocities committed against civilians in both Germany and the occupied territories. The Soviet contributors rightly mention the numbers murdered in the Soviet Union and eastern Europe and the concentration camps, but, while "Russians" and "Poles" are mentioned, one has to look hard to find in their papers any mention of the Jewish holocaust.

Professor Clark of Rutgers has contributed two papers, one concerning the drafting of the Charter provision on crimes against humanity and the interpretation thereof by the Tribunal (p. 177), and the other on the codification of the Nuremberg principles and subsequent development of international criminal law (p. 249). He provides an interesting insight into the "semi-colon protocol" amending Article 6(c) of the Charter, which he attributes to "a mechanical mistake in London" (p. 192). He also reminds us to remember, when assessing the Tribunal's contribution to the law on crimes against humanity, that the Tribunal confined itself to its own jurisdiction, indictment, and accused. "The opportunity open to the Tribunal to make a substantial contribution to the emerging norms on crimes against humanity *was simply not taken*" (p. 196, emphasis added). As to the significance of the Trial for the future, while recognizing that it indicated the reality of international criminal law, he points out that most post-1945 treaty developments are based not on universal jurisdiction, but on the "extradite or try" principle (p. 256).

In commenting upon the effects and lessons of Nuremberg, Professor Murphy of Villanova suggests that from an operational point of view, regardless of the position regarding war crimes and crimes against humanity, the concept of crimes against peace is a dead letter (p. 153). However, this was writtten before the International Law Commission drew up its draft on crimes against peace and security, adopting an approach far broader than that of the London Charter. Another view that has been overrun by events, especially the upsurge in neo-Nazism, is that of Professor Pomorski of Rutgers: "Through the accusation and conviction of the major

Hitlerite organizations, the Allies wanted to stigmatize Nazism as an enemy of civilization and thereby to prevent its revival. If one perceives a deterrent and preventive function of common law in a broad sense, if one views it as a consciousness-building factor, the idea of organizational prosecution fulfilled its tasks very well'' (p. 225).

Perhaps more significant is the assessment of the *nullum crimen* rule by Dr. Reshetov. He argues that there is no breach of the doctrine when international law proclaims criminality without postulating the form of trial or punishment (p. 113), especially since, more important than any such doctrine, is the rule that no serious crime should go unpunished (p. 112). Although he does not mention it, in this contention he is in agreement with the view adopted by Israeli authorities with regard to the prosecution of Eichmann.

It is not possible to comment on every contribution or view, however interesting. But those seeking to learn the background as well as the contribution of the Nuremberg Tribunal to such issues as international criminal jurisdiction and procedural law, the criminal responsibility of individuals, the concepts of crimes against peace, humanity, conspiracy, and the criminality of organizations, as well as some comments on war crimes per se, will find much to interest them in this collection of essays.

L. C. GREEN
University of Alberta, Edmonton

Mine Warfare at Sea. By Howard S. Levie. Dordrecht, The Netherlands: Martinus Nijhoff, 1991. Pp. 233 (U.S. $92.00).

Professor Levie, a professor of international law at the United States Naval War College who has published many books and articles on humanitarian law, has now written the first overall study of the military, legal, operational, and technological history of mine warfare at sea from its early beginnings to the present. The book is comprised of five chapters, three devoted to the history of mine warfare, one to the drafting of the 1907 Hague Convention on Mine Warfare at Sea, which remains the major instrument purporting to regulate this means of warfare, and one devoted to explaining technical matters in a manner understandable to the lay reader. There has been a reawakening of interest in the law of naval warfare within the last few years and this book is a very useful contribution to the debate among scholars and practitioners concerning the current state of customary law and the possible need for new treaty law.

The chapter devoted to the drafting of the 1907 Hague Convention includes an exploration of the reasons why a convention on mine warfare at sea was considered necessary. Essentially, it was because of damage caused by sea mines to commercial shipping uninvolved in the conflict during the Russo-Japanese War of 1904-6. It also contains an extended and thoughtful analysis of the negotiating history of the Convention and of the reasons why it failed to address a number of issues more effectively, in particular high seas mining, the mining of international straits, and the protection of commercial shipping. In short, this failure resulted from the fact that the two major naval powers of the time, Great Britain and Germany, had substantially different interests.

Great Britain, the pre-eminent naval power, wished to limit the use of mines so that it could enhance its control over water areas, exercise unimpeded naval mobility, and use the oceans to transport vast quantities of supplies and personnel in time of war. Germany, which was very clearly the second naval power, wished to impede Britain's ability to accomplish these objectives. As an illustration, Britain submitted a proposal that belligerents could use automatic submarine contact mines only in their territorial waters, those of their enemies, or within ten miles of fortified ports. Although there were extended discussions and the exploration of a variety of options, the Conference was unable to agree on any explicit limitations of areas outside neutral waters where mines could be used. Until the recent end of the Cold War, one might have envisaged a similar impasse between NATO members and members of the Warsaw Pact if attempts had been made to negotiate new and effective restraints on the use of mines at sea.

The 1907 Hague Convention refers explicitly merely to anchored and unanchored automatic contact mines. The chapter by Levie on technical issues discusses a wide variety of mines that function on the basis of other physical principles, in particular magnetic, acoustic, and pressure mines. It illustrates amply that when one is purporting to regulate new or emerging technology, it is unwise to utilize treaty definitions that are too narrow or that might be rendered obsolete within a few years after the treaty is drafted. Indeed, the discussion about whether the 1907 Convention applies to modern sea mines bears some resemblance to the recent and inconclusive debate over the proper interpretation of the ABM Treaty.

The chapters concerning the history of mine warfare place the law in context. The final chapter in particular, which contains brief case studies of several recent incidents in which sea mines have been used, including Vietnam (1972), the Red Sea (1984), Nicaragua (1984), and the Iran-Iraq War (1980-88), illustrates the continuing and unfilled requirement for effective legal regulation of this particular means of war.

Professor Levie concludes his chapter on the negotiating history of the 1907 Convention with the observation that "A new convention on mine warfare at sea is long overdue — but the likelihood of such a convention being drafted and becoming effective appears to be remote." With the end of the Cold War, it is possible that his conclusion is unduly pessimistic. Certainly, countries such as Sweden have been attempting to place proposals for new conventions to regulate mine warfare at sea on the agenda of a variety of fora within the last few years. Professor Levie's book, with its thoughtful analysis of both the law and the facts will have a significant impact when new conventions in this area are discussed. It also constitutes an excellent model for writers who wish to address the legal regulation of particular means and methods of war in the future.

COMMANDER W. J. FENRICK*
Commander, Director of Law for Operations and Training,
Office of the Judge Advocate General

* Views expressed in this review are those of the author only, and not of the Canadian government.

Maritime Terrorism and International Law. Ed. by Natalino Ronzitti. Dordrecht: Martinus Nijhoff, 1990. Pp. x, 185 (US $75.00) ISBN 0-7923-0734-8.

The hijacking of the *Achille Lauro* and the murder of Mr. Klinghoffer in October 1985 have stimulated a great deal of academic and other thought, particularly in Italy where the ship was registered. Since the hijacking did not satisfy the technical requirements for piracy *jure gentium* — a point cited by most of the contributors to this collection — it was recognized that there was a need to amend treaty law so that a similar act in the future could be adequately dealt with. Eventually, in 1988, the Rome Convention

on the Suppression of Unlawful Acts Against the Safety of Navigation and the Protocol for the Suppression of Unlawful Acts Against
the Safety of Fixed Platforms Located on the Continental Shelf were
adopted. The Convention, which is analyzed by Professor Treves of
the University of Milan (pp. 69-90) and the Protocol, analyzed by
Professor Ronzitti of the University of Pisa (pp. 91-96), reflect to a
great extent the provisions of the aerial terrorism conventions
adjusted to fit the maritime element.

In his opening paper, Professor Ronzitti reminds us that "maritime terrorism is quite a recent phenomenon compared to other
violent activities which may interfere with peaceful navigation"
(such as piracy or war) and, therefore, "it is useful to keep maritime terrorism separate from other forms of violence at sea in order
to avoid analogies which may prove to be false" (p. 1), and points
out that "terrorism and piracy are different phenomena, with the
consequence that rules on piracy cannot be applied" (p. 10).
Failure to appreciate these differences resulted in the United States
seeking to charge the hijackers with piracy *jure gentium*, despite the
comments of critics and the decision of Lord Stowell in *The Le Louis*
(1817), 2 Dods 210, which had pointed out that national definitions of a crime did not necessarily equate with the international
definition. Not only did the United States disregard international
law on this issue, but its action of forcing an Egyptian aircraft down
in Italy was considered "an act of armed force" and illegal (p. 12).

Questioning the rarity of maritime hijacking, Professor Menefee,
visiting at the University of Missouri, discusses in his paper a series
of takeovers, both piratical and political (pp. 43-68). One is
inclined to question his suggestion that the seizure of the *Santa
Maria* by Portuguese revolutionaries "may well have influenced the
seizure of the *Achille Lauro*" (p. 56), since the intention of the
terrorists in the latter incident had not been to seize the vessel; nor
is it clear on what basis he suggests that "publicity" may explain why
the *Santa Maria* takeover attracted "many legal commentators"
(p. 58), since this comment tends to ignore the political significance of that incident.

Professor Ronzitti makes some general comments on the right of
intervention when a maritime hijacking has taken place. Even
though a ship is under the jurisdiction of its flag state, he argues
that "with respect to its own nationals in mortal danger, a duty of
the flag State to intervene can be based only on the general duty to
protect human rights, which encompasses the fundamental right to

life. If the individuals in mortal danger are foreign citizens, a duty
to intervene can be grounded not only on the general principles
imposing the safeguard of human life, but on the more customary
international law rule which obliges States to protect foreigners"
(p. 7). However, the right to intervene is limited and "has to be
aimed not at punishing terrorists but at rescuing human beings. . . .
[Therefore,] an action which would not result in the rescue of
hostages but only in unnecessary massacre would be of a doubtful
legality" (p. 8). Unfortunately, Professor Ronzitti does not indicate
the legal basis for these views, which do not appear to coincide with
state practice when dealing with terrorist incidents.

Professor Ronzitti also suggests that when the hijacked ship is not
a flag ship of the intervening state, the intervention would normally
only be lawful if requested or permitted by the flag state. Nevertheless, if the latter was incapable of acting, intervention by the
national state of the hostages would probably be lawful (p. 8).

Closely related to the question of intervention is the paper by
Professor Gaja of Florence University, which says of terrorist acts
generally, "under certain circumstances, there may be a conflict
between the duty to fight terrorism and the duty to protect the life
and security of individuals. Moreover, the choice of one or the
other method must be viewed with regard to the risk of further
terrorist acts, which may be indirectly encouraged" (p. 18). But to
do nothing because of the risks is to suggest to terrorists that they
may operate without fear of opposition.

One of the issues that invariably arises when agreements are
made with terrorists is the extent to which they are binding and
should be observed. Professor Sacerdoti of Bergamo University has
no doubt that these agreements, like any made with kidnappers, are
"made under duress or out of necessity, and officials [should] try to
capture those responsible as soon as the hostages are out of danger
for purposes of prosecution and punishment. An obligation to do
so exists in the case of the taking of foreign hostages" (p. 29). Any
agreement with private hostage takers is, of course, not an international undertaking, but "just a set of unilateral reciprocal undertakings giving rise, at most, to 'natural obligations' and the only
sanction, in the case of non-compliance by one party, is non-compliance by the other party" (p. 31). He suggests that, although the
Egyptian safe-conduct in the *Achille Lauro* incident was probably in
breach of its obligations to both the United States and Italy, Egypt
was acting under duress to save lives; nevertheless, by the time of

the aircraft's departure with the hijackers on board, everyone was safe (p. 36).

The remaining three papers are somewhat related. Professors Leanza and Sico of Rome and Naples Universities respectively discuss the problem of compensation for victims of maritime terrorism (pp. 97-106), while the late Professor Goldie analyzes the legal proceedings in the United States arising from the *Achille Lauro* incident (pp. 107-28) and provides an interesting "excursus" on United States admiralty law concerning wrongful death (pp. 129-40). These papers should be read together with Appendices III-VI, which deal with the American court proceedings and include the text of the Memorandum by the Legal Adviser of the State Department — Judge Sofaer — on the matter. Finally, the Appendices include the texts of the Rome Convention and the Protocol, both of which may acquire major significance in the event of further acts of maritime terrorism.

From the point of view of the international lawyer, particularly the graduate student, this collection illustrates the variety of issues that a single incident may raise, and the manner in which these issues may be handled.

L. C. GREEN
University of Alberta

Settlement of International and Inter-State Water Disputes in India. By B. R. Chauhan. Published under the auspices of the Indian Law Institute. N. M. Tripathi Pvt. Ltd., Bombay, 1992. Pp. xviii, 346.

Dr. Chauhan, a distinguished Indian legal academic now retired, is an expert on international water resources law. He has studied the subject deeply, has published many works on it, and has also had practical experience as adviser to the Indian government and other bodies. In the book under review here, he revisits the subject. His objective in doing so was "to make a sound and reasonably appreciable contribution towards the solution of the problems involved in such [international and inter-state water] disputes, thereby tremendously accelerating the pace of socio-economic development in the concerned region and bestowing peace and prosperity upon the people affected thereby, including in particular the concerned under-privileged humanfolk" (Preface, p. v).

But Dr. Chauhan also set himself a more modest goal, saying that "even if this endeavour does not succeed in providing short-cuts and cut and dried solutions to all such . . . disputes in India, it will certainly make available sufficient amount of help material to successfully tackle these disputes in a flexible way. . . ." (*ibid.*). In fact, this lesser objective has been achieved; the endeavour does provide ample material for those faced with international water resources problems.

Part I of the book outlines the significance and scope of the problems of sharing water resources among states, and surveys some of the concepts and theories that have been proposed to solve these problems. Part II, entitled "International Arena," first canvasses the sources of international water resources law — juristic works, judicial decisions, the work of the leading international organizations (ILA, the Food and Agricultural Organization, the International Law Commission (ILC), and so forth); it then discusses India's water disputes with neighbouring states. Part III deals with the Indian experience with its inter-state rivers; this part starts at page 107 and continues until a few pages of the end of the book, with the exception of a short chapter on the practice of other states in dealing with their interstate or interregional water problems.

In Part III, the geographical features of seventeen Indian river basins are described first, and then there is a lengthy discussion of the history of the laws governing these rivers, from the Charter Act of 1833 until the present legal regime under the Indian Constitution of 1950. This is followed by a detailed examination of the decisions of the water dispute tribunals set up by the government of India to adjudicate five major interstate water disputes that have arisen since India gained its independence.

A particular strength of the book is found in the portion of Part III dealing with the work of the water dispute tribunals. The judgments of these tribunals are a rich source of knowledge about the legal principles and techniques that are appropriate for solving international and interstate water problems. For the most part, the tribunals held that the principle of equitable utilization and the other rules formulated by the International Law Association (ILA) in the Helsinki Rules of 1966 apply to interstate water disputes in India.

Another valuable feature is found in the concluding chapter of Part III, where Dr. Chauhan sums up the principles of law, equity, and state practice that have emerged from the decisions of the

Indian water dispute tribunals. He lists twenty-five guiding principles, thus providing, in a nutshell as it were, the essence of these decisions. Furthermore, also in this chapter, Dr. Chauhan makes a considerable number of "suggestions and recommendations" for strengthening the principles of law and the processes for settling water disputes between Indian states. His propositions apply generally, not just to India.

Notwithstanding its title, the book is really focused on India's internal water problems. India's international water problems and those of other states are discussed, but in too brief and cursory a manner. For example, the issues in dispute between India and Bangladesh over the Farakka barrage project are not adequately discussed; in fact, the reader gets no sense of the intensity of the dispute and of the legal issues raised by it.

A striking fact revealed by this work is the lack of concern about pollution and other environmental harm caused by the utilization of India's water resources. There is no mention of them in the discussion of the judgments of the water dispute tribunals, although one of the guiding principles that are said to have emerged from these judgments is that "some Tribunals have laid emphasis even on prevention of pollution of the concerned water resources" (p. 317). Dr. Chauhan recognizes this past lack of concern about environmental damage; in his recommendations, he remarks that "at present the contestant States lay their claims only to a specific quantum of water . . . but the time is approaching fast when the States will insist upon demanding a specific quantity of water with a specific quality free from all pollution, because practically every use of water needs water with specified minimum degree of qualitative purity" (p. 326). Hence, he recommends that the government of India enact "measures controlling management of water resources installations connected with inter-State rivers and river valleys for the purpose of environmental protection in general and prevention of water pollution in particular . . ." (*ibid.*).

This brief reference to pollution and environmental protection, coming only at the end of the book, points up a related gap in the discussion of the principles of international law on the subject, namely the inadequate treatment of the work of the ILC. For some twenty years the ILC has been engaged in the codification and progressive development of the law on the non-navigational uses of international watercourses and in 1991 adopted a set of draft articles on the topic. If these articles are finally adopted, they will change the law fundamentally, replacing the principle of equitable utilization, which is the rule applied in India, with the principle of "no appreciable harm." This issue has been a live one in the ILC since the mid-eighties. It is regrettable, therefore, that less than one page is devoted to the work of the ILC and that the only substantive work of the ILC referred to was done in 1980.

Apart from the shortcoming just mentioned, this book provides a valuable guide for those dealing with the problems involved in the utilization of India's interstate and international water resources. Moreover, the author's conclusions and recommendations should stimulate creative thinking in India and elsewhere on appropriate mechanisms and principles of law for the solution of these water problems.

CHARLES B. BOURNE
Faculty of Law, University of British Columbia

Yearbook of International Environmental Law, Vol. 1 (1990). Edited by Günther Handl. London, United Kingdom: Graham & Trotman, 1991. Pp. xxiv, 728 (U.S. $105.00); *Yearbook of International Environmental Law*, Vol. 2 (1991). Edited by Günther Handl. London, United Kingdom: Graham & Trotman, 1992. Pp. xxii, 784 (U.S. $195.00).

Günther Handl, long recognized as one of the top few scholars working in the field of international environmental law, has joined ranks with publishers Graham and Trotman to assemble a specialized international law yearbook that will be the envy of other subdisciplines of international law and a likely model for similar ventures in the future. Handl, his large editorial team (eight for the second volume), and a veritable college of contributors (ninety-six for the second volume) have compiled two exceedingly useful editions of the *Yearbook of International Environmental Law*. There can be no doubt that the *Yearbook* has succeeded, by its second volume, in meeting its own objective of "providing an authoritative as well as comprehensive review of internationally significant legal developments, in a format that makes information easily accessible" (p. xv, Volume 1). This review will concentrate on Volume 2, since it is the more honed publication and improves on the already fine Volume 1.

The *Yearbook* is divided into four parts. The first part is devoted to major articles. The second part, entitled "The Year in Review," contains short reports under thirteen different general headings and many more subheadings. A literature review, which constitutes the third part, is comprised of several short book reviews and a detailed bibliography of works published in the period covered by the *Yearbook*. The fourth part of the *Yearbook* is the documents section, in which selected instruments, decisions, and reports are reproduced in original form. Significantly, this documents section, beginning with Volume 2, is supplemented by computer diskettes, which contain those documents not reproduced in hard copy in the *Yearbook* itself.

The *Yearbook*'s self-designated flagship is the "Year in Review," which totals over four hundred pages in Volume 2. Taken collectively, the successive *Yearbooks* should become the researcher's first stop to get her or his bearings before going on to more detailed research. By and large, apart from being clearly written and organized, the reports can be described as insightful in the sense of passing on information and setting contexts to which the external observer and researcher would not otherwise be privy. Some of the reporters' comments on such matters as trendlines and expected actions by, and reactions of, various states would be undiscoverable through standard research methods short of contacting someone close to the process or events in question. This method of personal contact, which is almost peculiar to international law owing to the discipline's fluidity, cabal-like nature, and difficulty to research systematically, will not be displaced by the *Yearbook*. Nevertheless, the *Yearbook* will at the very least save some telephone calls and make much more informed the questions asked in others. The large majority of the almost one hundred contributors to the "Year in Review" are well-placed and well-respected scholars, practitioners, or legal counsel whose closeness to events outweighs any concern about bias that may result from that closeness.

While there are other sources (for example, *Environmental Policy and Law*) from which one can obtain reasonably current information on key events and developments in international environmental law, it is hard to overemphasize the comprehensiveness (in breadth and, for the most part, in detail) of the review reports in the *Yearbook*. These reports, in fact, are an up-to-date reference source for research on almost any imaginable environmental issue, with subtitles that include "Nuclear Waste Management," "Ozone

Layer," "'Civil Liability' and Other Forms of Transnational Accountability," and "Transboundary Movement of Hazardous Wastes." Furthermore, the Part 3 bibliography (thirty-eight pages in Volume 2) is co-ordinated with the "Year in Review" section in that they both use the same headings and subheadings for their entries. The *Yearbook* also contains a large number of reports on relevant developments in various countries or regions throughout the world and within international organizations and bodies. At this stage, the "Country/Region Reports" appear to be the biggest thorn in the side of the editors, who failed to receive eleven out of thirty-four expected contributions to this section in Volume 2. One suspects that this situation will improve relatively rapidly with successive *Yearbooks*.

Since Part 2, the "Year in Review," is the centrepiece of the *Yearbook* project, comprising well over half of Volume 2, evaluation of its "user-friendliness" is in order. As with all reference sources, it did take some time to determine how the information was organized. By and large, by combined reference to the index at the back of the *Yearbook* and to the detailed table of contents for the "Year in Review" reports, most topic searches with which this part was tested were successful. Nevertheless, there are gaps in both the index and the table of contents, and *Yearbook* users are strongly advised to use *both* of these tables under several different possible entries. For example, with respect to the recent GATT panel decision in the tuna-dolphin dispute, one index entry in Volume 2 of the *Yearbook* under "Trade/GATT/tuna-dolphin dispute, panel decision" missed coverage of the decision contained in Jay Johnson's report on "Fisheries/Marine Mammals" (at p. 210), while an index entry under "Tuna/dolphin dispute" caught the Johnson report but missed David Favre's discussion of the panel decision in his report on "Trade in Endangered Species" (at pp. 207-8). Furthermore, the table of contents for the "Year in Review" reports fails to fill in the gaps in the index entries, since neither the Johnson nor the Favre titles would necessarily suggest to a given researcher that information on the GATT panel ruling would be found in these reports. This is not, however, a serious criticism. Indeed, it represents a relatively isolated example in my testing of the referencing system, and is a picayune problem in view of the immense amount of information that is referenced in Volume 2. It is also, oddly enough, an indirect compliment to the interlocking richness of the various reports in the *Yearbook*. As Handl noted in his editorial to Volume 1, most issues are "addressed in overlapping fashion by two or more keyword entries" (p. xv). While he made this point to help mitigate any perceived bias brought about by the "close involvement of some reporters in the very developments they are called upon to analyze" (p. xv), his statement also draws attention to the value of having particular issues addressed from more than one personal or thematic perspective. Indeed, by reading each of the various treatments of the GATT panel decision in the tuna-dolphin dispute, one tends to get a more complete picture of the dispute and of the decision.

While the Part 2 "Year in Review" forms the core of the *Yearbook*, the Bibliography in Part 3 and the documents collection in Part 4 are important complementary features. The bibliography lists all forms of secondary literature, including journal articles, books, bibliographies, and edited volumes, itemizing the pieces contained in the latter sources. The inclusion of chapters from edited collections, in the manner begun only recently in the Max Planck Institute's *Bibliography of Public International Law*, should prove very useful, especially given the gap in many mainstream bibliographical services, which limit themselves to periodicals. Also, special issues of journals are treated similarly to edited collections in that "chapters" are listed together; this treatment avoids leaving the researcher to gather inductively that a particular journal issue includes several relevant articles. Finally, the section of the bibliography that corresponds to "Country/Region Reports" in the "Year in Review" is very much a comparative environmental law section and is not limited to publications that have a strictly international focus. In an era when public and private international law are increasingly entangled, as are international and municipal law, the inclusion of country-specific publications in this section is a wise choice.

Volume 2 of the *Yearbook* fulfilled the promise made by Editor-in-Chief Handl in Volume 1 to include an electronic storage service with future editions of the *Yearbook*. The subscriber to Volume 2 can order two double density 3.5" computer diskettes by sending a card (which is attached to the *Yearbook*) to the publisher. These two diskettes contain thirty-two documents which supplement the ten documents reproduced in the Part 4 Documents section of Volume 2. The table of contents for the Documents section indicates which documents are reproduced in the *Yearbook*'s pages and which are retrievable from the diskettes. The instructions are minimal; those coming with the diskettes state that they are usable on *most* IBM-compatible personal computers, while the editorial for Volume 2 indicates that they are usable on *any* such computer. There is no indication that the user's software program will make any difference, and the clear implication is that it will not — a situation that computer illiterates, such as this reviewer, may find fascinating. In any case, the diskettes worked perfectly on an IBM-compatible machine with WordPerfect 5.1 software. They were easily retrieved onto the screen, copied onto hard disk, and printed, although the latter did require going into the "Printer Control" function and then printing page by page. The possibilities surrounding this computer storage system are interesting. The documents can be easily edited and formatted for in-house handouts or materials for students, and for presentation sessions in other settings. Alternatively, sections can be copied into other documents in works-in-progress, eliminating the need to retype all the relevant sections as they are discussed and analysed.

This having been said, a number of improvements could be made to the *Yearbook*. First, the main table of contents at the beginning of the book does not include the more detailed table of contents for Part 2, "Year in Review." Rather, the latter is placed at the beginning of Part 2 (p. 55, Volume 2). It would seem useful to insert the detailed table of contents at the beginning of the volume, where it can be more easily relocated after a reader has turned to a report to determine if it contains information of interest. Since the bibliography in Part 3 uses the same entry scheme as the "Year in Review," the desirability of convenient reference to that scheme becomes even more marked. Also, from the contributor's as opposed to the researcher's point of view, it would seem appropriate to acknowledge all the contributors to each section in the "Year in Review" in the overall table of contents. One practical result of this system is that library cataloguers and compilers of periodical bibliographies who are unfamiliar with the structure of the *Yearbook* might be inclined to index those articles and book reviews whose authors are named in the main table of contents, but either leave out entirely the various reports or index them under the amorphous and anonymous general headings that appear in the main table of contents.

Apart from the relocation of the detailed table of contents for the "Year in Review," there is a need for a prominent statement preceding the bibliography to explain that it is organized on the same lines as the "Year in Review." In Volumes 1 and 2, the correspondence between these sections could easily be missed by a researcher who is unfamiliar with the *Yearbook*. The sole indication that the two sections have the same organizational headings is buried in a general statement from literature review editor Gretta Goldenman concerning all of the literature review in Part 3. Not only is this explanatory statement separated from the bibliography itself by three book reviews, but also it is misleadingly referenced in the main table of contents. The entry in the table of contents for the page in question is for "Book Reviews"; this entry is unlikely to inform researchers who are using the *Yearbook* only for its bibliography that they should consult this page before starting their search. It is likely that some researchers will end up haphazardly flipping through the bibliography with little sense of the organization of topics.

A further related point can be made about the ease of use of the bibliography. While this may strike the reader as petty, the editors and publishers might consider using a system of "headers" so that researchers can easily find the sections that they know are most likely to produce results. As it is, the researcher tends to get lost in the bibliography. For instance, told by the literature review editor Goldenman, in her above-mentioned statement, that scholarly bibliographies appear in section I.6 of the bibliography (headed "International Environmental Law in General"), this reviewer had to flip through the pages until eventually finding that section. Guidance from headers with indicators either by number (e.g., "I.6") or name (e.g., "International Environmental Law in General") would have made this search more efficient and less frustrating. The usefulness of these headers assumes, of course, that the researcher is aware that the organizational scheme of the bibliography is identical to that of the "Year in Review" and that she or he has been able to find the detailed table of contents of the latter for use in the bibliographical search.

With respect to the documents in Part 4, while the editors acknowledge that there will be disagreement over which documents appear in the *Yearbook* itself and which documents on the diskettes, they do not set out the criteria for that selection. It is not the purpose of this review to take issue with their choice. Rather, there are good arguments for including the most important documents in the *Yearbook* for more traditional reference and equally good arguments for putting them on the diskettes for more flexible and varied usage. For this reason, the Editors might consider placing the most important documents in the *Yearbook*, according to whatever criteria they specify, and putting *all* documents on computer diskette, including those that go into the *Yearbook*. Those users who find that a document is very important might, in fact, like computer access to the document for the reasons described above. The point could be taken further. Once the editors have received sufficient feedback about the usability of the diskettes in libraries and in settings that are less computer-accessible, they may wish to reduce the number of documents reproduced. This reduction of printed documents would be wise, in view of the exponential increase in their numbers in future and of the inevitable subjectivity around all but a few as to their importance. This would help keep *Yearbook* costs under control, a matter that will also be discussed in the last two paragraphs of this review. As a final suggestion, the diskettes might be shipped with the *Yearbook* rather than requiring the subscriber to make a separate request for the diskettes only after the *Yearbook* has been delivered.

A few additional, more general suggestions may be in order. Given the above-described problems related to awkwardness of use, it would seem desirable to have a clearly-designated "How to Use This *Yearbook*" section at the beginning of the book, along with cross-references to the instructions in this section at the start of each of the three research and reference parts (Parts 2–4). Also, the index should be made as comprehensive and accurate as follows. Those page numbers that refer to the main entry on any topic might be set in bold face type, and the index should clearly show where an entry is related to a corresponding document. Further, it might be better in the "Year in Review" reports for the editor to refer the reader to documents by using the indicator "doc" in bold letters rather than following the current system of bold face arrows, unless instructions that clearly explain the meaning of the arrows are included. Finally, consideration might be given to putting each year's bibliography on diskette along with the documents. A service of this type would greatly facilitate the compilation of each user's idiosyncratic personal research bibliography.

The only part not yet discussed is Part 1, which contains the major articles. Since this review has focused on the usefulness of the *Yearbook* as a research and reference tool, it is not intended to review each article beyond making the following few comments. All four articles, two in each volume, are theoretical or, at least, "big picture" pieces. In Volume 1, the two articles are Günther Handl's

"Environmental Security and Global Change: The Challenge to International Law" and Thomas Gehring's "International Environmental Regimes: Dynamic Sectoral Legal Systems." The two articles in Volume 2 are James Cameron and Jonathan Robinson's "The Use of Trade Provisions in International Environmental Agreements and their Compatibility with the GATT" and Kamen Sachariew's "Promoting Compliance with International Environmental Standards: Reflections on Monitoring and Reporting Mechanisms." The titles alone suggest the considerable ambitions of the articles and, by and large, each delivers. Some of the four pieces have proven useful in preparing various components of this reviewer's law school seminar on global environmental issues. In addition, each article has the strength of surveying a broad swathe of international environmental law in a way that is both theoretically challenging and likely to promote a greater ability of each reader to relate fundamental issues arising in her or his relatively limited subspecialty to more general theoretical and empirical considerations. Within the context of the strategic choice of the editors to make the *Yearbook* primarily a research and reference tool rather than a forum for article publishing, the choice to publish a small number of pieces of this ambitious nature makes sense. Not only is it clear what kinds of articles will get an editorial hearing (thereby rationing editorial resources), but also the *Yearbook* should attract high quality contributions as its selectivity on this score becomes recognized over time. The *Yearbook* should continue to carve out this niche and limit its articles to two or three "big picture" pieces a year.

The *Yearbook*'s editors and publishers should be praised for two relatively novel decisions. One is the "Year in Review" section's invitation to environmental non-governmental organisations (NGOs) to report on their activities as they bear on international environmental law, thereby explicitly providing a "platform for highlighting their own accomplishments" (p. xvi, Volume 1). This decision displays a healthy perspective that recognizes the importance of NGOs as transnational actors and their relative exclusion from academic and official fora. Within the two volumes, several organizations have provided NGO reports: namely, the Centre for International Environmental Law (CIEL, with offices in both London and Washington, D.C.), the Environmental Defense Fund, the International Union for the Conservation of Nature, Greenpeace International, and the Natural Resources Defense Council. To take one example, the CIEL (U.S.) entry in Volume 2 (p. 422) discusses its activities in relation to a "post-compliance" philosophy that seeks to promote a co-operative paradigm in the search for innovative and efficient solutions to international environmental problems. The second praiseworthy decision is that by Graham and Trotman to arrange for free-of-charge transfer of publication and distribution rights to publishers in developing countries, where costs of the *Yearbook* would otherwise be prohibitive even for institutional acquisitions. The explicit goal is to "ensure the availability of the *Yearbook* in those countries at a price that is truly affordable" (p. xvii, Volume 1).

A final comment should be made. The just mentioned effort to make the *Yearbook* more affordable in developing countries should not be taken to mean that the cost is not a concern in more affluent settings. It is a very expensive item. However, even at approximately $200 (Canadian), this reviewer has no hesitation in stating that the *Yearbook* is more than worth the annual investment for the institutional collections of governments, intergovernmental organizations, law libraries, law firms, corporations (whether transnational or national) that seek to track developments in environmental law, and environmental NGOs. As for non-institutional subscribers, the book is so useful as a constant reference source for those actively involved in the research, teaching, and practice of international environmental law that it is a shame that the cost cannot be less. The quality and overall usefulness of the *Yearbook* is such that this reviewer is almost tempted to say to those individuals seriously interested in international environmental law that the *Yearbook* is a must buy. Almost, but not quite. It is a purchase that should nonetheless tempt the reader and will tempt this reviewer each June or July as the *Yearbook* for the previous year comes out.

CRAIG SCOTT
Faculty of Law, University of Toronto

Basic Documents of International Environmental Law. 3 vols. Edited by Harald Hohmann. International Environmental Law and Policy Series. London: Graham & Trotman Ltd., 1992. Pp. xxxii, 1650 (U.S. $644.00).

Although several large collections of documents on environmental law and treaties already exist, the three volumes under review are justified on the grounds, first, that they include material of the sort not found in most of the other books, in particular the basic declarations by various international organizations and bodies, and second, that in any event they bring the material up-to-date.

Dr. Hohmann has included in his collection 200 documents that he considers to be the basic ones of international environmental law. His arrangement of them is especially convenient for the reader, for they are not set out chronologically but are grouped together according to subject matter. For example, in Volume I, which contains the important declarations, resolutions, or drafts of international organizations and other bodies, these documents are divided into seven groups: UNO/United Nations Environment Programme; "Recording Bodies" (ILA, IDI, and ILC); Economic Commission for Europe; OECD; Council of Europe; Declarations on the Protection of the Atmosphere/Climate Change and on Sustainable Development; and Important Drafts and U.S. Restatement.

The other two volumes deal with important international agreements, Volume II being devoted to water, namely the seas, rivers, and lakes, and Volume III to the soil (including the protection of species and nature) and to air (including the atmosphere). The basic data on each treaty, the date it was signed and came into force and the parties to it, are found in a separate section at the beginning of Volume II. This arrangement is not satisfactory; a reader who seeks the basic information about a document that he is examining in Volume III, for example, must turn to this section in Volume II for it.

The collection of documents is preceded in Volume I by a foreword by Professor Günther Handl, another foreword drawn from a speech by Hans-Dietrich Genscher, who was the Foreign Minister of Germany, an excerpt from a speech of H.R.H. the Prince of Wales, and a preface and an introduction by the author. Thus the importance of environmental protection and the documents dealing with it is emphasized.

As Dr. Hohmann points out in his introduction, some principles start out as "soft law" and in time become "hard law." If one may judge from what he wrote there, however, Dr. Hohmann, in his enthusiasm for environmental protection, tends to be quick in finding the emergence of a hard rule of customary international law. Consider, for example, some of his statements: "But all declarations reproduced here, even those with 'soft' formulations, have a legal meaning. The 'legal career' can be shown by comparing doc. 1 [Stockholm Declaration 1972] and doc. 7 [Cairo Guidelines and

Principles for the Environmentally Sound Management of Hazardous Wastes (UNEP), 1987]: While the legal principles in doc. 1 are very soft, they become ever harder during the next 15 years and many of them are established as customary duties in doc. 7" (pp. 1-2). Again, "The ILC-draft on the 'law of the non-navigational uses of international watercourses' (1991, doc. 18) may now be regarded as the most important codification of international water law, since the ILC has the official UN-mandate to promote the progressive development of international law and its codification, while the other two bodies [ILA and IDI] are private" (p. 5). This ignores the fact that the ILC has not yet finished its work on the Draft Articles and, moreover, that some of its proposals in the 1991 draft are controversial.

And then there is the statement that "the UN-Resolutions 2995, 3129 and 3281 (doc. 1b-1d) demonstrate the development of the duty to early consultations and regular information — a duty which to-day might be regarded as part of *jus cogens*" (pp. 2-3).

One agrees that there is a duty to exchange information and to consult other watercourse states about planned measures, but one would rest this opinion on firmer ground than these resolutions. Furthermore, the notion that these rules of customary international law are part of *jus cogens* is odd. Could watercourse states not agree to be governed by other rules?

Dr. Hohmann's views on what the principles of international environmental law are today and how they came into being are not relevant in judging the merit of his three volumes of documents; he has included in them all the basic documents in the field and each document will stand on its own feet, its significance for the evolution of international law being left to the informed judgment of the reader. Suffice it to say that these volumes will serve fully the needs of those who work in environmental law matters.

CHARLES B. BOURNE
Faculty of Law, University of British Columbia

Basic Legal Documents of the Russian Federation. Edited by William E. Butler. Dobbs Ferry: Oceana, 1992. Pp. v, 306. (US $75.00). ISBN 0-379-20308-1.

For some years now, Professor Butler and the Faculty of Laws at University College, London, have been placing scholars in their debt by publishing the English texts of some of the more important Soviet legal documents. With the death of the Soviet Union, comparative constitutional scholars will need to pay some attention to the basic legal documents of the Commonwealth of Independent States as well as of the various successor states. As a first step in this direction, Professor Butler has collected and translated the basic legal documents of the Russian federation.

Here can be found the Agreement on the Creation of the Commonwealth, together with the relevant subsidiary documents; in view of the interstate struggles now proceeding in the former Union, it is interesting to be reminded of the guarantees of frontiers and territorial limits that appear in this initial Agreement. While the member states have undertaken to co-operate in ensuring international peace and security and to fulfil the international obligations of the former Union, no provision is made for the succession by Russia to the seat in the Security Council of the former Union. There is, however, a Declaration of the Council of Heads of States of the Commonwealth to "support Russia so that it continues the membership of the USSR in the United Nations, including permanent membership on the Security Council, and other international organisations." The United Nations apparently accepted this statement without question, even though it would appear to be in breach of the Charter; this acceptance differed greatly from the fate of the similar statement embodied in the agreement between Malaysia and Singapore when the latter broke away from the former. It could be argued, of course, that either Georgia or Byelorussia as existing members of the United Nations, as distinct from Russia which had never been admitted, was perhaps more entitled to this position than was the newly independent entity.

Equally interesting are the documents on the Denunciation of the Treaty on the Formation of the USSR issued by Russia, as well as the Treaty on the Creation of an Economic Community, although it must always be remembered that only a minority of the states make up the Commonwealth.

As regards Russia itself, there are documents on the structure of the state, particularly relating to the liquidation of existing ministries; on property and privatization, especially of state and municipal enterprises; on company law, including joint stock societies; on restrictive practices, relating to competition and the limitation of monopolies; on foreign economic activities and entrepreneurship, with particular reference to Leningrad; and, finally, on the agreement with Ukraine on co-operation in foreign economic activity. However, in view of the current animosity between Russia and Ukraine, this agreement may be one of the first to be ignored.

In view of the tensions in Russia and the apparent efforts to remove President Yeltsin and his supporters with the possible restoration of a communist authority, it will be interesting to see how long any of these instruments remain more than papers of merely historic significance.

L. C. GREEN
University of Alberta, Edmonton

Aspects of Extradition Law. By Geoff Gilbert. Dordrecht: Martinus
   Nijhoff, 1991. Pp. xiii, 282 (Dfl 195). ISBN 0-7923-1162-0.

Traditionally, extradition has depended on bilateral treaties that expressly indicate the offences for which extradition may be granted. More recently, however, with the increase in international efforts to control terrorism and create new offences defined by international criminal law, the number of multilateral conventions providing for extradition, even in the absence of bilateral agreements, has multiplied. In addition, there has been a tendency in these bilateral agreements to indicate as extraditable those offences that are punishable by a declared minimum term of imprisonment. Further, as between members of the Commonwealth, the Fugitive Offenders Act, which has allowed for rendition without the normal processes of extradition, has been replaced in many countries by a Commonwealth Scheme for the Rendition of Fugitive Offenders of 1980, as amended in 1990; the text of this Scheme is reproduced as an Appendix to the work under review.

In view of these developments, many of the older authoritative works on extradition have lost much of their significance. Those interested in the topic must, therefore, be thankful to Geoff Gilbert for having provided them with this new survey, which has drawn on the jurisdictions of no fewer than twenty-five different countries, as well as the American and European Courts of Human Rights and other international tribunals such as the United States–Mexican Mixed Claims Commission and the United States Nuremberg War Crimes Tribunals.

Despite this internationalization of extradition, it is likely that not all practitioners will agree with the author that, because of the common factors in the various treaties and the cross references by national courts, "there is, in fact, an international law of extradition, even if it is applied by municipal courts" (p. 2). Their hesitancy to accept this view will be increased by the discretion that is retained by most executive authorities regardless of the decision of the national court — a discretion that is not confined to the protection of those pleading for political asylum (pp. 140, 162-64). Even where a court enforcing a local statute authorizes extradition or seeks to take advantage of an exclusion clause (for example, where the requesting state maintains the death penalty and the state requested does not), it is still possible for the executive to deny transfer (p. 36). See, especially, the cases of *Kirkwood* and *Soering* before the European Commission and Court of Human Rights relating to the death row syndrome (pp. 86-88).

Procedural as well as political considerations frequently tend to frustrate the demands of a requesting state. As a result, there is some suggestion that present extradition arrangements have become "out of date, [so that] alternative, less formal means of rendition have been employed, usually to enforce international crimes" (p. 3). These alternatives may be seen in the return of Barbie to France by Bolivia (pp. 193, 225 n2), or even in the abduction of Eichmann from Argentina (pp. 184-85). For those concerned with the enforcement of international criminal law or even desiring to ensure that criminals do not evade justice, "the overall objective [is] to design an efficient extradition law to expedite the prosecution of fugitives given certain protections which are necessary [from the standpoint of the protection of human rights] when a person is theatened with being removed from the safety of a state where he has committed no crime [and the local citizenry of which are not always aware of the fact that] extradition hearings do not determine the guilt or innocence of the fugitive, only his susceptibility to surrender" (pp. 7, 36). Notwithstanding the need to preserve human rights, "the balance between administrative convenience and the fugitive's rights is coming down firmly in favour of the former" (p. 68). Nevertheless, although the author suggests that "Conventional rights granted in respect of life and freedom from inhuman and degrading treatment . . . may well represent *ius cogens* which would prevent surrender of any fugitive under even the most watertight extradition treaty" (p. 81), he provides no evidence to support this view. On the other hand, promises made to the accused, such as "domestic dealings between the police and the fugitive [e.g., plea bargaining] could not override the international duties in the treaty" (p. 105).

Despite the tendency to replace the enumerative system by the length of sentence (pp. 38-39), the principle of double criminality is preserved, when "emphasis [should] be on the fugitive's acts or omissions, not on the precise requirements of the criminal laws of each state in some search for equivalence" (p. 52). This change of emphasis may be a way to avoid the general practice of denying extradition in fiscal cases, so that while extradition may not operate in the case of tax fraud, for example, the difficulty may be avoided by recourse to laws regarding theft or deception (p. 55).

Problems arise between Europe and the United Kingdom, because the latter demands evidence of a *prima facie* case, while civil law countries tend to be unwilling to extradite their own nationals. Gilbert points out that the European Convention on Extradition does not deal with this issue (pp. 58 *et seq.*), and suggests that since the Convention is silent, the European countries should reciprocate by allowing extradition of nationals (p. 97). This issue may become more significant after the further consolidation of Europe in 1993.

The most recent agreements regarding the extradition of terrorists have made great inroads into the well-established exception from extradition in regard to political offenders. The author points out that, if one bears in mind the historical reason for the introduction of this exception, this development does not appear so completely destructive of the principle. As he explains, "The exemption was aimed to protect people fighting for liberal democracy, yet the same language is still applied today to persons intent on destroying liberal democracy" (p. 115). While most western powers, at least, would almost certainly agree with this contention, those organizations that assert that their activities are directed to securing self-determination or overthrowing a so-called oppressive government would claim to be acting in the name of "liberal democracy." In this connection, the statement that Protocol II, 1977, "includes national groups seeking a change of government" is not supported by the text of the Protocol (p. 132). Before leaving the discussion of terrorism, one might express regret that Gilbert gives figures for terrorist acts provided by the United States (p. 134), but does not draw attention to the somewhat unique character of the United States' definition of terrorism, which is somewhat wider than that generally accepted.

Apart from the terrorism issue, the suggestion that the Swiss approach to the definition of a political offence based on "predominance and proportionality" (pp. 130-31, 149-52) is correct might well be supported in all circumstances, and in fact appears to be the manner in which the Irish and American courts are now approaching requests for extradition of IRA personnel submitted by the United Kingdom (see, for example, the discussion of *U.S.* v. *Doherty*, p. 126).

Perhaps some of the difficulties encountered with regard to extradition, whether or not the political offence defence is raised, could be avoided if all extradition treaties in the future included (as do most international criminal law conventions), the *aut dedere aut judicare* principle. The inclusion of this principle would recognize that the "fugitive has 'chosen' the asylum state [and] has voluntarily submitted himself to its jurisdiction" (p. 159). Thus, these treaties would give full effect to the time-honoured principle underlying the transfer of an accused — namely, that a criminal should not avoid judgment. At the same time, they would have the effect of internationalizing criminal law. Moreover, following this development, and "the growth of *ad hoc* extradition procedures in domestic extradition legislation, there should be less need for states either to abduct fugitives from other states or to connive with the asylum state to use deportation to obtain the fugitive's return [as was the case with *Soblen* (pp. 197-200)]. Nevertheless, at present there is evidence to suggest that methods of rendition other than extradition are frequently used in the so-called problem cases" (p. 183).

Such a policy might prevent another *Eichmann* case, in which "Israel merely relied on Anglo-American precedent which ignores international public order, violations of the fugitive's human rights and state sovereignty" (p. 185). One might inquire, however, whether the human rights of an accused against whom there is *prima facie* evidence of complete disregard of the human rights of his victims can really complain if he is abducted by a state that seeks to try him but is unable to do so because the asylum state fails to sign an extradition agreement or is politically sympathetic to the accused. Is it correct to suggest that forcible abduction, which "is rarely used" (p. 194), "might qualify as inhuman and degrading treatment" (p. 188) contrary to the European Convention on

Human Rights, and how does it differ from "'hot pursuit' which is undergoing a revival in Europe" (p. 195)?

The problem of the treatment of war criminals is once again topical, with the United States resorting to denaturalization and deportation, and the United Kingdom and Canada using criminal processes, although differing on the use of evidence taken abroad. In view of the difficulties being faced with regard to such prosecutions, the author makes the interesting suggestion that "to prevent Nazi war criminals enjoying immunity Israel should continue to prosecute and punish them, but this should only be where the state with territorial jurisdiction refuses to prosecute" (p. 222). This, of course, presumes that the territorial state will agree to extradite. In mentioning the possibility of the establishment of an international war crimes tribunal, the author refers to the *Breisach* trial of Peter of Hagenbach in 1474, cites (p. 229, n104) a paper read at the University of Southampton in 1989, and in the next footnote mentions Schwarzenberger's volume II published in 1968, which contains an entire chapter on the *Breisach* trial, first written about by Schwarzenberger in 1946!

No one purporting to be interested in problems relating to extradition can afford to ignore Gilbert's *Aspects of Extradition Law*.

L. C. GREEN
University of Alberta

International Labour Law Reports, Vols. 7, 8, and 9. Edited by Zvi H. Bar-Niv et al. Dordrecht/Boston/Lancaster: Martinus Nijhoff, Vol. 7, 1989. Pp. xxxvii, 647 (Can. $216.00); Vol. 8, 1990. Pp. xvi, 518 (Can. $208.00); Vol. 9, 1991. Pp. xix, 580 (CAN. $266.00).

The *International Labour Law Reports* is "intended primarily for the use of judges, labour law practitioners, industrial relations specialists and students who need or desire ready access to authoritative information of a comparative nature on problems arising in the field of labour law and industrial relations." The three volumes, 7, 8, and 9, under review here cover the period from October 1, 1987 to September 30, 1989.

The series draws predominantly upon the jurisprudence of individual states, but also includes decisions of the Court of Justice of the European Community and international bodies such as the European Court of Human Rights and the United Nations Human

Rights Committee. The list of nations represented has fluctuated slightly. Volume 7 contained sixteen: in alphabetical order, Argentina, Australia, Austria, Canada, France, Germany, Great Britain, Israel, Italy, Japan, The Netherlands, Norway, Spain, Sweden, Switzerland, and the United States. Finland was added in Volume 8, but Switzerland was dropped from Volume 9.

To produce a series of reports in the English language from such a broad spectrum of jurisdictions is a daunting task. The project is highly commendable, and the founding editor and editorial board have assembled a distinguished and experienced cast of labour law specialists for the purpose. One very helpful feature of the series is the practice of appending annotations to the reports, presumably written by the national reporters.

The reports do not follow the more common practice of reporting the decisions in date order, accessed by a comprehensive index. Instead the decisions are assembled by category under six broad headings or parts: "general principles of labour law and key concepts"; "basic rights pertaining to labour"; "manpower"; "individual employment relationships"; "collective labour relations"; and, finally, "administrative-judicial and general."

This structure has much to commend it, especially given the range of jurisdictions covered. However, its adoption entails a number of difficulties, mainly of an organizational or editorial character, that have to be overcome in order to maximize the utility of the service. On the basis of the three volumes received, the editors still have some way to go in order to achieve that goal.

Perhaps any classification of cases is bound to contain an element of arbitrariness. Sometimes it is difficult to find a structural slot in which to insert a particular topic. Opinions will differ. One wonders, for example, if the "right to privacy" is a "basic right pertaining to labour" of the same nature or charter as "freedom of association" or "political freedom"? Perhaps it would fit more comfortably under the "individual employment relationship."

Again, the "right to strike" may be characterized as a "fundamental right" and as a feature of the collective bargaining process. There is bound to be some overlap. When that occurs, the case is reported at one point, and a cross-reference given at the other location or locations. The cross-reference gives no more than the jurisdiction, the court, and the case name or reference: see, for example, Volume 8 at page 42 where the report simply refers to the decision set out at page 68. Since it is not the practice to paginate the first page of the decision, or the headings to the parts, one sometimes finds four or five pages in a row bearing no page number: in Volume 7, for example, the pagination jumps from 431 to 437. It is a curious feature, though it may cause less confusion as the reader becomes more familiar with the structure of the reports. It also appears strange in the case headings to find more prominence given to the jurisdiction and the court than to the name of the case.

Each volume of the reports provides a list of the cases reported, by jurisdiction. So far, so good. However, in order to comprehend the order in which the cases appear in the various parts, one needs more. They do not appear in date order, or jurisdiction by jurisdiction. The tool provided by the reports to chart one's way through the decisions is a list of "cases reported by subject matter." Unfortunately, the system is not entirely satisfactory. Of the three volumes reviewed only Volume 8 contains a list pertaining solely to it. The only "subject-matter" lists found in Volumes 7 and 9 are cumulative lists. That in Volume 7 covers Volumes 1-8, and that in Volume 9 covers Volumes 8 and 9. If the present organizational structure of the reports is to continue, it would be helpful to include a "subject-matter" list for each separate volume. Cumulative lists could appear at greater intervals.

The subject-matter lists would also be easier to use if the entries under the various parts or sections were placed in alphabetical order. Is there any particular reason, for example, why in Volume 7, page xxvii, "*t*rade dispute" should appear before "*s*trike," or a "*p*olitical" strike after the "*w*ildcat" variety? Or "*l*ock-out" after "*p*icketing"? At times the entries appear to be a motley collection of key words culled from those appearing under the case headings and reassembled in no particular order.

The subject-matter lists do provide helpful cross-references, but more could be done in that respect. Take, for example, the Canadian decision in *Re Public Service Employee Relations Act* reported in Volume 8. The case involved the "right to strike" and "freedom of association." It appears under the latter heading but not the former. The heading "right to strike" warns the reader to check "Collective Labour Relations: Conflict" but provides no cross-reference to "Freedom of Association." The decision does not appear under the "conflict" subject heading, though that heading does direct the reader back to "Basic Rights Pertaining to Labour: Right to Strike." A rather circuitous routing!

Given the multinational nature of the project, printing errors are rare: for example, scruting for scrutiny at the bottom of page 72 of Volume 7, and Wapping affair*e* on page 579. Occasionally the reports depart from the usual form of citation of English cases: square brackets should have been used for the appeal case cited at page 178 of Volume 7, for example.

These criticisms of the series, as reflected in the three volumes considered, do not relate to the concept, which is very worthwhile, nor to the selection of case reports. The problems that exist are of an organizational or editorial character. They are readily remediable. The series does help fill a void in the field of comparative labour law.

M. A. HICKLING
Faculty of Law, University of British Columbia

ANALYTICAL INDEX /
INDEX ANALYTIQUE

THE CANADIAN YEARBOOK OF
INTERNATIONAL LAW

1992

ANNUAIRE CANADIEN
DE DROIT INTERNATIONAL

(A) Article; (NC) Notes and Comments;
(PR) Practice; (R) Review
(A) Article; (NC) Chronique; (PR) Pratique;
(R) Recension de livre

Accord de libre-échange Canada-
États-Unis (ALÉ)
commerce, 317, 320-27
domaine des services, 291-300
investissement, 338
"Affaire de la délimitation maritime
Canada / France, L'," par
Ross Hornby et Valerie Hughes
(A), 3-41
Agence Internationale de l'Énergie
Atomique (AIEA), 137-63
Algerian conflict, 100-1
"Allocation of the Non-Navigational
Uses of International
Watercourses," by Patricia K.
Wouters (A), 43-88
"American Convention on Human
Rights, The," by Norman P.
Farrell (A), 233-60
American Declaration of the
Rights and Duties of Man,
234-35
Aspects of Extradition Law, by Geoff
Gilbert (R), reviewed by L. C.
Green, 458-62

Banque Crédit et Commerce Canada
(BCCC), 335
Banque Européenne pour la
reconstruction et le

Développement, la (BERD),
330, 345
Bar-Niv, Zvi H., editor, International
Labour Law Reports, Vols. 7, 8,
and 9, (R), reviewed by M. A.
Hickling, 462-65
Basic Documents of International
Environmental Law, edited by
Harald Hohmann (R),
reviewed by Charles B. Bourne,
454-56
Basic Legal Documents of the Russian
Federation, edited by William E.
Butler (R), reviewed by L. C.
Green, 456-58
Bayefsky, Anne F., International Human
Rights Law (R), reviewed by
L. C. Green, 433-35
Blais, Céline. See "Canadian Practice
in International Law / La
pratique canadienne en
matière de droit international
public: Treaty Action Taken by
Canada in 1991 / Mesures
prises par le Canada en
matière de traités en 1991"
(PR), 385-402
Blom, Joost. See "Canadian Cases in
International Law in 1991-92 /
La jurisprudence canadienne

en matière de droit
international en 1991-92"
(PR), 403-25
Boundary Waters Treaty, 52, 74, 76,
80, 85, 360
Boustany, Katia, "L'investigation dans
le programme nucléaire
irakien" (A), 137-63
Butler, William E., editor, *Basic Legal
Documents of the Russian
Federation* (R), reviewed by
L. C. Green, 456-58

"Cadres juridiques de la capitalisation
des dettes commerciales des
États, Les," par Vilaysoun
Loungnarath, Jr. (A), 197-232
Canada
abductions, transborder, 351-52
ALÉNA, 299-300, 342-43
architectes, processus de
consultation, 297-300
bilateral treaties, 341, 385-89,
393-97, 402
Canadian Charter of Rights and
Freedoms, 242, 250-51, 254-56
capitalisation des dettes
commerciales, 197-232
conflict of laws, 406-25
diplomatic relations, 369-71
extradition, 372-74
fisheries, 25-34, 374-76, 400, 402
France, boundary dispute with, 3-41
Free Trade Agreement, 352-55,
357-60
GATT, 317-20, 343, 352-56, 378-81
human rights, 233-34, 236-60,
365-67, 390, 399
inland waters, 43-88
institutions financières 291-96
institutions financières et le système
monétaire international,
329-36
international law at External
Affairs, 347-63
investissement, 337-45
multilateral treaties, 389-93,
398-402
labour, 301-15, 404-6
Loi sur les mesures économiques
spéciales, 349-50
NAFTA, 352-55, 381-83
National Defence Act, 244-45

OAS, 233, 259-60
"Open Skies" Treaty, 356-57
peacekeeping, 367-69
prisoners, conveyance of, 361
public international law, 403-6
Quebec, 166, 256, 292
Russia, 363
treaties, 357-63
U.S., relations with, 52-88, 298-300,
301-16, 361-62
War Measures Act, 256-57
water, transboundary, 43-88
wreckage and salvage, 361-62
See Accord de libre échange
Canada-États-Unis
Canada Labour Code, 309, 310, 313
Canada Labour Relations Board, 301,
303-4, 311, 313
"Canadian Cases in International Law
in 1991-92 / La jurisprudence
canadienne en matière de droit
international en 1991-92,"
compiled by / préparé par
Joost Blom (PR), 403-25
"Canadian Practice in International
Law / La pratique canadienne
en matière de droit
international public: At the
Department of External Affairs
in 1991-92 / Au ministère des
Affaires extérieures en
1991-92," compiled by /
préparé par Barry Mawhinney
(PR), 347-63
"Canadian Practice in International
Law / La pratique canadienne
en matière de droit
international public:
Parliamentary Declarations in
1991-92 / Déclarations
parlementaires en 1991-92,"
compiled by / préparé par
Maureen Irish (PR), 365-83
"Canadian Practice in International
Law / La pratique canadienne
en matière de droit
international public: Treaty
Action Taken by Canada in
1991 / Mesures prises par le
Canada en matière de traités
en 1991," prepared by /
préparé par Céline Blais (PR),
385-402

capitalisation des dettes commerciales
  acteurs, 198
  cadre réglementaire de l'État-
    débiteur, 218-19
  contraintes, 224-27
  contrat de rééchelonnement,
    211-18
  étapes, 198-200
  objectifs du cadre réglementaire
    national, 219-24
  réglementation bancaire, 207-11
  techniques, 227-30
Chauhan, B. R., *Settlement of
  International and Inter-State
  Water Disputes in India* (R),
  reviewed by Charles B. Bourne,
  443-46
China
  human rights, 365
"Chronique de Droit international
  économique en 1991 / Digest
  of International Economic Law
  in 1991: Le Canada et le
  système monétaire
  international en 1991,"
  préparé par / compiled by
  Bernard Colas (NC), 329-36
"Chronique de Droit international
  économique en 1991 / Digest
  of International Economic Law
  in 1991: Commerce," préparé
  par / compiled by Martin St-
  Amant (NC), 317-27
"Chronique de Droit international
  économique en 1991 / Digest
  of International Economic Law
  in 1991: Investissement,"
  préparé par / compiled by
  Pierre Ratelle (NC), 337-45
Colas, Bernard. *See* "Chronique de
  Droit international
  économique en 1991 / Digest
  of International Economic Law
  in 1991: Le Canada et le
  système monétaire
  international en 1991" (NC),
  329-36
Columbia River Treaty, 66-70
"Consultation Procedures under UN
  Rules for the Control of
  Restrictive Business Practices"
  by Franklyn P. Salimbene
  (NC), 273-90

debt
  developing countries, 221, 225-26,
    331-33
de Havilland, l'affaire, 339-41
délimitation maritime, Canada/
  France
  autres points, 34-38
  conclusions, 10-11, 39-41
  Convention de Genève (1958), 5-6,
    35-36
  différend, 5-8
  ligne établie, 11-19, 40
  opinions dissidentes, 38-39
  pêches, 25-34
  proportionnalité, 19-24, 40
  recherche d'hydrocarbures, 24-25
  Tribunal d'arbitrage, 8-10

East Timor
  human rights, 366-67
environment
  armed conflict, 347-48
  environmental law, 446-56
  fisheries, 25-34, 374-76, 390,
    400, 402
  GATT, 355-56
  International Environmental
    Agreements, 356
  parliamentary debates, 376-78
  treaties, 390-91, 398-401
  water, protection of, 46-49, 80-88
  wrecking and salvage, 361-62
European Community (EC)
  as an international organization,
    165, 168, 172-74, 181, 184-85,
    187, 191-94
European Convention, 238-39
European Court of Human Rights
  as an international organization,
    169, 170-71, 181
  right to life, 238-39
European Court of Justice, 168-69,
  170
extradition, 458-62

Falklands, 120
Farrell, Norman P., "The American
  Convention on Human
  Rights" (A), 233-60
France
  boundary dispute with Canada,
    3-41
  role in EC, 179

*From Coexistence to Cooperation:
International Law and
Organization in the Post-Cold War
Era*, edited by Edward
McWhinney, Douglas Ross,
Gregory Tunkin, & Vladlen
Vereshchetin (R), reviewed by
John N. Hazard, 427-30

GATT
  as an international organization,
     166, 171-74, 181-83, 188
  conflits et activités canadiens,
     317-21
  FTA, 354-56, 359
  Parliamentary declarations, 378-81
  Uruguay Round, 343, 44
Gilbert, Geoff, *Aspects of Extradition
  Law* (R), reviewed by L. C.
  Green, 458-62
Ginsburgs, George, *The Nuremberg
  Trial and International Law*
  (R), reviewed by L. C. Green,
  436-38

Haiti
  human rights, 366
Händl, Gunther, editor, *Yearbook of
  International Environmental Law*,
  Vols. 1 and 2 (R), reviewed by
  Craig Scott, 446-54
Harmon Doctrine, 54
Hohmann, Harald, editor, *Basic
  Documents of International
  Environmental Law* (R),
  reviewed by Charles B. Bourne,
  454-56
Hornby, Ross, "L'affaire de la
  délimitation maritime Canada/
  France" (A), 3-41
Hornby, Ross, "State Immunity. *Re
  Canada Labour Code*" (NC),
  301-16
Hughes, Valerie. *See* "L'affaire de la
  délimitation maritime
  Canada/France"
human rights
  American Convention on Human
     Rights, 233-60
  Canadian ratification of American
     Convention, 257-60
  compared to Canadian criminal
     law, 236-57

Inter-American Commission on
  Human Rights, 235, 240,
  250-54
Inter-American Court, 235, 240,
  242-43
  international, 431-35
  process, 235

India
  conflict with Pakistan, 94-99
  water, transboundary, 443-46
Institute of International Law,
  50-51
International Atomic Energy
  Association (IAEA)
  as an international organization,
     176
  Iraq, 138-63
"International Court as Emerging
  Constitutional Court and the
  Co-ordinate UN Institutions
  (Especially the Security
  Council), The," by Edward
  McWhinney (NC), 261-72
International Court of Justice
  emerging constitutional court,
     262-71
  as an international organization
     171
International Covenant on Civil and
  Political Rights (ICCPR) 234,
  238, 244, 246, 251-52,
  256-57
*International Human Rights: Problems of
  Law, Policy and Practice*, by
  Richard B. Lillich (R),
  reviewed by L. C. Green,
  431-33
International Human Rights Law, by
  Anne F. Bayefsky (R), reviewed
  by L. C. Green, 433-35
International Joint Commission
  water disputes, 53-88
International Labour Law Reports, Vols.
  7, 8, and 9, edited by Zvi H.
  Bar-Niv (R), reviewed by M. A.
  Hickling, 462-65
International Law Association, 49-50,
  74-75
International Law Commission (ILC)
  water, 43, 46-49
  as an international organization,
     169, 174

International Law in Theory and Practice,
by Oscar Schachter (R),
reviewed by Ivan L. Head,
430-31
International Monetary Fund (IMF)
as an international organization,
166-67, 174, 177-78, 183-84
debt stabilization, 224
international organizations,
effectiveness of,
Asia, 191-92
COMECON, 178
Commission on Refugees, 174
ECU, 186
EMU, 186, 192-94
effectiveness, 167-94
factors, 167-91
IAE, 176
ICAO, 173, 190
ICSID, 170
ILO, 176, 185-86
IMO, 190
League of Arab States, 188-89
OAU, 175, 178
OPEC, 175
UPU, 169, 174, 184, 190
World Bank, 174, 177, 178,
183-84
See also organizations by name; UN
"International Organizations," by
Bryan Schwartz and Elliot
Leven (A), 165-95
"Investigation dans le programme
nucléaire irakien, L'," par
Katia Boustany (A), 137-63
Iran
Iraq, 102-5, 125-29, 130
Lockerbie incident, 263
Iraq
claims against, 349-50
Iraq-Kuwait conflict, 89-90
investigation dans le programme
nucléaire, 137-63
sanctions against, 184, 349
See also Iran
Irish, Maureen. *See* "Canadian
Practice in International Law /
La pratique canadienne en
matière de droit international
public: Parliamentary
Declarations in 1991-92 /
Déclarations parlementaires en
1991-92" (PR), 365-83

Israel
Arab-Israeli conflicts, 91-94
Arab states, 189
U.S., 176-77

Jolivet, Christian, "Récents
développements dans le
domaine des services" (NC),
291-300

Kudriavtsev, V. N., editor. *See The
Nuremberg Trial and
International Law*

labour
international, 462-65
See also "State Immunity"
Law of the Sea
negotiations, 180
parliamentary debates, 374-76
treaties, 390-91, 398-99
Leven, Elliot. *See* "International
Organizations"
Levie, Howard S., *Mine Warfare at
Sea* (R), reviewed by
Commander W. J. Fenrick,
438-40
Lillich, Richard B., *International Human
Rights: Problems of Law, Policy
and Practice* (R), reviewed by
L. C. Green, 431-33
Libya
Lockerbie incident, 263-67
sanctions against, 349
Loungnarath, Vilaysoun, Jr., "Les
cadres juridiques de la
capitalisation des dettes
commerciales des États" (A),
197-232

McWhinney, Edward, editor, *From
Coexistence to Cooperation:
International Law and
Organization in the Post-Cold War
Era* (R), reviewed by John N.
Hazard, 427-30
McWhinney, Edward, "The
International Court as
Emerging Constitutional Court
and the Co-ordinate UN
Institutions (Especially the
Security Council)" (NC),
261-72

Mawhinney, Barry. *See* "Canadian
     Practice in International
     Law / La pratique canadienne
     en matière de droit
     international public: At the
     Department of External Affairs
     in 1991-92 / Au ministère des
     Affaires extérieures en
     1991-92" (PR), 347-63
Maastricht Treaty, 186, 194
*Maritime Terrorism and International
     Law*, edited by Natalino
     Ronzitti (R), reviewed by L. C.
     Green, 440-43
Mexico
     debts, 221, 225
     human rights, 243
     treaties, 386-87, 396
Mine Warfare at Sea, by Howard S.
     Levie (R), reviewed by
     Commander W. J. Fenrick,
     438-40
Montreal Convention (1971), 263-64,
     266-67, 269

naval warfare, law of
     Additional Protocol I, 115, 131-33,
        136
     exemptions, 110-13
     legal developments, 116-33
     military manuals, 105-15
     mine warfare, 438-40
     neutral states and vessels, 120-31,
        105-6, 113-15, 123-36
     state practice in various conflicts,
        89-105
     UN Charter, 116-23, 127, 134
Non-Proliferation Treaty (NPT),
     138-54, 162
North Atlantic Treaty Organization
     (NATO), 166, 172
*Nuremberg Trial and International Law,
     The*, edited by George
     Ginsburgs and V. N.
     Kudriavtsev (R), reviewed by
     L. C. Green, 436-38

Organization of American States
     (OAS)
     Canada, 259-60
     human rights, 233-34
     as international organization, 175,
        182

programme nucléaire irakien
     étendue et effet de l'investigation,
        154-63
     investigation, 138-49
     ONU, 137, 143-49, 153-62
     TNP, 138-54, 162
Public Service Alliance of Canada
     (PSAC), 301, 303-4

Ratelle, Pierre. *See* "Chronique de
     Droit international
     économique en 1991 / Digest
     of International Economic Law
     in 1991: Investissement"
     (NC), 337-45
"Récents développements dans le
     domaine des services," par
     Christian Jolivet (NC),
        291-300
Ronzitti, Natalino, editor, *Maritime
     Terrorism and International Law*
     (R), reviewed by L. C. Green,
        440-43
Ross, Douglas, editor. *See From
     Coexistence to Cooperation*
Russia
     agreement with Canada, 263, 342
     NATO, 172
     post-Cold War, 427-30, 456-58
     treaties, 389, 397
     UN, 261-62

St-Amant, Martin. See "Chronique de
     Droit international
     économique en 1991 / Digest
     of International Economic Law
     in 1991: Commerce" (NC),
        317-27
Salimbene, Franklyn P., "Consultation
     Procedures under UN Rules
     for the Control of Restrictive
     Business Practices" (NC),
        273-90
Salzburg Resolution, 51, nn. 30-32
Schachter, Oscar, *International Law in
     Theory and Practice* (R),
     reviewed by Ivan L. Head,
        430-31
Schwartz, Bryan, "International
     Organizations" (A), 165-95
*Settlement of International and Inter-
     State Water Disputes in India* by
     B. R. Chauhan (R), reviewed

by Charles B. Bourne,
443-446
Soviet Union. *See* Russia
State Immunity Act of Canada,
301-15
"State Immunity. *Re Canada Labour
Code*" by Ross Hornby (NC),
301-16

Treaties, 385-402
Tunkin, Gregory, editor. *See From
Coexistence to Cooperation*

Ukraine
recognition, 371-72
United Nations
as an international organization,
169, 171, 175, 185
Charter, 116-23, 127, 134
consultation procedures, 282-90
Convention on the Rights of the
Child, 239
end of Cold War, 261-62, 264
Iraq-Kuwait conflict, 90
programme nucléaire irakien
137-38, 143-49, 153-62
Resolution 687, 137-38, 144-49,
154-61
Resolution 707, 158-61
Resolution 715, 161
Resolution 731, 265
Resolution 748, 265-67, 270
restrictive business practices
(RBPs), 273-90
Security Council, 262-64,
269-71
UNCTAD, 281-82, 284-85
UNESCO, 174, 176-77, 184
treaties, 392-93, 400
WHO, 174

United States
federalism, 180
human rights, 240
waters, transboundary, 52-88
leaders, 186-87, 190
OAS, 79
Re Canada Labour Code, 303-8,
311-13, 404-6
treaties, 388-89, 394-95
UNESCO, 176-77, 184

Vereshchetin, Vladlen, editor. *See From
Coexistence to Cooperation*
Vietnam, 101-2, 120
"Visit, Search, Diversion, and Capture
in Naval Warfare" by Wolff
Heintschel von Heinegg (A),
89-136
von Heinegg, Wolff Heintschel,
"Visit, Search, Diversion, and
Capture in Naval Warfare"
(A), 89-136

water, transboundary
Canada-US case studies, 52-80
codification of allocation, 45-52,
80-88
India, 443-46
interpretation, 360
Wouters, Patricia K., "Allocation of
the Non-Navigational Uses of
International Watercourses"
(A), 43-88

*Yearbook of International Environmental
Law*, Vols. 1 and 2, edited by
Günther Handl (R), reviewed
by Craig Scott, 446-54
Yugoslavia
peacekeeping, 367-69

INDEX OF CASES /
INDEX DES AFFAIRES

Aanestad v. Saskatchewan, 410-11
Abbott v. Squires, 411
Acme Video Inc. v. Hedges, 417
Advance Diamond Drilling Ltd. v.
    National Bank Leasing Inc., 423
Aerial Incident at Lockerbie, 261-72
Alvarez Machain, 351, 374
Arbitrage franco-britannique, 7, 21,
    28 n. 48, 36-37
Auerbach v. Resorts International Hotel
    Inc., 417, 419-20

Bagnell v. Bagnell, 412
Boardwalk Regency Corp. v. Maalouf,
    417
Bosch v. Bosch, 425
Bow Valley Husky (Bermuda) Ltd. v.
    Saint John Shipbuilding Ltd., 413
Breisach trial, 462
Bridal Fair Inc. v. A. D. & D.
    Promotions Inc., 415
British Columbia (Director of Maintenance
    Enforcement) v. Fults, 418
Bushell v. T & N plc, 408-11

Caisse populaire Notre-Dame-de-Québec c.
    de Leeuw, 414
Canada (A. G.) v. Stuart, 434
Canastrand Industries Ltd., v. The "Lara
    S," 408
Cardel Leasing Ltd. v. Maxmenko, 421
Chadda v. Nolin, 412
Clarke v. Lo Bianco, 416
Columbia Trust Co. v. Skalbania, 405-7
Comaplex Resources Int'l Ltd. v.
    Schaffhauser Kantonalbank, 414
Compania Maritima Villa Nova S. A. v.
    Northern Sales Co., 418

D. & J. Coustas Shipping Co. S. A. v.
    Cia. de Navegaçao Lloyd Brasileriro,
    406
Daly c. Lalonde, 413-14
de Medeiros v. de Medeiros, 412

De Nicols v. Curlier, 424-25
Deutsch v. Law Society of Upper Canada
    Legal Air Fund, 251 n. 71

Eichmann case, 461

Fabrelle Wallcovering & Textiles Ltd v.
    North American Decorative Products
    Inc., 416-17, 418
Federal Deposit Ins. Corp. v. Vanstone,
    415
Fernandez v. Wilkinson, 432
Filartiga v. Pena-Irala, 432
Forsythe v. Forsythe, 411
Forti v. Suarez Mason, 432
Franford v. Franford, 412
Furlong v. Station Mont Tremblay Lodge
    Inc., 410, 421, 423

Garson Holdings Ltd., v. Norman Wade
    Co., 408
Goethe House New York, German Cultural
    Center v. N.L.R.B., 310-11
Golfe du Maine, l'affaire, 9, 18-19, 27, 30
Gourmet Resources Int'l Inc. v.
    Paramount Capital Corp., 415
Gouvernement de la République
    démocratique du Congo v. Venne, 302
    n. 4
Guinée/Guinée Bissau, l'affaire, 17

I Congreso del Partido, 309, 311, 312
Ireland v. United Kingdom, 432
Irwin Toy Ltd. v. A. G. Quebec, 237

Jordanov v. Filon, 418

Kirkwood case, 459
Kim v. Yun, 423
Kingwell v. Kingwell, 412
Krupp trial, 436-37

Libya v. United Kingdom, 264, 265
Libya v. United States, 264

Libye/Malte, l'affaire, 17, 1925, 40
Lietz v. Lietz, 411
Lorac Transport Ltd v. The Atra, 301 n. 4

McCulloch v. JPW Invts. Inc., 407
MacKay v. Hough, 412
McLean v. Pettigrew, 423
McMickle v. Van Straaten, 416
Marbury v. Madison, 262
Marfleet v. First City Trust Co., 408
May v. Greenwood, 408
Mer du Nord, l'affaire, 25, 30
Merasty v. Merasty, 412
Mithras Management Ltd. v. New Visions Entertainment Corp., 407, 423
Mohrbutter v. Mohrbutter, 411
Morguard Investments Ltd. v. De Savoye, 415-17
Moses v. Shore Boat Builders Ltd., 416

Narmi Establishment Vaduz c. Brooks Design Ltd, 414
Newgrade Energy Inc. v. Kubota America Corp., 410
Nicaragua case, 433
Northland Properties Ltd. v. Equitable Trust Co., 408

Ontario Bus Industries Inc. v. The Federal Calumet, 422
Ontario Inc., v. Deloitte & Touche Inc., 408

Palshnuk v. Palshnuk, 411
Pandalus Nordique Ltée v. Ulstein Propeller A/S, 410
Paterson v. Hamilton, 408
Paton v. United Kingdom, 239

R. v. Alegria, 404
R. v. Amway Corp., 237
R. v. Brydges, 250
R. v. Finta, 403-4

R. v. Keegstra, 434
R. v. Kopyto, 435
R. v. Martineau, 253
R. v. Milne, 251-52, 434-35
R. v. Morgentaler, Smoling and Scott, 241
R. v. Vaillancourt, 253
Re Canada Labour Code, 301-15, 311, 404-6
Rempel v. Reynolds, 411
Ronald A. Chisholm Ltd., v. Agro & Diverses Souscriptions Internationales — ADSI — S. A., 410

Sei Fujii v. California, 432
Schreter v. Gasmac Inc., 418
Sharp v. Sharp, 412
Shibamoto & Co. v. Western Fish Producers Inc. Estate, 421-22
Smallman v. Smallman Estate, 411
Smith v. R., 434
Soblen case, 461
Soering case, 432-33, 459
Southern Mills Invts. Ltd. v. Hamilton, 413
Suncor Inc. v. Canada Wire & Cable Ltd., 407

Terry v. Terry, 412
Texas Trading and Mill Corp. v. Federal Republic of Nigeria, 306, 311
Tezcan v. Tezcan, 424-25
Tolofson v. Jensen, 422-23
Trotter v. Trotter, 411
Tunisie/Libye, l'affaire, 19, 25, 27 n. 45, 37
Turbide c. Chevarie, 420-21

U.S. v. Doherty, 461

Velásquez Rodriguez, 432-33

Whalley v. Barsalou, 418
Wisconsin v. Illinois, 63 n. 96